NEW YORK STATE

JULIE SCHWIETERT COLLAZO

Contents

Discover New York State **6**
11 Top Experiences 8
Planning Your Trip 16
The Best of New York State 18
• State of the Arts 22
The Best of New York City 23
Fall Foliage Drives 24
Day Trips from New York City 27
• The Farm-to-Table Experience.... 29
Wild New York 30

New York City **33**
Sights 38
Entertainment and Events.......... 83
Shopping 88
Food 92
Accommodations 97
Information and Services 102
Getting There 104
Getting Around.................. 105

Long Island **108**
The North Shore 111
The North Fork and Shelter Island.... 121
The South Shore 128
The Hamptons 137

Information and Services 155
Getting There and Around 155

**The Hudson Valley
and the Catskills** **156**
Lower Hudson Valley.............. 161
Mid-Hudson Valley 186
The Catskills..................... 208
Upper Hudson Valley 221
Information and Services 228
Getting There and Around 228

**The Capital-Saratoga
Region** **229**
Albany.......................... 231
Saratoga Springs and Vicinity 242
Central New York................. 255
Information and Services 267
Getting There and Around 267

The Adirondacks **268**
Lake George and
  Adirondack Foothills............ 272
Champlain Valley................. 282
Lake Placid and High Peaks........ 289
Central Adirondacks 302

Northwest Lakes 310
The Thousand Islands 314
Information and Services 327
Getting There and Around 329

The Finger Lakes 330
Syracuse 334
Skaneateles Lake 341
Owasco Lake 343
Cayuga Lake 347
Ithaca 353
Seneca Lake 359
Elmira 366
Corning 370
Keuka Lake 374
Canandaigua Lake 378
Rochester 385
Little Finger Lakes 394
Information and Services 396
Getting There and Around 397

Buffalo and the
Niagara Region 398
Buffalo 403
Vicinity of Buffalo 414

Niagara Falls 416
North of Niagara Falls 422
Orleans County 428
South of Buffalo 430
Information and Services 434
Getting There and Around 434

Background 435
The Landscape 435
History and Government 437

Essentials 446
Transportation 446
Accommodations 448
Travel Tips 449
Information and Services 451

Resources 453
Suggested Reading 453
Internet Resources 456

Index 458

List of Maps 478

NEW YORK STATE

0 — 25 mi
0 — 25 km

CANADA

Peterborough

Kingston

Cape Vincent

Alexandria Bay

Watertown

Ogdensburg

Canton

Toronto

Lake Ontario

Oswego

Rome

Oneida Lake

Syracuse

Lewiston

Erie Canal

Rochester

Auburn

Otisco Lake

Batavia

Seneca Falls

Skaneateles Lake

Niagara Falls

Geneva

Finger Lakes

Owasco Lake

Buffalo

Canandaigua Lake

Cayuga Lake

Cortland

Letchworth State Park

Keuka Lake

Seneca Lake

Ithaca

Dunkirk

Watkins Glen

Binghamton

Chautauqua Lake

Salamanca

Olean

Wellsville

Corning

Elmira

Chautauqua

Allegany State Park

Jamestown

Bradford

Troy

Allegany Reservoir

PENNSYLVANIA

Oil City

Ridgway

Williamsport

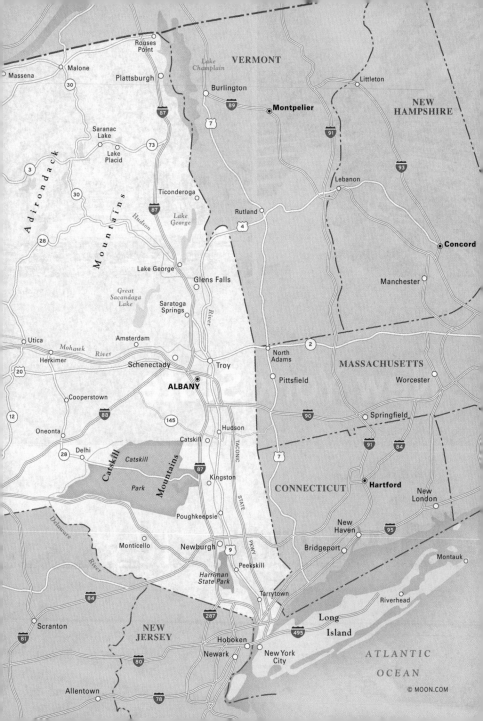

DISCOVER

New York State

New York. Even those who have never strolled the streets of the Big Apple can instantly conjure its magic, having long been fed stories of the city through movies, novels, plays, and melodies that stick in your head for much longer than a New York minute.

As amazing as it is, though, it's only a small part of what New York is.

No one can argue that Manhattan is the shiniest, most faceted jewel in New York's crown, but the gems hidden throughout the other 99 percent of the state are special, too. There are pockets of arts and culture in the Finger Lakes, culinary excellence in the Hudson Valley, and history to experience in Harriet Tubman's house in Auburn or Indian Field cemetery in Montauk.

Look for these along the state's labyrinth of scenic highways. Past the city's bright reflection, you'll see a breathtaking landscape of rivers, lakes, and mountains. Explore the rural communities of the Catskills, the sublime falls of Niagara, and the high peaks of the Adirondacks, waiting amid the largest semi-wilderness east of the Mississippi.

All of this is New York. Turn the page to discover all the gems of the Empire State's crown.

Clockwise from top left: Watkins Glen State Park; spring in New York City; lighthouse in Sleepy Hollow; charter boats on the Erie Canal; beach in Southampton; New York City skyline.

11 TOP EXPERIENCES

1 **Take a hike:** Watkins Glen State Park (page 364) offers easy, accessible trails with plenty of photogenic landscapes and waterfalls. And the Adirondak Loj trailhead (page 293) leads to many stunning hikes with incomparable views.

^
^
^

2 **Hit the beach:** Long Island's Jones Beach boasts plenty of sand for every sun-seeker, along with boardwalk lined with art deco facilities, Olympic-size pools, and refreshments (page 129).

3 **Learn about the fight for rights:** Discover how New York State was the cradle of activism at the Women's Right's National Historic Park (page 348), the Harriet Tubman Home (page 345), and the Niagara Falls Underground Railroad Heritage Center (page 419).

4 **Head off to the races:** Dress smart and place your bets for a proper summer experience at the Saratoga Race Course (page 245).

5 **See the NYC skyline:** It's not just from the top of the Empire State Building (page 63) or Rockefeller Center (page 64) where you can enjoy the New York City skyline. A cruise to and from Liberty or Ellis Islands (page 38) or a stroll across the Brooklyn Bridge (page 45) also offer stellar skyline views, especially at sunset.

>>>

6 **Root for a home team:** Buy some peanuts and cracker jacks, and celebrate America's pastime at a Yankees or Mets game (page 62), or at the National Baseball Hall of Fame and Museum (page 258).

>>>

7 **Discover your inner artist:** There's no shortage of art museums or sculpture gardens in the Empire State (page 22). You can even create your own piece of art by taking a glass-making class at the Corning Museum of Glass (page 371).

8 **Feel Niagara Falls:** There's plenty of room for everyone at the ever popular tourist destination. Climb aboard a boat to feel the mist of the falls (page 416).

9 **Get out on the water:** Canoe endless lakes in the Adirondacks (page 310), fly-fish the flowing rivers of the Catskills (page 218), or relive history on a cruise through the Erie Canal (page 428).

<<<

10 **Feast on farm fresh fare:** New York State is an agricultural hotspot for farm-to-table restaurants and markets (page 29).

>>>

11 **Raise a glass:** The wineries in the Finger Lakes (page 362) and Long Island (page 122) know how to pair delicious wines with beautiful scenery.

<<<

Planning Your Trip

Where to Go

New York City

This dazzling, shape-shifting metropolis belongs more to the world than the state. Great art, theaters, restaurants, nightlife, shopping, hotels, people—and, therefore, people-watching—are all here.

Long Island

This thin ribbon of land east of the city is home to popular **beaches** that stretch for miles along its southern coast. **Jones Beach** is the most popular, while **Fire Island** seashore may be the most unusual. **The Hamptons** are the summer playground of the rich and famous, while other seaside villages are filled with restaurants, inns, and B&Bs. The northern **Gold Coast** is lined with grand turn-of-the-20th-century mansions. There are also wineries and, in summer, roadside farm stands to be enjoyed here.

The Hudson Valley and the Catskills

North of the city, the Hudson Valley is rich with historical, cultural, and scenic sites, including sumptuous **Hudson River estates,** world-class art and history **museums, Revolutionary War sites,** and plenty of farm-to-table restaurants, resorts, and B&Bs. To the west rise the romantic

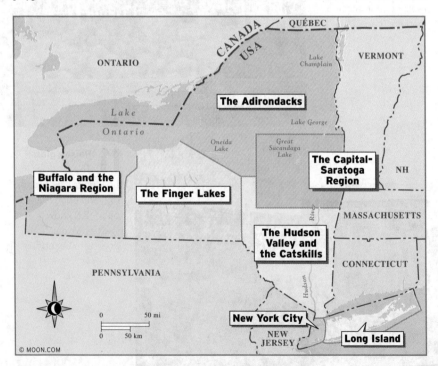

© MOON.COM

autumn display at Holiday Valley Resort in Ellicottville

and mysterious Catskills, where you'll find the fabled villages of **Woodstock, Saugerties,** and **Cooperstown,** home to the **National Baseball Hall of Fame and Museum.**

The Capital-Saratoga Region

Filled with tales of political intrigue, both historical and contemporary, the **capital city** of **Albany** is also host to the ambitious Empire State Plaza, as well as the Albany Institute of History & Art and the New York State Museum. This region is also famous for Victorian-era **Saratoga Springs,** host to the country's finest **horse racing** and home to **natural springs.** The **small towns** of central New York have interesting pasts matched by hopeful futures and robust **revitalization movements.**

The Adirondacks

North of Saratoga sprawls **Adirondack Park,** the East's greatest wilderness. Summer vacationers flock to its **vast forests, rugged peaks, gleaming lakes** and **ponds,** and **rushing rivers** and **streams.** Near the park's center is **Lake Placid,** site of the 1932 and 1980 Olympics. To the park's east is magnificent **Lake Champlain.** To the park's west is the **Thousand Islands** region, scattered over the St. Lawrence River and fascinating, small border towns.

The Finger Lakes

The long, narrow Finger Lakes are flanked by **vineyards,** stately **19th-century towns,** and a number of **historical landmarks,** many related to civil rights and women's history. **Auburn** was once home to abolitionists Harriet Tubman and William Seward; **Seneca Falls** was the site of the first women's rights convention.

Buffalo and the Niagara Region

Sublime **Niagara Falls** is the state's second-most popular tourist attraction (after New York City). The **Erie Canal** winds its way west through tiny canal towns. Western New York is also home to **Buffalo,** the state's second-largest city, once known for its steel industry.

The Best of New York State

Visit New York City for its cultural, historical, and commercial attractions. Travel to upstate New York for the outdoors—forests, mountains, rivers, and lakes—as well as historic sites and picturesque villages. Combine them to get the best of two very different worlds.

You could easily spend a month exploring this large, diverse state. With less time, you can combine a few days in New York City with another region: Long Island, the Hudson Valley, the Catskills, or the Adirondacks. More suggestions for spending time in New York City can be found on page 23.

The farthest reaches of the state, such as the Thousand Islands, Buffalo-Niagara, and western New York, are more accessible from Rochester or Buffalo. They are best explored as stand-alone summer getaways focused on outdoor recreation.

New York City

DAY 1

Start your day early with a visit to the **Statue of Liberty** and **Ellis Island.** Grab a slice of pizza or a simple lunch from a food truck to enjoy on **The High Line,** and take in the latest art installations at a gallery or two in **Chelsea** and the **Meatpacking District.** Browse in quirky boutiques or take a self-guided walking tour through Greenwich Village, SoHo, or other unique Lower Manhattan neighborhoods before having dinner at a popular local restaurant, such as upscale **Eleven Madison Park** or the more affordable, granddaddy of New York delicatessens **Katz's.** Cap off the evening with a cocktail at one of the city's rooftop bars, such as the one at **Hyatt Times Square,** the tallest in the city, with views of both the Hudson and East Rivers.

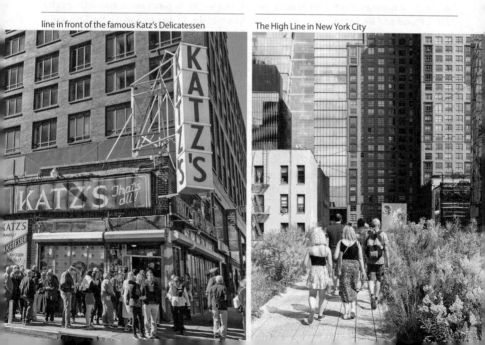

line in front of the famous Katz's Delicatessen

The High Line in New York City

Vanderbilt Mansion in Hyde Park

DAY 2

Spend the morning at the **Museum of Modern Art** before dipping into beautiful **Central Park.** From there, walk south on **5th Avenue,** shopping or window-shopping along the way. At night, brave the bustle of **Times Square** to take in a Broadway show and dinner in the Theater District. Visit the **Empire State Building,** open until 2am, to end the day with the lights of the city laid out before you.

DAY 3

Start the day on the Upper West Side, paying a visit to the iconic blue whale at the **American Museum of Natural History.** Then, stock up on road-trip snacks at **Zabar's,** or swap sides of the park to fill your art tank at the **Guggenheim Museum** or **Frick Collection,** both on the Upper East Side, before heading out of the city to explore other regions of the state.

The Hudson Valley

DAY 4

Let the city recede in your rearview mirror and head north on Route 9 to **Tarrytown.** Though it's just a 30-minute drive, you'll notice a dramatic transition between the throbbing energy of the city and the more pastoral, rural rhythms of the Hudson Valley. Here, you can tour the historic homes of Washington Irving at **Sunnyside,** John D. Rockefeller Sr. at **Kykuit,** and Jay Gould at **Lyndhurst.** If time permits, take a late afternoon walk through **Rockefeller State Park Preserve.** At night, dine in one of the area's many excellent restaurants, such as the farm-to-table **Blue Hill at Stone Barns.** If your budget permits, overnight at one of the Hudson Valley's castles; **Castle Hotel and Spa,** looming large over the Hudson River in Tarrytown, is one grand choice.

DAY 5

Head north on Route 9 to **Hyde Park,** where **The Culinary Institute of America** offers a tasty lunch at one of its signature restaurants. Nearby, you'll also find **FDR's Home, Library, and Museum** and lovely, free paths overlooking the Hudson within the **Vanderbilt Mansion**

Saratoga National Historical Park

property. Farther north is **Rhinebeck,** a town featuring indie bookshops, cafés, an organic and sustainable product farmers market on Sundays, or the unique Aerodrome classic biplane show on summer weekends.

The Capital-Saratoga Region

DAY 6

Continue north another 40 miles (64 km) or so to the historic town of **Hudson,** home to the Persian-style castle **Olana,** numerous antiques shops, and plenty of restaurants for lunch. Afterward, head on to **Albany,** about a half hour farther north on I-87. Stop at **Albany Heritage Area Visitor Center** for a good introduction to this historic region or go straight to the **New York State Museum** at **Empire State Plaza,** admiring impressive art and architecture en route. For a free, bird's-eye view of Albany, take an elevator to the observation level of **Corning Tower.**

DAY 7

Continue another 40 minutes north on I-87 to Saratoga Springs. In the morning, hit the track for breakfast and enjoy a behind-the-scenes tram tour, or drop some belongings to secure your seats or picnic table for afternoon races. Head downtown to shop and eat lunch along quaint Broadway, admiring the street's historic buildings. If you're not returning to the races, take in a spa treatment or go for a dip in one of the pools at **Saratoga Spa State Park,** or drive out to nearby **Yaddo** and stroll its calm, pretty gardens.

DAY 8

Before leaving Saratoga, make a stop at **Saratoga National Historical Park,** where battles that turned the course of the American Revolution were fought. From there, continue on Route 9 another half hour to **Glens Falls,** home to the **Hyde Collection,** a mansion filled with Old Masters paintings. Alternately, head to the town of **Cambridge** and the nearby **New Skete Monastery,** famous for its onion-domed structures and pay-by-honor-system cheesecake made by New Skete nuns.

The Adirondacks

DAY 9

Head back to Saratoga Springs and take I-87 north to Lake George. Along the way, stop at **Grant Cottage** to see the literal deathbed of the former U.S. president. Keep driving north along the shores of **Lake George** and **Lake Champlain.** In picturesque Westport, continue on Route 9N (which turns west), past the mountain villages of Elizabethtown and Keene, to Route 73, which leads to Lake Placid. Spend the rest of the day exploring **Lake Placid;** if time permits, observe feats performed year-round at the **Olympic Ski Jump Complex** or go snowless sledding with a bobsled experience on the Olympic track. If your interests are more historic, visit the **John Brown Farm State Historic Site.**

DAY 10

Drive 8 miles (12.9 km) south of Lake Placid and visit **Adirondak Loj** on the shores of Heart Lake. Set out from the lodge and spend the day hiking, snowshoeing, or cross-country skiing on **Adirondack trails,** depending on the season. If you have small children, head instead to nearby **Tupper Lake,** where **The Wild Center,** opened in 2015, will delight the whole family with its interactive nature exhibits.

DAY 11

Start heading south again, taking leisurely, scenic Route 30 through the heart of the Adirondacks. You can stop at **Adirondack Museum** along the way, but budget 3-4 hours for driving; your destination is the Catskills. Overnight at **The Graham & Co.,** a hip hotel in the town of **Phoenicia.**

The Catskills

DAY 12

Fuel up at one of Phoenicia's breakfast spots and then head east toward Woodstock and Saugerties. Along the way, you may want to stop for a ride on the **Catskill Mountain Railroad** or take a short detour to **Mount Tremper** to see the Kaatskill Kaleidoscope. **Woodstock** and **Saugerties** are both home to numerous restaurants, shops, and B&Bs. In Saugerties, be sure to visit outdoor sculpture park **Opus 40.**

DAY 13

From Woodstock and Saugerties, head south to explore the tiny canal town of **High Falls.** Along the way, take a break at one of the area's many organic farms to pick your own snacks of apples or raspberries, natural fuel to get you ready for climbing the Shawangunks before you check in at **Mohonk Mountain House and Preserve.** The Victorian mountaintop castle is more than 140 years old and the region's loveliest resort. Purchase a day pass to enjoy miles of gorgeous **hiking trails,** dotted with hand-hewn wooden gazebos for rest stops. If visiting in winter, take a cocoa break by the massive stone ice-skating pavilion's bonfire.

Stay for the night and take time to enjoy afternoon tea and cookies, a wealth of unique activities, or the resort's excellent spa. If more rustic accommodations are preferred, continue down the south side of the mountain past **New Paltz** and historic **Huguenot Street** to Bear Mountain State Park.

DAY 14

Take Route 9W south to **Bear Mountain State Park,** where you can take a short hike or drive to the top of Bear Mountain, where a clear day reveals the NYC skyline. Continue, depending on your interests, to **Washington's Headquarters, Storm King Art Center,** or **West Point.**

Then head back to New York City to finish the trip with a walk across the **Brooklyn Bridge.** Toast to the Empire State at one of the city's craft cocktail bars.

State of the Arts

You can easily lose yourself in the well-known wonders of New York City's art scene, but there are plenty of amazing arts institutions outside the city, too.

family viewing *Endeavor* by Lino Tagliapietra in the Corning Museum of Glass

LONG ISLAND

- **Parrish Art Museum** (page 140) is best known for its collection of paintings by northeastern artists such as William Merritt Chase and Jackson Pollock. Speaking of Pollock…

- **Pollock-Krasner House and Study Center** (page 149) in East Hampton preserves Pollock's paint-splattered studio and the home that he shared with artist Lee Krasner.

THE HUDSON VALLEY AND THE CATSKILLS

- **Dia:Beacon** (page 174) is a huge contemporary art museum. Just 30 minutes away is **Storm King Art Center** (page 183), a 500-acre setting for world-famous sculptures.

- **Opus 40** (page 207), near Saugerties, is a six-acre, hand-chiseled, bluestone sculpture, framed by views of the Catskills.

- **Maverick Concerts** (page 209) take place in a hand-hewn music chapel in Woodstock, created by Hervey White's artist colony in 1916.

THE CAPITAL-SARATOGA REGION

- **New York State Museum** (page 234) and **Albany Institute of History & Art** (page 235), both in the state capital, house strong collections of arts and crafts.

- Saratoga Springs has national museums dedicated to **dance** (page 247) and **racing** (page 244), but don't miss the **Tang Teaching Museum and Art Gallery** (page 243) at Skidmore College.

THE ADIRONDACKS

- As its name suggests, **Adirondack Museum** (page 304) is a trove of local artifacts.

- Glens Falls' **Hyde Collection** (page 272) is a robust collection of masterworks by the likes of Cézanne, Rembrandt, Picasso, and Van Gogh.

THE FINGER LAKES

- The **Corning Museum of Glass** (page 371) has the largest collection of glass in the world.

- The **Rockwell Museum of Western Art** (page 372) features multimedia from diverse periods, all about the American West.

BUFFALO AND THE NIAGARA REGION

- Buffalo's **Albright-Knox Art Gallery** (page 407) and Lewiston's **Castellani Art Museum** (page 424) both have fine contemporary art collections.

The Best of New York City

The city's most impressive attractions are packed within a short distance, allowing you to enjoy a classic New York experience in one whirlwind day.

- Start your day with a bagel with cream cheese and smoked fish at Upper West Side institution **Barney Greengrass.**

- Cross **Central Park** in a pedicab or taxi to explore Frank Lloyd Wright's final masterpiece, the **Guggenheim Museum.**

- Take the subway—itself a New York must—to Lexington Avenue. Grab a hot dog or pretzel as you walk over towards **Tiffany & Co.** on **5th Avenue,** and window-shop the renowned stretch of high-end fashion retail.

- At 53rd Street, hang a right and head toward the **Museum of Modern Art.**

- It's just a few blocks to **Rockefeller Center,** which features ice-skating and the famed Christmas tree during the winter and impressive floral displays in other seasons. Majestic **St. Patrick's Cathedral** is just across the street.

- Hail a taxi and travel down 5th Avenue to 34th Street, making sure to view every inch of the **Empire State Building** as you approach. Ride the elevators to the 86th-floor observatory to take in the magnificent views at twilight.

- Now that you've worked up an appetite, take a cab over to **Gramercy Tavern** for a classic New York City dining experience.

- Visit **Times Square** to gaze at the billboards, news tickers, and giant TV screens. They're so bright, you'll swear it's daytime.

- Top off the evening with a **Broadway show.** Be sure to buy tickets ahead of time—you can scout out discount tickets to same-day performances at the **TKTS** booth.

- Enjoy a nightcap at one of the bars in the elegant, wood-paneled **Algonquin Hotel.**

Sheep Meadow in Central Park

Fall Foliage Drives

New York's New England neighbors tend to grab more fall foliage headlines, but New York's autumn leaves are equally spectacular, and its backdrops even more magnificent.

Between late September and late October, the **Catskills** and **Adirondacks** are ablaze with flame-colored leaves, making these regions the obvious destinations to visit. But many other areas of the state offer leaf-peeping opportunities, too, and some of the best itineraries for optimal leaf-viewing are below.

What really sets New York State's leaf-peeping apart is the fact that you're not limited to road trips through these regions. In fact, name a mode of transportation, and you can probably find a fall foliage tour that will offer you a special view, the kind that can't be seen from the car. Possibilities include **Erie Canal boat rides,** either guided or self-piloted; **aerial leaf-peeping** from the **Whiteface Mountain Cloudsplitter Gondola** in Lake Placid; and **glider and biplane rides** at the **Harris Hill Soaring Center** in Elmira or the **Old Rhinebeck Aerodrome** in the Hudson Valley.

The New York State tourism website, **www. iloveny.com,** offers tips about prime fall foliage spots, as well as information about discounts, deals, and fall foliage packages.

Finger Lakes Fall Foliage Drive around Seneca Lake

Start/end: Geneva to Watkins Glen
Route: Rte. 14 and Old Corning Rd.
Distance: 35 miles (56 km)
Drive time: 45 minutes-1 hour

If you like your fall foliage reflected in the water and your drives punctuated with occasional stops for wine tastings, then this Finger Lakes drive will tick all the boxes. This drive is short but impressive, ideal for a time-crunched traveler. You'll start in **Geneva,** at the northern end of Seneca Lake, and drive south on Rte. 14 to **Watkins**

autumn colors on Whiteface Mountain

Kaaterskill Falls in Autumn

Glen, the southern end of Seneca Lake, tracing a path along the western side of the lake the entire way. Once in Watkins Glen, be sure to pull over into the parking lot for **Watkins Glen State Park.** Grab your camera, get out of the car, and take a quick hike along a trail that winds around craggy rock formations that have been eons in the making. Frame a shot of you and your traveling companions near one of the park's dozen waterfalls, with blazingly brilliant leaves edging the photograph.

Best of the Catskills

Start/end: Kaaterskill Wild Forest to Hunter Mountain
Route: Rte. 23A
Distance: 9 miles (14.5 km)
Drive time: 30 minutes

It's not the length of the drive; it's what there is to see along the way that matters when it comes to fall foliage. Plus, the short time in the car means you've got more time to explore by foot—and by air!—at each of the end points on this itinerary. Start in the **Kaaterskill Wild Forest,** where maples will show off their

impressive array of colors as you hike toward the **Kaaterskill Falls,** which has a 260-foot (80 m) drop. Once you've got your fill of hiking, hop back in the car and drive 9 miles (14.5 km) north to **Hunter Mountain,** where you can board the Scenic Skyride, a gondola that will slowly drift you up to a height of 3,200 feet (980 m). From there, you won't just enjoy the Catskills—you'll be able to take in the panoramic view of the leaves on the Berkshire Mountains of Massachusetts and the Green Mountains of Vermont.

Adirondacks Fall Show

Start/end: Lake George to Lake Placid
Route: Rte. 9N and Rte. 73W
Distance: 80 miles (129 km)
Drive time: 1.5 hours

This is the leaf peeping itinerary for travelers with plenty of time to wind through the twists and turns of Adirondack mountain roads. Start at the southwestern end of **Lake George** and make your way north, through **Lake Placid** and, finally, to **High Falls Gorge.** Along the route,

view from Bear Mountain State Park

you'll pass through iconic Adirondack scenery, beautiful any time of year, but especially in autumn.

That Long Island (Leaf) Life

Start/end: Sands Point to Greenport
Route: Rte. 495E
Distance: 85 miles (137 km)
Drive time: 1 hour and 45 minutes

Long Island isn't only for summer! Start at **Sands Point,** on **Long Island's Gold Coast** (which inspired F. Scott Fitzgerald's *The Great Gatsby*), where you'll breathe easier seeing yourself surrounded by the manicured gardens and the surrounding grounds. Hiking trails lined by maples and oaks eventually yield to the Long Island Sound—where else can you enjoy the beach and brilliant leaf color simultaneously, followed by (if you fancy it), a tour of one or more Gilded Age mansions? From here, drive out to **Greenport**, noting how beach towns and vineyards also change with the season, and end up in

Greenport, where you can enjoy the town's camera obscura, right on the waterfront.

Hudson Valley's Scenic Views

Start/end: Harriman State Park to Bear Mountain
Route: Seven Lakes Drive
Distance: 11 miles (17.7 km)
Drive time: 20 minutes

Seven Lakes Drive really will take you pass seven lakes, and that alone should sell you on this route. But there are so many bonus points for this fall foliage itinerary, too. If you take the train from New York City into the Hudson Valley, you'll hug the Hudson River and enjoy riverside fall foliage even before you take the wheel (just make sure you snag a window seat!). And once you've picked up a rental car to drive this deceptively short route from **Harriman State Park** to **Bear Mountain**, you'll soon see how the 20-minute drive can easily turn into a longer one, with all the charming Hudson Valley towns that Seven Lakes Drive winds through.

Day Trips from New York City

Oyster Bay

Distance from NYC: 33 miles (53 km)
Travel time: 1.5-2 hours
Mode of transportation: Train
Why go: Small-town Long Island charm with Gilded Age elegance

A popular day trip on Long Island's North Shore is Oyster Bay, home to **Sagamore Hill,** Theodore Roosevelt's former summer home. After touring the estate and its adjoining visitors center, have lunch in the village's Canterbury Ales Oyster Bar & Grill, or head east another 6 miles (9.7 km) to **Cold Spring Harbor.** Here you'll find a number of other good lunch spots, along with attractive shops and art galleries, a fish hatchery, and **The Whaling Museum**—all interesting places to while away the afternoon.

Tarrytown

Distance from NYC: 27 miles (43 km)
Travel time: 1 hour
Mode of transportation: Train
Why go: Gateway to Hudson Valley's Industrial Age-barons' mansions

One of the best day trips in the Hudson Valley is Tarrytown, home to a collection of mansions that once belonged to famous men, among them Washington Irving **(Sunnyside),** John D. Rockefeller **(Kykuit),** and Jay Gould **(Lyndhurst).** Visit one of the mansion museums in the morning and another in the afternoon, and have lunch in one of the village's many good restaurants. If time permits, make a stop at **Old Dutch Church and Burying Ground,** where Washington Irving found inspiration for *The Legend of Sleepy Hollow,* or **Union Church of Pocantico Hills,** holding nine stunning stained-glass windows by artist Marc Chagall. Splurge for dinner at Blue Hill at Stone Barns, the region's favorite farm-to-table restaurant. Plan in advance, though; reservations are always needed.

West Point and Storm King

Distance from NYC: 50 miles (81 km)
Travel time: 1.5 hours
Mode of transportation: Car
Why go: Military history, excellent eats, and outdoor art

Another good choice for a Hudson Valley day trip is **West Point,** perched on a cliff at a bend in the Hudson River, and nearby **Storm King Art Center.** Spend the morning at the **U.S. Military Academy,** where you'll find a fascinating museum of military history, a visitors center, and bus tours of the campus. Have lunch at the academy's **Thayer Hotel.** In the afternoon, take in Storm King Art Center, a stunning mountainside sculpture park featuring the work of world-famous artists spread out over 500 acres with great views. The center is open from early April to late November.

Marc Chagall's stained glass window in Union Church of Pocantico Hills

Old Dutch Church and Burying Ground

the grounds of Karma Triyana Dharmachakra

New Paltz to the Catskills
Distance from NYC: 56 miles (90 km)
Travel time: 1 hour and 10 minutes
Mode of transportation: Car
Why go: Historical and natural attractions

Fall is an especially good time to make a day trip to the Catskills; the foliage here is often spectacular. On your way north, stop in New Paltz, founded by French Huguenots in the late 1600s. The main sight here is **Huguenot Street,** known as "the oldest street in America with its original buildings." Official walking tours are offered May-October. New Paltz also holds many good lunch spots.

After lunch, continue north on Routes 213 and 209, past the scenic villages of High Falls, Stone Ridge, and Hurley. A bit farther north, pick up Route 28, which will bring you into **Catskill Park.** Take a scenic drive on Route 28A around **Ashokan Reservoir,** if time allows, and then head east to the artsy village of **Woodstock,** home to numerous shops, galleries, and good restaurants. From the village green, drive to the top of **Overlook Mountain** to explore the Tibetan monastery, **Karma Triyana Dharmachakra** (which has hosted the Dalai Lama), or take the steep but well-cleared carriage trail opposite the monastery to enjoy impressive views.

The Farm-to-Table Experience

Most of us may think of the Midwest as the bread-basket of the United States, but New York State is an agricultural hotspot, too, with farms, dairies, and orchards generating exceptional products for consumption, both locally and beyond. Read on for some favorite farm-to-table experiences.

NEW YORK CITY

- **Dirt Candy** (page 93): "Because vegetables are just candy from the dirt" is the tag line of this Lower East Side restaurant, which opened in 2008 and retains its title as NYC's "only vegetable restaurant." Reserve online, in advance, for a table at this hotspot, which is helmed by lauded chef Amanda Cohen.

LONG ISLAND

- **Perennial** (page 132): True, Long Island is one of New York's key wine-producing regions, but it's also, in summer months, one of the hot spots for local produce. Perennial offers all the best of Long Island's bounty, from local oysters to locally farmed fruits and vegetables.

THE HUDSON VALLEY AND THE CATSKILLS

- **Blue Hill at Stone Barns** (page 170): There are plenty of farm-to-table restaurants in this New York State farmland stronghold, but none is more (justifiably) popular than Blue Hill at Stone Barns. Is it pricey? YES. Do you need a reservation? Without a doubt. But when you pull up a seat at the table, you'll understand why Dan Barber has been one of *the* defining voices of the farm-to-table movement (including the voice and subject of an entire episode of the popular Netflix series, *Chef's Table*).

THE CAPITAL-SARATOGA REGION

- **Field Notes** (page 257): If a walk through this region's farmers markets leaves you hungry for more, look to Joan Porambo's and Kyle Macpherson's weekly dinners that feature locally grown and produced ingredients. Menus change regularly, but the common thread is the Capital-Saratoga ingredients and setting, where you can learn more about local farming.

locally farmed greens from the Finger Lakes

THE ADIRONDACKS

- **ADK Food Hub** (page 313): The growing season in the Adirondacks is short, but that's all the more impetus for restaurants to show off their stuff when it comes to locally grown and raised goods. In season, check out ADK Food Hub, which has a farmer's market and prepared food options, mostly featuring grab and go favorites—perfect for an ADK picnic.

THE FINGER LAKES

- **New York Kitchen** (page 380): No, the Finger Lakes aren't just for wine! At New York Kitchen, you don't just pull up to the table and claim your place setting; you can actually take cooking classes here, too, which feature the grown and raised bounty of this region of New York State.

BUFFALO AND THE NIAGARA REGION

- **Black Sheep Restaurant & Bar** (page 412): True, Buffalo is mainly known for Buffalo wings and its famed beef-on-'weck sandwich, but this northernmost region of the state is hardly an agricultural wasteland. At Black Sheep, you can taste the flavors of locally raised pork, as well as other meats, cheeses, and vegetables sourced in the region and New York State.

Wild New York

The Adirondacks, Catskills, and Finger Lakes are particularly well known for their wild places, but every region of the state offers something special.

The Hudson Valley and the Catskills

Nearest to New York City, find 5,000-acre **Bear Mountain State Park** and 46,000-acre **Harriman State Park.** Both offer excellent hiking.

Putnam County is home to **Constitution Marsh Audubon Center Sanctuary,** a 207-acre tidal marsh managed by the National Audubon Society. Farther north, in Columbia County, are **Taconic State Park** and **Lake Taghkanic State Park.**

Another premier outdoors area is **Catskill Park,** a 900-square-mile preserve. Day hikes are plentiful, especially in Greene County, with the park's highest peaks. The **Escarpment Trail** stretches for 24 miles (39 km) between Haines Falls and East Windham.

In Ulster County, the ancient **Shawangunk Mountains** are a mecca for rock-climbing enthusiasts. **Minnewaska State Park** holds two stunning glacial lakes, accessible by foot only.

The famous **Appalachian Trail** cuts through only a small section of New York in the **Hudson Highlands** for about 90 miles (145 km). The trail can most easily be picked up at **Harriman and Bear Mountain State Parks.**

The Adirondacks

Adirondack Park is a six-million-acre refuge with an unusual mixture of public and private lands. The 46 High Peaks tower in the park's center, most over 4,000 feet (1,220 m) high. Skiing and other winter sports make the **Lake Placid** area a four-season option for nature lovers.

You can also enjoy magnificent beauty by

sunrise in Letchworth State Park

Montauk Lighthouse

driving its many scenic highways and byways. **Blue Mountain Lake,** the northern part of **Lake George,** much of the western shores of **Lake Champlain,** and the **High Peaks** are especially scenic. If you're short on time, a visit to the region's recently opened **Wild Center** will give you a sense of the area's natural wonders.

The Finger Lakes

Between Cayuga and Seneca Lakes lies **Finger Lakes National Forest,** a 16,212-acre preserve laced with over 30 miles (48 km) of hiking trails. Though the terrain is largely flat, the forest contains some high hills with excellent vistas. The **Finger Lakes Trail** is a 560-mile (900 km) route that begins at the Pennsylvania border and runs to the Catskills.

The town of Ithaca is surrounded by deep gorges and thundering waterfalls. Some of the most stunning can be found at wild, rugged **Robert H. Treman State Park,** spread over 1,025 acres.

At the Finger Lakes' western edge lies 17-mile-long (27 km) **Letchworth Gorge,** dubbed the "Grand Canyon of the East," part of **Letchworth State Park.** All around grows a dense, thicketed forest laced with about 20 miles (32 km) of hiking trails.

Long Island

Most of 32-mile-long (52 km) Fire Island belongs to **Fire Island National Seashore** and is accessible by ferry and boat taxi only. Exceptions are **Robert Moses State Park** and **Smith Point County Park,** located at either end of the island.

Orient Beach State Park is a favorite among bird-watchers. **Hither Hills State Park** is known for its so-called walking dunes; its trails wind through cranberry bogs, beach terrain, and pine forests. **Montauk Point State Park,** at the very tip of the island, is an excellent fishing and bird-watching spot.

The Capital-Saratoga Region

John Boyd Thacher State Park, near Albany,

Cave of the Winds at Niagara Falls

is where you'll find the unusual Indian Ladder Geologic Trail, one of the richest fossil-bearing formations in the world. **Glimmerglass State Park,** on the shore of Otsego Lake in **Cooperstown,** features a swimming beach, hiking trails, and a grand neoclassical mansion. **Howe Caverns** offers glimpses of an underground New York filled with stalactites and stalagmites.

Buffalo and the Niagara Region

There are myriad ways to experience the world-famous falls at **Niagara Falls State Park.** Even in urban Buffalo, you can find plenty of opportunities for recreation: some of them are free and centered in the Canalside neighborhood, where you can ride bikes on land, water, or—in winter—ice, or take a turn around a section of the canal in a paddle or pedal boat.

New York City

When you're walking through Times Square or gazing at the skyline from atop the Empire State Building, New York City feels like the center of the universe. Most New Yorkers would insist it is. Not a shy bunch, they'll reel off the numbers: 8.6 million people speaking more than 200 languages; 305 square miles of everything you'd ever want, at any hour of the day or night.

Point out what an impossible place the city is and New Yorkers won't disagree. Instead, they'll regale you with stories of how bad it can be: the dirt, the heat, the humidity, the crowds! But there is pride in these stories, and more than a little wonder. The subtext is always that people

Sights 38
Entertainment
    and Events. 83
Shopping. 88
Food 92
Accommodations 97
Information
    and Services 102
Getting There 104
Getting Around 105

Highlights

Look for ★ to find recommended sights, activities, dining, and lodging.

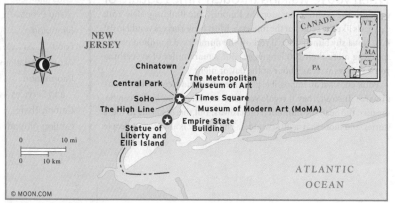

© MOON.COM

★ **Visit Lady Liberty:** Between 1882 and 1924, 12 million immigrants beheld the sight of the **Statue of Liberty** while passing through **Ellis Island** (page 38).

★ **Wander Chinatown:** Mott Street is the bustling heart of Chinatown, lined with restaurants, bakeries, tiny food stores, and cheery souvenir shops (page 46).

★ **Admire American architecture:** Check out **SoHo** not only for the chic boutiques and street vendors, but for its cast-iron buildings, which are this neighborhood's greatest treasure (page 49).

★ **Walk the line:** Constructed on an elevated railway, **The High Line** is a triumph of urban planning—and a magnet for tourists and locals alike (page 57).

★ **Feel the glow of Times Square:** The heart of the Theater District is a neon-splashed

spectacle best taken in after the sun goes down (page 62).

★ **Experience an iconic rooftop view:** The **Empire State Building** was erected in just 14 months. The result was a quintessential skyscraper with views that beg for everyone to go the top (page 63).

★ **Marvel at modern art:** With a recent $450 million renovation, the world-renowned **Museum of Modern Art** gained thousands of square feet to show off more contemporary and diverse masterworks (page 66).

★ **Explore Central Park:** Boating, ice-skating, carriage rides, concerts, and even a castle are just some of what can be found among the park's 843 acres of gorgeous scenery (page 67).

★ **Get to The Met:** The largest museum in the Western Hemisphere, **The Metropolitan Museum of Art** houses nearly three million works of art from all over the world (page 71).

prevail, and what's more, they do it in one of the most compelling places on earth.

New York is larger than life, a city of myth and legend. Much of what you've heard is true: The buildings are taller, the drivers are more obnoxious, the hipsters hipper, and the pace either exhausting or exhilarating, depending on your energy level. It's the country's center of commerce—between two and six billion shares are traded daily on the New York Stock Exchange—and its cultural heart. It draws people whose talent, ambition, and eccentricity are too big for any other place.

Much of what makes New York New York happens at street level, so the best way to see the city is on foot. Unless it's high summer, you can walk from the Empire State Building to Times Square and then to Central Park without breaking a sweat, and the spectacles you'll witness along the way will rival—and maybe even surpass—the city's famous sights. On the street, you'll be swept up in New York's controlled chaos; it's a city of pedestrians who surge across broad avenues, each alone in a crowd.

As for New Yorkers themselves, collectively they are a remarkably friendly and gregarious bunch, despite their reputation to the contrary. Talking to the cabdriver from Pakistan, the Japanese student with orange hair, or the street vendor from Brazil, you'll find the mosaic of people is what makes New York City a truly unique place.

So soak up some of the city's moxie and walk the walk. If your feet get tired, flag down one of the 13,587 yellow cabs, take a bus, or enter the 660-mile (1,060 km) subway system. Bundle up in the winter, peel down in the summer, and enjoy the mild "shoulder season" months of May, June, September, and October. Revel in the Big Apple, and star in a few New York stories of your own.

PLANNING YOUR TIME

You can see a lot of NYC in a few days. Manhattan, where most of the city's most famous attractions are located, is a compact place with an **excellent public transportation** system; it's also the best place in the world for **sightseeing on foot.**

First-time visitors will probably want to spend a day visiting the **Empire State Building** and **Metropolitan Museum of Art,** perhaps taking a wander through **Central Park** afterward.

The next day could be devoted to the **Statue of Liberty, Ellis Island,** and a short walking tour of **Lower Manhattan,** where highlights include Wall Street, South Street Seaport, the 9/11 Memorial Site and Museum, and the Observatory at One World Trade Center.

On your third day, explore the streets of **Chinatown, SoHo,** and **Greenwich Village.** At night, take in a **Broadway play,** visit a **jazz club,** and eat in one of the city's many restaurants representing cuisine from every corner of the globe.

If you have more time, spend a day at **The Museum of Modern Art** and take a stroll down **5th Avenue** and across East 42nd Street, visiting Rockefeller Center, St. Patrick's Cathedral, The New York Public Library, and Grand Central Terminal along the way. Or, explore the **American Museum of Natural History** and take the A train up to vibrant 125th Street in **Harlem.**

New York City

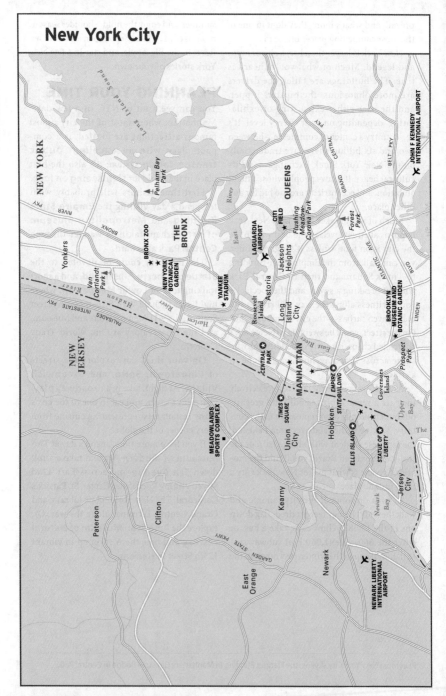

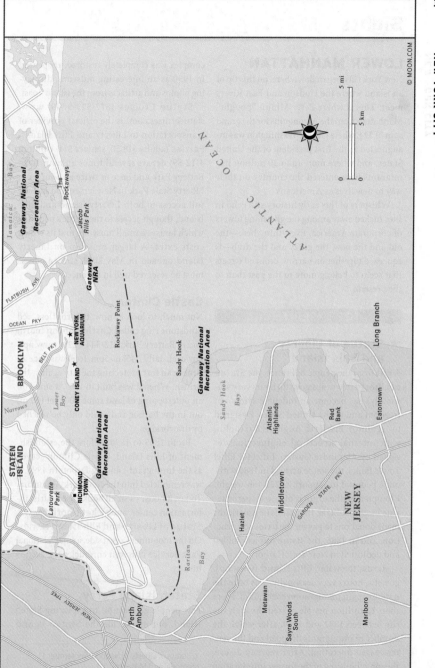

© MOON.COM

Sights

LOWER MANHATTAN

New York City began down here, on this tip of an island where the Hudson and East Rivers meet. This is where Peter Minuit "bought" Manhattan from the Algonquins for the grand sum of $24, where George Washington was inaugurated as the first president of the United States, and where more than 20 million immigrants have entered the country on their way to new lives as Americans.

Whispers of this early history still echo in sites tucked away among the glistening towers of corporate America. Everything here—the old and the new, the glitzy and the drab—is squeezed together on narrow, crooked streets that seem to belong more to the past than to the present.

TOP EXPERIENCE

★ Statue of Liberty and Ellis Island

A gift from the people of France, the **Statue of Liberty** (www.nps.gov/stli, hours vary seasonally) has become an indelible symbol of freedom and of the United States. Designed by sculptor Frédéric Auguste Bartholdi, with internal structural engineering designed by Alexandre Gustave Eiffel (of Eiffel Tower fame), the statue arrived in 1885 without a pedestal to support its 225-ton weight. Prompted by the urgings of newspaper magnate Joseph Pulitzer, thousands of Americans made donations to pay for the base's construction, and in 1886, the statue was assembled and dedicated in New York Harbor.

Across the water, **Ellis Island** (www.nps.gov/elis, hours vary seasonally) was once the nation's main immigration checkpoint. More than 12 million people passed through the site between 1892 and 1954, after which the number of immigrants dropped and the center ceased operation. After years of disuse, the main building of the former immigration complex was completely restored, reopening in 1990 as an interesting museum, displaying photos and artifacts from the island's past.

Statue Cruises (877/523-9849, www.statuecruises.com) is the official provider of transportation to Liberty and Ellis Islands. **Ferries** (adults $18.50, seniors $14, children 4-12 $9) depart several times an hour from Battery Park and once or twice an hour from Liberty State Park in New Jersey, and include full access to both Liberty Island and Ellis Island, though access to the statue's pedestal, which houses a small museum, and its crown costs extra. A larger museum on Liberty Island opened in May 2019. Crown access must be reserved well in advance.

Castle Clinton

Not much to look at now, this roofless, red sandstone ring called **Castle Clinton** (north end of Battery Park, 212/344-7220, www.nps.gov/cacl, daily 7:45am-5pm, free) was once an American fort protecting the city against the British. When it was built in 1807, it stood on an outcropping of land some 200 feet (60 m) out in the harbor and could only be reached by drawbridge.

From 1855 to 1890, before the establishment of Ellis Island, Castle Clinton served as the Immigrant Landing Depot. In 1896, it was remodeled into the New York Aquarium. Today, it houses a small bookstore, tourist information center, and **ticket booth for the Statue of Liberty and Ellis Island ferries.** On the monument's east side, a small National Park Service museum chronicles the castle's history.

Staten Island Ferry

Few people get around to exploring Staten Island, but many ride the **Staten Island**

1: Statue of Liberty 2: National September 11 Memorial and Museum

Manhattan

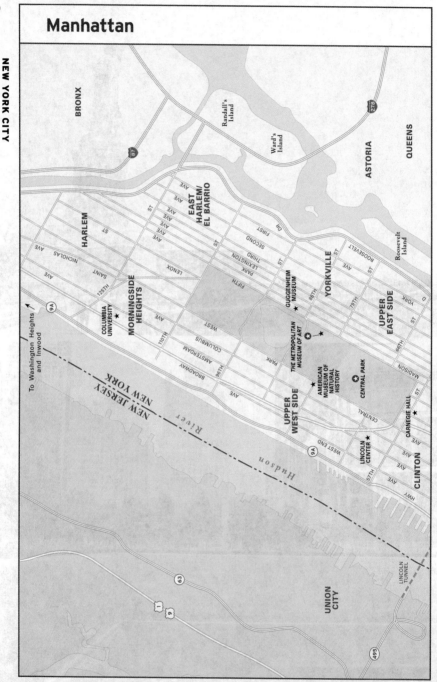

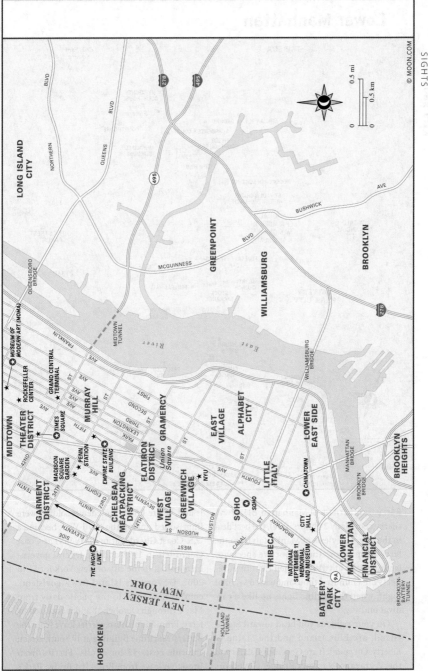

© MOON.COM

NEW JERSEY
NEW YORK

HOBOKEN

LONG ISLAND CITY

BLVD

NORTHERN

QUEENS BLVD

I-278

I-495

BLVD

MCGUINNESS

GREENPOINT

BUSHWICK

AVE

WILLIAMSBURG

BLVD

BROOKLYN

I-278

East River

MIDTOWN TUNNEL

QUEENSBORO BRIDGE

WILLIAMSBURG BRIDGE

MANHATTAN BRIDGE

BROOKLYN BRIDGE

BROOKLYN HEIGHTS

0.5 mi
0.5 km

★ Museum of Modern Art (MOMA)

MIDTOWN

★ Rockefeller Center

FRANKLIN

GRAND CENTRAL TERMINAL

★ Theater District

★ Times Square

Madison Square Garden

Penn Station

Empire State Building

42ND

34TH

MURRAY HILL

FIFTH AVE

PARK AVE
LEXINGTON AVE
THIRD AVE
SECOND AVE
FIRST AVE

GRAMERCY

Union Square

FLATIRON DISTRICT

GARMENT DISTRICT

TENTH
NINTH
EIGHTH
SEVENTH

23RD

CHELSEA/MEATPACKING DISTRICT

★ THE HIGH LINE

WEST VILLAGE

GREENWICH VILLAGE

NYU

14TH

EAST VILLAGE

ALPHABET CITY

AVE

LITTLE ITALY

SOHO

CHINATOWN

LOWER EAST SIDE

FOURTH

ELEVENTH

SIDE

HUDSON ST

HOUSTON

WEST

CANAL

BROADWAY

TRIBECA

CITY HALL

NATIONAL SEPTEMBER 11 MEMORIAL AND MUSEUM

LOWER MANHATTAN

FINANCIAL DISTRICT

BATTERY PARK CITY

9A

BROOKLYN-BATTERY TUNNEL

HOLLAND TUNNEL

Lower Manhattan

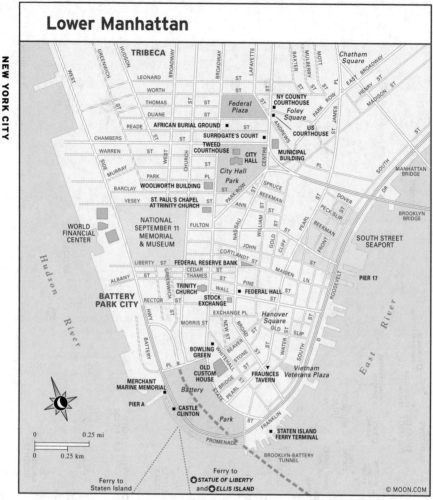

Ferry (southern tip of Manhattan, 311, www.siferry.com, daily 24 hours, free), the best deal in the city. The views of Manhattan from the ferry's trip across the harbor are spectacular, especially at twilight when the sunset reflects off a hundred thousand windows, or at night, when the skyline lights up like a carnival midway.

On your right, as you head toward Staten Island, are Ellis Island and the Statue of Liberty. On your left are Governors Island and the Verrazano-Narrows Bridge. Governors Island, where 1,500 Confederate soldiers were imprisoned during the Civil War, became a U.S. Coast Guard Station in 1966. The Coast Guard left in 1998 and the federal government sold it to the city of New York for $1 in 2002. **Governors Island** (www.govisland.com) is now open to the public daily from May 1 through October 31 and is accessed by ferry. From Manhattan, ferries leave from the Battery Maritime Building at 10 South Street; the ride costs $3 for adults. Ferries from Brooklyn leave from Brooklyn Bridge Park's

Pier 6. Check the island's website for activity and ferry schedules.

National Museum of the American Indian

At State Street and Battery Place is the stunning former U.S. Custom House, a 1907 beaux arts masterpiece designed by Cass Gilbert. Standing on the site of New York's first European settlement, the Custom House now houses the New York branch of the Smithsonian's **National Museum of the American Indian** (1 Bowling Green, 212/514-3700, www.americanindian.si.edu, daily 10am-5pm, Thurs. until 8pm, free). Inside the museum are displays holding some of the country's finest Native American art and artifacts, ranging in date of origin from 3200 BC to the present.

New Museum

Founded in 1977, **New Museum** (235 Bowery, 212/219-1222, www.newmuseum. org, Tue.-Wed. and Fri.-Sun. 11am-6pm, Thurs. 11am-9pm, adults $18, seniors $15, students $12, children under 18 free, pay what you wish Thurs. 7pm-9pm) offers frequent special events in addition to four ongoing exhibits focused on contemporary art by both U.S. and international artists working in a variety of media. Its small café is the perfect place for a quick, sweet bite or a cup of tea or coffee before exploring the surrounding neighborhood.

International Center of Photography

International Center of Photography (79 Essex St., 212/857-0000, www.icp.org, Tues.-Wed. and Fri.-Sun. 10am-6pm, Thurs. 10am-9pm, adults $14, seniors and students $12, children under 14 free, pay what you wish on Thurs. 6pm-9pm) includes spacious exhibit areas and a bookshop. Founded in 1974 by Cornell Capa, Robert Capa's brother (Robert Capa was a photojournalist killed in Vietnam), the center presents many of the city's most important contemporary photography exhibits, and opened in a new space in 2020.

Fraunces Tavern

Fraunces Tavern (54 Pearl St., 212/968-1776, www.frauncestavernmuseum.org) is a 1907 renovation of the historic pub where George Washington bade goodbye to his troops in 1783. The tavern, which still serves food, is a colonial setting and has a small **museum** (54 Pearl St., 212/425-1778, www.frauncestavern-museum.org, Mon.-Fri. noon-5pm, Sat.-Sun. 11am-5pm, adults $7, seniors, students, and children 6-18 $4, children under 6 free) with exhibits on early American history.

Wall Street

Wall Street is surprisingly narrow, shadowy, and short. Surrounded by towering edifices that block out the sun most of the day, the street stretches only about a third of a mile before bumping into the lacy, Gothic spires of Trinity Church. The wall for which Wall Street was named was erected by the Dutch in 1653 to defend the city against an expected attack by the British (Britain and the Netherlands were at war at that time). The street is one of New York's most famous thoroughfares, but it has a dark history. Established by the British in the late 1600s to accommodate the Royal African Company's growing human cargo, this was once the busiest slave market outside of Charleston, South Carolina. In the early 1700s, nearly 20 percent of New York City's inhabitants were enslaved people, and it was here they were examined and sold to the highest bidder.

Federal Hall National Memorial (26 Wall St., 212/825-6990, www.nps.gov/feha, Mon.-Fri. 9am-5pm, free), a fine Greek Revival building with a wide set of stairs that make a perfect perch for watching financial whizzes and fellow tourists go by, is near the western end of Wall Street. Beside the stairs is a bronze statue of George Washington, who took his inaugural oath of office here in 1789. Back then, the English City Hall stood on this site, and Washington spoke to the crowds from the building's second-story balcony.

Just south of Federal Hall National Memorial is an enormous building resembling a Roman temple: the **New York Stock Exchange** (11 Wall St., 212/656-3000, www. nyse.com). As a plaque on the building reads, the exchange's origins can be traced to 1792, when a group of 24 brokers drew up a trading agreement beneath a buttonwood tree on Wall Street. The Exchange has been closed to visitors since 9/11; barricades and security personnel guard its entrance.

Trinity Church (75 Broadway, 212/602-0800, www.trinitywallstreet.org, daily 7am-6pm, free tours Sun. after the 11:15am service) is one of the oldest and wealthiest churches in Manhattan. It has a small museum (free admission), documenting the church's history. Some of New York's most illustrious early residents, among them Alexander Hamilton, are buried in the church's cemetery.

The **Federal Reserve Bank of New York** (33 Liberty St., museum/tour entrance at 44 Maiden Ln., 212/720-6130, www.newyork-fed.org) is a massive, fortress-like structure of dark limestone that fills an entire city block and safeguards a huge pile of gold—497,000 bars of it, to be precise, the world's largest-known depository of monetary gold. Built in the style of an Italian Renaissance palace, the Federal Reserve is a "bank for banks," where cash reserves are stored. Foreign countries also keep gold bullion here, in vaults five stories underground. No one has ever attempted to rob the Fed, but if someone should, the entire building would shut down in 31 seconds. Free tours are offered two times a day, Monday-Friday (closed bank holidays), and include an informative video and a look at the vaults. Reservations must be made online in advance.

National September 11 Memorial and Museum

Ten years after the September 11, 2001, tragedy, the former World Trade Center site was reopened as the **National September 11 Memorial and Museum** (World Trade Center, 212/312-8800, www.911memorial. org, memorial open daily 7:30am-9pm, free; museum open Sun.-Thurs. 9am-8pm, last entry at 6pm, Fri.-Sat. 9am-9pm, last entry at 7pm, adults $26, seniors and students $20, children 7-12 $15). The eight-acre memorial site sits in the footprints of the original World Trade Center towers, which were destroyed in the 9/11 attacks. The somber memorial features two reflecting pools with the largest artificially constructed waterfalls in North America and bronze panels etched with the names of those who were killed in the 2001 terrorist attacks, as well as the earlier attack on the World Trade Center in 1993.

Security is tight in and around the memorial and museum. Bring photo ID and leave large bags and backpacks behind.

One World Observatory

It took nearly a decade to complete and plenty of New Yorkers were initially worried whether crowds would ever ascend to a sky-high observatory near the Twin Towers site, but **One World Observatory** (285 Fulton St., 844/696-1776, www.oneworldobserva-tory.com, daily 9am-8pm, summer 9am-10pm, $35), currently the tallest building in the Western Hemisphere, has been bustling since it opened in 2015. The observatory spans three floors.

Battery Park

To the immediate west of the World Trade Center Site is the **World Financial Center.** Though badly damaged during the September 11 attacks, it has since been restored to its former self: ultramodern office towers, complete with shops and restaurants, an outdoor plaza, and **Winter Garden at Brookfield Place** (230 Vesey St., 212/978-1673, www.bfplny. com), a glass-domed public space and the site of frequent free concerts, art exhibits, and other performing arts events.

At Manhattan's tip, breezy 25-acre **Battery Park** (State St., at Battery Place, 212/344-3491, www.thebattery.org) stretches south and north of the World Financial Center. Built on landfill, it's lined by the wide **Admiral**

George Dewey Promenade, a walkway within the park. Benches along the promenade make great places to relax in the sun and enjoy superb harbor views. Along the way are Castle Clinton, public art, an urban vegetable garden, restaurants, and play areas, including the **Sea Glass Carousel** (State St. and Water St., www.seaglasscarousel.nyc, Sun.-Thurs. 10am-7pm; Fri.-Sat. 10am-8pm, $5). The park also serves as the jumping-off point for visitors headed to Liberty and Ellis Islands. **Battery Park City Esplanade** (Battery Park City, 212/267-9700, www.bpcparks.org) is where weary Wall Streeters work off stress by jogging along the Hudson River. Benches provide rest spots with vistas of Lady Liberty and Ellis Island.

The Museum of Jewish Heritage (36 Battery Pl., at First Pl., 646/437-4202, www.mjhnyc.org, Sun.-Tues. and Thurs. 10am-5:45pm, Wed. 10am-9pm, Fri. 10am-3pm, adults $8, seniors and students $5, children under 13 free, Wed. 4pm-9pm free, special exhibits cost extra), overlooking the Hudson River, is a hexagonal building symbolic of the Star of David. The museum features thousands of moving photographs, cultural artifacts, and archival films documenting the inconceivable inhumanity of the Holocaust and resilience of the Jewish community.

South Street Seaport

Fulton Street meets the East River at **South Street Seaport** (www.seaportdistrict.nyc), one of the city's oldest, most historic areas. A thriving port during the 19th century, the seaport went into steep decline in the 20th century but was making a comeback by the 1980s, as a developer introduced restaurants and shops. The area is better than ever, thanks to a revitalization effort that followed damage wrought by Hurricane Sandy in 2012. An elevated park with an alfresco restaurant, a design market, Imagination Playground, and Citi Bike stations draw people in droves, especially during warmer months. The Seaport's historic sites are scattered throughout the 12-block district. Many of the sites are free, but to access the Seaport's galleries and 19th-century sailing ships or to join a walking tour, you'll need to purchase a ticket at the museum; prices vary based on experience.

Around City Hall

City Hall Park was first a cow pasture, then a gathering place for Revolutionary-era political meetings. Now it's the site of **City Hall** (311, www.nyc.gov), one of the finest federal-style buildings in New York. The City Hall area is full of impressive buildings (the park itself is lovely, with its flickering gas lamps). The very interested may take a tour of City Hall (call 311 or visit www.nyc.gov to make reservations).

The **Woolworth Building** (233 Broadway) stands at the edge of City Hall Park. Its glistening white walls and green copper roofs are best seen from a distance, where they can be appreciated in all their glory, but up close, the 1913 Cass Gilbert extravaganza is also a visual feast. Craggy-faced gargoyles peer down from a detailed neo-Gothic exterior, while mosaic-covered ceilings grace the lobby. One lobby caricature shows Frank Woolworth, king of the discount stores, counting his nickels and dimes. A farmer's son, Woolworth began as a salesman earning $8 a week. By the time he built his $13.5 million headquarters, however, he was able to pay for it *in cash.* Tours of the building's lobby reveal the architectural and cultural history of the magnificent skyscraper (203/966-9663, www.woolworthtours.com, $20-45).

TOP EXPERIENCE

Brooklyn Bridge

Until this celebrated link between Brooklyn and Manhattan was built, New Yorkers had to brave a perilous ferry to cross the East River. German-born engineer John Roebling designed the revolutionary suspension bridge using pressurized underwater chambers, or caissons, and twisted steel cable, a new invention that Roebling produced and later made popular throughout the world. Unfortunately, the bridge's creation was not without sacrifices. Approximately 20 workers died during its construction, including Roebling himself. After 14 years, the Brooklyn Bridge was completed in 1883, its opening attended by more than 150,000 people. At the time, the bridge's 1,595-foot (490 m) span was the longest in the world, and the towers anchoring it were taller than any other structure in North America. The bridge's completion—and permanence—are all the more fantastic considering it was built in a time when nearly a quarter of existing bridges ultimately collapsed.

The bridge remains a triumph of human ingenuity, reflected in its National Historic Landmark status. Its elevated walkway, shared by pedestrians and cyclists, offers exceptional views of the New York skyline. It also affords an up-close look at the bridge's construction, including narrow gaps in the path that show cars passing below. For a great view of the bridge itself, head to Brooklyn Bridge Park.

LOWER EAST SIDE

No region of New York has been home to more immigrants than the East Side between the Brooklyn Bridge and Houston Street. On an ever-gentrifying island, this is one of the few remaining districts where you can see and feel the immigrant vibrancy. Especially in Chinatown, streets teem with jostling crowds and bustling markets. Many New Yorkers visit Chinatown for lunch or dinner, and then head to Little Italy for dessert.

★ Chinatown

Crowded with restaurants and festive shops, **Mott Street** (at Canal Street) is a great spot for catching the flavor of Chinatown. Mott Street is the oldest Chinese-inhabited street in the city, and has many of Chinatown's oldest restaurants and Chinese stores. One store of note is **Yunhong** (50 Mott St., 212/566-8828), a tiny store dedicated to chopsticks. Be sure to explore the side streets off Mott, and take a walk into **Columbus Park** (at Mulberry and Bayard Sts.) to feel like you have left the streets of New York behind as

clusters of men play Chinese chess, checkers, and mah-jongg.

Museum of Chinese in America

The **Museum of Chinese in America** (215 Centre St., 212/619-4785, www.mocanyc.org, Tues.-Wed. and Fri.-Sun. 11am-6pm, Thurs. 11am-9pm, adults $12, seniors and students $8) examines the Chinese American experience in this nation of immigrants. Be sure to check out the museum's core exhibit, "With a Single Step: Stories in the Making of America." On sale in the museum's bookstore is an excellent *Chinatown Historical Map & Guide,* which provides insight into the neighborhood's history, as well as tips on what to order in Chinese restaurants, where to shop, and what to buy. The bookstore also carries many other titles by or about Asian Americans.

Little Italy

In contrast to Chinatown, Little Italy—at its zenith between 1890 and 1924—is a shadow of its former self. Only about 10 percent of the neighborhood's residents are of Italian ancestry, and the heart of its dining and shopping district has shrunk to just three short blocks along **Mulberry Street** just above Canal Street. Here, Italian restaurants and cafés line the street, with tables and striped umbrellas set out in warm weather. It's all very touristy, but it's also a lot of fun.

At the intersection of Mulberry and Grand Streets is a mother lode of great Italian food stores, including **Alleva Dairy** (188 Grand St., 212/226-7990, www.allevadairy.com), which claims to be the oldest Italian cheese store in the United States, and **Piemonte Homemade Ravioli** (190 Grand St., 212/226-0475, www.piemonteravioli.com), which has been turning out pasta since 1920.

Lower East Side Tenement Museum

Visit this museum to get a taste of what immigrant life was like in the 19th and early 20th

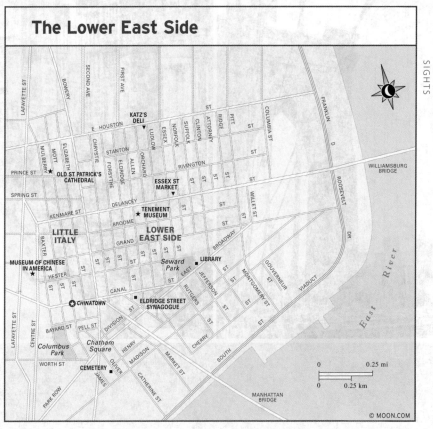

The Lower East Side

century. Start at the **Visitor Center and Museum Shop** (103 Orchard St., 877/975-3786, www.tenement.org, days, times, and prices vary by tour, call for details), then depart for a neighborhood walking tour or a guided visit through one of the immigrant apartments in a Lower East Side tenement building. The building, at 97 Orchard Street, is a deliberately dark and oppressive place; it originally had no windows, except in front, and no indoor plumbing. Declared illegal in 1935, it was sealed up and forgotten about until 1988, when historians looking for a structurally unaltered tenement building stumbled upon it.

Eldridge Street Synagogue

About four blocks south of the Tenement Museum is the 1886 **Eldridge Street Synagogue** (12 Eldridge St.). The first synagogue in New York built by Eastern European Jews, it's a large and startlingly elaborate building with beautifully carved wooden doors. Due to a dwindling congregation, the main sanctuary was sealed in the 1930s and not entered again for 40 years. In the early 1990s, restoration work began, and the synagogue now houses **Museum at Eldridge Street** (212/219-0302, www.eldridgestreet.org, tours Sun.-Thurs. 10am-5pm and Fri. 10am-3pm, adults $15, seniors and students $10, children $8, pay what you wish on Mon.). The museum can only be seen by guided tours, which start on the hour.

SoHo and TriBeCa

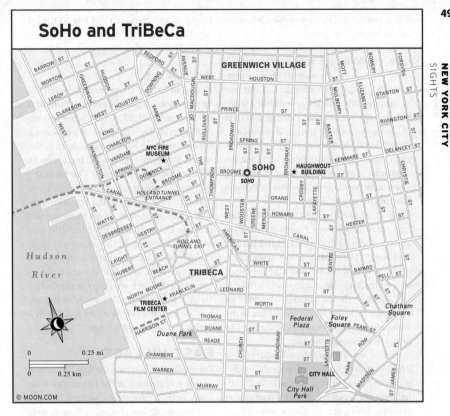

SOHO AND TRIBECA

Early on, SoHo (short for *So*uth of *Ho*uston) was a quiet residential suburb. By the 1870s, however, it was home to foundries, factories, warehouses, and sweatshops. In the 1960s, artists began moving in, attracted by low rents and high-ceilinged spaces. Soon thereafter, art galleries arrived, followed by shops and restaurants. SoHo became fashionable, so much so that artists could no longer afford high rents. SoHo is now primarily an upscale shopping and dining center. Within its 25 blocks, bounded by Houston and Canal Streets, Lafayette Street and West Broadway, beckon dozens of restaurants, bars, hotels, and shops.

1: Brooklyn Bridge 2: Chinatown 3: Washington Square Arch

Heading south out of SoHo and crossing over Canal Street, you'll enter TriBeCa, short for *Tri*angle *Be*low *Ca*nal. Encompassing about 40 blocks between Canal, Chambers, West, and Church Streets, the district is home to many of the city's toniest restaurants, yet large sections remain quiet and residential. Like SoHo, TriBeCa's main thoroughfares are Broadway and West Broadway, though some of its best cast-iron buildings are on side streets, especially White Street.

★ SoHo

SoHo is a compact neighborhood, perfect for just wandering about. **Broadway and West Broadway** are the main thoroughfares; **Prince and Spring Streets** hold an enormous array of shops. The intersections of

Prince and Spring Streets with West Broadway are the heart of the district.

As you walk through the neighborhood, check out the architecture. SoHo's cast-iron buildings remain its greatest treasure. Originally envisioned as a cheap way to imitate elaborate stone buildings, cast-iron facades were prefabricated in a variety of styles—including Italian Renaissance, French Second Empire, and Classical Greek—and bolted onto iron-frame structures. An American invention, the cast-iron building was erected primarily in New York, with SoHo boasting the largest collection.

Many of SoHo's finest cast-iron buildings can be found along Broadway. Foremost among them is Italianate **Haughwout Building** (488 Broadway). The magnificent edifice is five stories tall and nine bays wide on the Broadway side, and sports 92 windows, all flanked by Corinthian columns. Built for a merchant who once provided china to the White House, the store was the first in the city to install a passenger elevator.

Farther north is the **Singer Building** (561 Broadway), designed by the innovative architect Ernest Flagg in 1902. It's decked out with red terra-cotta panels, delicate wrought-iron detailing, and large plate-glass windows. Even farther north, note the maroon-and-white facade of **575 Broadway.**

Farther south, below Grand Street, is the so-called **"Queen of Greene Street"** (28-30 Greene St.), built in ornate Second Empire style.

New York City Fire Museum

Technically outside of SoHo to the west is the **New York City Fire Museum** (278 Spring St., 212/691-1303, www.nycfiremuseum.org, daily 10am-5pm, adults $10, seniors and students $8, children under 12 $5). Housed in a fire station that was active until 1959, the museum is staffed by ex-firefighters who enliven tours with personal anecdotes on request. It's filled with intriguing historical items, including a lifesaving net (which "caught you 75 percent of the time"), gorgeous 19th-century fire

carriages, and an exhibit that honors the fire department's courageous work following the World Trade Center attacks.

Art Spaces

Not all of SoHo's art galleries have left the neighborhood. **Ronald Feldman Fine Arts** (31 Mercer St., 212/226-3232, www.feldmangallery.com, days and hours vary by season), for one, has long been a mainstay in SoHo, with a focus on avant-garde installations. Another top art attraction is **The Drawing Center** (35 Wooster St., 212/219-2166, www.drawingcenter.org, Wed. and Fri-Sun. noon-6pm, Thurs. noon-8pm, adults $5, seniors and students $3, children under 12 free), the only nonprofit museum in the country to focus exclusively on historical and contemporary drawings. For a complete list of neighborhood galleries, pick up a copy of the *Gallery Guide*, a free listings guide, available at many bookstores. *Time Out New York* and *The New Yorker* also have good listings.

EAST VILLAGE

For much of its existence, the East Village was simply an extension of the Lower East Side. Then, in the 1950s, artists, writers, radicals, and counterculturists began arriving. Among them were artists Willem de Kooning, Paul Georges, and Joan Mitchell, followed by writers such as Norman Mailer, W. H. Auden, and Allen Ginsberg. Later, theaters, film festivals, dance halls, and punk rock clubs also found a home in this area. Though gentrification arrived in the 1980s, the neighborhood has not completely succumbed, and offers a thriving mix of artists and careerists, students and tourists. Nightlife thrives here in scores of restaurants and bars.

St. Mark's Church in-the-Bowery

Historic **St. Mark's Church in-the-Bowery** (131 E. 10th St., 212/674-6377, www.stmarksbowery.org, Mon.-Fri. 9am-4pm, Sun. 9am-1pm) stands near the former site of Peter Stuyvesant's farm. The church is a

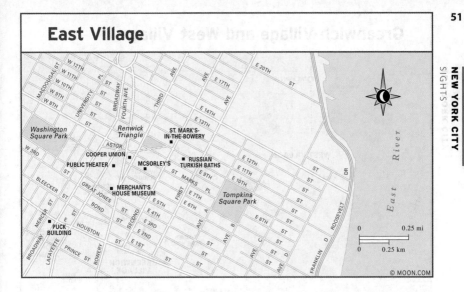

East Village

© MOON.COM

hodgepodge of architectural styles, made up of a 1799 base, an 1828 Greek Revival steeple, and an 1854 cast-iron Italianate porch. Buried in the bricked-in graveyard surrounding the church is "Petrus Stuyvesant" himself, the last and most colorful of the Dutch governors.

Today, St. Mark's is known primarily for its **poetry readings** (212/674-0910, www. poetryproject.org), **dance presentations** (212/674-8112, www.danspaceproject.org), and leftist politics.

St. Mark's Place

Raucous and run-down in spots, outrageously entertaining in others, St. Mark's Place is the heart of the East Village. Artists and musicians, students and tourists, hustlers and hipsters, all jostle each other, while the stores on either side sell everything from gourmet pretzels to frightening-looking leather goods. To get the full effect of it all, come after 10pm on a weekend night. The area today is leaning a bit toward touristy, so a better feel for the East Village might be found walking along 2nd Avenue.

Merchant's House Museum

The classic Greek Revival **Merchant's House Museum** (29 E. 4th St., 212/777-1089, www.merchantshouse.org, Thurs.-Mon. noon-5pm, adults $15, seniors and students $10) is furnished exactly as it was in 1835 when merchant Seabury Tredwell and his family lived here. It's the only remaining intact 19th-century family home in New York City, providing a rare glimpse into the lives of an affluent family of that period.

GREENWICH VILLAGE AND WEST VILLAGE

Once a hotbed of radical and artistic activity, the narrow winding streets of Greenwich Village and its western section, the West Village, now sometimes seem too tame, its restored buildings too cute, its shops and boutiques too name-brand. Only the well-to-do can afford to live here now, and nearly all the dingy old dives have gone safely commercial and mainstream. And yet, "the Village" (as the locals call this area) still has a bohemian soul lurking somewhere underneath. You can feel it sometimes in the old jazz clubs, or in Washington Square Park on a windy afternoon, or in the faces of some of the older residents, who haven't forgotten the neighborhood's roots.

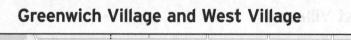

Greenwich Village and West Village

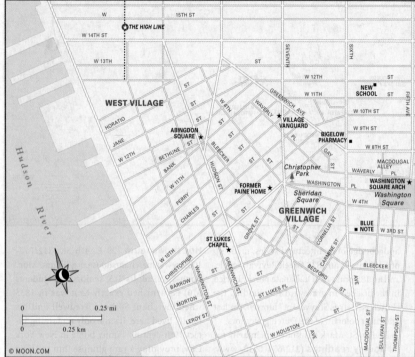

W 15TH ST
THE HIGH LINE
W 14TH ST
W 13TH
SEVENTH
SIXTH
W 12TH
ST
NEW SCHOOL
W 11TH
GREENWICH AVE
WAVERLY
FIFTH AVE
WEST VILLAGE
W 4TH
ST
VILLAGE VANGUARD
W 10TH ST
HORATIO
ABINGDON SQUARE
PL
BIGELOW PHARMACY
W 9TH ST
JANE
BLEECKER
GAY
W 8TH ST
W 12TH
HUDSON ST
MACDOUGAL ALLEY
BETHUNE
ST
WAVERLY
PL
BANK
Christopher Park
WASHINGTON
PL
WASHINGTON SQUARE ARCH
W 11TH
FORMER PAINE HOME
Sheridan Square
Washington Square
PERRY
W 4TH
GREENWICH VILLAGE
CHARLES
GROVE ST
CORNELIA ST
BLUE NOTE
W 3RD ST
Hudson River
ST LUKES CHAPEL
W 10TH
CHRISTOPHER
WASHINGTON ST
GREENWICH ST
CARMINE ST
BEDFORD
BLEECKER
AVE
BARROW
0   0.25 mi
MORTON
ST LUKES PL
LEROY ST
0   0.25 km
W HOUSTON
AVE
MACDOUGAL ST
SULLIVAN ST
THOMPSON ST
© MOON.COM

Artists and writers started coming to the neighborhood for its low rents, around 1910, and soon the area was teeming with artistic and political activity. Tearooms, literary bars, and basement poetry clubs sprouted up, and theater groups flourished. Among the Village residents during this period were Eugene O'Neill, Bette Davis, and e. e. cummings.

In the 1960s, folk clubs, antiwar rallies, and the civil rights movement brought to the Village Bob Dylan and Jimi Hendrix, Abbie Hoffman and Jerry Rubin. In 1969, the Village's Stonewall Riots marked the beginning of the national gay rights movement.

Nearly every street in the Village has something interesting to offer, and you can't go wrong just wandering about. Start at Washington Square Park, the eastern end of Greenwich Village and work your way west, crossing into the West Village at 7th Avenue. But be sure to **bring a map**—there's no grid system here.

Washington Square Park

Washington Square Park is the heart of Greenwich Village. On a sunny day you'll find everyone here, from kids on skateboards and students strumming guitars, to committed Hare Krishna spreading the word and old men taking in the sun. At the park's southwest corner are stone chess tables where the click-clack of pieces never seems to stop; near the center is the dog run, where Fidos of every conceivable shape and size dash madly to and fro.

Once marshland, the eight-acre park was purchased by the city near the end of the 18th century to be used as a potter's field. In the span of 1797-1825, at least 20,000 people were buried here.

The square was turned into a park in the late 1820s. Elegant town houses went up all around, including the still-standing, beautiful, redbrick Greek Revival town houses on the north side of the square. By the 1830s, Washington Square Park was considered to be the city's most fashionable residential neighborhood.

New York University (NYU) erected its first building on the park in 1837 and now occupies much of the park's periphery. Most of the old town houses have been replaced by institutional buildings, and the genteel old families replaced by students.

The park's biggest landmark is the marble **Washington Square Arch,** marking the north entrance. Eighty-six feet (26 m) tall, the arch replaced a temporary wooden one erected in 1889 to commemorate the centennial of George Washington's inauguration. Citizens liked the wooden arch so much that they decided to have it remade in marble. The designer was architect Stanford White, and the sculptor was A. Stirling Calder (father of famous mobile artist Alexander Calder).

Christopher Park and Sheridan Square

At Christopher Street and 7th Avenue South is Christopher Park, often mistaken for Sheridan Square. The latter is just southeast of Christopher Park at the triangle where Washington Place, Barrow, Grove, and West 4th Streets meet. The confusion is understandable as a statue of General Philip Sheridan stands in Christopher Park. Sheridan was a Union general best remembered for the racist (and often misquoted) line, "The only good Indians I saw were dead."

Next to the general is a George Segal sculpture depicting two gay couples—one male, the other female. Erected in 1991, the statue commemorates the Stonewall Riots, which took place across the street at Stonewall Inn on June 27, 1969. (The original **Stonewall** was

at 51 Christopher Street and is now gone; the bar called Stonewall at 53 Christopher is a namesake and, as of 2016, a State and National Historic Landmark.)

Across the street from Christopher Park is the former **home of Thomas Paine** (59 Grove St.), the Revolutionary War-era author of *Common Sense, The Crisis,* and *The Rights of Man.* It was Paine who wrote the famous words, "These are the times that try men's souls." Paine's house, marked with a plaque, is now the venerable gay piano bar **Marie's Crisis Cafe,** named partly as a tribute to Paine.

Children's Museum of the Arts

The **Children's Museum of the Arts** (103 Charlton St., 212/274-0986, www.cmany.org, Mon. and Wed. noon-5pm, Thurs.-Fri. noon-6pm, Sat.-Sun. 10am-5pm, adults $13, seniors and children under 1 free) is an experimental museum designed to expose kids to visual and performing arts by connecting them with working NYC artists. In the "Artist's Studio," youngsters can try their hand at sand painting, origami, and sculpture in a number of artist-monitored stations.

UNION SQUARE AND MADISON SQUARE PARK

The East Side between 14th and 42nd Streets is mostly residential, but it does have a considerable quiet charm and a number of quirky attractions sandwiched between brownstones and apartment buildings. Various neighborhoods make up this section of the East Side. **Union Square** begins at 14th Street and Broadway. **Madison Square** begins at 23rd Street and Broadway. Farther east is **Gramercy Park,** a residential square centered at 20th Street and Irving Place.

Union Square

Built over a central subway station, **Union Square** is a bustling urban center complete with sleek megastores, upscale restaurants, fashionable bars, and what may be the city's most popular **Greenmarket**

Union Square and Madison Square Park

Map labels:
MUSEUM OF MATHEMATICS
NEW YORK LIFE INSURANCE COMPANY
APPELLATE COURT
Madison Square Park
EATALY
METROPOLITAN LIFE BUILDING
FLATIRON BUILDING
GRAMERCY PARK
ROOSEVELT'S BIRTHPLACE
Gramercy Park
BARNES & NOBLE
Union Square
PETER COOPER VILLAGE
STUYVESANT TOWN
Stuyvesant Square
East River
FRANKLIN D ROOSEVELT DR

MADISON AVE, FIFTH AVE, BROADWAY, PARK AVE S, LEXINGTON AVE, PARK AVE, THIRD AVE, SECOND AVE, FIRST AVE, IRVING PLACE, PLACE

26TH ST, 25TH ST, 24TH ST, 23RD ST, 22ND ST, 21ST ST, 20TH ST, 19TH ST, 18TH ST, 17TH ST, 16TH ST, 15TH ST, 14TH ST, 13TH ST

0   0.25 mi
0   0.25 km

© MOON.COM

(212/788-7476, www.grownyc.org), open Monday, Wednesday, Friday, and Saturday.

Laid out as a park in 1815, Union Square was originally the province of prominent local families, such as the Roosevelts, who lived nearby. Then, in the mid-1800s, the city's entertainment and commercial industries moved in. The famous Academy of Music started on 14th Street, and department stores went up all along Broadway from 8th to 23rd Streets. This commercialism was short lived, however. By 1900, the theaters and shops had moved uptown to Madison Square at 23rd Street, and Union Square was home to garment factories and immigrants.

From the 1910s until after WWII, Union Square was a center for political demonstrations. Socialists, communists, and the Wobblies (members of the Industrial Workers of the World) protested here, while many

Union Square

left-wing organizations had headquarters on or near the square. One of the most dramatic protests took place on August 22, 1927, the night anarchists Nicola Sacco and Bartolomeo Vanzetti were executed. The police had machine guns mounted on a roof overlooking the square, but the demonstration remained peaceful. In recent years, the centrality of Union Square has again attracted protesters, especially during the Occupy Wall Street and Black Lives Matter movements.

Gramercy Park

Gramercy Park (between Park Ave. S. and 3rd Ave. and 20th and 21st Sts.) was bought and laid out in 1831 by lawyer and real estate developer Samuel Ruggles. As fashionable today as it was back then, the park consists of both stately buildings and an enclosed green to which only residents have access. Outsiders have to content themselves with peering in through an 8-foot-high (2.4 m) iron fence.

Broadway and Lower 5th Avenue

During the late 1800s, Broadway between 8th and 23rd Streets was known as **Ladies' Mile** because of the many fashionable department stores located there. The original stores are long gone, but their elaborate cast-iron facades remain.

The **Theodore Roosevelt Birthplace National Historic Site** (28 E. 20th St., 212/260-1616, www.nps.gov/thrb, Wed.-Sun. 9am-5pm, free) is a handsome, four-story brownstone and exact replica of Theodore Roosevelt's birthplace. It was rebuilt by Roosevelt's family and friends just after his death in 1919 and only a few years after the original building was torn down. The museum is filled with thousands of engrossing photographs and the world's largest collection of Roosevelt memorabilia, including TR's christening dress and his parents' wedding clothes.

Where 5th Avenue and Ladies' Mile meet at 23rd Street is one of Manhattan's most famous and idiosyncratic landmarks: The **Flatiron**

Building, designed by Chicago architect Daniel H. Burnham in 1902. Its nickname comes from its narrow triangular shape, only 6 feet (1.8 m) wide at the northern end.

Madison Square

Between 23rd and 26th Streets and 5th and Madison Avenues is Madison Square. Once a marsh, potter's field, and parade ground, the square became fashionable in the mid-1800s. In those days, expensive hotels stood along its west side, the old Madison Square Garden stood to the north, and the Statue of Liberty's torch-bearing right arm stood in the center of the square, awaiting funding for the monument's base. Today all those buildings and the arm are gone, but other graceful structures have taken their place.

Madison Square Park (E. 23rd-26th Sts., between 5th and Madison Aves., 212/538-1884, www.madisonsquarepark.org) is known for its ambitious public art exhibits. In summer months, the park hosts free concerts for children and families. At the southeast corner of the park, New Yorkers line up at **Shake Shack** (at E. 23rd St., 212/889-6600, www.shakeshack.com), which brings a fresh, locavore angle to fast food. You can also buy snacks or a full picnic across the street at **Eataly** (200 5th Ave., 212/229-2560, www.eatalyny.com).

On the park's east side between 23rd and 25th Streets is the 1932 **Metropolitan Life Insurance Company,** an enormous art deco building made of limestone that seems to change color with the day. On the north corner of 25th Street is the 1900 **Appellate Division of the New York State Supreme Court,** covered with an impossible number of marble sculptures. Taking up the whole block between 26th and 27th Streets is **New York Life Insurance Company,** an 1898 wedding cake extravaganza designed by Cass Gilbert.

At the north end of the park you'll find the **Museum of Mathematics** (11 E. 26th St., 212/542-0566, www.momath.org, daily 10am-5pm, adults $18 online or $19 at museum, seniors, students, and children over 2 $15 online

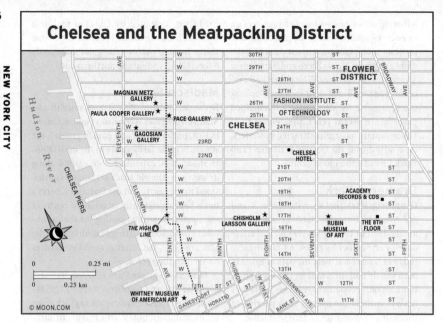

Chelsea and the Meatpacking District

(Map labels: W 30TH ST, W 29TH ST, W 28TH ST, FLOWER DISTRICT, BROADWAY AVE, MAGNAN METZ GALLERY, PAULA COOPER GALLERY, PACE GALLERY, W 27TH ST, W 26TH ST, FASHION INSTITUTE OF TECHNOLOGY, W 25TH ST, CHELSEA, GAGOSIAN GALLERY, ELEVENTH AVE, W 23RD, W 22ND, CHELSEA HOTEL, W 21ST ST, W 20TH ST, CHELSEA PIERS, ELEVENTH, W 19TH ST, ACADEMY RECORDS & CDS, W 18TH ST, Hudson River, W 17TH ST, CHISHOLM LARSSON GALLERY, THE HIGH LINE, RUBIN MUSEUM OF ART, THE 8TH FLOOR, W 16TH ST, TENTH, W 15TH ST, NINTH, EIGHTH, SEVENTH, SIXTH, FIFTH, W 14TH ST, W 13TH ST, 0 0.25 mi, 0 0.25 km, AVE, W 12TH ST, HUDSON ST, WHITNEY MUSEUM OF AMERICAN ART, GANSEVOORT, HORATIO, GREENWICH AVE, W 12TH ST, WASHINGTON ST, BANK ST, W 11TH ST, © MOON.COM)

or $16 at museum). The hands-on museum tries to inspire even the most entrenched math-phobe to fall in love with numbers. The museum is especially child- and teen-friendly, as every exhibit is interactive.

CHELSEA AND THE MEATPACKING DISTRICT

Heading north from the Village along Manhattan's west side, the buildings get taller and the landscape becomes more urban. Along the Hudson River, the pleasant, industrial-chic Meatpacking District straddles 14th Street, giving way to cosmopolitan Chelsea. Roughly stretching between 14th and 28th Streets, 6th Avenue and the Hudson River, Chelsea is made up of dozens of brownstones, row houses, tenements, and apartment buildings. West of 10th Avenue, former warehouses turned galleries comprise the largest commercial arts district in the city. Part residential, part industrial, this area has a solid, gritty feel and its share of attractions, among them The High Line, which offers fantastic views of Midtown's skyline.

Both neighborhoods are renowned for nightlife, with massive dance clubs and exclusive lounges clustered north of the galleries around 27th and 28th Streets.

West Chelsea Galleries

Even if you have little interest in contemporary art, it's worth visiting some of this neighborhood's exhibition spaces for their architectural exuberance alone.

Most of the galleries are in the West 20s between 10th and 11th Avenues, with an especially large collection located along West 22nd, 25th, 26th, and 29th Streets. Among them are such major names in the New York art world as **Pace** (508, 510, and 534 W. 25th St., 212/929-7000, www.pacegallery.com, Tues.-Sat. 10am-6pm), exhibiting works by the likes of Sol LeWitt and Julian Schnabel; the **Paula Cooper Gallery** (521 and 534 W. 21st St., 212/255-1105, www.paulacoopergallery.com, Tues.-Sat. 10am-6pm), representing such heavyweights as Carl Andre and Claes Oldenburg; and the **Barbara Gladstone Gallery** (530 W. 21st St. and 515 W. 24th St., 212/206-9300, www.gladstonegallery.

com, Tues.-Sat. 10am-6pm), specializing in painting, sculpture, and photography by established artists. The enormous **Gagosian Gallery** (522 W. 21st, 555 W. 24th St., and other locations in the city, 212/741-1111, www.gagosian.com, Tues.-Sat. 10am-6pm) is dedicated to artists such as Andy Warhol, Richard Serra, and David Salle. If you're interested in mixed media, installation, video, or conceptual sculpture, stop by **MagnanMetz Gallery** (521 W. 26th St., 212/244-2344, www. magnanmetz.com, Tues.-Sat. 10am-6pm), which often introduces artists from Cuba and elsewhere to New York audiences.

If you're short on time or tired of walking, maximize your gallery visits by going to some of the larger buildings that house multiple galleries. Two good bets include 547 W. 27th Street, home to, among others, **Aperture Foundation Gallery** (547 W. 27th St., 212/505-5555, www.aperture.org/gallery), featuring classic and contemporary photography, and **Ceres Gallery** (547 W. 27th St., 212/947-6100, www.ceresgallery.org), a nonprofit, artist-run gallery featuring contemporary work by women; and 210 11th Avenue, home to **Cavin-Morris Gallery** (210 11th Ave., 212/226-3768, www.cavinmorris.com), dedicated to eclectic global art, and **Sears-Peyton Gallery** (210 11th Ave., 212/966-7469, www.searspeyton.com), which represents a carefully selected handful of contemporary American artists.

To find out more about galleries, or about who's exhibiting where, pick up a copy of *Gallery Guide,* available in many bookstores and galleries. Or, check listings in *Time Out New York* or *The New Yorker.*

Rubin Museum of Art

Rubin Museum of Art (150 W. 17th St., 212/620-5000, www.rmanyc.org, Mon. and Thurs. 11am-5pm, Wed. 11am-7pm, Fri. 11am-10pm, Sat.-Sun. 11am-6pm, adults $19, seniors and students $14, children under 12 free) is a quiet, peaceful place that bills itself as the only museum in the world dedicated to Himalayan art. Opened in 2004, the Rubin

was founded by private collectors reluctant to donate their work to a larger institution that might let it gather dust in storage. The museum's stunning permanent collection includes paintings, sculpture, textiles, and prints ranging in age from the 2nd to the 19th centuries, and in origin from Nepal to southern Siberia. Housed in the former Barney's department store, the museum also offers films, lectures, concerts, and dance events in its state-of-the-art auditorium.

The same family that lent its name and its collection to Rubin Museum of Art established **The 8th Floor** (17 W. 17th St., 646/839-5908, www.the8thfloor.org, free), a smaller, more intimate gallery nearby. Its collection of contemporary Cuban art is especially strong.

★ The High Line

A triumph in innovative urban planning, **The High Line** (Gansevoort St. to W. 34th St., between 10th Ave. and 11th Ave., 212/500-6035, www.thehighline.org, hours vary by season) is a picturesque, 1.45-mile (2.3 m) stretch of public walkways, sundecks, and gardens built atop an elevated rail bed that runs along Manhattan's west side. Cutting through the Chelsea gallery district and offering views of Midtown skyscrapers on one side and the Hudson River on the other, the park is open year-round (and fully accessible by wheelchair) and, on warm days, is often packed with locals and tourists alike. A vestige of the neighborhood's industrial past, the elevated railway was built in the 1930s, replacing the street-level freight trains that carried goods from the Meatpacking District to the warehouses and docks farther north. After falling into disuse in the 1980s, the structure was threatened with demolition (most of the original 13 mi/20.9 km of track were demolished in the 1960s). In response, a local community-based organization, Friends of the High Line, launched a campaign for the structure's preservation.

Together with the city of New York, Friends of the High Line began long-term planning for a new public park atop the structure. The first segment of The High Line was opened to the public in 2009, with an additional northern stretch opening in June 2011. Since then, The High Line has become a focal point of the neighborhood, with a crop of trendy hotels, great restaurants, and shops opening along its route, in addition to ongoing public art projects sponsored by Friends of the High Line.

Whitney Museum of American Art

Whitney Museum of American Art (99 Gansevoort St., 212/570-3600, www.whitney. org, Sun.-Mon. and Wed.-Thurs. 10:30am-6pm, Fri.-Sat. 10:30am-10pm, adults $25, seniors and students $18, children under 18 free) opened in its new location in the Meatpacking District in 2015, a much anticipated architectural and artistic development. The new space is exceptionally spacious, the perfect setting for many of the museum's large-scale contemporary artwork, and is especially attractive because of its location on The High Line (it's at the park's southern entrance) and its proximity to a number of popular shops and restaurants in this vibrant neighborhood. The museum continues to host its always-provocative Biennial, which seems to specialize in controversial paintings and multimedia installations.

MIDTOWN AND TIMES SQUARE

Rush, rush, rush. Sometimes all the people in the world seem to be elbowing through Midtown. Most of Manhattan's skyscrapers are here, along with famous department stores and restaurants, and many visitor attractions. Fifth Avenue is the heart of Midtown, almost entirely lined with shops and office buildings. Shops in the upper 30s and lower 40s tend to be tourist traps selling discounted electronic gadgetry and souvenirs; in the upper 40s and 50s stand upscale boutiques and famous department stores. To see Midtown at its frenzied best, come on a weekday. Most visitor attractions are also open on weekends. With the exception of Times Square and the Theater District, much of Midtown closes after business hours.

Morgan Library

Morgan Library (225 Madison Ave., at 36th St., 212/685-0008, www.themorgan.org, Tues.-Thurs. 10:30am-5pm, Fri. 10:30am-9pm, Sat. 10am-6pm, Sun. 11am-6pm, adults $22, seniors $14, students and children 13-16 $13,

the High Line

Midtown and Times Square

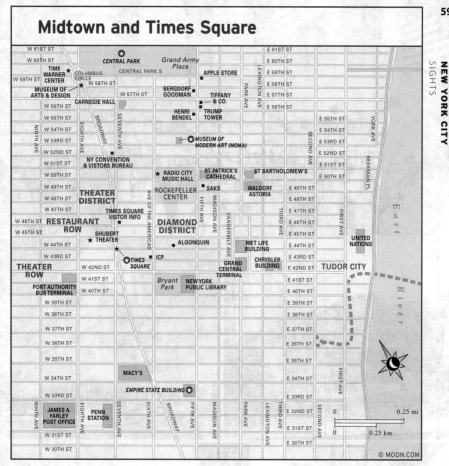

© MOON.COM

children 12 and under free, free Fri. 7pm-9pm), built between 1902 and 1906, began its life as the personal library of financier Pierpont Morgan, who spent a portion of his great fortune on illuminated, literary, and historical manuscripts, early printed books, as well as some drawings and prints. Designed by famed architectural team McKim, Mead, & White, the Italian Renaissance-style palazzo is considered among their finest work. In 1924, Morgan's son decided the collection was too fine and too important to remain restricted solely to the family's enjoyment, and it was opened as a public institution.

Over the years, Morgan Library has

expanded its physical structure, incorporating Morgan's brownstone residence and its collections. Its exhibits are always significant and ambitious, with recent shows featuring original manuscripts and ephemera of authors like Mark Twain, Edgar Allan Poe, and Charles Dickens.

Grand Central Terminal

Every day, roughly 750,000 people pass through **Grand Central Terminal** (42nd St., between Vanderbilt and Lexington Aves., www.grandcentral.com), home to the city's busiest subway station (seven lines pass through underground) and Metro-North

commuter trains. Completed in 1913 under the auspices of transportation magnate Cornelius Vanderbilt, the station is full of classical grandeur. The beaux arts facade on 42nd Street looks more like the entrance to a Roman coliseum than a rail station, with its pair of Corinthian columns supporting sculptures of Hercules, Minerva, and Mercury, the Roman god of speed and commerce. With its towering ceilings and famous four-sided Tiffany clock (rumored to be worth $10-20 million) at the center, the station's Main Concourse is one of the most spectacular public spaces in the world. It's almost always alive with activity—especially during rush hour, when commuters make a dash to catch the train. Above it all, the cerulean blue ceiling depicts zodiac constellations with fiber-optic lights that really twinkle.

Toward the end of the 20th century, Grand Central was considered an eyesore; years of wear and neglect had slowly robbed it of its splendor and significance. A decade of renovations brought the station back to its former glory—perhaps even surpassing it. Since the restoration was completed in 1998, Grand Central has become a destination unto itself, with an impressive food hall and a range of shops along the lower concourse. Many locals stop in, even if they aren't commuting, to eat at beloved **Grand Central Oyster Bar,** or pick up staples, flowers, or snacks at the Terminal's market.

To get the best view of Grand Central's busy lobby, ascend to the mezzanines on either the east or west side of the lobby. You can't loiter here, but you can stand here long enough to take in the scene and snap a photo.

The Chrysler Building

What the Empire State Building has in stature, the **Chrysler Building** (42nd St. and Lexington Ave., 212/682-3070), the quintessential art deco skyscraper, achieves in style. At the time of its construction, between 1928

and 1930, another building at 40 Wall Street was vying for the title of tallest in the city. To keep his competitors guessing, the building's architect, William Van Alen, hid his final plans for the top of the structure, which included a seven-story spire. At the last minute, workers raised the spire right through what spectators had assumed was the roof and riveted it into place. It was the first man-made structure to reach over 1,000 feet (300 m). However, its run at the top lasted only for about 40 days: When the Empire State Building was completed, it usurped Chrysler's title as the highest building in the world.

From the outside, the 1,046-foot (320 m) granite-and-glass structure, with its protruding gargoyles (designed to resemble the hood ornaments of Plymouth cars), is topped by distinctive crown ornamentation of stainless-steel cladding. The luxurious lobby (once a car showroom) is the only interior space open to the public, giving visitors a chance to peek past the security gates at the marble walls, the polished nickel chrome decorations that embellish the stairway railings, the *très* deco light fixtures, and the mural by Edward Trumbull, which depicts early-20th-century technological triumphs.

United Nations

In **United Nations Plaza** (extending from 42nd to 48th Sts. and from 1st Ave. to FDR Dr.) flags of 193 member states—each posted at equal height—flap in the breeze. Legally, the United Nations isn't part of New York at all, but is international territory. The United Nations has its own post office, postage stamps, and uniformed security force.

Reflecting the peace and serenity its organization seeks to promote, the U.N. headquarters stands on the banks of the East River, on a 17-acre plot donated by John D. Rockefeller in the mid-20th century. Built between 1950 and 1952, the complex is comprised of four structures: the 550-foot (170 m) glass Secretariat Building, the domed General Assembly, the Conference Building, and Dag Hammarskjöld

1: Grand Central Terminal 2: the Whitney Museum 3: view of Columbus Circle from the Time Warner Center 4: Times Square

Take Me Out to the Ball Game

Many New Yorkers like to believe that baseball was born right here. It's hard to say for certain, but what we do know is that a group of New York City men founded the New York Knickerbocker Baseball Club in 1845 and introduced new rules that distinguished what became American baseball from its antecedents, cricket and rounder.

Today, baseball remains a beloved pastime all around the state, from **Cooperstown,** home to the **National Baseball Hall of Fame and Museum** (page 258), to **New York City,** where not one, but two, teams compete for hometown favorite. The **Yankees** call the Bronx home, while the **Mets** rule the roost in Queens. Each year, the teams' rivalry comes to a head during the **Subway Series,** when fans shuttle between the two stadiums to witness the showdown.

Want to get in on the game? Here's what you need to know:

- **Yankees** (Yankee Stadium, One East 161st Street, Bronx, NY 10451, www.mlb.com/yankees/ballpark/information): Take the subway (4 train or D train) to 161st Street station. Travel time from Midtown Manhattan is 20-25 minutes.

- **Mets** (Citi Field, 41 Seaver Way, Flushing, NY 11368, www.mlb.com/mets/ballpark/information): Take the subway (7 train) to Mets-Willets Point station. Travel time from Midtown Manhattan is 20-30 minutes.

Many cities throughout the state have Minor League Baseball teams, too, including Rochester and Syracuse.

Library. An ambitious $2.15 billion renovation was completed in late 2015.

Outdoors, visitors can enjoy the United Nations sculpture garden, the highlight of which is the Japanese peace bell, rung at the start of each new session in September. If you want to look inside the United Nations, take the 45-minute **tour** (www.visit.un.org, adults $22, seniors and students $15, children 5-12 $12, children under 5 not allowed on tour), led by an international team of guides. A highlight is the General Assembly Hall, an 1,800-capacity room designed by 11 architects, where member nations meet. Along the way are donated objects and artwork from around the world, as well as displays that explain and document some of the missions of the United Nations.

★ **Times Square**

Times Square is best visited after sundown, when inventive street performers come out in droves and neon signs light up. By night, streets

are ablaze with huge panels of red, green, yellow, blue, and white. Not really a square at all, but rather two elongated triangles, it encompasses the intersection of Broadway and 7th Avenue between 42nd and 48th Streets.

Simultaneously New York's glitziest and seediest symbol, Times Square became the theater district in the 1910s and home to a thriving sex industry in 1960s. A cleanup effort in the 1990s made it far more tourist-friendly, with places like the Hard Rock Café and the Disney Store moving in. Today, there's even free wireless Internet and public restrooms at **Times Square Museum and Visitors' Center** (1560 Broadway, entrance on 7th Ave. between 46th and 47th Sts., 212/452-5283, www.timessquarenyc.org, daily 8am-8pm). Police and private security officers patrol the streets 24 hours a day.

An estimated one million revelers gather for the **New Year's Eve celebration** here, at which the famous crystal-covered ball drops from the flagpole at One Times Square. If you're considering rockin' with the crowds, be prepared: People start grabbing the best spots in the early afternoon, and, around 3pm, police start closing streets to traffic. There are no public restrooms available during the event, and no bags are allowed past the barricades.

Theater District

Most Broadway theaters are not on Broadway at all, but on side streets surrounding Times Square. The area is home to 41 legitimate theaters, 25 of which are city landmarks. West 44th and 45th Streets between 7th and 8th Avenues are especially rich blocks; here, you'll find the **Shubert, Helen Hayes, Booth, Majestic,** and **Minskoff** theaters, among others.

Next to the Shubert, connecting 44th and 45th Streets, is **Shubert Alley,** where unemployed performers once waited, hoping for a part. Today, a souvenir shop selling theater memorabilia is located here.

West 42nd Street

During the past 20 years, big changes have come to West 42nd Street, especially between 7th and 8th Avenues. For years a center for porn, this most-historic of theatrical streets has regained some of its former glory.

Most of the block's historic theaters have been restored. The Victory, opened by Oscar Hammerstein in 1900, is now **The New Victory** (209 W. 42nd St., 646/223-3010, www.newvictory.org), specializing in programming for young people. **The New Amsterdam** (214 W. 42nd St., www.newamsterdamtheatre.com), once home to the Ziegfeld Follies, is now owned by Disney. Movies and plays are on its docket.

Also on 42nd Street is **Madame Tussaud's New York** (234 W. 42nd St., 212/512-9600, www.madametussauds.com/new-york, Sun.-Thurs. 10am-8pm, Fri.-Sat. 10am-10pm, $29.95 and up if bought online, tickets bought on-site are more expensive), where you'll find waxy renditions of famous New Yorkers, past and present.

Intrepid Sea, Air, and Space Museum Complex

The Intrepid (W. 46th St., at 12th Ave., 212/245-0072, www.intrepidmuseum.org, spring and summer Mon.-Fri. 10am-5pm, Sat. 10am-6pm, winter daily 10am-5pm, adults $33, seniors and college students $31, children 5-12 $24, children 4 and under free), docked at Pier 86, is a former World War II aircraft carrier now serving as a military history museum housing lots of hands-on exhibits, most designed to appeal to kids. Decks feature small aircraft and space capsules. Permanent exhibits explore mysteries of satellite communication and ship design; special exhibits focus on such subjects as women pilots and Charles Lindbergh. Highlights are the Concorde and space shuttle *Enterprise.*

TOP EXPERIENCE

★ Empire State Building

One of the world's most famous buildings and an art deco landmark, the **Empire State Building** (350 5th Ave., at 34th St., 212/736-3100, www.esbnyc.com, daily 8am-2am, last elevator up at 1:15am, adults starting at $38, seniors $36, children 6-12 $32) was built during the Depression in an astonishing 14 months, at the rate of four stories a week. For years, it stood as the world's tallest building. That's no longer true, yet the Empire State remains the quintessential skyscraper and its stats remain impressive: 102 floors, 73 elevators, 6,500 windows, thousands of miles of telephone wire, and 1,860 steps. Visits to the two observation decks, one on the 86th floor, the other on the 102nd (additional fee), are so popular the lines are legendary, though an ultrapricey express ticket offers front-of-line access if time is tight. Another way to decrease the wait is to buy tickets online before your visit.

In 1933, Irma Eberhardt became the first person to commit suicide by jumping off the Empire State. That same year, the original classic film *King Kong* was made, showing a giant ape climbing the skyscraper. In 1945, a B-25 bomber struck the building's 79th floor, killing 14 people. And in 1986, two parachutists jumped from the 86th floor, but with a happier ending: They landed safely on 5th Avenue. Also, in case you're wondering, pennies thrown off the Empire State *cannot* kill pedestrians below, but they can cause severe burns.

New York Public Library

The lavish, 1911 beaux arts **New York Public Library—Stephen A. Schwarzman Building** (476 5th Ave., between 40th and 42nd Sts., 917/275-6975, www.nypl.org, Mon. and Thurs.-Sat. 10am-6pm, Tues.-Wed. 10am-8pm, Sun. 1pm-5pm), designed by Carrere and Hastings, houses one of the world's top five research libraries. The library's collection of over 15 million items—books, maps, and all manner of historical ephemera in more than 1,200 languages and dialects—occupies some 88 miles (142 km) of shelves above ground and 84 miles (135 km) below.

The library's grand entrance lobby, Astor Hall, is flanked by sweeping staircases; just beyond lies **Gottesman Hall,** where exhibits on subjects as diverse as Charles Dickens, New York City's culinary history, and Beat poets have been displayed. The 3rd floor is home to the library's **Main Reading Room,** big as a football field and sumptuous as the lobby of a luxury hotel. Books are ordered via a pneumatic tube system that sucks call slips down into the bowels of the stacks. It was in the library's Map Room that the U.S. Army planned the invasion of North Africa during World War II, and in the library's Science and Technology Room that Chester Carlson invented Xerox and Edwin Land invented the Polaroid camera.

The stone lions lounging outside the library were originally named "Leo Astor" and "Leo Lenox," after the library's founders, John Jacob Astor and James Lenox. In the 1930s, Mayor La Guardia dubbed the felines "Patience" and "Fortitude"—qualities he felt New York would need to survive the Depression.

Building tours (Mon.-Sat. 11am and 2pm, Sun. 2pm) and docent-led tours of **Gottesman Hall exhibits** (Mon.-Sat. 12:30pm and 2:30pm, Sun. 3:30pm) are free, and no reservations are needed. Meet at the main information desk in the lobby.

Bryant Park

Just behind the library is **Bryant Park** (www.bryantpark.org), filled with pretty flower beds, gravel paths, a stylish indoor-outdoor restaurant, and lots of benches that are usually packed with office workers at lunchtime. There's a reading room and a lovely carousel for children, as well as a variety of recreational games in spring, summer, and fall, including chess and table tennis.

The park is named after poet and journalist William Cullen Bryant, a great proponent of parks and one of the people most responsible for the creation of Central Park. Outdoor movies in the summer, free evening open-air concerts in spring and fall, and a scenic winter market featuring holiday-shopping stalls and a free ice-skating rink make this a nice four-season park.

Diamond District

Continuing north, you'll come to the **Diamond District** (W. 47th St. between 5th and 6th Aves.), where an estimated $400 million in gems are exchanged daily. Many of the dealers and cutters of the 2,500 companies crammed into this block are Hasidic Jews, identifiable by their long beards, earlocks, and black frock coats. As has long been their tradition, the Hasidim often negotiate their biggest deals in back rooms or on the sidewalk.

TOP EXPERIENCE

Rockefeller Center

The area between 48th and 51st Streets and 5th and 6th Avenues was once a notorious red-light district. Today, it's occupied

---

1: Bryant Park 2: the fountain at Rockefeller Center 3: Central Park 4: the Empire State Building

by **Rockefeller Center,** New York's most famous city within a city. Built by John D. Rockefeller during the height of the Depression, the magnificent art deco complex is comprised of 19 buildings, connected by plazas and underground passageways.

At the heart of the complex is the sunken **Lower Plaza,** home to an outdoor restaurant in summer, an ice-skating rink in winter, great people-watching year-round, and a gilded Prometheus watching over it all. At Christmastime, the famous Rockefeller tree is erected directly behind him.

NBC Studios (49th St. between 5th and 6th Aves., 212/664-3700, www.thetouratnbcstudios.com) are in Top of the Rock at 30 Rockefeller Plaza, where you can peer into the *Today* show studio window or take a tour. One-hour tours leave from **The NBC Experience Store** (every 15 minutes Mon.-Sat. 8:30am-5:30pm, Sun. 9:30am-4:30pm, adults $33, seniors and children 6-12 $29, children under 6 not permitted, reservations recommended). **Top of the Rock Observation Deck** (212/698-2000, www.topoftherocknyc.com, daily 8am-midnight, $32-38) on the 70th floor has the advantage of seeing the Empire State building.

Radio City Music Hall

Despite, or perhaps because of, its dated feel, **Radio City Music Hall** (6th Ave. and 50th St., www.radiocity.com) has been bringing families back for generations. An over-the-top creation with a stage as wide as a city block, it's the world's largest indoor theater.

Though the Music Hall has hosted many unusual performers over the years—including elephants and horses—its most famous are the Rockettes. Chorus girls—all between 5 feet 4 inches (163 cm) and 5 feet 7 inches (170 cm) in height—once appeared nightly. Now, the Rockettes kick and strut their stuff only during the Music Hall's two-month-long annual Christmas show.

Backstage tours (6th Ave. and 50th St., 212/247-4777, www.radiocity.com, daily 9:30am-5pm, adults $31, seniors and children under 12 $27) are offered and last 75 minutes.

★ The Museum of Modern Art (MoMA)

Holding the largest collection of modern art in the world, **MoMA** (11 W. 53rd St., between 5th and 6th Aves., 212/708-9400, www.moma.org, daily 10am-5:30pm, Fri. open until 9pm, adults $25, seniors $18, students $14, children 16 and under free) has a cool, elegant exterior that belies the many vibrant works on display inside. Founded during the Great Depression in 1929, the museum moved to this location on 53rd Street in 1939. The current 1939 building has gone through many alterations. The most recent one, completed in 2019, resulted in a massive expansion of square footage, allowing curators to completely reconceptualize how they show the museum's rich collections. The glass-sided walkways on the upper floors offer dramatic, sometimes vertigo-inducing views of the art and galleries below. In addition to the galleries, the museum has a film screening venue, a children's center, a hands-on creativity lab, and a fine-dining restaurant, The Modern.

The museum's collection includes over 200,000 paintings, sculptures, drawings, prints, photographs, and architectural models, and some 22,000 films, videos, and media works. Classic crowd-pleasers, such as Van Gogh's *Starry Night,* Rousseau's *The Sleeping Gypsy,* Monet's *Water Lilies,* and Picasso's *Les Demoiselles d'Avignon, are still on view, but the 2019 renovation brought with it the opportunity to introduce visitors to a much wider range of work and artists.*

Fifth Avenue

St. Patrick's Cathedral (5th Ave. between 50th and 51st Sts.) is perhaps the most iconic Roman Catholic cathedral in the United States, and sits directly across from Rockefeller Center. Designed by James Renwick, this elaborate Gothic creation with its soaring towers and lovely rose window took 21 years to build, replacing the old St. Pat's in Little Italy in 1879. Its grandeur attests to the success of New York's Irish Catholics who, at that time, were largely shunned by the city's predominantly Protestant upper classes.

Kitty-corner to St. Pat's, at the corner of 53rd Street, is another famous New York house of worship, **St. Thomas,** an Episcopal church completed in 1914. A French Gothic gem known for its lovely stonework and stained glass, the church has long been a favorite site for society weddings.

★ CENTRAL PARK

Between the Upper East and the Upper West Sides lies that most glorious of New York spaces: **Central Park** (between 5th and 8th Aves., 59th to 110th Sts., 212/310-6600, www.centralparknyc.org). Without this vast, rolling green estate—the lungs of the city—life in New York would probably become unbearable. Central Park is where New Yorkers go to escape cramped apartments, roaring traffic, and the cityscape of concrete and steel that makes one forget Manhattan is an island.

The Central Park, as it was once known, was the brainchild of poet-turned-newspaper editor William Cullen Bryant. Worried that the city was being smothered by block after block of relentless building, Bryant first called for the park's creation in the July 3, 1844, edition of his *Evening Post.* Landscape architect Andrew Jackson Downing and a number of politicians soon added their voices to Bryant's plea. Together, they hammered away at city government for 12 years until finally, in 1856, the city bought most of the land now comprising the park for five million dollars.

Frederick Law Olmsted and Calvert Vaux were the visionary landscape architects who turned Bryant's Central Park dream into reality. As Olmsted saw it, the park had two functions. One was to provide a place for the contemplation of nature. The other was to create a social tableau where the haves and have-nots could pass each other every day, providing an opportunity for the poor to become inspired by the rich.

The park took 20 years to complete. By the time it was finished, workers had shifted 10 million cartloads of dirt, imported a

Central Park

half-million cubic yards of topsoil, and planted 4-5 million trees. Central Park was an immediate success that led to a park movement across the United States and the world.

Central Park is 2.5 miles (4 km) long and 0.5 mile (.8 km) wide, covers 843 acres, and hosts 15-20 million visitors annually. Walking through it is like walking through a gigantic carnival site. You'll see scantily clad New Yorkers going running, biking, or inline skating; oblivious lovers; stroller-pushing nannies; students lounging with textbooks; cashmere-clad matrons; professional dog-walkers; and musicians playing everything from concertos to rap. Every size, shape, color, and make of humanity is here.

Generally speaking, the park is safe, but it's always advisable to stick to well-populated areas, especially during the week, when fewer people use the park. Avoid the park at night.

59th Street to 65th Street

Central Park South (59th St.) on the Plaza's north side is a gathering place for horse-drawn carriages and, farther west on 59th Street, pedicabs. For a **carriage ride,** simply walk along 59th Street and contract a carriage directly. Prices start around $57 for a 15-minute ride. **Central Park Tours** (347/746-8687, www.centralparktours.net) offers pedicab 50-minute and 2-hour tours; prices start at $47.

An excellent way to tour the park is by bike. Several vendors can be found on the west side of 59th Street, at the park's entrance off Columbus Circle. If you're keen to try a **Citi Bike** (www.citibikenyc.com), the city's bike share program launched in 2013, there are several docking stations on the park's periphery, including 59th Street, where you can purchase a 24-hour or 3-day pass.

If you're on foot, enter Central Park at 5th Avenue and 64th Street and you'll soon come to **Central Park Zoo** (830 5th Ave., 212/439-6500, www.centralparkzoo.com, early Apr.-early Nov. Mon.-Fri. 10am-5pm, Sat.-Sun. 10am-4:30pm, early Nov.-early Apr. daily 10am-4:30pm, adults $19.95, seniors $16.95,

children 3-12 $14.95). The small zoo groups its animals by climatic zones; polar bears cavort and swim, while penguins promenade in a snowy clime behind thick underwater viewing glass. An excellent open-air rain forest environment with netted walkways and tucked-away reptile tanks for various creepy crawlies tops the list. Crowds gather to watch the staff feed the sea lions, while the behavior presentation mimics *Madagascar* movie moments. At the zoo's northeast end is Delacorte Clock, where every half hour a parade of bronze animals marches around playing nursery tunes.

Nearby is **Wollman Rink** (212/439-6900, www.wollmanskatingrink.com, Mon.-Tues. 10am-2:30pm, Wed.-Thurs. 10am-10pm, Fri.-Sat. 10am-11pm, Sun. 10am-9pm, prices vary by day), packed in winter with exuberant ice-skaters.

North of the rink is the octagonal **Chess and Checkers House,** complete with 24 concrete game boards outside and 10 inside. Visitors can borrow pieces or bring their own and play for free.

The nearby **Dairy** houses a **Visitor Center and Gift Shop** (212/794-6564, daily 10am-5pm). Never a working dairy, the Victorian cottage was built to provide fresh milk and snacks for children and their caregivers visiting the park.

West of the Dairy is the 1908 **Carousel** (mid-park at 64th St., Apr.-Oct. daily 10am-6pm, call for hours in Nov.-Mar., $3.25), where 57 carved horses go round. Other amusement rides are here as well.

The sunken transverse road running from East 65th Street to West 66th Street is one of four such roads in the park (others are at 79th, 85th, and 97th Sts.). These roads were one of Olmsted's most brilliant innovations. Dynamited out of bedrock, they allow cars and buses to pass below the level of the park, while pedestrians pass on bridges above.

65th Street to 72nd Street

Heading a bit farther north and west, you'll come to **Sheep Meadow,** a huge expanse of lawn covered with thousands of semi-clad sun worshippers in warm weather. Real sheep grazed here until 1934. By then, the sheep were so inbred that many were malformed.

East of Sheep Meadow is **The Mall,** a promenade lined with trees and busts of famous men. This quarter-mile avenue was once a parade ground for the elite, who cruised up and down in the late afternoons, courting and showing off their fancy carriages. Today, The Mall is frequented by inline skaters, sidewalk artists, skateboarders trying to perfect their tricks, couples taking advantage of the romantic atmosphere to sit on the benches for heartfelt chats, and retirees working on their *New York Times* crosswords.

North of The Mall is the band shell at **Rumsey Playfield,** where a first-rate series of free outdoor concerts is presented every summer by **SummerStage** (212/360-1399, www.summerstage.org). Past performers have ranged from Patti LaBelle to Lila Downs to Youssou N'Dour.

72nd Street to 79th Street

Bethesda Terrace, just north of the band shell and the 72nd Street Transverse, is one of the park's grandest sights. The wide, brick-paved plaza centers on an ornate fountain; a semicircle of tiered steps cups the plaza's southern side. Lapping at the north end is **The Lake,** usually crowded with splish-splashing rowboats. These boats can be rented at the nearby **Loeb Boathouse** (212/517-2233, www.thecentralparkboathouse.com, daily 10am-dusk, $15 per hour, with a $20 cash deposit). You can also take a half-hour gondola ride here for $45.

West of Bethesda Terrace is **Strawberry Fields,** which Yoko Ono had landscaped into a Garden of Peace as a memorial to her husband, John Lennon, who was murdered outside The Dakota apartment building in 1980. Just inside the garden at 72nd Street is a circular marble mosaic spelling out the word *Imagine;* flowers brought by fans in tribute to Lennon often cover the mosaic, one of the park's most photographed landmarks.

East of Bethesda Terrace is **Conservatory Water,** aka the "model-boat pond." The pond is often dotted with miniature boats, most radio-controlled. During warm weather, model-boat regattas are held Saturday mornings. If you want to pilot a boat, you can rent one from **Sail the Park** (www.sailthepark. com, $11 for 30 minutes).

Two of the park's most famous statues are near Conservatory Water. *Alice in Wonderland,* by Jose de Creefts, perches

Bethesda Terrace in Central Park

on a mushroom to the north, while *Hans Christian Andersen,* by Georg Lober, sits with his *Ugly Duckling* to the west. Both statues are usually covered with adoring children.

West of the pond and north of The Lake is the 38-acre **Ramble,** a near-wild place crisscrossed with meandering paths. Far removed from city life, the Ramble is a favorite spot among bird-watchers; on a typical morning, about 15 kinds of warblers and 35 other species can be seen.

79th Street to 97th Street

North of the Ramble is the Gothic Revival **Belvedere Castle,** designed in 1858 by Calvert Vaux. Situated atop Vista Rock, one of the park's highest spots, the castle offers bird's-eye views of the Great Lawn and the Ramble. Downstairs is **Henry Luce Nature Observatory at Belvedere Castle** (midpark at 79th St., 212/772-0210, daily 10am-5pm, free).

Nearby are **Shakespeare Garden,** filled with plants and flowers mentioned in the playwright's work; **Swedish Cottage** (performance days, times, and prices vary), one of the last public marionette companies in the United States; and **Delacorte Theater,** where New York Public Theater has presented free **Shakespeare in the Park** performances (212/967-7555, www.shakespeareinthepark.org) each summer for more than 60 years. Two plays are usually featured, each running about a month. The free tickets for each day's show are handed out beginning at 6:15pm the same day; people start lining up in the early afternoon.

Abutting Delacorte Theater is the often dusty **Great Lawn.** Tens of thousands of New Yorkers spread out their blankets and picnic baskets on the lawn when the New York Philharmonic and the Metropolitan Opera Company perform here. The Lawn is often host to major personalities providing free concerts, lectures, or events. The Dalai Lama has spoken here several times and Simon and Garfunkel, Diana Ross, and Jon Bon Jovi have all played on the 55-acre lawn.

North of the Great Lawn is Central Park Reservoir, which holds about a billion gallons of water, most of which comes via aqueduct from the Catskills. Now known as **Jacqueline Onassis Reservoir** because the former first lady used to jog around its 1.58-mile (2.5 km) perimeter, it is one of the city's most popular jogging courses.

97th to 110th Street

As Frederick Law Olmsted originally intended, the northernmost section of Central Park, between 97th and 110th Streets, becomes more rugged and wild, filled with secret waterfalls and craggy cliffs. But at 105th Street near 5th Avenue is the lovely, formal **Conservatory Garden.** Actually three gardens in one, the Conservatory blooms from late spring through early fall. Its most popular spot is the Secret Garden, named after Frances Hodgson Burnett's classic children's book.

Just above the Conservatory is 11-acre **Harlem Meer.** Up until the mid-1990s, this lake—like much of the park above 97th Street—was avoided by New Yorkers fearful of crime. But since then, Central Park Conservancy has poured millions of dollars into the area, and it's been vastly improved. Harlem Meer is now stocked with some 50,000 bluegill, largemouth bass, and catfish, and is a favorite fishing ground for youngsters who can borrow free poles at **Charles A. Dana Discovery Center** (212/860-1370, daily 10am-5pm, free), which also houses natural history exhibits and hosts hands-on science programs.

UPPER EAST SIDE

Since the turn of the 20th century, the Upper East Side has been associated with wealth. Everyone from Andrew Carnegie to Gloria Vanderbilt has resided in this exclusive neighborhood, which is filled with brownstones and penthouses. In the early 1900s, the stretch of 5th Avenue facing Central Park became known as "Millionaire's Row." Many of these mansions have since been converted into museums and cultural institutions.

One particularly notable Upper East Side home is **Gracie Mansion** (Carl Schurz Park, east end of 88th St., 212/570-4773, www.graciemansion.org), an 18th-century federal-style manor house that has been the New York City mayor's official residence since 1942. Tours require reservations, but just walking the grounds, which overlook the Hell Gate Strait, is also pleasant.

But the Upper East Side is not only about the wealthy. It's also about more ordinary folk, who, as elsewhere in Manhattan, settled closer to the river. Stretching roughly from 59th Street to 100th Street and 5th Avenue to the East River, the long residential blocks are pleasant for strolling. Most of the sights and shops are along the north-south avenues rather than the east-west side streets. Madison Avenue is famed for its upscale shops, and 5th Avenue is dubbed "Museum Mile" for the 10 museums within its 82nd Street to 104th Street length.

The Frick Collection

The Frick Collection (1 E. 70th St., 212/288-0700, www.frick.org, Tues.-Sat. 10am-6pm, Sun. 11am-5pm, adults $22, seniors $17, students $12, children under 10 not admitted), like so many other New York cultural institutions, owes its creation to a wealthy robber baron hoping to whitewash questionable behavior with a hefty endowment to the arts. In this case, it was steel tycoon Henry Clay Frick, who broke up strikes with Pinkerton guards and narrowly avoided several assassination attempts. Upon Frick's demise (of natural causes) in 1919, a $15 million endowment and his posh 5th Avenue town house were donated to establish a museum displaying the primarily European artwork and furnishings he spent 40 years collecting; since then, the collection has grown to over 1,100 works, comprising one of the world's greatest private museums.

One of the Frick's most glorious rooms is West Gallery, a naturally lit hall that houses landscapes by Constable, Turner, and Corot, as well as portraits by Rembrandt, El Greco, and Velázquez. It is also the home of *Mistress and Maid,* one of three works by Vermeer in the collection. The indoor Garden Court, with a Romanesque fountain at its center, invites quiet reflection. Amid the palm fronds and stone frogs are Whistler's *Symphony in Grey and Green: The Ocean* and Corot's *The Boatman of Mortefontaine.*

★ The Metropolitan Museum of Art

One of the world's greatest museums is **The Metropolitan Museum of Art** (1000 5th Ave., 212/535-7710, www.metmuseum.org, Sun.-Thurs. 10am-5:30pm, Fri.-Sat. 10am-9pm, recommended admission adults $25, seniors $17, students $12, children under 12 free), on the east side of Central Park at 5th Avenue and 82nd Street. Housed behind an imposing beaux arts facade designed by Robert Morris Hunt, the main part of the museum spreads out over about 1.5 million square feet, holding nearly three million works of art in collections of everything from Egyptian sarcophagi to modern American paintings.

Directly up the staircase from the Great Hall is one of the Met's most stunning collections, **European paintings,** filling some 20-odd galleries. One room is filled with Rembrandts only; others house Vermeer, Van Dyck, Breughel, Rubens, Botticelli, El Greco, and Goya . . . and that's just for starters.

To the right of the Great Hall is the museum's famed **Egyptian collection,** displaying items as old as 4,000 years. The Met houses the largest collection of Egyptian art outside Egypt.

Three sides of the Met's original building are flanked by modern glass wings. At the back is the Robert Lehman Collection, housing an impressive collection of Old Masters and 19th-century French painters. On the south side are the Rockefeller and Acheson Wings. The Lila Acheson Wing is devoted to 20th-century art; on its roof is a sculpture garden with great views of Central Park.

On the Met's north side are the Sackler and

Upper East Side

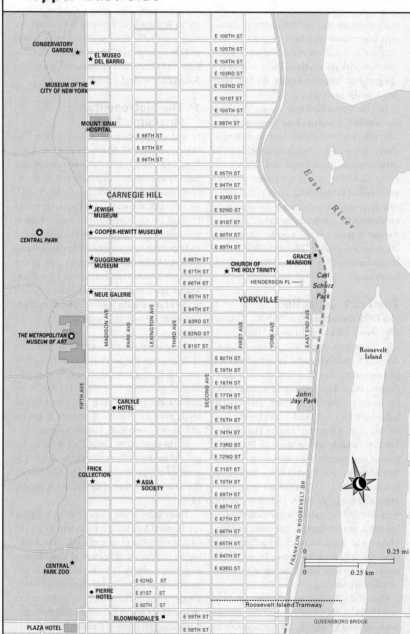

CONSERVATORY GARDEN ★

★ EL MUSEO DEL BARRIO

MUSEUM OF THE ★
CITY OF NEW YORK

MOUNT SINAI HOSPITAL

E 106TH ST
E 105TH ST
E 104TH ST
E 103RD ST
E 102ND ST
E 101ST ST
E 100TH ST
E 99TH ST
E 98TH ST
E 97TH ST
E 96TH ST

E 95TH ST
E 94TH ST

CARNEGIE HILL

★ JEWISH MUSEUM

★ COOPER-HEWITT MUSEUM

○ CENTRAL PARK

★ GUGGENHEIM MUSEUM

★ NEUE GALERIE

E 93RD ST
E 92ND ST
E 91ST ST
E 90TH ST
E 89TH ST
E 88TH ST
E 87TH ST
E 86TH ST
E 85TH ST

East River

GRACIE MANSION ■

Carl Schurz Park

CHURCH OF ★ THE HOLY TRINITY

HENDERSON PL

YORKVILLE

THE METROPOLITAN ○
MUSEUM OF ART

MADISON AVE
PARK AVE
LEXINGTON AVE
THIRD AVE
FIFTH AVE
SECOND AVE
FIRST AVE
YORK AVE
EAST END AVE

E 84TH ST
E 83RD ST
E 82ND ST
E 81ST ST
E 80TH ST
E 79TH ST
E 78TH ST
E 77TH ST
E 76TH ST
E 75TH ST
E 74TH ST
E 73RD ST
E 72ND ST
E 71ST ST
E 70TH ST
E 69TH ST
E 68TH ST
E 67TH ST
E 66TH ST
E 65TH ST
E 64TH ST
E 63RD ST

Roosevelt Island

John Jay Park

● CARLYLE HOTEL

FRICK COLLECTION ★

★ ASIA SOCIETY

FRANKLIN D ROOSEVELT DR

CENTRAL PARK ZOO ★

● PIERRE HOTEL

E 62ND ST
E 61ST ST
E 60TH ST

Roosevelt Island Tramway

BLOOMINGDALE'S ■

E 59TH ST

QUEENSBORO BRIDGE

PLAZA HOTEL

E 58TH ST

0   0.25 mi

0   0.25 km

© MOON.COM

American Wings. The Sackler Wing houses 15th-century-BC Temple of Dendur, carved in faded hieroglyphics. The American Wing contains exhaustive galleries of decorative arts, and many fine paintings by the likes of Gilbert Stuart, Thomas Eakins, John Singer Sargent, and Mary Cassatt.

If possible, come on a weekday morning, or on a Friday or Saturday evening when the candlelit Great Hall Balcony Bar is open and a jazz or classical quintet performs.

In 2016, a new building, called Met Breuer, opened; its concentration is modern and contemporary art. A ticket to the main building is valid for three days and provides admission to the Breuer, as well as to The Cloisters, a Met outpost in upper Manhattan.

Neue Galerie

Nearby is **Neue Galerie** (1048 5th Ave., at 86th St., 212/628-6200, www.neuegalerie.org, Thurs.-Mon. 11am-6pm, adults $25, seniors $16, students $12, children under 12 not admitted), devoted solely to fine and decorative arts of Germany and Austria from the first half of the 20th century. Housed in a renovated beaux arts mansion, the museum holds a large permanent collection of works by Gustav Klimt and Egon Schiele, a bookstore, design shop, and the smart Cafe Sabarsky, where you can indulge in Viennese coffee and a piece of Sacher torte.

Guggenheim Museum

Guggenheim Museum (1071 5th Ave., 212/423-3500, www.guggenheim.org, Sun.-Wed. and Fri. 10am-5:30pm, Sat. 10am-8pm, adults $25, seniors and students $18, children 12 and under free) was the final masterpiece of architect Frank Lloyd Wright, and the building makes as strong an impression as any of the artwork it houses. Its smooth plastered-concrete exterior has been compared to everything from a nautilus shell to a toilet bowl, but there's little doubt that the daring spiral design interrupted Manhattan's rectangular uniformity and has reshaped perceptions of art and architecture.

Designed to house Solomon R. Guggenheim's collection of nonobjective painting, the building was completed six months after Wright's death in 1959. The Guggenheim was the brainchild of mining magnate Solomon Guggenheim and Baroness Hilla Rebay von Ehrenwiesen, who dreamed of a new kind of museum that would suit the changing face of art. The collection began with works of 19th-century masters such as Cézanne and Van Gogh, but it is 20th-century artists like Marc Chagall, Paul Klee, Pablo Picasso, and Wassily Kandinsky for whom the Guggenheim is known. Today, the museum also champions contemporary artists, including Matthew Barney and Julie Mehretu.

Unlike many other New York museums, the Guggenheim does not overwhelm with the volume of its collections. A curved and continuous ramp connects a series of rooms that display works in the spare, minimalist way you would expect in a gallery. Several times a year, the entire museum is given over to an exhibition that surveys the work of single artists. In 2011, for example, the museum hung the entire collected work of contemporary artist Maurizio Cattelan from the ceiling of the central atrium.

Cooper-Hewitt National Design Museum

A branch of the Smithsonian Institution dedicated to design and decorative arts, **Cooper-Hewitt** (2 E. 91st St., 212/849-8400, www.cooperhewitt.org, Sun.-Fri. 10am-6pm, Sat. 10am-9pm, adults $18, seniors $12, students $9, children under 18 free, tickets cheaper if purchased online in advance) focuses on textiles, metalwork, wallpaper, ceramics, furniture, and architectural design. But half the story is the building itself; the museum occupies a 64-room mansion built by industrialist Andrew Carnegie.

The Jewish Museum

Housed in a magnificent French Gothic mansion once belonging to businessman Felix Warburg, **The Jewish Museum** (1109 5th

Ave., at 92nd St., 212/423-3200, www.the-jewishmuseum.org, Sat.-Tues. 11am-5:45pm, Thurs. 11am-8pm, Fri. 11am-4pm, adults $18, seniors $12, students $8, children under 18 free, free on Sat.) is the nation's largest Jewish culture museum. Changing, top-notch exhibits by famed Jewish artists such as Marc Chagall, as well as an outstanding permanent collection of ceremonial objects and cultural artifacts, are spread over three floors and a basement.

Museum of the City of New York

The renovated, neo-Georgian building on 5th Avenue between 103rd and 104th Streets houses the one-of-a-kind **Museum of the City of New York** (1220 5th Ave., 212/534-1672, www.mcny.org, daily 10am-6pm, suggested donation adults $20, seniors and students $14, children under 19 free). As its name suggests, the museum features "only in New York" exhibits, on topics both historical (Activist New York and The Gilded City: Beaux-Arts New York) and contemporary (Rising Waters: Photographs of Hurricane Sandy and From Bicycle Advocacy to Citi Bike: A Recent History of Bicycling in NYC). A strong emphasis on activism has defined many recent exhibits.

El Museo del Barrio

Dedicated to the art and culture of Puerto Rico and Latin America, **El Museo del Barrio** (1230 5th Ave., 212/831-7272, www.elmuseo.org, Wed.-Sat. 11am-6pm, Sun. noon-5pm, adults $9, students and seniors $5, children under 12 free) presents both contemporary and historical exhibits. Just a few blocks from Spanish Harlem, also called El Barrio, the museum is deeply committed to the local community and has many family-friendly cultural events. Most of its exhibits are temporary; on permanent display is

---

1: The Metropolitan Museum of Art 2: the Metropolitan Opera House at the Lincoln Center

a superb collection of *santos de palo* (carved wooden saints).

One block north of El Museo del Barrio at 105th Street is Central Park's truly lovely **Conservatory Garden,** most easily entered from 5th Avenue.

Asia Society

First-rate temporary exhibits, concerts, films, and lectures on various aspects of Asian culture and history are always on the calendar at **Asia Society** (725 Park Ave., 212/288-6400, www.asiasociety.org, Tues.-Sun. 11am-6pm, adults $12, seniors $10, students $7, children under 16 free). The museum is noted for its extensive collection of both traditional and contemporary work by Asian and Asian American artists, as well as a growing repository of video and new media work.

UPPER WEST SIDE

The Upper West Side is a mix of ornate 19th-century landmarks, solid pre-WWII apartment buildings, well-worn tenements, and some outstanding cultural institutions. The neighborhood is also known for its feisty liberal politics and love of culture. The best streets for wandering are Broadway and Columbus Avenue, both lined with shops. Streets running from east to west tend to be quiet and primarily residential.

Lincoln Center

The famed **Lincoln Center for the Performing Arts** (212/546-2656, www.lincolncenter.org) is actually a complex of buildings running from 60th to 66th Streets along Broadway, Columbus, and Amsterdam Avenues. As the home of The New York City Ballet, School of American Ballet, The New York Philharmonic, The Metropolitan Opera, and a host of other organizations and institutions, including Juilliard School of Music and Jazz at Lincoln Center, it's little wonder the center presents about 3,000 performances each year.

The fulcrum of Lincoln Center is a wide marble plaza featuring a circular fountain.

The **Metropolitan Opera House,** on the plaza's west side, is the center's most ornate building, graced with sparkling multistoried windows, brilliant chandeliers, and two vivid murals by Marc Chagall. **The David H. Koch Theater** (formerly known as The New York State Theater), on the plaza's south side, is home to the New York City Ballet.

The center's renovation, a massive, six-year project completed in 2012, cost more than one billion dollars. It made an already vital institution even more inviting and dynamic, uniting West 65th Street between Broadway and Amsterdam Avenue with the surrounding cityscape. The David Rubenstein Atrium at Lincoln Center became a public community and cultural space offering free performances, shady seating with free wireless Internet, information kiosks, a café, and discount ticket services. The renovation also created welcoming outdoor spaces in and around the main plaza, where in warmer weather, locals and visitors enjoy sitting and reading or sunning.

American Folk Art Museum

The **American Folk Art Museum** (2 Lincoln Sq./Columbus Ave., at 66th St., 212/595-9533, www.folkartmuseum.org, Mon.-Thurs. 11:30am-7pm, Fri. noon-7:30pm, Sat. 11:30am-7pm, Sun. noon-6pm, free) sits just across from Lincoln Center and exhibits a wide range of folk art, including quilts, toys, weather vanes, paintings, sculpture, handmade furniture, and the like. Temporary exhibits often focus on the work of individual self-taught artists.

The Dakota

Impressive buildings stand sentinel along Central Park West (CPW), the extension of 8th Avenue that borders Central Park. Most famous among them is **The Dakota** (northwest corner of 72nd St. and Central Park West). Built in 1884, The Dakota was financed by Edward Clark, heir to the Singer Sewing Machine fortune. At that time, the building stood so far north of the rest of Manhattan that it was said to be as remote as Dakota.

Clark liked that idea, and had the architect add ears of corn and an Indian's head above the entrance.

The Dakota's roster of famous tenants is long and includes Lauren Bacall, Roberta Flack, José Ferrer, Rosemary Clooney, John Lennon (who was murdered outside The Dakota), Yoko Ono, Gilda Radner, and William Henry Pratt, aka Boris Karloff, among many others.

New-York Historical Society

The **New-York Historical Society** (170 Central Park West, 212/873-3400, www.ny-history.org, Tues.-Thurs. and Sat. 10am-6pm, Fri. 10am-8pm, Sun. 11am-5pm, adults $22, seniors $17, students $13, children 5-13 $6, children under 5 free), founded in 1806, was one of the country's first cultural institutions. Today, it boasts a 17,000-square-foot gallery space featuring temporary exhibits that focus on all aspects of the city's history, from immigrants to board games, and a children's "museum within a museum," with interactive exhibits.

American Museum of Natural History

One of the city's greatest museums is the sprawling **American Museum of Natural History** (Central Park West at 79th St., 212/769-5100, www.amnh.org, daily 10am-5:45pm, adults $23, seniors and students $18, children 2-12 $13, shows and special exhibits cost extra). Behind its stone facade, the vast museum explores the wonders of Earth—its life, geology, and surroundings. Founded in 1869, the museum originally consisted of a few hundred mounted birds and mammals, but it quickly outgrew its first home, steadily acquiring an astonishing collection of rare gems; cultural artifacts from Asia, Africa, and the Americas; and the largest collection of dinosaur fossils in the world.

Among the many marvels in the Hall of Saurischian Dinosaurs is the fossilized skeleton of a *Tyrannosaurus rex* with a 4-foot-long

Upper West Side

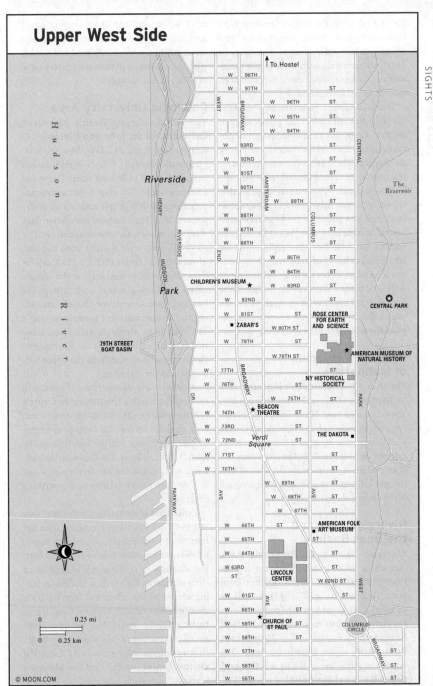

Hudson River

Riverside Park

Henry Hudson Parkway

79TH STREET BOAT BASIN

↑ To Hostel

WEST
BROADWAY
AMSTERDAM
COLUMBUS
CENTRAL

The Reservoir

W 98TH
W 97TH ST
W 96TH ST
W 95TH ST
W 94TH ST
W 93RD ST
W 92ND ST
W 91ST ST
W 90TH ST
W 89TH
W 88TH
W 87TH
W 86TH
W 85TH ST
W 84TH ST
★ CHILDREN'S MUSEUM W 83RD ST
W 82ND ST
CENTRAL PARK
W 81ST ST
■ ZABAR'S ROSE CENTER FOR EARTH AND SCIENCE
W 80TH ST
W 79TH ST
W 78TH ST
★ AMERICAN MUSEUM OF NATURAL HISTORY
W 77TH ST
W 76TH ST NY HISTORICAL SOCIETY
BROADWAY
W 75TH ST
★ BEACON THEATRE
W 74TH
W 73RD ST
Verdi Square
W 72ND ST ■ THE DAKOTA
W 71ST ST
W 70TH ST
W 69TH ST
W 68TH ST
W 67TH ST
W 66TH ST AMERICAN FOLK ART MUSEUM ■
W 65TH ST
W 64TH ST
W 63RD ST
LINCOLN CENTER
W 62ND ST
W 61ST ST
W 60TH ST
W 59TH ★ CHURCH OF ST PAUL ST
W 58TH ST
W 57TH ST
W 56TH ST
W 55TH ST
COLUMBUS CIRCLE
BROADWAY
PARK
WEST
AVE
DR
RIVERSIDE
END

0   0.25 mi
0   0.25 km

© MOON.COM

jaw (1.2 m), while the Hall of Ornithischian Dinosaurs features a stegosaurus and 65-million-year-old triceratops. The skeletons of extinct mammals, such as the woolly mammoth and saber-toothed tiger, have also been reconstructed and erected.

Inside Hayden Planetarium, an 87-foot (27 m) globe housed within the glass casing of the Rose Center for Earth and Space, you can take a three-dimensional tour of our galaxy and beyond. The museum's most-guarded attraction is the famed Star of India—a two-billion-year-old, 563-carat star sapphire that is part of the extensive gem and mineral collection; it was stolen in 1964 but recovered several months later. The Hall of Ocean Life, with its enormous fiberglass replica of a blue whale and exhibits of mammals from various continents, shows Earth's wildlife. Rooms dedicated to the cultures of the world add the human experience. With so much to see, it's impossible to fit it all into a single trip; explore the website to plan your visit.

Children's Museum of Manhattan

The always-busy **Children's Museum** (212 W. 83rd St., 212/721-1223, www.cmom.org, Tues.-Fri. and Sun. 10am-5pm, Sat. 10am-7pm, adults and children $15, seniors $12, free to children up to age one) is full of hands-on exhibits for kids ages 2-10. Here, children can draw and paint, learn crafts, drive an FDNY fire truck, listen to stories, or just explore one of the always-changing play areas.

Riverside Park and the Boat Basin

Riverside Drive abuts **Riverside Park** (stretching from 72nd to 153rd St. along the Hudson River), a long, narrow, sloping slice of green. Designed in the 1870s by Frederick Law Olmsted and Calvert Vaux, the park is a pleasant place with glorious views of the Hudson. Near the park's south end is **79th Street Boat Basin,** where houseboats dock. One important attraction in the park is **General Grant National Memorial** (Riverside Dr.,

at 122nd St., 212/666-1640, www.nps.gov/ gegr, free), a Greco-Roman-style mausoleum honoring the country's 18th president and his wife, Julia. Mosaics in the tomb portray some of Grant's historic battles.

Columbia University Area

The world's largest Gothic cathedral, **Cathedral of St. John the Divine** (1047 Amsterdam Ave., 212/316-7540, www.stjohndivine.org, daily 7:30am-6pm) is said to be large enough to fit both Notre Dame and Chartres inside. The church can accommodate some 10,000 people and is still under construction. The scheduled completion date, if enough money becomes available, will be 2050, 158 years after the first stone was laid. Three different **tours** (212/316-7540, call for days, times, and prices) meet at the visitors center and allow guests to walk through the bustling nave and serene chapels, including the unique **vertical tour,** involving a 124-foot (38 m) climb through spiral stone staircases to reach a view of the Morningside Heights neighborhood from the upper buttresses atop the cathedral.

Another lovely, historic house of worship in the neighborhood is **The Riverside Church** (490 Riverside Dr., 212/870-6700, www.trcnyc. org), modeled on the 13th-century cathedral in Chartres, France, and partially financed by John D. Rockefeller Jr. The Gothic-style landmark, with its soaring 24-story tower, is one of New York's most architecturally striking churches.

Columbia University (2960 Broadway, 212/854-1754, www.columbia.edu) stretches from West 114th Street to West 120th Street, between Amsterdam Avenue and Broadway. Founded as King's College in 1754, it educated some of the country's earliest leaders, including Alexander Hamilton and John Jay (first chief justice of the U.S. Supreme Court). Free **tours** (212/854-4900, Mon.-Fri. 1pm-2pm) are given year-round. Maps and other materials for self-guided tours are available in the **visitors center** (Room 213 of Low Memorial Library).

Outer Boroughs and Other Islands

Manhattan is the New York City you've come to know through movies, but there are four other boroughs and a few other islands that comprise New York. Exploring them is worth your time.

OUTER BOROUGHS

Brooklyn is replete with museums (Brooklyn Museum), music venues (Brooklyn Academy of Music, or BAM), parks, and, of course, Coney Island. Once considered New York's roughest, toughest borough, the rapidly gentrifying **Bronx** has Wave Hill, New York Botanical Garden, The Bronx Zoo, Bronx Museum of the Arts, Yankee Stadium, and Arthur Avenue Retail Market in Little Italy. **Queens** is New York's most culturally diverse borough, with the restaurants to prove it. And **Staten Island,** long neglected by visitors, is becoming a destination in its own right, with the massive Freshkills Park (ultimately slated to be 2,200 acres, or three times the size of Central Park) opening in phases between now and 2036.

the New York Botanical Garden in the Bronx

GOVERNORS ISLAND

Governors Island (www.govisland.com) opened to the public as a multiuse recreational site in 2005 after serving as a military installation for more than 200 years. Even before artillery and infantry troops were stationed here during the War of 1812, the island served as a coastal defense for both the state and the nation. In the 20th century, it became the base for the Atlantic Area Command of the U.S. Coast Guard, and served a number of diplomatic and ceremonial functions, including a United Nations-sponsored talk intended to lead to the restoration of democratic rule in Haiti.

Now, the island is open to the public as a cultural and recreational hub, with dozens of art exhibits, festivals, concerts, and events held throughout the summer. Some are quirky, like the Unicycle Festival, and some are nostalgic, like the Jazz Age Lawn Party. Plenty of visitors to the island take the ferry over to just enjoy the grounds, which are perfect for a picnic or a snooze in the sun.

RANDALL'S ISLAND

Neither as popular nor as easily reached as Governors Island, **Randall's Island** (www.randall-sisland.org), open year-round, is still worth a visit if you want a respite from Manhattan's hustle and bustle. It's an underrated spot for taking stellar photos of Manhattan's East Side skyline or for running and cycling on 8 miles (12.9 km) of underused, vehicle-free paths. The island is also home to a golf and tennis center, both of which are open to the public.

ROOSEVELT ISLAND

Roosevelt Island (www.rioc.ny.gov) has been an attraction for curious travelers since at least 1976, when a tramway connecting the island to Manhattan began operation, shuttling slowly over the East River at a peak height of 250 feet (75 m). The island is primarily residential, but visitors flock here to visit **Franklin D. Roosevelt Four Freedoms Park** (www.fdrfourfreedoms-park.org), opened in 2012. The park, nearly four decades in the making, is a quiet beauty and offers lovely views of both Manhattan's East Side and Queens's Gantry Plaza State Park in the Long Island City neighborhood.

HARLEM

Stretching roughly from 110th to 168th Streets, between the Harlem and Hudson Rivers, Harlem is one of the city's most historic and most diverse neighborhoods. During the 1920s and 1930s, this was the country's African American cultural center. The Harlem Renaissance attracted writers and intellectuals such as Langston Hughes and W. E. B. DuBois, while streets were jammed with jazz clubs, theaters, dance halls, and speakeasies. Duke Ellington played at Cotton Club, Chick Webb at The Savoy. Harlem lost much of this vibrancy during the Depression, when poverty began taking a stronger hold. In the 1960s, civil rights leaders like Malcolm X and Stokely Carmichael made it a mecca for Black consciousness. While it remains a vital center for the city's African American communities, Harlem is rapidly gentrifying. Prices have risen here to the point that beloved Harlem institutions have had to move or close completely in recent years.

The area is divided into West and Central Harlem, comprised mostly of African Americans, and East Harlem, home to many Latinos, hence its nickname: El Barrio (or "The Neighborhood" in Spanish). Here many numbered avenues take on proper names: 6th Avenue is Lenox Avenue or Malcolm X Boulevard; 7th Avenue is Adam Clayton Powell Jr. Boulevard (ACP Blvd.); and 8th Avenue is Frederick Douglass Boulevard.

125th Street

The heart of Harlem is 125th Street, always alive with vibrant colors, sights, and sounds. As the neighborhood's main commercial drag for decades, 125th Street has had many ups and downs. Today, it's riding an optimistic wave, with more businesses in operation now than at any other time in recent history. The street is home to two major cultural landmarks: The Studio Museum in Harlem and The Apollo Theater. Just south of 125th Street, on 5th Avenue, is **Marcus Garvey Park,** lined with elegant brownstones.

The Studio Museum in Harlem (144 W. 125th St., 212/864-4500, www.studiomuseum. org, Thurs.-Fri. noon-9pm, Sat. 10am-6pm, Sun. noon-6pm, suggested admission adults $7, students and seniors $3, children under 12 free) was founded in 1968 in a small factory loft. Today, it's a first-class institution spread over several well-lit floors of a turn-of-the-20th-century building. The "principal center for the study of Black art in America," the museum offers a permanent display of works by such masters as Romare Bearden, James VanDerZee, and Jacob Lawrence.

Perhaps the single most important landmark in the history of African American music, **The Apollo Theater** (253 W. 125th St., 212/531-5300, www.apollotheater.org) has hosted nearly every major jazz, blues, R&B, and soul artist to come along since the 1930s. Bessie Smith, Ella Fitzgerald, Billie Holiday, Duke Ellington, Louis Armstrong, Count Basie, Ray Charles, James Brown, Aretha Franklin, Diana Ross, and Michael Jackson all played The Apollo, and the list goes on and on. It is said that when a teenage Elvis Presley first came to New York, the one place he wanted to see was The Apollo. The same was later said of the Beatles.

Built in 1913, The Apollo was once Hurtig & Seamon's New Burlesque Theatre, which presented vaudeville to a Harlem that was then predominantly white. But by 1935, the neighborhood's racial mix had shifted, and the two-balconied theater, capable of seating 2,000, became famous for its Amateur Nights. Now a nonprofit enterprise, The Apollo continues to present a variety of entertainment, including a Wednesday amateur night. A small exhibit on the theater's early history is in the lobby. **Tours** (212/531-5337) are available for groups of 20 or more; otherwise, you may be able to join a group that has already booked.

Central Harlem

The Schomburg Center for Research in Black Culture (515 Malcolm X Blvd./Lenox Ave., 212/491-2200, www.nypl.org/locations/schomburg, Mon. and Thurs.-Sat. 10am-6pm,

Harlem

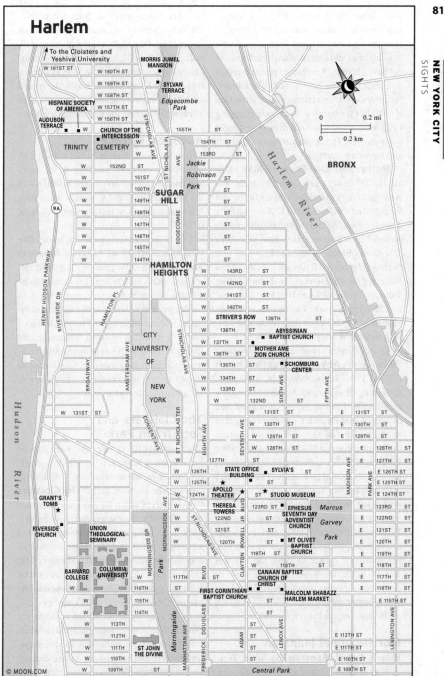

To the Cloisters and Yeshiva University

W 161ST ST
W 160TH ST
W 159TH ST
W 158TH ST
W 157TH ST
W 156TH ST

MORRIS JUMEL MANSION
SYLVAN TERRACE
Edgecombe Park

HISPANIC SOCIETY OF AMERICA
AUDUBON TERRACE
CHURCH OF THE INTERCESSION
TRINITY CEMETERY

155TH ST
154TH ST
153RD ST
W 152ND ST
151ST
150TH
149TH
148TH
147TH
146TH
145TH
144TH

ST NICHOLAS PL
ST NICHOLAS AVE

Harlem River

BRONX

0   0.2 mi
0   0.2 km

Jackie Robinson Park

SUGAR HILL

HAMILTON HEIGHTS

EDGECOMBE

143RD ST
142ND ST
141ST ST
140TH ST
STRIVER'S ROW 139TH ST
138TH ST
137TH ST
136TH ST
135TH ST
134TH ST
133RD ST
132ND ST

ABYSSINIAN BAPTIST CHURCH
MOTHER AME ZION CHURCH
SCHOMBURG CENTER

CITY UNIVERSITY OF NEW YORK

HENRY HUDSON PARKWAY
RIVERSIDE DR

9A

Hudson River

BROADWAY
AMSTERDAM AVE
HAMILTON PL
ST NICHOLAS AVE
CONVENT AVE
ST NICHOLAS AVE
EIGHTH AVE
SEVENTH AVE
SIXTH AVE
FIFTH AVE

W 131ST ST
131ST ST
130TH ST
129TH ST
128TH ST
127TH ST
126TH ST
125TH
124TH

STATE OFFICE BUILDING
SYLVIA'S
APOLLO THEATER
STUDIO MUSEUM

GRANT'S TOMB
RIVERSIDE CHURCH

UNION THEOLOGICAL SEMINARY

BARNARD COLLEGE
COLUMBIA UNIVERSITY

MORNINGSIDE DR
MORNINGSIDE AVE
Morningside Park
ST NICHOLAS AVE
CLAYTON POWELL JR BLVD
FREDERICK DOUGLASS BLVD
ADAM
LENOX AVE
MADISON AVE
PARK AVE
LEXINGTON AVE

THERESA TOWERS
EPHESUS SEVENTH DAY ADVENTIST CHURCH
MT OLIVET BAPTIST CHURCH
CANAAN BAPTIST CHURCH OF CHRIST
FIRST CORINTHIAN BAPTIST CHURCH
MALCOLM SHABAZZ HARLEM MARKET

Marcus Garvey Park

123RD ST
122ND ST
121ST ST
120TH ST
119TH ST
118TH ST
117TH ST
116TH ST
115TH ST
114TH ST
113TH
112TH
111TH
110TH
109TH ST

ST JOHN THE DIVINE

E 126TH ST
E 125TH ST
E 124TH ST
E 123RD ST
E 122ND ST
E 121ST ST
E 120TH ST
E 119TH ST
E 118TH ST
E 117TH ST
E 116TH ST
E 115TH ST
E 112TH ST
E 111TH ST
E 110TH ST
E 109TH ST

Central Park

© MOON.COM

Tues.-Wed. 10am-8pm, free) is a world-renowned institution founded by Arthur A. Schomburg, a Puerto Rican-born scholar, who as a child was told that African Americans did not have a history. A respected research center and branch of The New York Public Library, the center's most interesting visitor attraction is its **gallery**, where a wide array of changing exhibits about African and diaspora cultures are presented. The center also has a small gift and bookshop upstairs.

Mother AME Zion Church (140 W. 137th St., 212/234-1544), a neo-Gothic building, was New York City's first church organized by and for Blacks. It was founded in 1796—originally downtown at 156 Church Street—with money donated by a former slave. Also known as "Freedom Church" because of its connection to the Underground Railroad, the church has had many famous members, including Harriet Tubman, Frederick Douglass, Paul Robeson, and Sojourner Truth. The church welcomes visitors to participate in their music and worship services at 11am on Sundays.

One of Harlem's most famous addresses is the impressive **Abyssinian Baptist Church** (132 W. 138th St., 212/862-7474, www.abyssinian.org). It was founded in 1801 when a few members of the First Baptist Church refused to accept that church's racially segregated seating policy. The Abyssinian now has one of the country's largest Black congregations. The Reverend Dr. Calvin Butts III is Abyssinian's current pastor, and he continues the church's activist tradition. Sunday services, complete with gospel music, are held at 7am and 10am. Visitors are welcome at the latter service on a first-come, first-seated basis, and must enter at a specially designated tourist entrance on the southeast corner of West 138th Street and Adam Clayton Powell Jr. Boulevard. The church has specific policies regarding dress and behavior during the service, all of which are detailed on the church's website.

Morris-Jumel Mansion

Morris-Jumel Mansion (65 Jumel Terr., 212/923-8008, www.morrisjumel.org,

Tue.-Fri. 10am-4pm, Sat.-Sun. 10am-5pm, adults $10, seniors and students $8, children under 12 free) sits high over the city in a small, lush park. Manhattan's last remaining colonial residence, it was built in 1765 as a country home for British colonel Roger Morris and served as temporary headquarters for George Washington during the Revolutionary War.

Audubon Terrace

This monumental marble terrace is lined with impressive beaux arts buildings to the south and friezes and statuary to the north. All of the land once belonged to ornithologist John James Audubon; the terrace was built later, in 1904.

One of the beaux arts buildings houses **The Hispanic Society of America Museum and Library** (613 W. 155th St., 212/926-2234, www.hispanicsociety.org, Tues.-Sat. 10am-4:30pm, Sun. 1pm-4pm, free), one of the city's hidden treasures. Dark, somber, and mansion-like in feel and oddly big and hollow, it houses exquisite paintings by Goya, Velásquez, and El Greco, along with heavy Spanish furnishings, porcelain, and mosaics. Curators offer free 45-minute tours of the building and collections on Saturdays at 2pm.

The Cloisters and Fort Tryon Park

High on a hill at the northern tip of Manhattan is a surprising sight: a magical "medieval monastery," with wonderful views of the Hudson, called **The Cloisters** (99 Margaret Corbin Dr., inside Fort Tryon Park, 212/923-3700, www.metmuseum.org, open daily, hours vary by season, suggested admission, which includes admission to The Met, adults $25, seniors $17, students $12, children under 12 free). Financed in 1938 by John D. Rockefeller, The Cloisters house The Metropolitan Museum of Art's medieval collections. Incorporated into the building are the actual remains of four medieval cloisters, transported here from Europe, and the museum's most prized possessions, its 16th-century unicorn tapestries.

Entertainment and Events

Comprehensive entertainment listings can be found in *the New Yorker, New York,* and the Friday and Sunday editions of *the New York Times. Time Out New York,* which includes hundreds upon hundreds of listings, is especially useful. *Time Out* does a very good job of covering downtown; *the New Yorker* is the best source for capsule theater reviews; it also has a "Goings on about Town" app for smartphones that's good for information on the go, with search by location, dates, critics' picks, and event listings. For information on the ever-changing club scene, *Time Out* is again the most useful.

POPULAR VENUES

It's not the prettiest venue, but one of the biggest ones is **Madison Square Garden** (7th Ave. between 31st and 33rd Sts., 212/465-6741, www.msg.com), home to a packed schedule of concerts and other entertainment events, including the annual **Westminster Kennel Club Dog Show** (www.westminsterkennelclub.org), as well as the city's basketball and hockey teams, and world-class boxing matches.

Grand **Radio City Music Hall** (1260 6th Ave., at 50th St., 212/247-4777, www.radiocity.com) often presents popular national and international music acts, and, of course, the annual Christmas spectacular. Historic **Beacon Theatre** (2124 Broadway, at 74th St., 212/465-6225, www.beacontheatre.com) is a charming smaller venue that also hosts national and international musicians and performers; the roster of events is especially well represented by favorite stand-up comics. Recent performers have included Wanda Sykes, Bill Maher, John Legend, and Van Morrison. **The Town Hall** (123 W. 43rd St., 212/840-2824, www.thetownhall.org) is a National Historic Site that presents a variety of jazz, world, and traditional music in an intimate setting.

The atmospheric **Apollo Theater** (253 W. 125th St., 212/531-5305, www.apollotheater.org) offers mostly R&B, soul, and rap. On Wednesdays, the famed amateur-night tradition continues. Don't hesitate to venture up here at night; 125th Street is always bustling.

LIVE MUSIC

Long, dark **Mercury Lounge** (217 E. Houston, 212/260-4700, www.mercuryloungenyc.com) features an antique wooden bar, exposed brick walls, heavy red drapes, and an excellent sound system. Hip rock and jazz acts play here. **The Bowery Ballroom** (6 Delancey St., 212/533-2111, www.boweryballroom.com) is one of the city's few midsize venues. Complete with a balcony, it presents a wide variety of music acts.

City Winery (155 Varick St., 212/608-0555, www.citywinery.com) is a posh, airy, blond-wood-floored performance space and restaurant that often features big names in pop, rock, jazz, and folk.

The oldest and arguably best jazz club in the city is **Village Vanguard** (178 7th Ave. S., at 11th St., 212/255-4037, www.villagevanguard.com), a dark, wedge-shaped basement room filled with rickety tables and fading photographs. Established in 1934, Vanguard has booked all the greats, from Miles Davis and Dinah Washington to Wynton Marsalis and Terence Blanchard. Jazz lovers also trumpet **Blue Note** (131 W. 3rd St., 212/475-8592, www.bluenotejazz.com). Though pricey, with overly commercial decor and mediocre food, the club has attracted jazz luminaries since 1981; nightly sets are at 8pm and 10:30pm. Less well-known but also good is **Fat Cat** (75 Christopher St., 212/675-6056, www.fatcatmusic.org), a spacious subterranean bar packed with locals playing pool, table tennis, shuffleboard, foosball, and board games. Three nightly sets of top-notch live jazz keep the party rocking until the 5am closing. Another basement jazz joint is **Smalls Jazz**

Club (183 W. 10th St., 212/252-5091, www. smallslive.com), with an old-school Village vibe and stuffed to standing-room-only on weekends. Multiple sets each evening (one cover admits you to them all) often focus on young talent.

After a Latin-inspired dinner, ditch your table for the nearby dance floor at S.O.B.'s (204 Varick St., 212/243-4940, www.sobs. com), New York's premier world music showcase, hosting everything from hip-hop and bhangra to the beats of Brazil, the Caribbean, Africa, and beyond.

Manhattan School of Music (120 Claremont Ave., 212/749-2802, www.msmnyc.edu), a competitive world-renowned music conservatory, offers degrees up to the doctoral level in the areas of classical and jazz performance and composition. The wealth of talent here is exhibited in free jazz and classical and orchestral concerts and performances throughout the year.

CLASSICAL MUSIC AND OPERA

Classical music thrives in New York City, especially at **Lincoln Center for the Performing Arts** (between 62nd and 65th Sts., and between Columbus and Amsterdam Aves., 212/546-2656, www.lincolncenter. org). The center presents an astonishing 3,000 performances a year. On its north side is 2,700-seat **Avery Fisher Hall,** home to The New York Philharmonic (Sept.-May), Great Performers Series (Oct.-May), and Mostly Mozart Festival (July-Aug.).

Just north of Avery Fisher, above 66th Street, is 1,096-seat **Alice Tully Hall,** where The Chamber Music Society of Lincoln Center performs.

A dozen or so blocks from Lincoln Center is Manhattan's other major classical music venue, **Carnegie Hall** (7th Ave. and 57th St., 212/247-7800, www.carnegiehall.org). Saved from demolition by Isaac Stern and others in the early 1960s, this legendary hall remains a favorite spot among musicians of all genres.

On the west side of Lincoln Center is the grand **Metropolitan Opera House** (Lincoln Center, 212/362-6000, www.metopera.org), home of the Metropolitan Opera Company. A good seat here costs over $100, but under-$20 seats and standing-room tickets are often available in the upper balcony (bring binoculars).

THEATER

Attending a Broadway show is a quintessential New York experience. There's nothing quite like hurrying down the neon-splashed streets of Times Square along with thousands of other theatergoers, most of whom always seem to be running late. Among Broadway's many gorgeous, historic venues—most located just off Times Square—are the **Shubert** (225 W. 44th St., 212/239-6200, www.shubert.nyc), **Booth** (222 W. 45th St., 212/239-6200, www. booth-theater.com), **Nederlander** (208 W. 41st St., 212/921-8000, www.nederlander-theatre.com), **Majestic** (245 W. 44th St., 212/239-6215, www.majestic-theater.com), **Belasco** (111 W. 44th St., 212/239-6200, www.shubertorganization.com), and **Lyceum** (149 W. 45th St., 212/239-2949, www.shubert-organization.com).

Discount tickets to same-day performances are sold daily at three **TKTS** (www. tdf.org) booths in the city, run by the Theater Development Fund. The **Times Square** location (under the red steps in Father Duffy Square on Broadway and 47th St., Mon. and Wed.-Sat. 3pm-8pm, Tues. 2pm-8pm, Sun. 3pm-7pm) sells tickets for evening performances. On days when matinee tickets are available, the booth opens at 10am. There is also a **South Street Seaport** location (corner of Front and John Sts., Mon.-Sat. 11am-6pm, Sun. 11am-4pm) and one at Lincoln Center (located in the David Rubenstein Atrium at 61 W. 62nd St., Mon.-Sat. noon-7pm, Sun. noon-5pm).

DANCE

New York is home to two major ballet companies. **American Ballet Theater** (890 Broadway, 212/477-3030, www.abt.org),

Best of Broadway and Beyond

There's nothing like seeing a Broadway show to really top off a full day in NYC. Times Square's garish lights beckon you to escape reality for a few hours through the work of the world's best actors and performers in some of the country's most beautiful, historic theaters.

Most visitors to New York City know they want to see a Broadway show, but many are intimidated by the process of choosing a show and buying tickets. And they may not know some of the most basic terms and tips for making the most of their Broadway experience. Here, then, is a Broadway primer:

"Broadway," "Off-Broadway," and "Off-Off-Broadway" are terms that refer to different types of theaters in Manhattan. Not determined solely by the theater's physical location on or off Broadway, the terms also take into account the number of seats a theater has and whether the actors are union or nonunion. The general rule of thumb? **"Broadway"** shows occur in theaters between 40th and 54th Streets and 6th and 8th Avenues; these theaters have more than 499 seats. **"Off-Broadway"** shows play in theaters with 100-499 seats. And **"Off-Off-Broadway"** shows play in theaters with fewer than 100 seats. Broadway productions lean toward the mainstream, and Off-Broadway productions almost equally so—despite having begun in the 1930s as a rebellion against Broadway values. Off-Off Broadway theater was a 1960s rebellion against the rebellion; its shows are often quirky and experimental.

"Stage door" refers to the door that actors and other employees use to enter and leave the theater. As such, it's the place you'll want to post yourself after the show if you hope to glimpse your favorite actor or try to get an autograph.

Broadway isn't just for adults. In addition to long-running kid-friendly shows like *The Lion King* and *Wicked,* there are productions designed especially with kids in mind. If you're traveling with little ones, check the show schedule for **The New Victory Theater** (www.newvictory.org). This theater for kids features plays, puppetry performances, and much more, with shows for children as young as four months. Another kid-friendly tip? Once a year, **"Kids' Night Out"** (www.kidsnightonbroadway.com), which actually takes place over several nights, offers free tickets to select Broadway shows for kids 6-18.

For discount tickets any time of the year, check Theatre Development Fund's **TKTS booths** (www.tdf.org) in the middle of Times Square, at Lincoln Center, or in the South Street Seaport. Here, you can score legit, day-of-show tickets for up to 50 percent off their regular price.

once directed by Mikhail Baryshnikov, and **New York City Ballet** (www.nycballet.com), founded by George Balanchine and Lincoln Kirstein, both perform at **David H. Koch Theater** in Lincoln Center (212/496-0600).

NIGHTLIFE
Lower Manhattan
Jeremy's Ale House (228 Front St., 212/964-3537, www.jeremysalehouse.com) is a jovial bar whose "Beer isn't the only thing for breakfast anymore" bumper stickers pretty much say all you need to know about this spot. Happy hour specials include 32-ounce Styrofoam cups of beer and half-price well drinks.

One of the city's most popular cocktail bars is **The Dead Rabbit Grocery and Grog** (30 Water St., 646/422-7906, www.deadrabbitnyc.com), whose unpleasant name belies its many charms, including craft cocktails that harken back to another era.

Macao Trading Company (311 Church St., 212/431-8750, www.macaonyc.com) is a sexy subterranean lounge with Eastern-influenced cocktails and a 1930s Macao theme. Food from the upstairs restaurant is served until 3:30am.

Lower East Side
Lower East Side nightlife ranges from laid-back bars and lounges, some of which are holes-in-the-wall, to more

upscale, see-and-be-seen, well, scenes. The domestic-sounding **Pianos** (158 Ludlow St., 212/505-3733, www.pianosnyc.com) is less precious than Beauty & Essex (146 Essex St., 212/61400146, www.beautyandessex. com), which, while seemingly modest with its pawn shop storefront, gets distinctly fancier once you've been permitted past the velvet rope.

SoHo and TriBeCa

Stop by **Spring Lounge** (48 Spring St., 212/965-1774, www.thespringlounge.com), aka the Shark Bar (so named for stuffed sharks mounted on walls), to enjoy a pint or two in a dive bar-chic spot where drinking starts at 8am.

The classic bar in SoHo is **Fanelli's Cafe** (94 Prince St., 212/226-9412), an 1876 pub complete with beveled-glass doors, tiled floors, and heavy, dark wood. Passable bar food is served on worn wooden tables. At **Pegu Club** (77 W. Houston St., 212/473-7348, www.peguclub.com), colonial Asian decor characterizes this upscale cocktail bar where the mixologists produce beautiful drinks harking back to yesteryear.

Once an artists' hangout, **Puffy's Tavern** (81 Hudson St., 212/227-3912, www.puffystavern.nyc) now attracts everyone from bankers and bikers to police and firefighters. **Walker's** (16 N. Moore St., 212/941-0142, www.walkersnyc.com) is an 1890s saloon that serves tasty pub grub and Guinness on tap.

East Village

McSorley's Old Ale House (15 E. 7th St., 212/473-9148, www.mcsorleysoldalehouse. nyc) is one of New York's oldest bars and was once a hangout of *New Yorker* writer Joseph Mitchell, who wrote of the place in his book *McSorley's Wonderful Saloon*. Inside, find a potbellied stove, old gas lamps, a carved mahogany bar, and pressed tin ceilings. Also in the neighborhood is **Angel's Share** (8 Stuyvesant St., 212/777-5415), a speakeasy-style bar tucked away in the restaurant Village Yokocho.

Greenwich Village and West Village

Sturdy old **White Horse Tavern** (567 Hudson St., 212/989-3956, www.whitehorsetavern1880.com) was once a writer's hangout; Dylan Thomas drank himself to death here. Now the tavern caters mostly to a college crowd. Outdoor picnic tables are set up in summer.

Blind Tiger Ale House (281 Bleecker St., 212/462-4682, www.blindtigeralehouse.com) is considered one of New York's top craft beer bars with a prodigious selection of draft beers and an upscale bar menu.

They take libations seriously at **Little Branch** (20 7th Ave. S., 212/929-4360), a cozy nightspot where mixologists craft first-rate cocktails with ultrafresh ingredients, hand-chipped ice, and chilled glasses. There's live jazz Sunday-Thursday.

Among gay bars, **Stonewall Inn** (53 Christopher St., near 7th Ave. S., 212/488-2705, www.thestonewallinnnyc.com) was named a State and National Landmark in 2016. Across the street is **The Monster** (80 Grove St., 212/924-3558, www.monsterbarnyc. com), featuring a drag cabaret. **Henrietta Hudson** (438 Hudson St., 212/924-3347, www.henriettahudson.com) is a popular lesbian bar, said to be New York City's oldest, drawing largely professional crowds.

Chelsea and the Meatpacking District

Founded by two beverage consultants whose goal is to "help the world drink better," **The Tippler** (425 W. 15th St., basement level of Chelsea Market, 212/206-0000, www.thetippler.com) is a trendy spot with classic architectural elements and artisanal cocktails.

Jungle Bird (174 8th Ave., 646/868-8422, www.junglebirdnyc.com) is, at its name suggests, a bar where the decor and drinks are both inspired by the tropics, and definitely made for the Instagram era. As interesting (if not more so) than the drinks is the full menu, with dishes inspired by Vietnam and neighboring countries. This is definitely a spot to

Craft Cocktails

Forget cosmos, appletinis, and any drink tinged blue with curacao; now, New Yorkers want their cocktails artisanally titled and mixed, preferably with handcrafted, small-batch ingredients, the more locally sourced, the better. It's not enough, anymore, to stock trendy liquors, prepped in cocktail shakers, and strained into martini glasses or, worse, the grossly oversized, bowl-shaped margarita glass, rimmed with—gasp!—plain old salt. Now, New Yorkers out on the town for a drink expect bespoke glasses, special or vintage bar gear, and homemade garnishes (no shriveled orange peel or jarred Maraschino cherry, please) for specific, inspired drinks . . . all served by a bespectacled, mustachioed, vest-and-suspenders-wearing barkeep.

A growing number of the city's bartenders are happy to indulge these customers. After all, they're the ones who gave rise to the craft cocktail movement. Mixing bitters in their basements and cutting their own ice cubes, these drink artisans spawned the current craze for cocktails that can average $16 a pop. Here's a sampling of the best craft cocktails in Manhattan.

- **Angel's Share** (8 Stuyvesant St., 212/777-5415), East Village

- **The Dead Rabbit Grocery and Grog** (30 Water St., 646/422-7906, www.deadrabbitnyc.com), Lower Manhattan

- **Little Branch** (20 7th Ave. S., 212/929-4360), West Village

- **Refinery Rooftop** (63 W. 38th St., 646/664-0310), Midtown

- **The Tippler** (425 W. 15th St., basement level of Chelsea Market, 212/206-0000), Chelsea

pop into if you're with a bunch of friends; order the Jungle Bird Bowl, a punch bowl of the house cocktail that will serve 4-6 people.

Bar Americano (518 W. 27th St., 212/525-0000) is a popular option in Chelsea's gallery/High Line district. The downstairs bar is all sleek lines and low lights for the see-and-be-seen set.

Midtown

Midtown is *the* neighborhood to experience the city's best rooftop bars, among them **bar 54** (135 W. 45th St., 646/364-1234 www.timessquare.hyatt.com, Sun.-Thurs. 5pm-1am, Fri.-Sat. 5pm-2am). Its sweeping river-to-river views are thanks to its perch on the 54th story of the Hyatt Centric Times Square. Indoor and outdoor fireplaces create a cozy ambience in colder weather, and creative cocktails and a full wine list are served year-round.

Refinery Rooftop (63 W. 38th St., 646/664-0310, www.refineryrooftop.com), atop Refinery Hotel, focuses on cocktails made of natural ingredients using

biochemistry techniques. The bar has an indoor area with seats, an outdoor terrace, and an indoor-outdoor patio with retractable glass roof. For a drink in the city's only revolving bar, overlooking Times Square, take an elevator to the top of glitzy Marriott Marquis for the aptly named **The View** (1535 Broadway, 212/704-8900). Yes, it's an overpriced tourist attraction, but it's hard to beat the 360-degree view.

Back on ground level, elegant, wood-paneled **Algonquin Hotel** (59 W. 44th St., 212/840-6800, www.algonquinhotel.com), near the Theater District, offers several bars and lounges.

P. J. Clarke's (915 3rd Ave., 212/317-1616, www.pjclarkes.com) is an out-of-time saloon sporting brass railings, worn wood, and sawdust on the floor. Featured in the 1945 movie *The Lost Weekend* and in the television show *Mad Men*, P. J.'s also serves pricey burgers and sandwiches.

In the postmodern Four Seasons Hotel is **TY Bar** (57 E. 57th St., 212/758-5700, www.fourseasons.com/newyork), serving classic cocktails that hark back to the 1920s and 1930s. Drinks at posh St. Regis Hotel's **King Cole Bar and Lounge** (2 E. 55th St., 212/753-4500) don't come cheap, but the room's stunning historic mural by Maxfield Parrish makes it worthwhile.

Upper West Side

Amsterdam Avenue between 79th and 85th Streets is teeming with bars. Mostly a younger twentysomething crowd prevails, but a quieter choice is tiny **Dead Poet** (450 Amsterdam Ave., 212/595-5670, www.thedeadpoet.com).

Harlem

Many of Harlem's classic nightspots closed long ago, including famed Lenox Lounge, but several new bars and restaurants suggest a coming resurgence. Popular **Corner Social** (321 Lenox Ave., 212/510-8552, www.cornersocialnyc.com) is one of several newer bar-restaurants that have both enjoyed and contributed to Harlem's gentrification. Crowds of young professionals drink and eat here, often spilling out onto the sidewalk, where a handful of tables are set up in warmer months.

Right across the street from Corner Social is **Red Rooster** (310 Lenox Ave., 212/792-9001, www.redroosterharlem.com), one of the many projects of ambitious chef-preneur Marcus Samuelsson. Upstairs, the restaurant serves Southern-U.S.-inspired dishes like fried chicken; downstairs, Ginny's Supper Club operates as "part raucous speakeasy, part debonair jazz lounge."

Shopping

If you can't find it—whatever the "it" is—in New York City, it either doesn't exist or you don't need it. Whether you're looking for vintage clothes, custom cookware, rare or specialized books, or notions of 900 sorts, you can probably find it in Manhattan . . . as long as you know where to look.

LOWER EAST SIDE

The Lower East Side is a destination for shoppers searching for vintage, handmade clothes, and accessories at chic, if small, boutiques. Don't expect bargains, but you will find one-of-a-kind pieces, especially on Orchard and Rivington Streets. If you're in need of undergarments, **Orchard Corset Center** (157 Orchard St., 212/674-0786, www.orchardcorset.com) sells them, including, as its name indicates, corsets. And as long as you're thinking about that part of the body, a visit to **Babeland** (94 Rivington St., 212/375-1701, www.babeland.com) might be in order; the sex shop is New York's cleanest and most professional.

SOHO AND TRIBECA

SoHo and TriBeCa are among the city's most popular neighborhoods for shopping, boasting a variety of clothing, novelty, design, and niche-interest shops. The area is especially known for trendy clothing stores, many very expensive, and gift and home furnishings shops. Chic designer stores sit near vintage shops like **What Comes Around Goes Around** (351 W. Broadway, 212/343-1225, www.whatgoesaroundnyc.com), which claims to sell the best luxury vintage goods.

SoHo and TriBeCa also have a number of bookstores, a favorite of which is the hip **McNally Jackson Books** (52 Prince St., 212/274-1160, www.mcnallyjackson.com), a two-level bookstore in SoHo, complete with café and a station where aspiring authors can print their own books.

If you're something of a writer yourself, then treat yourself to a pen at **Fountain Pen Hospital** (10 Warren St., 212/964-0580, www.fountainpenhospital.com), a fix-it shop in TriBeCa that also sells new, fine pens.

EAST VILLAGE

Shops in the East Village stay true to the neighborhood's punk and alt-everything roots, with vintage clothes and accessories and counterculture books and goods all on offer here. **Screaming Mimi's** (382 Lafayette St., 212/677-6464, www.screamingmimis. com) is known for 1950s-, 1960s-, and 1970s-era duds. **Stock Vintage** (143 E. 13th St., 212/505-2505) is one of the few vintage stores that specializes in menswear; it also has exceptional accessories, such as jewelry and cigarette cases.

GREENWICH VILLAGE AND WEST VILLAGE

The Village has loads of interesting shops of all sorts and has, so far, managed to stave off the big name brands that would colonize the neighborhood with boutique-size outlets. One is **C. O. Bigelow Apothecaries** (414 6th Ave., 212/533-2700, www.bigelow-chemists.com), New York's oldest continuously operating pharmacy; the official historic landmark was established in 1838 and still sports its original oak fittings and gaslight fixtures. For intellectual stimulation, visit **Three Lives & Co.** (154 W. 10th St., 212/741-2069, www.threelives.com), one of the city's top literary bookstores and host of frequent readings by well-known authors. **Bookbook** (266 Bleecker St., 212/807-8655, www.bookbooknyc.com) has an excellent selection of sale books and an extensive cookbook selection.

UNION SQUARE AND MADISON SQUARE PARK

Like the Village, the neighborhoods in and around Union Square and Madison Square Park offer plenty of neat, independently owned businesses; especially well represented are bookstores and foodstuffs and home decor shops. Many of the city's nonprofit, social service organizations and cultural organizations have thrift stores that funnel proceeds of sales back to their respective causes. One of the most popular is **Housing Works** (157 E. 23rd St., 212/529-5955, www.housingworks. org), which has more than a dozen thrift stores spread across the city. You can find one of them, along with thrift stores of several other nonprofits, along E. 23rd Street between 2nd and Park Avenues. A neighborhood novelty is New York's largest and oldest hat store, **J. J. Hat Center** (310 5th Ave., 212/239-4368, www.jjhatcenter.com). Established in 1911, J. J.'s stocks over 15,000 men's hats, including fedoras, Stetsons, homburgs, and caps.

Cooks and food lovers will enjoy the area, too. Venerable **Kalustyan's** (123 Lexington Ave., 212/685-3451, www.kalustyans.com) was the first store to import Indian foodstuffs into the city; the shop features spices, staples, and specialty items from many countries around the world.

So you've got ingredients . . . now, in what vessels should you serve your inspired meals? **Fishs Eddy** (889 Broadway, 212/420-9020, www.fishseddy.com) can help; it's filled with retro and retro-inspired dinnerware. The shop features restaurant and diner overstocks—much of it NYC-themed—as well as its own line of dishes and glassware.

Some of the city's best-loved bookstores are in the Union Square-Madison Square Park neighborhood, including the granddaddy of them all, **Strand Book Store** (828 Broadway, 212/473-1452, www.strandbooks.com, daily 9:30am-10:30pm). The institution cherished by book-loving New Yorkers is the only one of 48 bookstores that used to line so-called "Book Row," which ran from Union Square to Astor Place. The Strand boasts 18 miles (29 km) of shelves, which are loaded with more than 2.5 million new and used books. A rare books room is on the store's top floor.

CHELSEA AND THE MEATPACKING DISTRICT

Shops in Chelsea and the Meatpacking District tend to be trendy, expensive, and a little bit precious, but you can stay grounded by popping into **Chelsea Market** (75 9th Ave., 212/243-6005, www.chelseamarket. com), a winding maze of gourmet butchers,

A Day in Brooklyn

Brooklyn Bridge Park

One day is hardly sufficient to explore and enjoy one of New York City's four outer boroughs, but with 8-12 hours, you can pack in plenty of Brooklyn's best experiences.

Start your day at **Dough** (448 Lafayette Ave., 347/533-7544, www.doughdoughnuts.com, daily 6am-9pm), a popular doughnut shop in the Bed-Stuy neighborhood. Mexican American pastry chef Fany Gerson blends the flavors of her two countries and cultures in treats like the horchata doughnut and the dulce de leche doughnut. Don't worry about the sugar or fat; you'll walk plenty today!

From Dough, head to the **Brooklyn Museum** (200 Eastern Pkwy., 718/638-5000, www. brooklynmuseum.org, Wed. and Fri.-Sun. 11am-6pm, Thurs. 11am-10pm, adults $16, students and seniors $10, children under 19 free), NYC's third-largest art museum. Here, you'll find a heady hodge-podge of works that span a dizzying array of eras and genres. Feminist and Black art, however, are the strengths of the museum's collection.

Next, head to Greenpoint. Fully in the midst of gentrification, this traditionally Polish neighborhood still retains some of its old-school shops and restaurants, including **Jaslowiczanka Bakery** (163 Nassau Ave., 718/389-0263, daily 10am-8pm). This cash-only spot sells delectable pastries, which should be enjoyed after lunch at **Tørst** (615 Manhattan Ave., 718/389-6034, www. torstnyc.com, Sun.-Thurs. noon-midnight, Fri.-Sat. noon-2am), a Nordic restaurant whose menu is a mash-up of Brooklyn's cultural diversity. There are Mexican-inspired black bean tortas with Oaxacan cheese and avocados, as well as Polish-inspired hot dogs topped with Korean kimchi. Somehow, it works… deliciously.

After you're sated, head southwest (you can take a water taxi or ferry!) to **Brooklyn Bridge Park,** the borough's ultimate playground. Depending upon the season, you'll find everything from a kids' carousel and bathing beach to the under-the-radar music lovers' attraction, **Bargemusic** (Brooklyn Bridge Park, 718/624-4924, www.bargemusic.org), a concert venue located in—you guessed it!—a barge, which has been going strong since 1977. Before ending your day by catching the sunset from the park, pop over to **Fornino at Pier 6** (Brooklyn Bridge Park, Pier 6, 718/422-1107, www.fornino.com) for a wood-fired pizza, or book in advance a table at classy **River Café** (1 Water St., 718/522-5200, www.rivercafe.com), where gents are required to don jackets. Walk off your dinner by taking a hike across the **Brooklyn Bridge,** a must-do item on the NYC bucket list.

cheesemongers, bakers, grocers, and vintners, as well as cute cafés and snack shops. The market also has a branch of **Posman Books,** featuring an excellent selection of New York City-themed books, and **Bowery Kitchen Supply,** where you're likely to spot a famous chef. Chelsea Market also hosts regular pop-up shops, selling everything from boutique and brand-name clothing to jewelry and fancy wineglasses.

If you know where to go, you can score some collectibles in these neighborhoods, too. **Academy Records and CDs** (12 W. 18th St., 212/242-3000, www.academy-records.com) sells pretty much every American genre on CDs and LPs.

Chelsea Flea Market (29 W. 25th St. between Broadway and 6th Ave., www.annexmarkets.com) features 125+ vendors selling mid-century modern and other vintage items every Saturday and Sunday.

MIDTOWN AND TIMES SQUARE

Midtown and Times Square represent a large swath of shopping pleasure in Manhattan, home to the city's most iconic department stores. The king of them all, of course, is **Macy's** (151 W. 34th St., 212/695-4400, www.macys.com). Ten stories high and a full block wide, the store was founded in 1858 by Rowland Hussey Macy, a Quaker from Nantucket. More of a do-it-yourself kind of person? You can buy fabric and notions at **M&J Trimming** (1008 6th Ave., 212/391-6200, www.mjtrim.com), with a huge selection of beads, buttons, lace, and feathers.

Deep-pocketed visitors looking to add to their jewelry boxes should head to 5th Avenue, home to **Tiffany & Co.** (727 5th Ave., 212/755-8000, www.tiffany.com). In Truman Capote's *Breakfast at Tiffany's,* character Holly Golightly opines, "Nothing bad can ever happen to you at Tiffany's," and she may be right. A recent addition to the store is a café where, yes, you too can have breakfast at Tiffany's.

In the technology and electronics realm, **B&H** (420 9th Ave., 212/444-6615, www.

bhphotovideo.com) holds the undisputed title as *the* most popular electronics store in New York City—or *anywhere* for that matter. The scene is quintessential New York: The megastore, run by Hasidic Jews, is abuzz with customers from around the world, their purchases shuttling from storage to the ground-floor pay and pick-up area via an overhead trolley system. Free seminars on topics as wide-ranging as basic photographic techniques to advanced video editing are offered in the store's Event Space venue.

Museum shops are also good places to find unique gifts, and at **The New York Public Library** (inside the main branch, the Schwarzman Building, at 42nd St. and 5th Ave., 212/930-0641, www.shop.nypl.org), you'll find a solid selection of New York City-themed items.

UPPER EAST SIDE

Be prepared to spend a pretty penny in this tony neighborhood, where you'll find a number of exclusive clothiers and retailers on Madison, Park, and 5th Avenues. Among them are **Polo Ralph Lauren** (men's flagship: 867 Madison Ave., 212/606-2100; women's/home flagship: 888 Madison Ave., 212/434-8000), with its classic, upscale American fashion.

Food lovers will enjoy neighborhood institutions like **Schaller & Weber** (1654 2nd Ave., 212/879-3047, www.schallerweber.com), a 1937 German butcher shop that will mail sausages anywhere in the world. If you want to don your own apron, **Kitchen Arts & Letters** (1435 Lexington Ave., 212/876-5550, www.kitchenartsandletters.com) stocks recent and hard-to-find cookbooks and literary titles related to food.

Other popular shopping spots in this neighborhood include **Star Magic** (1256 Lexington Ave., 212/988-0300, www.starmagic.com), which sells a range of fun space-age gifts, including science kits, mobiles, prisms, kaleidoscopes, and books, and **The Manhattan Art & Antiques Center** (1050 2nd Ave., 212/355-4400, www.the-maac.

com), a complex with about 100 small antiques shops.

UPPER WEST SIDE

While it's not as interesting or as varied as the Village, nor as expensive as the Upper East Side, the Upper West Side has plenty to offer shoppers; this *is* still New York, after all.

Broadway, Amsterdam Avenue, and **Columbus Avenue** are the main thoroughfares here. **Off Broadway Boutique** (139 W. 72nd St., 212/724-6713) sells secondhand clothes once worn by stars. If the city itself impresses you more than its celebrities, pop into the gift shop at **The New-York Historical Society** (170 Central Park West, 212/485-9203, www.nyhistorystore.com) for Big Apple-themed gifts and postcards.

Food lovers shouldn't skip **Zabar's** (2245 Broadway, 212/787-2000), one of the city's most beloved food stores. Dating back to the 1930s, Zabar's sells over 10,000 pounds of coffee, 10 tons of cheese, and 1,000 pounds of salmon a week, not to mention pots and pans, microwave ovens, vacuum cleaners, and the like. Some 10,000 customers are said to pass through its friendly portals on a Saturday afternoon. The best time to come is weekdays before 5pm.

GreenFlea (Columbus Ave., between W. 76th and 77th Sts., 212/239-3027, www.greenfleamarkets.com, Sun. 10am-5:30pm) has a mix of new and used goods as well as a green market; it bills itself as the city's largest flea market. Nearby is the delightful **Book Culture** (450 Columbus Ave., 212/595-1962, www.bookculture.com), where, in addition to buying new releases and bestsellers, you can pull a chair up to their writer's desk and pen a postcard—postage is on them!

HARLEM

Running from east to west, 125th Street cuts across Harlem and is one long line of discount clothiers and chain retailers. Look to some of the surrounding streets, then, for unique purchases. One such spot is **Malcolm Shabazz Harlem Market** (52 W. 116th St., between Lenox and 5th Ave., 212/987-8131), where dozens of vendors sell T-shirts, Kente cloth, African art, wool skullcaps, Gambian drums, African music, and hair-braiding services.

For informative and interesting Harlem-themed books and gifts, visit the shop at The New York Public Library's **Schomburg Center for Research in Black Culture** (103 W. 135th St., 212/491-2200).

Food

New Yorkers love to brag about the thousands of eating establishments in their city. Some come and go almost overnight; others have been around for decades. A few rules of thumb: the East Village is an excellent neighborhood for cheaper eats and ethnic restaurants; SoHo, TriBeCa, and Columbus Avenue boast lots of trendy spots; and Midtown and the Upper East Side are home to some of the city's most venerable, expensive restaurants.

CHINATOWN

Chinatown is home to over 300 restaurants serving various cuisines, including Hunan, Szechuan, Shanghai, Cantonese, Vietnamese, and Thai. You can't go wrong with most of the restaurants here, especially those catering to a large Asian clientele. All are inexpensive to moderately priced, with the average entrée less than $12.

A half-dozen or so cavernous, gaily decorated restaurants serve dim sum from mid-morning until late afternoon, and fixed-price banquets thereafter. One of the largest and best of these eateries is **Golden Unicorn** (18 E. Broadway, 212/941-0911, www.goldenunicornrestaurant.com, Mon.-Fri. 10am-10:30pm, Sat.-Sun. 9:30am-10:30

pm, $19), where waiters use walkie-talkies to communicate. Arrive early, as there's often a long wait.

Chinatown also has sweets. Try **Chinatown Ice Cream Factory** (65 Bayard St., 212/608-4170, www.chinatown icecreamfactory.com, daily 11am-10pm, $5), where you can buy every flavor of ice cream from ginger to mango.

LITTLE ITALY

Though Little Italy is generally *not* the place to go for good Italian food, it does hold some bargain-priced eateries, cheery cafés, and a few noteworthy dinner restaurants.

For an old-school feel, grab a table at **Da Nico** (385 Broome St., 212/343-1212, www. danicoristorante.com, Sun.-Thurs. noon-10:30pm, Fri.-Sat. noon-11:30 pm, $24), which has a garden out back where you can sit in summer months. Excellent coal-oven pizza and savory roasted meats and fish are their specialty.

For an afternoon snack, try cozy, tile-floored **Caffe Roma** (176 Mulberry St., 212/226-8413, Sun.-Thurs. 8am-10pm, Fri.-Sat. 8am-midnight, $7.50), a wonderful espresso and pastry café that was once a hangout for opera singers and has turned out sweets since 1891.

LOWER EAST SIDE

The granddaddy of New York delicatessens is **Katz's** (205 E. Houston St., 212/254-2246, www.katzsdelicatessen.com, Mon.-Wed. 8am-10:45 pm, Thurs. 8am-2:45am, Fri.-Sat. 24 hours, Sun. open until 10:45pm, $22), a huge, cafeteria-style place where you take a number at the door. Overhead hang WWII-era signs reading "Send a salami to your boy in the Army."

Russ & Daughters (179 E. Houston St., 212/475-4880, www.russanddaughters.com, Mon.-Wed. and Fri.-Sun. 8am-6pm, Thurs. 8am-7pm, $14) is a bustling place filled with smoked fish and dried fruits, all arranged in neat rows.

Yonah Schimmel's (137 E. Houston St., 212/477-2858, www.knishery.com, daily 10am-7pm, $3.50) is a rickety old storefront selling some of the best knishes in New York.

Dirt Candy (86 Allen St., 212/228-7732, www.dirtcandynyc.com, Tues.-Sat. 5:30pm-11pm, tasting menu $65-99), which opened in 2008, retains its title as NYC's "only vegetable restaurant." Reserve online, in advance, for a table at this hotspot, which is helmed by lauded chef Amanda Cohen.

SOHO AND TRIBECA

Once too hot for its own good, **Balthazar** (80 Spring St., 212/965-1414, www.balthazarny. com, Mon.-Fri. 7:30am-midnight, Sat. 8:30am-4pm and 5:30pm-1am, Sun. 8:30am-4pm and 5:30pm-midnight, $32), a large and bustling brasserie, still draws a sleek, celebrity-studded crowd.

Dark and stylish ★ **Raoul's** (180 Prince St., 212/966-3518, www.raouls. com, Sun.-Thurs. 5:30pm-midnight, Fri.-Sat. 5:30pm-1am, brunch served Sat.-Sun. 11:30am-3:30pm, $34), a French bistro, is a downtown hot spot and with good reason: The food and ambience are top-notch.

Reserve months in advance to get a seat at **Nobu** (105 Hudson St., 212/219-0500, www. noburestaurants.com, Mon.-Fri. 11:45am-2:15pm, Sun.-Thurs. 6pm-10:15pm, Fri.-Sat. 6pm-11:15pm, $40), arguably the most famous Japanese restaurant (with Peruvian touches) in the United States. Partly owned by Robert DeNiro, and a favorite among celebrities, the sleek eatery offers lots of innovative fare created by acclaimed chef Nobu Matsuhisa.

EAST VILLAGE

The East Village has traditionally been known for its cheap, Eastern European eateries, where the average main course costs $12. One legendary 2nd Avenue spot is **Veselka** (144 2nd Ave., 212/228-9682, www.veselka.com, daily 24 hours, $18), the place to go for borscht, pierogi, and scrumptious poppy-seed cake.

The East Village is also known for inexpensive Indian restaurants, most of which lie along 6th Street between 1st and 2nd Avenues.

Follow That Food Truck!

New York City is fully in the age of the food truck. Despite the constant threat of parking tickets and the stress of working in claustrophobic mobile kitchens, food trucks have allowed many entrepreneurial chefs who can't afford a brick-and-mortar restaurant the chance to build their own mini-culinary empires. For the city's office workers, food trucks offer a welcome alternative to the uninspired sandwich. For travelers, they offer a chance to experience New York City's cultural and culinary diversity without securing coveted reservations or footing the bill for expensive sit-down meals.

Practically every cuisine imaginable is served from food trucks: Jamaican and Colombian, Mexican and Korean—even Mexican/Korean—and everything in between. You can wash your meal down with a juice from **Green Pirate Juice Truck** and then head to the next truck for dessert: Cupcakes, ice cream, doughnuts, cookies, brownies, and crepes are just some of the sweet treats on wheels.

Many food trucks cluster around 48th and 49th Streets and Park Avenue during lunchtime. Simply walk up and down the street to see what strikes your fancy. Most food trucks use the social media site Twitter to broadcast their locations and daily specials. And if you're in New York in September, consider attending **The Vendy Awards** (www.streetvendor.org/vendys). Started in 2004, Vendys are the Oscars of street food. Street cart and food truck vendors participate in a cook-off for attendees and judges as they vie for an award.

Panna II (93 1st Ave., 212/598-4610, www.pannatwo.com, daily noon-midnight, $22) is one fabulously festive BYOB spot covered in Christmas and chili pepper lights.

One of the oldest pastry shops in the East Village is **Veniero's** (342 E. 11th St., 212/674-7070, www.venierospastry.com, Sun.-Thurs. 8am-11:45pm, Fri.-Sat. 8am-12:45am, $6). Established in 1894, it features classic Italian treats.

GREENWICH VILLAGE AND WEST VILLAGE

Corner Bistro (331 W. 4th St., 212/242-9502, www.cornerbistrony.com, Mon.-Sat. 11:30am-4am, Sun. noon-4am, $12), a dark pub with creaky wooden booths and an excellent jazz jukebox, has been turning out burgers and other diner hits for decades.

Widely considered one of the city's best pizzerias, ★ **John's** (278 Bleecker St., 212/243-1680, www.johnsbrickovenpizza.com, Sun.-Thurs. 11:30am-11pm, Fri.-Sat. 11:30am-midnight, $21) draws long lines for its thin, crispy, and non-greasy New York-style pies. Pizza is sold by the whole pie only, no slices.

Pearl Oyster Bar (18 Cornelia St., 212/691-8211, www.pearloysterbar.com, Mon.-Thurs. noon-2:30pm and 5:30pm-10:30pm, Fri. noon-2:30pm and 6pm-11pm, Sat. 6pm-11pm, $30) is a New England clam shack in the heart of the Village. Try the sublime lobster roll.

CHELSEA AND THE MEATPACKING DISTRICT

Numerous restaurants, many with outdoor tables in summer, line 7th and 8th Avenues between 14th and 23rd Streets. Among them is **Cafeteria** (119 7th Ave., 212/414-1717, www.cafeteriagroup.com, daily 24 hours, $16), serving excellent brunches and a wide range of American fare.

Haven's Kitchen (109 W. 17th St., 212/929-7900, www.havenskitchen.com, Mon.-Sat., hours vary by season, $12) is a popular "farm to fork" café, cooking class center, and supper club.

For a taste of late-19th-century New York, visit **Keens Steakhouse** (72 W. 36th St., 212/947-3636, www.keens.com, Mon.-Fri. 11:45am-10:30pm, Sat. 5pm-10:30pm, Sun. 5pm-9:30pm, $55), an atmospheric multiroomed pub with a crackling fireplace in winter.

There's a happening scene at **The Standard Grill** (848 Washington St., 212/645-4100, www.thestandardgrill.com, Sun.-Wed. 7am-11:30pm, Thurs.-Sat. 7am-12:30am, $32) in hip The Standard hotel, where showy dishes like saffron pappardelle with braised rabbit draw a trendy crowd. There's outdoor seating.

UNION SQUARE AND MADISON SQUARE PARK

The refined, oak-lined **Gramercy Tavern** (42 E. 20th St., 212/477-0777, www.gramercytavern.com, Sun.-Thurs. 11:30am-11pm, Fri.-Sat. 11:30am-midnight, $36) serves award-winning, seasonal American fare, with an emphasis on local ingredients. Dinner is prix fixe in the dining room, but there are à la carte lunch options in the low-key, no-reservations front room.

Pricey—and, most agree, worth every penny—is **Eleven Madison Park** (11 Madison Ave., 212/889-0905, www.elevenmadisonpark.com, Mon.-Wed. 5:30pm-10pm, Thurs.-Sun. 5:30pm-10:30pm, $315), whose multicourse tasting menu features New York State-sourced fare.

MIDTOWN AND TIMES SQUARE

If you're planning to eat in the Theater District before a show, make reservations or give yourself plenty of time. Many restaurants are packed 6:30pm-8pm. During warm weather, both Bryant Park (between 40th and 42nd Sts., 5th and 6th Aves.) and the steps of The New York Public Library are good spots for lunch. Nearby vendors sell everything from hot dogs to gourmet fare.

At the **'wichcraft** kiosk in Bryant Park, you can pick up sandwiches and soups to enjoy at one of the park's tables. For something a bit more upscale, make your way to **Bryant Park Grill** and the **Bryant Park Cafe** (25 W. 40th St., 212/840-6500, www.arkrestaurants.com, daily 11:30am-3:30pm and 5pm-11pm, $32) overlooking The New York Public Library's back lawn. Both serve imaginative American fare in a handsome setting, but the grill is somewhat more formal. In summer, a rooftop terrace opens up.

In the Theater District, across from the Shubert Alley is legendary **Sardi's Restaurant** (234 W. 44th St., 212/221-8440, www.sardis.com, Tues.-Sun. lunch and dinner, $30), its walls lined with caricatures of celebrities. Once frequented by theater folks, Sardi's now attracts mostly tourists, but is still a fun, lively spot serving varied international cuisine.

Nearby, you'll find the area known as Restaurant Row on West 46th Street between 8th and 9th Avenues. Many of the restaurants here will have pre-theater prix fixe menus or after-show specials, or both. One such spot, located inside a charming brownstone, is **Hourglass Tavern** (373 W. 46th St., 212/265-2060, www.hourglasstavern.com, Sun.-Tue. 4pm-11pm, Wed.-Sat. 4pm-midnight, Sat.-Sun. brunch 11am-3pm), whose $27 prix fixe dinner menu includes bread, soup or salad, an entrée, and dessert.

Ninth Avenue between 42nd and 59th Streets is lined with one restaurant after another. Among them is the **Afghan Kebab House** (764 9th Ave., 212/307-1612, www.afghankebabhouse1.com, daily 11:30am-11pm, $15), serving succulent kebabs in exotic surroundings. And airy, well-lit **Uncle Nick's** (747 9th Ave., 212/245-7992, www.unclenicksgreekcuisine.com, daily 11:30am-11pm, $20), one of Manhattan's few Greek restaurants.

One of the most recent additions to the Midtown dining scene is the multi-concept market/restaurant of superstar chef José Andrés, whose ★ Mercado Little Spain (10 Hudson Yards, www.littlespain.com, daily 7am-11pm, prices vary by restaurant/stall) includes a churros stand, a cocktail bar, a sandwich stall, a pastry shop, a seafood spot, and, among others, a restaurant specializing in dishes cooked over a wood fire. Despite being deluged by enthusiastic customers at all hours, the service here is particularly attentive and friendly, thanks to intensive training.

For a classic New York lunch, eat at Grand Central Terminal's ★ **Oyster Bar** (89 E. 42nd St., inside Grand Central, lower level, 212/490-6650, www.oysterbarny.com, Mon.-Sat. 11:30am-9pm, $34), complete with red-checked tablecloths and a vaulted ceiling. Adjoining the main restaurant is a cheaper counter area, where dishes average $13. Note that the counter closes earlier.

UPPER EAST SIDE

The soon to be a centenarian **Lexington Candy Shop** (1226 Lexington Ave., 212/288-0057, www.lexingtoncandyshop.net, Mon.-Fri. 7am-7pm, Sat. 8am-7pm, Sun. 8am-6pm, $12) may make you think this spot sells nothing but sweets, but it's actually an old-fashioned luncheonette founded in 1925.

Good Persian food can be found at **Persepolis** (1407 2nd Ave., 212/535-1100, www.persepolisnewyork.com, Sun.-Thurs. noon-11pm, Fri.-Sat. noon-11:30pm, $24), offering succulent kabobs, fragrant, deeply spiced stews, and sour cherry rice.

Candle Cafe (1307 3rd Ave., 212/472-0970, www.candlecafe.com, Mon.-Fri. 11:30am-10pm, Sat. 11am-10pm, Sun. 11am-9:30pm, $20) offers scrumptious vegan food even a carnivore can enjoy.

Daniel (60 E. 65th St., 212/288-0033, www.danielnyc.com, Mon.-Sat. 5pm-10:30pm), named for chef Daniel Boulud, wins kudos from food critics for its superb French cuisine, discerning wine list, and impeccable decor. The four-course prix fixe tasting menu is $158; a wine pairing is extra. There is also a seven-course tasting menu. Note that this restaurant has a dress code.

UPPER WEST SIDE

For good people-watching during the summer, stake out an outdoor table in one of the many eateries located directly across from Lincoln Center.

Funky **Gray's Papaya** (2090 Broadway, 212/799-0243, www.grayspapayanyc.com, daily 24 hours, $3) sells some of the city's best cheap hot dogs—to be eaten standing up. Hole-in-the-wall **La Caridad 78** (2199 Broadway, 212/874-2780, www.lacaridad78.com, $12) is the best of the Cuban Chinese restaurants in this part of town—just look at the long line of cabdrivers out front.

The Upper West Side is a bit of a brunch destination, due in no small part to restaurants like **Sarabeth's** (423 Amsterdam Ave., 212/496-6280, www.sarabethsrestaurants.com, daily 8am-10pm, $28). **Epicerie Boulud** (1900 Broadway, 212/595-9606, www.epicerieboulud.com, Mon. 7am-10pm, Tue.-Sat. 7am-11pm, Sun. 8am-10pm, $12) is also an option, with soups and sandwiches, cheese and charcuterie, an oyster bar, and lots of luscious pastries. Note that there isn't much seating here, however.

Barney Greengrass (541 Amsterdam Ave., 212/724-4707, www.barneygreengrass.com, Tue.-Fri. 8:30am-4pm, Sat.-Sun. 8:30am-5pm, $45) is best known for its traditional bagels and lox, and has been a favorite in this neighborhood for over 100 years. The sit-down restaurant has pricey (but delicious) smoked fish platters.

HARLEM

Skip the famous Sylvia's, which has become overrun with tourists dispatched by the busload, in favor of **Miss Mamie's Spoonbread Too** (366 W. 110th St., 212/865-6744, www.spoonbreadinc.com, Mon.-Fri. 2:30pm-9:30pm, Sat. 11:30am-10:30pm, Sun. 11:30am-9:30pm, $20), which serves up heaping portions of tasty Southern dishes.

In a part of Harlem known as Little Senegal, **Africa Kine Restaurant** (2267 Adam Clayton Powell Jr. Blvd., 212/666-9400, www.africakine.com, daily noon-2am, $14) serves delectable Senegalese food. Share the grilled meats and stews, which come with bowls of rice.

The Coffee That Fuels the City That Never Sleeps

There's a Starbucks on practically every corner in New York City, but many coffee-loving locals prefer to patronize hometown cafés and coffeehouses. Here are a few favorites:

- **Blue Bottle Coffee** (450 W. 15th St.) advertises "a six-stool counter where we feature a selection of single origin coffees prepared on Manhattan's first Lucky i. Cremas siphon bar, along with nel drip-style coffee." In other words, this is not a venti fat-free soy latté kind of place. It's for serious coffee intellectuals.

- **Café Grumpy** (224 W. 20th St.) has a silly name that belies its serious coffee. Selections are noted not only by the micro-region in which the single-origin beans were harvested, but also by who roasted them. Selections are then prepared in an $11,000 Clover machine, which brews each cup individually, not only adjusting to the ideal water temperature but tailoring the process to that particular bean. Starbucks has since bought the company that makes Clover machines and stopped sales to any other coffeehouse, so Café Grumpy remains one of only several hundred owners of this specialized brewmaster. They enforce a strict no Wi-Fi policy—better to enjoy your coffee without digital distractions.

- **Pennylane** (305 E. 45th St.) is a welcome addition to a neighborhood once blighted by bad coffee. Thanks to this minimalist café's location a stone's throw from the United Nations, it's popular among diplomats. You might feel out of place among all the well-tailored suits and multilingual conversations, but these regulars are a friendly bunch. If you can't find a seat, there's ample space at Dag Hammarskjöld Plaza, just around the corner on 47th Street.

- **Stumptown Coffee Roasters at the Ace Hotel** (18 W. 29th St.) is good for an artisanal cup to go or, if you prefer, to be enjoyed in the trendy hotel's lobby, a de facto office for hip young entrepreneurial types.

On Harlem's east side, **Patsy's Pizzeria** (2287 1st Ave., 212/534-9783, www.thepatsyspizza.com, Mon.-Sat. 11am-midnight, Sun. 11am-11pm, $16) was the country's first coal-stoked brick-oven pizzeria. A Frank Sinatra favorite, it was established in 1932. Note that this is a cash-only establishment.

The traditional **Hungarian Pastry Shop** (1030 Amsterdam Ave., 212/866-4230, Mon.-Fri. 7:30am-11pm, Sat.-Sun. 8:30am-11pm, $4) sells mouthwatering strudel and other sweet treats. It's been a favorite haunt of Columbia University faculty, staff, and students since the 1960s.

Accommodations

With real estate values continually spiraling upward, cheap sleeps are not readily available in New York City. An "inexpensive" room costs $100-150 per night, while a moderately priced one with "nothing special" costs $150-250. The average hotel room now runs over $300 per night. It is likely to be small and cramped, with minimal amenities.

At the other end of the scale, New York is a glittering wonderland, home to some of the world's grandest hotels. The Plaza, Pierre, Four Seasons, Mandarin Oriental, and St. Regis are among the reigning monarchs. Even if you can't afford to stay in these elegant properties, they're well worth stepping into for afternoon tea, a cocktail, or just a look-see.

NYC & Company (800/NYC-VISIT or 212/484-1200, www.nycgo.com), the city's

NYC's Discount Weeks

"Budget-friendly" isn't exactly the first adjective that comes to mind when you think of planning a trip to New York City. Budget travelers shouldn't be discouraged from visiting, however. Visitors can cut costs by taking advantage of one of the city's special discount weeks. Often running at least nine days and as long as nearly a month, these "weeks" offer deep markdowns or two-for-one specials on typically expensive services or experiences, ranging from meals and Broadway shows to hotel accommodations and spa services.

- **Hotel Week:** Each January, dozens of hotels—many of them trendy boutique properties where standard nightly rates can exceed $500—sign on to offer travelers rooms at $100, $200, or $300 per night.

- **Broadway Week:** Since launching in 2011, Broadway Week has been wildly successful, selling more than 300,000 tickets through its two-for-one pricing system. It typically runs for the first two weeks in September and again for two weeks in late January/early February.

- **Off-Broadway Week:** Like Broadway Week, Off-Broadway Week runs for nearly two weeks in winter, offering two-for-one-priced tickets for popular and lesser-known shows at off-Broadway venues.

- **Comedy Week:** If you prefer stand-up, sketch, or improv comedy to dramas and musicals, time your visit to coincide with Comedy Week, which spans two weeks in late October-early November. Expect two-for-one tickets for well-known acts and emerging talent.

- **Spa Week:** Participating spas offer $50 treatments during this discount week, which is held each spring and fall.

- **Restaurant Week:** The original discount week and one of the city's favorites is Restaurant Week, which is held twice a year and typically runs as long as three weeks. Participating restaurants offer prix fixe lunch and dinner menus at far more comfortable prices.

For information about all of these discount weeks, visit NYC & Company's website (www.gonyc.com). Get deeper discounts—or even freebies—by following the city's tourism organization, NYC & Company, on twitter (www.twitter.com/nycgo). During discount weeks, trivia questions spotlighting business participants are tweeted out; followers who respond correctly may win a free meal, tickets, or a service.

official convention and visitors bureau, sponsors Hotel Week each January, a discount program intended to promote tourism in the slower winter months by making hotel rooms more affordable. Rooms that typically go for $300 and up may go as low as $100, with special amenities added as incentives to book.

Another option for saving money is booking online. Expedia.com, Orbitz.com, Hotels.com, and Hotwire.com are among the most popular, though many hotel managers say they will meet or beat these booking engines' rates if you call the hotel directly and inquire.

Keep in mind that in addition to the room rate, you'll also have to pay a hefty hotel tax of 14.75 percent.

LOWER MANHATTAN
$150-300

As far as location goes, it's pretty hard to beat **Conrad Hotel** (102 North End Ave., 212/945-0100, www.hilton.com, $250 and up), which is steps from both the Hudson River (some rooms overlook the waterway) and a massive complex of shops and restaurants.

Over $300

W New York Downtown (8 Albany St., 646/826-8600, www.wnewyorkdowntown.

com, $485 and up) took a gamble with this location: Would people want to stay so close— practically atop—the site where the 9/11 terrorist attacks occurred? The answer has been a clear "Yes." Guests love the bird's-eye view of the gleaming new One World Trade Center. The terrace bar is pretty spectacular, and the hotel is just a short walk from multiple subway lines.

LOWER EAST SIDE
Under $150

The **Chelsea Center** (83 Essex St., 646/669-8495, www.chelseacenterhostel.com, $35 pp bunk, $100 private room) is a small, friendly hostel with dorm-style accommodations, free luggage storage and a safe, and a light continental breakfast. All rooms share bathrooms. Note that this is a cash-only establishment.

Over $300

All of the 110 rooms at sleek and minimalist 20-story **Hotel on Rivington** (107 Rivington St., between Essex and Ludlow Sts., 212/475-2600, www.hotelonrivington.com, $375-580) are wrapped in glass, offering stunning views of Manhattan. Velvet couches, heated-tile bathroom floors, private terraces, and in-room spa services are among the hotel's attractions, not to mention its hot location.

SOHO AND TRIBECA
Over $300

When it opened in 1996, 370-room ★ **SoHo Grand** (310 W. Broadway, at Grand Ave., 212/965-3000 or 800/965-3000, www.sohogrand.com, $400-550) was SoHo's first hotel since the 1800s. Sleekly done up in industrial metals, oversize lamps, columns, and sofas in its lobby, the hotel has become a chic, minimalist haven for well-heeled fashionables and Europeans. Custom-designed guest rooms feature muted grays. Adjoining the lobby is a classy, high-ceilinged bar.

The Mercer (147 Mercer St., at Prince St., 212/966-6060 or 888/918-6060, www.mercer-hotel.com, $550-760) is a stylish spot, located in the middle of SoHo. Each of its 75 understated rooms is done up in furniture made of African woods and features a large bathroom with a tub made for two. Downstairs is Mercer Kitchen restaurant.

EAST VILLAGE
Over $300

From the moment you approach **The Bowery** (335 Bowery, 212/515-9100, www.theboweryhotel.com, $420-500) and the red-vested, black-bowler-hatted doorman welcomes you in, you feel as if you've slipped back into Old New York. With exceptional, warm service and public areas that are so inviting, you'll be tempted to tuck into a heavy leather chair before the crackling fire or greenery-filled courtyard and hide from the world, sipping a martini in the smokeless period bar. It really seems wasted on a city that has so much to offer outside the lobby doors. There are also floor-to-ceiling factory-style windows and generous tubs built for two.

GREENWICH VILLAGE AND WEST VILLAGE
Under $150

The Jane (113 Jane St., 212/924-6700, www.thejanenyc.com, $105-135) is a lively, hip boutique hotel with an amazing bar housed in a century-old building, offering great amenities (free wireless Internet, robes, flat-screen TV with DVD) and rooms reminiscent of a luxury train car. Larger "Captain's Cabins" offer private baths.

$150-300

Though small, the lobby of family-owned ★ **Washington Square Hotel** (103 Waverly Pl., 212/777-9515, www.washingtonsquarehotel.com, $201-351) is stunning with all black-and-white tiles, lacy iron grillwork, gilded adornments, and Audubon prints. Rooms feature art deco touches, and you can't beat the location, just off Washington Square Park.

UNION SQUARE AND MADISON SQUARE PARK
$150-300

No one seems to mind the tiny rooms at the trendy **Ace Hotel** (20 W. 29th St., 212/679-2222, www.acehotel.com/newyork, $199 and up). Design aficionados love the bold touches here, and the hotel's lobby is always buzzing with locals, who use the dark, café-like space as their personal office. An outlet of the popular Stumptown Coffee is just off the lobby.

Over $300

At the stylish **W Union Square** (201 Park Ave. S, at 17th St., 212/253-9119, $300-1,000), you'll find well-appointed rooms filled with ultracomfortable furnishings and a lively lobby-bar filled with beautiful people. This is one of several W hotels in the city.

CHELSEA AND THE MEATPACKING DISTRICT
$150-300

Modernist with a nautical theme, **The Maritime Hotel** (363 W.16th St., 212/242-4300, www.themaritimehotel.com, $265-345) is a 126-room boutique hotel whose 5-foot-diameter (1.5 m) porthole windows add a decorative charm to the boldly decorated rooms, as well as views out onto Midtown and the Hudson River. An on-site restaurant and the Tao Downtown nightclub have made this a popular place in the neighborhood for both guests and visitors alike.

Over $300

The Standard (848 Washington St., 212/645-4646, www.standardhotels.com/new-york-city, $300-400) hits an architectural high note straddling the elevated High Line park. Floor-to-ceiling windows in the guest rooms, knockout views, and the outdoor biergarten don't hurt.

MIDTOWN AND TIMES SQUARE
$150-300

Charming ★ **Affinia Shelburne** (303 Lexington Ave., 212/689-5200, www.affinia.com, $230-299) in the Murray Hill neighborhood is boldly modern. Upstairs are spacious suites with two double beds and well-equipped kitchens, making this a good value for the money.

Built in 1901, the spiffy, neo-art deco

Bikes are an amenity at The Maritime Hotel in Chelsea.

★ **Kixby** (45 W. 35th St., between 5th and 6th Aves., 212/947-2500 or 800/356-3870, www. kixby.com, $250-380) offers 195 recently renovated guest rooms and a large, comfortable lobby. An exercise room and lively rooftop terrace are on the top floor, where drinks are served in summer.

Still deliciously old-fashioned, with lots of wood paneling and brocaded chairs, is the 1902 ★ **Algonquin** (59 W. 44th St., between 5th and 6th Aves., 212/840-6800 or 800/555-8000, www.algonquinhotel.com, $270-500). Each floor has a different color scheme, and the inviting rooms offer plump beds, comfy armchairs, and bathrooms equipped with plenty of amenities. Downstairs, where Dorothy Parker and friends once met, are several snug lounges perfect for afternoon tea, cocktails, or aperitifs.

$300-500

Hyatt Times Square New York (135 W. 45th St., 646/364-1234, www.timessquare-hyatt.com, $399) is a newer, 487-room hotel in a mirror-like 54-story tower that literally reflects the city. Rooms are surprisingly large for a Midtown hotel (even bigger than some New Yorkers' apartments!), and are enlivened with New York City-themed pop, minimalist, and conceptual artwork. After you check in by iPad, you can explore on-site amenities, including a chic rooftop lounge, trendy diner, fitness center, and the only hotel spa in the neighborhood.

The European-styled ★ **Hotel Elysée** (60 E. 54th St., between Madison and Park Aves., 212/753-1066 or 800/535-9733, www.elysee-hotel.com, $439-500) is furnished in dark woods, plush carpets, and Asian antiques. Most of the rooms have Italian marble bathrooms, and adjoining the lobby is the classy Monkey Bar, its walls covered with murals. Among the famous residents who once lived in the Elysée are Joe DiMaggio, Tallulah Bankhead, and Tennessee Williams.

UPPER EAST SIDE
$300-500

Downstairs at the small and stylish **Franklin** (164 E. 87th St., between Lexington and 3rd Aves., 212/369-1000, www.franklinhotel.com, $330-490) is a tiny streamlined lobby done up in black and burnished steel with mirrors and fresh flowers. Upstairs are 53 cozy guest rooms featuring beds with billowing canopies, cherrywood furnishings, and a fresh flower at each bedside.

Over $500

A magnificent slice of the Old World can be found at the ★ **Pierre Hotel** (5th Ave., at 61st St., 212/838-8000 or 800/749-7734, www. thepierreny.com, $600-1,400). The stunning lobby is adorned with chandeliers, fresh flowers, silks, and damasks, while the guest rooms are lavishly furnished with antiques. A good way to sample the Pierre, even if you can't afford to stay, is to stop in at the baroque-styled Rotunda for an elegant afternoon tea.

UPPER WEST SIDE
$150-300

The friendly ★ **Hotel Beacon** (2130 Broadway, at 75th St., 212/787-1100 or 800/572-4969, www.beaconhotel.com, $245-295) offers good value for the money. Its rooms are large and attractive and equipped with two double beds and kitchenettes. The lobby gleams with black-and-white marble and brass.

HARLEM
Under $150

Efuru Guest House and Suites (106 W. 120th St., 212/961-9855, www.efuru-nyc.com, $85-129) is comprised of two brownstones in the heart of historic Harlem. Homey, deluxe rooms and studio apartments have full kitchens, and each accommodation is equipped with cable TV and wireless Internet, as well as access to the shared courtyard.

Information and Services

TOURIST INFORMATION

New York City's Official Visitor Information Center (810 7th Ave., 212/484-1222, www.nycgo.com, Mon.-Fri. 8:30am-6pm, Sat.-Sun. 9am-5pm), run by NYC & Company, New York's tourism marketing organization, is open 365 days a year. Maps, brochures, and events calendars are available. The center also runs a visitor information kiosk in **Macy's Herald Square** (151 W. 34th St., 212/484-1222).

When out of town, written information can be ordered by calling **NYC & Company** (800/NYC-VISIT or 212/484-1200).

Downtown Alliance (212/566-6700, www.downtownny.com) can provide you with information about Lower Manhattan. Various business partnerships operate carts stocked with tourist brochures near such visitor-heavy sites as Grand Central Terminal and the Empire State Building.

TOURS

No matter where your interests lie—in architecture, ethnic foods, or social history—you can find a tour tailor-made for you. Walking tours abound all over the city, especially in spring and fall, with each one more imaginative than the next (for example, "Famous Murder Sites" and "Edith Wharton's New York"). Most are reasonably priced.

City Tours

One of the best ways to get an overview of the city is to take a **Circle Line** cruise (Pier 83, W. 42nd St. and Hudson River, 212/563-3200, www.circleline.com, prices vary by tour). Boats cruise daily year-round. Standard daytime cruises last three hours; "express" and evening cruises last two hours.

Gray Line Sightseeing (777 8th Ave., 212/445-0848, www.graylinenewyork.com, prices vary by tour) offers over a dozen bus tours lasting anywhere from two hours to a full day. Tours are offered year-round. Gray Line also offers sightseeing cruises.

For a spectacular bird's-eye view of the city, try **Liberty Helicopter Tours** (212/967-6464, www.libertyhelicopter.com, $200 and up pp, reservations required).

Walking Tours

The Municipal Art Society (111 W. 57th St., 212/935-3960, www.mas.org) runs an extensive series of walking tours almost daily year-round. Most of the tours focus on architecture and history.

Context Travel (800/691-6036, www.contexttravel.com) offers walking tours on various topics, including architecture, art, and urban history; all are led by scholars. Groups are intimate, never booking more than six people.

Big Onion Walking Tours (888/606-9255, www.bigonion.com), founded by two Columbia University graduate students, offers some of the city's most fun and well-researched tours. Many of the tours concentrate on New York's immigrant history and on neighborhoods below 14th Street.

The 92nd Street Y (1395 Lexington Ave., 212/415-5500, www.92y.org), a leading cultural institution, offers many excellent walking and bus tours. They're very popular and must be reserved weeks in advance.

In Harlem, **Harlem Spirituals** (212/391-0900, www.harlemspirituals.com) specializes in visits to gospel services and soul food restaurants, as well as historic sites. **Harlem Heritage Tours** (212/280-7888, www.harlemheritage.com) offers many different tours, ranging from "jazz nights in Harlem" to gospel walking tours.

Downtown, the **Lower East Side Tenement Museum** (103 Orchard St., 212/982-8420, www.tenement.org) sponsors walking tours of old immigrant neighborhoods. For a hip tour of the East Village and environs, check out Rock Junket Tours (212/209-3370, www.rockjunket.com). "Rocker guides" lead participants past legendary rock, punk, and glam sites from the 1960s to the present.

Other unique tours focus on niche interests, including food, and nature. Foods of New York Tours (212/913-9964, www.foodsofny.com, prices vary by tour, tastings included) explores some of the most famous restaurants and food shops in Greenwich Village, the West Village, Chelsea, and Chinatown. Worth watching out for are free nature walks offered in all five boroughs by the Urban Park Rangers (212/360-2774 or 866/692-4295, www.nyc.gov/parks).

The Big Apple Greeter (212/669-8159, www.bigapplegreeter.org) matches visitors with enthusiastic volunteers eager to introduce the city to out-of-towners. The service is completely free and especially helpful to the disabled and tourists interested in visiting off-the-beaten-track spots.

TIPS FOR TRAVELERS
Tipping
A 15-20 percent tip is customary for waiters and taxi drivers. Hotel bellhops expect $1-2 a bag, porters $1-2 for hailing a cab, and room attendants $3-5 per person per night.

Restrooms
Finding a place to use the bathroom in Manhattan can be challenging when you're out and about; most restaurants and cafés post signs warning that bathrooms are for paying customers only. Some of the most accessible public restrooms in Manhattan are at Grand Central Terminal (42nd St. and Park Ave.), the main branch of The New York Public Library (5th Ave. and 42nd St.), on the southeastern edge of Madison Square Park (E. 23rd St. and Park Ave S.), and Barnes and Noble and Whole Foods (various locations).

Safety
As in most big cities, crime in New York can be a problem, and in the past, New York had a bad reputation for all sorts of crime. In recent years, however, New York has consistently ranked as one of America's safest large cities. Statistically, your chances of being mugged are less than 30,000 to 1. To avoid being that one:

Act as if you know where you're going, especially when passing through empty neighborhoods. New Yorkers, forever blasé, keep up a brisk, disinterested pace at all times. When unsure if you are headed the correct way, better to circle the block walking purposefully to head back in the correct direction than to flaunt your confusion.

Don't carry large quantities of cash or large bills, but do carry something; $20 is recommended.

Avoid parks at night, and be extra careful around transportation centers such as Port Authority and Penn Station.

In residential neighborhoods, stick to blocks where other people are in sight or at least where cars are passing by. At night, on empty streets, walk near the curb, away from dark overhangs.

LGBTQ Travelers
Founded in 1983, The Lesbian, Gay, Bisexual & Transgender Community Center (208 W. 13th St., between 7th and 8th Aves., 212/620-7310, www.gaycenter.org) houses the National Museum and Archive of Lesbian and Gay History and hosts numerous events that are open to the public. Everything from dances to movies is presented here. Free information "Welcome Packets" about the city are also available for travelers.

Travelers with Disabilities
New York is difficult for visitors with disabilities to navigate, as much of the city's core infrastructure is so old, but information and support are available. One source is the Mayor's Office for People with Disabilities (311), which puts out a free Access Guide.

For more general information, contact Society for Accessible Travel and

Hospitality (212/447-7284, www.sath.org), a nationwide nonprofit membership organization that collects data on travel facilities around the country.

The **Big Apple Greeter** program (212/669-8159), available free to all visitors, matches out-of-towners with New Yorkers eager to share their hometown. Of the 300+ volunteer "Big Apple Greeters," many are specifically trained to help people with disabilities enjoy the city.

All of New York's buses are wheelchair accessible, but only a handful of subway stations are (the number is growing, however). **New York City Transit** (718/596-8585, www.mta.info) maintains information about stations with elevators and escalators on its website, as well as service outages. The city also runs the Accessible Dispatch program for wheelchair users to call for **accessible taxis** (646/599-9999).

EMERGENCIES

Dial 911 for emergency **police, ambulance,** or **fire department** response. For the location of the nearest police precinct, call 311.

Private hospitals with 24-hour emergency rooms include **Mount Sinai Beth Israel Medical Center** (1st Ave., at 16th St., 212/420-2000), **New York University Langone Medical Center** (1st Ave., at 34th St., 212/263-7300), **Mount Sinai West** (9th Ave., at 58th St., 212/523-4000), **New York-Presbyterian/Weill Cornell Medical Center** (York Ave., at 68th St., 212/746-5454), and **Mount Sinai Medical Center** (5th Ave., at 100th St., 212/241-6500).

Getting There

AIR

New York is serviced by three airports. **John F. Kennedy International Airport** (www.jfkairport.com) is about 15 miles (24 km) from Manhattan in Queens. It's the largest of the three and handles primarily international flights. **La Guardia Airport** (www.laguardiaairport.com), also in Queens, is about 8 miles (12.9 km) from Manhattan and handles primarily domestic flights. **Newark Liberty International Airport** (www.newarkairport.com), across the Hudson River in New Jersey, handles domestic and some international flights. Kennedy is generally the most congested of the three airports, Newark the least; however, ongoing construction at La Guardia means that incoming and outgoing travelers should build in extra time to get in and out of this airport.

Public transportation from the airports into Manhattan and the other boroughs is excellent; call 800/247-7433 for general information.

A **taxi ride** into Manhattan from La Guardia takes 20-30 minutes and costs about $45, including tolls and tip. The fare is a standard metered fare, so prices will vary based on traffic and time of day. The ride from Kennedy to Manhattan takes 30-45 minutes and costs a flat fare of $52, plus tolls, tip, and some obligatory surcharges (when going the other way, from Manhattan to Kennedy, the trip is metered, but usually costs about the same). The 45-minute ride from Newark usually runs about $65. Cabs leave from well-marked stands staffed by dispatchers, just outside the flight arrival areas at all airports. Avoid "gypsy" cabs and drivers asking "Taxi? Taxi?" near baggage claim areas and just outside the terminal.

NYC Express Bus (718/777-5111, www.nycairporter.com) offers frequent bus service to and from LaGuardia ($16 one-way) and Kennedy ($19 one-way). Stops are made near Grand Central Terminal (Park Ave. between 41st and 42nd Sts.), inside the Port Authority

Bus Terminal (42nd St. and 8th Ave.), and near Penn Station (33rd St. and 7th Ave.).

Newark Airport Express (212/964-6233 or 877/894-9155, www.newarkairportexpress. com) offers frequent bus service between Newark Airport and Manhattan ($17 one-way, $30 round-trip). Buses leave every 15 minutes and make three stops in Manhattan: near Grand Central Terminal (41st St. and Park Ave.), next to Bryant Park (northwest corner of 42nd St. and 5th Ave.), and inside the Port Authority (42nd St. and 8th Ave.).

SuperShuttle (212/209-7000, www.supershuttle.com) offers door-to-door pick-up van service from homes and hotels to any of the three area airports. Fares start around $24.

Of course, rideshare services like **Lyft** and **Uber** also offer transportation to and from all three airports. Consult the app upon arrival or departure for current pricing.

TRAIN

Manhattan has two main railroad stations: **Pennsylvania Station** (33rd St. and 7th Ave.), commonly referred to as Penn Station, and **Grand Central Terminal** (42nd St. and Park Ave.). All **Amtrak** trains (800/872-7245) arrive and depart from Penn Station. **New Jersey Transit** (973/762-5100) and **Long Island Rail Road** (718/217-5477) also offer passenger-train service out of Penn Station. **Metro-North** (212/532-4900) runs commuter trains to suburban New York and Connecticut from Grand Central. Both stations are well serviced by buses, subways, and taxis.

BUS

Port Authority (8th Ave. between 40th and 42nd Sts., 212/564-8484) is the world's largest bus terminal, serving both commuter and long-distance travelers. Major bus lines departing from the terminal include **Greyhound** (800/231-2222, www.greyhound.com), **Peter Pan** (800/343-9999, www.peterpanbus.com), and **New Jersey Transit** (973/762-5100 or 800/772-2222, www.njtransit.com).

CAR

If you must drive into Manhattan, be prepared to pay a steep price for parking at a garage (often $20 or more an hour) or to spend 20 minutes or more looking for street parking. Street meters are disappearing in the city, but don't think that means they're free; each block has one or two machines where you make your payment via credit or debit card. Be sure to get the receipt, which must be displayed on the driver's side of your car's dashboard.

Getting Around

Most of Manhattan is laid out in a grid pattern, which makes it easy to find your way around. Avenues run north-south, streets east-west, and most are one-way. Fifth Avenue, which marks the city's center, separates the East and West Sides. Street addresses are labeled accordingly (1 E. 50th St., 1 W. 50th St.), with numbers increasing as you head away from 5th Avenue. Broadway, following an old Algonquin trail, cuts through the city on a diagonal.

Neighborhoods not laid out in a numbered grid pattern—essentially everything south of 14th Street—are more difficult to navigate; it helps to have a good map. The same applies in the other boroughs, where it's also a good idea to get exact directions to your destination before you set out.

If you don't know how to get where you're going, you can use mapping and directions services on the MTA's website (www.mta.info).

Walking is by far the best way to see New York City. In Manhattan, calculate about a minute to walk each north-south block and two minutes for each east-west block.

SUBWAY

Subways are the easiest and quickest way to get around town. Service is frequent, at least in Manhattan, and the trains run 24 hours a day, 7 days a week, year-round.

To ride the subways, you'll need a MetroCard, an electronic fare card, which can be purchased at kiosks in subway stations and can be bought in either value or time increments (7 day or 30 day). Basic fare is $2.75. Fees change regularly; access www.mta.info for up-to-date information.

Subway maps are usually posted in each station, and free copies are sometimes available at service booths. You can also see the map online at www.mta.info.

Three main subway lines service the city, each with multiple trains and routes. The IRT runs north-south on either side of Manhattan; the IND runs along 6th and 8th Avenues; and the BMT runs from Lower Manhattan to Brooklyn and Queens. A new line, the Second Avenue subway, opened in late 2016.

Subway lines have numbers and colors, but New Yorkers typically refer to the trains they take by number, not color. They also don't typically use the terms IRT, IND, or BMT. Lines used most frequently by visitors are the No. 6 train, which makes local stops along the East Side of Manhattan, and the No. 1 train, which makes local stops along the West Side. There's also a Grand Central-Times Square Shuttle connecting the east and west sides on 42nd Street.

Over 5.7 million passengers travel the nearly 700 miles (1130 km) of active subway track every day without mishap. Still, crime is an occasional problem and you should take certain precautions. Keep a close eye on your belongings, especially during rush hours when the crush of the crowd makes pickpocketing easy. Don't wear expensive jewelry or have electronics, such as smartphones, visible. Avoid empty or near-empty cars, even during the day, when the subways are theoretically the safest. Sit in the center car, which has a conductor and is usually the most crowded car on the train. Finally, although many New Yorkers ride the subways at all hours, it's not especially advisable to take them after midnight.

BUS

Buses run 24 hours a day uptown along 10th, 8th, 6th, Madison, 3rd, and 1st Avenues, and downtown along 9th, 7th, 5th, and 2nd Avenues. East-west crosstown service can be found on Houston, 8th/9th, 14th, 23rd, 34th, 42nd, 49th/50th, 57th, 66th, 72nd, 79th, 86th, 96th, 116th, and 125th Streets. Bus stops are usually located every two blocks, and signs or shelters mark the spots.

The fare is $2.75, payable with either exact change (no bills) or the electronic MetroCard. Free transfers are available between uptown-downtown buses and crosstown buses, enabling you to make any one-way trip in Manhattan on a single fare. Good bus service is also available in the outer boroughs. Fees change regularly. Access the website for up-to-date information: www.mta.info. Also, note that the "Select Bus" service was introduced in 2010, turning some routes into "skip-stop" service. For these buses (indicated by "Select Bus" written on the front), fares are paid via machine at the bus shelter using your MetroCard. (You'll need to hold on to the receipt as proof of payment; uniformed and undercover officers on board spot-check for fare evaders.)

BIKE

It's never been a better time to cycle New York City, thanks to nearly 1,300 miles (2090 km) of bike lanes and an additional 1,000 miles (1610 km) of car-free lanes. Citi Bike (www. citibikenyc.com) is the city's bike share program; visitors can use the service as often as they'd like, using the pay-as-you-go system. Download the Citi Bike app for a map of bike stations. Be sure to wear a helmet; it's the law, as is following the same traffic rules as cars.

TAXI AND CAR SERVICE

Another mode of New York City transportation is the taxicab, all painted yellow with lighted signs on their roofs. When the sign is lit, the cab is available and may be hailed and taken anywhere. Fares begin at $2.50 for the first 0.25 mile, then jump $0.50 for each additional 0.2 mile and for every 60 seconds of waiting time or slow traffic. A $1 surcharge is added to rides begun between 4pm and 8pm; a $0.50 surcharge is added to rides begun between 8pm and 6am; and a $.30 surcharge is added as an "improvement" fee. A 15-20 percent tip is the norm and can be added automatically to the fare by the passenger when using a debit or credit card.

In late 2013, the city introduced a new series of taxis designed especially for the "outer" boroughs. The so-called "Boro Taxis" are "apple green," and can only be hailed in the boroughs *or* in Manhattan above E. 96th Street on the East Side and W. 110th Street on the West Side.

For decades, New Yorkers have often preferred to use a car service rather than taxi when making certain trips, especially trips to airports. Popular services include **Dial 7** (212/777-7777, www.dial7.com) and **Carmel** (866/666-6666, www.carmellimo.com). Many New Yorkers also use smartphone app-based services like **Uber** (www.uber.com) and **Lyft** (www.lyft.com). Though convenient, such service can be more expensive than the other taxi or car service options listed here.

BOAT AND FERRY SERVICE

Sometimes, especially when you're in the midst of the concrete jungle, it's easy to forget that you're surrounded by water in New York City. As such, plenty of "if by sea" (or river, as the case may be!) travel options are available. An insider tip? They're often the fastest and easiest way to get around, too!

NYC Ferry (www.ferry.nyc) rules the East River, the waterway dividing Manhattan from Queens. With fares matching those of the NYC subway system, the $2.75 zip across the river is a bargain, free from many of the annoyances of the subway system.

New York Waterway (www.nywaterway.com) owns Hudson River routes, on Manhattan's West Side, connecting, especially, New York and New Jersey. Fares vary based on destination.

New York Water Taxi (www.nywatertaxi.com) tends to cater more to visitors than residents of the city, offering sightseeing jaunts. Locals use the water taxi primarily for shopping trips to Ikea. Fares vary based on destination.

water taxi and ferry

Long Island

The North Shore 111
The North Fork
    and Shelter Island. . . .121
The South Shore 128
The Hamptons. 137
Information
    and Services 155
Getting There
    and Around. 155

Long Island stretches east from New York City

for about 120 miles (193 km). Remarkably, given its proximity to the city, much of the island is still farmland, dunes, and beach.

At the westernmost end of the island are the New York City boroughs of Brooklyn and Queens. So, in common parlance, Long Island begins at the Queens-Nassau County border. The farther east you travel, the more the island resembles its Algonquin name, Paumanok, said to mean "the island with its breast long drawn out and laid against the sea." Long Island's shape has often been compared to a whale. Its eastern bulk, never much more than 20 miles (32 km) wide, splits at the 80-mile (129 km) point into two curving spits of land, or "flukes,"

Highlights

Look for ★ to find recommended sights, activities, dining, and lodging.

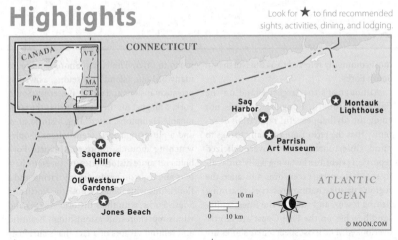

© MOON.COM

★ **Roam the Old Westbury Gardens:** Resplendent as it is, the mansion isn't the main attraction at this estate; it's the nation's finest English gardens that surround it (page 113).

★ **Tour Sagamore Hill:** The former summer home of Theodore Roosevelt is packed with fascinating memorabilia (page 114).

★ **Beat the heat at Jones Beach:** The state's most famous (and crowded) white sand beach, boardwalk, and art deco facilities lie just 25 miles from Midtown Manhattan (page 129).

★ **Visit the Parrish Art Museum:** 34,000 square feet are packed with exceptional modern and contemporary art (page 140).

★ **Stroll Sag Harbor:** The lively old port holds a fascinating whaling museum, 19th-century sea captains' homes, and a wharf with great views of a busy harbor (page 146).

★ **Climb a lighthouse tower:** Commissioned by George Washington in 1792, the **Montauk Lighthouse** stands sentinel on a lonely bluff at Long Island's easternmost tip (page 152).

Long Island

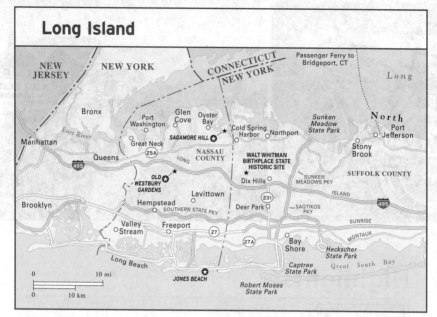

most commonly referred to as the North and South Forks.

Although it's the largest island on the Eastern Seaboard, Long Island does not enjoy the idyllic, peaceful reputation of serenity that the term *island* usually brings to mind. Unfortunately, due to overpublicized reports of celebrities behaving badly and reality shows flaunting excess over substance, the region's pristine nature preserves, charming fishing towns, and some of the finest white-sand beaches on the East Coast are largely overlooked. The most spectacular shores are along the southern coast, where white sands and dunes stretch out for an incredible, all-but-unbroken 123 miles (198 km). Most beaches along the northern coast front the gentle waters of Long Island Sound and are small and pebbly. Sailors satisfy their lust for wind, birders and anglers connect with the quiet, natural side of the island, and surfers ply the waves.

Beaches aside, both shores and forks have much to offer. The North Shore is home to many of Long Island's museums, as well as private mansions and nature preserves. South Fork, a magnet for the jet set, boasts the fashionable Hamptons, interesting historic sites, and a glittering social scene where people-watching abounds. More rural North Fork holds yet more historic sites, picturesque harbors and bays, orchards, organic farms, and a flourishing wine industry. Both the North and South Forks, with their historic villages and windswept shores, are astonishingly beautiful and remind visitors of a fact that's curiously easy to forget: This really is an island, with an idiosyncratic culture very different from that of the mainland.

PLANNING YOUR TIME

Each of Long Island's four sections—North Shore, North Fork, South Shore, and South Fork—can easily be explored in a day or two, depending on how many stops are made. Alternately, they can be combined into one

Previous: Montauk Lighthouse; bikes in the Hamptons; beach houses on the Hamptons' shore.

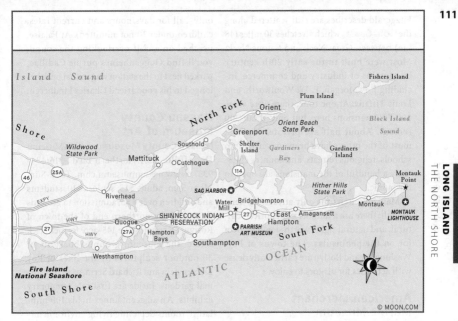

long loop that begins and ends in New York City. If you do make the 120-mile (193 km) trip from New York City to either busy **South Fork** or quieter **North Fork,** you'll want to spend at least two nights on the island. A five-day trip ensures enough time to explore both

forks and make stops at the North Shore's **Oyster Bay** and **Cold Spring Harbor** on the way back. Oyster Bay and Cold Spring Harbor make for good day trips from New York City, as do **Jones Beach, Fire Island, Northport,** and **Port Jefferson.**

The North Shore

The farther east you travel along the North Shore, the more rural the landscape becomes. Traffic thins out considerably around Oyster Bay, and by the time you reach Centerport—less than 20 miles (32 km) from the Queens-Nassau border—you'll feel like you've left the city far behind.

Route 25A, also known as Northern Boulevard (and, in Nassau County, as North Hempstead Turnpike), is the northernmost major route that traverses Long Island. It's the best option for unhurried exploring. Long Island Expressway (LIE), or I-495, runs parallel to Route 25A to the south. It is the quicker route (except during rush hour) and therefore

good to use when driving directly to a specific site.

GREAT NECK AND PORT WASHINGTON PENINSULAS

Heading into Long Island, you'll immediately cut across the bases of two large peninsulas: Great Neck and Port Washington. F. Scott Fitzgerald and his wife Zelda once lived at 6 Gateway Drive, Great Neck, and it was on these two thick thumbs of land that he modeled his West and East Eggs of *The Great Gatsby.*

Many opulent estates such as the ones

Fitzgerald describes are still scattered along the Gold Coast, which stretches 30 miles (48 km) between Great Neck and Eatons Neck. Most were built in the early 20th century by captains of industry and commerce, including J. P. Morgan, F. W. Woolworth, and Louis Tiffany. At one time, there were some 600-700 mansions here, but only about 200 remain. About half are privately owned; most of the others have been converted into schools, religious retreats, and country clubs. Only a handful of the mansions are open to the public.

Mansions aren't the only attractions here, though; there are a number of historical, cultural, and natural sights worth slowing down for on the peninsulas. The towns of Port Washington and Roslyn are particularly dense with activities for visitors to enjoy.

American Merchant Marine Museum

American Merchant Marine Museum (300 Steamboat Rd., 516/726-6047, www.usmma.edu/museum, Tues.-Fri. 10am-3pm, free), on the campus of the U.S. Merchant Marine Academy, showcases such odd treasures as models of well-known passenger liners and a life-size model of a cargo ship, used to train students during World War II. The academy's grounds offer good views of Throgs Neck Bridge, City Island, and the Bronx.

Sands Point Preserve

Just beyond Port Washington at the tip of the peninsula is 216-acre Sands Point Preserve (127 Middle Neck Rd., 516/571-7900, www.sandspointpreserveconservancy.org, days and hours vary by season, $10-15 pp), filled with woods, shoreline, nature trails, ball fields, and several castle-like buildings.

Sands Point was originally developed by railroad heir Howard Gould, and later purchased by the Guggenheims. Between the two families, they built three mansions: the immense Tudor-style Hempstead House, the much smaller Mille Fleures, and the Norman-style château, Falaise (guided tours

only, call for days/hours and current rates, children under 10 not admitted). At Falaise, perched on a cliff overlooking the sound, you'll find Guggenheim's purple Cadillac, parked next to the station wagon that once belonged to his good friend Charles Lindbergh.

Nassau County Museum of Art

Nassau County Museum of Art (Museum Dr., off Rte. 25A/Northern Blvd., 516/484-9337, www.nassaumuseum.com, Tues.-Sun. 11am-5pm, adults $15, seniors $10, students and children over 4 $5; admission to grounds free) is at the northern end of the town of Roslyn. Occupying the 145-acre former Frick estate, the museum grounds boast about 30 outdoor sculptures by the likes of Roy Lichtenstein and Richard Serra, as well as formal gardens. Inside are first-rate temporary exhibits. An adjacent annex holds 100 miniature rooms depicting living environments from the 18th century to the present.

Food and Accommodations

Plush, elegant ★ Roslyn Hotel (1221 Old Northern Blvd., 516/625-2700, www.theroslynhotel.com, $215-290) offers 77 well-appointed guest rooms decorated in deep roses and greens. Breakfast, Internet access, and parking are all complimentary.

There are a couple of notable places to eat in Roslyn. Hendrick's Tavern (1305 Old Northern Blvd., 516/621-1200, Mon.-Wed. 5pm-10pm, Thurs.-Fri. 5pm-11pm, Sat. 11:30am-11:30pm, Sun. 11:30am-10pm, $35), located in a historic building where George Washington once ate breakfast, offers a menu heavy on steak and seafood dishes. On the other end of the cuisine and budget spectrum is plain and simple local favorite Chicken Kebab (92 Mineola Ave., 516/621-6828, www.chickenkebab.com, Mon.-Thurs. 11:30am-10pm, Fri.-Sat. 11:30am-11pm, Sun. noon-10pm, $12), serving Greek and Middle Eastern specialties.

For a town its size, Port Washington has a surprising number of restaurants. One

The North Shore (Western Section)

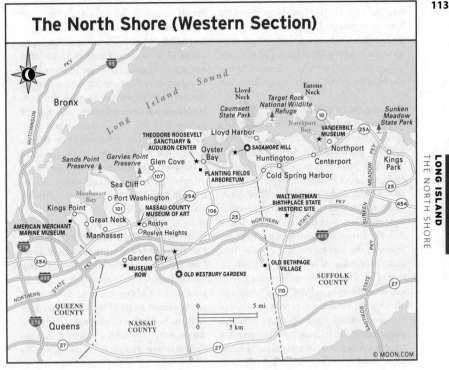

popular spot is **Louie's Oyster Bar & Grill** (395 Main St., 516/883-4242, www.louiessince1905.com, Mon.-Thurs. 11:30am-10pm, Fri.-Sat. 11:30am-11pm, Sun. 11:30am-3:30pm, $30), a local institution offering classic seafood dishes and great views of Manhasset Bay.

★ OLD WESTBURY GARDENS

One of Long Island's most sumptuous mansions, now known as **Old Westbury** (71 Old Westbury Rd., 516/333-0048, www.oldwestburygardens.org, days and hours vary by season, adults $12, seniors $10, children 7-17 $7), is just a few miles beyond Roslyn, near the Long Island Expressway. Built in 1906 in a palatial Charles II style, this grand edifice was once home to John S. Phipps and his wife Margarita Grace heirs to steel and shipping fortunes.

The mansion is magnificently furnished with 18th-century antiques, but it's the 88 acres of formal gardens out front and back that draw crowds. Considered to be the finest English gardens in the United States, Old Westbury's grounds are filled with tree-lined walks, grand allées, ponds, statuaries, architectural "follies," and hundreds of species of plants, including historic varieties and new hybrids.

OYSTER BAY

In the mid-1700s, both the English and Dutch inhabited picturesque Oyster Bay, which accounts for the fact that the place has two main streets just a block apart. East Main Street was once controlled by the Dutch, West Main Street by the English. Named for Oyster Bay's most prominent resident, Theodore Roosevelt Memorial Park is a charming little downtown park along the water on Long Island Sound.

The towns of Oyster Bay, Cold Spring Harbor, and Old Bethpage can be combined into one nice day trip from New York City. Start at Sagamore Hill in Oyster Bay, stop for lunch in Cold Spring Harbor, and move on to the Whaling Museum or Old Bethpage Village to round out the tour. To reach Oyster Bay from Route 25A, head north on Route 106.

★ Sagamore Hill

Sagamore Hill National Historic Site (20 Sagamore Rd., 516/922-4788, www.nps. gov/sahi, grounds: daily dawn-dusk, staffed buildings: Wed.-Sun. 9am-5pm, adults $10, children under 16 free; fee is for Roosevelt Home only) is the rambling hilltop estate that was once the summer home of Theodore Roosevelt. It sits on the outskirts of Oyster Bay. The former U.S. president, assistant secretary of the Navy, governor of New York State, police chief of New York City, and author of 30-odd books came here with his wife and six children to indulge in the "strenuous life": hiking, swimming, playing tennis, and horseback riding. Roosevelt never forgot his public duties while living here, however; out front is a wide porch with its railing removed so he could more easily address crowds who often assembled to hear him speak.

Theodore Roosevelt Sanctuary and Audubon Center

Across the street from Sagamore Hill, 13-acre **Theodore Roosevelt Sanctuary and Audubon Center** (134 Cove Rd., 516/922-3200, www.ny.audubon.org, daily dawn-dusk, free) was established in 1923 as the first Audubon Songbird Sanctuary in the United States. The trees, shrubs, and vines planted on the grounds have been chosen to attract birds. A small **visitors center** (Mon.-Fri. 9am-4pm) features exhibits on the area's wildlife and Roosevelt's extensive involvement in the conservation movement. Visitors are also welcome to walk the sanctuary's trails between dawn and dusk.

Raynham Hall

Among Oyster Bay's notable historic homes-turned-museums is **Raynham Hall** (20 W. Main St., 516/922-6808, www.raynhamhallmuseum.org, Tues.-Sun. 1pm-5pm, adults $7, students and seniors $5, children under 6 free), once the home of prosperous Revolutionary War-era merchant Samuel Townsend. Townsend was a suspected Tory, but his son was George Washington's chief spy in New York City. When the war broke out, Raynham Hall was confiscated by the British, though Townsend's daughter Sally remained in the house. There, she overheard the British discussing Benedict Arnold's planned betrayal of West Point and conveyed that information to colonists.

Planting Fields Arboretum

Planting Fields Arboretum State Historic Park (1395 Planting Fields Rd., 516/922-9200, www.plantingfields.org, daily 9am-5pm, $8 per car), west of Oyster Bay, is a lush affair on the former estate of insurance executive William Robertson Coe. Some 160 acres of the property's 409 acres are planted with ornamental trees and shrubs, while about 200 other acres are preserved in their natural state.

At the heart of Planting Fields is **Coe Hall** (1395 Planting Fields Rd., 516/922-9200, www.plantingfields.org, Apr. 1-Sept. 30, daily 11:30am-3:30pm, adults $5, children under 12 free), a Tudor Revival stone mansion. The 1918 house is furnished with European antiques to give it the feel of an old English country manor.

Food and Accommodations

For overnight stays, **East Norwich Inn** (6321 Northern Blvd., 516/922-1500, www.eastnorwichinnli.com, $125-150) is a pleasant, upscale motel offering comfortable rooms with double beds. Wireless Internet and continental breakfast are included in the room rate.

For dining in downtown Oyster Bay, there's **Wild Honey** (1 E. Main St., 516/922-4690, www.wildhoneyrestaurant.com, Tues.-Fri. 11:30am-2:45pm and 5pm-close, Sat.-Mon. 5pm-close, $24), which serves American food with a creative flare in a beautiful historic building that formerly served as Teddy Roosevelt's executive office.

Canterbury's Oyster Bar & Grill (46 Audrey Ave., 516/922-3614, www.canterburysobg.com, $28) specializes in the Bay's namesake oysters. Various fish entrées, lobster, and pasta are also on the menu.

COLD SPRING HARBOR

During the mid-1800s, Cold Spring Harbor was a busy whaling port. Its main street, now Route 25A, was once called Bedlam Street for the cacophony of foreign languages heard there during whaling's heyday. The village's taverns were full of exotic objects sailors brought back from all ends of the earth. On the village's outskirts was Bungtown, a small settlement producing barrels for whale oil.

Today, the boats bobbing in the harbor and the town's Whaling Museum recall the port's rich, adventurous past. The small, tourist-oriented village also offers shops, galleries, historic buildings, and a few other museums.

The Whaling Museum

The Whaling Museum (301 Main St., 631/367-3418, www.cshwhalingmuseum.org, Memorial Day-Labor Day daily 11am-5pm, winter Tues.-Fri. noon-4pm, Sat.-Sun. 11am-5pm, adults $6, seniors and children 4-18 $5) is a small, friendly institution founded in 1936. Exhibits in the trim, whitewashed building include a large collection of scrimshaw, a fully rigged whaleboat from the 19th century, huge iron cauldrons used to process whale blubber, thousands of journals and letters, and a great collection of historical photographs.

The museum also highlights the role that race played in whaling, explaining that whaling was the first racially integrated American industry. As early as the 1810s and 1820s, Caucasian and African American sailors, captains, shipbuilders, and shipowners were working alongside each other. One boat, the *Industry*, out of Nantucket, Massachusetts, was captained and crewed entirely by African Americans.

SPLIA Gallery

The small but excellent **Society for the Preservation of Long Island Antiquities Gallery** (161 Main St., 631/692-4664, www.splia.org, hours vary seasonally, $5 suggested donation) features changing exhibits tracing the island's social and cultural history. SPLIA was founded in 1948 in response to postwar changes on Long Island, namely suburbanization. The organization advocates historic preservation and strives to inform the public about Long Island's storied past through exhibits and events.

Cold Spring Harbor Fish Hatchery and Aquarium

Cold Spring Harbor Fish Hatchery and Aquarium (1660 Rte. 25A, 516/692-6768, www.cshfha.org, daily 10am-5pm, adults $6, seniors and children 3-12 $4), established in 1883, is just a few miles south of the village center. Until the early 1970s, this small plant produced about 100,000 brook trout a year, which were shipped upstate to stock the waters of the Adirondacks and the Catskills.

The hatchery suspended such mammoth operations in 1979, following the construction of larger facilities upstate, but it still functions as an educational institution. A half-dozen pools teem with hundreds of thousands of growing trout, all swimming together in one direction at one moment, switching to another the next. You'll also see a hatch house where eggs are incubated; a warm-water pond stocked with bass, bowfin, catfish, carp, bluegill, and the like; a turtle pond; and aquariums holding about 30 species of freshwater fish native to New York State.

Food

Grasso's (134 Main St., 631/367-6060, www.grassosrestaurant.com, Mon.-Sat. noon-3:30pm and 4pm-10pm, Sun. 11:30am-2:30pm and 3pm-9pm, $32) is a popular spot where live jazz accompanies upscale New American and Italian dishes. **Honu Kitchen and Cocktails** (363 New York Ave., 631/421-6900, www.honukitchen.com, Tues.-Thurs.

Walt Whitman: Birth of an American Poet

A few miles south of Huntington proper stands a farmhouse that's now preserved as the Walt Whitman Birthplace State Historic Site (246 Old Walt Whitman Rd., South Huntington, 631/427-5240, www.waltwhitman.org, days/hours vary by season, adults $6, seniors $5, students $4, children under 5 free). For all the congestion surrounding it, the Walt Whitman House sits in serene isolation behind a tall hedge.

Setting foot into its snug, sunny hall is like stepping into a well-crafted poem. Whitman's father built this house, and everything in it is meticulously designed and constructed, from hand-hewn beams held together with wooden pegs to innovative storage closets built into the fireplace walls.

Whitman only lived here until he was five, when his family moved to Brooklyn. But he came back to Long Island as a young man to teach school, and the museum does a good job of chronicling his entire life. A short movie covers the highlights of his career, while upstairs and in an interpretive center next door are exhibit rooms filled with his papers, early editions of *Leaves of Grass*, and his schoolmaster's desk.

Other sites connected with Walt Whitman are located throughout the West Hills region. Some are buildings, while others are hills or hollows through which the poet liked to meander on his frequent trips back to the village of his birth. Ask at the Walt Whitman Birthplace for a copy of the booklet and trail map outlining these sites.

5pm-10pm, Fri.-Sat. 5pm-11:30pm, Sun. 11:30am-8pm, $32) claims to have Long Island's longest bar. It also serves seasonal, contemporary American fare with plenty of surf and turf options.

OLD BETHPAGE VILLAGE RESTORATION

About 10 miles (16.1 km) south of Cold Spring Harbor is Old Bethpage Village (1303 Round Swamp Rd., 516/572-8400, www.obvrnassau.com, Wed.-Sun. 10am-4pm, adults $14, seniors and children 5-12 $8), a restored 19th-century village filled with craftspeople and interpreters in period dress. A blacksmith shop, general store, hat shop, tavern, working farm, and about 45 other pre-Civil War buildings, most moved here from other locations on the island, are spread out over the village's 209 acres.

Thematic programming is offered throughout the year. In May, you'll spot Union soldiers training in the fields. Come in August for baseball games played according to 1860

1: Sagamore Hill 2: Sunken Meadow State Park
3: docks along the North Shore's Manhasset Bay
4: the Old Westbury Gardens

rules. In December, you'll witness a 19th-century Christmas.

Camping is available nearby at 64-site Battle Row Campground (1 Claremont Rd., 516/572-8690, $54-58/night), which also has a recreation center on-site.

Food and Accommodations

Large, full-service Melville Marriott (1350 Walt Whitman Rd., Melville, 631/423-1600, www.marriott.com, $169-289) has 357 rooms and an indoor pool, fitness center, business center, and restaurant.

If you're in the mood for Italian, Jonathan's Ristorante (15 Wall St., Huntington, 631/549-0055, www.jonathan-sristorante.com, Tues.-Sat. noon-3pm and 5pm-10:00pm, Sun. 4pm-9pm, $29) is a bistro serving eclectic Italian fare, including a wide range of pastas.

SUNKEN MEADOW STATE PARK

The main attraction at popular 1,266-acre Sunken Meadow State Park (Rte. 25A and Sunken Meadow Pkwy., near Kings Park, 631/269-4333, www.parks.ny.gov/parks/37, daily dawn-dusk, parking $8-10)

The North Shore (Eastern Section)

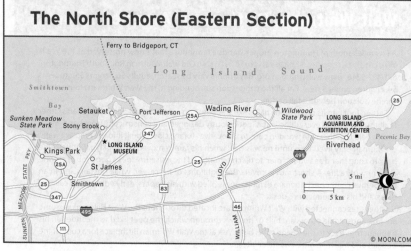

is a mile-long (1.6 km) beach, often packed in summer with thousands of sun worshippers tanning, swimming, napping, and playing. Three golf courses, lots of hiking trails, a salt marsh, and a small natural history museum are also within the park. Visitors can also enjoy the **Long Island Greenbelt Trail** (631/360-0753, www.ligreenbelt.org), which runs the 32-mile (52 km) width of Long Island from Heckscher State Park to Sunken Meadow.

ST. JAMES

Continuing east on Route 25A, through large, traffic-clogged Smithtown, you'll soon come to tiny St. James. The town's biggest claim to fame is the **St. James General Store** (516 Moriches Rd., 631/854-3740, daily 10am-5pm), listed in the National Register of Historic Places. Used continuously since 1857, the creaky store is a hodgepodge affair stuffed to bursting with old-fashioned candy, scented soaps, historic postcards, and the like.

STONY BROOK

Built on a hill sloping down to the water is the restored 18th-century village of Stony Brook. Just outside town is Stony Brook University, part of the State University of New York

(SUNY) system, which adds to the vitality of the village.

Although it's a popular tourist destination, complete with shopping malls and an ultra-clean feel, Stony Brook has managed to retain its rural character. Much of Stony Brook's charm is due to a man named Ward Melville, owner of the Thom McAn shoe company. Back in the 1940s, Melville—concerned about encroaching suburbia—had the village rebuilt along historical lines while successfully fighting for strict zoning codes. He paid for much of the rebuilding himself.

Along Main Street are the **harbor** and **village center** (www.stonybrookvillage.com), where well-marked signs point the way to shops and historic sites. To one side is an old **U.S. post office** (129 Main St.), equipped with a mechanical eagle that flaps its wings every hour on the hour. To the other side is **Mirabelle at Three Village Inn** (150 Main St., 631/751-0555, www.lessings.com), built in 1751.

Beyond the post office is **All Souls Episcopal Church,** designed by architect Stanford White and built in 1889. Pitched on the steep slope of a small hill, the tiny church, complete with zigzagging steps and a narrow steeple, has a fairy-tale quality, as if it were built for elves.

Continue walking a few blocks past the church to wide, dark Mill Pond and the gray-shingled **Stony Brook Grist Mill** (100 Harbor Rd., 631/751-2244, Apr.-Nov. Sat.-Sun. noon-4:30pm, adults $2, children $1). Built in 1751, the restored mill still grinds corn.

Long Island Museum of American Art, History and Carriages

This nine-acre complex of the **Long Island Museum of American Art, History and Carriages** (1200 Rte. 25A, 631/751-0066, www.longislandmuseum.org, Thurs.-Sat. 10am-5pm, Sun. noon-5pm, adults $10, seniors $7, children 6-17 $5) on the outskirts of town focuses on American history and art. Foremost among its buildings is renowned Carriage House, which contains about 90 horse-drawn vehicles, ranging from hand-painted coaches and firefighting equipment to elaborate sleighs and a rare Roma wagon. Roma wagons seldom survive because of the culture's custom of burying all of a person's possessions—even wagons—after his or her death.

The art museum holds both changing exhibits and a large collection of works by William Sidney Mount, a 19th-century African American painter from Stony Brook who depicted rural Long Island life. The Bayman's Art Gallery features hand-carved antique decoys and 15 miniature period rooms. Also on-site are a blacksmith's shop, barn, one-room schoolhouse, and other 19th-century buildings.

Food and Accommodations

Built in 1751 and once the home of Captain Jonas Smith, Long Island's first millionaire, ★ **Mirabelle at Three Village Inn** (150 Main St., 631/751-0555, www.lessings.com, $129-399) is now a lovely inn with 21 rooms and a full-service restaurant. The rambling white house features period antiques, fireplaces, ceiling beams, and plenty of colonial atmosphere in a setting overlooking the water. Some rooms are housed in the historic white-clapboard main building; others are in an attractive modern wing. The adjoining **Restaurant Mirabelle** (150 Main St., 631/751-0555, weekends only 5pm-9:30pm, $38) specializes in New American cuisine; in addition to à la carte options, a tasting menu is available. **Mirabelle Tavern** (breakfast daily 8am-10am, lunch Mon.-Fri. noon-3:30pm, Sat. noon-3pm, dinner Mon.-Thurs. 5pm-9pm, Fri.-Sat. 5pm-9:30pm, Sun. 4pm-8:30pm) is the other on-site restaurant; as its name suggests, tavern favorites, like fish-and-chips and burgers, are its menu staples.

PORT JEFFERSON

Just beyond Stony Brook, Port Jefferson was once a thriving shipbuilding community and then home to several lace factories and gravel pits. Today, it's the main destination for visitors to the North Shore, catering mostly to the tourist trade.

A number of historic homes are downtown. Most are privately owned, but **Mather House Museum** (115 Prospect St., 631/473-2665, www.portjeffhistorical.org, May-Oct. Wed.-Sun. noon-4pm, suggested donation), once owned by a shipbuilder, is open to the public. Inside, find an eclectic collection of 19th-century garments, Native American artifacts, and model boats. Out back are herb gardens, a marine barn, and a crafts house.

Downtown also offers several small tourist-oriented malls as well as some one-of-a-kind shops, including **Village Chairs & Wares** (40311 W. Broadway, 631/331-5791, www.villagechairs.com, appt. only), which specializes in handmade chairs and tables inspired by Shaker and Farmhouse styles.

The **ferry** (631/473-0286, www.88844ferry.com) to Bridgeport, Connecticut, leaves from Port Jefferson's docks. For brochures and a map of the village, stop by **Port Jefferson Chamber of Commerce** (118 W. Broadway/Rte. 25A, 631/473-1414, www.portjeffchamber.com, year-round Mon.-Fri. 10am-4pm, June-Sept. Sat.-Sun. noon-4pm).

The Pine Barrens

Much of the eastern end of Long Island, from just east of Port Jefferson to Hampton Bays, is covered by a 100,000-acre pine-barren wilderness. Five times larger than Manhattan, the Pine Barrens sits over what is said to be the purest underground drinking-water supply on the island. In its scruffy wooded growth, dominated by pitch pine and scrub oak, are several rare plant and animal species, including unusual stands of dwarf pine.

For many years, the Pine Barrens were at the center of an intense environmental debate that pitted conservationists against builders and local government officials. In 1989, an environmental group, the Long Island Pine Barrens Society, sued Suffolk County for approving building projects in the wilderness area without studying the environmental impact. The New York State Court ruled no study was required but said the state needed to draw up a plan to protect the area. A Central Pine Barrens Joint Policy and Planning Commission was created, and, in 1994, they proposed establishing a 53,000-acre core area where building would be banned, surrounded by a 47,000-acre area open to controlled development.

The plan became law in July 1995 and is a major environmental victory. The Pine Barrens are now New York's third forest preserve, following the Adirondacks and the Catskills.

To access a 5-mile (8.1 km) trail that leads through the Pine Barrens, head south of the Riverhead traffic circle on Route 104 for about 2 miles (3.2 km) and watch for signs. The trail should be avoided during hunting season, October-February. For more information, contact the **Long Island Pine Barrens Society** (547 E. Main St., Riverhead, 631/369-3300, www.pinebarrens.org), which has a downloadable trail guide on its website.

Food and Accommodations

Large and always bustling ★ **Danfords Hotel and Marina** (25 E. Broadway, 631/928-5200, www.danfords.com, $159-389) serves as a de facto anchor for downtown Port Jefferson. Many rooms have balconies and views of the water; some have working fireplaces. The inn's upscale restaurant, **Wave Seafood Kitchen** (25 E. Broadway, 631/928-5200, www.danfords.com, lunch and dinner daily, hours vary by season, $38), also overlooking the water, serves seafood and contemporary New American fare. During warm weather, guests can eat on the outside "Admiral's Deck."

WILDWOOD STATE PARK

Continuing northeast from Port Jefferson, past the small town of Wading River, you'll find **Wildwood State Park** (790 Hulse Landing Rd., 631/929-4314, www.parks.ny.gov/parks/68, daily dawn-dusk, parking $8-10). Surrounded by farm country, Wildwood is blissfully empty during the off-season, but crowded during summer. Within its 600 acres are nearly 2 miles (3.2 km) of beach, 12 miles (19.2 km) of hiking trails, bathhouses, picnic areas, ball fields, refreshment stands, and a 314-site **campground** (Sun.-Thurs. $18 tent sites, $30 trailer sites, Fri.-Sat. $22 tent sites, $34 trailer sites).

RIVERHEAD

Riverhead lies on the shore of Peconic Bay, right between the North and South Forks. The Suffolk County seat since 1727, Riverhead was once a thriving commercial center that benefited from the area's many farms. In more recent years, it suffered an economic downturn but is now experiencing something of a renaissance, thanks in part to the popular Long Island Aquarium and Exhibition Center. Downtown Riverhead is also home to a number of lovely old brick buildings. Its revitalized waterfront is a good place for a summer stroll.

Long Island Aquarium and Exhibition Center

State-of-the-art **Long Island Aquarium** (431 E. Main St., 631/208-9200, www.longisland-aquarium.com, daily 10am-5pm, adults $33, seniors $27, children 3-12 $24, children under 3 free) houses everything from native Long Island fish to moray eels, Pacific octopuses, piranhas, stingrays, and seals. A large living coral reef is awhirl with colorful tropical fish, and an underwater cavern houses more than a dozen sharks. Visitors can also embark on a simulated submarine dive or take in a seal show.

Partner institution New York Marine Rescue Center (NYMRC, formerly the **Riverhead Foundation for Marine Research**, 467 E. Main St., 631/369-9840, www.nymarinerescue.org) maintains several exhibits on-site. Among them are a rescue center for rehabilitating injured seals, sea turtles, and other marine life, and a touch tank where children can handle starfish, crabs, snails, and small fish. NYMRC also offers seal-watching cruises that depart from Point Lookout on the South Shore and naturalist cruises down the Peconic River.

Suffolk County Historical Society

At the other end of Riverhead's Main Street is **Suffolk County Historical Society** (300 W. Main St., 631/727-2881, www.suffolkcounty-historicalsociety.org, Wed.-Sat. 10am-4:30pm, adults $5, seniors $3, children under 18 $1). This large, rambling museum filled with eclectic treasures is an excellent place in which to get a sense of Suffolk County's past. Browse the good-size collections of Native American artifacts, colonial furniture and ceramics, and other examples of early craftsmanship. There's also an excellent bookstore on-site.

The North Fork and Shelter Island

Like better-known South Fork across Great Peconic Bay, the North Fork was first settled in 1640 by colonists from New England. That heritage flavors everything from the look of its villages to the independent mind-set of its people. It is still predominantly rural. Expect fertile farms and rolling vineyards, as well as one-stoplight towns with white-steepled churches, colonial saltboxes, and village greens.

The North Fork can be easily explored in a day, but it is so achingly beautiful, especially near the beaches of Orient Point, that it's worth lingering. Highlights include historic villages of Cutchogue, Southold, and Orient; the bustling harbor town of Greenport; and 4-mile-long (6.4 km) Orient Beach.

Accommodation options are limited to simple beachfront resort motels and B&Bs. Shelter Island has several historic inns. As in other shore areas, rates tend to be on the high side in season (Memorial Day-Labor Day) and reasonable the rest of the year. Two- or three-night minimum stays are often required in summer, especially on weekends.

Two major roads traverse the North Fork. Route 25 to the south is the more popular route and can get congested on summer weekends. Sound Avenue/Route 48 to the north is a good alternative.

SOUND AVENUE

Heading east onto the North Fork via the northern route of Sound Avenue (which turns into Route 48), you'll soon come to **Briermere Farms** (4414 Sound Ave., 631/722-3931, www.briermere.com, daily from April to Christmas Eve, 9am-5pm). Known for homemade pies, Briermere features about 15 different varieties on any given day, ranging from standards like blueberry and peach to blends like blackberry-apple and strawberry-rhubarb.

Near the intersection of Sound Avenue and Herricks Lane is **Hallockville Museum Farm** (6038 Sound Ave., 631/298-5292, www.hallockville.com, late May-late Oct., Sat. 11am-3pm, adults $7, seniors and children $5), a 102-acre farm that was owned by the Hallock family for over 200 years. Now a museum listed in the National Register of

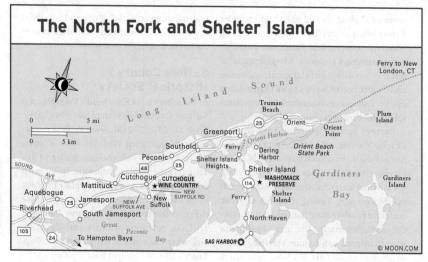

The North Fork and Shelter Island

Historic Places, Hallockville centers around a 1765 homestead, a large barn, a smokehouse, and a shoemaker's shop (where Capt. Zachariah Hallock made over 1,700 pairs of shoes between the years 1771 and 1820). The museum also stages frequent crafts demonstrations, festivals, and workshops.

CUTCHOGUE WINE COUNTRY

One of the prettiest North Fork hamlets, Cutchogue is filled with white churches, leafy trees, and weathered, shingled homes. The town is named after a Native American word for "principal place." **Historic wooden buildings** (Rte. 25, 631/734-7122, www.cutchoguenewsuffolkhistory.org, late June-early Sept. Sat.-Mon. 1pm-4pm, call for off-season hours, donations welcome), operated by the Cutchogue-New Suffolk Historical Council, cluster around the village green.

The most interesting of the group is **Old House**, which dates to 1649. Dark and cozy inside, it's outfitted with all the luxuries of its day, including wood paneling, leaded-glass windows, and a fluted chimney. The house was "lost" for close to 100 years, but was rediscovered in the 1930s by a WPA worker who noticed its unusual chimney.

Next to Old House are 1840 **Old**

Schoolhouse Museum and **Wickham Farmhouse,** equipped with furniture and farm implements from the early 1700s. Across the street is **Village Library,** housed in a lovely New England-style church. The church was built in 1862 because of a schism within its congregation. The Presbyterian minister was an ardent abolitionist who preached against slavery week after week until the church elders got tired and threw him out. The minister then gathered his followers and built the new church.

Wine Tasting

Cutchogue—along with Peconic, just down the road—is the center of Long Island's wine-producing country. In general, wineries are open for tastings daily 11am-5pm; but during the off-season, it's best to call in advance. Tours can usually be arranged by appointment.

Before you even reach Cutchogue, you'll pass the sign saying "Entering Wine Country," and almost immediately you'll spy **Palmer Vineyards** (5120 Sound Ave., 631/722-9463, www.palmervineyards.com, Sun.-Fri. 11am-5pm, Sat. 11am-6pm, tasting fees $25 pp plus 20 percent gratuity). One of Long Island's largest vineyards, it attracts hundreds of visitors on a summer's day. Palmer offers self-guided tours, a tasting room that looks like an English pub, and an outdoor deck overlooking its vineyards.

Off Route 25 east of Cutchogue is **Pugliese Vineyards** (34515 Main Rd., 631/734-4057, www.pugliesevineyards.com, Mon.-Sat. 11am-5pm, Sun. 11am-6pm, $15), which features a lovely collection of hand-painted bottles containing a chardonnay, blanc de blanc sparkling wine, cabernet sauvignon, and merlot, among other varietals.

Along Route 25 closer to Peconic is 500-acre **Pindar Vineyards** (37645 Main Rd., 631/734-6200, www.pindar.net, daily 11am-5:30pm, wines sold by the glass), the largest vineyard on the island. Over 20 different wines are produced here annually, and tours run continuously throughout the day. Also popular is nearby **Lenz Winery** (Main Rd., 631/734-6010, www.lenzwine.com, Nov.-May daily 10am-5pm, Memorial Day to mid-Oct. daily 10am-6pm, $24), a 70-acre vineyard with a striking modern main building.

To the north, along Route 48 in Cutchogue, is **Castello di Borghese-Hargrave Vineyard** (17150 Rte. 48, 631/734-5111, www.castellodiborghese.com, daily 11am-5pm,

wines by the glass), the oldest vineyard on the island, founded in 1973.

Food

Not quite as old as the historic buildings in town, vintage, chrome-laden **Cutchogue Diner** (Main Rd./Rte. 25, 631/734-7016, www.cutchoguediner.com, Mon.-Fri. 7am-3pm, Sat.-Sun. 6:30am-3pm, $13) near the village green dates to the 1920s. The diner's pancakes and meat loaf are especially good. Also nearby is **Braun Seafood Co.** (30840 Main Rd., 631/734-6700, www.braunseafood.com, Mon.-Sat. 8am-6pm, Sun. 8am-5pm), where you can purchase clam pies, an East End specialty (these can't be eaten on the spot; they must be cooked).

SOUTHOLD AND VICINITY

Settled in 1640, Southold is one of the oldest communities of European origin in New York State. The earliest settlers to arrive here came from New Haven, Connecticut, starting up the industries of farming and whaling. Though the latter is no longer practiced, farming remains an important activity. You'll see plenty of roadside stands tempting you with fresh-from-the-garden fare. Some of the

Cutchogue wine country

The Algonquins

Thirteen Algonquin tribes—including the Canarsees, Rockaways, Merricks, Massapeaques, Shinnecocks, Montauks, and Setaukets—occupied Long Island before the arrival of the Europeans. Today, many of the island's villages, harbors, and bays are named for these early peoples.

Algonquins fished in coastal waters, harvested quahog clams (producing much of the wampum used by northeastern Native Americans from the shells), and grew corn, pumpkin, melon, and tobacco. According to one settler's journal, "[The Algonquins] were a tall, proud, and handsome people with grace of walk, active of body, carried straight as arrows."

Montauk chief Wyandanch, the grand sachem of Long Island tribes, befriended the settlers who began arriving in the 1640s. Ninicraft, chief of the Narragansetts who lived across the sound, tried to enlist Wyandanch's help in killing off the settlers in 1652. When Wyandanch refused, the Narragansetts declared war on the Montauks and nearly destroyed them.

Within a century after the arrival of the Dutch and English, only about 400 Native Americans remained on Long Island. Most had died of diseases introduced by Europeans; those who survived were subject to innumerable indignities. In 1759, for example, Native Americans had to beg for the right to cut firewood.

Today, a small Algonquin community of about 700 Shinnecocks still lives on Shinnecock Reservation near Southampton. Each Labor Day weekend, they celebrate their heritage with a three-day powwow that attracts Native Americans from across the country.

prettiest hamlets on Long Island, including Greenport and Orient, are part of Southold.

Sights

Standing testimony to the town's long history is a **museum complex** (54325 Main Rd., 631/765-5500, www.southoldhistoricalsociety.org, days and hours vary by season and by installation within the complex, suggested donation $5) conveniently located in the middle of low-key downtown. Among the many historic buildings here are the weathered 1750 **Thomas Moore House,** lavishly furnished Victorian **Currie-Bell House,** and lovely, hand-hewn **Pine Neck Barn.** Also on the museum grounds are a working blacksmith shop, a buttery, and a millinery filled with an assortment of 19th- and early-20th-century hats. A map and more information about the museum complex can be picked up at 19th-century **Prince Building,** where the Southold Historical Society is headquartered. Also in the building is the **Museum Shop** (Mon.-Fri. 10am-3pm), selling books and handcrafts.

Run by the Long Island chapter of the New York State Archaeological Association, the **Southold Indian Museum** (1080 Main Bayview Rd., 631/765-5577, www.southoldindianmuseum.org, year-round Sun. 1:30pm-4:30pm, June-Aug. only Sat. 1:30pm-4:30pm, adults $2, children $0.50) houses an extensive array of Algonquin artifacts. Here you'll find the country's largest collection of Algonquin pottery (from 3000 BC to colonial times).

Just north of downtown Southold is the striking **Horton Point Lighthouse** (off Lighthouse Rd., 631/765-5500 or 631/765-2101, Memorial Day-mid-Sept. Sat.-Sun. 11:30am-4pm, adults $5 or $10 per family), which stands high on a bluff at the end of Lighthouse Road. The first lighthouse on this site was commissioned by George Washington in 1790. The current lighthouse was built in 1857 and is still operational. Painted in stark white and surrounded by rhododendrons, the building overlooks a lonely stretch of beach. Lighthouse tours take visitors through the keeper's quarters and the working light tower. Downstairs is a small museum filled with artifacts, paintings, and "treasures" from sunken ships.

Food and Accommodations

North Fork Table and Inn (57225 Main Rd., 631/765-0177, www.northforktableandinn.

com, $250-275) offers lovely accommodations. **The Table** (Mon. and Thurs. 5:30pm-8pm, Fri. 5:30pm-9:30pm, Sat. 5pm-9:30pm, Sun. 5pm-8pm, $34) at the inn prepares seasonally inspired dishes featuring locally grown biodynamic and organic produce, fresh local seafood from Peconic Bay and Long Island Sound, North Fork artisanal cheese, and a well-thought-out wine list. Prix fixe and tasting menus are available for lunch and dinner. Check the website for special events, such as beer pairing meals or harvest celebrations.

GREENPORT

North Fork's principal commercial center is bustling Greenport, laid out in neat squares that slope down to the harbor. Greenport has been a boating community since before the Revolutionary War. In the 1700s, cargo ships from the West Indies docked here to unload molasses and rum. Later, the port became a center for whaling and the oyster trade. Even today, an estimated two-thirds of Greenport's population earns its living from boats and related industries. The harbor is always full of fishing boats and pleasure craft, and the streets are lined with restaurants and shops, some tourist-oriented, some not.

Sights

Waterfront **Mitchell Park** (115 Front St., 631/477-2200, www.greenportvillage.com) is a great place to watch all the maritime activity. Children will enjoy a ride on the 1920s **Mitchell Park Carousel** (days and hours vary by season, $2) or a peek inside the public access **camera obscura** (summer daily daylight hours, off-season weekends and holidays daylight hours).

East End Seaport Museum and Maritime Foundation (end of 3rd St., 631/477-2100, www.eastendseaport.org, June 30-Labor Day daily 1pm-5pm, Memorial Day-June 30 and Labor Day-mid-Oct. Sat.-Sun. 1pm-5pm, Nov.-Apr. by appointment only, suggested donation) is loaded with artifacts from the fishing and boatbuilding industries.

Changing exhibits focus on such subjects as women and the sea and yacht racing.

Railroad buffs will want to visit the **Railroad Museum of Long Island** (440 4th St., 631/477-0439, www.rmli.us, Sat.-Sun. 11am-4pm, adults $12, children 5-12 $6). The museum, housed in what was once a freight station, traces the history of railroading on the island. One highlight is the 20 foot (6 m) model of the Greenport freight yard as it looked in 1955; another is a ride on the Allan Herschell G-16 miniature train that Long Island sent to the 1964-1965 World's Fair.

Food

★ **Claudio's** (111 Main St., 631/477-0627, www.claudios.com, hours vary seasonally, $32), a huge, rambling seafood restaurant, dominates the harbor area. Established by a Portuguese sailor in 1870, Claudio's bills itself as the "oldest same family owned restaurant in the United States." Design details include heavy carved wood, stained glass, and an enormous bar brought to the restaurant by barge from a New York City hotel in 1885. Near Claudio's, **Aldo's** (103-105 Front St., 631/477-6300, www.aldos.com, daily 8am-5:30pm, $15) is a café and bakery serving strong espresso.

Accommodations and Camping

The main building at ★ **Townsend Manor Inn** (714 Main St., 631/477-2000, www.townsendinn.com, $160-235 in summer, $100-155 off-season) is a historic 1835 Greek Revival house complete with restaurant, old-fashioned cocktail lounge, and cozy living room. Guest rooms are located in several modern additions, and a pool is nearby as well.

Popular 1950s-era **Silver Sands Motel** (Rte. 25 at Silvermere Rd., 631/477-0011, www.silversands-motel.com, $150 standard room, $1,400/week apartments, $2,500/week cottages) is set on a quarter mile of private beach. It offers a variety of accommodations, ranging from motel rooms to apartments and beach cottages. Also a good choice, with a variety of accommodation options, is smaller **Sunset Motel** (62005 Rte. 48, 631/477-1776, www. sunsetmotelgreenport.com, $225 summer, $140-175 off-season). At ★ **Sound View Inn** (58855 North Rd./Rte. 48, 631/477-1910, www. soundviewinn.com, $195-255 summer, $130-155 off-season), also on the beach, all rooms have balconies, and some have kitchenettes. Tennis courts and a pool are on the grounds. All three motels are closed in winter.

Camping is available at the 150-site **Eastern Long Island Kampgrounds** (690 Queen St., 631/477-0022, www.easternlikampground.net, $50-70). On-site are a camp store, laundry facility, and playground. The campground also has wireless Internet.

ORIENT

At the far, far end of the North Fork is Orient, a tiny historical town set on one of the most glorious spots on the island. On this narrow piece of land, you'll find gentle beaches, osprey nests, and only a few buildings, including houses that still fit the description in the 1930s WPA guide: "The little weathered shingle houses, few more than one-and-a-half stories high, sit primly behind picket fences. In sun or storm the Atlantic winds roll in. . . ."

To reach Orient proper, cross a narrow isthmus. To the left are crescent-shaped Truman Beach and Long Island Sound, to the right, Orient Harbor and Gardiners Bay.

The town centers around an old-fashioned post office and **Orient Country Store.** The former is still equipped with turn-of-the-20th-century stamp windows, while the latter sells groceries, sandwiches, home-baked treats, and arts and crafts made by locals.

Sights

Oysterponds Historical Society (1555 Village Ln., 631/323-2480, www.oysterpondshistoricalsociety.org, July-Sept. Wed.-Fri. and Sun. 2pm-5pm, Sat. 11am-5pm, free), at the end of Village Lane, is a group of six well-preserved historic buildings. **Webb**

House is a pre-Revolutionary War inn, while **Village House** is a 19th-century home containing memorabilia from the 1800s, when Orient was a popular resort with two big hotels. Temporary exhibits are showcased in **Schoolhouse Building,** the only building open year-round.

If you continue down Village Lane to King Street and turn onto Narrow River Road, you'll come to an early **slave burial ground,** in a pretty spot overlooking the sea. Twenty slaves are buried here, along with Dr. Seth Tuthill and his wife Maria. "It was [the Tuthills'] wish that they be buried with their former slaves," reads a plaque near the cemetery.

Orient Point and Beach

A few miles beyond Orient, at the very tip of North Fork, is Orient Point, where ferries dock on their way to and from New London, Connecticut. Abutting the point is **Orient Beach State Park** (N. County Rd., off Rte. 25, 631/323-2440, www. www. parks.ny.gov/parks/106, daily dawn-dusk, parking $8-10), one of the finest beaches on Long Island. Stretching west over a long finger of land, the 357-acre park features miles of white, ocean-washed sands. It's especially popular among bird-watchers and nature lovers, who appreciate the park's rare maritime forest. Facilities include a bathhouse, refreshment stand, horseshoe court, and hiking trails.

SHELTER ISLAND

In the middle of the bay between the North and South Forks is Shelter Island, a quiet retreat of wooded hills, uncrowded beaches, and expensive vacation homes, some dating back to the Victorian era. The island's first European resident was Nathaniel Sylvester, one of four businessmen who bought the island in 1651. Thanks to Sylvester, the island subsequently became a haven for Quakers fleeing persecution in Massachusetts. Sylvester gave the Quakers shelter—hence the island's name—and allowed them to practice their religion here.

Shelter Island has an exclusive air about it, due partly to its moneyed population and partly to the fact that it can be reached only by ferry. The high cost of the very short ferry ride ($12 one-way) keeps out the hoi polloi.

Sights

For day visitors, Shelter Island is the sort of place that's fun to explore without any particular destination in mind. Many roads wander past sun-splashed meadows and bays, dark woods, and historic homes. Near the North Ferry dock is **Shelter Island Heights,** filled with steep streets and Victorian-era gingerbread cottages. Across the bay from the Heights is **Dering Harbor,** the smallest incorporated village in the state, boasting a number of impressive mansions along Shore Road. At just 2.1 square miles, the year-round population hovers in the double digits.

History buffs might also want to stop at **Havens House** (16 South Ferry Rd./Rte. 114, 631/749-0025, www.shelterislandhistorical.org, Apr.-Oct. Wed.-Sat. 10am-2pm, donation), a 1743 home in the National Register of Historic Places. The five-room house, run by the Shelter Island Historical Society, is outfitted with period furnishings and features a nice collection of antique dolls and toys.

Mashomack Preserve

Shelter Island's major treasure is **Mashomack Preserve** (79 S. Ferry Rd., 631/749-1001, www.nature.org/mashomack, days and hours vary by season, suggested donation adults $3, children $2), operated by The Nature Conservancy. Occupying nearly a third of the island, the preserve spreads out over 2,039 acres of oak woodlands, marshes, freshwater ponds, tidal creeks, and 12 miles (19.3 km) of shoreline. One of the East Coast's largest concentrations of nesting ospreys is within its confines, along with everything from ibis and hummingbirds to harbor seals and terrapins.

Nature trails and hikes 1.5-11 miles (2.4-17.7 km) in length meander through the preserve. The entrance to the preserve is about a mile from South Ferry dock.

Food and Accommodations

Built on bluffs overlooking Coecles Inlet is the 1929 ★ **Ram's Head Inn** (Ram Island Dr., 631/749-0811, www.theramsheadinn. com, $150-350 in summer, with breakfast, closed Nov.-Apr.), boasting its own private beach, small boats, tennis courts, restaurant, and wide porch with wicker furniture. Most of the 17 rooms are filled with lots of light and simple antiques. Lunch and dinner (average entrée $38) consist of seasonal, local ingredients served in a high-ceilinged room hung with paintings.

Friendly, turn-of-the-20th-century **House on Chase Creek** (3 Locust Ave., 631/749-4379, www.chasecreek.com, $130-245 summer, $85-175 off-season) offers three comfortable guest rooms and a suite year-round. **Maria's Kitchen** (55 N. Ferry Rd., 631/749-5450, www.mariaskitchenshelterisland.com, daily 8am-8pm, $14), also in town, serves tacos and Mexican-inspired dishes.

Getting There and Around

To reach Shelter Island from the North Fork, take **North Ferry** (631/749-0139, www.northferry.com), which leaves from Route 114 at the foot of 3rd Street in Greenport. From the South Fork, take **South Ferry** (631/749-1200, www.southferry.com), which leaves from Route 114 in North Haven, about 3 miles (4.8 km) north of Sag Harbor. Both ferries operate every 10-15 minutes from about 6am to 1:45am during summer. The North Ferry costs $12 one-way for a car and driver, plus $2 for each passenger. The South Ferry costs $15 one-way for a car and driver. Less expensive round-trip tickets to and from Greenport or to and from North Haven are available but cannot be applied to a trip that combines the two ferry services.

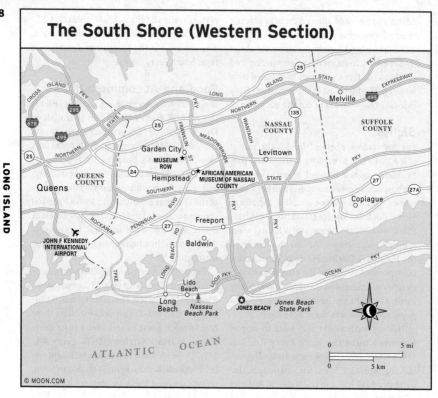

The South Shore (Western Section)

© MOON.COM

The South Shore

The South Shore is unbearably congested near New York City. However, just off its coast, the cityscape recedes into a long line of barrier islands and white sands. Beaches, beaches, and more beaches stretch out against the pounding surf. Nearest to the city are Lido Beach, Long Beach, and famed Jones Beach, followed by Fire Island and South Fork.

FREEPORT

Heading into Nassau County on Sunrise Highway (Rte. 27), you'll soon come to Freeport, a busy fishing and boating community that's the largest town on the South Shore. Freeport's most famous native son is Canadian American violinist and bandleader

Guy Lombardo. A long avenue named in his honor runs through downtown.

Freeport's main visitor attraction is its "Nautical Mile," located along **Woodcleft Canal,** bordered by a street of the same name. Much of Freeport was built on landfill, and Woodcleft is one of several canals in town. Along it, you'll find lots of shops, many selling arts and crafts, a plethora of seafood restaurants, and fishing boats sporting signs advertising "Half-day Flounder." On summer evenings, music beckons from outdoor bars while party boats set sail for dinner and moonlight cruises.

For more information on Freeport, contact the **Freeport Chamber of Commerce**

Bay Houses

If you pay close attention while driving along the Wantagh, Meadowbrook, or Loop Parkways linking Jones Beach and Point Lookout to the mainland, you'll spot small cottages perched on platforms and surrounded by marshland and water. At one time, there were hundreds of such bay houses, as they are called, in the town of Hempstead. Now there are only about 15; 20 were destroyed by Hurricane Sandy in 2012.

The building of the bay houses began in the early 1700s when the island's farmers, needing hay for their cattle, hired baymen to row out to remote marshlands and bring back hay for their animals. The journey often took several hours each way, so it wasn't long before baymen began building shacks in which to overnight. At first, these shacks were crude constructions. But as the years went by, baymen developed them into cozy cabins that they could also use for recreation and for the planting and harvesting of oysters and clams.

In the early 1900s, recreational anglers discovered the South Shore, and the bay houses developed yet another purpose: bait stations. Then, a decade or two later, Prohibition arrived. Some baymen, writes folklorist Nancy Solomon in her book *On the Bay,* "played an indispensable role in rum running, smuggling, via their bay houses, illegal booze from large cargo ships offshore to hotels...."

All this history was almost lost in 1993, when the baymen's lease on their bay houses—last renewed by Hempstead in 1965—ran out. The town government had voted to have the houses destroyed, but Solomon's book, together with the efforts of the South Shore Bayhouse Owners' Association, convinced the town board of the homes' historic value. Their leases have since been extended virtually indefinitely.

Although the bay houses can be seen from the parkways, the best way to view them is by boat. Charter fishing boats that run out of Freeport pass close by.

Approximately 40 other bay houses are located in Suffolk County opposite Captree State Park near Captree Island, Sexton Island, and Havermeyer Island.

(46 N. Ocean Ave., 516/377-2200, www. freeportny.com). For more information on sportfishing, call **Freeport Boatmen's Association** (540 Guy Lombardo Ave., 516/378-4838, www.freeportboatmens.com).

Food and Accommodations

The Freeport Inn and Marina (445 S. Main St., 516/623-9100, www.freeportinn.com, $125-325), just north of Jones Beach, is a recently renovated property popular with boaters and landlubbers alike.

One of the best restaurants along Nautical Mile is **Hudsons on the Mile** (340 Woodcleft Ave., 516/442-5569, www. hudsonsonthemile.net, days and hours vary by season, closed in winter, $32), serving seafood, sushi, and steak. Clientele here tend to be young and trendy. In summer, bands play on a crowded outdoor deck.

TOP EXPERIENCE

★ JONES BEACH

Just 25 miles (40 km) from Midtown Manhattan, **Jones Beach** (1 Ocean Pkwy., Wantagh, 516/785-1600, www. www.parks. ny.gov/parks/10, daily dawn-dusk, parking $8-10) is Long Island's most famous and most accessible stretch of sand. Although its 6.5 miles (10.5 km) are packed cheek by jowl on a hot summer's day, the beach is so magnificent that it still manages to impress. And talk about good people-watching!

City Parks Commissioner Robert Moses, who shaped much of the modern landscape of New York, approached Jones Beach with the goal of transforming a sandbar off a reef into the finest public beach in the United States. He largely succeeded, in an engineering feat that took two years to complete. Finished in

1929, the beach boasts an enormous number of well-worn but first-class facilities, including two lovely art deco bathhouses, wading and Olympic-size pools, ball fields, pitch-and-putt golf, shuffleboard courts, basketball courts, picnic areas, refreshment stands, a restaurant, a wide, weathered boardwalk, and a 200-foot-high (70 m) water tower shaped like an obelisk. **Jones Beach Theater** (Jones Beach, Wantagh, 516/221-1000, www.jonesbeach.com), which presents big-name music acts in summer, is also here.

Jones Beach is open year-round, but lifeguards are only on duty Memorial Day-Labor Day. To reach Jones Beach, take the Wantagh State or Meadowbrook State Parkways south off Sunrise Highway (Rte. 27), and watch for signs. Traffic is typically terrible in summer. If you're coming from New York City, consider taking the **Long Island Rail Road** (718/217-5477 or 516/822-5477, www.mta.info/lirr). The train travels to Freeport, where shuttle buses operate to and from the beach.

West of Jones Beach are several smaller beaches, including **Long Beach** and **Lido Beach,** that are often less crowded and fun to explore. To reach these locales, take Meadowbrook State Parkway to Loop Parkway.

Food and Accommodations

Allegria Hotel (80 W. Broadway, 516/889-1300, www.allegriahotelny.com, $139-319), a beachfront luxury hotel in Long Beach, has 143 guest rooms offering views of the Atlantic Ocean and New York City skyline. If that's not enough, there's also a 10,000-square-foot rooftop infinity pool. The hotel's restaurant, **Atlantica** (80 W. Broadway, 516/889-1300, www.allegriahotel.com, daily 7am-10am and 11am-10pm, $30), specializes in seafood options and has an extensive wine list. The hotel also an on-site lounge, L'Onda.

CENTRAL NASSAU COUNTY

Heading into Long Island on Southern State Parkway, you'll pass one of the state's only African American museums and two historic residential communities, Garden City and Levittown. Neither of the towns is a tourist attraction in the traditional sense, but both have played an interesting role in suburban development in the United States.

African American Museum of Nassau County

The **African American Museum of Nassau County** (110 N. Franklin St., Hempstead, 516/572-0730, www.theaamuseum.org, Tues.-Sat. 10am-5pm, ages 5 and up $5) is on a scruffy main drag in sprawling downtown Hempstead. It's a small but active institution where exhibits change every 8-10 weeks. Most exhibits are arts or history oriented, and range from locally produced shows to traveling Smithsonian productions. Past exhibits have included the role of African Americans at NASA and Black royals.

Museum Row

The hangars of Mitchel Field, a former airfield just outside Garden City, have been transformed into **Museum Row.** At the heart of the project is the impressive **Cradle of Aviation Museum** (Charles Lindbergh Blvd., 516/572-4111, www.cradleofaviation.org, Tues.-Sun. 9:30am-5pm, adults $16, seniors and children $14). Biplanes and fighter planes seem to soar up into the atrium, while all around are dozens of rare aircraft documenting the history of flight. Many major aviation events took place on Long Island; Charles Lindbergh's 1927 nonstop transatlantic flight, for instance, departed from nearby Roosevelt Field (now a shopping mall). An IMAX theater and Red Planet Cafe, designed to look like a futuristic Mars space base, are other fixtures in the museum.

Long-established **Long Island Children's Museum** (11 Davis Ave., 516/224-5800, www.licm.org, days and hours vary by season, adults and children over age 1 $14, seniors $13) has hands-on exhibits for kids of

---

1: Jones Beach **2:** Fire Island Lighthouse

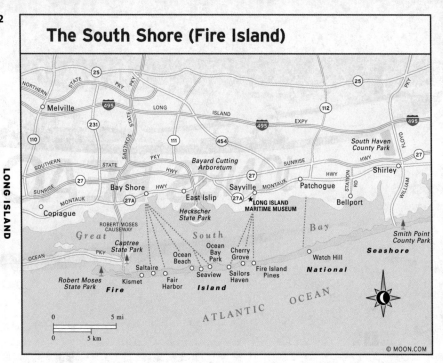

The South Shore (Fire Island)

all ages. Topics range from art to science, with plenty of activities, like bubble blowing, that are just plain fun.

The **Nassau County Firefighters' Museum and Education Center** (1 Davis Ave., 516/572-4177, www.ncfiremuseum.org, Tues.-Sun. 10am-5pm, adults $5, seniors and children $4) is also in Museum Row. This is a fun museum for families that features some antique fire engines, as well as interactive activities appropriate for kids.

Food

Long Island is one of New York's hot spots for local produce. **Perennial** (990 Franklin Ave., Garden City, 516/743-9213, www.perennial-restaurant.com, daily 5pm-10pm, $30) offers all the best of Long Island's bounty, from local oysters to locally farmed fruits and vegetables.

FIRE ISLAND

A long skinny stick of land stretching 32 miles (52 km) parallel to Long Island's south shore, Fire Island is a near-mythic place, known for its wildness—both in terms of its wilderness landscape and its party atmosphere.

Four distinct visitor areas and 17 resort communities make up the island, but it's all part of the National Seashore system. No cars are allowed on most of Fire Island, where park rangers administer a number of magnificent white-sand beaches.

Take note of posters describing precautions to avoid poison ivy and deer ticks; both are abundant here and can quickly ruin a vacation. As long as you stick to beaches and boardwalks, or wear long pants when exploring grasses and woodlands, you shouldn't have a problem.

Free, excellent maps of Fire Island are available at various visitors centers on the island or from **Fire Island National Seashore Headquarters** (120 Laurel St., Patchogue, 631/687-4750, www.nps.gov/fiis, hours seasonal). Another helpful website is www.fireisland.com.

Welcome to the 'Burbs

Long Island is the archetypal American suburb. Early suburbs began springing up in western Nassau County in the 1920s. But the island's real transformation came with World War II, when factories producing aircraft and specialized weapons systems turned Long Island into an important manufacturing center. After the war, large housing tracts were built to accommodate returning soldiers. The most famous of these tracts was Levittown, the result of the transformation of potato fields into 17,447 inexpensive ranch homes by developer William Levitt in 1949. The largest housing development ever created by a single builder, Levittown was the American Dream come true for the working class, as well as the butt of countless jokes about "ticky-tacky houses" all looking just the same.

Levittown was originally built exclusively for GIs returning from World War II, but was later opened to the general public. Each preassembled house was built in five days using a 27-step process. Each had a living room, two bedrooms, a kitchen and bath, an attic, washing machine, barbecue grill, and television set. The cost to young families was $60 a month, no money down.

In the end, the individuality and imagination of Levittown's residents foiled many of the community's detractors. Drive down the streets here today and you'd be hard-pressed to find any house that closely resembles another. Some owners have added rooms and second floors, others have changed the facades or added driveways. To reach Levittown from Hempstead, head east on Hempstead Turnpike (Rte. 24).

Between 1950 and 1960, Long Island's population doubled from 670,000 to 1.3 million, and between 1960 and 1980 it doubled yet again. The island's population continues to swell; currently, more than 7.5 million people call Long Island home—and those are just year-round residents.

Resort Communities

Fire Island wasn't declared a National Seashore until 1964, by which time 17 resort communities had already been established. These communities were allowed to remain, as long as they didn't grow beyond their designated boundaries. Today, they are popular vacation spots, especially among Manhattanites.

Each Fire Island community has its own distinct character. Cherry Grove and Fire Island Pines are the island's two gay retreats; Kismet and Fair Harbor attract a large singles crowd; Saltaire and Seaview cater primarily to families.

Most of these communities are not designed for the casual visitor. Their vacationers tend to rent or share houses—usually for the entire summer—and often arrive via hired water taxi. Most of these communities also do not offer bathhouses or other public facilities.

Two communities that *do* welcome day-trippers and overnight visitors are Ocean Beach and Ocean Bay Park. Ocean Beach attracts many families, Ocean Bay Park many singles. Both are friendly, middle-class communities equipped with public facilities and serviced by Fire Island Ferries (Bay Shore, 631/665-3600, www.fireislandferries. com, adults round-trip $21, children round-trip $6-11, depending on age).

Cherry Grove also welcomes casual visitors. Older, smaller, less expensive, and more exuberant than its sister community, the Pines, it centers around Grove Hotel, which always teems with a gay crowd, talking, drinking, and partying. Cherry Grove is serviced by Sayville Ferry Service (River Rd., Sayville, 631/589-8980, www.sayvilleferry.com, adults round-trip $18, children round-trip $8.50).

Robert Moses State Park

At Fire Island's westernmost end is 1,000-acre Robert Moses State Park (off Robert Moses Cswy., 631/669-0470, daily dawn-dusk, parking $8-10), one of only two sections of the island that can be reached by car. A public beach since 1898, the park feels like a smaller, less crowded version of Jones Beach. The park, which is also a National Seashore, has bathhouses, shops, and snack bars.

The South Shore (Eastern Section)

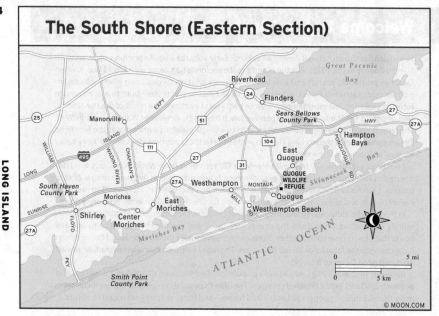

© MOON.COM

At the park's western end is the black-and-white-striped **Fire Island Lighthouse** (4640 Captree Is., 631/661-4876, www.fireislandlighthouse.com, call for days and hours), built in 1827 to prevent shipwrecks. The current lighthouse dates to 1858. At its base is a **visitors center** (631/661-4876, days and hours vary by season). The lighthouse tower was restored in 2013, and **tower tours** (adults $8, seniors and children 12 and under $4) are available by advance reservation.

Sailors Haven

One of the island's most interesting beaches for day visitors is **Sailors Haven,** reached via ferry from Sayville. Sailors Haven is part wild beach and boardwalk, part dunes and grasses, and part **Sunken Forest**—a scrappy 300-year-old maritime forest located below sea level between two lines of sand dunes. A weathered gray boardwalk leads from the ferry dock through the 40-acre forest, lush with oak, maple, red cedar, and sour gum trees, as well as sassafras, bayberry, inkberry, and cattail. Due to the island's strong winds and salty air, none of the trees can grow taller

than the dunes, even though freshwater extends as deep as 40 yards (36.6 m) beneath their roots. Essential to the forest's existence, this freshwater exists because the island's annual rainfall exceeds its annual evaporation.

Sailors Haven, a National Seashore, has several facilities, including bathhouses, a snack bar, and a **visitors center** (631/597-6183, www.nps.gov/fiis, seasonal). Ferries are operated by **Sayville Ferry Service** (River Rd., Sayville, 631/589-8980, www.sayvilleferry.com, adults round-trip $16, children round-trip $8.50).

Watch Hill

Another National Seashore **visitors center** (631/597-6455, www.nps.gov/fiis, seasonal), similar to but larger than the one at Sailors Haven, is located at **Watch Hill,** on the eastern end of Fire Island. Remote and lonely in feel, Watch Hill is filled with dunes and an often-unpopulated beach; adjacent to it is a National Wilderness Area that visitors are welcome to explore. Spring and fall are especially good times to come, as Fire Island is on the Atlantic Flyway, a major avian migratory route. Watch Hill also has bathhouses, a snack bar, and nature trails.

Ferries are operated by **Davis Park Ferry Co.** (West and Division Sts., Patchogue, 631/475-1665, www.davisparkferry.com, adults round-trip $20, children round-trip $13, cash only).

Smith Point County Park

East of Watch Hill and its adjacent National Wilderness Area is another beach park accessible by car. Like Robert Moses State Park, **Smith Point County Park** (William Floyd Pkwy., 631/852-1313, www.nps.gov/fiis) has plenty of bathhouses and concession stands and attracts large crowds on summer weekends. Technically speaking, the park is not part of the National Seashore, but since it's located next to **Smith Point West,** which *is,* and both are lined with the same wide and wonderful beach, it all feels the same. Smith Point West also has a National Seashore **visitors center** (631/281-3010, seasonal) and a self-guided nature trail.

Smith Point County Park and Smith Point West are at the southern end of William Floyd Parkway, off Sunrise Highway (Rte. 27). In summer months, parking costs $10.

William Floyd Estate

As you drive down William Floyd Parkway to and from Smith Point, you'll pass signs for **William Floyd Estate** (245 Park Dr., 631/399-2030, www.nps.gov/fiis, seasonal, free), now part of the National Seashore. Floyd was a Revolutionary War general and one of the signers of the Declaration of Independence. After his death, his family's estate grew to include over 600 acres of forests and meadows, along with a grand 25-room mansion and 12 outbuildings. The estate remained in the Floyd family's hands until 1977 when Cornelia Floyd Nichols signed it over to the National Park Service one year before her death. Guided tours of the house are available.

Accommodations

One of the few hotels on Fire Island is simple but comfortable ★ **Fire Island Hotel and Resort** (25 Cayuga Walk, Ocean Bay Park, 631/583-8000, www.fireislandhotel.com, summer weeknight $230-345, weekend $285-543), housed in converted U.S. Life Saving Service buildings. The hotel caters primarily to families, but rooms go very fast. Reserve well in advance; weekend reservations require a three-night minimum stay. Another good choice for families is comfortable, air-conditioned, 1940s-era **Cleggs Hotel** (478 Bayberry Walk, Ocean Beach, 631/583-9292, www.cleggshotel.com, weeknight $165, weekend $395).

Grove Hotel (Ocean Walk, Cherry Grove, 631/597-6600, www.grovehotel.com, summer weeknight $75-160, weekend $500-750 for two-night minimum) caters to the gay community. Rates drop significantly during the off-season.

BAY SHORE AND VICINITY

Several Fire Island ferries leave from the town of Bay Shore. The ferry docks at the foot of Maple Avenue, and on summer days, beachgoers stream down the thoroughfare, armed with coolers, beach chairs, and umbrellas. Few of them stop at **Gibson-Mack-Holt House** (22 Maple Ave., 631/665-1707, www.bayshorehistoricalsociety.org, Tues. and Sat. 1pm-4pm, free), but the very attractive historical home is well worth a look. Several rooms have been restored to their original 1820 condition, while other house memorabilia are from the town's turn-of-the-20th-century heyday. The house is run by the Bay Shore Historical Society and was restored almost entirely by volunteers.

Sightseeing cruises around Great South Bay are offered by **South Bay Cruises** (631/750-5359, www.laurenkristy.net, Apr.-Oct.). The cruises leave from Bay Shore Manor Park at the foot of Clinton Avenue.

Heckscher State Park

Heckscher State Park (off Heckscher State Pkwy., East Islip, 631/581-2100, www.parks.ny.gov/parks/136, daily dawn-dusk, parking

Stop for a Gander

Big Duck

Sitting all by itself by the side of the road on Route 24 in Flanders, the pure white bird—with its orange bill and bright red eyes made from Model-T taillights—makes the **Big Duck** look like a simple child's drawing come to life. The only giveaway that something else is afoot is the dark outline of a door just beneath the duck's throat.

The 20-foot-high (6 m), 30-foot-long (9 m) Big Duck was built in 1931 by an ambitious duck-raising farmer who hoped to attract more customers and was inspired after a stop at a coffeepot-shaped coffee shop during a trip through California. Ducks were big business on Long Island at that time; in 1939, there were 90 duck farms in Quogue alone. Ducks and eggs were sold from a shop within the building, seen as a model for large-scale advertisement-building across the country. So influential was the Big Duck that the term "duck" is still used in architecture whenever a building is made into a literal translation of an object.

Today, the Big Duck is listed in the National Register of Historic Places, and it's open daily, year-round. The tourist stop is made complete by a shop with—what else?—duck books, duck T-shirts, duck coffee mugs, postcards, and books.

$8-10) is a 1,500-acre spread east of Bay Shore. The park is an especially good place for families to go swimming because the water is calm, protected by the bay. Facilities include three beaches, a pool, bathhouses, nature trails, and a 69-site campground.

Long Island Greenbelt Trail, maintained by **Long Island Greenbelt Trail Conference** (631/360-0753, www.ligreenbelt.org), runs 32 miles (52 km), from Heckscher State Park on the South Shore to Sunken Meadow State Park on the North Shore. The trail follows the Connetquot and Nissequogue

River Valleys through wetlands, pine barrens, and forest.

Bayard Cutting Arboretum

One of the greatest estates along the South Shore is **Bayard Cutting Arboretum** (440 Montauk Hwy., Great River, 631/581-1002, www.bayardcuttingarboretum.com, Apr.-Oct., Tues.-Sun. 10am-5pm, Nov.-Mar. Tues.-Sun. 10am-4pm, parking $8), once owned by railroad magnate William Bayard Cutting. The 690-acre estate was designed by Frederick Law Olmsted, the famed landscape architect who also designed New York City's Central Park.

The arboretum centers on a dark baronial Tudor mansion. Inside are a few natural history exhibits and Hidden Oak Cafe, serving light lunch fare, but the place feels oddly empty. Perhaps that's because compared to the estate's glorious grounds, the mansion seems almost an afterthought.

Just outside the mansion is a verdant lawn, stretching 600 feet (180 m) down to the Connetquot River. On either side stand huge old black oak trees, spreading out their leafy branches. All around are specialized gardens: the azalea garden, rhododendron garden, lilac garden, and holly garden.

Parts of the arboretum were badly hit by Hurricane Gloria in 1985. An estimated 1,000 trees were lost during that storm, including about 20 of Long Island's oldest trees and 80 of the 120 species originally planted by Cutting. Younger trees were planted in their stead, but it will be many years before they reach their predecessors' 90-foot (25 m) heights.

Long Island Maritime Museum

Laid-back **Long Island Maritime Museum** (86 West Ave., West Sayville, 631/854-4974, www.limaritime.org, Mon.-Tues., Thurs.-Sat. 10am-4pm, Sun. noon-4pm, adults $8, seniors and children $6) occupies an idyllic spot overlooking Great South Bay. Housed in shipshape buildings, the museum holds the largest collection of small craft in Long Island. On display is everything from oyster vessels and sailboats to ice scooters and clam boats.

A historic oyster house and an 1890s bayman's cottage, both of which were moved here from elsewhere on the island, are also on display. The oyster house holds an extensive exhibit on the harvesting of shellfish. Next door is a working boat shop where volunteers build new boats and restore old ones.

Food

Wine bar and bistro **fatfish** (28 Cottage Ave., Bay Shore, 631/666-2899, www.fatfish.info, seasonal, $30) has an extensive menu with plenty of fish, seafood, poultry, and meat options. Another excellent option is **The Lake House** (240 W. Main St., Bay Shore, 631/666-0995, www.thelakehouserest.com, Tues.-Thurs. 5pm-10pm, Fri.-Sat. 5pm-11pm, Sun. 4pm-10pm, $34), which specializes in upscale New American dishes.

The Hamptons

The South Fork is perhaps best known for the Hamptons, New York City's playground. The rich and influential, the middle-class and obscure, all flock here during summer to rent weathered cottages, poke around in picture-perfect towns, indulge in fast-paced nightlife, and, most of all, explore magnificent beaches.

But the South Fork also has a culture all its own that has nothing to do with tourists. Farmers and fisherfolk continue to practice their livelihoods here as they have for hundreds of years. Humble fields adjoin multimillion-dollar second homes, and fishing boats share harbors with pleasure craft.

The English first arrived in Southampton from Lynn, Massachusetts, in 1640. Much of their reason for coming was the fact that the Algonquins made wampum (beads) on the island. Wampum could be exchanged for valuable beaver and other furs, and the English wanted to get access to the beads before the Dutch. The Algonquins welcomed the English, and in a matter of decades, English villages were flourishing, with village greens, white-steepled churches, and colonial saltboxes—many of which still stand today. Tourists started arriving in the 1800s, soon followed by hotels, and the railroad, marking the beginning of the end of sleepy village life.

Note that several Hamptons locales

The Hamptons

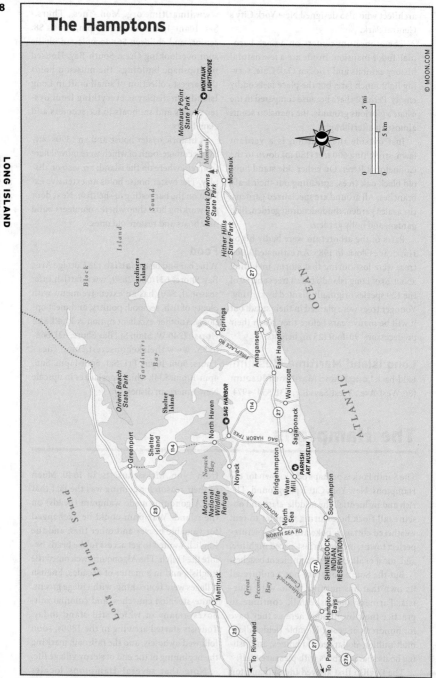

(Westhampton Beach, Quogue, Hampton Bays) are actually west of the South Fork, but when people speak of the "Hamptons," they're generally referring to those towns east of Shinnecock Canal.

PRACTICALITIES
Beach Parking

Although all South Fork beaches are open to the public, parking can be a major problem. Many village and town beaches require parking permits (good for the entire summer), which usually cost nonresidents over $100. However, some excellent public beaches have daily parking fees; the best of these are Atlantic Beach in Amagansett, Main Beach in East Hampton, and the beach at Hither Hills State Park in Montauk. Many hotels and motels also offer low-cost day-parking passes to their guests or include parking permits as an amenity; inquire when you book.

Parking illegally is not a good idea. Rules are strictly enforced, and violators will be ticketed with a heavy fine or towed. Most parking rules apply during summer only.

Nightlife

The South Fork is noted for its nightlife, which runs the gamut from casual bars to discos. In general, the nights get going as late in the Hamptons as they do in major urban centers—say 11pm—and don't shut down until 2am or even 4am on weekends. A few favorite spots to see and be seen include **AM Southampton** (125 Tuckahoe Ln., 516/492-0346), particularly strong with rap and hip-hop, and **The Leo** (44 Three Mile Harbor Rd., 631/324-3332), which says it aims to "bring sophistication" back to the Hamptons nightclub scene. Meanwhile, out on Montauk, the wildly popular **Surf Lodge** (183 Edgemere St., 631/238-5190) has featured performers as diverse as Patti Smith and Willie Nelson.

Accommodations

As in other resort areas, peak-season accommodations in the Hamptons don't come cheap. Peak-season rates usually apply from mid-June through Labor Day, and minimum two- or three-night stays are often required, especially on weekends. Rates drop dramatically during the off-season.

Along the beach near Montauk, you'll find simple family-style resort motels that are more moderately priced. Rates listed for South Fork are for double rooms, but many places also offer family packages. Meanwhile, historic inns and B&Bs are plentiful throughout the region. Most resort motels are closed in winter; most inns and B&Bs are open year-round.

QUOGUE

Turning south off Sunrise Highway onto Montauk Highway around Sayville or Patchogue will save you time and take you past a number of pretty villages. One of the prettiest is Quogue, a tiny place filled with big old shingled homes and wide empty streets.

Geographically part of the Hamptons, Quogue established itself as an autonomous village in 1928, allowing it, in the words of its village government, "to proudly stand apart from the 'Hamptons Scene'" to focus "on wholesome family oriented activities." True, it's not as popular as the Hamptons, but it *is* wholesome and family-friendly. Though the number of activities here is not boundless, two attractions are worth a stop.

Old Schoolhouse Museum

Quogue's **Old Schoolhouse Museum** (114 Jessup Ave., 631/996-2404, www.quoguehistory.org, hours vary seasonally, donations welcome) is a shingle-sided house built in 1822 and in use until 1893 as Quogue's first school. It is believed to be the oldest schoolhouse in Suffolk County, and its longevity may be attributed to the fact that it has always been well cared for compared to other schools, which tended to be neglected within their communities. The schoolhouse has been operating as a museum since 1949.

Quogue Wildlife Refuge

Long Island has a number of beautiful, ecologically important wildlife refuges, one of which is in Quogue. **Quogue Wildlife Refuge** (3 Old Country Rd., 631/653-4771, www.quoguewildliferefuge.org, grounds open daily dawn-dusk, Nature Center open Tues., Thurs., and Sat.-Sun. 11am-4pm, free) was established in 1934. It is notable for its rare dwarf pines and, especially, for its Distressed Wildlife Complex, where wild animals with permanent injuries receive ongoing care. The refuge also offers over 7 miles (11.3 km) of trails spread out across its 305 acres.

Food and Accommodations

Dockers Waterside (94 Dune Rd., 631/653-0653, www.dockerswaterside.com, brunch, lunch, dinner, hours vary seasonally, $40) is a bustling restaurant on the waterfront, serving everything from steak to seafood. Live music is often featured on the weekends.

For accommodations right by the beach, ★ **Hampton Ocean Resort** (30 Dune Rd., East Quogue, 631/653-3600, www.hamptonoceanresort.com, $225-600) is a hidden treasure. It offers warm and over-the-top service, including an excellent crew of polite, friendly staff who set up private cabanas and loungers for each room, hand-pack personalized coolers filled with snacks and drinks, fire up the barbecue, and deliver everything from fresh beachside drinks and frozen treats to veggie burgers and hot dogs, all complimentary, so you never have to take your toes out of the sand or pull out your wallet. Two-bedroom cottages ideal for families or couples traveling together feature a fully equipped kitchen and an outdoor covered patio with a large dining table. Resort highlights are the seemingly endless stretch of white sand with nary a hotel in sight and moonlight bonfires on the beach (s'mores included).

SOUTHAMPTON

The oldest of the Hamptons' villages is Southampton, a pristine and deceptively simple-looking town attracting a high quotient of socialites and the nouveau riche. Downtown is just a few blocks long, but it's lined with leafy trees, posh boutiques, and expensive cars. Its winding wooded lanes are dotted with splashy second homes, most of which are protected from prying eyes by tall privacy hedges.

Southampton, settled in 1640, was first called Conscience Point; its name was later changed to honor the earl of Southampton. The town centers on the intersection of Main Street and Job's Lane. Walking maps and brochures can be picked up at the **Southampton Chamber of Commerce** (76 Main St., 631/283-0402, www.southamptonchamber.com, Mon.-Fri. 10am-4pm, Sat.-Sun. 11am-3pm).

★ Parrish Art Museum

The **Parrish Art Museum** (279 Montauk Hwy., 631/283-2118, www.parrishart.org, Wed.-Mon. 10am-5pm, with late hours on Fri. until 8pm, adults $12, seniors $9, children under 18 free) houses a notable collection of 19th- and 20th-century American art. William Merritt Chase and Fairfield Porter, both of whom spent much time in the area, are especially well represented. Out back, find an arboretum and a sculpture garden shaded by rare trees. In summer, the museum presents many lectures, concerts, films, and other special events.

Southampton Historical Museum

Southampton Historical Museum (17 Meeting House Ln., 631/283-2494, www.southamptonhistory.org, Wed.-Sat. 11am-4pm, adults $5, children under 17 free) administers a number of historic buildings. The museum is centered at **Rogers Mansion** (17 Meeting House Ln.), a Greek Revival home built by a whaling captain in 1843. Inside the home are period furnishings, a Shinnecock exhibit, and Revolutionary War artifacts. Out back is a cluster of historical buildings, including a one-room schoolhouse, blacksmith's shop, carpenter's shop, and cobbler. The 1648

1: a beach in the Hamptons **2:** general store in the Hamptons

Thomas Halsey Homestead (249 S. Main St.) is the oldest building in Southampton, a tiny gray cottage sitting primly behind a fence, oblivious to the modern world. Built by one of the town's original settlers, the house is still in excellent condition and is furnished with 17th- and 18th-century antiques. Nearby **Pelletreau Shop** (78 Main St.) is the only 1600s-era trade shop in the United States that has been in continuous use; today, it is occupied by a jeweler who offers workshops to visitors.

Shinnecock Reservation

Just west of town, **Shinnecock Reservation** (631/283-6143) is home to about 700 Native Americans and the **Shinnecock Nation Cultural Center and Museum** (100 Montauk Hwy., 631/287-4923, www.shin-necockmuseum.com, Fri.-Sat. 11am-4pm, adults $8, seniors $5.50, children 5-12 $4.75). Opened in 2001, the museum showcases historic birch-bark canoes and farm implements, beadwork, basketry, weavings, photographs, and an informative video.

Visitors are also welcome to attend the annual **Shinnecock Indian Powwow** (www.shinnecockindianpowwow.com), held on Labor Day weekend. This major event attracts Native Americans from all over the country. Traditional dances, foods, and arts and crafts are featured.

Beaches

Southampton's main public beach is **Coopers Beach** (268 Meadow Ln., 631/283-0247, $50 a day parking fee), with full facilities including concessions, bathhouse, and chair and umbrella rental. No parking permit is required at the often-uncrowded **Old Town Beach** (end of Old Town Rd.). There are only about 30 parking spaces, however, and no facilities.

Food

The Golden Pear Cafe (99 Main St., 631/283-8900, www.goldenpearcafe.com, daily 6:30am-6pm, $12) offers homemade baked goods, sandwiches, and pasta. If you're looking to pick up food, try **The Village Gourmet Cheese Shoppe** (11 Main St., 631/283-6949, www.villagecheeseshoppe. com, Mon.-Sat. 7am-6pm, Sun. 7am-5pm, $12) for takeout.

More serious meals can be had at ★ **Le Chef Bistro** (75 Job's Ln., 631/283-8581, www. lechefbistro.com, hours vary seasonally), a French restaurant with a lively bar to one side, and dining to the other. A three-course prix fixe dinner menu is offered for $35.

Accommodations

Tudor-style ★ **Southampton Inn** (91 Hill St., 631/283-6500, www.southamptoninn. com, summer $389-489, Sept.-June $129-489) offers 90 spacious rooms decorated with English country-style accents. The inn has a heated outdoor swimming pool, a library with Steinway piano and fireplace, and tennis courts. The resort is especially popular with families and wedding parties.

WATER MILL AND BRIDGEHAMPTON

A few miles east of Southampton is the small village of Water Mill, named for the big grist-mill near the town center. The village's first gristmill was built in 1644. The current one dates to 1800 and now operates as **Water Mill Museum** (41 Old Mill Rd., 631/726-4625, www.watermillmuseum.org, hours vary seasonally, adults $3, seniors $2.50). During the summer, the mill still grinds corn and wheat with its all-wooden gears, shafts, and wheel. A number of art exhibits and events are held here during the summer.

A few miles east of Water Mill is Bridgehampton, named for a small bridge that was built over Sagg Pond in 1686. During the 1800s, Bridgehampton was known for helping distressed ships at sea. The first headquarters of the Life Saving Service of Long Island was founded here in 1878; it merged with the Coast Guard in 1915. Today, Bridgehampton is another picture-perfect Long Island town. Big redbrick buildings line its Main Street, along with a number of antiques shops.

Food

In Bridgehampton, sit indoors or outdoors at **Bobby Van's** (2393 Montauk Hwy., 631/537-0590, www.bobbyvans.com/bridgehampton.html, Mon.-Fri. 11:30am-10:30pm, Sat. 11:30am-11pm, Sun. 11:30am-10pm, $45), a place to see and be seen. It was once frequented by the literati and is now popular with celebrities. Classic steakhouse fare is what you can expect here.

Another expensive-but-worth-it option is **Topping Rose House** (1 Bridgehampton-Sag Harbor Tpke., 631/537-0870, www.toppingrosehouse.com, breakfast daily 8am-10:30am, lunch Mon.-Fri. 11:30am-3pm, dinner Sun.-Thurs. 5:30pm-9pm, Fri.-Sat. 5:30pm-10pm, Sat.-Sun. brunch 11:30am-3pm), whose menu was designed by star chef Jean-Georges. Most of the ingredients are sourced from the sea and nearby farms, including the hotel-restaurant's own plot, Topping Rose Farm.

EAST HAMPTON

At the center of the Hamptons lies East Hampton, an old-money stronghold now better known for its famed artists and writers, actors and directors, publishers and media moguls. East Hampton has been a mecca for successful "creative types" since the 1870s, when artists William Merritt Chase, Childe Hassam, and others summered here.

In the late 1970s, the now-defunct *Saturday Evening Post* ran a contest asking readers to vote for the most beautiful town in America. East Hampton won, and it's not hard to see why. Even more than Southampton, East Hampton is an idyllic New England village that seems to have stepped out of time. Perfect colonial homes, emerald-green lawns, and white picket fences are everywhere. Nothing seems quite real, but who cares? What could possibly go wrong in a world such as this?

A pond, village green, and Old Burying Ground split Main Street at the western end, while at the eastern end, in isolated splendor on a plush lawn, stands weathered Old Hook Mill. Between these two landmarks lie most of the town's shops, restaurants, and historic sites, all of which can be explored on foot. To catch a glimpse of the area's many posh summer homes, take a drive along Ocean Avenue or Lily Pond Lane.

East Hampton Chamber of Commerce (58B Park Pl., 631/324-0362, www.easthamptonchamber.com, June-Sept. Mon.-Sat. 10am-4pm, off-season hours vary) is well stocked with brochures and maps. **East Hampton Historical Society** (101 Main St., 631/324-6850, www.easthamptonhistory.org) sponsors walking tours of downtown and the cemetery in summer and fall. Many are led by guides dressed in colonial garb. Reservations are required.

Historic James Lane

At the western end of the village are Town Pond—once a watering hole for East Hampton's cattle—and the snug **Home Sweet Home** (14 James Ln., 631/324-0713, May-Sept. Mon.-Sat. 10am-4pm, Sun. 2pm-4pm, adults $4, children $2), a nicely restored 1650 saltbox that was the boyhood home of John Howard Payne, composer of the song "Home Sweet Home." Inside the house is a good collection of English ceramics and early American furniture; out back are a windmill and garden.

Next door to Home Sweet Home is a complex of restored weathered buildings known as **Mulford Farm** (10 James Ln., 631/324-6850, Memorial Day weekend-mid-Oct. Sat. 10am-5pm, Sun. noon-5pm, or by appointment, adults $4, seniors $3, children $2). Owned by the same family from 1712 to 1944, the four-acre homestead includes a farmhouse, barn, garden, and various outbuildings. Costumed guides lead tours in summer.

Historic Main Street

Just east of James Lane stands **Clinton Academy** (151 Main St., 631/324-6850, www.easthamptonhistory.org, Memorial Day weekend-mid-Oct. Sat. 10am-5pm, Sun. noon-5pm, free), a large wood-and-brick building dating to the late 1700s. The

building, which once housed the first prep school in the state and one of the first coed schools in the country, has also served as a theater and the office of the local newspaper. Today, it is a historical museum open to the public for tours.

Town House (149 Main St., 631/324-6850, www.easthamptonhistory.org, Memorial Day weekend-mid-Oct. Sat. 10am-5pm, Sun. noon-5pm, suggested donation adults $4, seniors $3, students $2), located next to Clinton Academy, is an elfin, one-room schoolhouse with a potbellied stove. The building also once served as the town hall and is the only remaining colonial-era town government meeting place still in existence.

Old Hook Mill (631/324-0713, July-Aug. Mon.-Sat. 10am-4pm, Sun. 2pm-4pm, adults $2, children under 12 $1), on the other end of Main Street, is the best surviving example of the many windmills that once dotted the South Fork. (Most of the few remaining windmills are not open to the public.) It was built by Nathaniel Dominy V, an innovative designer who included several then-unheard-of labor-saving devices, including a grain elevator, in his remarkably efficient mill.

Guild Hall

Across the street from Clinton Academy is **Guild Hall** (158 Main St., 631/324-0806, www.guildhall.org, days and hours vary by season, free), one of the premier art institutions on Long Island. Inside its three large galleries are temporary exhibits featuring top contemporary artists such as Chuck Close. Also part of Guild Hall is **John Drew Theater,** which presents dance, theater, and music performances, as well as literary readings by some of the famed authors who summer in the Hamptons. Every August, **The Clothesline Art Sale** presents work by both established and emerging artists.

1: Old Hook Mill in East Hampton **2:** Hedges Inn **3:** shops in Southampton

Beaches

East Hampton has five beaches, all of which are owned and overseen by the village. From Memorial Day until the last Saturday in June and again from Labor Day until September 30, East Hampton's beaches are open only on weekends and holidays. From the last Saturday in June until Labor Day, beaches are open daily. Main Beach and Two Mile Hollow Beach are the only East Hampton beaches offering **day parking** ($30 per weekday, purchase at Main Beach's pavilion, Mon.-Fri. 9am-4pm). A useful, up-to-date resource for beachcombers seeking more information is the village of East Hampton's website (www.easthamptonvillage.org).

Large crowds enjoy gorgeous **Main Beach** (101 Ocean Ave., 631/324-0074), which is staffed by lifeguards during the busy summer season. Facilities include bathhouses and concession stands. **Two Mile Hollow Beach** (Two Mile Hollow Rd.) is in the middle of a nature sanctuary and has no facilities. All the other beaches in East Hampton are usually less crowded, but require a resident parking permit.

Food

★ **Bostwick's Chowder House** (277 Pantigo Rd., 631/324-1111, www.bostwick-schowderhouse.com, Sun.-Thurs. 11:30am-10pm, Fri.-Sat. 11am-11pm, $26) is a casual, festive place specializing in fresh seafood.

East Hampton also has its share of posh eateries, where getting a reservation is no mean feat. One of them is **Nick & Toni's** (136 N. Main St., 631/324-3550, www.nickandtonis.com, daily 5:45pm-close, $36), which offers Mediterranean and rustic Italian cuisine in a sophisticated yet relaxed setting.

As expected, some of the hotels and inns in town offer good dining options. The hotel at the Maidstone has **The Living Room** (207 Main St., 631/324-5494, www.themaidstone.com, daily breakfast, lunch, and dinner, $38), where the Slow Food philosophy informs the New American dishes on the menu, and **The 1770 House** (143 Main St., 631/324-3504, www.1770house.com, dinner, $42) has two on-site dining options: an upscale contemporary American restaurant featuring local ingredients and a tavern.

Accommodations

Among the more moderately priced inns in this expensive town is **Bassett House Inn** (128 Montauk Hwy., 631/324-6127, www.bassetthouseinn.com, $145-375 July-Aug.), a large home built in 1830. It offers 12 guest rooms, all decorated with antiques. Some of the less expensive rooms share baths; some of the more expensive ones have fireplaces, and one has a whirlpool.

Boutique hotel **The Maidstone** (207 Main St., 631/324-5006, www.themaidstone. com, $450-550 summer, $225-295 off-season) is housed in a 150-year-old Greek Revival home that was once a tannery. From the 1920s until the first decade of the 2000s, the house served as an inn. In 2008, it was bought by a Swedish hotelier who brought the property up to date and introduced his Scandinavian design sensibility and luxe amenities for a modern boutique hotel stay. In addition to organic linens and high-end toiletries, summer guests love the coveted beach parking permit that comes with each room. The hotel's Slow Food-certified restaurant, The Living Room (breakfast, lunch, dinner, $40), focuses on fresh, local, organic ingredients.

Among the oldest accommodations on the South Fork is **Hedges Inn** (74 James Ln., 631/324-7101, www.thehedgesinn.com, $675-1,100 summer, $205-425 off-season). Built by one of the town's founding families, with sections dating back to more than three centuries, the inn features 13 nicely restored rooms, some overlooking Town Pond.

Another historic accommodation is **The Huntting Inn** (94 Main St., 631/324-0410, www.thepalm.com/Huntting-Inn, $250-750 summer, $195-450 off-season), with comfortable rooms and attentive staff. Its convenient location is noteworthy: The Hampton Jitney bus service stops directly across the street and it's a three-minute walk to Main Street's

shops and restaurants. Beach passes, towels, and chairs are included in the room rate in summer months.

★ SAG HARBOR

Driving north from East Hampton along Route 114, through lush, fertile farm country, you'll soon come to the old whaling port of Sag Harbor. During its heyday, Sag Harbor was a bustling, bawdy commercial town, and some of that lively atmosphere—so different from the elegance of much of the Hamptons—lingers.

Sag Harbor is a good town to explore on foot. Lower Main Street is filled with shops and restaurants, while upper Main and side streets hold dozens of 19th-century homes and huge old trees. At the foot of Main Street is the weather-beaten 1,000-foot (300 m) Long Wharf, which offers close-up views of the harbor.

Plentiful parking is available near the waterfront, especially between Main and Meadow Streets. Traffic usually doesn't get quite as congested here as it does in the Hamptons, but it can still be daunting.

In summer, **Sag Harbor Chamber of Commerce** (55 Main St., 631/725-0011, www.sagharborchamber.com) runs a **visitor information center** (July-Aug. daily 9am-4pm) in the old windmill at the entrance to Long Wharf.

Sag Harbor Whaling and Historical Museum

One of the most interesting buildings in town is **Sag Harbor Whaling and Historical Museum** (200 Main St., 631/725-0770, www. sagharborwhalingmuseum.org, May 15-Oct. 1 Mon.-Sat. 10am-5pm, Sun. 1pm-5pm, adults $8, seniors and students $6, children under 11 $3), its entrance marked with tall Corinthian columns and the impressive, large jawbones of a whale. The mansion was built in 1845 by architect Minard Lafever for whaling-ship owner Benjamin Huntting.

The hodgepodge of jumbled exhibits—some absolutely fascinating, others looking suspiciously like junk—makes exploring the museum a lot of fun. On display you'll find everything from wooden boats and tools used by whalers to ostrich eggs and a centuries-old soda cracker.

Custom House

Around the corner from the whaling museum is the **Custom House** (Main St. and Garden St., 631/692-4664, www.splia.org/custom-house, Memorial Day weekend-mid-Oct. Sat.-Sun. 10am-5pm, adults $6, seniors and students $5, children 6-11 $3), the former home of 18th-century customs inspector Henry Packer Dering. Dering's job was to record all the goods entering the harbor and collect entry taxes. He used his front room as an office; the room is equipped with wooden window shields that Dering shut whenever he wanted to count money.

Other Historic Sites

All along Main Street near Custom House stand impressive **sea captains' houses,** and nearby is **Old Whaler's Church** (44 Union St., 631/725-0894, www.oldwhalerschurch.org, daily 9am-3pm). Designed in 1844 by Minard Lafever, the church is built in an unusual Egyptian Revival style, and has a soaring interior.

Wildlife Refuge

About 4 miles (6.4 km) west of Sag Harbor is 187-acre **Elizabeth A. Morton National Wildlife Refuge** (2595 Noyack Rd., 631/725-7598, www.fws.gov, daily dawn-dusk, parking $4). The refuge overlooks Peconic and Noyack Bays, and features sandy and rocky beaches, wooded bluffs, ponds, and nature trails. The refuge is open year-round, but much of the beach is closed April-mid-August to protect nesting birds, including the piping plover, which is a threatened species.

Shopping

Locals gripe about the gentrification of their town, epitomized by Main Street, where familiar urban retailers and restaurateurs are setting up South Fork outposts. For a town that has embraced its moniker "The Unhamptons," the quickening creep of nonlocal brands and stores is a nuisance.

A few locals hang on, though, attempting to stave off takeovers. **Sag Harbor Variety Store** (114 Main St., 631/725-9706, www.sagharborvariety.com) was established as

Sag Harbor Whaling and Historical Museum

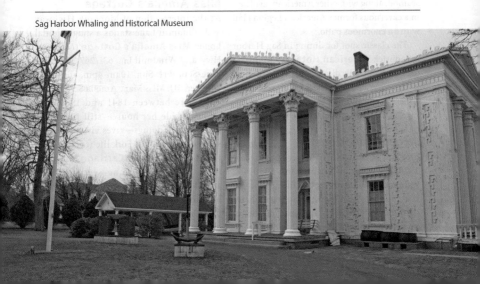

an old-fashioned five-and-dime with lots of odds and ends. Today, its wares tend more toward dollar store-type items, but it's still fun to poke around the aisles and rifle through the bins here. **The Wharf Shop** (69A Main St., 631/725-0420, www.wharfshop.com) sells gifts and toys as well as Sag Harbor-themed souvenirs: postcards, magnets, ornaments, and fine chocolates inspired by the area. **Annyx** (150 Main St., 631/725-9064, www.annyxsagharbor.com) is a home decor shop with unique recycled, vintage, and handmade accessories and gifts.

Food

A classic seafood shack, appropriately named **The Dockhouse** (1 Long Wharf, 631/725-7555, www.dockhouseny.com, daily 10:30am-9pm, $18), sits among bobbing yachts right on the pier. If you can't get a seat inside, take your lobster roll and wander to nearby park benches. The Dockhouse is also an excellent spot to pick up the freshest seafood for your own clambake as it doubles as a fish market. Check their chalkboard for prices.

For dinner and a view, check out ★ **Dockside Bar & Grill** (26 Bay St., 631/725-7100, www.docksidesagharbor.com, hours vary seasonally, $28), serving lots of seafood, along with other American favorites, in a cavernous former American Legion Hall with an enormous patio.

The classic spot for dining in Sag Harbor is redbrick **American Hotel** (49 Main St., 631/725-3535, daily dinner, $42), which despite its name has a European feel and serves French American cuisine. The restaurant has won numerous awards for its extensive wine list.

Accommodations

Sag Harbor Inn (45 W. Water St., 631/725-2949, www.sagharborinn.com, $260-442 summer, $139-219 off-season, includes breakfast), on the edge of downtown, is a modern, two-story hotel with 42 clean, spacious rooms, many with balconies overlooking the harbor.

Similar in style is ★ **Baron's Cove Inn** (31 Water St., 631/725-2100, www.baronscove.com, $190-480 summer, $80-280 off-season), an upscale resort with 67 rooms, most decorated with a nautical theme. Guests appreciate the hotel's complimentary beach shuttle, which eliminates the need for coveted beach parking permits, and pet owners love to book the pet-friendly rooms.

Historic 1846 ★ **American Hotel** (49 Main St., 631/725-3535, www.theamericanhotel.com, $250-400 summer, $135-250 off-season) dates back to the town's whaling era. Built of redbrick with a white porch out front, the hotel is a member of the Historic Hotels of America. Upstairs are eight guest rooms done up in Victorian antiques; downstairs is an acclaimed restaurant. The hotel's location is convenient to all the shops and restaurants on Main Street.

AMAGANSETT

Small, picturesque Amagansett takes its name from the Algonquin word for "place of good waters." Native Americans traveling between East Hampton and Montauk often stopped here for fresh water. A monument and plaque on Bluff Road mark the spot.

Miss Amelia's Cottage

At the intersection of Montauk Highway and Windmill Lane stands a snug colonial home: **Miss Amelia's Cottage** (Montauk Hwy. and Windmill Ln., 631/267-3020, late June-Sept. Fri.-Sun. 10am-4pm, adults $3, children $1). Miss Mary Amelia Schellinger lived here between 1841 and 1930, and a look inside her house—still furnished with her belongings—gives visitors a good sense of what South Fork life was like back then. **Roy K. Lester Carriage Museum** (631/267-3020, late June-Sept. Fri.-Sun. 10am-4pm, donations accepted), just behind the cottage, contains about 30 restored carriages, including a surrey with a fringe on top.

Jackson Pollock and Lee Krasner

artists' studio at Pollock-Krasner House

In 1988, the unassuming 19th-century farmhouse where artists Jackson Pollock and Lee Krasner lived opened to the public as the **Pollock-Krasner House and Study Center** (830 Springs Fireplace Rd., East Hampton, 631/324-4929, www.pkhouse.org, guided tour by appointment only May-Oct.). Art workshops, changing exhibits, and lectures are held at **The Fireplace Project** (851 Springs Fireplace Rd., www.thefireplaceproject.com), just north of the Pollock-Krasner House.

The house, built in 1879 and since designated a National Historic Landmark, displays the artists' collection of Victorian furniture, books, and jazz records. Guests can also visit the barn where Pollock created many of his greatest works; the proof is on the floor, splattered in Pollock's signature style. In 1956, after a tragic car accident took Pollock's life less than a mile from their home, Krasner moved her own studio into the barn and continued her artistic career. She died in 1984.

On Accabonac Road, not far from Pollock's old residence, is **Green River Cemetery** (Accabonac Rd., just south of Old Stone Hwy.), which has recently become one of the Hamptons' odder tourist attractions. Pollock is buried in the cemetery beneath a boulder marked with an engraving of his signature. Since his death, numerous other creative luminaries—including visual artist Stuart Davis, poet Frank O'Hara, and art critic Harold Rosenberg—were also buried in Green River. Visitors often drop by to show their respects, sometimes leaving tributes such as paintbrushes behind.

East Hampton Town Marine Museum

Long, creaky **East Hampton Town Marine Museum** (301 Bluff Rd., 631/267-6544 or 631/324-6850, www.easthamptonhistory. org, days and hours vary by season, adults $8, children $5) is on the outskirts of town, filled with artifacts relating to whaling, fishing, and the sea. Boats and more boats, along with an exhibit on shipwrecks, are displayed on the first floor; upstairs are exhibits on shellfish harvesting, scalloping, ice fishing, harpooning, and whaling. The museum also offers great views of the dunes and the Atlantic Ocean.

Beaches

A wide and wonderful public beach is at the end of **Atlantic Avenue** (off Rte. 27, Amagansett, 631/324-2417). It was once known as "Asparagus Beach" because it attracted bunches of singles who stood together watching everyone else. Staffed by lifeguards and feeding hungry crowds from a large concession stand, the beach now attracts a more mixed crowd. Parking is fee-based on weekdays, but a permit is required on weekends.

Wildlife Refuge

Merrill Lake Sanctuary (off Springs Fireplace Rd., 631/329-7689, daily dawn-dusk, free), run by The Nature Conservancy, is an easily accessible salt marsh especially good for bird-watching. A trail leads through the refuge. Ospreys nest here in late June and early July.

Nightlife

The oldest and most beloved of nightspots on the South Fork is **Stephen Talkhouse** (161 Main St., 631/267-3117, www.stephentalkhouse.com), where first-rate musicians—everyone from Bob Dylan to Bo Diddley, and Patti Smith to Percy Sledge—have played for decades. The place has a nice, laid-back feel, with worn wooden tables and friendly waitstaff.

Food and Accommodations

★ **Mill-Garth Country Inn** (23 Windmill Ln., 631/267-5229, www.hamptonsweb.com/millgarth, $225-375, breakfast included) is a romantic and eclectic B&B comprised of cozy cottages and studios clustered around small patios. Part of the property dates to 1840. Lush vegetation and wicker furniture are everywhere. The beach is about a half mile away, so guests especially appreciate that room rates include a beach pass and parking permit.

Clam Bar at Napeague (2025 Montauk Hwy., 631/267-6348, www.clambarhamptons.com, $28) is the best spot to pull over and snag a picnic table for an unpretentious, satisfying meal of fried clams, lobster rolls, or clams on the half shell and a bucket of beer.

MONTAUK

I stand as on some mighty eagle's beak,
Eastward the sea absorbing, view-
ing, (nothing but sea and sky,)
The tossing waves, the foam,
the ships in the distance,
The wild unrest, the snowy, curling caps—
that inbound urge and urge of waves,
Seeking the shores forever.

Walt Whitman, "From Montauk Point"

The drive from Amagansett to Montauk is only about 10 miles (16.1 km), but the landscape changes dramatically along the way. Near Amagansett, the South Fork still feels like a well-tended region of small towns and farms; near Montauk, the terrain becomes windswept, barren, and wild. Despite all the tourists who flock here in summer, Montauk remains a somewhat isolated fishing village surrounded by dunes and a sandy beach. Commercial fishing is still big business here, though the introduction of new catch limits in recent years has forced some smaller commercial fishing operations to diversify their businesses by adding charter services to their roster of activities.

Montauk proper centers around a circular green with a weathered gazebo. On one side of the green, known as Village Plaza, is **White's Drug and Department Store** (631/668-2994, daily, hours vary seasonally), a creaky old variety store where you can buy everything from postcards and sunglasses to small appliances and 14-karat-gold jewelry.

North of Montauk proper is **Montauk Harbor,** always teeming with fishing and pleasure craft and home to a number of restaurants. Every June, the harbor hosts the festive Blessing of the Fleet, in which hundreds of boats receive prayers for a safe season.

Montauk is a welcome respite after the heady, moneyed land of the Hamptons. Though it, too, now has its share of trendy hot spots, Montauk's main attraction remains the sea and shore.

Two-lane Montauk Highway is the only road that runs all the way from Southampton

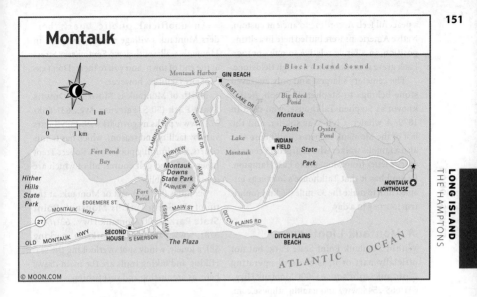

Montauk

© MOON.COM

to Montauk. During the summer and on weekends, it often gets unbearably congested, but there is no alternate route.

Montauk Chamber of Commerce (742 Montauk Hwy., 631/668-2428, www.montaukchamber.com, Mon.-Fri. 10am-5pm, Sat.-Sun. 10am-2pm) is well stocked with brochures and maps. Parking is usually available in lots along Main Street or on side streets.

Second House Museum

The oldest building in Montauk is **Second House Museum** (Second House Rd., off Montauk Hwy., 631/668-5340, www.montaukhistoricalsociety.org, hours vary seasonally, adults $5, children $2), a dark and long-ceilinged affair, first built in 1746 and rebuilt in 1797. Inside, you'll find period furniture and small, casual exhibits on Montauk history.

One of the most interesting displays concerns Samson Occom, a Mohegan born in Connecticut. Occom came to Montauk in 1744 after converting to Christianity. He married a Montauk woman and became a noted preacher, as well as the author of several hymns still sung today. Together with two settler ministers, Occom went to England in the 1760s to raise money for indigent Native

Americans. The earl of Dartmouth was so impressed with Occom's powerful preaching that he donated £10,000 to the cause. Back in North America, however, the other two ministers took over administration of the funds, which they used to found Dartmouth College in 1769. Occom withdrew from village life, a disillusioned, discouraged man.

Third House

Third House is a big, rambling property several times the size of Second House. Set in the middle of what is now **Montauk County Park** (off Rte. 27 east of the village center, 631/852-7878, www.montaukhistoricalsociety.org, June-Sept. Wed.-Sun. 10am-5pm, free), it was used by Teddy Roosevelt and his Rough Riders in 1898, and currently functions as the park headquarters. A small exhibit on Roosevelt and his troops, along with early Montauk artifacts, are on display here.

Indian Field

At the end of Pocahontas Lane, off East Lake Drive, is **Indian Field,** a burial ground. The last piece of land owned by the Montauks on Long Island, Indian Field today sits surrounded by modern homes, but still retains a peaceful feel. According to ancient custom, Native Americans were buried here in a sitting position, in a circle relative to one another. Each grave is marked with a rough fieldstone.

The cemetery's largest and only engraved stone belongs to Stephen Pharaoh, better known as Stephen Talkhouse, who died in 1879. A whaler, Civil War soldier, and the last of the Montauk sachems, Talkhouse was also a famous walker who charged 25 cents to carry a letter from Montauk to East Hampton. Legend has it that Talkhouse's long legs enabled him to make the 35-mile (56 km) roundtrip journey in a day.

★ Montauk Lighthouse

Within Montauk Point State Park, but not officially part of it, is the still-operating Montauk Lighthouse (2000 Montauk Hwy., 631/668-2544, www.montauklighthouse.com, hours vary seasonally, adults $12, seniors $8, children 12 and under $5, children under 41 inches tall not admitted to climb tower, parking $8), one of the most popular visitor attractions on Long Island. The lighthouse—the oldest in New York State and the fourth-oldest active lighthouse in the country—was commissioned by George Washington in 1792 and has been protecting vessels traveling the transatlantic trade route ever since. At one time, the lighthouse burned whale oil. Today it's automated and no longer requires a keeper. The Coast Guard still runs the technical end of the lighthouse but leases the building to the Montauk Historical Society.

Beaches and Parks

About 3 miles (4.8 km) west of Montauk is Hither Hills State Park (164 Old Montauk Hwy., 631/668-2554, www.parks.ny.gov/parks/122, daily dawn-dusk, parking $10). Home to the only official public beach in Montauk where you can park without a permit, Hither Hills has a bathhouse, general store, picnic area, and campground with 168 sites. The park is also laced with hiking trails leading into isolated dunes, which offer wonderful views of the ocean and bay.

An unofficial public beach borders Montauk's village center. Just park in Montauk, walk south down South Essex Street at the end of town, and you're there. Don't expect any facilities, however.

North of Montauk is Montauk Downs State Park (50 S. Fairview Ave., 631/668-3781, www.parks.ny.gov/parks/29, daily, hours vary by facility and season), which has tennis courts, a swimming pool, and a Robert Trent Jones-designed golf course, all of which are open to the public.

Six miles (9.7 km) east of Montauk, at the tip of the South Fork, is Montauk Point State Park (2000 Montauk Hwy., 631/668-3781, www.parks.ny.gov/parks/61, parking $8), a lonely, windy spot overlooking the sea. Hiking and biking trails are the main draws here, as are surfing and surf fishing.

Other Recreation

The nation's oldest cattle ranch, established in 1658, is Deep Hollow Ranch (Montauk Hwy., 3 mi/4.8 km east of village center, 631/668-2744, www.deephollowranch.com). Modern-day visitors can take guided trail rides through 3,000 acres of parklands, pastures, and beach.

Sportfishing is one of Montauk's major attractions. "Party boats" take out large groups of anglers daily. To sign on, call Viking Fishing Fleet (631/668-5700, www.vikingfleet.com). Viking Fishing Fleet also offers whale-watching cruises departing from Montauk Harbor in July and August.

Food

For brunch, John's Pancake House (721 Main St., 631/668-2383, daily 6am-3pm, $10) serves a solid breakfast at a good price, though service can be spotty. Still, their pancakes, waffles, and crepes bring in a crowd, so be prepared for a line. The Naturally Good Foods & Cafe (779 Montauk Hwy., 631/668-9030, www.naturallygoodcafe.com, hours vary seasonally, $9 breakfast, $14 lunch) is a

---

1: Montauk Lighthouse **2:** the Hampton Jitney

Farming and Fishing

The Dutch were the first European settlers to arrive on Long Island and were quickly followed by the English, who began settling the North and South Forks in 1640. Unlike many colonial settlers elsewhere, those who established themselves on Long Island had it easy. The land was flat, rich, and easy to cultivate; the sea was brimming with seafood and shellfish. Soon, dozens of small communities were flourishing.

During the Revolutionary War, Long Island was occupied by the British, and many settlers chose to flee rather than remain under the king's rule. But postwar, the island prospered once again. Cattle ranching (in Montauk) and whaling (in Cold Spring Harbor, Sag Harbor, and Greenport) joined farming and fishing as important industries. In the mid-1800s, the Long Island Rail Road was built and agriculture became big business. To this day, Suffolk County remains one of New York's most productive farming regions.

While still an important player in commercial fishing in the United States, Long Island's fishing industry has not fared as well as the farming industry. Quotas introduced in the 2000s to protect waters from overfishing have impacted small commercial fishing operations on Long Island negatively, forcing them to establish side businesses, such as chartering themselves out as pleasure boats, to survive.

Long Islanders never go down without a fight, however, and the importance and influence of fishing are still visible across the island, especially in Montauk and other towns on the South Shore.

small natural-foods store that serves oatmeal, granola, and burritos for breakfast and salads, sandwiches, and wraps for lunch.

Surfside Inn (685 Old Montauk Hwy., 631/668-5958, www.surfsideinnmontauk. com, lunch and dinner, $40) sits high above the ocean, offering great views from its porch and patio. The restaurant specializes in farm-to-table New American fare, and its friendly bar is a favorite among locals.

Bustling ★ **Gosman's Dock** (500 W. Lake Dr., 631/668-5330, www.gosmans.com, daily noon-10pm, $30) is a Montauk institution, an enormous dockside restaurant that serves consistently fresh fare. Three dining rooms, all of which overlook the harbor, range in price from the cheap clam bar where you can grab a sandwich and a seat at the outside tables, to the Topside restaurant.

★ **Dave's Grill** (468 W. Lake Dr., 631/668-9190, www.davesgrill.com, May-Oct. daily from 5:30pm, $35) is a classy, intimate bistro specializing in grilled fish. During the summer, there's often a long wait, but it's worth it.

Accommodations

★ **Hither Hills State Park** (164 Old Montauk Hwy., 631/668-2554, www.parks. ny.gov/parks/122) has 168 popular campsites that must be reserved in advance. In peak season, sites can be reserved by the week only. The cost for New York State residents is $31 per night on weekdays, $35 per night on weekends; for nonresidents, it's $62 per night on weekdays, $70 per night on weekends.

There are many resort motels in and near Montauk. One half mile west of the village is **Breakers at Montauk** (769 Old Montauk Hwy., 631/668-2525, www.breakersmtk.com, $150-210 summer, $105 off-season), which offers studios and one- and two-bedroom cottages, all of which face the beach and come with parking permits for the town beach.

Royal Atlantic Beach Resort (126 S. Emerson Ave., 631/668-5103, www.royalatlantic.com, $105-1,240 summer, $70-105 off-season) offers a variety of accommodations, including studios, one-bedroom suites, and "two-story luxury beach houses." All units have kitchenettes and private terraces.

Modern, gray-shingled ★ **Surf Club Resort** (20 Surfside Ave., 631/668-3800, www.surfclubmontauk.com, $255-510 summer) is on the edge of Montauk village, by the beach. This condominium resort also rents one- and two-bedroom duplexes. The condos are built around an attractive pool.

Rooms at the hip **Surf Lodge** (183 Edgemere St., 631/483-5037, www.thesurflodge.com, $275-400) open onto a private sundeck, complete with hammocks for lazy afternoon siestas. Along with iPod docks, a complimentary bar of "sex wax" (which, of course, gives surfers a better grip on their boards) is provided in each room. A stylish bar and restaurant are on-site. Each summer, the hotel plays host to an array of activities, including an impressive concert series, outdoor surf cinema, and live art installations.

Information and Services

For general information on Long Island, contact **Long Island Convention and Visitors Bureau and Sports Commission** (330 Motor Pkwy., Ste. 203, Hauppauge, 631/951-3440 or 877/386-6654, www.discoverlongisland.com). For more information on attractions in Nassau County, contact **Nassau County Industrial Development Agency** (1550 Franklin Ave., Ste. 235, Mineola, 516/571-1945 www.visitnassaucounty.com). For information on attractions in Suffolk County, visit the website of **Suffolk County Government** (www.suffolkcountyny.gov) and look for the visitors' section. For more information on any of the state parks or campgrounds, visit www.parks.ny.gov.

Getting There and Around

The major west-east thoroughfares traversing Long Island are Routes 25 and 25A to the north; Long Island Expressway (LIE), or I-495, mid-island; and Sunrise Highway/Route 27 and Montauk Highway (Rtes. 27A and 80) to the south. Southern State Parkway also traverses the South Shore but ends mid-island, at Heckscher State Park.

Keep in mind that traffic on Long Island is often slow and tangled, especially in summer. Avoid Long Island Expressway during rush hour and on summer Friday afternoons, when thousands of city dwellers head for the Hamptons.

A good alternative to driving is taking public transportation. Many Long Island communities, including those on the North and South Forks, can be reached from Manhattan via **Long Island Rail Road** (718/217-5477 or 516/822-5477, www.mta.info/lirr). Fares are reasonable, and taxis and rideshares are usually available at stations. There is bus service between New York City and the Hamptons; **Hampton Jitney** (631/283-4600, www.hamptonjitney.com) and **Hampton Luxury Liner** (631/537-5800, www.hamptonluxuryliner.com) service the Hamptons.

Ferries operate between Connecticut and Long Island. **Cross Sound Ferry** (631/323-2525 or 860/443-5281, www.longislandferry.com) travels between New London, Connecticut, and Orient Point, New York. **Bridgeport/Point Jefferson Ferry** (631/473-0286, www.88844ferry.com) shuttles between Bridgeport, Connecticut, and Port Jefferson, New York. From Port Jefferson, it's an easy one-hour drive to the west of the North Fork.

The Hudson Valley and the Catskills

Lower Hudson Valley...161
Mid-Hudson Valley.....186
The Catskills 208
Upper Hudson Valley...221
Information
    and Services.........228
Getting There
    and Around..........228

It's hard to believe, but to the immediate north of honking, teeming, steaming New York City lies some of the most splendid scenery in the Northeast.

The beauty begins at the edge of the Bronx, where for a 21-mile (34 km) stretch the blue-gray Palisade cliffs drop precipitously into the Hudson River. Farther north and to the west sprawl scrappy Ramapo Mountains, while to the east you'll glimpse the long, dark, silent reservoirs of New York City's water system. Midway up the valley begin the Hudson Highlands, an extension of the Appalachian Mountains made up of steep cliffs, craggy bluffs, and brooding blue-black peaks. Lush, loamy farmland, heavy with fruits and vegetables, spreads across the regions to the east, west, and north of the Highlands.

Highlights

Look for ★ to find recommended sights, activities, dining, and lodging.

★ **Walk among giants:** The stunning park of **Storm King Art Center** is filled with giant sculptures by the likes of Louise Bourgeois, Alexander Calder, Mark di Suvero, and David Smith (page 183).

★ **Walk over the Hudson:** This rehabilitated railroad bridge spanning the Hudson River is the longest elevated pedestrian walkway in the world (page 188).

★ **Dine at the Culinary Institute of America:** This lovely foodie haven features several award-winning, chef-student-staffed restaurants open to the public. Tours and a culinary bookstore round out the offerings (page 193).

★ **Look up in the sky:** In addition to antique shops and an organic farmers market, the picturesque village of **Rhinebeck** has airshows at the Aerodrome and hosts the Hudson Valley Hot-Air Balloon Festival (page 194).

★ **Go back in time:** Tour historic **Huguenot Street,** the oldest street in America with its original buildings (page 202).

★ **Unwind at Mohonk Mountain House and Preserve:** The storybook setting of this mountain resort evokes bygone days, along with scenic hikes, s'more roasting, and movies under the stars (page 204).

★ **Hike Minnewaska State Park:** Located high in the Shawangunk Mountains, this park is filled with panoramic views, glacial lakes, and hiking trails for all expertise levels (page 204).

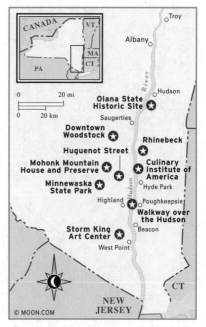

★ **Get in the groove:** Let your inner hippie loose and commune with the crowd on the village green in **Downtown Woodstock** (page 209).

★ **Pay a visit to Olana:** It's hard to pick a favorite among the Hudson Valley's epic estates, but this State Historic Site is particularly remarkable because of its unusual architecture and decor (page 224).

The Hudson Valley and the Catskills

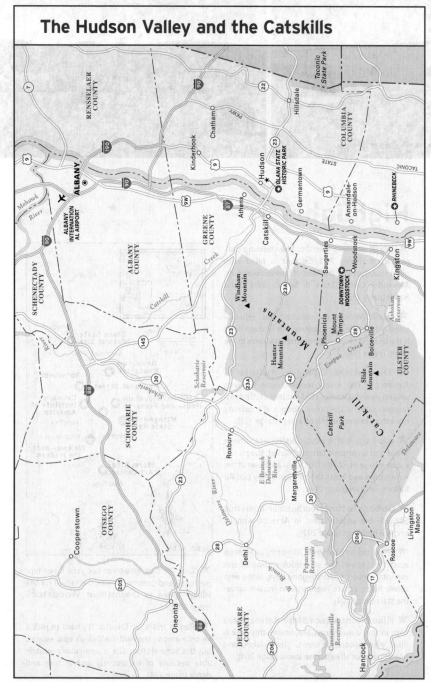

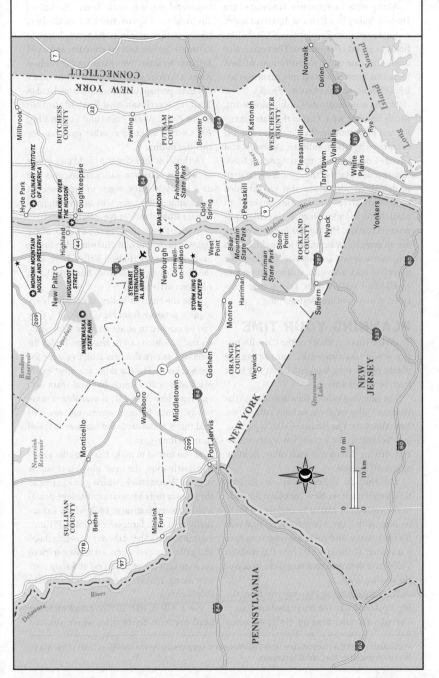

Along with its seductive landscape, the Hudson Valley lays claim to dozens of major historic sites, from Revolutionary War battlefields to grand river estates. The region also offers first-rate cultural institutions, offbeat museums, gourmet restaurants, luxurious hotels and inns, and glorious state parks.

No less majestic are the Catskill Mountains, which lie to the west. One of the state's many natural playgrounds, the Catskills region is comprised by Ulster, Sullivan, Delaware, and Greene Counties, encompassing nearly 6,000 square miles. Many of those miles are covered by densely wooded mountains and threaded by rushing rivers and streams, making an ideal destination for visitors who enjoy outdoor recreation. Hiking, fishing, and biking are all popular in summer, while skiing and other snow sports are popular in winter. For more laid-back activities, visitors can explore small-town main streets, take scenic train rides, or enjoy autumn leaf-peeping.

PLANNING YOUR TIME

To do the Hudson Valley or the Catskills justice would take two weeks, but you can see plenty over a long weekend or on day trips from New York City.

The gateways to both the Catskills and the Hudson Valley are about an hour's drive from New York City. The Hudson Valley is particularly accessible, with many key sights within easy driving distance of each other, most on or just off Route 9.

The Hudson Valley is well serviced by trains arriving from New York City. But once in the region, it's easiest to explore all that's on offer with a car. Many travelers find that it's both easier and more affordable to take a train out of the city and into the Hudson Valley and then pick up a rental car in one of the smaller towns.

For a good one- or two-day trip from the Big Apple, stick to the lower Hudson Valley. **Tarrytown and Sleepy Hollow,** home

to several major historic homes, including Sunnyside and Kykuit, make for an ideal day trip. Another option is **Beacon,** home to cutting-edge Dia:Beacon museum, and **Cold Spring,** an attractive village on the Hudson River. Outdoor lovers might want to take a day hike, perhaps on the famous Appalachian Trail, in **Harriman and Bear Mountain State Parks. West Point** and **Storm King Art Center** make up another good one- or two-day outing.

A three- or four-day trip could take in one of the lower Hudson Valley sights, plus two days in **Hyde Park,** home to the Roosevelt and Vanderbilt estates, with an overnight in or near **Rhinebeck** or **New Paltz.**

With six days, travel to two or three of the sights in lower and mid-Hudson Valley before heading to upper Hudson Valley. Here, visit the historic city of **Hudson,** home to Olana, a Persian-style castle.

Like the Hudson Valley, the Catskills are a quick getaway from New York City; they can be reached in about an hour, depending on traffic, which can be heavy on Friday afternoons as city-dwellers look to escape for the weekend. The Catskills are most easily reached by car, though bus and train service from New York City is available to some towns. Once here, however, visitors will find that a rental car is the best way to travel through the region.

If you intend to make the Catskills a day-trip destination, the most obvious choice is to go to **Woodstock,** which gained fame as the gateway to its namesake music-love-peace-and-happiness festival in 1969 (which was actually held on a farm over 50 miles (81 km) away in Bethel). Spend the day browsing shops and galleries or see a concert at **Maverick** to get a sense of the area, and eat and shop your way along Tinker Street, the town's main thoroughfare.

For 2-4 days, start in Woodstock and then head north to **Boiceville,** where you can both see and stay at the impressive Onteora Mountain House, former home of mayonnaise magnate Hellman. From Boiceville, go west on Route 28 to **Mount Tremper,** where you can take a look at the Kaatskill Kaleidoscope, said to be the world's largest. Continue west on Route 28 and overnight in Phoenicia; the next day, you can either take a ride on the Catskill Mountain Railroad or, depending on the weather, go tubing on the river. After Phoenicia, you could choose to go southwest and explore the wilds of Catskill Park or make the loop back to Woodstock by taking Route 212 East.

Lower Hudson Valley

First-time visitors will probably want to concentrate on Hudson River towns and villages, which are small, accessible, and charming. To explore them by car, follow Route 9, or Broadway, which is an extension of Manhattan's Broadway. To reach Route 9 from Manhattan, take the West Side Highway (Route 9A) north and watch for signs.

To head for destinations west, cross the George Washington Bridge on the upper level, taking the Palisade Parkway exit to your immediate right at the end of the bridge. Don't be alarmed by "Welcome to the Garden State" signs; this route takes you on a quick jog through New Jersey before you reenter the Empire State.

YONKERS

Yonkers, on the Hudson just north of New York City, takes its name from *youncker* (young nobleman) Adriaen Van Der Donck, who first acquired it from the Dutch West India Company in the early 1600s. With a population of over 196,000, Yonkers is actually the fourth-largest city in New York State, but its identity is tied to New York City, and it serves as a sort of scruffy extension of its much larger neighbor to the south.

Originally a Lenape village, Yonkers became an important manufacturing center in the second half of the 19th century. Among its chief products were textiles, carpets, patent medicines, insulated wire and cable, and elevators. Yonkers inventor Elisha G. Otis introduced the world's first "perpendicular stairway"—or elevator—in 1853.

Hudson River Museum

Yonkers' biggest visitor attraction is the **Hudson River Museum** (511 Warburton Ave., 914/963-4550, www.hrm.org, Wed.-Sun. noon-5pm, adults $8, seniors and students $5, children $4), partially housed in an impressive stone mansion overlooking the Hudson. Built by financier John Bond Trevor in 1876, Glenview Mansion is still outfitted with its original Victorian furnishings and art. Next door is a large, modern museum wing that presents first-rate exhibits on everything from regional flora and fauna to Hudson River history. Also at the museum are the exuberant *The Bookstore*—an "environmental sculpture" designed by Red Grooms—and the all-digital, full-dome **Andrus Planetarium** (adults $5, seniors $4, and children $3), equipped with a Zeiss star machine.

Philipse Manor Hall State Historic Site

A few miles south of the Hudson River Museum is grand **Philipse Manor Hall State Historic Site** (29 Warburton Ave., 914/965-4027, www.parks.ny.gov, Apr.-Oct. Tue.-Sat. noon-4:30pm, Nov.-Mar. Tue.-Sat. noon-3:30pm, adults $5, seniors and students $3, children under 12 free), built in the 1680s for Frederick Philipse, who came to New York to work as a carpenter for Governor Peter Stuyvesant. Through his own skills and a strategic marriage, Philipse became one of the most powerful men in the Hudson Valley. By the end of his life, he owned an estate

Biking the Bridges

Rail trails and scenic biking abound in the Hudson Valley. The following bikeable bridges are just some of the options cyclists have for crossing the Hudson. All bridges offer lovely views and connections to scenic rides on both sides of the river. Bridges and walkways are listed from south to north.

NEWBURGH-BEACON BRIDGE

From dawn to dusk, cyclists are welcome to ride on the south sidewalk of the bridge, which offers views of Storm King Art Center. Take care, as the surface of the sidewalk is metal with a strong texture and can become slippery when wet.

MID-HUDSON BRIDGE

Bicycles may be taken across the north walkway from dawn to dusk. Ride down Church Street to approach from the east; from the west, look for the "Bicycle Route" signs to the walkway.

WALKWAY OVER THE HUDSON

This multiuse recreational path was created from an abandoned railroad bridge; it is now the longest elevated pedestrian bridge in the world (though cyclists are welcome, too). Visitors can approach from the Highland or Poughkeepsie end of the bridge; for specific directions visit the walkway's website (www.walkway.org).

RIP VAN WINKLE BRIDGE

The roadway is open to cyclists, while the walkway on the south side is for pedestrians.

GREAT FREEDOM ADVENTURES HUDSON VALLEY BIKE TOURS

Longer cycling trips in the Hudson Valley are offered by Great Freedom Adventures (www.greatfreedomadventures.com). During its six-day Hudson Valley Bike Tour, guides lead cyclists on scenic routes, with stops at historic sites like Olana; award-winning restaurants like those at the Culinary Institute of America; and shops and farms of artisanal producers.

that covered virtually all of modern-day Westchester County.

A prominent Loyalist, Philipse was one of the 200-plus colonial New Yorkers who signed the Declaration of Dependence, swearing allegiance to King George III shortly after those 56 other Americans signed the Declaration of Independence. Documents and artifacts from that era are on display, along with an excellent collection of American portraits by Gilbert Stuart and other artists.

Empire City Casino at Yonkers Raceway

Nighttime harness racing can be seen year-round at Yonkers Raceway (810 Central Ave., 914/968-4200, www.empirecitycasino.com, post time Mon.-Tues. and Thurs.-Sat. 6:50pm). The current track dates back to 1958, but the first Yonkers track was built in 1898 and was long known as the "poor man's racecourse." In addition to the raceway, Empire City Casino (810 Central Ave., 914/968-4200, www.empirecitycasino.com, daily 9am-4am) is here. Now owned by MGM, it operates from the clubhouse and features three restaurants, cocktail lounges, live entertainment, 5,300 slot machines, and electronic table games, including baccarat, craps, and roulette.

Food

If you want to eat in town, La Bella Havana (35 Main St., 914/920-9777, www.labellahavana.com, daily 11:30am-midnight,

Lower Hudson: Westchester County

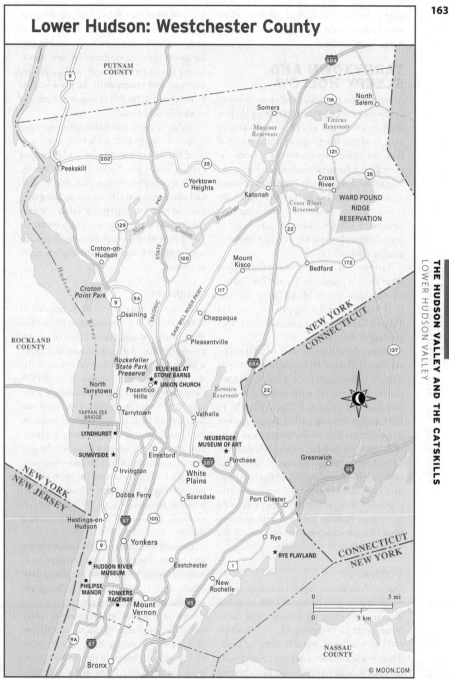

© MOON.COM

$25) offers mojitos and *el sabor de Cuba* with fusion foodie flair via respected chef Alexandre Cheblal.

TARRYTOWN AND SLEEPY HOLLOW

Among the most popular visitor destinations in this area are Tarrytown and Sleepy Hollow. Washington Irving, one of the area's prominent residents from bygone times, quipped that the name Tarrytown came from the early Dutch farmers' tendency to linger too long at the village tavern. But most historians agree that "tarry" is a corruption of *tarwe*, the Dutch word for "wheat." Despite being busy commuter villages, the towns are home to several major historic sites and a handful of smaller ones.

Tarrytown is located at one of the Hudson River's widest points, the Tappan Zee. Tappan were an Algonquin tribe and *Zee* means "sea" in Dutch. Across the Tappan Zee runs the Tappan Zee Bridge, its graceful silver lines glinting in the sun.

Many of the historic sites in Tarrytown and Sleepy Hollow are operated by **Historic Hudson Valley** (914/631-8200, www.hudsonvalley.org), an educational institution founded by John D. Rockefeller Jr. in 1951 and originally called Sleepy Hollow Restorations. The philanthropist and preservationist Rockefeller, owner of the nearby Kykuit estate, acquired area properties of cultural, historical, and architectural significance and saved them from the wrecking ball. The organization changed its name to Historic Hudson Valley in 1987 and continues to operate several historic sites in the Hudson Valley.

Sunnyside

One of Tarrytown's earliest commuters was writer Washington Irving. In 1835, he moved into an old village farmhouse, now called **Sunnyside** (3 W. Sunnyside Ln., 914/591-8763 on weekends, 914/631-8200 on weekdays, www.hudsonvalley.org, hours vary seasonally, adults $12, seniors $10, children

3-17 $6), where he felt he could find the quiet he needed for his work, yet still be within easy reach of New York City. Almost immediately upon moving into his new abode, Irving began remodeling it, adding gables, dormers, and towers until the place was, as he described it, "as full of angles and corners as an old cocked hat."

Today, 17-room, wisteria-draped Sunnyside is open to the public. It's a fairy-tale place, complete with costumed guides, a landscaped garden, and a pond with a bevy of swans. Much of Irving's furniture, including his desk and woodstove, is still in the house, along with many of his books. Just below Sunnyside runs the Hudson River Railroad, which Irving allowed to be built through his property on the condition that it stop to pick him up whenever he pleased.

Lyndhurst

Less than a mile north of Sunnyside is **Lyndhurst** (635 S. Broadway, 914/631-4481, www.lyndhurst.org, closed Jan.-Mar., ticket prices vary based on season and tour type), a magnificent Gothic Revival mansion designed by Alexander Jackson Davis in 1838. Originally built for William Paulding, a former New York City mayor, Lyndhurst was later owned by the unscrupulous financier Jay Gould. Among Gould's many questionable acts were his attempt to corner the gold market, which resulted in the disastrous panic of Black Friday, September 24, 1869, and his engineering of a deal that ruined his former business associate, Cyrus W. Field. Not surprisingly, none of this history is discussed at the site.

Covered with gables and chimneys, turrets, and towers, the exterior of Lyndhurst has a magical aspect. Inside, however, it feels dark. Much of the Goulds' heavy furnishings and art collection are still in place.

Surrounding the mansion are 67 acres, complete with formal gardens, a children's playhouse, a bowling alley, nature paths, and spectacular views of the Hudson. Don't miss the romantic ruins of an enormous

Great River Estates

- **Philipse Manor Hall,** Yonkers: This mansion, built for Frederick Philipse III, was confiscated by the state and sold at an auction after George Washington ordered Philipse arrested for his Loyalist beliefs. The state reacquired the house in 1908; today, it is a museum devoted to 18th-century history, art, and architecture.

- **Sunnyside,** Tarrytown: Writer Washington Irving's former abode, full of gables and towers, sits beside a pond with swans. Guides in period dress take you back to the mid-19th-century during a house and grounds tour.

- **Lyndhurst,** Tarrytown: The magnificent Gothic Revival estate, designed by the great Alexander Jackson Davis in 1838, was home to a mayor, a merchant, and a railroad magnate. It is now managed by the National Trust for Historic Preservation, whose staff offers guided tours of the house and grounds.

- **Philipsburg Manor,** Sleepy Hollow: This reconstructed 17th- and 18th-century manor house, which relied heavily upon enslaved people for its operation, is complete with a functional water-powered gristmill and guides in period dress.

- **Kykuit,** Sleepy Hollow: The former Rockefeller estate is famed for its magnificent grounds and collection of modern art, including works by Picasso and Calder. Staff offers guided tours.

- **Van Cortlandt Manor,** Croton-on-Hudson: This lovely 18th-century stone-and-clapboard house is not as well known as the Tarrytown mansions and therefore a good place to visit on summer weekends. Guides show visitors one of the largest and best-equipped 18th-century kitchens in the United States, as well as colonial and federal period furniture.

- **Locust Grove,** Poughkeepsie: The romantic octagonal villa was once the summer home of artist-scientist-philosopher Samuel Morse, inventor of the telegraph. It is now a museum and 200-acre nature preserve.

- **Springwood,** Hyde Park: Perhaps the most interesting of the Hudson River estates, Springwood is FDR's former home, a deeply personal place. Adjoining it is a first-rate library-museum. Nearby is Eleanor Roosevelt's equally personal Val-Kill. Together, they comprise the Franklin D. Roosevelt National Historic Site, operated by the National Park Service.

- **Vanderbilt Mansion,** Hyde Park: This was the most extravagant Hudson River estate, built in a posh beaux arts style. Go here to drool over lavish furnishings, gold-leaf ceilings, Flemish tapestries, and the like.

- **Staatsburgh State Historic Site,** Staatsburg: The vast, 65-room mansion sits on a hill overlooking the Hudson River and Catskill Mountains. Edith Wharton based the Trenor estate in *The House of Mirth* on this place.

- **Wilderstein,** Rhinebeck: This whimsical, all-wooden Queen Anne mansion with interiors by Tiffany and grounds designed by Calvert Vaux is one of the smaller estates. Visitors can enjoy house tours and exploring the 3 miles (4.8 km) of trails crisscrossing the estate.

- **Montgomery Place,** Annandale-on-Hudson: Though the classical revival-style mansion is impressive, the grounds here are the main draw; 380 acres feature woodland trails with views of the Hudson River and Catskill Mountains, as well as carefully groomed gardens.

- **Clermont State Historic Site,** Germantown: This grand mansion has an especially fine front lawn lined with black locust trees. Historic house tours are offered, or visitors can simply wander the 500 acres of grounds.

- **Olana State Historic Site,** Hudson: This eccentric Persian-style castle, perched high on a hill, was built by Hudson River School painter Frederic Church in 1870. The landscaped grounds are considered as impressive as Church's artwork.

greenhouse, the 14 rooms of which once housed a renowned orchid collection.

Tarrytown Music Hall

Built in 1885, Tarrytown Music Hall (13 Main St., 914/631-3390, www.tarrytownmusichall.org) is the oldest live theater in Westchester County and a National Historic Landmark. Top-notch jazz, folk, and blues concerts are performed here; plays, musicals, operas, comedies, dance, and films are also on the schedule.

Old Dutch Church and Burying Ground

In Sleepy Hollow, the Old Dutch Church (540 N. Broadway, 914/631-1123, www.rctodc.org, cemetery gates close at 4:30pm daily) dates back to 1685 and is believed to be the oldest church in continuous use in New York State. But except for its thick walls, little of the structure is original.

Surrounding the church is a Dutch cemetery that early settlers believed was haunted by a headless Hessian ghost. That local tale later became the inspiration for Washington Irving's *The Legend of Sleepy Hollow*. Irving took many of his characters' names from the cemetery's tombstones.

Adjacent to the Old Dutch cemetery is newer Sleepy Hollow Cemetery (540 N. Broadway, 914/631-0081, www.sleepyhollowcemetery.org, daily 8am-4:30pm), a scenic and peaceful place where Washington Irving, Andrew Carnegie, William Rockefeller, and other early movers and shakers are buried. Walking tours and photography tours are offered in warmer months; check the website for the current schedule.

Philipsburg Manor

Across the street from the Old Dutch Church is Philipsburg Manor (381 N. Broadway, 914/631-3992, www.hudsonvalley.org, hours vary seasonally, adults $12, seniors $10,

children 3-17 $6), a carefully reconstructed 17th- and 18th-century manor house, complete with a working gristmill and small farm. Once owned by Frederick Philipse of Yonkers, the estate is now often jammed with tour buses and groups of schoolkids; of all the Historic Hudson Valley properties, this one is best for families. Costumed guides describe life in colonial times as visitors pass through the main stone house, gristmill, Dutch barn, and other buildings.

Kykuit

Just northeast of Sleepy Hollow in the elite village of Pocantico Hills, Kykuit (KYE-cut, visitor's center at Philipsburg Manor, 381 N. Broadway, 914/631-8200, www.hudsonvalley.org, hours vary seasonally, admission fees vary by type of tour and day of the week) served as the weekend home for three generations of the Rockefeller family. Compared to many of the estates along the Hudson, the beaux arts Kykuit, built in 1908, is a relatively modest affair, decorated with 18th- and 19th-century antiques. The house tour doesn't become especially interesting until it descends to Nelson Rockefeller's astonishing subterranean art gallery, filled with more than 100 works by such modern masters as Picasso, Motherwell, Warhol, and Léger.

Even more wonderful are Kykuit's 87 acres of meticulously landscaped grounds, offering glorious views of the Hudson and Palisades. The gardens—complete with boxwood hedges, romantic arbors, and linden allées—are whimsically dotted with yet more modern-art masterpieces, including sculptures by Gaston Lachaise, Aristide Maillol, and Alexander Calder.

Kykuit tours leave from Philipsburg Manor (381 N. Broadway). Five different kinds of tours are offered and reservations for most tours are not required; same-day tickets are sold on a first-come, first-served basis starting at 9am.

1: Kykuit estate 2: Sunnyside 3: Philipsburg Manor
4: Lyndhurst mansion

Union Church of Pocantico Hills

Union Church of Pocantico Hills (555 Bedford Rd., 914/631-8200, www.hudsonvalley.org, Mon. and Wed.-Sat. 11am-4pm, Sun. noon-4pm, $7) is a serene attraction. Inside are nine stunning stained-glass windows by Marc Chagall and a luminous rose window by Henri Matisse. The Chagall windows depict biblical scenes. The Matisse window—a leafy swirl of green, yellow, and blue—was the final work completed by the artist before his death. Visitors can admire the windows on their own or request a guided tour.

Rockefeller State Park Preserve

Once part of the Rockefeller estate, the well-kept 750-acre **Rockefeller State Park Preserve** (off Rte. 117 near Rte. 9, Mount Pleasant, 914/631-1470, www.parks.ny.gov/parks/59, daily dawn-dusk, parking $6) is filled with meadows and woodlands, a small lake, a peony monument that was a gift of Japan, and over 14 miles (22.5 km) of mostly level paths. The preserve is designated as an Important Bird Area by the National Audubon Society because more than 180 bird species have been documented here. Maps are available at the entrance.

Teatown Lake Reservation

Just a short drive from Tarrytown is peaceful 875-acre **Teatown Lake Reservation** (1600 Spring Valley Rd., 914/762-2912, www.teatown.org, trails daily dawn-dusk, visitors center daily 9am-5pm), with a shimmering lake, hiking trails, an interpretive museum in two colonial buildings, and wildflowers galore in spring, summer, and fall. Most of the 230 species of native and endangered flowers grow on an isolated two-acre island in the middle of the park, accessible only by tour ($6 pp, reservations required, children under 12 not permitted on island).

Van Cortlandt Manor

In Croton-on-Hudson, 18th-century **Van**
Cortlandt Manor (525 S. Riverside Ave., 914/631-8200, www.hudsonvalley.org, hours vary seasonally, adults $12, seniors $10, children 3-16 $6) is another splendid estate managed by Historic Hudson Valley. Oloff Van Cortlandt arrived in this county in 1638, and his son, Stephanus Van Cortlandt, became the first native-born mayor of New York City. The Van Cortlandt family once owned 87,000 acres of land stretching from Croton all the way east to Connecticut. They were staunch supporters of the Revolution, and among their many famous guests were Generals Washington and Lafayette.

The deed to the Van Cortlandts' property still hangs in the house, along with original family portraits. Also on display are period furnishings and a working kitchen where guides concoct colonial recipes. Outside, a long, brick-paved walk flanked with flower beds leads to a restored 18th-century inn.

Food

Mint Premium Foods (19 Main St., 914/703-6511, Tues.-Thurs. 11am-9pm, Fri.-Sun. 11am-10pm) is a must-stop for gourmands or anyone else really. The tiny shop stuffed with gorgeous international delicacies, hot and cold, makes this takeout a top option for foodies, especially considering the vast array of scenic picnicking spots in the area. **Horsefeathers** (94 N. Broadway, 914/631-6606, www.horsefeathersny.com, Sun.-Wed. 11:30am-9pm, Thurs.-Sat. 11:30am-10pm, $24) is a cozy local institution, known for home-style food, good burgers, sweet potato fries, and an extensive bar.

Ultraromantic **Equus Restaurant** (400 Benedict Ave., 914/631-3646, www.castle-hotelandspa.com, daily breakfast, lunch, and dinner, $50 average dinner entrée) at Castle Hotel and Spa is spread out over several elegant rooms, including The Garden Room, The General's Bar, and Tapestry Lounge. It features unique and creative Auberge-style

---

1: Old Dutch Church in Sleepy Hollow **2:** Union Church of Pocantico Hills

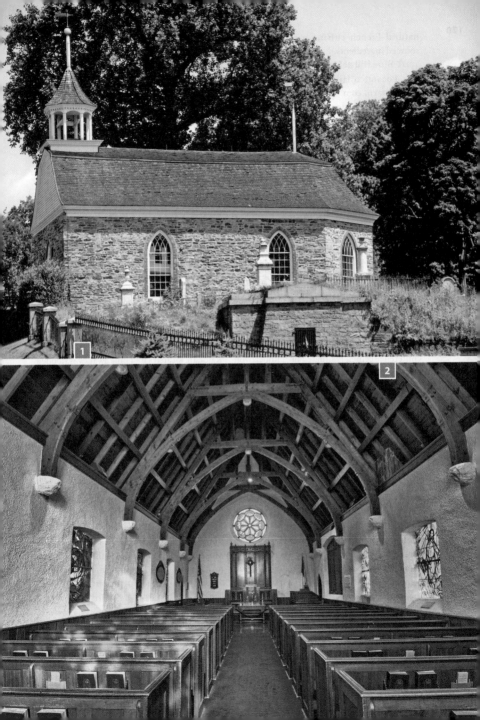

natural French cuisine based on locally sourced ingredients.

★ **Blue Hill at Stone Barns** (630 Bedford Rd., Pocantico Hills, 914/366-9600, www. bluehillfarm.com, tasting menu $278) is a branch of Manhattan's Blue Hill. Owner Dan Barber is a major figure in the locavore movement and a James Beard Outstanding Chef of the Year-award winner. His Hudson Valley outpost is in a beautifully restored barn located at **Stone Barns Center for Food and Agriculture** (914/366-6200, www.stonebarnscenter.org), a nonprofit education center and 80-acre farm. Known for being an experience where food is truly honored, the venue has no set menu; tasting menus are designed around the day's harvest, and range in price. Reservations are required.

Accommodations

Doral Arrowood (975 Anderson Hill Rd., Rye Brook, 914/939-5500, www.doralarrowood.com, $199-249), a 114-acre resort and conference center, is situated on a Robert von Hagge-designed nine-hole golf course and offers a Hot Stix facility, which uses a golfer's "swing DNA" for personalized club-fitting. A driving range, pool, tennis, squash, racquetball and sand volleyball courts are also available. Though largely used for meetings, the resort offers good deals and is a great location to use as a base for exploring the area.

Scoring high in the romance department is ★ **Tarrytown House Estate & Conference Center** (49 E. Sunnyside Ln., 800/553-8118, www.tarrytownhouseestate. com, $209-399), housed in two pristine 19th-century estates: one a Greek Revival mansion once owned by B&O Railroad executive Thomas King, the other a sprawling "castle" that belonged to tobacco heiress Mary Duke Biddle. Together, the estates boast lavish gardens, a well-equipped health club, and a billiard room.

One of the most romantic hideaways in Westchester County is ★ **Castle Hotel and Spa** (400 Benedict Ave., 914/631-1980, www. castlehotelandspa.com, $285-355). Perched on

a hill overlooking the Hudson, this authentic castle, with its 75-foot-high (23 m) main tower, was built near the turn of the 20th century by the son of a Civil War general. Now a luxury establishment that's a member of the Small Luxury Hotels of the World and National Trust Historic Hotels networks, it offers 31 luxurious accommodations, some with working fireplaces. On the premises is Sankara Spa and the acclaimed Zagat five-star Equus Restaurant.

NORTHEASTERN WESTCHESTER
Katonah

The well-heeled, picturesque village of Katonah is about 10 miles (16.1 km) east of the Hudson River, where Route 35 meets I-684. There are 55 historic homes on broad, tree-lined Bedford Street alone, all part of an area that's in the National Register of Historic Places. The homes were moved here between 1895 and 1897 when the original village of Katonah, located a half mile away, was flooded to create Cross River Reservoir. That event is known locally as "the Inundation."

Katonah Avenue, running parallel to Bedford Street, is also lined with Victorian-era buildings that were moved from the old village. Among them are the creaky, old-fashioned **Charles Department Store** (113 Katonah Ave., 914/232-5200, www.charlesdeptstore.com), still operated by descendants of the original owners.

Museum Mile

Route 22, just outside Katonah, is known as Museum Mile because of the three major cultural institutions found here. Most famous among them is the **Caramoor Center for Music and the Arts** (149 Girdle Ridge Rd., 914/232-5035, www.caramoor.org). An overgrown and romantic estate built in the 1930s by financier Walter Tower Rosen, Caramoor presents a highly acclaimed outdoor **music festival** (box office 914/232-1252) every summer, featuring many top names in classical music and opera and some top names in jazz.

Originally built by Rosen to house his outstanding art collection, **Caramoor Rosen House** (149 Girdle Ridge Rd., 914/232-5035, www.caramoor.org, $15) is well worth visiting. The fascinating main house was created by combining entire rooms from historic European buildings and surrounding them with a Mediterranean-style shell. One of the bedrooms comes from a 1678 French château; the exquisite music room was originally part of a 16th-century Italian villa. Meanwhile, all around the house are sunbaked courtyards and deserted gardens strewn with weathering statuary. Reservations to visit the Rosen House must be made in advance.

Down the street from Caramoor is **John Jay Homestead** (400 Jay St., 914/232-5651, www.johnjayhomestead.org, days and hours vary by season, adults $10, seniors $7, children under 12 free). Jay was president of the Continental Congress, first chief justice of the U.S. Supreme Court, and coauthor of both the Federalist Papers and the Treaty of Paris (which ended the American Revolution). He retired here after leaving public office in 1801. The large wooden house with shutters and an inviting veranda is filled with period antiques and memorabilia. Surrounding the house are landscaped gardens and a farm.

Near John Jay's former home is the small but exceedingly lovely **Katonah Museum of Art** (134 Jay St., 914/232-9555, www.katonahmuseum.org, Tues.-Sat. 10am-5pm, Sun. noon-5pm, adults $10, seniors and students $5, children under 12 free). Designed by Edward Larrabee Barnes, the museum features unusual temporary exhibits by major contemporary artists such as Milton Avery and Mark Rothko.

Cross River

A few miles east of Katonah is 4,315-acre **Ward Pound Ridge Reservation** (Rtes. 35 and 121, 914/864-7317, daily 8am-dusk, parking $10), the largest park in Westchester County. Laced with 35 miles (56 km) of good, fairly rugged hiking trails, the park also features two rivers for fishing and a small

Trailside Nature Museum (Tue.-Sat. 9am-4pm). Year-round camping under lean-tos is available.

Chappaqua

About 8 miles (12.9 km) south of Katonah is one of Westchester's more unusual lodgings, the 12-bedroom ★ **Crabtree's Kittle House Restaurant and Inn** (11 Kittle Rd., 914/666-8044, www.crabtreeskittlehouse.com, $167, with continental breakfast). Over 200 years old, the building has been a carriage house, roadhouse, girls' school, guesthouse for the Mount Kisco Little Theater, restaurant, and inn. Henry Fonda and Tallulah Bankhead were among the actors who overnighted here.

Attached to the inn is a **restaurant** (11 Kittle Rd., 914/666-8044, www.crabtreeskittlehouse.com, Mon.-Fri. lunch and dinner, Sat. dinner, Sun. brunch and dinner, $36). The farm-to-table restaurant has a tasting menu available. Live jazz is often played on the weekends. Reservations are recommended for this popular spot.

SOUTHEASTERN WESTCHESTER
Purchase

Despite its bland appearance, the wealthy community of Purchase is home to two remarkable cultural sites. **Neuberger Museum** (735 Anderson Hill Rd., 914/251-6100, www.neuberger.org, Wed. noon-8pm, Thurs.-Sun. noon-5pm, adults $5, seniors and students $3, children under 12 free), on the campus of Purchase College, State University of New York, is a first-rate art museum with an outstanding collection of modern works by such masters as Georgia O'Keeffe, Jackson Pollock, Henry Moore, Frank Stella, Mark Rothko, Edward Hopper, and—especially—Milton Avery. Avery was the favorite painter of the museum's founder, Roy Neuberger, and 20 of his canvases are on display.

Just down the street from Neuberger are **Donald M. Kendall Sculpture Gardens at PepsiCo** (700 Anderson Hill Rd., 914/253-2000, pepsico.com/sculpture-gardens, Mar.

30-Oct. 31, Sat.-Sun., 10am-4pm, free). An impressive outdoor sculpture garden is filled with works by Alexander Calder, Jean Dubuffet, George Segal, Claes Oldenburg, and many others. More than 40 works are on display, installed on carefully landscaped grounds complete with dramatic fountains. A path winds through the area, and a map is available at the entrance.

To reach either the museum or the gardens from I-684, take the State University of New York exit and follow the signs.

Constitution Marsh
Constitution Marsh Audubon Center Sanctuary (127 Warren Landing Rd., Garrison, 845/265-2601, https://constitution.audubon.org, year-round Tues.-Sun. 9am-dusk), a 207-acre tidal marsh, is managed by the National Audubon Society. An interpretive nature trail and boardwalk run through the preserve, while at river's edge is a **visitors center** (May-Oct. Tues.-Sun. 9am-5pm, free). The sanctuary is rich with birds—194 species have been spotted—and wildflowers.

The preserve also has canals created by farmers who hoped to use the marshlands to grow rice. Once a day at high tide, from May through early October, Audubon Society runs guided canoe trips through these canals. Trips are free and enormously popular; reservations must be made weeks in advance.

Manitoga
Heading north on Route 9D—watch closely for signs—you'll come to **Manitoga** (584 Rte. 9D, Garrison, 845/424-3812, www.visitmanitoga.org, trails: early May-late Oct. daily dawn-dusk, prices vary based on tour type). Created by industrial designer Russel Wright over a period of about three decades beginning in 1947, Manitoga is designed, as the artist put it, to "bring to American culture an intimacy with nature." Throughout the center run three hiking trails that Wright carefully manipulated to their best natural effect. Some parts are reminiscent of a Japanese garden; others are considerably wilder.

At Manitoga's center is Wright's glass-walled home and studio, **Dragon Rock,** built on the edge of a small quarry. Wright rerouted a waterfall to turn the quarry into a pond.

Food
One of the few old-fashioned drive-ins left in the region is the ever-popular **Red Rooster Drive-in** (1566 Rte. 22, Brewster, 845/279-8046, Mon.-Thurs. 10am-11pm, Fri.-Sat. 10am-1am, Sun. 10am-midnight, $8), always crowded with families and enthused kids.

COLD SPRING
Legend has it that the quaint village of Cold Spring was first named by George Washington after he took a sip of the local waters. The village didn't flourish, however, until the 1800s when the federal government created an iron foundry here. Around the same time, tourists traveling by steamboat first discovered the glories of the Hudson Valley. Cold Spring, with the granite dome of Storm King Mountain looming across the way, was a favorite overnight stop.

Today, much of Cold Spring still embodies the spirit and look of its Victorian heyday. Throughout the area are a number of old inns and restored 19th-century buildings housing attractive antiques, and gift shops line Main Street. **Walking tours** (845/265-4010, www.putnamhistorymuseum.org) of the village are offered by Putnam History Museum.

At the foot of Main Street is the Hudson River, but you can't get there without first detouring south, under the Metro-North train tracks (a sign marks the way). Once at the shore, you'll find the **Riverfront Bandstand and Dock,** the latter jutting out into the river and offering outstanding views.

Putnam History Museum
Originally a school for children of the Irish immigrants employed by Cold Spring's foundry, this small 1820 building is now **Putnam History Museum** (63 Chestnut St., 845/265-4010, www.putnamhistorymuseum.

Lower Hudson: Putnam County

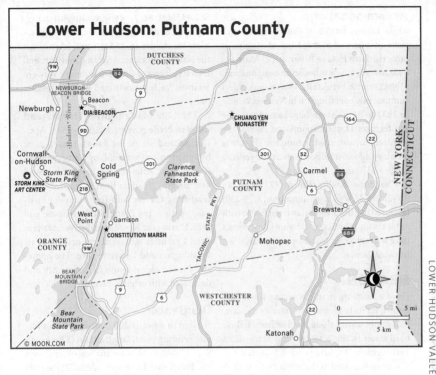

org, Wed.-Sun. noon-4pm, adults $10, seniors and students $5). Run by the Putnam County Historical Society, the museum houses a re-created foundry room, schoolroom, country store, and country kitchen, along with a dug-out canoe, horse-drawn sleigh, and historic photographs.

Chuang Yen Monastery

Take a detour east from Cold Springs on Route 301 to view the largest indoor statue of the Buddha in the Western Hemisphere at the largest monastery in the eastern United States, **Chuang Yen Monastery** (2020 Rte. 301, Carmel, 845/225-1445, www.baus.org, Apr. 1-Jan. 1 daily 9am-5pm, free). Standing 37 feet (11 m) tall, the Buddha sits surrounded by 10,000 small Buddha figurines in the Great Buddha Hall. Gravel walkways lead to several smaller halls, a lovely lake, and the Woo-Ju Library, a circulating library with titles in English and Chinese.

Food

Friendly **Cold Spring Depot** (1 Depot Sq., 845/265-5000, www.coldspringdepot.com, Sun.-Thurs. 11:30am-9pm, Fri.-Sat. 11:30am-10pm, $26) is a casual joint housed in an old railroad station. **Foundry Cafe** (55 Main St., 845/265-4504, Mon.-Tue. and Thurs.-Fri. 6am-3pm, Sat.-Sun. 8am-5pm, $10) special-izes in naturally healthy foods and regional American cooking, including soups, home-baked goods, and grain dishes.

On the shores of the Hudson River you'll find historic ★ **Hudson House Restaurant** (2 Main St., 845/265-9355, www.hudson-houseinn.com, Mon.-Thurs. 11:30am-4pm and 5pm-9pm, Fri.-Sat. 11:30am-3:30pm and 4pm-10pm, Sun. 11am-3:30pm, $36) at Hudson House River Inn. The restaurant serves fresh seafood and regional American cuisine. An outdoor dining area opens in summer, and many tables have great views of the river.

Accommodations

Right on the banks of the Hudson, with close-up views of Storm King Mountain, is boxy **Hudson House River Inn** (2 Main St., 845/265-9355, www.hudsonhouseinn.com, $170-250 with breakfast), the second-oldest continuously operating inn in New York. Built in 1832 to house steamboat passengers, the inn features 11 guest rooms and two suites, all nicely furnished with antiques. On-site is an airy indoor-outdoor restaurant serving lunch and dinner.

Charming ★ **Pig Hill Inn** (73 Main St., 914/265-9247, www.pighillinn.com, $170-250) is housed in a brick Georgian town house with antiques for sale. Six of the nine guest rooms have a fireplace or woodstove. Out back is a terraced garden.

BEACON

Once a bustling manufacturing town best known for its brick and hat factories, Beacon, like many towns along the Hudson, fell on hard times in the 20th century. Many of its 19th-century buildings were boarded up. The town was used as the setting for the 1995 movie *Nobody's Fool,* starring a down-and-out Paul Newman. However, since then, revitalizing change has come to town, thanks largely to Dia:Beacon, a major contemporary arts museum that opened in 2003. During its first year of operation, Dia:Beacon attracted nearly 100,000 visitors, twice as many as projected. Main Street is now spiffy with artsy clothing boutiques, bistros, and antiques shops, while second-home owners have contributed to the increase in real estate prices.

Mount Beacon towers over the city and has played an important role in its history. During the Revolutionary War, colonists set signal fires on the summit to warn compatriots of British troop movements. During the early 1900s, a casino serviced by a funicular sat atop the mountain; the tracks remain visible today.

Historic Houses

At **Mount Gulian Historic Site** (145 Sterling St., 845/831-8172, www.mountgulian.org, days and hours vary by season, adults $8, seniors $6, children 6-18 $4), you'll learn about the Native American, African American, and Dutch cultures of the Revolutionary War-era Hudson Valley. Costumed guides conduct tours.

The 1709 **Madam Brett Homestead** (50 Van Nydeck Ave., 845/831-6533, Apr.-Dec. second Sat. of the month 1pm-4pm or by appointment) was built by Catheryna and Robert Brett. After the death of her husband by drowning, Madam Brett succeeded in establishing the region's first thriving business venture: the Frankfort Storehouse and Mill. During the Revolutionary War, Madam Brett's granddaughter entertained Generals Washington and Lafayette here. The homestead is the oldest house in the county and decorated with original furniture.

Dia:Beacon

Housed in a nearly 300,000-square-foot former printing plant, **Dia:Beacon** (3 Beekman St., 845/440-0100, www.diabeacon.org, days and hours vary by season, adults $15, seniors and students $12, children under 12 free) displays the permanent collection of the Dia Art Foundation, an innovative arts institution based in New York City. Among the highlights are Andy Warhol's 1979 *Shadows,* composed of 102 paintings; Richard Serra's monumental Torqued Ellipses series; a large-scale sculpture by Walter De Maria; a series of fluorescent light works by Dan Flavin; and Agnes Martin's 1999 suite of paintings *Innocent Love,* created specifically for the institution.

Redesigned from a factory into a museum by artist Robert Irvin, Dia:Beacon sits on 34 landscaped acres with flowering fruit trees. The museum is within walking distance of Metro-North train station; on weekends, the Beacon Shuttle provides transportation to various stops in town.

Food

The in-house restaurant at **The Roundhouse at Beacon Falls** (2 E. Main St., 845/440-3327,

Lower Hudson: Rockland County

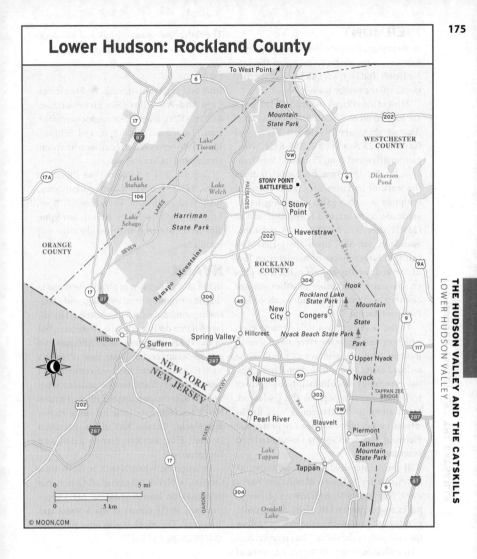

To West Point ↗

Bear Mountain State Park

WESTCHESTER COUNTY

Lake Tiorati

Lake Stahahe

STONY POINT BATTLEFIELD ■

Dickerson Pond

Lake Welch

Stony Point

Lake Sebago

Harriman State Park

Haverstraw

ORANGE COUNTY

ROCKLAND COUNTY

Hook

Rockland Lake State Park

Mountain

New City

Congers

State

Hillburn

Suffern

Spring Valley

Hillcrest

Nyack Beach State Park

Park

Upper Nyack

NEW YORK
NEW JERSEY

Nanuet

Nyack

TAPPAN ZEE BRIDGE

Pearl River

Blauvelt

Piermont

Lake Tappan

Tallman Mountain State Park

Tappan

0   5 mi

0   5 km

Oradell Lake

© MOON.COM

www.rhbeacon.com, Fri.-Sat. 5pm-10pm, Sun. 11am-3pm, $30) is a top choice for upscale dining in Beacon and especially favored by art lovers who find themselves hungry after visiting Dia:Beacon. Dishes on the menu are seasonal, featuring local ingredients, and draw raves from guests, who also enjoy waterfall views from the restaurant's floor-to-ceiling windows.

Accommodations

Roundhouse (2 E. Main St., 845/765-8369, www.roundhousebeacon.com, $189-439) is a 23-room boutique hotel in a former factory that sits on Fishkill Creek, with many rooms looking out on the creek's waterfall. Windows are floor to ceiling, offering a mesmerizing, meditative experience. The hotel is a short walk from Beacon's restaurants and shops.

PIERMONT

In its heyday, Piermont was a bustling commercial center at the terminus of the Erie Railroad. Today, it's a quieter, less touristy version of the nearby town of Nyack.

Most of the village's shops and art galleries are located on or just off Piermont Avenue. Among them are **Piermont Flywheel Gallery** (223 Ash St., 845/365-6411, www.piermontflywheel.com, Thurs. and Sun. 1pm-6pm, Fri.-Sat. 1pm-9pm, free), which features the work of its co-owners, all artists and sculptors. Another gallery featuring handmade objects by artisans is **The Outside In** (249 Ferdon Ave., 845/398-0706, www.theoutside.in, Sat.-Sun. 10am-6pm). Here, you can find larger pieces of handcrafted furniture and smaller objects suitable as gifts or souvenirs. A number of other vintage clothing boutiques and sundries shops line Piermont Avenue.

In the center of town is **Piermont Pier,** which extends into the river about a mile. Built by Chinese immigrants to allow the railroad easier access to Hudson River ships, the pier today is delightfully overgrown with cottonwoods, poplars, and goldenrod. From along its length you'll have unobstructed views of the Tappan Zee Bridge and Piermont Marsh, a 950-acre wetland and bird sanctuary.

If you're interested in visiting **Piermont Marsh,** enter **Tallman Mountain State Park** (off Rte. 9W, 845/359-0544, www.parks.ny.gov/parks/119, daily dawn-dusk, parking $6), just south of the pier and follow the bike path to the shore. The preserve, covered with wildflowers in the spring, is one of the most important fish-breeding areas along the Hudson and an excellent bird-watching spot.

Nightlife

One of the Hudson Valley's oldest and best-loved music clubs is **Turning Point** (468 Piermont Ave., 845/359-1089, www.turningpointcafe.com, tickets $15-35) in Piermont.

The club presents mostly folk and folk rock, along with some jazz and blues.

Food

Informal yet sophisticated ★ **Freelance Cafe and Wine Bar** (506 Piermont Ave., 845/365-3250, www.freelancecafe-piermont.com, Tues.-Sun. noon-3pm and 5:30pm-10pm, $30) serves eclectic cuisine with Asian, French, and Italian influences.

Tequila Sal y Limon (468 Piermont Ave., 845/680-6741, www.tequilany.com, Mon.-Wed. noon-9pm, Thurs. noon-9:30pm, Fri.-Sat. noon-10:30pm, Sun. noon-9pm, $16) serves Mexican favorites like tacos and enchiladas.

NYACK

In the 1800s, the town of Nyack was home to thriving shipping, boatbuilding, and shoe- and cigar-manufacturing industries. The village fell into decline after the Depression, but in the 1970s was reborn as an antiques and arts-and-crafts center. Today, most of Nyack's Victorian downtown has been restored, and homes of the rich and famous perch on steep wooded hills surrounding the village. Famous Nyack residents have included Helen Hayes, Ben Hecht, Carson McCullers, Jonathan Demme, Ellen Burstyn, Harvey Keitel, and Toni Morrison.

In summer, when Nyack is flush with tourists, a Nyack Chamber of Commerce **information booth** (845/353-2221) operates daily at the corner of Main Street and Broadway. The booth is also open on weekends in spring and fall.

Edward Hopper House Art Center

The birthplace and home of painter Edward Hopper (1882-1967) is a two-story clapboard house in downtown Nyack now called the **Edward Hopper House Art Center** (82 N. Broadway, 845/358-0774, www.edwardhopperhouse.org, Wed.-Sun. noon-5pm or by appointment, adults $7, seniors $5, children under 17 free). The son of a prosperous dry-goods merchant, Hopper grew up in Nyack and held title to the house until his death, even though he left the village in 1910 to live in New York City. Hopper is buried in Nyack's Oak Hill Cemetery.

The rooms of the Hopper House are wonderfully evocative, filled with a clean white light reminiscent of the artist's work. Only a small section of one room is devoted to Hopper's art. Most of the house is a gallery showcasing the work of local artists; out back is a picturesque garden where summer jazz concerts are presented.

Recreation
Riverfront **Memorial Park,** off Main Street in the village center, offers great views of the Hudson. Two miles (3.2 km) farther north is **Nyack Beach State Park** (off N. Broadway, 845/268-3020, www. parks.ny.gov/parks/156, daily dawn-dusk, parking $6), a riverfront stretch offering hiking, fishing, and more great views.

Hook Mountain State Park (845/268-3020, www.nynjtc.org, daily dawn-dusk, parking $6), at the steep northern end of North Broadway, offers bird's-eye views of the Hudson, along with hiking and biking trails. Once a favorite campground among Native Americans, the park is said to be haunted by the Guardian of the Mountain, a medicine man who appears every September during the full moon to chant the ancient harvest festival. A hawk watch is held in the park in the spring and fall.

Entertainment
Entertainment and nightlife options include lively, rollicking **O'D's Tavern** (66 Main St., 845/358-0180, www.ods-nyack.com, Mon. 5pm-9:30pm, Tue.-Thurs. noon-9:30pm, Fri.-Sat. noon-10pm, Sun. noon-8:30pm), with farm-to-table fare. Live Irish bands perform on Monday nights.

Nyack also hosts many street fairs and festivals. Three of the biggest, all featuring about 200 vendors, are **Art, Craft & Antiques Dealers' Fairs** (www.acadaofnyack.com), usually held on the third Sunday of May, July, and October.

Shopping
Most of the village's shops are found along Main Street and South Broadway. **Hickory Dickory Dock** (43 S. Broadway, 845/358-7474, www.hickorydock.com) sells clocks, handmade toys, and collectibles. **Saffron Trading Company** (14 S. Broadway, 845/353-3530, www.saffrontradingcompany.com) and **Maria Luisa Boutique** (77 S. Broadway, 845/353-4122, www.marialuisaboutique.com) are fun to browse for beautiful home accents and other lifestyle accessories.

Food
Simple, casual **Strawberry Place** (72 S. Broadway, 845/358-9511, daily 7am-4pm, $11) is a local favorite that's especially good for breakfast. For after-meal treats, **Temptations Cafe** (80 Main St., 845/353-3355, www.temptationscafe.com, Mon.-Fri. 11:30am-9pm, Sat.-Sun. 8am-8:30pm, $5 average dessert) is the place to go for ice cream and desserts.

King & I (91-93 Main St., 845/358-8588, www.kingandinyack.com, Tue.-Thurs. noon-3pm and 5pm-9pm, Fri. noon-3pm and 5pm-10pm, Sat. noon-10pm, Sun. noon-9pm, $15) is known for its fresh, authentic Thai food. Asian-fusion cuisine is the order of the day at sleek, stylish ★ **Wasabi** (110 Main St., 845/358-7977, www.wasabichi.com, Mon.-Fri. noon-2:30pm and 5pm-10pm, Sat. noon-11pm, Sun. 4pm-9:30pm, $28).

For dinner in a historic setting, try ★ **Hudson House of Nyack** (134 Main St., 845/353-1355, www.hudsonhousenyack.com, Tue.-Thurs. 5:30pm-10pm, Fri.-Sat. 5:30pm-11pm, Sun. 5pm-9:30pm, $30), housed in an old town hall and former jailhouse with pressed tin walls and ceilings. On the menu is eclectic American cuisine and lots of homemade desserts. Patio dining is featured in summer.

Accommodations

The Time Nyack (400 High Ave., 845/675-8700, www.thetimehotels.com/nyack, $230), is a 133-room hotel located in a former factory overlooking the Hudson River and Tappan Zee Bridge. Free wireless Internet and complimentary parking are perks. Other on-site services include a gym and restaurant.

TAPPAN

Tappan was the first town in New York State to establish an official historic district. Its Main Street is flanked with many nicely restored 18th- and 19th-century buildings, and in the town center is a village green that once held public stocks and a whipping post.

Revolutionary War Sites

Tappan is associated with both the beginning and the end of the planned betrayal of West Point by Benedict Arnold and British major John Andre during the Revolutionary War. It was in the DeWint House on Livingston Avenue that Washington entrusted West Point to Arnold, and it was in the Mabie House on Main Street that Andre—after his capture in Tarrytown—was imprisoned before being hanged.

Both buildings are still standing and open to the public. **DeWint House,** also known as **Washington's Headquarters** (20 Livingston Ave., 845/359-1359, www.dewinthouse.com, Tues.-Sun. 10am-4pm, free) is now a bona fide museum holding Washington memorabilia, artifacts regarding Masonic history, and information about the Andre trial. Washington was headquartered here in 1780 and 1783, and was a Mason for 47 years. On the day of Andre's execution, Washington closed the shutters to his room.

Mabie House is now better known as **The '76 House** (110 Main St., 845/359-5476, www.76house.com); it's a dark, low-ceilinged establishment that has functioned as a tavern and restaurant since 1800. Andre's former bedroom is now a dining room.

Also connected with Andre is **Andre Monument** (Old Tappan Rd. at Andre Hill Rd.). Here, a large crowd of spectators, held back by 500 infantrymen, watched Andre's execution on October 2, 1780. Only upon seeing the hangman's noose did Andre realize that his request to be shot as a soldier, rather than hung as a spy, was not to be granted. Impatient with his slow-moving hangman—a sympathetic fellow prisoner—Andre placed the noose around his own neck and the handkerchief around his own eyes. "All I request of you gentlemen," he said before the final signal was given, "is that you bear witness to the world that I die like a brave man."

Food

The '76 House (110 Main St., 845/359-5476, www.76house.com, Mon.-Thurs. 11:30am-3pm and 5pm-9pm, Fri. 11:30am-3pm and 5pm-9:30pm, Sat. 11:30am-3pm and 5pm-10pm, Sun. 11:30am-3pm and 4pm-9pm, $30), complete with exposed beams, Dutch tiles, and fireplaces, specializes in traditional American fare for lunch and dinner, along with some unusual game specialties. A jazz vocalist or pianist often performs on the weekends.

RAMAPO MOUNTAINS

Near the western edge of Rockland County rise the craggy foothills of the Ramapo Mountains. Nearly 600 million years old, the Precambrian Ramapos, which spill over into New Jersey, are one of the oldest landmasses in North America. At one time, their slopes, now eroded and dotted with erratics left during the Ice Age, constituted a mountain system as grand as the Rockies.

In New York, most of the Ramapos fall within two very popular state parks: Harriman and Bear Mountain. The parks were created largely through the efforts of Mrs. E. H. Harriman, widow of railroad tycoon Edward Harriman and mother of the late statesman W. Averell Harriman. When the state proposed building a prison at Bear Mountain in 1908, Mrs. Harriman offered to give the Palisades Interstate Park Commission 10,000 acres in return for dropping the project. The proposal was accepted, and since then the parks have been significantly enlarged through other gifts and purchases.

Harriman State Park

Straddling Rockland and Orange Counties is the second-largest state park in New York: **Harriman State Park** (off Rte. 17 or Palisades Pkwy., Exits 17 or 18, 845/786-2701, www. parks.ny.gov/parks/145, open daily, hours vary by section of park, $6-10 vehicle fee, depending upon sites visited), a 46,000-acre preserve that is considerably less developed than its better-known neighbor to the north, Bear Mountain State Park. **Seven Lakes Drive,** which hugs the shores of only a small portion of the many bodies of water to be found in this preserve, runs through the heart of the park. Two of the park's most spectacular lakes are crystal-clear **Lake Tiorati** and **Lake Sebago.** Ironically, their Native American names—bestowed upon them by others eager to create a romantic atmosphere—are not local, but rather names that come from Western tribes. Both of the large, artificially constructed lakes have swimming beaches.

About 200 miles (320 km) of **marked trails** loop through Harriman and its neighbor, Bear Mountain. Basic information on some of these trails can be picked up at the headquarters of the **Palisades Interstate Park Commission** (Bear Mt., Rte. 9W, 845/786-2701). For more detailed information and maps, stop at the superb **Park Visitor Information Center** (between Exits 16 and 17 on the Palisades Pkwy., 845/786-5003) or contact the **New York-New Jersey Trail Conference** (201/512-9348, www.nynjtc. org). The park also offers an excellent, 200-site **campground** (call 800/456-2267 for reservations).

Just south of the park, on a mountaintop near Hillburn, is ★ **Mount Fuji** (296 Old Rte. 17, 845/357-4270, www.mtfujirestaurants. com, Mon.-Thurs. noon-2:30pm and 5pm-10pm, Fri. noon-2:30pm and 5pm-11pm, Sat. 5pm-11pm, Sun. 5pm-10pm, $36), a big, glitzy Japanese steakhouse offering stunning views

of the valley below. On the western border of the park are Clove Furnace Historic Site, Tuxedo Park, and Sterling Forest.

Bear Mountain State Park

When New Yorkers think about getting out of the city for a day hike, they tend to think about **Bear Mountain State Park** (Palisades Pkwy., Exit 19, and Rte. 9W, 845/786-2701, www.parks.ny.gov/parks/13, daily 8am-dusk, parking $10), one of the most popular recreational areas in the region. Abutting Harriman to the north, the park offers dramatic views of the Hudson River and—on exceptionally clear days—New York City skyscrapers. Because Bear Mountain can get very crowded on weekends, it's best to come during the week. This is also no place for the outdoors purist; almost every inch of the 5,000-acre park has been trodden over many times.

To hike to the top of Bear Mountain and back takes 3-4 hours. For those who prefer to drive to the summit, **Perkins Memorial Drive** (open Mar.-Oct.) offers stunning overlooks and historic markers that tell of Revolutionary War battles that took place here. Legend has it that Hessian Lake was named for the many dead Hessian soldiers whose bodies were weighted and dumped there after the battle of Fort Clinton. The fort's ruins are nearby.

Though overrun with crowds on summer weekends, ★ **Bear Mountain Inn and Overlook Lodge** (55 Hessian Dr., 845/786-2731, www.visitbearmountain.com, $95-145) is a charming spot, just over 100 years old. The inn's rooms are divided among the Main Inn, four small stone cottages, and Overlook Lodge, a 24-room property near Hessian Lake. Come on a weekday in fall and you'll have the place to yourself! The inn also has restaurants serving global cuisine made with locally sourced ingredients. Sunday brunch is also a popular dining event here.

Route 17 South

Route 17 runs along the western edge of Harriman State Park. In an earlier incarnation, Harriman was mining country, and its mountains are still pocked with mine shafts and foundries. A small museum documenting the area's mining history now stands at **Clove Furnace Historic Site** (21 Clove Furnace Dr., Arden, 845/351-4696, Mon.-Fri. 9am-11am and 1pm-4pm, free).

Just behind the museum is romantic, ivy-covered Arden House, which served as the residential estate of the Harriman family until 1972. Local lore has it that Edward Harriman built his mansion on this mountain site because he'd been shunned by the exclusive nearby community of Tuxedo Park and wanted his wife to be able to look down on it daily. Note that the privately owned house is not open to the public.

Continuing south on Route 17, you'll come to Route 17A. Travel west on the road about 2 miles (3.2 km) to reach the dark, quiet woods of **Sterling Forest State Park** (845/351-5907, www.parks.ny.gov/parks/74, daily dawn-dusk). The spacious visitors center has historical and nature exhibits, as well as a small gift shop. Special weekend hikes and events launch from here.

Nearby, popular **New York Renaissance Faire** (600 Rte. 17A, 845/351-5174, www.renfair.com, adults $29.95, seniors $25.95, children 5-12 $13) is presented on weekends in August-September. During the festival, which attracts about 175,000 visitors annually, knights in shining armor joust on horseback, minstrels strum love songs, a human chess game is played, and Shakespearean plays are staged. A special ShortLine bus leaves for the festival from Manhattan (800/631-8405).

Farther south on Route 17, you'll catch a glimpse of **Tuxedo Park.** Watch for a high stone wall and gatehouse on the right. The residential community was designed in the 1880s as a millionaires' refuge and is filled with turreted mansions. Etiquette maven Emily Post lived here for many years, and it was in Tuxedo Park that the formal dinner jacket of the same name was first introduced.

STONY POINT

South of Bear Mountain is **Stony Point Battlefield** (Park Rd., off Rte. 9W, 845/786-2521, www.parks.ny.gov, hours vary seasonally and by installation, parking $5), where the British army threatening West Point was based in the summer of 1779. Stony Point was captured by Americans in a daring midnight raid led by General "Mad" Anthony Wayne. A tour of the battlefield takes visitors through a small interpretive museum, past the ruins

Lower Hudson: Orange County

of the British fortifications, and past the oldest lighthouse on the Hudson River. Beautiful countryside surrounds the site.

WEST POINT

The section of the Hudson Valley between Dunderberg Mountain to the south and Storm King Mountain to the north is known as **Hudson Highlands.** Along this 15-mile (24 km) stretch, the Hudson River, narrowing and deepening, cuts through the Appalachian Mountain Range, creating a spectacular rocky gorge.

About halfway up this stretch, where the river takes a sharp turn, is a rocky outcropping known as West Point. With its strategic views of both sides of the river, it's easy to see why it was such an important stronghold during the Revolutionary War. Today, West Point is best known as the home of the U.S. Military Academy, authorized by Congress in 1802.

U.S. Military Academy

About 4,400 cadets are enrolled at the **U.S. Military Academy** (www.westpoint.edu) each year. Graduates have included Generals Grant, Lee, Pershing, MacArthur, and Eisenhower; misfits have included James Whistler and Edgar Allan Poe.

Near the Thayer Gate entrance to the Gothic, fortress-like academy is a giant **visitors center** (Rte. 218, 845/938-2638, daily 9am-4:45pm). The center stocks brochures and maps, holds a large gift shop, and screens a short movie about cadets' lives.

Next door to the visitors center is **West Point Museum** (Rte. 218, 845/938-2203, daily 10:30am-4:15pm, free), filled with a wide and fascinating array of exhibits on military history. Here, you'll find everything from a Stone Age ax to weapons used in Vietnam and the Gulf War; dioramas of famous battles fought between the 16th and 20th centuries; the letter that Einstein wrote to President Roosevelt urging him to begin research on the uses of plutonium; and a pistol that once belonged to Adolf Hitler. One philosophical panel, simply entitled "Reflections," includes quotes by

famous military leaders throughout history, from Thucydides to Eisenhower.

The academy can only be visited via escorted **tours** (adults $17-20, children 5-12 $13-16), which leave from the visitors center throughout the day, except during special events such as football games. Tour highlights include **Cadet Chapel,** lined with lovely stained-glass windows donated by graduated classes; the **Plain,** where the cadets march out in formation at precisely 12:20pm every day; and **Trophy Point,** where you'll find unforgettable views of the blue-gray Hudson. Also at the point are links of the "Great Chain" that the patriots once stretched across the river here to prevent the passage of British ships.

Constitution Island

One of the more unusual spots at West Point is **Constitution Island** (845/265-2501, www.constitutionisland.org, hours vary seasonally, adults $15, seniors and students $10, children under 6 free, reservations required), accessible only by boat, which leaves from West Point's South dock. Strategically important during the Revolution, the island later became the home of Susan and Anna Warner, two 19th-century writers who taught Bible classes at West Point. Susan was the author of the popular 1850 novel *The Wide, Wide World;* Anna was best known for writing the words to the hymn "Jesus Loves Me." The sisters lived in **Warner House,** a 17-room Victorian mansion built on the island by their father in 1836. One wall of the mansion dates back to Revolutionary War days, and the whole house is furnished more or less as it was when the sisters lived here. At present, the house is under restoration and is not open to the public, but boat trips still leave you at the island to stroll the grounds and gardens.

Food and Accommodations

On the academy grounds just inside Thayer Gate off Route 218 stands the big, gray, castle-like ★ **Thayer Hotel** (674 Thayer Rd., 845/446-4731 or 800/247-5047, www.thethayerhotel.com, $190-230), where the

rooms are outfitted in the style of late-19th-century Americana. Some rooms overlook the Hudson, others the West Point campus. The lobby and restaurant are outfitted with marble floors and iron chandeliers. Outside is a pleasant terrace with more great views of the Hudson. The hotel's upscale **MacArthur's Riverview Restaurant** (674 Thayer Rd., 845/446-4731 or 800/247-5047, www.thethayerhotel.com, breakfast, lunch, and dinner, average dinner entrée $34) serves traditional American and continental cuisine.

★ STORM KING ART CENTER

Storm King Art Center (Old Pleasant Hill Rd., off Rte. 32 a few miles south of Vails Gate, 845/534-3115, www.stormking.org, early Apr.-late Nov. Wed.-Sun. 10am-5pm, adults $18, seniors $15, students and children over 5 $8) is a breathtakingly beautiful sculpture park built on a hilltop. About 120 permanent works and many more temporary ones are scattered over green lawns and wheat-blond fields, while in the distance are the dusk-blue Shawangunks. Nearly every major post-WWII sculptor is represented here, including Alexander Calder, Henry Moore, Louise Nevelson, Isamu Noguchi, and Richard Serra. A map of the 500-acre park and its sculptures is available at the gate. An imperial Norman-style building that was originally the home of lawyer Vermont Hatch stands in the center of the park; it houses temporary exhibits. An open-air café sells light fare made from locally sourced ingredients. There's live music in the summer.

Accommodations

★ **Storm King Lodge** (100 Pleasant Hill Rd., 845/534-9421, www.stormkinglodge.

1: Storm King Art Center, view of the south fields. All works by Mark di Suvero. L to R: *Pyramidian*, 1987/1998. *She*, 1977-78. *Mon Père, Mon Père*, 1973-75. *Mother Peace*, 1969-70. *For Chris*, 1991. Except where noted, all works gift of the Ralph E. Ogden Foundation **2:** view of the Hudson River from the U.S. Military Academy at West Point

com, $175-195) offers excellent views of Storm King Mountain. Housed in a converted carriage house and centered around an expansive common room with a stone hearth, the lodge offers four cozy guest rooms, two of which have private fireplaces. There is also a cottage available for rent.

CORNWALL-ON-HUDSON

Storm King Highway (Rte. 218) runs from West Point north to the tidy village of Cornwall-on-Hudson; it's a twisting, narrow roadway that hugs the cliffs of the Hudson River Gorge, offering stunning views of the landscape below. It's a particularly fine drive in fall, when the hills are ablaze with turning leaves.

Hudson Highlands Nature Museum

Hudson Highlands Nature Museum (25 Boulevard, 845/534-7781, www.hhnaturemuseum.org, Mon.-Fri. 8:30am-4pm, $5 for ages 2 and up), founded in 1959, is one of the oldest environmental museums in the country and notable for its hands-on, down-to-earth feel. At its Wildlife Education Center, visitors can see living animals in re-created habitats. At the museum's second site, the **Outdoor Discovery Center** (100 Muser Dr., Cornwall, 845/534-5506, Sat.-Sun. noon-4pm, $5 for all visitors over 3), visitors can enjoy nature programs and trail walks on the grounds of this former 174-acre horse farm.

Food and Accommodations

A Cornwall institution since 1985, ★ **Painter's Restaurant** (266 Hudson St., 845/534-2109, www.painters-restaurant.com, Mon.-Fri. 11am-10pm, Sat. 10am-10pm, Sun. 10:30am-9pm, $22) offers an eclectic array of sandwiches and burgers, salads and pasta, along with some Italian, Japanese, and Mexican specialties. Walls are hung with works by local artists. Upstairs, at the **Painter's Inn,** are seven B&B guest rooms ($95-135).

Luxurious ★ **Cromwell Manor Inn** (174 Angola Rd., 845/534-7136, www.

cromwellmanorinn.com, $185-410) is an elegant 1820s B&B with nine guest rooms, some equipped with working fireplaces, whirlpool tubs, or steam rooms. There is also a four-room cottage available for rent. Listed in the National Register of Historic Places, the manor is situated on a seven-acre estate surrounded by mountains and has its own formal gardens and croquet courts.

NEWBURGH AND VICINITY

North of Cornwall-on-Hudson, Route 9W leads to the small city of Newburgh. Once a thriving whaling port and later an important factory town manufacturing everything from lawn mowers to handbags, Newburgh spent much of the late 20th century in a sorry state. Fortunately, Newburgh is coming out of its postindustrial slump, and now boasts a revitalized waterfront, Newburgh Landing, flush with restaurants, bars, and shops. Here, you can catch a narrated two-hour river cruise with **Hudson River Adventures** (845/220-2120, www.prideofthehudson.com, May-Oct.).

Washington's Headquarters State Historic Site

Washington's Headquarters State Historic Site (84 Liberty St., 845/562-1195, www.parks.ny.gov, Apr.-Oct. 31 Wed.-Sat. 10am-5pm, Sun. 1pm-5pm, adults $4, seniors $3, children under 12 free), the nation's first public historic site, sits at the far edge of downtown, on bluffs overlooking the Hudson. The general spent the last six months of the war here while his officers and troops waited farther south. It was from this headquarters—originally a farmhouse built by the Hasbrouck family—that Washington issued a victorious order for a "cessation of hostilities," bringing about an end to the Revolutionary War on April 19, 1783.

Now a state park, Washington's Headquarters has been restored to reflect his stay, and the place has a very personal feel. Its small, whitewashed rooms are simply furnished with cots, firearms, and facsimiles of Washington's account books, along with the desk he once used. The general remained in the house for about a year after the war ended, waiting for the British to leave New York. During much of that time, he was restless, bored, and resentful of public demands upon his time.

Surrounding the house are a wide lawn and high stone wall. An excellent visitors center with new interactive displays is at the entrance, while the 53-foot (16 m) Tower of Victory, built to commemorate the 100th anniversary of the war's end, sits near the bluffs.

Crawford House

History buffs might also want to visit the 1830 **Captain David Crawford House** (189 Montgomery St., 845/561-2585, www.newburghhistoricalsociety.com, Apr.-Oct. Sun. 1pm-4pm, also open by appointment, $5), just a few blocks away from Washington's Headquarters. The home of the Historical Society of Newburgh Bay and the Highlands, the house is filled with period antiques, Hudson Valley paintings, and an intriguing series of photo exhibits documenting Newburgh's more prosperous days.

Motorcyclepedia

Newburgh has added a modern twist to its cultural offerings with **Motorcyclepedia** (250 Lake St., 845/569-9065, www.motorcyclepediamuseum.org, Fri.-Sun. 10am-5pm, adults $15, seniors $12, children 12-18 $10, children 7-11 $5, children under 7 free), the largest motorcycle museum in the United States. More than 600 motorcycles—some more than 100 years old—are displayed in the 85,000-square-foot space; collection highlights include rare vintage bikes, police and military bikes, sidecars, and more than 100 Indians, the first motorcycles produced in the United States, starting in 1901.

New Windsor Cantonment

Several other Revolutionary War sites are located within a few miles of Washington's

Headquarters, in the town of New Windsor. Most interesting among them is **New Windsor Cantonment** (374 Temple Hill Rd., New Windsor, 845/561-1765, www.parks. ny.gov, Apr.-Oct. Tue.-Sat. 10am-5pm, Sun. 1pm-5pm, free), where the general's 7,000 troops, accompanied by some 500 women and children, waited out the last months of the war. Here they lived in log huts during a long, hard winter—a situation that almost led to rebellion. Today's cantonment re-creates the lives of the Continental Army's soldiers and camp followers.

National Purple Heart Hall of Honor

Right next to New Windsor Cantonment, the **National Purple Heart Hall of Honor** (374 Temple Hill Rd., New Windsor, 845/561-1765, www.thepurpleheart.com, hours vary seasonally, single admission free, $3 fee pp for groups of 10 or more) is a tribute to recipients of this prestigious military service award. Staff is devoted to collecting, preserving, and sharing stories of Purple Heart recipients, whose names are listed in a searchable electronic database that spans every war from the Civil War to present conflicts. Visitors can watch the film *For Military Merit,* as well as listen to interviews.

Gomez Mill House

Four miles (6.4 km) north of Newburgh is the 1714 **Gomez Mill House** (Mill House Rd., off Rte. 9W, Marlboro, 914/236-3126, www. gomez.org, Apr.-Oct. Wed.-Sun. 10am-4pm, adults $10, seniors $7, and children 6-18 $4), the oldest extant house of a Jewish family in the nation. Continuously occupied between 1716 and 1998, the Mill House was home to fur traders, merchants, Revolutionary War soldiers, farmers, artisans, and statesmen.

The house was originally built by Louis Moses Gomez, who bought 6,000 acres along the Hudson after fleeing the Spanish Inquisition. Several Native American paths converged on his property, and Native Americans once gathered near his home to hold ceremonial rites. In the early 20th century, Dard Hunter, a renowned craftsperson and papermaker, lived in the house.

Wineries

Seven wineries are in the area, including **Brotherhood** (100 Brotherhood Plaza Dr., Washingtonville, 845/496-3661, www. brotherhood-winery.com, Sun.-Thurs. 11am-5pm, Fri. 11am-6pm, Sat. 11am-7pm, $10 tasting fee, $15 tour and tasting pass, $8 tour-only pass), the oldest winery in the United States. Tours of the largest underground wine cellars in the country are given daily in April through December and on weekends the rest of the year. **Warwick Valley Winery and Distillery** (114 Little York Rd., Warwick, 845/258-4858, www.wvwinery.com, daily 11am-6pm, $5-10 tasting fee) is open daily all year, making a variety of wines and Doc's Hard Apple Cider, which is distributed throughout the country.

Food

If your sweet tooth is aching, stop at **Commodore's** (482 Broadway, 845/561-3960, Mon.-Sat. 9am-7pm, Sun. 10am-6pm), famous for its handmade chocolates.

Yobo (1297 Rte. 300, 845/564-3848, www. yoborestaurant.com, Mon.-Thurs. 11:30am-10pm, Fri. 11:30am-11pm, Sat. 12:30pm-11pm, Sun. 12:30pm-10pm, $17) serves a wide variety of dishes from China, Korea, Indonesia, and other Asian countries in an artificially constructed atmosphere of babbling brooks and waterfalls.

One of the area's most popular Italian restaurants is ★ **Il Cena'Colo** (228 S. Plank Rd., 845/564-4494, www.ilcenacolorestaurant. com, Mon. and Wed.-Thurs. noon-2:30pm and 5pm-9pm, Fri. noon-2:30pm and 5:30pm-11pm, Sat. 5:30pm-11pm, Sun. 4pm-9pm, $29), which serves Tuscan-style and Northern Italian fare. Among the tasty specials are oyster stew, fried baby artichokes, and gnocchi with venison sauce.

In downtown Marlboro, near the Gomez Mill House just north of the Orange-Ulster

County border, is lively **Raccoon Saloon** (1330 Rte. 9W, 845/236-7872, www. raccoonsaloonmarlboro.com, Mon.-Thurs. 11:30am-10pm, Fri.-Sat. 11:30am-11pm, Sun. 11:30am-9pm, $23). On the menu is an enormous selection of tasty burgers and beers, along with homemade ice cream.

The Wherehouse (119 Liberty St., 845/561-7240, www.thewherehouserestaurant.com, Tues.-Thurs. noon-11pm, Fri.-Sat. noon-midnight, Sun. noon-9pm, $11) is a casual, affordable spot close to Washington's Headquarters. Almost 50 different kinds of burgers are on the menu, alongside hot dogs, sandwiches, and chili.

Newburgh Brewing Company (888 S. Colden St., 845/569-2337, www.newburghbrewing.com, Wed. 4pm-9pm, Thurs. 4pm-10pm, Fri. 4pm-midnight, Sat. noon-midnight, Sun. noon-5pm, $12), a craft brewery housed in a renovated box factory that dates to the 1850s, has a beautiful tasting room that affords panoramic views of the Hudson River. Newburgh beer, local wine, and a menu of traditional beer-paired foods are served.

Mid-Hudson Valley

Many of the Hudson Valley's top attractions are clustered in the mid-Hudson region. Most of the grand riverfront estates for which the area is famous are located here, as are Vassar and Bard Colleges, the historic town of Rhinebeck, The Culinary Institute of America, and myriad country villages, pick-your-own farms, public gardens, and excellent restaurants and lodgings.

The historic museum-estates are all in a 20-mile (32 km) riverfront stretch between Hyde Park and Clermont that in 1990 was declared a National Historic Landmark District, the second-largest such district in the United States.

The district contains some 2,000 buildings, only a handful of which are open to the public. Of these, Franklin Delano Roosevelt's estate, Springwood, is by far the most personal and popular, and can be combined with a visit to Val-Kill, Eleanor Roosevelt's retreat. Between the two homes and nearby FDR Library and museum, you'll come away with a good sense of both the Roosevelts and the times in which they lived. Of the other museum-estates, Vanderbilt Mansion is the most lavish, Montgomery Place the most beautiful, Mills Mansion the most cavernous, Clermont the most elegant, and Wilderstein the smallest and least known.

South of Hyde Park is the river city of Poughkeepsie. While it has fallen on hard times, it has interesting historic and cultural sites to offer. A few miles east of Route 9, the expansive rural countryside is dotted with small villages, wineries, produce stands, and horse farms. The entire Hudson Valley is a major horse-breeding area, with about half of its horse farms located in Dutchess County.

POUGHKEEPSIE

Poughkeepsie (Wappinger for "reed-covered lodge by the little water place"), the seat of Dutchess County, was founded in 1683 and designated the state capital in 1777. From the mid-1800s through the mid-1900s, the town was a major industrial center. It then served as home base for IBM following World War II. But the late 20th century was not kind to Poughkeepsie. Many of its factories closed down and urban renewal ravaged the city, destroying many of its historic 19th-century brick buildings. In the 1990s, IBM laid off thousands of employees.

Today, Poughkeepsie is poised for its comeback, as a revitalization project focuses on Main and Market Streets as a hub for commercial and cultural development. Near the river and railroad station, where Union and Academy Streets intersect Main and Mill,

Mid-Husdon: Dutchess County

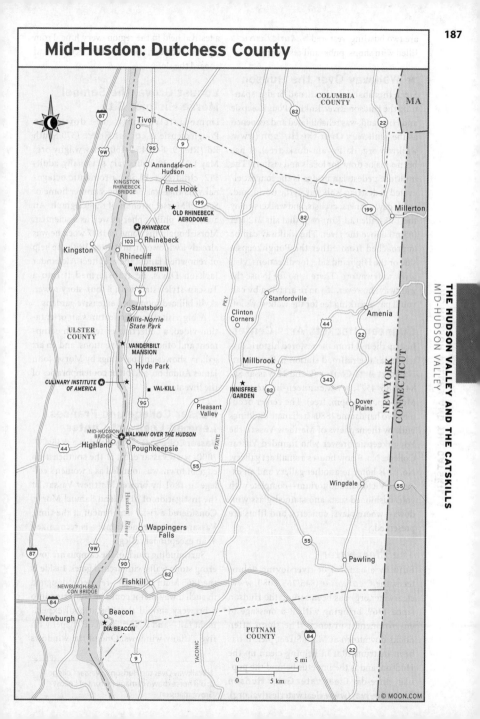

COLUMBIA COUNTY

MA

Tivoli

Annandale-on-Hudson

Red Hook

OLD RHINEBECK AERODOME

Millerton

RHINEBECK

Rhinebeck

Rhinecliff

WILDERSTEIN

KINGSTON RHINEBECK BRIDGE

Kingston

ULSTER COUNTY

Staatsburg

Mills-Norrie State Park

VANDERBILT MANSION

Hyde Park

CULINARY INSTITUTE OF AMERICA

VAL-KILL

Stanfordville

Clinton Corners

Amenia

Millbrook

INNISFREE GARDEN

MID-HUDSON BRIDGE

WALKWAY OVER THE HUDSON

Highland

Poughkeepsie

Pleasant Valley

Dover Plains

Wingdale

NEW YORK

CONNECTICUT

Hudson River

Wappingers Falls

Pawling

NEWBURGH-BEACON BRIDGE

Fishkill

Newburgh

Beacon

DIA:BEACON

PUTNAM COUNTY

TACONIC

0   5 mi

0   5 km

© MOON.COM

are two bustling, restored historic districts filled with shops, pubs, and restaurants.

★ Walkway Over the Hudson

Since this abandoned railroad bridge spanning the Hudson River, linking Poughkeepsie and Highland, was rehabilitated and reopened as the Walkway Over the Hudson (www.walkway.org, daily 7am-dusk, free), it has been a major draw for locals and visitors. The multiuse pedestrian bridge is the longest elevated pedestrian walkway in the world, and, every day, runners, cyclists, and walkers enjoy the 1.28-mile (2.1 km) path that sits 212 feet (65 m) above the river. The walkway can be approached from either the Poughkeepsie side or the Highland side; for directions, visit www.walkway.org. There is no fee to use the walkway; however, if you're arriving by car, you'll pay a parking fee for the walkway's lot.

Cunneen-Hackett Arts Center

Just up the hill from the restored historic district near the railroad station is Cunneen-Hackett Arts Center (9 and 12 Vassar St., 845/486-4571, www.cunneen-hackett.org, Mon.-Fri. 9am-5pm, free). The center occupies two handsome 1880s Italianate buildings built by the nephews of Matthew Vassar, the Poughkeepsie brewer who founded Vassar College. No. 9 now houses a small art gallery; No. 12 is home to another gallery and an exquisite Victorian auditorium—complete with gold-cushioned seats and stained-glass windows—where plays, concerts, and films are presented.

The *Clearwater*

Built by a handful of river-loving volunteers, the *Clearwater* (845/265-8080, www.clearwater.org) has been sailing the Hudson since 1969, bringing with it a message of environmental urgency. The sloop often docks downtown at Main Street pier. It has been instrumental in helping clean up the Hudson, and is the impetus behind the popular, three-day Clearwater Great Hudson River Revival (www.clearwaterfestival.org),

a festival held in the region every June. From April to October, you can buy a ticket to sail aboard the sloop.

Locust Grove, the Samuel Morse Historic Site

Immediately south of downtown Poughkeepsie is Locust Grove (370 South Rd./Rte. 9, 845/454-4500, www.lgny.org, May 1-Nov. 30, hours vary seasonally, adults $12, children 6-10 $6), a romantic octagonal villa that was once the summer home of Samuel Morse, inventor of the telegraph. An artist and philosopher as well as a scientist, Morse bought his home in 1847 when he was already a widower in his fifties. With the help of renowned landscape architect Alexander Jackson Davis, he transformed it into a Tuscan-style estate with a four-story tower, skylit billiard room, and extensive gardens.

A big visitors center features an orientation video, a collection of telegraph equipment and other Morse inventions, and an art gallery showcasing paintings by Morse, John James Audubon, and other contemporaries of the inventor.

Vassar College and Frances Lehman Loeb Art Center

Vassar College (124 Raymond Ave., 845/437-7000, www.vassar.edu), at the southeastern edge of town, was founded as a women's college in 1861 by brewer Matthew Vassar, at the instigation of his friend Samuel Morse. Considered a risky experiment at the time, Vassar—now coeducational—is recognized as an exceptional college.

Surrounding much of the campus are towering stone walls with arched gates. Inside is the 1865 Main Building—reputedly designed in such a way that it could be converted into a brewery should the educational experiment fail—and a Norman-style chapel with five Tiffany windows. One of the windows

---

1: Walkway Over the Hudson 2: Vassar College 3: old horse drawn carriage in front of Locust Grove mansion

depicts Elena Lucrezia Cornaro Piscopia, the first woman to receive a doctorate (from the University of Padua in 1678).

Near the main gate stands **Frances Lehman Loeb Art Center** (124 Raymond Ave., 845/437-5632, www.fllac.vassar.edu, Tues.-Wed. and Fri.-Sat. 10am-5pm, Thurs. 10am-9pm, Sun. 1pm-5pm, free), designed by Cesar Pelli. Vassar was the first college in the country to have its own art gallery, and today owns more than 12,500 works ranging in origin from ancient Egypt to modern-day New York. Especially strong are the collections of Hudson River landscape paintings, Old Master prints by Dürer and Rembrandt, and contemporary European and American art.

Entertainment

The local premier performing arts venue is **Bardavon 1869 Opera House** (35 Market St., 845/473-2072, www.bardavon.org). One of the oldest theaters in the country, it presents everything from top-caliber opera to serious drama. Two small but interesting professional theater groups connected with Vassar College are **New Day Repertory Co.** (29 N. Hamilton St., 845/485-7399) and **Powerhouse Theatre** (124 Raymond Ave., 845/437-5907, www.powerhouse.vassar.edu).

For live music, stop into **The Chance** (6 Crannel St., 845/471-1966, www.thechancetheater.com), where nationally known artists play everything from country to R&B. The weekend editions of the *Poughkeepsie Journal* contain good entertainment listings.

Food

For tasty baked goods in the historic district, try **Caffé Aurora** (145 Mill St., 845/454-1900, www.caffeaurora.com), which has been serving sweet treats since 1941.

Rosticceria Rossi and Sons (45 S. Clover St., 845/471-0654, www.rossideli.com, Mon.-Fri. 7:30am-6pm, Sat. 8am-5pm, $10) is a popular Italian deli selling panini, salads, and lunch standards like chicken, veal, and eggplant parmesan.

Accommodations

One of the nicest places to stay in Poughkeepsie is ★ **Best Western Plus The Inn and Suites at the Falls** (50 Red Oaks Mill Rd., 845/462-5770, www.bestwestern.com, $145-230, with breakfast), which overlooks Wappingers Creek on the outskirts of town. Rooms are handsomely outfitted in contemporary European and country styles.

Downtown, you'll find the attractive, upscale **Poughkeepsie Grand Hotel and Conference Center** (40 Civic Center Plz., 845/485-5300, www.pokgrand.com, $110-165, with full American breakfast). Popular among couples tying the knot, the hotel also has spacious suites for families and business travelers.

MILLBROOK AND VICINITY

About 12 miles (19.3 km) northeast of Poughkeepsie on Route 44 is moneyed Millbrook, surrounded by large estates and horse farms. Though it seems hard to believe today, in this village of pricey antiques stores and gift shops, Timothy Leary once ran his League for Spiritual Discovery out of the old Danheim estate on Franklin Avenue. The estate, located about a mile from the village green, is recognizable by its large stone Bavarian-style gatehouse. Others who have made Millbrook their home in more recent years are Mary Tyler Moore, Daryl Hall, and Liam Neeson.

Innisfree Garden

The serene 200-acre **Innisfree Garden** (362 Tyrrel Rd., 845/677-8000, www.innisfreegarden.org, early May-mid-Oct. Wed.-Sun. 10am-5pm, $10 adults, $5 seniors and children) is landscaped around a small glacial lake just outside Millbrook. Founded by painter Walter Beck and his wife Marion and designed according to Eastern principles, the so-called "cup garden" is actually a series of many little gardens, each arranged to draw attention to one especially beautiful object at its center. One of the small gardens focuses on a lotus pool, another on a group of "purple smoke trees," a third on a hillside cave. The Dragon, the Turtle, and the Owl—three large rocks standing sentinel over the preserve—sit on a spit of land jutting out into the lake.

Despite the garden's careful design, it has a wild and natural feel. Spreading out over a series of small hills and dales, dappled by sunlight, it features many isolated spots where visitors can linger.

Cary Institute of Ecosystem Studies

A few miles west of Millbrook is a 1,900-acre preserve that's home to both the **Mary Flagler Cary Arboretum** (Rte. 44A, just off Rte. 44, 845/677-5359, Mon.-Sat. 9am-4pm, Sun. 1pm-4pm, free) and the **Cary Institute of Ecosystem Studies** (Rte. 44A, just off Rte. 44, 845/677-5343, www.caryinstitute. org, trails: daily dawn-dusk, internal roadways: Apr. 1-Oct. 31 daily 8:30am-7pm). The arboretum is open to the public, as is much of the institute's grounds, where ecological research is being conducted. Both are affiliated with the prestigious New York Botanical Garden in New York City.

Visitors to the arboretum must stop first at the **Gifford House Visitor and Education Center** to pick up a visitor permit, information, and maps. Directly behind the center are the perennial gardens, filled with over 1,000 species of plants. Among these gardens is a daffodil bed with 12 kinds of daffodils, a poisonous plants bed, and a garden specifically planted to attract butterflies. Surrounding the gardens are short hiking trails that lead past meadows, fern glens, and pine and hemlock forests.

Wing's Castle

One of the oddest sites in the Hudson Valley is whimsical **Wing's Castle** (717 Bangall Rd., 845/677-9085, www.wingscastle.com, Memorial Day weekend-Labor Day weekend Wed.-Sun. noon-4:30pm, adults $12, children under 12 $8), set atop a rolling green hill with a panoramic view of the Hudson Valley. Built by Peter and Toni Wing and

family, the castle has been a work in progress since 1970, lovingly put together out of everything from antique barn doors to toilet-bowl floats. Much of its stone came from abandoned railroad bridges.

It all began in the late 1960s when Peter, just back from Vietnam, and his wife Toni needed a place to live. They owned a piece of land but had only $1,100 between them. The solution? They'd build the place themselves, out of salvaged materials; never mind the fact that they had no construction experience whatsoever.

Everyone told them it couldn't be done, but today the castle stands, quirky and proud. Each part is designed in a different style—Asian, Tibetan, Germanic, French—and it all works beautifully, with bits of colored fiberglass winking in the walls and a water-filled moat leading to an inviting hot tub. Inside is a hodgepodge collection of military artifacts, carousel animals, Native American arts, and the Wings' personal possessions.

The Wings turned part of their property into a two-room bed-and-breakfast in 2011. Children are not allowed at the bed-and-breakfast.

Wineries

Millbrook Vineyards and Winery (26 Wing Rd., at the Shunpike/Rte. 57, 845/677-8383, www.millbrookwine.com, Labor Day-Memorial Day daily noon-5pm, $12.50-25 tasting fee) is spread out over 130 acres just below Wing's Castle. Known for its chardonnay, Millbrook also produces a pinot noir, cabernet franc, and other wines.

About 10 miles (16.1 km) northeast of Millbrook is award-winning **Cascade Mountain Winery** (835 Cascade Rd., Amenia, 845/373-9021, www.cascademt.com, Sat.-Sun. 11am-5pm, tasting fees vary). The family-owned winery produces whites, reds, and roses.

Food

Vintage, stainless-steel **Millbrook Diner** (3266 Franklin Ave., 845/677-5319, www.

millbrookdiner.com, daily 6am-9pm, $13) serves dependable diner fare and especially good breakfasts. **Serevan Restaurant** (6 Autumn Ln., Amenia, 845/373-9800, www. serevan.com, Thurs.-Mon. 5pm-10pm, $34) earns raves from diners for Chef Serge Madikians's Mediterranean-Middle Eastern fusion flair, enhanced by local, organic, and free-range ingredients.

Accommodations

Camping is available at the 27-site **Wilcox Memorial Park** (Rte. 199, off Taconic Pkwy., Stanfordville, 845/758-6100, $34/night tent sites, $35/night RV sites), which has two lakes and a complex of farm buildings dating back to the 18th century.

HYDE PARK AND VICINITY

Hyde Park's most popular destinations are the former homes of Franklin Delano Roosevelt, Eleanor Roosevelt, and a branch of the Vanderbilt family. Despite its blue-blood ancestry, the sprawling village is a downscale affair filled with aging shopping malls, tour buses, traffic jams, and motels named after the village's famous former residents.

Hugging the riverbank between the Vanderbilt Mansion and the Roosevelt homes is **Hyde Park Trail,** a 10-mile (16.1 km) (and growing) system of easy hiking trails, well marked by white-and-green signs. Maps of the trails can be picked up at the **Wallace Center** (4079 Albany Post Rd./Rte. 9, 845/229-5320 or 800/FDR-Visit, www.nps.gov/hofr, daily 9am-5pm).

Henry A. Wallace Visitor and Education Center

The **Wallace Center** at the **Franklin D. Roosevelt Presidential Library and Museum** (4079 Albany Post Rd./Rte. 9, 845/229-5320 or 800/FDR-Visit, www.nps. gov/hofr, daily 9am-5pm, adults $10, seniors $6, children under 16 free) is the best first stop for visitors to Hyde Park. The center provides a good, comprehensive orientation to the

Roosevelt and Vanderbilt sites through exhibits and an introductory film. Visitors can buy tickets and get directions here; a large café and museum shop are also on-site.

FDR's Home, Library, and Museum

Franklin Delano Roosevelt was born and raised at **Springwood** (4079 Albany Post Rd., 845/229-5320, www.nps.gov/hofr, daily 9am-5pm, adults $18, children under 16 free, advance reservations required), a low-lying Georgian-style mansion along the Hudson. Later, he and his wife Eleanor raised their five children here, while Franklin rose through the political ranks. In 1928, he was elected governor of New York, and in 1932, president of the United States.

Now a National Historic Site, FDR's home has been restored to look much like it did during his presidential days. It has a very intimate feel. In the living room are the leash and blanket of his dog, Fala; in the "snuggery" are furnishings once belonging to his domineering mother, Sara Delano Roosevelt; in his office are books and magazines he was reading during his last visit here in March 1945. At the eastern end of the estate is **Top Cottage** (adults $10, children under 16 free), where Roosevelt entertained his closest friends.

Of at least equal interest is the adjacent **Franklin D. Roosevelt Presidential Library and Museum** (4079 Albany Post Rd./Rte. 9, 845/486-7770 or 800/FDR-Visit, www.fdrlibrary.marist.edu, days and hours vary by season, adults $20, children under 16 free), which houses a superb series of exhibits on the family and their times. Here you'll find everything from FDR's christening dress and early political speeches to Eleanor's diary entries describing the enormous pain she felt upon learning of her husband's extramarital affairs.

Tickets to the FDR sites often sell out on fall weekends; to make a reservation, call 800/967-2283. Note that combination tickets for the library and home are available.

Val-Kill

By 1924, Eleanor Roosevelt had had enough of both her husband's political cronies and her mother-in-law, so she built a weekend retreat for herself 2 miles (3.2 km) east of the family estate. She moved there permanently after FDR's death in 1945.

Surrounded by fields and woodlands, the **Eleanor Roosevelt National Historic Site,** aka **Val-Kill** (54 Valkill Park Rd., 845/229-9115, www.nps.gov/elro, daily 9am-5pm, adults $10, children under 16 free) is a simple and rustic place that, compared to Springwood, attracts relatively few visitors. The former first lady's tastes were delightfully unassuming; she used regular china, set up card tables for extra guests at Christmas, and hung family photographs helter-skelter over the cottage's rough-hewn walls. Nonetheless, it was in this simple setting that Mrs. Roosevelt drafted the U.N. Declaration of Human Rights and entertained important world leaders such as Nikita Khrushchev, Haile Selassie, Adlai Stevenson, and John F. Kennedy. A photograph of a 40-something JFK and a 70-something Eleanor is prominently displayed in the living room.

Vanderbilt Mansion

Two miles (3.2 km) north of the Roosevelt homes is the extravagant **Vanderbilt Mansion National Historic Site** (119 Vanderbilt Park Rd., 845/229-9115, www.nps.gov/vama, daily 9am-5pm, free), built in a posh beaux arts style complete with lavish furnishings, gold-leaf ceilings, Flemish tapestries, and hand-painted lampshades. Built between 1896 and 1898 by Frederick and Louise Vanderbilt, the mansion, designed by McKim, Mead & White, cost what was then a whopping $2.5 million. Nonetheless, it was the smallest of the Vanderbilt estates and was used only in spring and fall.

Next door to the mansion are extensive formal gardens and a coach house (not open to the public) in which the Vanderbilts housed six limousines that were always at their guests' disposal. The gardens have glorious views of the Hudson, with the smoky Shawangunk Mountains rising behind.

Staatsburgh State Historic Site

In Staatsburg, about 5 miles (8.1 km) north of the Vanderbilt Mansion, reigns the **Staatsburgh State Historic Site** (75 Mills Mansion Rd., 845/889-8851, www.parks.ny.gov/historic-sites/25, Thurs.-Sun. 11am-5pm, adults $8, seniors and students $6, children under 12 free). Also known as **Mills Mansion,** the vast 65-room hilltop hideout is in a continual process of being restored. Guides take visitors through a series of cavernous rooms, some plush with Louis XIV, XV, and XVI furnishings, others filled with craftspeople busy at restoration work. The most beautiful room is the long dining room, flanked with Flemish tapestries and large windows overlooking the Hudson.

Parts of Mills Mansion date back to 1825, but most of the house was built in 1896 by McKim, Mead & White. Once owned by financier Ogden Mills, the mansion was frequented by Edith Wharton, who used it as the model for the Trenor estate, Bellomont, in *The House of Mirth.*

Surrounding Mills Mansion is **Mills-Norrie State Park** (9 Old Post Rd., 845/889-4646, www.parks.ny.gov/parks/171, daily dawn-dusk), a 1,000-acre preserve with a marina, campground, small environmental museum, and two nine-hole golf courses. Scenic hiking trails run along the west side of the park, overlooking the Hudson. The park also has a 46-site **campground** (tent sites Sun.-Thurs. $15 for New York State residents, $20 for nonresidents, Fri.-Sat. $19 for residents, $24 for nonresidents) and 10 **cabins** ($94.50/night and $378/week for New York State residents, $102.50/night and $406/week for nonresidents, 2-night minimum required) for rent (reservations 800/456-2267, May-Oct.).

★ The Culinary Institute of America

A half-mile south of Hyde Park proper is

The Culinary Institute of America, or CIA (1946 Campus Dr., 845/452-9600, www.ciachef.edu, daily, tour $6), the nation's most prestigious cooking school, founded in 1946. Housed in a former Jesuit seminary on 170 acres overlooking the Hudson River, the institute trains about 1,850 students at a time, in a 21-month program that includes courses in everything from pork butchering to provisions purchasing. Between classes, students hurry about campus dressed in traditional white chefs' tunics and white-and-gray checked pants.

The CIA is open daily and visitors are welcome to stroll the grounds, browse the well-stocked Craig Claiborne Bookstore, take a tour, or eat in one of several first-rate, student-staffed restaurants.

Entertainment

The Hyde Park Drive-In Theatre (4114 Albany Post Rd., 845/229-4738, www.hydeparkdrivein.com, May-Sept. nightly, $10 adults, $7 children 5-11, show starts at dusk) features two screens. The drive-in is always bustling with friendly crowds. Bring blankets and lawn chairs or just recline the driver's seat to enjoy the classic 1950s atmosphere.

Food

Hyde Park's best restaurants are at The Culinary Institute of America (1946 Campus Dr., 845/471-6608, www.ciarestaurants.com); reservations are essential. Each of the restaurants has its own distinct style. The most casual is Apple Pie Bakery Cafe (Mon.-Fri. 7:30am-6pm, $12), which specializes in delicious desserts but also has a café menu. The most elegant is The Bocuse Restaurant (Tues.-Sat. 11:30am-1pm and 6pm-8:30pm, $30-50), named for master chef Paul Bocuse, whose "updated French" menu offers novel interpretations on classic bistro and provincial cuisine. Food can be ordered à la carte or from the tasting menu. In between are Ristorante Caterina de Medici (Mon.-Fri. 6pm-8:30pm, $39), featuring contemporary and traditional Italian specialties, and

American Bounty Restaurant (Tues.-Sat. 11:30am-1pm and 6pm-8:30pm, $26), dedicated to regional American dishes. Be aware that the restaurants are closed during school breaks; call ahead to avoid disappointment.

Accommodations

Directly across from Vanderbilt Mansion is attractive Journey Inn Bed & Breakfast (1 Sherwood Pl., 845/229-8972, www.journeyinn.com, $115-205), filled with antiques and memorabilia from the owners' international travels. The inn offers seven comfortable air-conditioned guest rooms, each done up to reflect a different destination, including Kyoto, Mombasa, and Tuscany.

Hyde Park has an abundance of decent budget motels, many of which cater to families and tour groups. Among them is the family-owned, 25-room Roosevelt Inn (4360 Albany Post Rd., 845/229-2443, www.rooseveltinnofhydepark.com, $95-120), where you can choose between "deluxe" or "rustic" style rooms.

★ RHINEBECK

Continuing north along Route 9, you'll come to the picturesque village of Rhinebeck, the shady streets of which are lined with restored Victorian buildings. Rhinebeck was first settled in 1686 by Dutch immigrants and has been home to five illustrious Hudson Valley families: the Beekmans, Livingstons, Astors, Montgomerys, and Schuylers.

Rhinebeck Area Chamber of Commerce operates a Visitor Information Booth (23F E. Market St., 845/876-5904, www.rhinebeckchamber.com, Mon.-Sat. 10am-4pm, Sun. noon-4pm).

Built in 1766, the famed Beekman Arms (6387 Mill St., 845/876-7077, www.beekmandelamaterinn.com, main building $140-150) is said to be the oldest inn in continuous operation in America. Everyone from George Washington and Aaron Burr to William

---

1: the Culinary Institute of America
2: Old Rhinebeck Aerodrome

Jennings Bryan and FDR once ate or slept here. Even if you're not planning to do so yourself, the place is worth a look. Inside are low ceilings, heavy beams, wide floorboards, walk-in fireplaces, and benches dating to the Revolutionary War. The inn consists of a cluster of several small buildings, as well as the handsome, American Gothic **Delamater Inn** ($100-250), designed by Alexander Jackson Davis.

Next door to Beekman Arms is a tiny **U.S. post office** (6383 Mill St.), a WPA project built in 1939 as a replica of the first home built in Rhinebeck. Inside are artifacts from the original building along with murals depicting the town's history.

Across the street from the post office stands **Rhinebeck Reformed Church** (6368 Mill St., 845/876-3727, www.rhinebeckreformed. org, office open daily 9am-1pm), designed by Robert Upjohn in 1808. Next to the church is a picturesque graveyard with tombstones that date to the 1700s.

Old Rhinebeck Aerodrome

Most summer Saturdays and Sundays at the storybook **Old Rhinebeck Aerodrome** (9 Norton Rd., 845/752-3200, www.oldrhinebeck.org, May 1-Oct. 31 daily 10am-5pm), Sir Percy Good Fellow climbs into his biplane to fight the Evil Black Baron for the heart of Trudy Truelove. Cheering the adversaries on as the rotary engines roar and the castor oil burns are excitable Madame Fifi, dashing Pierre Loop-da-Loop, and a crowd of early-21st-century citizens who have donned WWI-era hats, scarves, dresses, and coats at the gate.

Appearances to the contrary, this charming aerodrome—holding a hodgepodge of hand-painted signs and rickety hangars—is a serious place. On its grounds are about 75 historic airplanes dating back to the early 1900s. Among them are a 1911 Curtiss D, a 1929 Sopwith Camel, and a 1908 Voisin whose double canvas wings, light as gossamer, resemble those of a giant dragonfly. Summer weekends feature an air show reenacting historic flights. At the aerodrome you can visit a **museum**

(May 1-Oct. 31 daily 10am-5pm, adults $12, seniors and children 6-17 $8, children under 5 free) or attend the **air shows** (mid-June-mid-Oct. Sat.-Sun, 2pm-4pm, adults $25, seniors $20, children 6-17 $12, children under 5 free, includes museum admission). **Flights** (summer Sun. from 10am, $100 for a 15-minute ride) over the Hudson River in a 1929 open-cockpit biplane are offered during the summer.

Wilderstein

Whimsical all-wooden Queen Anne mansion **Wilderstein** (330 Morton Rd., 845/876-4818, www.wilderstein.org, May-Oct. Thurs.-Sun. noon-4pm, adults $11, seniors and students $10, children under 12 free) sits in the middle of a 19th-century estate designed by Calvert Vaux, one of the two men who designed Central Park. *Wilderstein* means "wild man's stone" and was named after a Native American petroglyph found on the property. Inside the 1852 house—adorned with dormers, gables, and a magnificent, five-story tower—are lavish interiors by J. B. Tiffany. Outside are 40 acres of meadows and woods, including roads and trails offering great views of the Hudson.

Entertainment and Events

Upstate Films (6415 Montgomery St., 845/876-2515, www.upstatefilms.org) is a revival movie theater screening foreign, independent, and documentary films, along with classics. The **Center for the Performing Arts at Rhinebeck** (661 Rte. 308, 845/876-3080, www.centerforperformingarts.org) offers theater, children's shows, concerts, jazz under the stars, and other events.

Rhinebeck's **Dutchess County Fairgrounds** (6550 Spring Brook Ave., 845/876-4000, www.dutchessfair.com) hosts a number of events throughout the year. Among them are an **Antiques Fair** in May, **crafts fairs** in October, the **Hudson Valley Hot-Air Balloon Festival** in July, and the six-day **Dutchess County Fair** in the summer. The latter is the largest county fair in the state, second in size only to the New York State Fair held in Syracuse.

Shopping

Rhinebeck is known for its antiques stores and galleries, many of which are located along Route 9 or Market Street. One popular site is **Beekman Arms Antique Market** (Beekman Square at the Beekman Arms, 845/876-3477, daily 11am-5pm), which houses more than 30 vendors in an old red barn.

Tucked in between the newer stores are two creaky village institutions: **Rhinebeck Department Store** (1 E. Market St., 845/876-5500, www.rhinebeckstore.com) and **A. L. Stickle Variety Store** (13 E. Market St., 845/876-3206). Both are veritable time capsules from the 1940s. **Oblong Books and Music** (Montgomery Row, 845/876-0500, www.oblongbooks.com) is a great indie bookshop. Stop by to catch an author reading or grab some tunes for the road.

Open air **Rhinebeck Farmers' Market** (summer location 61 E. Market St., www.rhinebeckfarmersmarket.com, Sun. 10am-2pm) is a meeting spot for local farmers, crafters, and the community, a pleasant mix of city weekenders and village residents. Live music provides a nice background against which vendors sell raw honey, local wines, sheep and goat cheese, cut flowers, free-range farm-raised pheasant, venison and lamb, and organic potted herbs and greenery.

Food

A good place for burgers and fries, sandwiches, and salads is **Foster's Coach House Tavern** (6411 Montgomery St., 845/876-8052, www.fosterscoachhouse.com, Tues.-Thurs. and Sun. 11am-9pm, Fri.-Sat. 11am-10pm, $19). Housed in an actual former coach house, Foster's is filled with wacky horse paraphernalia, including horseshoes, a horse carriage that's now a telephone booth, and mock horse stalls.

If you're in the mood for Mediterranean or European cuisine, a couple of restaurants fit the bill. Lively, noisy **Gigi Trattoria** (6422 Montgomery St., 845/876-1007, www.gigihudsonvalley.com, Tues.-Thurs. noon-9:30pm, Fri. noon-10pm, Sat. 11:30am-10pm, Sun. 11:30am-9pm, $28), housed in what was once an automobile showroom, bills itself as "Hudson Valley Mediterranean." On the menu are flatbread pizzas and lots of pasta dishes. ★ **Le Petit Bistro** (8 E. Market St., 845/876-7400, www.lepetitbistro.com, Mon., Wed., Thurs., Sun. 10:30am-3pm and 5pm-9:30pm, Fri.-Sat. 5pm-10pm, $28) is a classy yet casual bistro and bar with worn pine floors. The menu focuses on tasty French cuisine prepared with fresh local ingredients. **Tavern** (6387 Mill St., 845/876-1766, www.beekmandelamaterinn.com/dining, Mon.-Thurs. 11:30am-3:30pm and 4pm-9pm, Fri.-Sat. 11:30am-3:30pm and 4pm-10pm, Sun. 10:30am-3:30pm and 4pm-9pm, $28) at Beekman Arms is partially in the historic inn and partially housed in a greenhouse room filled with plants and flowers. The restaurant serves solid American fare with an emphasis on regional foods.

Accommodations

Famed **Beekman Arms** (6387 Mill St., 845/876-7077, www.beekmandelamaterinn.com, $100-300) is an inn that includes a cluster of several small buildings. Rooms in the historic main building ($140-150) have plenty of atmosphere, but are small; those in the handsome, American Gothic ★ **Delamater Inn** ($100-250), designed by Alexander Jackson Davis, are the most splendid and popular. Also at Delamater are six guesthouses perfect for families. Rooms in the other buildings cost $100-300.

The Rhinecliff Hotel (4 Grinnell St., 845/876-0590, www.therhinecliff.com, $160-190), an 1854 renovated rooming house, offers all the modern luxury amenities you could need, including wireless Internet, whirlpool tubs, and views of the Hudson from every room. This boutique country hotel has been touted for its authentic sense of place and features a restaurant and bar worthy of a pop in.

Delightful ★ **Whistle Wood Farm** (52

Pells Rd., 845/876-6838, www.whistlewood.com, $120-325) is on the outskirts of town, surrounded by fields and woodlands. Both a working horse farm and a friendly B&B, Whistle Wood boasts a whirlpool tub, decks overlooking the corral and fields of wildflowers, and plenty of in-room amenities. Stay in the main house or in the Carriage House, divided into two suites.

Motels in town include tiny, eight-room **Rhinebeck Motel** (6938 Rte. 9, 845/876-5900, www.rhinebeckmotel.biz, $120) and family-owned **Rhinebeck Village Inn** (6260 Rte. 9, 845/876-7000, www.rhinebeckvillageinn.com, $80-98). Both are clean and friendly.

NORTH OF RHINEBECK
Red Hook

Five miles (8.1 km) north of Rhinebeck is Red Hook, a small, low-key village filled with a surprising number of restaurants, inns and B&Bs, and historic buildings, such as **Octagonal House** (7444 S. Broadway), which now houses the **Red Hook Library** (www.redhooklibrary.org).

Anchoring the village is handsome, federal-style **Red Hook Inn** (7460 S. Broadway, 845/758-8445, www.theredhookinn.com, $180-275), sporting a wide front porch. Inside are nine guest rooms and a restaurant (five-course prix fixe $99-119) serving fresh fare with international influences.

The striking, blue **Grand Dutchess Bed and Breakfast** (7571 Old Post Rd., 845/758-5818, www.granddutchess.com, $165-195), a Victorian Italianate mansion offering six light-filled guest rooms, is within walking distance of downtown. All rooms have private baths and air-conditioning, and antiques are everywhere.

A good spot for breakfast, lunch, or a simple dinner is the wonderful old **Village Diner** (7550 N. Broadway, 845/758-6232, www.historic-village-diner.com, daily 6am-9pm, $11). Built in 1927, the art deco-style eatery is still family owned and operated. Try the homemade doughnuts, soups, and egg creams. The Hudson Valley region in general has

been a supplier of cut flowers since Victorian times, and Dutchess County in particular was once the violet and anemone capital of the world. One of the oldest nurseries still around is **F. W. Battenfeld & Sons** (856 Rte. 199, 845/758-8018, www.anemones.com), just outside Red Hook. The best time to visit is October-May, when the anemones are in bloom. Also of note near Red Hook is the large, family-owned **Greig Farm** (223 Pitcher Ln., 845/758-1234, www.greigfarm.com, July-Oct. daily 9am-7pm), where you can pick your own apples, pumpkins, peaches, and berries.

Annandale-on-Hudson

Three miles (4.8 km) west of Red Hook, in Annandale-on-Hudson, is **Montgomery Place** (River Rd., off Rte. 9G, 845/758-5461, www.american-arcadia.hudsonvalley.org, seasonally daily dawn to dusk, free; house tours: early May-late Oct., admission by timed tour, adults $10). One of the loveliest mansions along the Hudson, this quiet, 1802 federal-style gem was remodeled in the 1860s by famed Alexander Jackson Davis. Every line of the classical structure and every inch of the romantic grounds seem perfectly in place. Stunning views of the Hudson and the Catskills beyond can be had from the mansion's circular, columned portico.

Montgomery Place was home to the prominent Livingston family for almost 200 years. Members of the family continued to live in the house until the 1980s, and it is still almost entirely furnished with their treasures.

Surrounding Montgomery Place are landscaped grounds laced with walking trails. Just outside the estate's gates are its still-thriving **Montgomery Place Orchards** (4330 Rte. 9G, 845/758-6338, www.mporchards.com, June-Oct.), where you can pick your own fruits and berries.

Abutting Montgomery Place is **Bard College** (Rte. 9G at Annandale Rd., 845/758-6822, www.bard.edu), an idyllic 540-acre campus stippled with gardens and wooded groves. Once owned by Columbia University in New York City, Bard is now an independent institution known for its creative arts programs. Cutting-edge exhibits are showcased in its **Center for Curatorial Studies** (845/758-7598, www.bard.edu/ccs, Thurs.-Sun. 11am-6pm, free). Concerts and the critically acclaimed Bard Music Festival (which focuses on a different composer each year) are presented in the dramatic, brushed-stainless-steel **Richard B. Fisher Center for Performing Arts** (845/758-7900, www.fishercenter.bard.edu, tours Mon.-Thurs., call for appointment), designed by architect Frank Gehry and acoustical designer Yasuhisa Toyota. Daily tours show how the center's swooping lines reflect the surrounding landscape. The **SummerScape SpiegelTent** (845/758-7900, www.bard.edu/pac/summerscape) is a seven-week-long extravaganza of performing arts programming.

Tivoli

If you continue north of Annandale-on-Hudson on Route 9G to Route 78 and head west, you'll come to the hamlet of Tivoli. Henry Hudson is thought to have anchored offshore here in 1609, and nearby Cruger Island may once have been an important meeting ground for the local Wappingers and upstate Iroquois.

Today, Tivoli is a popular hangout for Bard College students and professors, hence its many restaurants and bars. Among the most popular is boisterous ★ **Santa Fe** (52 Broadway, 845/757-4100, www.santafetivoli.com, Tues.-Thurs. 4pm-9:30pm, Fri.-Sat. 4pm-10pm, Sun. 1pm-9pm, $18), offering Southwestern and Mexican food. In summer, a small outdoor dining area opens upstairs. Also a favorite, serving tasty, high-quality sushi, tempura, and noodles in a more relaxed setting is **Osaka** (74 Broadway, 845/757-5055, www.osakasushi.net, Mon.-Thurs. 11:30am-2:30am and 4:30pm-9pm, Fri.-Sat. 11:30am-2:30pm and 4:30pm-10pm, Sun. 3pm-9pm, $18).

Clermont State Historic Site

Just north of the Dutchess County border is **Clermont State Historic Site** (Woods Rd., off Rte. 9G, Germantown, 518/537-6622, www.friendsofclermont.org, grounds: year-round daily dusk-dawn, free; house tours: mid-Apr.-Oct. 31 Wed.-Sun. 11am-4pm, Nov. 1-late Dec. Sat.-Sun, 11am-3pm, adults $7, seniors and students $6, children under 12 free), a grand historic estate that was once home to seven generations of the Livingston family. The Georgian manse sits on the edge of a wide lawn lined with enormous black locust trees. Views from the estate are superb; down below is the Hudson River, and in the distance are the high Catskill Mountains peaks that inspired the estate's name. *Clermont* is French for "clear mountain."

The 35-room mansion holds many of the Livingstons' heirlooms, including period furniture and family portraits by Gilbert Stuart and others. Robert R. Livingston (1746-1813) was arguably the most famous of the clan. He administered the first oath of office to George Washington, helped draft the Declaration of Independence, and served as minister to France under Thomas Jefferson.

Landscaped grounds include a Lilac Walk (in bloom in May), formal gardens, and many acres of fields, forests, and wetlands laced with carriage paths and hiking trails. On the front lawn near the river is a plaque honoring inventor Robert Fulton, whose steamboat, the *Clermont,* first traveled up the Hudson from New York City to Albany in August 1807.

Lake Taghkanic State Park and Vicinity

To the east of Clermont, amid rolling hills, is pristine **Lake Taghkanic State Park** (1528 Rte. 82, Ancram, 518/851-3631, www.parks.ny.gov/parks/38, daily dawn-dusk, parking $10), centering on cool, blue Lake Taghkanic, a 1,569-acre body of water ringed with bathing beaches and boat launches. Hiking trails climb small peaks to offer splendid views of the valley below. Also in the park are a top-rated **campground** (reservations 800/456-2267, May-Oct. Sun.-Thurs. $15/night, Fri.-Sat. $22/night) with 60 campsites, picnic areas, a boat-rental shop, ball field, and fitness trail.

Not far from Lake Taghkanic State Park is the classic ★ **West Taghkanic Diner** (1016 Rte. 82, 518/851-7117, www. wtdinerny.com, Thurs. 8am-3:30pm, Fri.-Sat. 8am-3:30pm and 5pm-9pm, Sun. 8am-3:30pm, $15), where old-school diner aesthetic meets American modern food and the Instagram era.

Taconic State Park

Not to be confused with Lake Taghkanic State Park, much larger **Taconic State Park** (253 Rte. 344, off Rte. 22, Copake Falls, 518/329-3993, www.parks.ny.gov/parks/83, daily 8am-sunset, parking $7) is another lovely preserve. It's on the New York-Massachusetts border, set against the Taconic Mountains, a small range that extends northward into Vermont. Two separate recreation areas—Rudd Pond and Copake Falls—are in the 5,000-acre park, which features hiking trails, beaches, campsites, boat rentals, picnic areas, and playgrounds.

The park's greatest attraction is Bash-Bish Glen, where Bash-Bish Brook cascades down a striking series of waterfalls. A craggy outcropping known as Eagle Cliff stands at the top of the cataract; local legend has it that several Native Americans once fell to their deaths over its edge. Among them was a woman named Bash Bish, after whom the brook was named. Her spirit is said to still inhabit the area. An ice-cold, 40-foot-deep (12 m) quarry pool is also nearby.

The park also has **camping** facilities (reservations 800/456-2267, May-Oct. Sun.-Thurs. $19/night, Fri.-Sat. $24/night).

Copake Falls

On the edge of Taconic State Park is the serene village of Copake Falls, centered around a handful of historic wooden buildings and a small traffic circle with a historic four-faced clock. One of the county's most popular weekend events, attracting everyone from farmers to second-home owners, is the weekly **Copake Auction** (266 E. Main St., Copake, 518/329-1142, www.copakeauction. com).

Hillsdale

Winter brings skiers and snowboarders to Hillsdale's **Catamount Ski Area** (Breezy Hill Rd., off Rte. 23, 518/325-3200, www.catamountski.com). The ski resort offers more than 35 slopes and trails and eight lifts, along with a laid-back atmosphere that makes it especially good for families. It also claims to have the longest zipline in North America.

Comfortable **Swiss Hutte** (Breezy Hill Rd., off Rte. 23, 518/325-3333, www.swisshutte.com, $150-220) sits in the middle of the Catamount Ski Area, overlooking the slopes. On-site are a cozy wood-paneled bar and separate dining room (bar dishes $16, restaurant entrées $35) that serve Swiss-American fare.

The rambling, near-legendary **Rodgers Book Barn** (467 Rodman Rd., 518/325-3610, www.rodgersbookbarn.com, Apr. 1-Oct. 31 Thurs.-Mon. 11am-5pm, Nov. 1-Mar. 31 Fri.-Sun. 11am-5pm) is filled with books, books, and more books—over 50,000 titles, all secondhand. They're housed in a two-story barn with lots of nooks and crannies, and an adjacent annex.

Falcon Ridge Folk Festival (Dodds Farm, 44 Rte. 7D, 860/364-2138, www.falconridgefolk.com) comes to Hillsdale every late July-early August. On tap are top folk performers from around the country.

NEW PALTZ

Between the Hudson River and the Shawangunk Mountains lies the small town of New Paltz. New Paltz was founded in 1677 by a group of French Protestants who came to the New World seeking religious freedom. The Huguenots first settled just north of New Paltz, in Kingston and Hurley. But in June 1663, the area's indigenous Esopus raided the two small settlements, kidnapping 45 women and children. That September, a Huguenot search party found and freed the hostages. While embracing his family, one member of the party—Louis DuBois—noticed the

Mid-Hudson and the Catskills: Ulster County

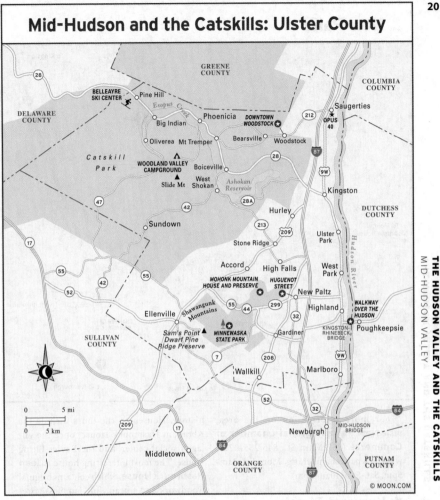

fertile land around him. He returned in 1677 with 11 others to buy and patent a 33,000-acre tract of land, and the next year, the 12 families settled along what is now known as Huguenot Street.

The new town was governed by a kind of corporation called the Duzine, referring to the 12 partners. That arrangement continued until well after the Revolution, by special permission of the New York State legislature. The system apparently worked well; one later commentator wrote, "So fine and free from animosity and greed has been the life of the people of New Paltz that previous to 1873 no lawyer ever found a permanent residence here."

Today, the center of New Paltz lies just east of historic Huguenot Street, along Chestnut and Main Streets. Here, you'll find a clutch of attractive stores and restaurants. New Paltz is also home to a State University of New York (SUNY) branch that offers an especially strong arts department, which helps account for the town's strong cultural scene.

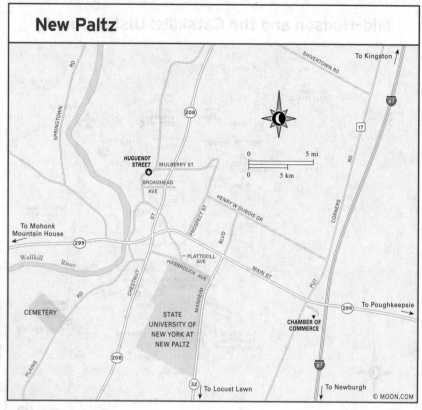

New Paltz

For more information on the area, visit **New Paltz Regional Chamber of Commerce** (257 Main St., 845/255-0243, www.newpaltzchamber.org, Mon.-Fri. 9am-5pm, Sat.-Sun. 10am-3pm).

★ Huguenot Street

This National Historic Landmark is said to be the oldest street in America with its original buildings. Along its cool and shady time-ripened blocks stand six stone houses built in the early 1700s, as well as a reconstructed 1717 French church and cemetery, a 1799 house, a library, and museum.

All official walking tours of the street begin at the **1705 DuBois Fort Information Center** on Huguenot Street between Broadhead Avenue and North Front Street. A small museum here documents the street's

history. Houses on the tours include the Abraham Hasbrouck House, once the village's social center, and the Bevier-Elting House. The most interesting house is **Jean Hasbrouck House,** which contains original woodwork and a beautiful "jambless" fireplace. Downstairs are rooms that once served as a tavern and general store, while upstairs are period furnishings, including a "senility cradle" used for the old and infirm.

Huguenot Street is run by the **Huguenot Historical Society** (88 Huguenot St., 845/255-1660, www.huguenotstreet.org, days and hours vary by season, tours $15), which includes among its members many descendants of the original families. The society offers walking tours of the street; the standard tour lasts 90 minutes. During the **Colonial Street Festival** (Huguenot St., second Sat.

in Aug.) all the houses are open and various colonial-era skills, such as quilting and musket firing, are demonstrated.

Locust Lawn

Four miles (6.4 km) south of New Paltz are more historic sites administered by the Huguenot Historical Society. Most important among them is **Locust Lawn** (436 S. Rte. 32, Gardiner), an elegant federal-style mansion built by Revolutionary War hero Colonel Josiah Hasbrouck in 1814. After the war, the colonel became one of the wealthiest men in Ulster County. He filled his home with fine period furniture, magnificent china, and paintings by the likes of Ammi Phillips and John Vanderlyn.

Nearby is considerably more rustic **Terwilliger House,** built in 1738. A wonderful example of Huguenot and Dutch architecture combined, the stone-and-wood cottage features a wide central hallway, long sloping roof, and creaky front porch.

To arrange a tour of either site, call the **Huguenot Historical Society** (88 Huguenot St., 845/255-1660, www.huguenotstreet.org).

Wineries

Wine enthusiasts might want to visit **Adair Vineyards** (52 Allhusen Rd., www.adair-wine.com, May-Oct. Sat.-Sun. 11am-6pm, Nov.-Apr. Sat.-Sun. 11am-5pm), which centers on a National Historic Landmark dairy barn that's more than 200 years old. The tasting room is in the old hayloft.

Or, head east to **Route 9W,** which hugs the shores of the Hudson River. Many small wineries are located along the route between West Park and Marlboro. Most famous among them is **Benmarl Winery** (156 Highland Ave., Marlboro, 845/236-4265, www.benmarl. com, Apr. 1-Dec. 31 Sun.-Thurs. noon-6pm, Fri. noon-8pm, Sat. 11am-8pm, mid-Jan.-Mar. 31 Thurs.-Sun. noon-5pm, $10 tasting fee). First planted as a vineyard in the late 16th century—and thus claiming to be America's oldest winery—it sits on a hilltop with great views of the river. The winery produces award-winning varietals, including chardonnays and cabernets.

Entertainment and Events

Concerts and plays are often on tap at **The State University of New York at New Paltz** (Rte. 32, just south of New Paltz, 1 mile (1.6 km) west of I-87, 845/257-2121), with many staged at the university's **Parker Theatre** (845/257-3880).

Though now primarily a casual restaurant, **P&G's** (91 Main St., 845/255-6161, www.pandgs.com, Mon.-Wed. and Sat. 11am-10pm, Thurs. 11am-9:30pm, Fri. 11am-8pm, Sun. 11am-9pm, $20) began as a dance hall in the 1900s and still presents live local bands on the weekends.

The **Ulster County Fair** (249 Libertyville Rd., 845/255-1380, www.ulstercountyfair. com, early Aug.) is held on the Ulster County Fairgrounds. The fairgrounds also host the **Woodstock-New Paltz Art & Crafts Fairs** (249 Libertyville Rd., 845/516-389-3712, www. quailhollow.com, Memorial Day and Labor Day weekends).

Food

With its outdoor café and homemade treats, **The Bakery** (13A N. Front St., 845/255-8840, www.ilovethebakery.com, daily 7am-6pm, $9) is a good spot for breakfast or a simple lunch. Main Street also offers a number of dining options. Popular ★ **A Tavola** (46 Main St., 845/255-1426, www.atavolany.com, Thurs.-Mon. 5:30pm-10pm, $28), complete with skylights, cooks up innovative Italian fare.

Accommodations

Rocking Horse Ranch (600 Rte. 44/55, 845/691-2927, www.rockinghorseranch. com, $100-260), a family-owned resort and dude ranch, is east of Highland proper. The Rocking Horse sits beside a lake and features indoor and outdoor pools, saunas, tennis courts, activities for kids, nighttime entertainment, and trail rides. In winter, the ranch offers cross-country skiing, ice-skating, snowshoeing, and sleigh rides.

In Wallkill, between Walden and New Paltz on Route 208, is the 1740 Audrey's Farmhouse (2188 Brunswick Rd., 845/895-3440, www.audreysfarmhouse.com, $205-300). The B&B offers comfortable guest rooms with feather beds, a swimming pool, library, and splendid views of the Shawangunks. Well-behaved dogs are welcome.

THE SHAWANGUNKS

Just west of New Paltz rise the Shawangunk Mountains, a tilted ridge of translucent quartz conglomerate cemented into sedimentary rock. One-tenth the age of the earth, the Shawangunks are often mistakenly assumed to be an extension of the Catskills, but are a distinct, separate range. The Shawangunks' steep escarpments make them a favorite spot for rock climbers. One local rock-climbing guide service and school is HighXposure Adventures (800/777-2546, www.high-xposure.com). Beginners are welcome.

★ Mohonk Mountain House and Preserve

High in the heart of the Shawangunks is Mohonk Mountain House (1000 Mountain Rest Rd., 855/883-3798, www.mohonk.com, $200-500 rooms, $389-735 including three meals per day, unlimited activities, and free kids' club), an enormous castle-like structure on the edge of a deep-blue glacial lake. Built by Quaker twins Albert and Alfred Smiley in 1870, Mohonk is the last of the magnificent resort hotels that once lined the Hudson.

In its heyday, Mohonk hosted a long line of distinguished guests, including Presidents Hayes, Taft, and Wilson. Albert Smiley was deeply concerned about the welfare of Native Americans, and, from 1883 to 1916, numerous important Friends of the Indian conferences were held here.

Mohonk is an ultraromantic place, bursting with gables and chimneys, turrets and towers. The grounds offer lovely scenic hikes, natural cave spelunking, impressive gardens (with English maze), mountain biking, and crystal-clear lake swimming. Trails, dotted with more than a hundred tiny gazebo-like sitting spots, provide resting places to enjoy the view or a good book. Numerous activities are scheduled throughout the day, ensuring guests every possibility to tailor a visit to their interests. A sense of family and pride is pervasive among the excellent staff, who offer warm smiles and assurances that your needs will be met. Bonfires (where staff offers preloaded s'mores roasting sticks), square dancing, movies under the stars, logrolling competitions, and other classic vacation activities make you feel as if you've stepped back in time.

To jump back into the present, hit the top-rated spa and outdoor mineral bath overlooking the mountains. Four-season fun means snow-tubing, Nordic skiing, snowshoeing, and ice-skating in the gorgeous stone pavilion or on Lake Mohonk.

The adjacent 5,600-acre Mohonk Preserve (845/255-0919, www.mohonkpreserve.org, daily dawn-dusk, grounds day pass: adults $15 for hikers, $20 for climbers, bikers, and horseback riders, children under 12 free) is ideal for outdoor adventure. Over 30 miles (48 km) of trails and carriage roads crisscross the preserve. The visitors center is free, but use of the grounds is fee-based, and day passes do not permit access to the Mountain House or its facilities.

★ Minnewaska State Park

If the idea of spending $15-20 per person to hike the Mohonk Preserve sounds a bit steep, head farther west through fertile farmland to Minnewaska State Park (5281 Rte. 44/55, 845/255-0752, www.parks.ny.gov/parks/127, hours vary seasonally and by park facility, parking $10). Also located high in the Shawangunks, the park is filled with panoramic views, hiking trails, paved carriage roads, waterfalls, and lakes.

Near the center of the park is deep-blue Lake Minnewaska—Iroquois for "floating waters"—surrounded by white sandstone

1: gazebo on Lake Mohonk 2: Opus 40 3: Mohonk Mountain House and Preserve

cliffs. The lake was created during the Ice Age when a glacier sliding by pulled out a hunk of soft sandstone. Lake Minnewaska has a sandy beach area where swimming is permitted, but if you like your bathing more secluded, hike the 3-mile (4.8 km) trail to **Lake Awosting.** This mile-long (1.6 km) lake can only be reached on foot and is an idyllic spot surrounded by dark, piney woods.

Just minutes away from Minnewaska State Park is popular ★ **Minnewaska Lodge** (3116 Rte. 44/55, Gardiner, 845/255-1110, www.minnewaskalodge.com, $135-319). Catering to outdoors enthusiasts, the 26-room lodge features rooms with cathedral ceilings and decks overlooking the 'Gunks, along with Mission-style furniture, oversize picture windows, and a wood-burning stove. Works by local artists hang on the walls.

After visiting the park, you might want to step into the old-fashioned, family-owned **Mountain Brauhaus** (junction of Rtes. 299 and 44/55, Gardiner, 845/255-9766, www.mountainbrauhaus.com, Wed.-Sat. 11:30am-9pm, Sun. 11:30am-8:30pm, $22) for a frothy mug of German beer and a plate of *rouladen* or *kassler rippchen.* The roadhouse sits at the base of the Shawangunks and offers spectacular views.

Ellenville

Southwest of Minnewaska State Park, where Route 209 meets Route 52, is the village of Ellenville. Located at the western base of the Shawangunks, Ellenville was once known for its Jewish boardinghouses and mega-resorts. Most of these are gone now, but the town still has plenty of fine colonial and Greek Revival buildings, and a few remaining kosher shops and restaurants. Among them is **Cohen's Bakery** (89 Center St., 845/647-7620, daily 6:30am-6pm), famed locally for its first-rate raisin-pumpernickel bread.

The Ellenville area also has a reputation for good hang gliding. **Mountain Wings Hang Gliding Center** (77 Hang Glider Rd., 845/647-3377, www.mtnwings.com) rents equipment and offers introductory one-day hang gliding courses.

Accommodations

For the most popular resort in the area, head to **Mohonk Mountain House** (1000 Mountain Rest Rd., 855/883-3798, www.mohonk.com, $200-500). The massive resort, which has been in operation since 1869, looks like a fairy castle; inside are many different room types, many with working fireplaces. Activities abound, and the gorgeous landscape—pond, mountains, woods (particularly spectacular in fall)—ensures you'll never get bored. A restaurant and spa are on-site as well.

NORTH ON ROUTE 209

Today's Route 209 closely parallels Old Route 209, reputedly the oldest highway in America. Originally known as the Old Mine Road, the old route ran between copper mines near Pahaquarry, New Jersey, and Kingston-on-the-Hudson, and was built sometime in the early 1600s. Many old homes and markers commemorating Native American raids are situated along Old Route 209, which runs concurrently with today's route in many places.

High Falls and Vicinity

Take Route 209 north to Route 213 east to High Falls, where the **D&H Canal Museum** (23 Mohonk Rd., 845/687-9311, www.canalmuseum.org, May-Oct., Sat.-Sun. 10am-4:30pm, donation) tells the story of the Delaware and Hudson Canal. Built in the 1820s, the canal was used to ship coal from the mines of Pennsylvania to the factories of New York. Later, it was used to ship cement made in the High Falls area to New York City. The museum has dioramas of the canal, working models of locks, and maps, photos, and artifacts.

For a simple meal, try **The Egg's Nest** (1300 Rte. 213, 845/687-7255, www.theeggsnest.com, Mon. and Thurs. noon-9pm, Fri. noon-10pm, Sat. 9am-10pm, Sun. 9am-9pm, $20), an eccentric spot offering tasty sandwiches and soups.

Stone Ridge

Stone Ridge Orchard (3012 Rte. 213, 845/687-2587, www.stoneridgeorchard.com, farmstand open daily Mar.-Oct. Wed.-Sun. 9am-6pm) and **Davenport Farms** (3411 Rte. 209, Stone Ridge, 845/687-0051, www.davenportfarms.com, daily 7am-7pm) offer country fresh prepared baked goods; you-pick apple, raspberry, and peach acreage; and farm activities like cider pressing or hayrides on busy summer weekends.

Bed-and-breakfast fans have an excellent choice in Stone Ridge. **Hasbrouck House** (3805 Rte. 209, 845/687-0736, www.hasbrouckhouseny.com, $195-425) is an elegant 18th-century colonial mansion. It offers nine guest rooms, an antique billiard room, 40 acres of gardens and woods, and a lake.

Hurley

Off Route 209 on the outskirts of Kingston lies this small village of 24 meticulously restored stone cottages. Almost all are private homes open to the public only once a year, during **Hurley Stone House Day** (www.stonehouseday.org), but they're also interesting to view from afar.

Hurley dates to 1651, when French Huguenots built wooden homes along Esopus Creek. The settlers didn't treat the indigenous Esopus well and, in 1663, the Esopus retaliated by burning down the Huguenot settlement. Six years later, the settlers rebuilt, this time in stone.

Self-guided walking tour maps of Hurley can be picked up at the post office at the town's entrance, at the Hurley Library, or Elmendorf House, both on Main Street. A plaque with a town map also stands by the library.

Elmendorf House is believed to be the oldest house in Hurley. Known as the Half-Moon Tavern in Revolutionary days, it now houses a small museum run by the **Hurley Heritage Society** (52 Main St., 845/338-1661, www.hurleyheritagesociety.org, hours vary seasonally). The Heritage Society can also arrange tours of other historic buildings: **Polly Crispell Cottage,** also on Main

Street, is equipped with a "witch catcher," or set of iron spikes set into the chimney; west of Main Street is the **Hardenberg House,** where abolitionist and suffragist Sojourner Truth, born a slave in Ulster County, spent her first 11 years.

SAUGERTIES

About 15 miles (24 km) north of Kingston, where Route 212 meets Route 9W, is Saugerties, filled with turn-of-the-20th-century brick buildings. Saugerties was once a river port known for its packet-trade and racing steamers. Most famous among them was the *Mary Powell,* the fastest ship on the Hudson between 1861 and 1885.

Opus 40

Between Saugerties and Woodstock is one of the most unusual spots in Ulster County, an environmental sculpture known as **Opus 40** (50 Fite Rd., 845/246-3400, www.opus40.org, mid-May-Nov. Thurs.-Sun. 10am-5pm, adults $10, seniors and students $7, children 6-12 $3). Created by artist Harvey Fite over a period of 37 years, Opus 40 covers more than six acres of an abandoned bluestone quarry. Its pools and fountains, sculptures and walkways, all center on a towering blue-gray monolith reminiscent of Stonehenge. The dark crest of Overlook Mountain rises behind Opus 40.

Fite, a professor at Bard College, created his monumental work using traditional quarrier's tools. Adjacent to the site is **Quarryman's Museum,** itself a work of art. The museum is filled with hammers and screws, chains and wagon wheels, with everything arranged according to size and shape. A seven-minute video on the site is featured.

Shopping

Downtown Saugerties is full of antiques shops, most of which are located along Main and Partition Streets. Some are serious affairs. One of the largest emporiums is **Saugerties Antique Center & Auction House** (220 Main St., 845/246-8234), which houses about

25 dealers. A guide to the town's antiques stores can be picked up in many shops.

Food

Black-Eyed Suzie's Upstate (230 Partition St., 845/247-3069, www.blackeyedsuziesupstate.com, $22) is a homey, welcoming spot that showcases local farm fare in dishes like the lentil mushroom burger and chickpea and veggie stew. Don't skip dessert (sticky toffee pudding, chocolate fondue for two!). In warmer months, an outdoor dining area is a big draw for out-of-towners and locals alike.

Accommodations and Camping

The largest campground in Saugerties is **Rip Van Winkle** (149 Blue Mountain Rd., 888/720-1232, www.ripvanwinklecamp-grounds.com, $10 pp), offering 170 sites. The

Saugerties-Woodstock KOA (882 Rte. 212, 845/246-4089, www.koa.com/campgrounds/Saugerties, rate varies by site type) offers 100 sites and camping cabins.

At ★ **Saugerties Lighthouse B&B** (168 Lighthouse Dr., 845/247-0656, www.saugertieslighthouse.com, $250, plus $40 per additional guest), adventurous guests can watch boats pass by on the Hudson from their basic second-story rooms. From the parking lot, it's a 10-minute walk to the lighthouse, though this can be a wet experience.

Three bedrooms and a spacious two-room suite are the accommodations at **B&B Tamayo** (91 Partition St., 845/246-9371, www.saugertiesbedandbreakfast.net, $150-230), which started its life as a popular restaurant. It is open May-October. The B&B owners (who also owned the restaurant) now host occasional dinner parties and cooking classes.

The Catskills

Glancing at a map, Hudson Valley and the Catskills may look like one continuous, largely indistinguishable mass. Drive, bike, hike, or paddle through the region, though, and you'll begin to discern some differences. While neighbors, the two regions each have a unique composition and character. Hudson Valley is chock-a-block with farm stands and farm-to-table restaurants, art galleries, and old estates-turned historical sites. And while there's more rambling land here than New York City, to be sure, your wanderings in the Hudson Valley will inevitably involve encounters with local characters.

In the Catskills, meanwhile, it's easy to take a side road and find yourself alone in the wild, whether on or off the beaten path of the 1,000+ square miles that comprise the Catskills – and that's just the park. While art—especially music—and history can be found in the Catskills, the outdoors is the best reason to make your way to this

region, especially in the summer and fall months, when recreational options abound and the changing colors of leaves take your breath away.

WOODSTOCK AND VICINITY

The famed arts colony of Woodstock is still a picturesque and unusual spot, inhabited by an idiosyncratic bunch of artists and crafts-people, individualists and ne'er-do-wells. But the place is often so overrun with tourists that it's hard to tell.

Woodstock the town dates to the 1700s. But Woodstock the arts colony dates to 1902, when a wealthy Englishman, freethinker, and lover of the arts named Ralph Radcliffe Whitehead came here to set up an arts-and-crafts community. A student of John Ruskin who railed against the evils of the Industrial Revolution, Whitehead envisioned his colony as living apart from the modern world, surrounded by scenic splendor, and supporting itself with its arts and crafts.

Whitehead went in with two partners, bought 1,300 acres, and built a small village, Byrdcliffe, just above Woodstock. A few years later, one of his followers, poet Hervey White, became fed up with Whitehead's authoritarian demands and started a second arts community, Maverick, on the south side of town. Then, in 1906, the Art Students League of New York City arrived, opening a summer school in Woodstock's downtown. The village was thronged with ever-increasing numbers of painters, potters, weavers, poets, dancers, musicians, novelists, hangers-on, and tourists eager to "see the artists."

By mid-century, folk singers Pete Seeger, Joan Baez, and Peter, Paul, and Mary had discovered Woodstock, and in the 1960s, Bob Dylan moved in, buying a farm on an isolated mountaintop. The town's first recording studio was built, and a series of small concerts, the Woodstock Soundoffs, was staged. The Soundoffs were the immediate forerunner of the legendary 1969 Woodstock Music Festival that took place in Bethel, 60 miles (97 km) away. The concert organizers wanted to hold the event closer to home, but Woodstock had no open space large enough, and last-minute ordinances imposed by nervous officials prevented the concert from taking place in Saugerties as originally planned.

★ **Downtown Woodstock**

For all its renown, Woodstock remains a small village, with a population of about 6,000. Its main thoroughfare is Tinker Street, which according to legend is named after a tinker's wagon that sank into the mud here one fine spring day.

Where Tinker Street meets Rock City and Mill House Roads is the village green, where you may spot a resurgence of tie-dyed clothing, making you wonder what year it is. Nearby is the Millstream, immortalized in Tell Taylor's classic song, "Down by the Old Millstream."

Dozens of small shops, restaurants, galleries, and museums crowd the streets of Woodstock. Among the oldest is **Woodstock Artists Association and Museum** (28 Tinker St., 845/679-2940, www.woodstock-art.org, Sun., Wed. and Thurs. noon-5pm, Fri.-Sat. noon-6pm), which has exhibited the works of area artists since 1920 and is lovingly referred to as "the local Louvre." First-rate **Center for Photography at Woodstock** (59 Tinker St., 845/679-9957, www.cpw.org, Wed.-Sun. noon-5pm) is housed in what was once the Espresso Café, where Bob Dylan, Janis Joplin, and other 1960s-era icons performed. Tinker Street is also home to **The Golden Notebook** (29 Tinker St., 845/679-8000, www.goldennotebook.com), a good bookstore.

Overlook Mountain

Looming behind Woodstock is Overlook Mountain, the summit of which offers splendid views of the valley and river below. To reach the mountain from town, take Rock City Road to Meads Mountain Road; the trailhead is opposite **Karma Triyana Dharmachakra** (335 Meads Mountain Rd., 845/679-5906, www.kagyu.org, days and hours vary based on scheduled events, guided monastery tour each Sat. at 1:30pm, free), a Tibetan Buddhist monastery. In its shrine room is a 13-foot-high (4 m) statue of the Buddha, which was used by Martin Scorsese in his film *Kundun,* about the life of the Dalai Lama.

The 2-mile (3.2 km) walk to the top of the mountain follows an old roadbed, and is of easy-to-moderate difficulty and takes about an hour. Along the way you'll pass the ruins of the Overlook Mountain House, once a popular resort that was anchored to the mountain by strong cables to keep it from being blown away. Plaques tell the resort's fascinating history.

Entertainment

Founded by poet Hervey White, the **Maverick Concerts** (120 Maverick Rd., 845/679-8217, www.maverickconcerts.org, mid-July-late Sept.) are the oldest chamber music series in the country, featuring top musicians in a relaxed woodsy setting. The remarkable "music chapel," hand-hewn in 1916, boasts perfect acoustics and seats only 400. It's changed little since its creation. The concerts attract an eclectic crowd, drawing from New York City's metro music lovers as well as those who remember Woodstock because they were there. Following a nearly century-old tradition, very little reserved seating is available. Join excited concertgoers for first-come seating under the rustic chapel's dome or on handmade wooden benches decorated with woven branches under the canopy of leafy trees.

The **Colony** (22 Rock City Rd., 845/679-8639, www.colonycafewoodstock.com, Thurs.-Mon. 7pm-close) presents local, regional, and national performers in a building that dates to 1929 and was renovated in 2017 by new owners who viewed the venue as "an antique that needed to be restored." In addition to music performances, there's an on-site café that serves beer, wine, coffee, and dessert.

Housed in the 1902 Byrdcliffe art colony is **Woodstock Byrdcliffe Guild** (34 Tinker St., 845/679-2079, www.woodstockguild.org), an arts center featuring performance art, theater,

and film. Since 2000, Woodstock has been home to the **Woodstock Film Festival** (www.woodstockfilmfestival.org), held each fall.

To find out what's going on in the area, check the **Woodstock Times** (www.hudsonvalleyone.com) or listen to Woodstock's independent radio station, Radio Woodstock, WDST, FM 100.1.

Food

One of Woodstock's oldest restaurants is the hole-in-the-wall **Joshua's** (51 Tinker St., 845/679-5533, www.joshuaswoodstock.com, Mon.-Tues. and Thurs.-Fri. 11am-close, Sat.-Sun. 10am-close, $26), serving simple but tasty Middle Eastern-inspired food. **The Garden Café** (6 Old Forge Rd., 845/679-3600, www.thegardencafewoodstock.com, Mon. and Wed.-Fri. 11:30am-9pm, Sat.-Sun. 10am-9pm, $14) on the village green serves up vegetarian and vegan fare even carnivores can appreciate.

Another local favorite is **The Red Onion** (1654 Rte. 212, 845/679-1223, www.redonionrestaurant.com, Sun.-Thurs. 5pm-9pm, Fri.-Sat. 5pm-10pm, $27). Housed in an 1830s farmhouse on the outskirts of town, the restaurant serves an eclectic international menu.

view from a lookout tower on Overlook Mountain

By the Time They Got to Woodstock...

By the time they got to Woodstock . . . they had to keep going for over 50 miles (81 km). The famed 1969 Woodstock Music Festival actually took place on Max Yasgur's farm in Bethel, as opposed to the Catskill mountain town that provided its name.

To get to Bethel from Route 52, head east on Route 17B, through mile after mile of scenic farm country. The former Yasgur farm is off Hurd Road. Signs off Route 17B point the way to an enormous lime-green field sloping down to borders of dark green trees. A horizontal stone marker near the road reads: "This is the original site of the Woodstock Music and Arts Fair held on Aug. 15, 16, 17, 1969." It also lists the festival's many performers: Richie Havens, Arlo Guthrie, Joan Baez, Joe Cocker, Ravi Shankar, Santana, and Janis Joplin, to name a few.

Bethel Woods Center for the Arts (200 Hurd Rd., 866/781-2922, www.bethelwoodscenter.org) opened in 2006 with a performance by the New York Philharmonic. The $65 million center was built on the site of the 1969 Woodstock Festival and features the pavilion amphitheater, outdoor stage area, theater, interpretive center with impressive multimedia interactive exhibits about the 1969 festival, and a seasonal craft and farmers market.

The venue attracts an ambitious lineup of performers ranging from the New York Philharmonic to ballet troupes, jazz greats, and pop music stars, as well as arts workshops and film festivals. During big concerts, area campgrounds are the first to fill, though the Bethel Woods Center for the Arts website offers a comprehensive directory of additional accommodations. Those visiting the museum on concert days should buy advance tickets to avoid disappointment.

Not far from Bethel Woods Center for the Arts is exquisite **Lake Superior State Park** (Dr. Duggan Rd., off Rte. 17B, 845/794-3000, ext. 5002, www.parks.ny.gov/parks/87, May-Oct. daily 9am-dusk, parking $7 in summer), an all-but-untouched recreation area open for swimming, picnicking, boating, and fishing. Boats are available for rent.

Accommodations

Twin Gables (73 Tinker St., 845/679-9479, www.twingableswoodstockny.com, $159-224) has functioned as a homey guesthouse since the 1920s and claims to be the oldest house in Woodstock. Some rooms share baths.

Also downtown, you'll find the attractive **Woodstock Inn on the Millstream** (48 Tannery Brook Rd., 845/679-8211, www.woodstock-inn-ny.com, $169-375), an upscale property with a variety of room types. The inn is in walking distance of Millstream, a natural brook and swimming hole and a favorite cooldown spot in the summer.

Built as the home of Woodstock artist Jo Cantine, the elegant hideaway **Woodstock Country Inn** (185 Cooper Lake Rd., 845/679-9380, www.woodstockcountryinn.com, $185-300) offers four guest rooms filled with light and antiques. There is also an outdoor pool and great mountain views.

WEST ON ROUTE 28

Route 28 runs right through the heart of **Catskill Park** and **Catskill Forest Preserve** (no entrance fee). Just past Boiceville, the land turns wooded, wild, and wonderful, with mountains rising to the left and right. Five of the Catskills' highest peaks are located in Ulster County.

Twelve-mile-long (19.3 km) **Ashokan Reservoir** begins near the park's entrance. Built between 1909 and 1919, despite fierce local opposition, the reservoir displaced eight communities, 2,600 graves, 64 miles (103 km) of road, and 11 miles (17.7 km) of railroad. Around the reservoir runs Route 28A, a marvelous **scenic drive** that skirts Ashokan Dam, fountains, and a picnic area. Peaks rising to 3,000 feet (910 m) surround the western end.

To either side of Route 28 are small, wistful villages that were once major resort destinations but now aren't much more than

The Roxbury Experience

For those who didn't get enough of the wonderfully weird Woodstock experience, the village of Roxbury, which lies right up Route 28W, has plenty to offer. Between the Roxbury Arts Group's (venues vary, 607/326-7908, www.roxburyartsgroup.org) gallery and single-day workshops in felting and clay-work, walking tours (Town of Roxbury Department of Community Resources, 607/326-3722) of town led by costumed historical figures, and Roxbury Nine Vintage (www.roxburyny.com) baseball games played by 19th-century rules, you will quickly understand why the entire town was placed in the National and State Registers of Historic Places.

Perhaps the best reason to visit is The Roxbury Motel (2258 County Hwy. 41, Roxbury, 607/326-7200, www.theroxburymotel.com, $99-698), the grooviest boutique hotel in the Catskills. A stay in "Maryann's Coconut Cream Pie" will find you dreaming of whipped meringue kisses and leave you wondering why you ever sleep in a staid chain hotel. Fortunately, the owners' incredible attention to detail pulls off this trip back to the 1960s and '70s with style and class. Stop at the local bakery to buy your own to-die-for coffee cake, part of the motel's impressive continental breakfast spread, as you head back out on the road to reality.

clutches of well-worn buildings, huddled together against the modern world. The original Route 28 once ran through their centers; the modern route bypasses them completely.

Boiceville

On the outskirts of Boiceville is ★ Onteora Mountain House (96 Piney Point Rd., 845/657-6233, www.onteora.com, $225-265), a noteworthy B&B. Onteora sits high on a mountaintop overlooking Catskill Park. Once the posh retreat of mayonnaise mogul Richard Hellman, the home features huge picture windows, cathedral ceilings, and a massive stone fireplace. The B&B offers seven guest rooms, all with private baths and most with magnificent views.

The very popular Bread Alone Bakery & Cafe (3962 Rte. 28, 845/657-3328, www.breadalone.com/boiceville, daily 7am-5pm, $10) offers much more than just great fresh bread baked in a wood-fired oven. Also on the menu are homemade soups, sandwiches (try the roasted cauliflower!), pastries, and coffees.

Mount Tremper

One of the odder attractions in the Catskills is Emerson (5340 Rte. 28, 877/688-2828, Sun.-Fri. 9am-5pm, Sat. 9am-6pm, adults $5, children under 11 free), where you'll find the world's largest kaleidoscope, housed in a former grain silo. Inside the nearly 60-foot-tall (18 m) tower, visitors stare straight up into myriad images multiplied by 254 facets covering about 45 feet (14 m). Also in the complex are shops selling kaleidoscopes, furniture, clothing, books, and gifts.

Catskill Rose (5355 Rte. 212, 845/688-7100, www.catskillrose.com, Thurs.-Sun. 5pm-9pm, $26) serves dishes inspired by a variety of culinary traditions and countries, prepared by a husband-and-wife team.

The Emerson resort includes the Woodnotes Grille (5340 Rte. 28, 845/688-2828, www.emersonresort.com, breakfast daily from 7am-noon, dinner Sun.-Thurs. 5pm-9pm, Fri.-Sat. 5pm-10pm, $26), which serves new American fare with locally sourced ingredients in a setting overlooking Esopus Creek and Mount Tremper; the family-friendly Emerson Resort Lodge (5340 Rte. 28, 877/688-2828, www.emersonresort.com, $190-300), furnished in upscale log-cabin-style decor, and adults-only Emerson Resort Inn (5340 Rte. 28, 877/688-2828, www.emersonresort.com, $299-399). There is also a spa on the premises.

A good area campground is Kenneth L. Wilson Campground (859 Wittenberg Rd., 1 mi/1.6km off Rte. 28, 845/679-7020, reservations 800/456-2267, $22/night for New York State residents, $27/night for nonresidents), which has 71 sites, picnic areas, showers, boat rentals, and mountain bike trails for advanced riders. Reservations should be made well in advance.

Phoenicia

One of the most prosperous villages along Route 28 is Phoenicia, known for its trout fishing, kayaking, and tubing, all done on Esopus Creek, which runs through the town. From May to September, floating down the creek on huge black inner tubes is one of the county's most popular activities. Several tube rental shops are located at the entrance to Phoenicia; among them is **Town Tinker** (10 Bridge St., 845/688-5553, www.towntinker. com, Memorial Day-Sept. 30).

Less than a mile away, housed in the old railroad station at the town's east end is the **Empire State Railway Museum** (70 High St., 845/688-7501, www.esrm.com, Memorial Day-Oct.31 weekends and holidays 10:30am-4:30pm, $3), which documents the history of the five different railroads that serviced the Catskills between the late 1860s and the 1940s.

Between the railroad museum and nearby Mount Pleasant runs **Catskill Mountain Railroad** (845/688-7400, www.catskillmountainrailroad.com, hours vary seasonally). Scenic train rides along Esopus Creek are still chugging along and are particularly popular during fall foliage in September-October.

Phoenicia's Main Street is short, which makes it easily walkable. On it, you'll find a handful of shops like **The Tender Land Home** (64 Main St., 845/688-7213, www.tenderlandhome.com), selling handcrafts and home accessories, and the self-described "antique emporium and odditorium," **Homer & Langley's Mystery Spot** (72 Main St., 845/688-7868, www.mysteryspotvintage. com), a "shrine to clutter" that is "packed to the rafters" with "knick-knacks and doodads" curated by artist Laura Levine.

★ **Sweet Sue's** (49 Main St., 845/688-7852, www.sweetsue1984.wixsite.com, Fri.-Mon. 8am-1pm, $12) is Phoenicia's obligatory spot for breakfast and brunch. Over a dozen types of pancakes are on the menu. **Brio's** (68 Main St., 845/688-5370, www.brios.net, Sun.-Thurs. 7am-10pm, Fri.-Sat. 7am-11pm, $16) is a dependable pizzeria that also serves pasta and salads and more than 20 beers on tap.

"Catskills vs. Hamptons" read buttons sitting in a bowl on the check-in desk at **The Graham & Co.** (80 Rte. 214, 845/688-7871, www.thegrahamandco.com, $198), Phoenicia's boutique hotel. You'll be forgiven if you feel confused about your coordinates when you glance at the cool kids lounging around the pool here: Might Phoenicia be the next East Hampton? Twenty rooms are spare on design but perfectly comfortable; some even have kitchenettes. A bunkhouse is intended for snowboarders and skiers. A pool, bikes, and a fire pit round out the on-the-grounds amenities at this hip hotel.

Woodland Valley

Off Route 28 1 mile (1.6 km) west of Phoenicia, Woodland Valley Road turns off to the left and leads through Woodland Valley, one of the deepest and most romantic valleys in the Catskills. Four miles (6.4 km) in, the road comes to a parking lot at **Woodland Valley State Campground** (1319 Woodland Valley Rd., 845/688-7647, reservations 800/456-2267, $20/night for New York State residents, $25/night for nonresidents), where reservations should be made well in advance.

There is also a well-marked trail that takes hikers to the top of Wittenberg Mountain. The 3.4-mile, 2,800-foot (5.5 km, 850 m) ascent takes about three hours. It's steep near the beginning and again near the top, but only of moderate difficulty most of the way. The spectacular view from the summit—one of the best in the Catskills—encompasses almost all of Ashokan Reservoir.

From Wittenberg Mountain, a short, narrow trail leads via a connecting ridge to Cornell Mountain, which offers good views of Slide Mountain, the highest peak in the Catskills. The hike from Wittenberg to Cornell takes about 30 minutes.

Pine Hill and Highmount

Good downhill skiing can be found in Highmount at New York State-owned **Belleayre** (Belleayre Rd., off Rte. 28, Highmount, 845/254-5608, www.belleayre.com). There are more than 45 trails for skiers of all skill levels. The vertical drop is 1,404 feet (430 m). The longest run is over 12,000 feet (3,660 m). During the off-season, you can hike or take a chairlift to the summit.

Anchoring the small village nearby is **Pine Hill Arms Hotel** (288 Main St., Pine Hill, 845/254-4012, www.pinehillarms.com, $95-200), a once old-fashioned, slightly stuffy spot that recently underwent an update. A beautiful old bar remains, a coffee shop was added, and the restaurant's menu was given an overhaul, too. One of the most economical places to stay in all of the Catskills is the friendly **Belleayre Lodge and Cabins** (15 Hostel Dr., Pine Hill, 845/254-4200, www.belleayrelodge.com, $100-350), which offers cabin-style accommodations.

WEST ON ROUTE 23A

Some of the most dramatic scenery in the Catskills lies west of Route 32 on Route 23A. For about 4 miles (6.4 km), between Palenville and Haines Falls, the road winds steeply up nearly 1,500 feet (460 m), past craggy cliffs and rocky streams, forested walls and outstanding views. The incline continues at a gentler angle between Haines Falls and Hunter, then levels out to run along Schoharie Creek.

Kaaterskill Falls

Off Route 23A about 3 miles (4.8 km) west of Palenville, in the Kaaterskill Wild Forest, are **Kaaterskill Falls,** marked with a sign and roadside parking lot. At 260 feet (80 m)—compared to Niagara's 167 feet (51 m)—these are the highest waterfalls in the state. During the Romantic Age, everyone from Thomas Cole and Asher Durand to James Fenimore

1: a tube rental shops in Phoenicia **2:** the Graham & Co. hotel in Phoenicia **3:** the Catskill Mountain Railroad **4:** Kaaterskill Falls

Cooper and William Cullen Bryant were inspired by this long glittering torrent. The falls were portrayed in countless paintings, illustrations, and poems until they became an icon for the American wilderness. Near the top of the falls once stood Catskill Mountain House, the nation's first mountain resort.

To reach the lower basin of Kaaterskill Falls, follow the trail on the north side of Route 23A. The hike, which begins at Bastion Falls, takes less than an hour round-trip, and although there are steep spots, the trail is mostly level.

Escarpment Trail

The **Escarpment Trail** stretches 24 miles (39 km) between Route 23A in Haines Falls and Route 23 in East Windham without crossing a single highway. Parts of the trail have been used for more than 150 years, as initials and dates carved along its ledges attest.

To access the popular section of the Escarpment Trail that leads past the former site of the Catskill Mountain House, continue about 2 miles (3.2 km) past the Kaaterskill Falls parking area and take the first right onto County Road 18, following signs to North-South Lakes Campground. At the end of this 4-mile (6.4 km) road, just before the campground, turn right onto Scutt Road, where you'll find a parking area and a blue-marked trail.

Follow the trail through a forested area, past Spruce Creek and a four-way intersection, toward Layman Monument and Sunset Rock. Soon after the intersection, the trail skirts along the top of the Great Wall of Manitou. The terrain here is fairly level and all along the way are overlooks offering magnificent views. Near the Layman Monument you can see Kaaterskill Clove ("clove" comes from the Dutch word for "gorge"), with Hunter Mountain behind.

About 1.5 miles (2.4 km) past Inspiration Point is a red-marked cutoff trail leading to the site of the former Catskill Mountain House. Take this shorter trail, or continue on the more scenic blue trail past Split and

Boulder Rocks. Either way, in 20-30 minutes you'll reach the large open ledge upon which the famed resort once stood. An informative plaque marks the spot.

To hike from the parking lot to the Catskill Mountain House site takes about an hour and a half. From there, you can return the way you came or take the service road back to the parking lot.

Catskill Mountain House Site

Don't miss the view from the **Catskill Mountain House site,** just east of Haines Falls. The whole world seems to lie at your feet. Straight ahead, in the distance, are the gray-blue Taconic and Berkshire Mountains; below is the Hudson, shrunk to a slim silver line. The view is perhaps best described in James Fenimore Cooper's *The Pioneers,* one of his Natty Bumppo tales: "'What see you when you get there?' asked Edwards. 'Creation!' said Natty, . . . 'all creation, lad.'"

The site can be reached by driving into **North-South Lakes Campground** (County Rd. 18, Haines Falls, 518/589-5058, closed late Oct.-mid-May, $24.75/night for New York State residents, $29.75/night for nonresidents). Drive to the end of the service road. The short trail that leads to the site is located at the far end of the parking lot. For those with more time and more stamina, the site can also be reached by hiking the 24-mile (39 km) Escarpment Trail.

North-South Lakes

According to legend, North and South Lakes are the two eyes of a great reclining giant, Onteora; nearby Lake Creek was made from his tears. South Lake, formerly known as Sylvan Lake, was one of Thomas Cole's favorite subjects. He painted his well-known *Lake With Dead Trees* and *Catskill Lake* here.

The 219-site **North-South Lakes Campground** (County Rd. 18, Haines Falls, 518/589-5058, reservations 800/456-2267, closed late Oct.-mid-May) is part of a state park by the same name, where you'll find two long, pristine lakes ringed by deciduous trees that erupt with fiery color in fall, a sandy beach, bathhouses, and hiking trails. Rowboats can be rented, and fishing is good.

Tannersville

Part scruffy mountain village, part cheery tourist town, Tannersville—named for its once-extensive tanning industry—is now home to a few shops and cafés, several inns and B&Bs, and more than its fair share of tattoo parlors. In the village center, you'll find **Maggie's Krooked Cafe** (6000 Main St., 518/589-6101, www.krookedcafe.com, daily 7am-7pm, $17), offering home-cooked specialties such as pancakes and beer-battered shrimp. Another café on Main Street, **Last Chance Antiques and Cheese Cafe** (6009 Main St., 518/589-6424, www.lastchanceon-line.com, daily 11am-close, $16), is a combination store/café featuring overstuffed sandwiches, homemade soups, cheeses, and chocolates. There are plenty of gluten-free and vegan options on the menu.

Hunter Mountain

In winter, New York City residents by the thousands flock to the slopes of Hunter Mountain Ski Area, the Catskills' best-known ski center. In summer and fall, Hunter Mountain Festivals are staged here. Annual events include the German Alps Festival, the International Celtic Festival, and Oktoberfest, among others.

Before becoming a ski town, Hunter was known first for its tannery and then for its chair factory. Today you'll find lodges and restaurants along its Main Street, many done up in ersatz Swiss motifs. Many shut down during the off-season.

SKIING

Hunter Mountain Ski Area (off Rte. 23A, 518/263-4223, www.huntermtn.com) actually covers three mountains, with 67 trails, 13 lifts, and 100 percent snowmaking capability. On summer weekends, **Summer Sky Ride** (Memorial Day Weekend-Oct., adults

Upper Hudson

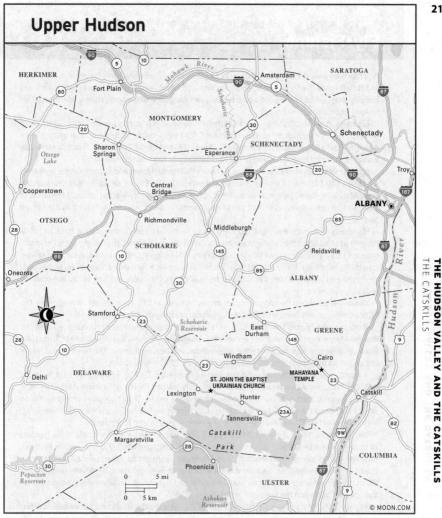

$14, seniors $10, children 7-12 $10) travels to the mountain's summit.

HIKING

A number of good, well-marked hiking trails crisscross the area around Hunter Mountain. Many start at the back of the mountain on Old Spruceton Road. To get here, continue west on Route 23A past the Ukrainian church and turn left onto Route 42 South. Continue to the hamlet of Westkill, turn east onto County Road 6, and follow it 6 miles (9.7 km) through pastoral Spruceton Valley. You'll find two parking lots and the trailheads at the end, after the road has become dirt.

The main trail leading to Hunter's summit is of moderate difficulty, covers 7.2 miles (11.6 km) round-trip, and takes about 6-7 hours. Along the way is a mile-long (1.6 km) spur leading to **Colonel's Chair,** a northern protuberance of the mountain supposedly resembling a giant armchair. The chair was named

Fly-Fishing

At a roadside park deep in the Catskills, a plaque quoting the Fisherman's Prayer says it all: "God grant that I may live to fish until my dying day, and when it comes to my last cast I then most humbly pray, when in the Lord's safe landing net I'm peacefully asleep, then in His mercy I be judged good enough to keep."

Livingston Manor, on the banks of the Willowemoc, is primarily known for its superb trout fishing. The Willowemoc offers nearly 7 miles (11.3 km) of public water from Livingston Manor downstream to Roscoe, and the Beaverkill's 15 miles (24 km) below Roscoe are all public and easily wadable. Covered bridges dating to the mid-1800s span the trout streams.

Appropriately situated about midway between Livingston Manor and Roscoe is state-of-the-art **Catskill Fly Fishing Center and Museum** (1031 Old Rte. 17, 845/439-4810, www.cffcm. com, Mar.-Nov. daily 10am-4pm, donations accepted). Started by a group of local fisherfolk in 1981, the center does an excellent job of documenting the history of fly-fishing in the United States.

Hundreds of meticulously crafted flies, along with rods, reels (some dating back to 1850), historic photos, and other artifacts are on display. To the uninitiated, that might sound ho-hum, but don't pass judgment until you've seen the bumble puppy, midge, quill gordon, wet spider, cow dung, or red ant. Fly-tying is a bona fide folk art, and each fly is an intricate affair, individually designed and named. At one time, flies were made out of feathers and furs; today, the material is usually synthetic.

The center also hosts fly-tying demonstrations, lectures, and fly-tying classes for beginners. The Willowemoc, usually lined with fisherfolk in waders casting their lines, runs out front.

Roscoe, aka **Trout Town U.S.A.,** is considerably larger and more sophisticated than Livingston Manor, but its raison d'être is the same. American fly-fishing was developed at **Junction Pool,** just west of Roscoe, where the Willowemoc and Beaverkill meet. The town boasts five of the country's best trout streams and plenty of other fishable waterways.

A number of expert fly-tiers still live and work nearby. **Dette Trout Flies** (13 Main St., 845/439-1166, www.dettetroutflies.com) is a family-owned fly-tying business started in 1928. Among anglers, the Dette name is known around the world. The shop gives straight intel on what to expect throughout the area in their Daily Report (online and by phone at 607/498-5350), including river flows, temperatures, turbidity, insect hatches, and local weather.

Continuing farther up Lewbeach Road, you'll enter Catskill Park and soon come to the hamlets of Beaverkill and Lewbeach. State-run **Beaverkill Campground** (792 Berrybrook Rd. Spur, 845/439-4281, $20/night for New York State residents, $25/night for nonresidents) is situated on the banks of Beaverkill River, another world-famous trout-fishing stream. The 52-site campground (20 of them, river sites) has a picnic area with grills and hot shower facilities. Keep an eye out for the covered bridge on the property, which dates to 1865.

Wulff School of Fly Fishing (845/439-5020, www.wulffschool.com), in Lewbeach, offers weekend trout-fishing and fly-casting workshops May-June. Run by Joan Wulff, a champion angler and author, the school is set on 100 acres and includes a private stretch of the Beaverkill River.

after Colonel William Edwards, an early tanner who made his fortune decimating the area's hemlock forest. It was Edwards who first put Hunter, then known as Edwardsville, on the map.

One of the easiest hikes in the Catskills, leading to Diamond Notch Falls, also begins at the parking lots. The gently inclining trail is about a mile long and runs alongside West Kill Creek. Wildflowers and birds are abundant.

For more information on hiking Hunter Mountain, stop in at the main **Hunter Mountain Ski Area** (off Rte. 23A in the heart of the village, 518/263-4223, www.huntermtn. com).

FISHING

In summer, anglers can be found **trout fishing** in Schoharie Creek along Route 23A, while hikers take to the slopes of Hunter Mountain.

ACCOMMODATIONS AND CAMPING

Charming ★ **Fairlawn Inn** (7872 Main St., 518/263-5025, www.fairlawninn.com, $159-250) is a three-story Victorian inn with nine attractive guest rooms, many with brass or four-poster beds. Stained-glass windows, parquet floors, 19th-century antiques, wraparound porches, and a stunning central staircase add to the ambience.

The modern ★ **Scribner Hollow Lodge** (13 Scribner Hollow Rd., 518/263-4211, www.scribnerslodge.com, $115-340 pp, with breakfast and dinner) is a full-service lodge with 38 guest rooms, an outdoor pool, an unusual indoor grotto, saunas, and fireplaces. Each of the rooms is furnished differently, and artwork is everywhere.

Near the base of Hunter Mountain is chalet-style **Hunter Mountain Inn** (7433 Main St., 518/263-3777, www.hunterinn.com, $100-180), whose bar is a favorite haunt of the après-ski crowd; live music is often featured on weekends. The inn holds 42 rooms, which feature cathedral ceilings and whirlpool tubs.

Four miles (6.4 km) south of town is the 24-site **Devil's Tombstone Campground** (Rte. 214, 845/688-7160, reservations 800/456-2267, $16/night for New York State residents, $21/night for nonresidents), one of the oldest campgrounds in the Catskills and an ideal base camp for skilled hikers.

Lexington

Continuing west on Route 23A, you'll pass through the nondescript hamlets of South Jewett and Jewett Center before coming to the startlingly beautiful **St. John the Baptist Ukrainian Catholic Church** (Rte. 23A just east of Lexington, 518/263-3862, www.brama.com/stjohn). The church was built in 1962 in memory of Ukrainians killed by Communists in World War II. The entire edifice, with its rich brown cedar shingles, onion domes, and steeply pitched roofs, was constructed without nails in the traditional Ukrainian manner. The interior features a stunning hand-carved altar, along with wood carvings and icons. On Saturday evenings in July and August, classical chamber music concerts are presented in the adjacent *Grazhda,* or community center, and on Sunday, a brunch buffet with dumplings, borscht, and other Ukrainian specialties is laid out after Mass.

EAST ON ROUTE 23

Route 23A cuts east to west across the northern part of the Catskill Mountains. If you want to loop back to Palenville, passing through some spectacular scenery along the way, take Route 23 east from Lexington.

Ashland

Heading east along Route 23, you'll pass a wide and wonderful waterfall on the right known as **Red Falls.** At its base is a deep, dark swimming hole. From the waterfall, Route 23 winds through the hamlet of Ashland, an excellent place to stop to take photographs of the iconic Catskills scenery.

Windham

Route 23 continues past Ashland to the busy ski resort village of Windham. More upscale than Hunter, Windham is filled with Greek Revival buildings, ski lodges, and restaurants.

Windham Mountain Resort (33 Clarence D. Lane Rd., 518/734-4300, www.windhammountain.com) is considerably smaller than Hunter Mountain, but it's also less hectic. The resort offers 54 trails, a 3,100-foot (940 m) summit, and 97 percent snowmaking capability.

There are numerous dining options in Windham. The restaurant concepts themselves, as well as hours, vary by season, so check the website (www.windhammountaininn.com) for current restaurants and service hours.

★ **Albergo Allegria B&B** (43 Rte. 296, off Rte. 23, a half mile east of Windham,

518/734-5560, www.albergousa.com, $99-179), a charming Victorian manor house that feels more like an inn than a B&B, is in a rural setting on the outskirts of town. Twenty-one guest rooms are nicely done up in period antiques. Downstairs is a comfortable lounge with overstuffed couches and a fireplace… and don't miss the guest pantry, which is stocked with homemade cookies and other snacks.

Cairo

Between Windham and Cairo (KAY-ro), Route 23 turns from scenic to spectacular as it traverses the big wide slopes of Windham High Peak, Burnt Knob, and Acra Point. Expansive Helderberg Valley opens up below, while the Green Mountains of Vermont and the White Mountains of New Hampshire make themselves visible on the horizon. A scenic overlook is located midway.

At Acra, you can continue east directly into Cairo, or loop south through the community of Round Top, once known for its German resorts, one or two of which are still in operation. The hamlet's foremost accommodation, however, is the wonderful ★ **Winter Clove Inn** (2965 Winter Clove Rd., Round Top, 518/622-3267, www.winterclove.com, $110-145 pp including all meals, weekly rates available), a big white colonial sitting on a hillside. Owned by the same family since 1830, Winter Clove has swimming pools, tennis courts, a nine-hole golf course, hiking trails, and an antique bowling alley.

Buddhist Temple

Just beyond the town of Cairo, off Route 23B, is Ira Vail Road and signs that will lead you to the **Mahayana Temple at South Cairo** (700 Ira Vail Rd., 518/622-3619, www.mahayana.us, daily 8:30am-6pm), the retreat of the Eastern States Buddhist Temple of America, based in New York City. The red-and-gold enclave sits in a peaceful woodsy area at the end of a dirt road. Not far from the red-gated entrance are the serene Lake of Fortune and Longevity and the Pagoda of Jade Buddha.

To one side are the Grand Buddha Hall and several smaller temples.

A plaque at the Grand Hall tells the story of the Yings who immigrated to the United States from China in 1955, only to find no organized Buddhist temple in New York. Seven years later they founded the first, at 64 Mott Street in New York City's Chinatown, and soon thereafter built the Mahayana retreat.

Inside the Grand Hall is an altar laden with three golden Buddhas, fruit, and flowers. Two monks in orange robes sit against one wall. The retreat actively welcomes visitors, as the many unobtrusive donation boxes attest.

Don't leave the Mahayana retreat without visiting the fascinating Five Hundred Arhats Hall. Here, 500 golden Buddhas, each one different from the next, sit in a darkened room lit only with small spotlights.

EAST DURHAM

On Route 145, about 5 miles (8.1 km) northwest of Cairo, is the village of East Durham. At first, nothing seems too out of the ordinary in this scenic spot surrounding by rolling hills, but then you start to notice one shamrock after another, one green building after another, one Irish name after another: O'Sullivan, Kelly, McGrath, McGuire, O'Connor, McLaughlin, Ryan, O'Shea. Ethnic resorts may be dying out in the Catskills, but someone forgot to tell East Durham.

Variously nicknamed Ireland's 33rd County, the Irish Catskills, or the Irish Alps, East Durham and environs have been an Irish resort since the late 1800s, when immigrants living in New York City escaped the summer heat by coming up here to the hills that reminded them of home. Much of this tourist trade died down in the 1970s with the advent of affordable flights to Ireland, but it's recently begun to enjoy a resurgence, thanks to a new wave of Irish immigrants to New York.

Guaranteed Irish

One unique stop in the village center is **Guaranteed Irish** (2220 Rte. 145, 518/634-2392, Apr.-Dec. daily, Jan.-Mar. weekends only), which bills itself as "the largest Irish import store in the United States." Inside this sprawling building you'll find everything from Irish sweaters and china leprechauns to an excellent selection of Irish music and literature. Most everyone who shops here seems to have at least a touch of Irish brogue, so even if you don't intend to buy, it's great fun just to listen.

Entertainment and Events

The **MJQ Irish Cultural & Sports Centre** (2267 Rte. 145, 518/634-2286, www.mjqirish-culturalcenter.com) presents theater, music, dance, and sporting events.

Irish music can also be heard at many of the casual pubs along Route 145, or the more formal lounges situated in the village's resorts.

The popular **East Durham Irish Festival** (518/634-2286, www.eastdurhamirishfesti-val.com), featuring Irish bands, bagpipes, and dancers, takes place over Memorial Day weekend.

Food and Accommodations

Gavin's Irish Country Inn (118 Golden Hill Rd., off Rte. 145, 518/634-2582, www.gavins.com, $99-269) offers lodging and meals, as well as live music several nights a week. **Shamrock House** (2388 Rte. 145, 518/634-2897, www.shamrockhouse.com, $75-189, rates depend upon guest's desire to include meals), owned by the Kellegher family since 1938, is a well-kept motel with a restaurant, pub, and live Irish music on weekends.

Upper Hudson Valley

The quiet Upper Hudson Valley feels distinct from both the Lower Hudson Valley and the Catskills. In fact, it feels like a perfect blend of the two. In the small towns of the Upper Hudson, you'll still find river villages with stellar views, gorgeous estates dating back to an earlier era which you can tour with a guide, and quaint shops and galleries where you can shop for everything from local literature to sculptures hewn from the region's wood. The overall atmosphere is pastoral, the pace unhurried, and the natural and artificially constructed attractions always worth pulling over for.

CATSKILL

The town of Catskill, the Greene County seat, sits on the sloping banks of the Hudson River at the mouth of Catskill Creek. The natural harbor here helped the town grow steadily after its founding in the late 1600s. By the early 1900s, Catskill was the prosperous home of small knitting factories, brickyards, and distilleries.

During Prohibition, the town was known for its "retailers of liquid damnation." Catskill applejack was brewed in the hills surrounding town and buried in jugs whenever the law came around. The lucrative moonshine trade coupled with the inaccessible hills made Catskill a favorite haunt of New York City gangsters Legs Diamond and Vincent Coll. Diamond was once tried in the **Greene County Courthouse,** an imposing neoclassical building that still stands at the corner of Main and Bridge Streets.

Today, the town feels worn around the edges, but it retains a distinct charm. Besides the courthouse, **Main Street** showcases one big wooden building after another, many housing friendly, old-fashioned businesses. **Catskill Gallery** (398 Main St., 518/943-3400, www.greenearts.org, Mon.-Fri. 10am-5pm, Sat. noon-5pm, free), run by the Greene County Council on the Arts, presents exhibits, concerts, readings, and plays throughout the year. Running parallel to Main Street is **Spring Street,** a treasure trove of Victorian homes. In the summer, check out the **Hi-Way Drive-In Theater** (10699 Rte. 9W, Coxsackie,

Upper Hudson: Columbia County

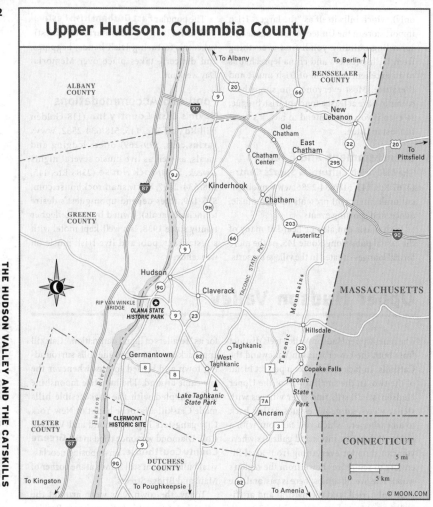

518/731-8672, www.hiwaydrivein.com, May-Oct. nightly, $10 adults, $5 children 3-11, show starts at dusk), which offers four screens and FM radio-generated audio for the double features shown nightly, complete with dancing popcorn and games of chance during intermission.

Cedar Grove

The father of the Hudson River School, Thomas Cole, lived in Catskill much of his adult life. Born in England in 1801, Cole came

to New York City in 1818. He taught himself to paint landscapes, and in 1825 took his first sketching trip up the Hudson. The works he produced on that trip won him instant recognition.

Cole's former home, **Cedar Grove** (218 Spring St., 518/943-7465, www.thomascole. org, days, hours, and rates vary by season) is a big yellow-and-white house with a wide veranda overlooking the Hudson. The house features exhibits on Cole and his family, other Hudson River artists such as Frederic Church,

Hudson

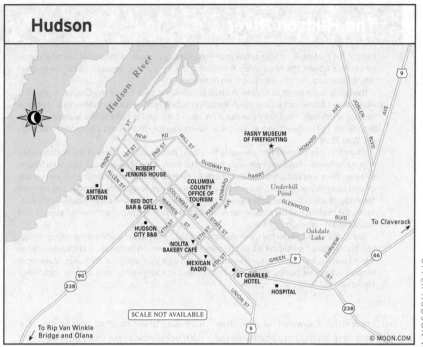

and the Catskills. Also on display are a few small works by Cole and memorabilia such as his paint box and Bible. Out back is Cole's old studio, housed in what were once enslaved people's quarters.

ATHENS

About 4 miles (6.4 km) north of Catskill on Route 385 is the attractive village of Athens. At one time or another, the town has been a center for brick-making, shipbuilding, ice-harvesting, and mushroom-growing (grown in icehouses, after the advent of refrigeration).

Today, Athens feels like a smaller, sleepier version of Catskill. Its streets, too, are lined with big old wooden buildings, many of them from the Victorian age. Route 385 south of Athens parallels the Hudson at water level, offering splendid views of the river and the 1874 **Hudson-Athens Lighthouse** (located in the Hudson River, 518/828-5294, www. hudsonathenslighthouse.org, tours offered in summer, adults $25, children $15).

Downtown, right on the Hudson's shore, is the Victorian **Stewart House** (2 N. Water St., 518/567-1642, www.stewarthouse.com, lunch $15, dinner $24). Downstairs is a formal dining room and a more casual bar/bistro area where contemporary American fare is served. There is also a small **hotel** ($249-349) on the property. Its nine rooms each feature views of the Hudson River and have queen beds.

HUDSON

Hudson is one of the most interesting towns along its namesake river. Once a whaling port and 19th-century boomtown, the town has been gentrified by New Yorkers seeking second homes. Today, amid handsome antiques stores and weathered Victorian buildings, proud descendants of whalers and Manhattan weekenders live side by side.

The Dutch began arriving in Hudson in the 17th century, but the town wasn't really settled until the 1780s, when a group of seafaring New Englanders seeking a harbor safe

The Hudson River

Most of the Hudson River isn't a river at all but an estuary, or arm of the sea; ocean tides run as far north as Albany. The Algonquins, recognizing this natural phenomenon, called the Hudson "Muhheakantuck," or "the river that flows both ways."

Navigable as far north as Albany, the Hudson begins at Lake Tear of the Clouds atop Mount Marcy in the Adirondacks. Only 315 miles (505 km) long from its source to New York Harbor, it varies in width from 2 feet (0.6 m) to about 2 miles (3.2 km), and in depth from a few inches to 216 feet (66 m). The Hudson's widest point is at Haverstraw Bay; its deepest is between Newburgh and West Point.

When European settlers first arrived in New York, they found the banks of the Hudson—like all the Northeast—lined with primeval forest. The trees were of gargantuan size, with foliage so dense there was virtually no undergrowth. By the mid-1800s, most of those trees were gone, cleared away for agriculture. Then came the Industrial Revolution, and cities, towns, and factories sprang up all along the river, bringing with them increasingly toxic levels of pollution. By the early 1970s, the Hudson had become, in the words of one local newspaper, a "flowing cesspool that was the shame of the Empire State."

Today, thanks largely to the Clean Water Act of 1972 and the work of the nonprofit organization Riverkeeper, the Hudson is a much cleaner place. Towns no longer spew untreated sewage into its waters, and factories have significantly reduced their chemical discharge. Much work remains to be done, but the Hudson is now regarded as a "recovering" river with an "improving" environmental condition.

from British attack discovered the area's deep waters and steep bluffs. They purchased the land in 1783; by the following spring, several families had arrived and built homes.

Many of the new settlers were Quakers who carefully designed their new city to be a shipping center, complete with straight main streets, a shipyard, wharves, and warehouses. In 1785, Hudson received the third city charter granted in New York State, and by 1790, 25 schooners—most in the whaling business—were registered in the city. In 1797, Hudson missed becoming the capital of New York State by one vote.

By the mid-1800s, the whaling industry had all but disappeared, but the coming of the railroads enabled an industrial transformation. Business boomed until the early 1900s, when industrial demands changed and Hudson began a slow decline. In the 1980s, the city was rediscovered by New Yorkers seeking refuge and began its rebirth.

Warren Street

The heart of downtown Hudson and the gentrification process is Warren Street, lined

with one historic building after another. On the block closest to the river, there's a Greek Revival mansion with a "widow's walk" that once belonged to a whaling captain (No. 32). Along the 100 block alone are a federal-style brick house with "eyebrow" windows (No. 102), a Queen Anne clapboard house with attractive trim (No. 114), and a rare Adam-style house with an ornamental marble frieze (No. 116).

The 1811 **Robert Jenkins House** (113 Warren St., 518/828-9764, Apr.-Oct. Sat. 1pm-5pm, or by appointment, $4 suggested donation) is home to a small local history museum. Exhibits include paintings by several lesser-known Hudson River School artists, the jawbone of a whale, General Grant's "personal table," and other curious odds and ends.

★ Olana State Historic Site

Perched high on a hill just south of Hudson is **Olana State Historic Site** (5720 Rte. 9G, 518/828-0135, www.olana.org, grounds: year-round daily 8am-sunset, parking fee may apply in summer and fall; house: mid-May-early Nov. Tues.-Sun. 10am-5pm, hours vary off-season, adults $15, seniors and students $8, children under 12 free; $5 vehicle fee May-Oct. Sat.-Sun.), an eccentric, Persian-style castle built in 1870 by landscape artist Frederic Church, with the help of architect Calvert Vaux. Church was then at the height of his career and had just returned from a trip to the Middle East, a land with which he had fallen in love.

A tour of Olana begins in the formal greeting room, which is hung with a dozen paintings, including one by Church's teacher and the founder of the Hudson River School, Thomas Cole. Here, a guide explains that one of the largest contributions the Hudson River School made to the United States was its portrayal of the wilderness as something approachable and worth preserving; before, it had been regarded as hostile and dangerous. One of Church's most famous paintings, of Niagara Falls, was used to spearhead a movement to save the falls from destruction.

Throughout the castle, painted in deep blues, reds, and yellows, are romantic arched doorways, wide-open windows, stenciled Persian lettering, and plush Persian rugs. Every room is filled with unique objects carefully picked out by the artist, who one critic said had the "best taste of his time." Each room also houses a number of Church's majestic, luminous canvases. The dining room is an amazing picture gallery, hung floor to ceiling with hundreds of canvases from the 16th to 18th centuries.

FASNY Museum of Firefighting

The delightful, spit-and-polish **FASNY Museum of Firefighting** (117 Harry Howard Ave., 518/822-1875, www.fasnyfiremuseum.com, daily 10am-4:30pm, adults $10, children 3 and older $5, family $25) boasts the nation's largest collection of firefighting equipment and related paraphernalia, including dozens of exquisite old horse-drawn fire carriages, many equipped with fairy-tale finery. Several carriages sport engraved lanterns and velvet-covered seats. One even has silver- and gold-plated hubcaps.

Part of the museum's charm is its location on the grounds of New York's retirement home for volunteer firefighters. You'll see the retirees hanging out on the porch as you drive up, and you'll meet them as you tour the museum. From them you'll learn that 80 percent of New York State's firefighters are still volunteers, a fact that poses a serious problem,

Olana State Historic Site

as the demands of firefighting are not compatible with busy modern-day lives.

Shopping

In recent years, Warren Street has become a destination for antiques lovers; dozens of stores of varying quality are located here, most between 5th and 7th Streets. Among them are **Theron Ware Gallery** (548 Warren St., 518/828-9744, www.theronwarehudson.com), specializing in classic Americana and ornate European antiques, and **Ornamentum** (506 Warren St., 518/671-6770, www.ornamentumgallery.com), part jewelry store and part art gallery. The two-story **Carrie Haddad Gallery** (622 Warren St., 518/828-1915, www.carriehaddadgallery.com) exhibits paintings, photographs, and sculpture by both established and up-and-coming artists.

Food

As the commercial hub of the community, it's not surprising that the area's best restaurants are along Warren Street. A good place for breakfast is **Nolita Bakery Cafe** (454 Warren St., 518/828-4905, daily 7:30am-4pm, $9).

At the sleek and trendy ★ **Red Dot** (321 Warren St., 518/828-3657, www.reddotrestaurant.com, Mon. and Wed.-Sun. 5pm-10pm, Sat.-Sun. 11am-3pm, $22), you can order everything from calamari to Thai curried vegetables.

Accommodations

The Victorian ★ **Hudson City B&B** (326 Allen St., 518/822-8044, www.hudsoncitybnb.com, $125-175) was built by Joshua Waterman, a former Hudson mayor, in the 1860s. Outside, find a wide veranda lined with wicker chairs. Inside, find a parlor with a fireplace and guest rooms filled with antiques.

Built in the late 1800s, the redbrick **St. Charles Hotel** (16-18 Park Pl., 518/822-9900, www.stcharleshotel.com, $105-139, with continental breakfast) offers simple, adequate rooms.

KINDERHOOK

The charming village of Kinderhook, or "children's corner," was first settled by the Dutch, a fact reflected in the town's neat tree-lined streets, historic wooden buildings, and laid-back atmosphere. The village's most famous native son was Martin Van Buren, and signs directing visitors to the former president's birth site, home, and gravesite are everywhere. It is to Van Buren, nicknamed "Old Kinderhook," that we owe the expression "O.K."

To reach Kinderhook from Hudson, take Route 9 north about 10 miles (16.1 km).

Martin Van Buren National Historic Site

Martin Van Buren, a tavern owner's son who rose to hold the highest office in the land, spent the last 21 years of his life in this large yellow house surrounded by linden trees, now called the **Martin Van Buren National Historic Site** (1013 Old Post Rd., 518/758-9689, www.nps.gov/mava, grounds: daily 7am-dusk, free; house: late May-Oct. 31 9am-4pm daily, free). Before Van Buren bought the property in 1839, Washington Irving had often visited here, sometimes even tutoring the former residents' children.

A visit to Lindenwald, as the house is known, begins with a short film on the "Little Magician" (Van Buren was only 5 ft 6 in/168cm), who avidly supported Jeffersonian democracy, served as vice president under Andrew Jackson, and established the country's independent treasury. In his day, Van Buren was regarded as a cool and competent diplomat who operated most effectively behind the scenes, "row[ing] to his object with muffled oars."

A fine collection of musical instruments is in the sitting room, all done up in elegant gold and light blue. A magnificent French wallpaper mural depicting a hunting landscape is in the banquet room, which is kept dark at all times to preserve the mural, which can only be viewed by flashlight.

Luykas Van Alen House

Also off Route 9H, just north of Lindenwald, is the **Luykas Van Alen House** (Rte. 9H, 518/758-9265, www.cchsny.org, early July-mid-Oct. Sat.-Sun. noon-4pm, $12 ticket includes visit to Ichabod Crane School House, $15 ticket includes visit to Ichabod Crane School House and James Vanderpoel House, see below), a 1737 Dutch farmhouse complete with a steeply pitched roof, wide chimneys, delft tile, and sturdy furnishings. If the place looks familiar, it's because it was used in Martin Scorsese's film *The Age of Innocence*, based on the Edith Wharton novel.

In front of the farmhouse is a dark and peaceful pond that's home to several swans; to one side is the one-roomed **Ichabod Crane School House.** Washington Irving apparently based his famous character on a schoolteacher from Kinderhook; the building has been restored to look as it did in the 1920s.

Downtown Historic Sites

The 1820 **James Vanderpoel House** (16 Broad St., 518/758-9265, by appointment, see above for ticket prices) is by the village green. Vanderpoel, a contemporary of Martin Van Buren, was a prominent attorney, state assemblyman, and judge. The house is an excellent example of federal-style architecture and contains an interesting collection of period furnishings and paintings by early area artists.

Nearby is **Columbia County Historical Society Museum and Library** (5 Albany Ave., 518/758-9265, Mon.-Wed. and Sat.-Sun. 10am-4pm and by appointment, free), housed in what was once a Masonic temple. Changing exhibits focus on the county's history and culture.

Food and Accommodations

The log cabin **Carolina House** (59 Broad St., 518/758-1669, www.carolinahouserestaurant.com, Tue.-Thurs. 5pm-9pm, Fri.-Sat. 5pm-10pm, Sun. 4:30pm-9pm, $24) is a family-owned local favorite that attracts diners from miles around. Contemporary American fare is featured on the menu, which also has a vegetarian and gluten-free section.

Housed in an 1852 colonial farmhouse is **Mile Hill B&B** (2461 Mile Hill Rd., 917/691-8757, www.milehillbandb.com, $150-255), offering two guest rooms and a pool on the grounds.

THE CHATHAMS

To the east of Kinderhook, in a countryside of rolling hills and horse farms, are the Chathams: the village of Chatham, Chatham Center, East Chatham, North Chatham, and Old Chatham. Old Chatham, settled in 1758, is little more than a crossroads; the village of Chatham is the Chathams' commercial hub. During the late 1800s, over 100 trains a day passed through here on their way to Albany or Boston. The streets are still lined with Italianate brick storefronts dating back to that era.

Near East Chatham is **Librarium** (126 Black Bridge Rd., 518/392-5209, www.thelibrarium.com, hours vary seasonally), a homey book barn with over 35,000 used titles. There are also picnic tables on-site where you can enjoy your lunch should you so choose.

Columbia County Fair (junction of Rtes. 66 and 203, 518/392-2121, www.columbiafair.com) comes to the Chatham fairgrounds over Labor Day weekend. It's the nation's oldest continuously running county fair.

Accommodations

The **Inn at Silver Maple Farm** (1871 Rte. 295, East Chatham, 518/781-3600, www.silvermaplefarm.com, $129-389) is an 1830s dairy farm turned lovely B&B where a Shaker aesthetic meets modern amenities. Complete with pine floors, exposed beams, and hand-painted murals, the inn is surrounded by fields and woods. The rooms are airy and comfortable, while a deck offers scenic views of the Berkshire Mountains.

Camping is available in nearby Austerlitz at the 200-site **Woodland Hills Campground** (386 Fog Hill Rd., 518/392-3557, www.whcg.net, $36/night).

Information and Services

For general information on the region, contact **Hudson Valley Tourism** (845/615-3860, www.travelhudsonvalley.com).

County tourism offices and websites include the following:

- **Westchester County Tourism** (148 Martine Ave., Ste. 104, White Plains, 914/995-8500 or 800/833-9282, www.visitwestchesterny.com)

- **Rockland County Tourism** (18 New Hempstead Rd., New City, 845/708-7300, www.explorerocklandny.com)

- **Orange County Tourism** (124 Main St., Goshen, 845/615-3860 or 800/762-8687, www.orangetourism.org)

- **Putnam County Visitors Bureau** (110 Old Rte. 6, Carmel, 845/225-0381, www.putnamcountyny.com)

- **Dutchess County Tourism** (3 Neptune Rd., Poughkeepsie, 845/463-4000, www.dutchesstourism.com)

- **Columbia County Tourism** (401 State St., Hudson, 518/828-3375, www.columbiacountytourism.org)

Hudson Valley (www.hvmag.com) is a glossy monthly magazine about the region, available at area newsstands. Its restaurant and shop listings are especially useful. *Edible Hudson Valley* (https://ediblehudsonvalley.ediblecommunities.com) is another regional magazine, with information about local food, restaurants, and attractions such as wineries.

Getting There and Around

The easiest way to explore the Hudson Valley is by car. However, many towns along the east bank of the Hudson River and some in Westchester's Harlem Valley are reached by trains that depart from Grand Central in Manhattan. On the west banks of the Hudson, communities in Rockland and Orange Counties (Tuxedo, Harriman, Salisbury Mills, Campbell Hall, Middletown, Otisville, and Port Jervis) are serviced by **Metro-North Railroad** (212/532-4900 or 800/638-7646, www.mta.info/mnr), which leaves from Manhattan's Penn Station. Taxis are usually available at the villages' railroad stations. **Amtrak** (800/872-7245, www.amtrak.com) provides rail service between New York City and more than 40 stations in the Hudson Valley.

If traveling up Metro-North's Hudson Line, sit on the left-hand side of the train car. The railroad hugs the eastern shoreline and offers spectacular views.

Trailways (800/225-6815, www.trailways.com) and **ShortLine Bus** (800/631-8405, www.coachusa.com/shortline) offer daily bus service between Manhattan's Port Authority Bus Terminal and many Hudson Valley communities.

Travelers can opt to fly into either New York City's JFK or LaGuardia airports or Stewart International or Albany International Airport. Among the major airlines flying into Stewart are **Delta** (800/221-1212), **JetBlue** (800/538-2583), and **USAir** (800/428-4322); those flying into Albany are **Delta** (800/221-1212), **Southwest** (800/435-9792), **United** (800/241-6522), and **USAir** (800/428-4322).

The Capital-Saratoga Region

Central New York State benefits from both the glory days of Hudson River and Erie Canal commerce, as well as the beauty of its riparian landscapes. Plus, there's Albany's political intrigue and Saratoga's social strutting during summer horse-racing season. And it's close enough to New York City for a quick getaway.

Still, residents tend to feel slighted by travelers, who aren't quite sure where the region begins and ends, much less what single characteristic sets it apart from better-known getaways like the Hudson Valley, the Catskills, and the Adirondacks. Because it doesn't have a singular, cohesive identity, it's easy to skip the region altogether.

That would be a mistake. This part of the state is worth visiting

Albany.................231
Saratoga Springs
    and Vicinity..........242
Central New York.......255
Information
    and Services.........267
Getting There
    and Around..........267

Highlights

Look for ★ to find recommended sights, activities, dining, and lodging.

★ **Take in the view:** Love it or hate it, you've got to appreciate the sheer, Rockefeller-ian ambition that made the **Empire State Plaza** possible, especially when viewed from Corning Tower's observation deck (page 234).

★ **See the State Capitol Building:** The centerpiece of the stunning castle-like edifice is its stone staircase, hand-carved with 300 tiny faces, each different from the next (page 235).

★ **Head off to the races:** For more than 150 years, the **Saratoga Race Course** has turned an entire town into a summer destination, sweeping up all of its visitors in its equine traditions (page 245).

★ **Get in the water at Saratoga Spa State Park:** There's more to this park than its Grand Georgian hotel. It also boasts 2,200 acres filled with mineral baths, swimming pools, and hiking trails (page 247).

★ **Have dessert at New Skete Monastery:** This region of New York gave rise to many spiritual and utopian communities. This one is alive and well and worth a visit for its cheesecake, which you buy on the honor system (page 253).

★ **Root for your home team:** The massive and enthusiastic **National Baseball Hall of**

Fame and Museum wins over even those who don't root, root, root for a home team (page 258).

because so much history happened here, and it's documented and shared so passionately. This is where the United States claimed the first major victory of the Revolutionary War. Nearly 60 years later, this is where New York's abolitionist movement was fostered. It's where both state and national political careers have been born (and died). It's where passionate folks in tiny towns build museums and shrines to the people and creeds they believe in, from the most secular (baseball and boxing) to the most sacred (the Eastern Orthodox religion). To travel the region is to be treated to the full throes of these passions, which can't help but rub off on you.

PLANNING YOUR TIME

The Capital-Saratoga region doesn't appear as road-trip friendly as some of the state's other regions, mainly because the key attractions look like random scatter plots on a map. Visitors shouldn't be discouraged by this fact, however; well-maintained interstates (including I-87 and I-90) and secondary roadways connect noteworthy cities and towns, making for fast travel. Most of the top spots to visit are clustered in and just around downtown zones. Comfortable accommodations are often right alongside them, making it easy for travelers to maximize their time and get the most out of a visit.

Albany is the ideal stopover, an urban home base for exploring the region. Though not exactly equidistant to the other main points of interest, it's just off the interstate, allowing quick access to other towns and cities recommended here. Plus, the capital's hotels, restaurants, and services offer lots of options for a range of budgets.

The Capital-Saratoga region is increasingly promoting itself as a four-season destination, and, in fact, there *is* plenty to see and do here year-round. Keep in mind, though, that summer months are when the region really shines. It's this season when most attractions are open daily, with longer hours, and when the area's most famous sights and experiences—especially Saratoga's horse racing—are polished up for an influx of visitors. Plan on three full days to see the highlights of Capital-Saratoga, which could be an extension of a Hudson Valley visit or your gateway to the Adirondacks or Catskills.

Albany

From a distance, Albany looks like just another average, midsize city clustered around a handful of high-rise office buildings, but beneath its calm surface you'll find a surprisingly complex soul. Albany, as William Kennedy writes in *O Albany!*, is "as various as the American psyche itself, of which it was truly a crucible."

The oldest city in New York and one of the oldest in the nation, Albany is located at the head of the navigable portion of the Hudson River. This strategic position has shaped much of its history, both colonial and industrial. Explorer Henry Hudson arrived in 1609, and by the mid-1600s, the Dutch settlement of Fort Orange had become a flourishing trading post. The Erie Canal and the railroad cemented Albany's role as a hub of early American industry. Irish immigrants settled here while building the canal, and thousands more Irish and Germans arrived with the coming of the Industrial Revolution. Factories manufacturing everything from checkers and dominoes to textiles and woolens lined the Hudson during this manufacturing boom. The WPA's *A Guide to the Empire*

Previous: New York State Capitol Building in Albany; the gardens at Yaddo; Cooperstown's Main Street.

The Capital-Saratoga Region

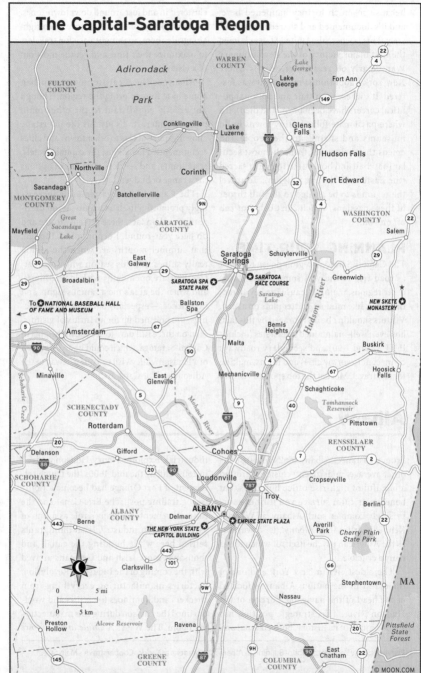

FULTON COUNTY

WARREN COUNTY

Adirondack

Park

Lake George

Lake George

Fort Ann

22
4

149

Conklingville

Lake Luzerne

Glens Falls

Hudson Falls

30

Northville

Corinth

87

Fort Edward

Sacandaga

MONTGOMERY COUNTY

Batchellerville

9N

32

4

Mayfield

Great Sacandaga Lake

SARATOGA COUNTY

9

WASHINGTON COUNTY

22

Salem

30

East Galway

29

Saratoga Springs

Schuylerville

29

29

Broadalbin

SARATOGA SPA STATE PARK

SARATOGA RACE COURSE

Saratoga Lake

Greenwich

Hudson River

NEW SKETE MONASTERY

To ★ NATIONAL BASEBALL HALL OF FAME AND MUSEUM

Ballston Spa

5

Amsterdam

67

Bemis Heights

Buskirk

90

50

Malta

67

Hoosick Falls

Minaville

East Glenville

Mechanicville

Schaghticoke

5

40

Tomhannock Reservoir

SCHENECTADY COUNTY

9

87

Pittstown

Rotterdam

Mohawk River

RENSSELAER COUNTY

20

Gifford

Cohoes

7

2

Delanson

20

90

Loudonville

Cropseyville

88

SCHOHARIE COUNTY

787

Troy

Berlin

ALBANY COUNTY

Delmar

ALBANY

Empire State Plaza

Averill Park

22

443

Berne

THE NEW YORK STATE CAPITOL BUILDING

Cherry Plain State Park

MA

443

66

101

Clarksville

Stephentown

0   5 mi

9W

Nassau

0   5 km

Alcove Reservoir

Ravena

20

Pittsfield State Forest

Preston Hollow

145

GREENE COUNTY

9H

87

90

East Chatham

22

COLUMBIA COUNTY

© MOON.COM

Albany

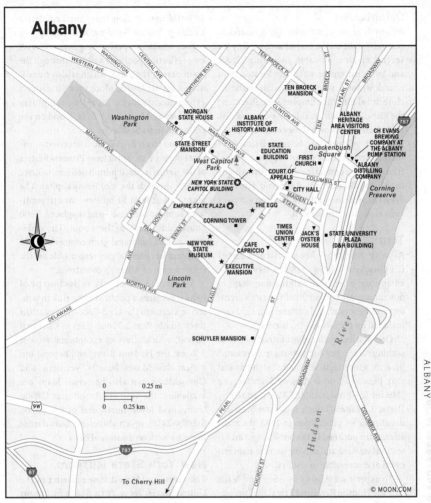

State reported that Albany's population doubled between 1820 and 1830.

It's not surprising, then, how many famous figures got their start in Albany. The city was an early home to writers Herman Melville, Bret Harte, and Henry James. Presidents Martin Van Buren, Millard Fillmore, Grover Cleveland, Theodore Roosevelt, and Franklin Roosevelt all got their starts here, and President Chester A. Arthur is buried here.

Today, Albany is home to a large branch of the State University of New York (SUNY), and as part of New York's "Tech Valley," it's diversifying its traditional economic base. As the state capital, though, Albany's main business is government. Come here at lunchtime when the legislature is in session and you'll see thousands of workers hurrying out for a sandwich and a few moments of sun. Alliances are made and deals are forged over meals and drinks; this is a city notorious for political wheeling and dealing.

Orientation

Albany is an easy city to navigate, thanks to generally light traffic and its accessibility via several major interstates, including 87, 88, and 90. Most visitor sights are located in or near downtown, where the most dramatic architectural lures are Empire State Plaza and the Capitol, which sit side by side on a hill. From here, downtown slopes eastward to the river, whose banks are being reclaimed for recreation. Hudson River Way is a pedestrian bridge connecting downtown Albany to Albany Riverfront Park and Corning Preserve, and the Mohawk Hudson Bikeway runs along the river as well.

Tours

Albany Heritage Area Visitor Center (25 Quackenbush Sq., 518/434-0405, www. albany.org) offers free walking tour maps of downtown. More than 20 of the city's architectural, historical, and cultural highlights are included on the self-guided itinerary.

One of Albany's foremost attractions is its architecture. A few highlights are mentioned here; for a thorough, self-guided architectural tour, pick up a copy of *Albany Architecture* (Mount Ida Press, 518/426-5935), edited by Diana S. Waite. Though it has not been updated since its publication in 1993, the main attractions outlined in the book's eight architectural walking and driving tours remain relevant and accessible to visitors.

To experience Albany by water and learn why the Hudson River and Erie Canal were so central to the city's early growth, take a tour with **Dutch Apple Cruises** (boarding at Broadway and Quay St., 518/463-0220, www. dutchapplecruises.com).

SIGHTS
★ Empire State Plaza

Dominating downtown Albany is **Empire State Plaza** (between Eagle and Swan Sts., Madison Ave. and State St.), the extravagant brainchild of Governor Nelson Rockefeller. An enormous marble platform sitting atop a hill, the plaza covers 98.5 acres and includes 10 buildings, among them the Legislative Building, Justice Building, and The Egg—a round, whimsical performing arts center. A long reflecting pool cuts a ribbon through the main part of the plaza, which is also a destination for art lovers. More than 90 abstract expressionist works, including sculptures by Calder and Noguchi, can be found on the plaza and in its buildings.

Legend has it Rockefeller conceived of the plaza during a 1959 visit from Princess Beatrix of the Netherlands: It humiliated him to drive royalty through the moldering capital. The plaza cost at least $1 billion—an extraordinary sum for the time—and displaced 3,600 households, many of them poor. The ambitious project generated great controversy, but the plaza has been largely responsible for the rejuvenation of Albany's downtown.

Visitors can relax by the **reflecting pool** (which becomes a public skating rink in winter) or ascend to the 42nd-floor **observation deck** (daily 9am-2:30pm, free) in **Corning Tower,** which offers an exceptional view of Albany, the Hudson River, and beyond (on a clear day, Massachusetts, Vermont, and Connecticut can also be seen). Maps are available at the **Visitors Assistance Office** (concourse level, north end of the plaza, 518/474-2418), which also offers tours during the workweek on a seasonal basis.

New York State Museum

The oldest and largest state museum in the United States, **New York State Museum** (222 Madison Ave., 518/474-5877, www.nysm. nysed.gov, Tues.-Sun. 9:30am-5pm, suggested donation $5) is located on Madison Avenue at the southern end of Empire State Plaza. Spread out over a maze of high-ceilinged rooms, it's packed with life-size dioramas, multimedia shows, historical artifacts, and scientific specimens of all types.

• As might be expected, a large part of the museum's collection is comprised of artifacts and ephemera from "New York's natural and human heritage." Permanent exhibits are dedicated to topics as diverse as Native

Americans, birds of New York, the Harlem Renaissance, and the 2001 terrorist attacks on the World Trade Center; the museum also hosts about a dozen temporary exhibits annually. One popular stop for visitors with kids is The Carousel, which features 40 animals, two chariots, and a round tub. It's free and runs every 15 minutes during museum hours.

★ New York State Capitol Building

The stunning **State Capitol Building** (tours: 518/474-2418, Mon.-Fri. 10am, noon, 2pm, and 3pm, free, reservations recommended) sits on State Street at the northern end of Empire State Plaza. Begun in 1867, the castle-like edifice required 32 years and $25 million to complete; it is one of only a handful of capitols in the United States that does not have a dome. A clutch of architects, including Thomas Fuller, Henry Hobson Richardson, and Frederick Law Olmsted, participated in the design, which explains its diverse—but ultimately cohesive—collage of architectural styles.

Capitol tours lead visitors past gold-leaf walls of the Senate Chamber and granite columns of the Assembly Chamber before culminating at the "Million Dollar Staircase." Here, 300 tiny, hand-carved faces smile, glare, or stare at passersby. Seventy-seven of the faces are of famous figures, including Susan B. Anthony, Frederick Douglass, Abraham Lincoln, and Walt Whitman, but most are anonymous, and each is different from the next.

Free tours and free self-guided audio tours are available. Be prepared to pass security clearance and present an ID.

Albany Institute of History & Art

One of the oldest museums in the United States, founded in 1791, **Albany Institute of History & Art** (125 Washington Ave., 518/463-4478, www.albanyinstitute.org, Wed. and Fri.-Sat. 10am-5pm, Sun. noon-5pm, adults $10, seniors and students $8, children

6-12 $6, children under 6 free) is housed in an elegant beaux arts building and contains some wonderful gems, including many paintings by artists of the Hudson River School. Early works of American portraiture are in the museum's collection, along with Dutch ceramics, Albany-made silver, and New York-made furniture. Changing exhibits on the Hudson Valley and Capital District are also featured.

Discover Albany Visitor Center

The **Discover Albany Visitor Center** (25 Quackenbush Sq., at Broadway and Clinton Ave., 518/434-0405, www.albany.org, Mon.-Fri. 9am-4pm, Sat. 10am-3pm, Sun. 11am-3pm) is a good place to learn about Albany's history and culture. This large, refurbished water pumping station contains informative exhibits on everything from the city's ethnic heritage to its industrial past, as well as cultural curiosities, such as the tale of the modern billiard ball, invented in Albany in 1868.

Albany Distilling Company

The city's first licensed distillery since Prohibition, **Albany Distilling Company** (ADC, 78 Montgomery St., 518/621-7191, www.albanydistilling.com, free tours on Sat. must be reserved in advance, online) is a small but passionate operation where craft spirits are made. Local New York State ingredients go into ADC's bourbon and whiskey, while their rum is made from Caribbean molasses. The founders and distillers give tours and offer tastings on Saturdays and by appointment; their facility is adjacent to the wildly popular C. H. Evans Brewing Company at Albany Pump Station.

USS *Slater*

Albany's waterfront is home to the country's only restored World War II destroyer escort, the **USS *Slater*** (Broadway and Quay St., 518/431-1943, www.ussslater.org, Apr.-Nov. Wed.-Sun. 10am-4pm, adults $9, seniors $8, children 6-14 $7, children under 6 free), which is open to the public for guided

tours. The galley and mess hall, officers' and sailors' quarters, and watch and battle stations all have objects from the destroyer's active period.

Albany Riverfront Park and Corning Preserve

From downtown Albany, walk across the Hudson River Way, a pedestrian bridge, to reach these two Hudson River parks. In them you'll find walking/biking trails, picnic tables, exercise stations, and panoramic views of the Hudson, often busy with fishing boats, college crew teams, private yachts heading to and from the Erie Canal, and, at times, the *Half Moon*, an exact replica of the ship Henry Hudson used to reach Albany in 1609. Free concerts are presented during summer at the 1,000-seat riverfront amphitheater. A restaurant on a barge is at Corning Preserve's north end.

The entrance to Hudson River Way is off Broadway, not far from the visitors center; note the lampposts, each of which tells about a different episode in Albany history.

New York State Executive Mansion

One block south of Empire State Plaza is the governor's mansion, New York State Executive Mansion (138 Eagle St., tours: 518/473-7521, Sept.-June Thurs. only, 11am, noon, 1pm, and 2pm, free), open to the public by reserved tour only. An impressive Italianate building with a wraparound porch, the mansion dates to 1856, when it was constructed as a private residence. The state purchased the property in 1877, and each successive governor has put his stamp on it: Theodore Roosevelt built a gym; FDR sunk a pool; and animal lover Al Smith installed a zoo.

Free tours of the mansion are arranged through Empire State Plaza's visitor services center. Reservations must be made two weeks in advance of the tour.

1: Empire State Plaza in Albany **2:** USS *Slater* **3:** New York State Capitol Building **4:** the Tulip Festival at Washington Park

Schuyler Mansion

The gracious 1761 Georgian Schuyler Mansion (32 Catherine St., 518/434-0834, May-Oct. Wed.-Sun. 10am-5pm, adults $5, seniors $4, children 5-12 free) is perched on a hill that once offered a great view of the Hudson. The home, now a State Historic Site, was built by Philip Schuyler, a leading Albany citizen and general during the Revolutionary War. Daniel Webster once honored Schuyler as "second only to Washington in the services he performed for his country," but Schuyler was relieved of his duties and court-martialed for ordering the evacuation of Fort Ticonderoga. A probable victim of political infighting, Schuyler was eventually acquitted, though he resigned his post.

Schuyler Mansion hosted major political players of the day—Benjamin Franklin, Benedict Arnold, George Washington, Aaron Burr—and served as a prison for General Burgoyne following the British surrender at Saratoga. Schuyler's daughter Elizabeth married Alexander Hamilton here.

Historic Cherry Hill

To the south of downtown Albany stands homey, colonial-era Historic Cherry Hill (523 S. Pearl St., 518/434-4791, www.historiccherryhill.org, tours on Wed. and Sat. afternoons, adults $5, seniors $4, students $2, children 6-17 $1), which recently underwent a decade of extensive renovation. Built in 1787 by Philip and Mary van Rensselaer, the house was home to five generations of the van Rensselaer and Rankin families; the last member died in 1963.

The frugal van Rensselaers had a hard time throwing anything away. Inside, you'll find an odd assortment of furnishings from all five generations. Highlights include early Dutch tiles, a striking sleigh bed, turn-of-the-20th-century swimming trunks, 1920s postcards, and an early Castro convertible. The kitchen is equipped with both a colonial-era wall oven and a freestanding gas stove.

Lark Street

Two blocks west of Empire State Plaza is Lark Street, Albany's bohemian hub, lined with an eclectic array of small shops, restaurants, and nightclubs. Most are located in the eight blocks between Madison and Washington Avenues. Lark Street sits on the edge of Center Square, a prosperous residential neighborhood notable for its fine architecture. Some of the best examples stand along State Street between Lark Street and Empire State Plaza. In these two short blocks you'll find one opulent 19th-century home after another, many designed by Albany architects Charles Nichols, Albert Fuller, and Ernest Hoffman.

Washington Park and State Street

Continue another block west of Lark Street to **Washington Park,** a lush green oasis considered an "Olmstedian" style park, given the influence of famed landscape architect Frederick Law Olmsted on its design. Curved roads, wooded glades, open meadows, ornate gardens, and Washington Lake can all be found on its 90 acres. Though not original to the park's 1870s beginnings, **Lake House,** an extravagant terra-cotta affair with pink terrazzo floors and wrought-iron chandeliers, is also found here.

State Street's opulence continues along the north side of the park. Highlights include **Grange Sard Jr. House** at No. 397, designed by Henry Hobson Richardson, and No. 441, the work of William Ross Proctor.

Ten Broeck Mansion

The imperial, federal-style **Ten Broeck Mansion** (9 Ten Broeck Pl., between Ten Broeck and N. Swan Sts., 518/436-9826, www.tenbroeckmansion.org, May-Oct. Thurs.-Fri. 10am-4pm, Sat.-Sun. 1pm-4pm, Nov.-Apr. by appointment, adults $5, seniors and students $4, children 5-12 $3) stands on the north side of Albany, in the city's Arbor Hill neighborhood. It was built for Abraham Ten Broeck and his wife Elizabeth van Rensselaer in 1797-98. Ten Broeck served as a general in the Continental Army and later as state senator, judge, and mayor of Albany.

Now owned by Albany County Historical Association, the mansion contains a fine collection of period furniture and showcases changing historic exhibits. Tours, free with admission, are given on the hour. Curiosities include a snug wine cellar that wasn't rediscovered until the 1970s. Its rare contents were sold for $42,000; proceeds were used to restore the house.

Nipper

All along Broadway in northern Albany hulk old factory buildings dating back to the city's era of industrial activity. A highlight is the former **RTA Building** (991 Broadway, at Loudonville Rd.). RTA was a distributor of RCA electrical appliances, and on the building's roof sits a 25-foot-high (8 m), four-ton statue of Nipper, the canine symbol of the RCA-owned Victor Company. Nipper's head is cocked to the side and he wears a quizzical expression, as if to ask, "What am I still doing here?" The statue was built in Chicago around 1858 and shipped in five sections on railroad flatcars.

ENTERTAINMENT

The city's best sources for information about entertainment are the Thursday and Sunday editions of *The Times-Union* (518/454-5694, www.timesunion.com).

Performing Arts and Film

The Egg (Empire State Plaza, Madison Ave. and Swan St., 518/473-1845, www.theegg.org), named for its shape, is the capital's premier arts venue. It houses two theaters; one has 982 seats and the other is more intimate with 450 seats. Both present a wide range of music, theater, and dance.

The **Capital Repertory Theatre** (111 N. Pearl St., 518/445-7469, www.capitalrep.org) presents classical, contemporary, and world-premiere works October-June. The company performs in the 286-seat Market Theater, formerly a grocery store.

The Shakers

Brought "across the pond" from England, 19 official Shaker communities sprang to existence in the United States in the 18th century, with most in Ohio, Kentucky, and parts of the Northeast, including the communities of New Lebanon and Albany. American Shakers lived a pacifist communal life and believed in equality of the sexes, common ownership of property and goods, innovation in agriculture and manufacturing, confession of sins, simplicity in their own mannerisms and dress, and celibacy. Living in rural colonies consisting of several "families" of non-blood-related members who occupied separate quarters based on sex, Shakers sought to avoid corruption in the outside world.

New Lebanon, in the capital region's Columbia County, is just a few miles from the New York-Massachusetts border. Established in 1785, New Lebanon was one of the earliest Shaker communities and an organizational, architectural, and spiritual model for those that followed. Though no Shakers live at Mt. Lebanon Shaker Village (202 Shaker Rd., New Lebanon, 518/794-9100, www.shakerml.org, mid-June-early Oct. Fri.-Mon. 10am-4pm, adults $10, seniors $8, children under 13 free) today (the last Mt. Lebanon Shaker died in 1947), the site is a National Historic Landmark with a museum open to the public. Visitors can learn more about the community through guided tours that lead visitors through the North, Center, and Church Family buildings, as well as the Meetinghouse, which has a unique arched roof.

Watervliet Shaker National Historic District (25 Meeting House Rd., 518/456-7890, www.shakerheritage.org, Tues.-Sat. 9:30am-4pm, $5 suggested donation), just outside Albany in the town of Colonie, is the capital region's other significant Shaker community and North America's first Shaker settlement, established in 1776. It too is a national historic site open to the public. During its height, this Shaker settlement was active not only in the women's rights movement, but in abolition, and recent research confirmed that Watervliet was a safe haven for fugitive enslaved people.

In Watervliet, eight sturdy, clean-lined Shaker buildings still stand, grouped around a crossroads. The splendid 1848 Meeting House has been converted into a visitors center, where you'll find a small exhibit area, a gift shop offering Shaker crafts, and a large hall where Shakers once held their meetings. Bleacher-style rising seats in back were set aside for "World's People"—nonbelievers—who often came to meetings to watch and listen to the Shakers' music. Today, the hall is used for Shaker concerts, workshops, and crafts shows. One of the most important features of this site is its cemetery, where spiritual leader Mother Ann Lee is buried. Visitors can also take self-guided tours, picnic on the grounds, and browse or pick up a free walking tour map in the gift shop.

The 1931 Palace Theatre (19 Clinton Ave., 518/465-3334, www.palacealbany.com), which seats 2,800, was once an opulent movie palace. Today, it's home to the Albany Symphony Orchestra and host to touring concert acts, Broadway shows, and movies.

Tiny Albany Civic Theater (235 2nd Ave., 518/462-1297, www.albanycivictheater.org), occupying a converted turn-of-the-20th-century firehouse, presents four theater productions every year. Each runs just three weeks; tickets sell out quickly.

Times Union Center (51 S. Pearl St., 518/487-2000, www.timesunioncenter-albany.com) is a multipurpose facility with adaptable seating arrangements that can accommodate crowds ranging in size from 6,000 to 17,500. Concerts, family shows, sporting events, and trade shows are presented.

Nightlife

On Lark Street, long Albany's center for nightlife, you'll find a wide variety of restaurants and bars, including Bomber's Burrito Bar (258 Lark St., 518/463-9636, www.bombersburritobar.com, daily 11am until at least 12:30am), featuring a tequila and beer bar in addition to burritos. LGBTQ-friendly Oh

Bar (304 Lark St., 518/463-9004, www.ohon-lark.com, Mon.-Wed. 2pm-3am, Thurs.-Sat. 2pm-4am, Sun. 2pm-3am) features an outdoor patio and garden.

Other LGBTQ-friendly bars in Albany are found on Central Avenue, including the city's oldest gay bar, Waterworks (76 Central Ave., 518/465-9079, www.waterworkspub.com, daily 1pm-4am), and Rocks (77 Central Ave., 518/472-3588, www.rocks77.com, daily 2pm-4am).

Lark Tavern (453 Madison Ave., 518/694-8490, www.albanylarktavern.com, Mon. 3pm-2am, Tue.-Sat. 11am-2am, Sun. noon-2am) hosts live music acts and has trivia and comedy nights each week; it also has a full-service dining room where lunch and dinner are served.

Albany's Warehouse District is a popular place to spend the evening. All of the following watering holes are located on Broadway between Clinton and Pleasant Streets: The Olde English Pub and Pantry (683 Broadway, 518/434-6533, www.theoldeenglish.com, Mon.-Sat. 10am-2am, Sun. 10am-midnight), German-style Wolff's Biergarten (895 Broadway, 518/427-2461, www.wolffsbiergarten.com, Mon.-Fri. 11am-2am, Sat. 9am-2am, Sun. 9am-midnight), and Irish pub Graney's Stout (904 Broadway, 518/427-8688, www.graneysbarandgrill.com, Mon.-Tue. 11:30am-1am; Wed.-Thurs. 11:30am-2am; Fri.-Sat. 11:30am-4am; Sun. noon-1am).

EVENTS

Albany celebrates its Dutch heritage with the impressive Tulip Festival (518/434-1217), held in early May.

Throughout the summer, free concerts (518/474-2418) and other special events are staged at Empire State Plaza. Park Playhouse (518/434-2035) presents free musicals and plays at Lake House in Washington Park in July and August.

Fairgrounds in the nearby village of Altamont (fairs: 518/861-6671, www.

altamontfair.com) host some of the region's top special events. Among them are the Old Songs Festival of Traditional Music and Dance in June, Altamont Fair in August, and Capital Region Scottish Games in early September. The fairgrounds also host local craft beer and wine fests in the fall.

FOOD

★ Jack's Oyster House (42 State St., 518/465-8854, www.jacksoysterhouse.com, daily 11:30am-10pm, $34) is a classic downtown seafood restaurant frequented by legislators. Run by the same family for more than 100 years, the restaurant serves up lunch and dinner against a backdrop of white tablecloths, tiled floors, and big pane-glass windows. Reservations are recommended.

New World Bistro Bar (300 Delaware Ave., 518/694-0520, www.newworldbistrobar.com, Sun.-Thurs. 5pm-9:30pm, Fri.-Sat. 5pm-10pm, $28), near Lark Street, offers "global soul food" using seasonal and sustainable products, many from regional farms. There's an extensive small plate menu, as well as a number of gluten-free and vegan options.

C. H. Evans Brewing Company at the Albany Pump Station (19 Quackenbush Sq., 518/447-9000, www.evansale.com, Mon.-Thurs. 11:30am-11pm, Fri.-Sat. 11:30am-midnight, Sun. noon-8pm, $23) is a popular microbrewery and full-service restaurant (think pasta, beef, and burgers) with a 120-year family heritage. It's located in the building that once housed the original pumping station for Albany Water Works.

Modern, upscale Cafe Capriccio (49 Grand St., 518/465-0439, www.cafecapriccio.com, Sun.-Thurs. 5pm-9pm, Fri.-Sat. 5pm-10pm, $28) is a local favorite specializing in Northern Italian fare. Angelo's 677 Prime (677 Broadway., 518/427-7463, www.677prime.com, Mon.-Fri. 11:30am-2pm and 5:30pm-10pm, Sat. 5:30pm-10pm, $39) is Albany's go-to upscale restaurant for steak and seafood. Its wine list features more than 400 varieties.

Yono's (25 Chapel St., 518/436-7747, www.

yonos.com, Mon.-Sat. 5:30pm-11pm, $36) is headed up by a husband-wife team whose menu features Indonesian specialties alongside French and continental dishes inspired by Chef Yono's travels. Diners can order à la carte or enjoy the chef's tasting menu accompanied by a vintage from the 600-bottle-strong wine list.

ACCOMMODATIONS

There's much to recommend about the **Hilton Albany** (40 Lodge St., 518/462-6611, www.hiltonalbany.com, $169-285). First is the hotel's unbeatable location, within comfortable walking distance to Empire State Plaza, the Capitol, and numerous downtown restaurants and attractions. Size (385 rooms and suites), service (extensive breakfast buffet), and amenities, including free wireless Internet, are also notable. Some higher-floor rooms and suites have exceptional views of the Hudson River, Capitol, or other architectural stunners, like the Albany Home Savings Bank building.

Elegant, 19th-century **Morgan State House** (393 State St., 518/427-6063, www.statehouse.com, $160-260) on Washington Park has both rooms and full suites. If traveling with children, this inn is not a good option, as kids under 16 are not allowed.

Neoclassical **State Street Mansion** (281 State St., 518/462-6780, www.statestreetmansion.com, $105-175) dates to 1881. It offers seven guest rooms; several are "European plan," which means they share a bathroom with another room. All guests receive a free continental breakfast each morning.

Historic **Century House** (997 New Loudon Rd./Rte. 9, Latham, 518/785-0931, www.thecenturyhouse.com, $129-149), a third-generation family-run property with a pool and tennis court, is just outside Albany in the town of Latham. The mansion makes use of an 1800s public house as the base for its handsome restaurant and federal-style tavern, serving hearty, tasty meals with a gourmet flair and great attention to detail. The hotel features a complimentary hot country breakfast buffet with chef on hand for special requests. A 1.5-mile (2.4 km) nature trail is also on-site.

★ **Desmond Hotel and Conference Center** (660 Albany-Shaker Rd., 518/869-8100, www.desmondhotels.com, $145-185), a lovely hotel-inn filled with period furnishings, artwork, rich dark-wood paneling and warm, top-quality service, is convenient to Albany's airport. Faux Colonial Williamsburg villages form charming interior courtyards around airy fountains, garden seating, and poolside lounging. Many rooms feature balconies or private patios. The large property has two heated indoor pools, a health club, and several dining options, including Simpson's Grille and The Tavern, both serving casual American fare. Wireless Internet, parking, and an airport shuttle are all free for guests.

About 15 minutes east of Albany is ★ **Gregory House Country Inn** (3016 Rte. 43, Averill Park, 518/674-3774, www.gregoryhouse.com, $115-125), a gracious homestead and modern inn with 12 nicely appointed guest rooms. On-site are a popular Italian restaurant called La Perla. Wireless Internet and continental breakfast are included in the room rate.

VICINITY OF ALBANY
John Boyd Thacher State Park

For terrific views of the Hudson and Mohawk Valleys, head 18 miles (29 km) west of Albany to **John Boyd Thacher State Park** (1 Hailes Cave Rd., Voorheesville, 518/872-1237, www.parks.ny.gov/parks/128, daily 7am-sunset, nature center open Tues.-Sun. 9am-5pm, parking $6). Here, you'll also find the unusual **Indian Ladder Geologic Trail** (May-mid-Nov. daily, weather permitting), a half-mile-long ledge that is one of the richest fossil-bearing formations in the world.

For most of the year, Saratoga Springs is a charming Victorian town known for its first-rate arts scene, grand romantic architecture, sophisticated shops and restaurants, and therapeutic mineral springs. Come summer, though, the town turns itself upside down with buyers and sellers of dreams. From dawn until dusk, and then from dusk until dawn, gossiping socialites, shrewd business-people, and innocent tourists mix with breeders, trainers, and grooms . . . all for the love of horses.

The Saratoga Race Course, built in 1864, is the country's oldest racetrack, and it has long represented the very best of what racing has to offer. Louisville may have its Kentucky Derby, Baltimore its Preakness, but serious horse fans come to Saratoga for six weeks of exclusive racing. Attendance at the sprawling, Victorian-era grandstand—complete with striped awnings, clapboard siding, and gilded cupolas—swells the town's population of 28,000 to one million during summer months.

Saratoga is slower but no less interesting once the horses are back in their stables. Arts thrive at the Saratoga Performing Arts Center, Skidmore College, and Yaddo, a renowned artists' retreat. The town also supports several fine museums, Saratoga Spa State Park, and a number of good hotels and B&Bs, as well as a robust local food culture. Surrounding Saratoga is lush, rolling countryside offering more cultural, historical, and scenic attractions. Best known among them is the Saratoga National Historical Park, where the 1777 battles that turned the course of the Revolutionary War were fought.

Orientation
Saratoga Springs is a compact city. The main avenue is Broadway, lined with bustling shops and restaurants. At one time, Broadway was flanked with one grand hotel after another. Today, only the 1877 Adelphi (365 Broadway, www.theadelphihotel.com) remains. Other buildings worth noting along Broadway include the 1916 classical revival Adirondack Trust, No. 473, adorned with Adirondack symbols and bronze Tiffany doors, and the 1910 beaux arts post office, No. 475. At Lake Avenue, across from the post office, is the 1871 Italian palazzo city hall, birthplace of the American Bankers Association and the American Bar Association.

The track lies to the east of downtown, off Union Avenue, while Saratoga Spa State Park is to the south, off South Broadway (Rte. 9). The Thruway (I-87) passes within a few miles of the city.

Park downtown in large, free lots between Broadway and Circular Street.

The **Saratoga County Chamber** (28 Clinton St., 518/584-3255, www.saratoga.org) operates an **information booth** (Broadway near the entrance to Congress St., June-Sept. daily 9am-5pm, extended hours during racing season).

SIGHTS
Heritage Area Visitor Center
A good place to start a tour of Saratoga is at the **Heritage Area Visitor Center** (297 Broadway, 518/587-3241, www.saratogaspringsvisitorcenter.com, May-Nov. Mon.-Sat. 9am-6pm, Sun. 10am-3pm, free), housed in Drink Hall, where mineral waters were once sold. Back then, different waters were recommended for different times of the day: Hathorn in the morning, Coesa before dinner, and Geyser in the evening.

Today, the beaux arts hall with its barrel-vaulted ceiling is filled with history exhibits and racks bursting with tourism brochures. Free walking tour maps pinpointing the area's springs and other points of interest can be picked up here.

Congress Park

Congress Park (Broadway and Congress St., 518/587-3241), directly across from the visitor center, is a small jewel of a retreat filled with lawns, graveled walkways, and flowering plants. In the center of it all reigns the Italianate redbrick Canfield Casino, now home to Saratoga Springs History Museum.

One of the oldest parks in the country, Congress Park dates back to 1792 when Nicholas Gilman, a member of the first U.S. Congress, "discovered" and named Congress Spring. Then along came Gideon Putnam, who in 1806 bought swampland next to the spring, siphoned off some of its waters, and built Saratoga's first mineral-water bathhouse. In 1876, Frederick Law Olmsted completely redesigned the park, replacing old structures with high Victorian Gothic buildings. Tours of the park are offered in summer.

Canfield Casino

Lavish **Canfield Casino** in Congress Park was built by John Morrissey in 1870 as an adjunct to his new racetrack. One writer of the day described the place as having "gorgeously furnished toilet rooms, faro parlors, and drawing rooms."

Fabulous sums were won and lost in the casino's gaming rooms, and many "Monte Carlo suicides" were said to have been committed. Before the casino was shut down in 1907, Canfield purportedly netted the then-enormous profit of $2.5 million.

Today, the casino houses **Saratoga Springs History Museum** (1 E. Congress St., Congress Park, 518/584-6920, www.saratoga-history.org, Feb.-Mar. Sat.-Sun. 10am-4pm, Apr.-May Wed.-Sun. 10am-4pm, Memorial Day-Labor Day daily 10am-4pm, adults $8, seniors $7, students $5, children under 12 free). Downstairs, temporary exhibits focus on the history and culture of Saratoga. Upstairs are period rooms and an oddball collection of artifacts, including Egyptian spears, bullets from Battles of Saratoga, and old gaming tables.

Tang Teaching Museum and Art Gallery

The dynamic **Tang Teaching Museum and Art Gallery** at Skidmore College (815 N. Broadway, 518/580-8080, www.tang.skidmore.edu, Tues.-Wed. and Fri.-Sun. noon-5pm, Thurs. noon-9pm, suggested donation adults $5, seniors $2, children over 12 $3, children under 12 and students free) hosts contemporary art exhibits and cultural events, all

Victorian architecture along Union Avenue in Saratoga Springs

Saratoga Springs

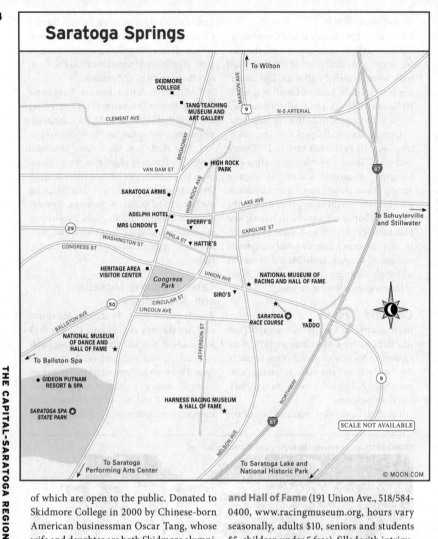

To Wilton

SKIDMORE COLLEGE

TANG TEACHING MUSEUM AND ART GALLERY

CLEMENT AVE

MARION AVE

N-S ARTERIAL

BROADWAY

VAN DAM ST

HIGH ROCK PARK

HIGH ROCK AVE

SARATOGA ARMS

87

ADELPHI HOTEL

MRS LONDON'S

29

SPERRY'S

LAKE AVE

To Schuylerville and Stillwater

CAROLINE ST

WASHINGTON ST

PHILA ST

HATTIE'S

CONGRESS ST

HERITAGE AREA VISITOR CENTER

Congress Park

UNION AVE

NATIONAL MUSEUM OF RACING AND HALL OF FAME

50

CIRCULAR ST

LINCOLN AVE

SIRO'S

JEFFERSON ST

SARATOGA RACE COURSE

YADDO

BALLSTON AVE

NATIONAL MUSEUM OF DANCE AND HALL OF FAME

To Ballston Spa

9

GIDEON PUTNAM RESORT & SPA

HARNESS RACING MUSEUM & HALL OF FAME

NORTHWAY

87

SARATOGA SPA STATE PARK

NELSON AVE

SCALE NOT AVAILABLE

To Saratoga Performing Arts Center

To Saratoga Lake and National Historic Park

© MOON.COM

of which are open to the public. Donated to Skidmore College in 2000 by Chinese-born American businessman Oscar Tang, whose wife and daughter are both Skidmore alumni, the museum is dedicated to "fostering interdisciplinary thinking." The permanent collection includes works in a wide range of media, while temporary exhibits focus on everything from pop art to site-specific installations.

National Museum of Racing and Hall of Fame

Even non-racing fans will want to step into the one-of-a-kind **National Museum of Racing** **and Hall of Fame** (191 Union Ave., 518/584-0400, www.racingmuseum.org, hours vary seasonally, adults $10, seniors and students $5, children under 5 free), filled with intriguing exhibitions on the history and mechanics of thoroughbred racing. Learn why all thoroughbreds trace their origins to one of three Arabian progenitors and how, at a full gallop, a horse takes in five gallons of air a second. Exhibits on racing champs tell stories of Man o' War and Secretariat, Seattle Slew and Affirmed, while exhibits on Saratoga tell of the resort town's gambling heyday.

In summer, the museum offers **tours**

The Wickedest Summer Resort

Saratoga Springs didn't really take off until the 1860s, when prizefighter, gambler, and general roustabout John Morrissey built the Saratoga Race Course. The track was a near-instant success and was soon joined by elaborate gambling casinos and posh, block-long hotels where fluttering socialites danced with hard-nosed gamblers beneath crystal chandeliers.

Saratoga regulars included prominent horsemen such as William R. Travers, financiers such as J. Pierpont Morgan, actresses such as Lillian Russell, and high rollers such as Diamond Jim Brady, who sometimes wore as many as 2,548 diamonds with his evening outfits. New York City reporters, including intrepid Nellie Bly of the *New York World,* were dispatched to Saratoga to file stories about the country's "Wickedest Summer Resort."

By the early 1900s, the vice-fueled fun seemed to be over. A reform movement closed down casinos, some springs dried up due to excessive commercial pumping, and the fashionable crowd moved on.

New York State intervened, establishing a state reservation to preserve the largest cluster of springs in 1909. Over the next 25 years, the state transformed the reservation into Saratoga Spa State Park, complete with a hotel and two magnificent bathhouses. Saratoga's golden era of the spa began, with people coming from all over to take "the cure": drinking mineral waters, soaking in baths, and exercising. Casinos were also in full swing again, this time under control of gangsters like Lucky Luciano and Dutch Schultz.

Saratoga suffered another decline after World War II as interest in spa therapy declined and casinos were shut down again, this time for good. Only the racecourse mustered on, with races held every August without fail.

Saratoga's many charms were rediscovered by a new generation in the 1960s, when old Victorian buildings were snatched up and renovated, and a new wave of socialites and vacationers moved in.

(summer Wed.-Sun. 8:30am, $10 pp) of the training track.

TOP EXPERIENCE

★ Saratoga Race Course

The nation's oldest thoroughbred track, **Saratoga Race Course** (267 Union Ave., 518/584-6200, www.nyra.com/saratoga), comes to life every mid-July through early September. Most U.S. tracks present one weekly stakes race, featuring top-of-the-line horses; Saratoga has one every day. The meet's highlight is the Travers Stakes, held on the fifth Saturday; other big events are the Whitney, the Alabama, and the prestigious Fasig-Tipton yearling sales.

Saratoga, filled with striped tents and bright flowers, remains one of the world's best tracks for a close-up view of the horse-racing world. Thoroughbreds are walked through the crowd before being saddled in the paddock, and jockeys stop to talk and sign autographs between races.

Breakfast at the track is a race-day tradition. Early access and the long-standing honor system policy of reserving a shaded picnic table with a personal item ensure visitors a comfortable spot to enjoy the day. A buffet breakfast is served 7am-9:30am on the Porch of the Clubhouse. Thoroughbreds prepare for races in sight, with workout commentary offered during the meal. A much-anticipated bonus of the breakfast is the free 45-minute tram and walking tour of the historic stable area post-toast. The first tour leaves the main Clubhouse entrance at 7:30am; additional trams leave approximately every 15 minutes until 9am. Trams run on a first-come, first-served basis and often fill to capacity early.

Yaddo

Just east of the racetrack lies the artists' retreat **Yaddo** (312 Union Ave., 518/584-0746,

YADDO

SARATOGA
CASINO AND
RACEWAY

www.yaddo.org, garden and grounds tours $10, days and hours vary by season), housed in a Victorian Gothic mansion that was once home to Spencer and Katrina Trask. Spencer was a New York financier and philanthropist, Katrina a poet.

Artists come to Yaddo to get away from the noisy outside world and work in uninterrupted peace. About 4,000 writers, composers, and visual artists have enjoyed residencies here since the program began in 1926, including James Baldwin, Sylvia Plath, and Laurie Anderson.

The house is off-limits to the public, but visitors are welcome to stroll through an Italian garden, featuring over 100 varieties of roses, and a rock garden planted with flowering perennials. Wistful marble statues and a picturesque fountain provide other photo ops.

Saratoga Casino and Raceway

South of the main track stretches the half-mile-long **Saratoga Casino and Raceway** (342 Jefferson St., 518/682-8888, www.saratogacasino.com), a foremost trotting track. Opened in 1941, the track features evening racing February-December with a short break in January. Some of the track's top races take place during the thoroughbred meet.

On-site is also **Saratoga Harness Hall of Fame** (352 Jefferson St., 518/587-4210, July-Sept. Tues.-Sat. 11am-3pm, hours vary off-season, free). On display are antique horseshoes, racing silks, high-wheel sulkies, and other memorabilia. One exhibit honors Lady Suffolk, the "Old Grey Mare" of folk-song fame, who raced in Saratoga in 1847.

National Museum of Dance and Hall of Fame

South Broadway leads out of downtown and past the **National Museum of Dance and Hall of Fame** (99 S. Broadway, 518/584-2225, www.dancemuseum.org, June-Oct.

Tues.-Sun. 10am-4:30pm, adults $10, seniors and students $8, children under 12 $5), the only museum in the country devoted exclusively to professional American dance, including ballet, modern dance, vaudeville, and tap. Housed in Saratoga Spa State Park's former Washington Bathhouse, the museum spreads out over four spacious halls filled with blown-up photographs and plaques. Temporary exhibits hang near the entrance, while TV monitors screening famous performances are featured throughout. The museum also has an interactive kids' wing.

★ Saratoga Spa State Park

More European than American in feel, **Saratoga Spa State Park** (off S. Broadway, just south of downtown, 518/584-2535, www.parks.ny.gov/parks/saratogaspa, hours vary by facility and season, parking $10) spreads out over 2,200 pristine acres, every one of which was meticulously planned. At one end is Avenue of the Pines, flanked with towering green-black trees. At the other, Loop Road leads past a half-dozen mineral springs, each with a different taste, depending on its mineral content.

Saratoga's springs gurgle up from ancient seas trapped in limestone layers sealed by a solid layer of shale. A geological fault line runs through the layers, cracking the shale and allowing water to escape to the surface. The limestone enriches the water with minerals, and carbon dioxide adds natural carbonation. Most of the springs bubble up in Congress Park, High Rock Park, and Saratoga Spa State Park. Some are marked by pavilions, others by fountains, and each has its own distinct taste. A complete guide to the springs and their reputed therapeutic values can be picked up at Saratoga Springs' **Heritage Area Visitor Center** (297 Broadway, 518/587-3241, www.saratogaspringsvisitorcenter.com).

The mineral baths remain the heart of the park. **Roosevelt Baths** (518/584-3000 or 800/452-7275, www.gideonputnam.com, daily 9am-7pm, treatments $35-410), within walking distance of Gideon Putnam Hotel,

1: one of Saratoga's many springs 2: the entrance to Yaddo 3: the Union Avenue entrance of Saratoga Race Course

Racing Season

Saratoga Race Course, the country's oldest racetrack, is a cultural and historical gem enjoyed by thoroughbred horse-racing aficionados and betting novices alike. With an attendance capacity of 50,000, this hot spot was named one of the top 10 sporting venues in the world by *Sports Illustrated,* and it retains its old-world charm. Here are some tips to make the most of your day at the races.

Track Basics: The 40-day season starts in mid- or late July and runs through early September. Races are held daily, except Tuesdays. The venue opens at 11am weekdays, 10:30am weekends, and post time is 1pm. General admission is $7; clubhouse admission is $10. A dress code is enforced for box seat and clubhouse ticket holders; details are available on the course's website (www.nyra.com).

For general information during the meet, call Saratoga Race Course at 518/584-6200. For advance ticket sales, contact **New York Racing Association** (718/641-4700, www.nyra.com).

Parking and Traffic: New York Racing Association maintains large parking lots across from the track; prices vary according to proximity. Parking is also available in many private lots surrounding the track. You can park for free at Saratoga Casino and Raceway, which has ample lots, and take the free shuttle to the racecourse. If you're *not* planning to go to the track, avoid traffic-clogged Union Avenue between noon and 1pm, and again around 5:30pm.

Seating: Most of the nearly 7,000 reserved seats in the grandstand and clubhouse are sold by mail in January. However, about 1,000 grandstand seats go on sale every race day at the track's Union Avenue entrance. On weekdays, tickets are often available until post time; on weekends, they're typically gone by 10 or 11am.

Many fans bring lawn chairs, blankets, and coolers to the shady grounds behind the track, which are equipped with large, flat-screen TVs. Others watch the races on their feet, then retreat to benches near the betting windows.

How to Bet: Easy-to-follow instructions are printed inside *Post Parade,* the daily program, available at the gate. Minimum bets are $1.

After the Races: The most popular racetrack hangout is **Siro's** (168 Lincoln Ave., 518/584-

includes a fitness center and private rooms and tubs, where clients relax in bubbling golden-brown waters, indulge in algae body wraps, and enjoy muscle-relief treatments.

Victoria Pool (late June-early Sept. daily 10am-6pm, adults $8, children $4), embellished with colored tiles, romantic archways, and a small café, is near the park's center. Even on the hottest days, the pool often remains uncrowded, partly because the park also boasts a second, larger pool—**Peerless Pool** (late June-early Sept. Wed.-Mon. 10am-6pm, free), adjoined with diving and wading pools. **Catherine's in the Park** (58 Roosevelt Dr., 518/583-4657, Mon.-Tues. 11am-6pm, Wed.-Sun. 11am-6:30pm, $12) is a convenient lunch spot near the pools, offering soups and sandwiches.

ENTERTAINMENT
Performing Arts
Saratoga Performing Arts Center (108 Ave. of the Pines, 518/584-9330, www.spac. org) is an outdoor amphitheater with a capacity of 25,000 spectators. As the preeminent performing arts center of the Capital-Saratoga region, SPAC presents the New York City Opera, the New York City Ballet, the Philadelphia Orchestra, and well-known rock, pop, and jazz stars throughout the summer. Picnicking before performances is a Saratoga tradition.

Nightlife
Saratoga has a lively nighttime scene, thanks largely to the presence of Skidmore College and the racetrack. **Caroline Street**

Saratoga Race Course

4030, www.sirosny.com), adjacent to the south side of the track. A long bar is set up beneath a striped canvas tent, and live bands play until about 8:30pm, when the party then moves inside.

Polo Matches: Coinciding with racing season, world-class **polo matches** (518/584-8108, www.saratogapolo.com) take place on Fridays and Sundays at **Saratoga Polo Field** (Bloomfield and Denton Rds.). Most games begin at 5:30pm; gates open at 4pm.

Accommodations: Most hotels and B&Bs double their prices during racing season, and many of the most popular places are booked solid months in advance. Even if you arrive at the last minute, however, you will find something. **Saratoga County Chamber** (www.saratoga.org) maintains an updated list of available rooms.

is especially known for its many clubs and bars, most catering to twentysomethings. **Desperate Annie's** (12-14 Caroline St., 518/587-2455, www.desperateannies.com, daily 4pm-4am), aka DA's, is a popular college and local hangout, complete with pool table. Around the corner, **9 Maple Ave.** (9 Maple Ave., 518/583-2582, www.9mapleave.com, daily 4pm-3am) is the place to go for serious jazz.

Caffe Lena (47 Phila St., 518/583-0022, www.caffelena.com, Wed. 7pm-9:30pm, Thurs. 7pm-11pm, Fri-Sat. 8pm-10:30pm, Sun. 7pm-9:30pm) is the oldest continuously run coffeehouse in the United States, founded in 1960 by Lena Spencer. Little wonder that it was named Best Small Venue in North America by the International Folk Alliance: Bob Dylan played here on his first tour of the East, and Don McLean first played "American Pie" on the café's small stage. Lena is gone now, but her legacy continues with a lineup of top acoustic acts—Odetta, Jimmie Dale Gilmore, Tom Paxton, and others. Small plates, coffees, and desserts are served up alongside music at weekend concerts; self-serve refreshments are offered during "emerging artist" shows.

Big, boisterous **Parting Glass** (40-42 Lake Ave., 518/583-1916, www.partingglasspub.com, Mon.-Thurs. 11am-1am, Fri.-Sat. 11am-2am, Sun. 11am-midnight) has 170 beers and Guinness on tap, along with a wide selection of pub grub. Live music and poker nights keep regulars and visitors entertained.

Lively bar scenes can also be found at many restaurants, including **Siro's** (168 Lincoln

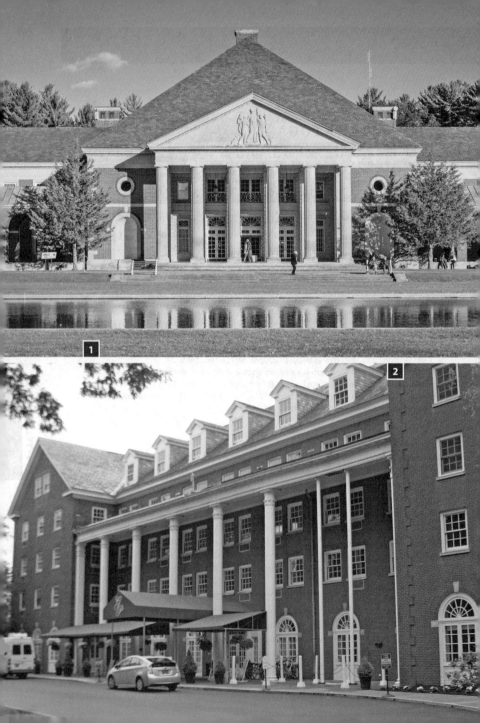

Ave., 518/584-4030, www.sirosny.com, Mon.-Thurs. 11:30am-10:30pm, Fri. 11:30am-11pm, Sat. 5pm-11pm, Sun. 5pm-10:30pm), Cantina (430 Broadway, 518/587-5577, www.cantinasaratoga.com, Sun.-Mon. and Wed.-Thurs. 11:30am-9pm, Tues. and Fri.-Sat. 11:30am-10pm), and Olde Bryan Inn (123 Maple Ave., 518/587-2990, www.oldebryaninn.com, Sun.-Thurs. 11am-10pm, Fri.-Sat. 11am-11pm).

SHOPPING

Broadway is Saratoga's main shopping street, though its side streets hold treasures, too. Lyrical Ballad Bookstore (7 Phila St., 518/584-8779, www.lyricalballadbooks.com), housed in the old Saratoga National Bank building, is a packed-to-the-rafters antiquarian shop that stocks about 30,000 books. Rare volumes are stored in the bank's old safe-deposit vault. Back on Broadway, G. Willikers (461 Broadway, 518/587-2143, www.gwillikerstoys.com) upholds its decades-long tradition of selling toys (plenty of horse-themed games, figurines, and books, of course!), alongside newer specialty shops like Saratoga Olive Oil Co. (484 Broadway, 518/450-1308, www.saratogaoliveoil.com).

FOOD
Bakeries, Breakfast, and Diners
Mrs. London's (464 Broadway, 518/581-1652, www.mrslondonsbakery.com, daily 7am-6pm) offers a mouthwatering selection of desserts, baked goods, and gourmet coffees.

Shirley's Restaurant (74 West Ave., 518/584-4532, Mon.-Sat. 6:30am-8pm, Sun. 7am-1:30pm), open since the 1960s, is a good spot for breakfast, lunch, homemade pies, and Canadian poutine.

Gideon Putnam (24 Gideon Putnam Rd., 518/584-3000, www.gideonputnam.com, Sun. 10:30am-1:30pm, $27.95) is well known for its Sunday brunch buffet. Cheese and pastry options are offered, while egg and carvery stations serve up brunch favorites. Expect an enormous array of options.

Restaurants
★ Hattie's (45 Phila St., 518/584-4790, www.hattiesrestaurant.com, daily 5pm-10pm, $20) has been a Saratoga institution since 1938. This is the place to go for tasty fried chicken, barbecued ribs, catfish, and sweet potato pie.

Another institution is casual Olde Bryan Inn (123 Maple Ave., 518/587-2990, www.oldebryaninn.com, Sun.-Thurs. 11am-10pm, Fri.-Sat. 11am-11pm, $26), housed in a rustic 1825 stone house with dark, thick-beamed ceilings and a big, comfortable bar. The extensive menu features American pub fare and comfort food favorites.

Only open during racing season, ★ Siro's (168 Lincoln Ave., 518/584-4030, www.sirosny.com, Mon.-Thurs. 11:30am-10:30pm, Fri. 11:30am-11pm, Sat. 5pm-11pm, Sun. 5pm-10:30pm, $34-52) boasts the best after-track bar scene, as well as the most exclusive restaurant in town. Featured are both innovative and traditional continental dishes. Reservations are essential.

Max London's Restaurant and Bar (466 Broadway, 518/587-3535, www.maxlondonsrestaurant.com, Sun. 9am-10pm, Mon.-Thurs. 3pm-10pm, Fri.-Sat. 9am-10:30pm, $26) serves consistently tasty pizzas and pastas in a hip atmosphere, as well as a popular weekend brunch.

Cantina (430 Broadway, 518/587-5577, www.cantinasaratoga.com, Sun.-Mon. and Wed.-Thurs. 11:30am-9pm, Fri.-Sat. 11:30am-10pm, $16) is a Victorian barroom with patio seating serving good Mexican cuisine and occasional live music. Ask about Taco Tuesday specials.

The Wine Bar (417 Broadway, 518/584-8777, www.thewinebarofsaratoga.com, Mon.-Sat. 4pm-last call, $19) offers nearly 50 wines by the glass, live music, a smoking lounge, patio dining in season, and a broad menu of small plates and half entrées. An impressive suite with oversize bedroom and full amenities is also available.

1: Roosevelt Baths in Saratoga Spa State Park **2:** the Gideon Putnam hotel in Saratoga Spa State Park

A little pricier than the others, candlelit **Chianti Il Ristorante** (18 Division St., 518/580-0025, www.chiantiristorante.com, Mon.-Thurs. 5pm-9:30pm, Fri.-Sat. 5pm-10:30pm, Sun. 5pm-9pm, $26) is known for authentic Northern Italian cuisine and an award-winning wine list.

ACCOMMODATIONS
Hotels

Well-maintained grounds and friendly staff make **Roosevelt Inn and Suites** (2961 S. Broadway/Rte. 9, 800/524-9147, www.rooseveltsuites.com, $79-99 off-season, $195-255 racing season) a solid choice for reasonably priced lodging. Located a few miles out of town, the hotel has two tennis courts, a pool, health club, and day spa, all of which make this a popular spot for an off-season getaway. **Longfellows** (500 Union Ave., 518/587-0108, www.longfellows.com, $145-165 off-season, $225-265 racing season), with its airy loft rooms built inside a renovated 1915 dairy barn, offers modern amenities and on-site dining.

It's hard to beat **Gideon Putnam** (24 Gideon Putnam Rd., 866/890-1171, www.gideonputnam.com, off-season $99-269, racing season $325-479) for location; the hotel enjoys pride of place in a particularly peaceful part of Saratoga Spa State Park, but is still close to downtown (a five-minute drive when there's no traffic). Rooms are large and comfortable, and a restaurant is on-site for guests who don't feel like venturing out for a meal. The hotel also manages the Roosevelt Baths; spa treatments can be booked directly through the concierge.

Bed-and-Breakfasts

Downtown Saratoga has a plethora of Victorian-era B&Bs. One of the most spectacular is the high Victorian Gothic **Batcheller Mansion Inn** (20 Circular St., 518/584-7012, www.batchellermansioninn.com, $160-245 off-season, $335-425 racing season), which offers nine spacious guest rooms, including one that features a pool table. Equally unique

is the 1901 Queen Anne **Union Gables Inn** (55 Union Ave., 518/584-1558, www.uniongables.com, $165-190 off-season, $335 racing season), notable for its wonderful wide porch, rose garden, and pool. Each guest room has a private bath and small refrigerator; several of the rooms are pet-friendly.

The Brunswick at Saratoga Bed & Breakfast (143 Union Ave., 518/584-6751, www.brunswickbb.com, $109-149 off-season, $229-335 racing season) is a Gothic Victorian home built in 1886; it is particularly popular with horse lovers, as the B&B is directly across the street from the racetrack.

EXCURSIONS FROM SARATOGA
Cambridge

About 25 miles (40 km) east of Saratoga Springs, Cambridge is the official birthplace of pie à la mode. The historic moment occurred one evening in the mid-1890s when Professor Charles Watson Townsend, dining at Hotel Cambridge, ordered ice cream with apple pie; a neighbor eating at the next table dubbed the concoction "pie à la mode." The professor ordered it by its new name during a subsequent visit to Delmonico's in New York City. The waiter had never heard of it and called for the manager, who declared in consternation, "Delmonico's never intends that any other restaurant shall get ahead of it. . . . Forthwith, pie à la mode will be featured on the menu every day." A *New York Sun* journalist, overhearing the conversation, reported it the next day; before long, pie à la mode was a fixture on menus across the country.

Today, Hotel Cambridge sits empty on Main Street, waiting hopefully for a new owner to restore it to its former glory. The hotel's neighbors, however, are evidence of vibrant small-town life and the trend of Main Street restoration movements around the state and country. A prime example is indie bookstore **Battenkill Books** (15 E. Main St., 518/677-2515, www.battenkillbooks.com), which features new titles on a range of topics, as well as magazines, gifts, toys, and a remarkably full schedule of readings, book club meetings, and other events. The bookstore's neighbors include **Cambridge Food Co-Op** (1 W. Main St., 518/677-5731, www.cambridgefoodcoop.com), featuring local, natural, and organic food. There's also **Hubbard Hall** (25 E. Main St., 518/677-2495, www.hubbardhall.org), a rural opera house dating to 1878. Today, the restored hall is host to a wide range of music, dance, and theater events throughout the year, including the popular **Music from Salem** classical series held during the summer, which has featured renowned international chamber music performers.

★ New Skete Monastery

If you wonder whether you've driven into a cultural and geographical warp hole when you happen upon gold, onion-domed structures on a thickly wooded hilltop between Cambridge and Vermont, don't worry: You've just stumbled upon the Eastern Orthodox **New Skete Monastery** (273 New Skete Ln., 518/677-3928, www.newskete.org, grounds: Tues.-Sun. dawn-dusk). Home to a handful of brothers, the monastery centers around a rough-hewn wooden chapel filled with icons painted by the monks. A more elaborate church presides nearby.

Apart from its religious mandate, New Skete's secular claim to fame is dogs. Monks began breeding and training German shepherds shortly after moving here in 1966, when it became apparent they could not support themselves by farming. The business took off, especially after 1978, when one of the brothers wrote a best-selling, award-winning book, *How to Be Your Dog's Best Friend* (Little, Brown). The 2007 TV series *Divine Canine* introduced the New Skete monks to a new generation, renewing public interest in the monastic community.

Though kennels are off-limits to the public, guests can visit the chapel and gift shop. The nuns of New Skete, famous for their cheesecake, run a similar **gift shop** (343 Ash Grove Rd., 518/677-3810). When no staff is present,

the gift shops run on an honor system. New Skete also offers accommodations and meals for visitors who want a quiet retreat of two or more days; reservations must be made in advance and the suggested donation is $70-80 per night. The main church is open during Sunday morning services only.

Stillwater

Battles that turned the course of the American Revolution were fought about 12 miles (19.3 km) southeast of Saratoga. The former battlefield is now part of **Saratoga National Historical Park** (648 Rte. 32, 518/664-9821, www.nps.gov/sara, May-Oct. daily 9am-dusk, weather permitting, free).

In October 1777, British general Burgoyne and his forces marched south from Canada to take control of the Hudson River. They planned to meet Colonel Leger and his forces in Albany and continue to New York City to join General Howe. Instead, just outside Saratoga, General Burgoyne came upon the American forces, 9,000 strong. Led by General Horatio Gates and General Benedict Arnold, the Americans defeated the British in two fierce battles.

A tour of the park begins at the **visitors center** (May-Oct. daily 9am-5pm), where you can watch an informative film. Beyond the center is a 9-mile (14.5 km), self-guided driving tour past strategic points equipped with audio recordings, plaques, and maps. Only a few bunkers remain, but the countryside is exceptionally lovely, especially in late afternoon, when mists roll in from the nearby Hudson River.

Schuylerville

Continue north of the battlefield on Route 4 for about 8 miles (12.9 km) to reach Schuylerville, lined with worn white buildings and empty storefronts. Just south of the Route 32 intersection stands **Schuyler House** (Rte. 4, 518/664-9821, June-Sept. Wed.-Sun. 10am-4pm, free). Also part of the Saratoga National Historical Park, the house once belonged to the Schuyler family, who ran a self-sufficient estate here that employed about 200 people. The house was burnt by Burgoyne during the Battles of Saratoga but was rebuilt that same year.

Take Route 32 west of Schuyler House about a half mile to reach **Saratoga Monument** (Rte. 32, late May-early Oct. 10am-12:30pm and 1pm-4pm, free), a beautifully restored gray obelisk on a hill. The third part of Saratoga National Historical Park, the monument features four niches honoring the battles' American leaders—General Philip Schuyler, General Horatio Gates, Colonel Daniel Morgan, and General Benedict Arnold. Statues stand in the first three niches; the fourth stands deliberately empty.

Ballston Spa

Before the Civil War, Ballston Spa outranked Saratoga as a fashionable resort and watering hole. After the war, however, the racetrack and casinos drew the crowds away, and Ballston Spa turned to knitting mills and tanneries. Today, little evidence of any of these industries remains except at Saratoga County Historical Society's **Brookside Museum** (6 Charlton St., 518/885-4000, www.brooksidemuseum.org, Wed.-Fri. 10am-4pm, Sat. noon-4pm, free). Housed in what was once a resort hotel, Brookside showcases exhibits on the town's 19th-century spas, 20th-century amusement parks, early African American settlers, and dairy farming.

Also in Ballston Spa is the eclectic **National Bottle Museum** (76 Milton Ave., 518/885-7589, www.nationalbottlemuseum.org, June-Sept. daily 10am-4pm, Oct.-May Mon.-Fri. 10am-4pm, donation). Thousands of antique and handmade bottles are displayed, most without signage; a video on antique bottles is featured. The museum hosts the annual Saratoga Antique Bottle Show and Sale, an impressive event where aficionados have their goods appraised or trade and sell bottles. It has also opened a small glassworks studio in a nearby facility, where visitors can take classes.

Wilton

One of the oddest and most moving house museums in New York State is **Grant Cottage** (off Ballard Rd., 518/584-4353, www.grantcottage.org, Memorial Day-Labor Day Wed.-Sun. 10am-4pm, Labor Day-mid-Oct. Sat.-Sun. 10am-4pm, adults $6, seniors and children 6-18 $5), a state historic site.

President Ulysses S. Grant came to Mount McGregor in June 1885. Afflicted with throat cancer, he spent the last six weeks of his life here, completing his memoirs. Grant had become bankrupt paying back the money he had urged friends to invest in his son's company; the company went belly-up after his son's partner absconded with the funds. As a result, Grant was working frantically to finish his book so his family would have something to live on after he was gone. At the time, Mount McGregor was home to popular Hotel Balmoral, owned by W. J. Arkell. Arkell, an admirer of Grant, lent the general his cottage when he learned that New York City's summer heat was preventing Grant from finishing his memoirs. Grant—often sleeping as few as two hours a night—did succeed in finishing his memoirs just four days before his death on July 23, 1885. They are considered to be among the finest ever written by an American general and earned the family half a million dollars in royalties.

The house remains as it was when Grant and his family left it. In one room are Grant's toothbrush, his nightshirts, and a half-empty bottle of medicinal cocaine. In another are wreaths sent by mourners, preserved in beeswax more than a century ago, and the bed where Grant died, the bedspread stained with flowers brought by mourners.

The cottage currently shares land with Mt. McGregor Correctional Facility; to access the cottage, guests must stop at a guard booth and enter a walled minimum-security complex topped with barbed wire. The New York State's governor's office has announced that the prison is likely to be closed, which may result in even easier access to the historic site.

Bed-and-Breakfasts

In Schuylerville, the wood-frame, federal-style **Dovegate Inn** (184 Broad St., 518/695-3699, www.dovegateinn.com, $110-130 off-season, $185-200 racing season) is a welcoming B&B offering three spacious guest rooms with private baths. A small restaurant and gift shop are also on-site.

The Mansion Inn (801 Rte. 29, Rock City Falls, 518/885-1607, www.themansion saratoga.com, $140-225 off-season, $250-499 racing season) lies 7 miles (11.3 km) west of downtown Saratoga. This 1866 Victorian mansion sits on four acres, built by 19th-century industrialist George West, known as the Paper Bag King, and is listed in the National Register of Historic Places. Modern conveniences and luxury amenities make this a good out-of-town lodging for racing season.

Central New York

Often overlooked in favor of the regions that bookend it, Central New York's defining features may be harder to see at first glance. Don't speed through this area, though, especially if you're interested in science, history (and the history of industry in the United States, specifically), or baseball—yes, baseball!—as this part of New York is home to the National Baseball Hall of Fame and Museum. Summer and fall are the best months to visit, with the abundant outdoor recreation opportunities and the beautiful scenery.

SCHENECTADY

Schenectady is best visited for its history. The oldest European settlement in the Mohawk Valley, the city boasts one of the largest and best collections of 18th-century buildings in New York—the **Stockade,** the state's first historic district. Visitors walking along this district's quiet, crooked streets, heavy with trees, will be transported back to a gentler age.

Museum of Innovation and Science and Suits-Bueche Planetarium

The **Museum of Innovation and Science** (15 Nott Terrace Hts., off Nott Terrace, 518/382-7890, www.misci.org, June-Sept. Mon.-Sat. 10am-5pm, Sun. noon-5pm, off-season hours vary, adults $12, seniors $10, children 3-12 $8) is a modern, interactive, and kid-friendly spot, whose mission is to foster understanding of how technology and science affect modern-day visitors in their daily lives. The museum is also known for its 30-foot-high (9 m) **planetarium;** an additional fee is charged at admission for guests who want to see a planetarium show.

Stockade District

Along the banks of the Mohawk River, in the triangle formed by State and North College Streets, lies the **Stockade** (www.historicstockade.com), one of the nation's oldest continuously occupied neighborhoods. Settled in 1661 by Dutch merchants and fur traders, the outpost flourished until 1690, when a party of French Canadians and their Native American allies burnt it to the ground, massacring most of the inhabitants and marching the rest to Québec.

Native Mohawks encouraged the Dutch to rebuild, and two years later the Stockade was flourishing once again. During the next two centuries, all of Schenectady's most important families settled here. Today, the residential district is a wonderful spot, filled with architectural landmarks of all styles and periods. The oldest are churches and graveyards dating back to the 1690s; the newest are homes built in the 1930s.

Plaques pinpointing some of the Stockade's more interesting sites are located

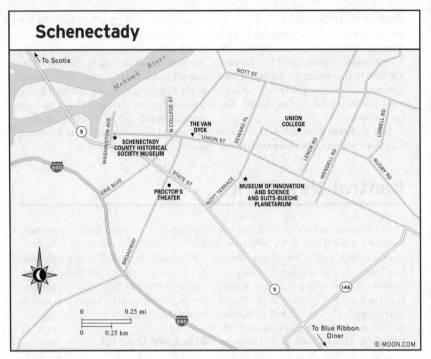

Schenectady

throughout the district. Maps are available in the Schenectady County Historical Society Museum on the southern edge of the Stockade.

Schenectady County Historical Society Museum

On display in the friendly, three-story **Schenectady County Historical Society Museum** (32 Washington Ave., 518/374-0263, www.schenectadyhistorical.org, Mon.-Fri. 9am-5pm, Sat. 10am-2pm, adults $5, children free) is everything from antique dolls and guns to period costumes and furniture. Highlights include an elaborate dollhouse that once belonged to the family of Governor Yates and the notebooks and letters of GE's electrical genius, Dr. Charles Steinmetz.

Union College

The first planned college campus in the United States, **Union College** (807 Union St., 518/388-6000, www.union.edu) was designed in 1814 by classical landscape architect Joseph Jacques Ramee. Filled with broad lawns and giant elms, Union admitted only men until 1970.

At the center of the campus is high Gothic **Nott Memorial,** the only 16-sided building in the Northern Hemisphere. Nearby are **Jackson's Gardens,** beautifully landscaped formal gardens first planted in the early 1800s by math professor Isaac Jackson.

Union College is located between Lenox Road, Seward Place, Union Avenue, and Nott and Union Streets. Parking is available in the lots at Nott Street and Seward Place.

Entertainment

Try to catch a show at historic **Proctor's Theatre** (432 State St., 518/346-6204, www. proctors.org), an architectural gem built in 1926. Once a vaudeville palace, it also hosted the first public demonstration of the television and has seen the likes of Cab Calloway and Duke Ellington performing in the ornate, 2,700-seat auditorium, which features a 1931 Golub Mighty Wurlitzer Organ. The events calendar is packed with Broadway musicals, concerts, operas, dance troupes, and classic movies.

Food and Accommodations

In the Stockade, head to **Blue Ribbon Restaurant and Bakery** (1801 State St., 518/393-2600, www.blueribbonrestaurant. com, Sun.-Thurs. 7am-10pm, Fri.-Sat. 7am-11pm, $15), especially known for its cheesecake. Before dessert, you can get a heaping plate of diner-style food.

If a walk through this region's farmers markets leaves you hungry for more, look to **Field Notes** (204 Lishakill Rd., Colonie, 518/400-2024, www.fieldnotes-ny.com, hours vary seasonally) where Joan Porambo's and Kyle Macpherson's weekly dinners feature locally grown and produced ingredients. Menus change regularly, but the common thread is Capital-Saratoga ingredients, where you can learn more about local farming.

Overlooking the Mohawk River across from Schenectady is ★ **Glen Sanders Mansion** (1 Glen Ave., Scotia, 518/374-7262, www.glensandersmansion.com, $154-350), an upscale inn housed in a historic stone home with original Dutch floors and doors. The inn's on-site restaurant, **The Lounge** (1 Glen Ave., Scotia, 518/374-7262, www.glensandersmansion.com, Sun.-Wed. 4pm-9:30pm, Thurs.-Sat. 4pm-10pm, $14), serves modern pub cuisine. Ten standard guest rooms offer double queen-size beds; 10 suites offer king-size beds and sitting areas, some with fireplaces.

SCHOHARIE COUNTY

Schoharie County, like much of central New York, is defined by its picturesque farmland. It's beautiful enough, but if you're driving through without knowing the county's less visible attractions, you'll miss out. Many of the best sights in Schoharie County can't even be seen at eye level; you'll have to go underground to discover them. Schoharie's prehistoric caves and 100-foot (30 m) underground waterfall are two of the county's subterranean wonders.

Howe Caverns (255 Discovery Dr., Howes Cave, 518/296-8900, www.howecaverns.com, May-Oct. daily 9am-6pm, Nov.-Apr. Fri.-Sun. 10am-3pm, adults $25, seniors $22, children ages 12-15 $21, children ages 5-11 $13, children under 5 free) is a living, limestone cave carved out by an underground river over the course of six million years. Today, it's a veritable amusement park. Passing through the somewhat touristy offerings at the surface (geode cracking and gemstone, arrowhead, or fossil panning) brings you to a lobby where groups wait for their timed tour. Hopping in an elevator drops you down 15 stories to explore the cavern, which includes an underground boat ride and a particularly lovely passage called the "winding way." Visitors looking for something out of the ordinary can take a two-hour adventure spelunking tour through areas not accessible to the general public or explore the old-fashioned way—by lantern, the way Lester Howe might have done it when the caverns were discovered in 1842 . . . by his cow, Millicent. In addition to cave tours, visitors can also zip-line, rock climb, or test out a ropes course during warmer months.

Secret Caverns (671 Caverns Rd., Howes Cave, 518/296-8558, www.secretcaverns. com, hours and admission fees vary seasonally) may not actually be a secret, but they are less commercialized and crowded than Howe. Secret Caverns are also smaller than Howe, with formations that may not seem as impressive until you see the 100-foot (30 m) waterfall that helped form the caverns in the first place.

Once underground but now housed safely in **Gilboa Museum** (122 Stryker Rd., Gilboa, 607/588-9413, www.gilboafossils.org, early June-early Sept. Sat.-Sun. noon-4:30pm, donations accepted) are nine of the world's oldest tree fossils and the first fossil tree stumps that were documented in North America. An amateur naturalist made the initial discovery of these Devonian Period fossils, which were found in a tree trunk in Schoharie Creek after a flood. Seventy years later, an expedition from New York State Museum found almost 50 more; some were retained for the museum's collection, and others were shipped near and far to other collectors and institutions. Though the nine fossils at this museum represent just a portion of the museum's interests and collection, they comprise its most compelling exhibit.

The caverns and the Gilboa Museum are about halfway between Albany and Cooperstown, and can be taken in as day trips from either city or as interesting stops when traveling between the two. For an excellent lodging and dining option in Schoharie County, there's **American Hotel** (192 Main St., Sharon Springs, 518/284-2105, www.americanhotelny.com, $150-175 Nov.-May, $215-235 June-Oct.). Built in 1847, it sat vacant for nearly a third of the 20th century until it was bought and restored by its current owners in 1996. Nine comfortable rooms feature Frette linens, free wireless Internet, and breakfast; the on-site restaurant sources most of its produce from nearby farms.

COOPERSTOWN

With its friendly, old-fashioned Main Street, population of about 1,800 residents, and, of course, the National Baseball Hall of Fame and Museum, Cooperstown likes to think of itself as the most famous small town in America. To the north are the still waters of Otsego Lake; to the south, east, and west are the rolling, forested hills of Leatherstocking Country.

Cooperstown was first settled in 1790 by William Cooper, father of James Fenimore, America's first internationally recognized author. Fiercely ambitious Cooper Sr. obtained the land through unscrupulous means during the chaos following the Revolutionary War, then immediately set about establishing himself as a grand gentleman. Within a decade he'd built the largest private home west of Albany, won widespread respect for his skill as a land developer, and established

Cooperstown as the Otsego County seat. Later, he became a county judge and representative to Congress.

James Fenimore Cooper wrote about Cooperstown in his novel *The Pioneers,* and set many of his Natty Bumppo tales on the shores of "The Glimmerglass"—Otsego Lake. After travels at sea and abroad, he settled down in his hometown and took over where his father had left off, playing lord of the manor. Cooper was buried in the town's Christ Church Cemetery in 1851.

In the late 1800s, Cooperstown became home to the Clark family, who'd made a fortune with Singer Sewing Machines. Edward Clark, the family patriarch, built a miniature castle called Kingfisher Tower on Otsego Lake in 1876. In the late 1930s and 1940s, one of his descendants, Stephen C. Clark, established the town's three famous museums—the National Baseball Hall of Fame, Farmers' Museum, and Fenimore Art Museum.

On summer days, Cooperstown's population swells by the thousands. Tourists wearing baseball caps and T-shirts are everywhere, and parking can be a problem. The best approach is to park in one of the park-and-ride lots on Routes 80 and 28 and ride the free trolley into town. During the off-season, street parking is generally available.

TOP EXPERIENCE

★ National Baseball Hall of Fame and Museum

The National Baseball Hall of Fame and Museum (25 Main St., 607/547-7200, www.baseballhall.org, June-Sept. daily 9am-9pm, Oct.-May daily 9am-5pm, adults $25, seniors $20, children 7-12 $15) was established in 1939 as an homage to America's favorite pastime. It's loaded with state-of-the-art displays covering every aspect of the sport, from famous ballparks and women's baseball, to the World Series, Negro League, and baseball in the Caribbean. Aficionados and collectors crowd displays to see such memorabilia as Jackie Robinson's warm-up jacket, Hank Aaron's

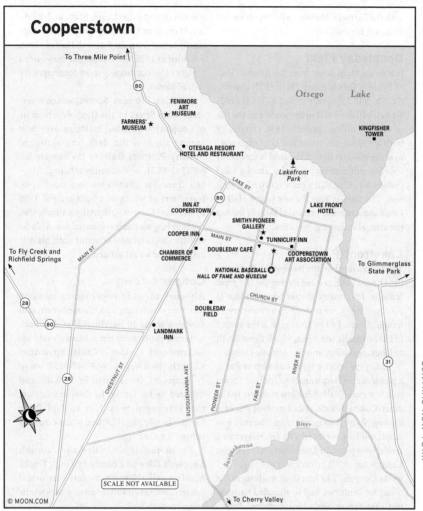

Cooperstown

To Three Mile Point

Otsego Lake

FENIMORE ART MUSEUM

FARMERS' MUSEUM

KINGFISHER TOWER

OTESAGA RESORT HOTEL AND RESTAURANT

Lakefront Park

LAKE ST

INN AT COOPERSTOWN

LAKE FRONT HOTEL

SMITHY-PIONEER GALLERY

COOPER INN

MAIN ST

TUNNICLIFF INN

To Fly Creek and Richfield Springs

MAIN ST

CHAMBER OF COMMERCE

DOUBLEDAY CAFÉ

COOPERSTOWN ART ASSOCIATION

To Glimmerglass State Park

NATIONAL BASEBALL HALL OF FAME AND MUSEUM

CHURCH ST

DOUBLEDAY FIELD

LANDMARK INN

CHESTNUT ST

SUSQUEHANNA AVE

PIONEER ST

FAIR ST

RIVER ST

River

Susquehanna River

SCALE NOT AVAILABLE

© MOON.COM

To Cherry Valley

locker, Willie Mays's glove, Yogi Berra's catcher's mitt, and that rarest of all baseball cards, the Honus Wagner 1909 T-206 tobacco card, recalled at the request of the nonsmoking ballplayer.

Occupying three floors and 60,000 square feet, the museum begins with a cavernous Hall of Fame honoring the greats. A ramp to one side leads to exhibits on such subjects as "Scribes and Mikemen" and "Baseball at the Movies," while stairs lead to the 2nd and

3rd floors, where the heart of the collection is housed. One room honors Babe Ruth; another, baseball in the 19th century; a third, "Today's Game." Separate exhibit cases are devoted to such major players as Hank Aaron, Jackie Robinson, and Ty Cobb. A 13-minute multimedia show, "The Baseball Experience," is presented throughout the day, while film and audio clips supplement exhibits' visuals. Daily trivia games and educational programs are also featured. Combination tickets with the Farmers' Museum and Fenimore Art Museum are available.

Doubleday Field

Just down Main Street from the Baseball Hall of Fame is **Doubleday Field** (1 Doubleday Ct., 607/547-2270, year-round daily), the oldest baseball diamond in the world and the site of the first official game in 1839. Originally built for 8,000 spectators and later expanded to accommodate 10,000, the field is now available for rent and very popular among local groups, meaning that a game is often in progress. The field is also the site where Hall of Fame inductees are presented awards during the annual Induction Weekend.

Lakefront Park

Two blocks north of the Baseball Hall of Fame lies Otsego Lake, created during the last great Ice Age. Like many glacial lakes, Otsego is cool and deep, with steep banks and overhanging trees. Fed by springs, it is the source of the Susquehanna River, which flows south to Chesapeake Bay and the Atlantic Ocean.

Along the lake's edge is **Lakefront Park,** a pleasant spot frequented by families. To one side is a statue called *Indian Hunter;* to the other, **Council Rock,** once a meeting place for various Native American tribes. The rock was employed by Cooper in *The Deerslayer* as a rendezvous point for Deerslayer and his friend Chingachgook. "The rock was not large . . . ," wrote Cooper, "The incessant washing of the water for centuries had so rounded its summit, that it resembled a large beehive." Today, a flight of stone steps leads down to a terrace overlooking the rock.

From the park you can see 60-foot-high (18 m), 1907 **Kingfisher Tower,** designed in the style of a European castle by architect Henry Hardenbergh, who also designed The Plaza Hotel in New York City. The miniature castle/tower is not open to the public.

Galleries

The galleries of the **Cooperstown Art Association** (22 Main St., 607/547-9777,

www.cooperstownart.com, Mon. and Wed.-Sat. 11am-4pm, Sun. 1pm-4pm, free) are diagonally across from the Baseball Hall of Fame. Founded in 1928, the association showcases a variety of works ranging from contemporary to traditional.

Flanking **Pioneer Street,** which intersects Main Street by the flagpole, are some of Cooperstown's oldest buildings. Foremost among them is the dark, low-ceilinged **Smithy-Pioneer Gallery** (55 Pioneer St., 607/547-8671, www.smithyarts.org, May-Oct. Tues.-Sat. 10am-5pm, Sun. noon-5pm, free), part of which was built around 1786 by William Cooper. Originally a storehouse, the building was later converted into a blacksmith's shop and now contains both historic artifacts and an art gallery.

Cooper's Town

Although the old Cooper family mansion was torn down long ago, Cooperstown still contains about 20 buildings that date back to James Fenimore's time. Most closely associated with Cooper is **Christ Episcopal Church** (46 River St., 607/547-9555, www.ceccoop.net), consecrated in 1810 on land donated by his father. In Cooper's fiction, the church appears as "New St. Paul's"; the Cooper family plot is located in the cemetery behind the church.

For more Cooper-related sites, consult *Cooper's Otsego County* by Hugh Cooke MacDougall (New York State Historical Society, 607/547-1400, available at www.jf-coopersociety.org).

Farmers' Museum

Just outside downtown Cooperstown is the second of its famous museums, **Farmers' Museum** (5775 State Hwy. 80/Lake Rd., 607/547-1450, www.farmersmuseum.org, early May-mid-Oct. daily 10am-5pm, hours vary off-season, adults $12, seniors $10.50, children 7-12 $6), composed of meticulously

---

1: National Baseball Hall of Fame and Museum
2: Farmers' Museum in Cooperstown

restored pre-Civil War buildings. Run by the New York State Historical Association, this is not just another living history museum; rather, it's the granddaddy of them all. Founded in 1944, it was the first open-air museum in New York State and one of the first in the country.

The museum is spread along one looping street, lined with a general store, blacksmith's shop, printing office, doctor's office, and druggist's shop. In the Main Barn near the entrance hang imaginative exhibits on early rural life; skillful guides roam about in period dress, some demonstrating such arts as broom-making and open-hearth cooking. Sheep graze in the village common. Fat cows wander a nearby hill.

One of the museum's odder exhibits is the 2,900-pound Cardiff Giant. Supposedly unearthed in nearby Cardiff in 1869 by the hitherto unassuming William Newell, the sleeping stone man with the mysterious smile soon drew visitors from all over the country. A Harvard professor claimed the Giant dated back to Phoenician times; Oliver Wendell Holmes drilled a hole behind his left ear to see if the brain was petrified. Only after Newell had raked in tens of thousands of dollars was the statue proven to be a hoax.

Combination tickets with the Baseball Hall of Fame and Fenimore Art Museum are available.

Fenimore Art Museum

Directly across the street from Farmers' Museum is the third of Cooperstown's museum triumvirate. **Fenimore Art Museum** (5798 State Hwy. 80/Lake Rd., 607/547-1400, www.fenimoreartmuseum.org, mid-May–mid-Oct. daily 10am-5pm, hours vary off-season, adults $12, seniors $10.50, children 12 and under free), also run by the New York State Historical Association, holds the state's premier collection of folk art, fine art, and Native American art. Highlights include Thomas Cole's *Last of the Mohicans,* Gilbert Stuart's *Joseph Brandt,* a version of Edward Hicks's *Peaceable Kingdom,* and an eclectic

collection of weather vanes, trade signs, cigar-store Indians, and decoys.

One wing of the museum houses the Eugene and Clare Thaw Collection of American Indian Art. Perhaps the most important privately owned collection of its kind, it includes about 700 works spanning 2,500 years of native North American culture. Among the many stunning items on display are a flowing Blackfoot headdress, a Lakota-painted horsehide, and a brilliant blue Heiltsuk moon mask.

A first-rate bookstore is also on-site, as is a café serving light lunch with a view of Otsego Lake. Combination tickets with the National Baseball Hall of Fame and Farmers' Museum are available.

Recreation

You'll find good swimming at public beaches on Otsego Lake at **Glimmerglass State Park** (off County Rd. 31, 607/547-8662, www.nysparks.com/parks/28, $7 vehicle entrance fee); **Three Mile Point** (East Lake Rd., 607/547-2777), off Route 80; and **Fairy Springs** (East Lake Rd., 607/547-2150), off County Road 31.

On summer Saturday nights, the bleachers are always filled with families and fans of stock car racing at **Lebanon Valley Speedway** (1746 Rte. 20, 518/794-9606, www.lebanonvalley.com). Racing season runs April-October.

Entertainment

Glimmerglass Festival is an acclaimed musical event taking place every July-August at **Glimmerglass Opera** (7300 State Hwy. 80), a partially open-air theater by Otsego Lake. Three operas and a musical typically comprise the festival's musical menu, rounded out with backstage tours and symposia. The **box office** (18 Chestnut St., 607/547-2255, www.glimmerglass.org) is downtown. Apart from the festival, chamber music concerts, lectures, and plays take place regularly in **Hyde Hall** (Glimmerglass State Park, 607/547-5098, www.hydehall.org).

For an elegant evening out, step into Templeton Lounge of **Otesaga Resort Hotel** (60 Lake St., 607/547-9931, www.otesaga.com). Live music and dancing are offered Thursday-Saturday evenings (8:30pm-11:30pm).

Shopping

Numerous shops occupy Cooperstown and the surrounding area. A few miles south of Cooperstown is **Fly Creek Cider Mill** (288 Goose St., 607/547-9692, www.flycreekcidermill.com, open year-round, but days and hours vary by season), where apples are pressed in a 19th-century wooden cider mill. The mill is water-powered, and all original equipment is used. Also on-site is an extensive gift shop and a snack bar selling lots of tasty homemade treats, including cider doughnuts and cider floats and slushes. A duck pond and play area will delight kids.

Among the region's more unusual stores is **Wood Bull Antiques** (3920 Rte. 28, 607/286-9021, www.woodbullantiques.com), in a large barn 8 miles (12.9 km) south of Cooperstown. According to the owners, the merchandise has been gathered from over four decades of attic rummaging and thousands of auctions.

Breweries

Cooperstown has two breweries offering tastings and tours. **Brewery Ommegang** (656 County Rd. 33, 607/544-1800, www.ommegang.com, daily noon-5pm, adults $5 for tour, $10 for tasting) was built on an old hops farm in 1997 and has been brewing Belgian-style beer ever since. Belgian-inspired food is served in an on-site café. **Cooperstown Brewing Company** (110 River St., Milford, 607/286-9330, www.cooperstownbrewing.com, Mon.-Sat. 10am-6pm, Sun. noon-5:30pm, adults $3, children free) is a small, independently owned brewery making beer from homegrown hops. Tasting pours are generous and label names reflect Cooperstown's baseball history: Nine Man Ale, Old Slugger, and Strike-Out Stout.

Food

High-ceilinged ★ **Doubleday Cafe** (93 Main St., 607/547-5468, www.doubledaycafe.com, daily 7am-9pm, $13) has a friendly small-town feel, with a counter bar to one side and lots of tables and chairs in back. The menu has a nice variety of sandwiches, salads, and simple entrées.

Otesaga Resort Hotel's **Hawkeye Bar & Grill** (60 Lake St., 607/544-2524, breakfast, lunch, and dinner, hours vary seasonally, $22) is especially good for lunch in summer, when lakeside patio seating opens up. Sandwiches and soups are staple lunch fare; the dinner menu is more elaborate.

★ **Nicoletta's Italian Cafe** (96 Main St., 607/547-7499, www.nicolettasitaliancafe.com, daily 4pm-9:30pm, $16), housed in an airy, high-ceilinged former storefront, is a local favorite. Specialties include tasty pasta dishes made from fresh, local ingredients and classics like veal piccata.

A variety of international dishes are offered at the lovely lakeside ★ **Blue Mingo Grill** (Sam Smith's Boatyard, 6098 Hwy. 80, 607/547-7496, www.bluemingogrill.com, hours vary seasonally, $14). Lunch dishes include salads, grilled fish, and pizzas, while the dinner menu changes weekly and can include anything from Thai dishes to fresh lobster.

Accommodations

The 1902 ★ **Otesaga Resort Hotel** (60 Lake St., 607/547-9931, www.otesaga.com, $465-550 with full breakfast, dinner, and afternoon tea) is a delicious grande dame of a hotel, affiliated with Historic Hotels of America. Stately white columns tower out front. Out back, a long, circular porch with rocking chairs overlooks the lake. Facilities include a romantic ballroom with a 20-foot-high (6 m) coffered ceiling, a main dining room, the appealing Hawkeye Bar & Grill, tennis courts, and first-rate Leatherstocking Golf Course. All rooms are outfitted with period furnishings.

The Otesaga also operates **The Cooper Inn** (Main and Chestnut Sts., 607/547-2567, www.cooperinn.com, $265 summer, $110-160 off-season, breakfast included), built between 1813 and 1816. Reigning over its own little park in the heart of the downtown, the luxurious inn offers 15 handsomely decorated rooms and the use of all Otesaga facilities.

★ **Inn at Cooperstown** (16 Chestnut St., 607/547-5756, www.innatcooperstown.com, $187 summer, $115-375 off-season, breakfast included) is all that an inn should be—big, creaky, lined with a wide porch, and shaded with magnificent trees. All 18 guest rooms have private baths and queen or double beds. The two-story luxury suite features a king bed, hydro spa tub, and wet bar.

Cooperstown's oldest inn, now somewhat worn but still atmospheric, is 1802 **Tunnicliff Inn** (34-34 Pioneer St., 607/547-9611, www.tunnicliffinn.net, $155-375 summer, $89-200 off-season). Here, you'll find 17 guest rooms, a restaurant, and a historic bar. A hot breakfast buffet is included in the room rate.

Among the many inviting B&Bs in Cooperstown is stately ★ **Landmark Inn** (64 Chestnut St., 607/547-7225, www.landmarkinncooperstown.com, $200-295 July-Aug., $115-210 off-season), in an 1856 Italianate mansion. Beautifully restored, the inn offers a plush parlor complete with fireplace, hardwood floors polished to a high gleam, a game room, various cozy sitting areas, and 11 spacious guest rooms, many named after writers or artists, and each with a feather duvet bed, refrigerator, air-conditioning, cable TV, wireless Internet, and antiques.

Cooperstown also has a number of good, clean motels. Forty-five-room **Lake Front Hotel** (10 Fair St., 607/547-9511, www.cooperstownlakefronthotel.com, $169-259 summer, $85-189 off-season) is in the heart of the village, overlooking Otsego Lake. An on-site restaurant serves breakfast, lunch, and dinner; a deck overlooks the lake.

Seven miles (11.3 km) north of Cooperstown is ★ **Lake 'N Pines Motel** (7102 Rte. 80, 607/547-2790, www.lakenpines motel.com, $130-165 summer, $65-105 off-season). As its name suggests, it is also on the lake. Here, guests can choose between motel rooms and cottages. On-site are indoor and outdoor pools and a small beach with paddleboats. Breakfast is included in the room rate.

In addition to **Glimmerglass State Park's campground** (1527 Hwy. 31, 607/547-8662), camping options include **Cooperstown Beaver Valley Campground** (138 Towers Rd., Milford, 607/293-7324, www.beavervalleycampground.com), which offers tent sites ($36-40/night), RV sites ($48-56/night), camping cabins ($895-995/week), three beaver ponds (one with catch-and-release fishing), a pool, baseball field, and playground. **Cooperstown Shadow Brook Campground** (2149 Hwy. 31, 607/264-8431, www.cooperstowncamping.com) offers tent sites ($24-35/night) and RV sites ($45-62/night) as well as cabin lodging ($79-98/night). There's also a heated pool. The commercial campgrounds have wireless Internet and all the campgrounds are open May-October.

GLIMMERGLASS STATE PARK

Glimmerglass State Park (1527 Hwy. 31, 607/547-8662, www.nysparks.com/parks/28, daily 8am-dusk, parking $7) occupies the northern end of Otsego Lake. Features of this peaceful green oasis include a swimming beach, plenty of hiking and biking trails, a playground, and a 43-site **campground** ($15-25/night for New York residents, $20-30/night for nonresidents).

Grand neoclassical **Hyde Hall** (607/547-5098, www.hydehall.org, June-Oct. daily 10am-5pm, adults $12, seniors and children $10) stands in the heart of the park. Once home to the Clarke family, the mansion had fallen into serious disrepair but has been undergoing restoration for several years. Admission includes a guided tour, offered on the hour beginning at 10am and ending at 4pm.

HERKIMER

There's not gold in them thar hills, but there are diamonds…sort of. The town of Herkimer is known for its diamond mines, but wait! The diamonds are actually quartz crystals, so named because of both the color and faceting of the quartz that look similar to a cut and polished diamond.

Families, especially, may want to make a stop in Herkimer to do some mining, which is an exciting activity for kids. Several campgrounds, including **Ace of Diamonds** (84 Herkimer St., 315/891-3855, www. herkimerdiamonds.com, $20-35/night) and **Herkimer Diamond KOA Resort** (4626 State Rte. 28, 315/891-7355, www. herkimerdiamond.com/koa-campground, $39-49 for tent sites, $90-267 for cottages) offer both accommodations and the opportunity to go **diamond mining.** The latter is particularly thrilling for families, as one of the cabins has a built-in observatory, and another is a treehouse-style accommodation.

UTICA

If ever a city deserved its nickname, it's Utica. The "Second Chance City" is a smaller burg flecked with gems most travelers miss. Utica, though, is accustomed to having its potential overlooked. Located halfway along the Erie Canal corridor, it seems the city should have been—and should be—more important than it ever has been. Because it's also on the shallowest part of the Mohawk River, however, it's never been able to benefit from the robust commerce other canalside towns enjoyed. Still, Utica has been a stopover point for plenty of travelers, including Mark Twain, and an attractive home for many refugees arriving in the United States, a demographic trend that has made the city remarkably diverse. That diversity is reflected most of all in the city's culinary scene, which boasts everything from Bosnian to Cuban cuisine. In addition to fantastic food from far-flung lands, you'll also find a surprising amount of impressive art in Utica, primarily at Munson Williams Proctor Arts Institute.

Sights

Munson Williams Proctor Arts Institute (310 Genesee St., 315/797-0000, www.mwpai. org, Tues.-Sat. 10am-5pm, Sun. 1-5pm, free) houses 20 galleries exhibiting American and European paintings and decorative objects from its 25,000-item collection, which spans genres and generations. Notable pieces include work by Dalí, Picasso, and Pollock.

Stanley Center for the Arts (261 Genesee St., 315/724-1113, www.thestanley. org) was designed by Thomas Lamb, a 20th-century architect renowned for theaters and cinemas. The Stanley opened as a movie house in 1928 and is one of just three remaining "Lamb theaters" in the country (all three are in New York). Today, it hosts year-round performances of Broadway shows, Utica Symphony Orchestra concerts, and visiting musical and comedic acts.

FX Matt Brewing Company, also known as **Saranac Brewery** (830 Varick St., 800/765-6288, www.saranac.com, tours Fri.-Sat., adults $5, must make reservation by phone), is a family-owned brewery offering tours and a tasting tavern; it also hosts numerous community events throughout the summer, including a concert series. Tour guides get rave reviews for being friendly and knowledgeable.

Food and Accommodations

The Tailor and the Cook (94 Genesee St., 315/793-7444, www.thetailorandthecook.com, Wed.-Sat. 5pm-9:30pm, $30) is Utica's most celebrated farm-to-table restaurant. Two executive chefs share responsibility for the kitchen and seasonal menu changes. Many plates have hints of global influences, such as Jamaican blue crab and scallion dumpling and North African chickpea stew.

The Pratt-Smith House (10497 Cosby Manor Rd., 315/732-8483, $75-90) is a federal-era colonial brick home that was once a working farm. Today, it's a welcoming B&B whose owners are consistently commended by guests for their friendly warmth. Affordability and a generous breakfast make up for areas that are crowded with knickknacks and the mattresses that could use an update.

Rosemont Inn Bed and Breakfast (1423 Genesee St., 866/353-4907, www.rosemontinnbb.com, $109-189) is an Italianate Victorian home in a central downtown location, just a few minutes from both Stanley Center for the Arts and Munson Williams Proctor Arts Institute. All seven guest rooms have private baths and one has a working fireplace.

ONEIDA

If the name of this small New York town between Utica and Syracuse sounds familiar, it probably is. Like the famous china and silver manufacturer, it took its name from the Native American Oneida tribe. The town's history is a curious one. Like many villages along the Erie Canal, Oneida owes its founding and initial flourishing to both the waterway and the railroad. By the late 19th century, the town had become the home of a utopian socialist commune called the Oneida Community, whose own manufacturing activities preceded those of the Oneida china and flatware empire. Today, the stories of these varied chapters in the town's history are told at historic parks, museums, and other sites of interest.

Sights

Old Erie Canal State Historic Park (315/637-6111, www.nysparks.com/parks/17) is a 36-mile (58 km) section of the 360-mile-long (580 km) Old Erie Canal, straddling Oneida and Madison Counties. You can dip into the park at various points. To get there, take NYS Thruway Exit 34 (Canastota); turn left on North Peterboro Street, then left on East North Canal Street. The **Erie Canalway Trail** (www.ptny.org), a multi-use national recreation trail paralleling the canal, also runs through the park. Several small, canal-themed museums can be found in the park, including **Chittenango Landing Canal Boat Museum** (7010 Lakeport Rd., Chittenango, 315/687-3801, www.chittenangolanding.org, days and

hours vary by season, adults $6, seniors $5, children $3) and **Canastota Canal Town Museum** (122 Canal St., Canastota, 315/697-5002, www.canastota.com, days and hours vary by season, adults $3, children 12 and under free). The former is dedicated to the watercraft that plied the canal, while the latter emphasizes just how profoundly the canal shaped the small towns along its banks through trade.

Cross Island Chapel (Pond, off Sconondoa Rd.) is reputed to be the smallest church in the United States and was once the smallest church in the world before being ousted by a slightly smaller house of worship in Switzerland. Though it's open to the public by appointment, it may be better appreciated as a photo op, since just two people can fit inside it at the same time. The church, which dates back only to 1989, is just shy of 29 square feet in size and can only be reached by boat, as it's in the middle of a pond.

Shako:wi Cultural Center (5 Territory Rd., 315/829-8801, www.oneidaindiannation.com/shakowiculturalcenter, Mon., Wed., Fri., 9am-5pm, free) offers visitors the opportunity to learn about Oneida tribal history and culture through exhibits that were established and are managed by the Oneida nation. A shop with authentic, handmade crafts is also on-site.

Food and Accommodations

It's amazing that the oddly-named, 93,000-square-foot, 19th-century **Oneida Community Mansion** (170 Kenwood Ave., 315/363-0745, www.oneidacommunity.org, $115-200) even functions as a B&B, given its national historic landmark status and its dual existence as a museum. The former home of the utopian experiment, the Oneida Community, this property sits on 33 acres of old-growth trees and gardens. Room rates include a tour of the mansion, as well as modern amenities like free wireless Internet.

Turning Stone Resort (5218 Patrick Rd., Verona, 800/771-7711, www.turningstone.

com, rates vary by accommodation type) is a massive complex with a variety of accommodation types (hotel rooms and suites and RV sites, among others), a dozen bars and restaurants, a casino, spa, and five golf courses, three of which are championship courses. It's like Vegas . . . but in central New York.

Information and Services

For information on the state parks mentioned in this chapter, visit the website of the **New York State Office of Parks, Recreation, and Historic Preservation** (www.parks.ny.gov). The major cities and counties also have their own tourist information offices and websites:

- **Albany Heritage Area Visitor Center** (25 Quackenbush Sq., Albany, 518/434-0405, www.albany.org)

- **The Saratoga County Chamber** (28 Clinton St., Saratoga Springs, 518/584-3255, www.saratoga.org)
- **Oneida County Tourism** (www.oneidacountytourism.com)
- **Schenectady County Visitors Agency** (www.discoverschenectady.com)
- **Schoharie County Tourism** (www.visitschohariecounty.com)

Getting There and Around

If you want to reach the area by air, **Albany International Airport** (junction of I-87 and I-90, 518/242-2200, www.albanyairport.com) is the region's biggest and most central airport; however, the region is also easily reached by **trains** (Amtrak, 800/872-7245, www.amtrak.com) or **buses** (Trailways, 800/858-8555, www.trailways.com) departing New York City. Once here, however, travelers will find that a car is the best way to get around and see the area's highlights. Major national car rental chains have rental outposts at the airport.

If arriving by car, visitors will find it's easy to reach the region's main cities and secondary towns, as major interstates, including I-87 and I-90, facilitate accessibility.

The Adirondacks

Lake George and
  Adirondack
  Foothills 272
Champlain Valley 282
Lake Placid and
  High Peaks 289
Central Adirondacks . . . 302
Northwest Lakes 310
The Thousand Islands . . 314
Information
  and Services 327
Getting There
  and Around. 329

Nearly one-third of New York State is a big, blank space on the map. Most of it is contained within Adirondack Park, a six-million-acre refuge that includes vast, silent forests, thousands of gleaming lakes and ponds, hundreds of rugged smoke-blue peaks, and miles of rushing rivers and streams. During the region's short summers, vacationers flock here by the thousands to canoe, fish, camp, and hike.

Once the hunting grounds of the Iroquois and Algonquin, the Adirondacks were largely overlooked by early settlers. Military outposts went up along the shores of Lakes George and Champlain in the mid-1700s, but the rest of the region remained the haunt of hunters and trappers until well into the 1800s. In 1837, New York State

Highlights

Look for ★ to find recommended sights, activities, dining, and lodging.

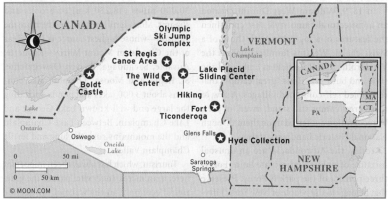

★ **Meet the masters:** The **Hyde Collection** features important works of Old Masters, including Rembrandt, El Greco, and Degas, housed in this 1912 mansion styled as a Renaissance villa (page 272).

★ **Uncover history at Fort Ticonderoga:** The French, British, and Americans all once held control of this meticulously restored fort, which counts a lock of Washington's hair among its objects on display (page 283).

★ **Get an Olympian's perspective:** The **Olympic Ski Jump Complex** offers a gasp-worthy view of the high jumps from a sky deck, while the nearby freestyle aerial training center boasts a year-round training and competition site for freestylers (page 292).

★ **Ride a bobsled:** At **Lake Placid Sliding Center,** bobsleds passenger rides are given year-round on the 1980 Olympic track.

Don't worry, professional drivers are included (page 292).

★ **Hit the trail:** The **Adirondak Loj** trailhead leads to many stunning trails that ascend the region's incomparable peaks. Its information center will advise you in selecting the right trail (page 293).

★ **Canoe:** Consisting of over 18,000 acres of lakes and ponds, the **St. Regis Canoe Area** is the largest such area in the Northeast U.S., offering a vast variety of canoeing experiences for all expertise levels (page 310).

★ **Go wild:** With a highly interactive museum, 81 acres of outdoor space, and a "Wild Walk" trail of treetop bridges, visitors can easily spend an entire day at the **Wild Center** (page 311).

★ **Visit a castle:** If you can't live in your own castle, visiting **Boldt Castle**—built at the bidding of George Boldt in honor of his wife— is probably the next best thing (page 322).

commissioned a natural-history survey of the wilderness, led by geologist and botanist Ebenezer Emmons. Accompanying Emmons was artist Charles Cromwell Ingham, whose paintings of the Adirondacks astonished the general public. Few realized that so great a wilderness remained in the Northeast. Soon outdoor enthusiasts discovered the region. Most famous among them were the members of the Philosophers' Camp. Organized by William Stillman of Cambridge, Massachusetts, the camp included such eminent men as Ralph Waldo Emerson and Louis Agassiz, who came to hike, fish, canoe, botanize, talk, and write.

In 1879, William West Durant created an architectural camp style that combined the features of a log cabin with those of a Swiss chalet. Wealthy families such as the Vanderbilts and Rockefellers embraced the style and built luxurious "great camps" that resembled self-contained villages. A few of these great camps still stand, saved, in part, by recognition conferred upon them through National Historic Landmark status.

Today, the Adirondacks are an unusual mixture of public and private land. Forty-three percent of the park is Forest Preserve that belongs to the people of New York. Fifty-seven percent is privately owned by industries and individuals and devoted primarily to forestry, agriculture, and recreation. Within Adirondack Park live about 128,000 people in 103 towns and villages, many of which have populations of fewer than 1,000.

Contrary to popular belief, the Adirondacks are not an extension of the Appalachian Mountains, but rather are part of the vast Canadian Shield. Nearly twice as old as the Appalachians, the Adirondacks are composed of Precambrian igneous and metamorphic rock thrust upward about 10 million years ago. Atop the summits is a bluish, erosion-resistant bedrock that, at 1.2 million years old, is among the oldest exposed bedrock in the world.

Also contrary to popular perception, much of the Adirondacks is not mountainous. Most of the area lies between 1,000 and 2,000 feet (1,610 and 3,220 m) above sea level, with the western and southern sections composed of gentle hills strewn with lakes, ponds, and streams. Most of the highest summits, known as the High Peaks, are in the northeastern section, around Lake Placid. Forty-two of the 46 High Peaks are over 4,000 feet (1,220 m); Mount Marcy, at 5,344 feet (1,629 m), is the highest.

Throughout the Adirondacks run 1,200 miles (1,930 km) of rivers fed by an estimated 30,000 miles (48,280 km) of brooks and streams. Most significant among them are the Hudson—whose highest source is Lake Tear of the Clouds on Mount Marcy—Raquette, Ausable, Sacandaga, Beaver, Oswegatchie, St. Regis, and Moose. The park also contains about 3,000 lakes and ponds, including the large and well-known Lake George and Lake Champlain. Between Lake Champlain and the mountains runs the long and fertile Champlain Valley.

Tourism, which has always been important here, is an increasingly vital part of the year-round economy. In the wake of the decline of the factory, logging, and commercial fishing work that were the traditional economic mainstays here, more businesses in the tourism industry are looking for ways to extend the appeal of the region to all four seasons.

PLANNING YOUR TIME

A minimum of four or five days is necessary to explore the highlights of the Adirondacks. One to two weeks allow for more leisure and flexibility, especially if you want to do some hiking or canoeing. **Lake Placid** and **Saranac Lake** make good bases of operations. From these two scenic villages amidst the **High Peaks**, it's an easy drive to attractions and good hiking trails. Alternatively, to tack the Adirondacks onto

---

Previous: hiker in Adirondack Mountains; the grounds of Boldt Castle; Mirror Lake.

The Adirondacks

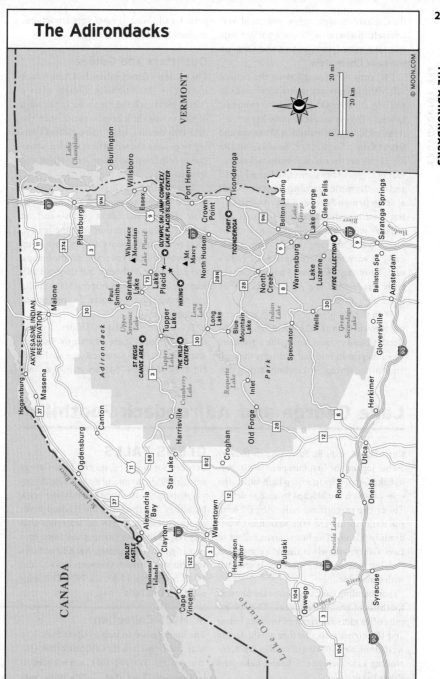

© MOON.COM

the Capital-Saratoga region, you could base yourself in charming **Saratoga Springs** and take overnight trips to **Lake George** and **Lake Champlain.**

I-87 runs north-south along the eastern side of the Adirondack region; local roads 28 and 28N cut across the mountains from east to west, offering access to some key attractions, including **Adirondack Museum** and **Great Camp Sagamore.** Roads 73 and 86 are in the northeastern Adirondacks, providing access to top sights like **Lake Placid** and the **Olympic Training Center,** as well as **John Brown Farm** and **Adirondak Loj.** But travelers who stick only to roads and villages will get a one-sided sense of the place. While offering superb views, roads make it easy to underestimate the park's vast, haunting wildness. The only way to truly experience the Adirondacks is by water or on foot.

With the exception of ski resort areas and major towns such as Lake Placid, much of the North Country closes during the off-season, which begins in mid-fall and runs through mid-to-late spring. If traveling during that period, call ahead to make sure attractions, restaurants, and hotels are open.

Outfitters and Guides

The guide is a firmly entrenched Adirondack institution. Traditionally thought of as a crusty, plaid-jacketed man wise in the ways of the woods, he's been around since the mid-19th century, when naive visitors coming to explore the wilderness needed someone to help them find their way around and stay alive.

The Adirondack Guides Association was formed in 1891 to establish a uniform pay scale. Today, hundreds of guides—and not just men—operate throughout the region. They're not as necessary as they once were, thanks to well-marked trails, detailed maps, and regional guidebooks, but they can still lead you to out-of-the-way spots. Many guides offer group trips, too; some also rent or sell outdoor gear.

For a complete list of guides, contact the **New York State Outdoor Guides Association** (1936 Saranac Ave., Lake Placid, NY 12946, 866/469-7642, www.nysoga.com).

Lake George and Adirondack Foothills

Christened Lac du St. Sacrement in 1609 by Father Jogues, the first European to discover it, Lake George lies in a deep fault valley, the ends of which are blocked by glacial debris. Thirty-two magnificent miles long (52 km), the dark, spring-fed lake surrounds hundreds of islands. The busy tourist village of Lake George sprawls at the lake's southern end, but otherwise the shoreline is crowded with dense pine.

Surrounding Lake George are the forested foothills of the Adirondacks. Their summits offer glorious views of the lake below and the higher peaks farther north. To the west gleam a smattering of smaller lakes, including Lake Luzerne, Schroon Lake, and Brant Lake.

GLENS FALLS

Between Saratoga Springs and Lake George lies Glens Falls, a town of wide, empty downtown streets, dotted with handsome brick buildings. Nearby flows the Hudson River and a 60-foot-high (18 m) waterfall that was responsible for turning the town into an early industrial center. An Adirondacks **information booth** (between Exits 17 and 18 off northbound I-87, 518/792-2730) is located in Glens Falls.

★ Hyde Collection

The main reason to stop in Glens Falls is to tour the first-class **Hyde Collection** (161 Warren St., 518/792-1761, www.hydecollection.org, Tues.-Sat. 10am-5pm, Sun.

Lake George and Southeastern Adirondacks

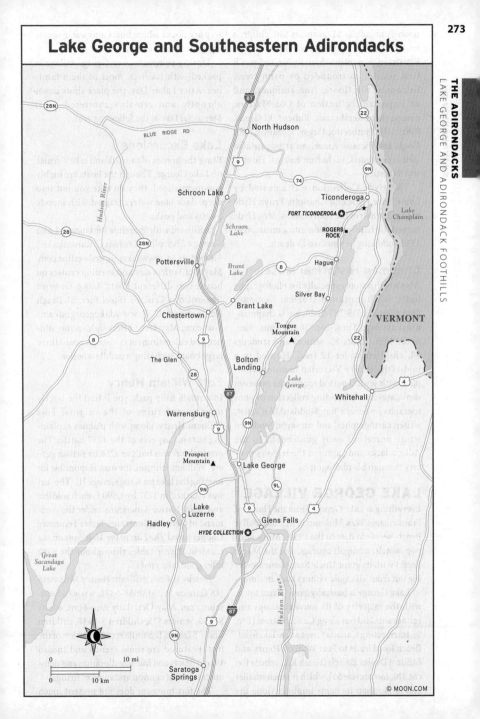

© MOON.COM

noon-5pm, adults $12, seniors $10, children under 12 free), housed in a 1912 American Renaissance mansion. Step inside and you'll find yourself surrounded by palm trees, balconies, tile floors, fine antiques, and an important collection of Old Masters, among them Rembrandt, Rubens, El Greco, Botticelli, Tintoretto, Degas, Cézanne, Van Gogh, and Picasso. American artists are also well represented, including Eakins, Homer, and Whistler.

The Hyde Collection was amassed by Louis Fiske Hyde and Charlotte Pruyn Hyde in the first half of the 20th century. Mrs. Hyde turned the family mansion into a museum in 1952, following her husband's death.

Chapman Historical Museum

Also worth a stop, especially for photography buffs, is **Chapman Historical Museum** (348 Glen St., 518/793-2826, www.chapman-museum.org, Tues.-Sat. 10am-4pm, Sun. noon-4pm, adults $5, seniors and students $4, children under 12 free). Housed in a mid-19th-century Victorian mansion, complete with several period rooms, the museum showcases an outstanding collection of photographs by Seneca Ray Stoddard. An artist, writer, cartographer, and surveyor, Stoddard wrote numerous early guidebooks to the Adirondacks and captured the region's majesty through his photographs.

LAKE GEORGE VILLAGE

Everything at Lake George, from the House of Frankenstein Wax Museum to Million Dollar Beach, seems to date to the 1950s. Mom-and-pop motels, minigolf courses, and the Magic Forest with its giant Uncle Sam statue towering out front all cajole visitors back in time.

Lake George is basically a one-street town, with the majority of its souvenir shops and restaurants laid out along Canada Street (Rte. 9). Intersecting Canada Street at the lakefront, Beach Road leads to Fort William Henry and **Million Dollar Beach** (Beach Rd., vehicle fee: car $10, motorcycle $5), which is *much* smaller and tamer than its name implies. Along the

way are docks where boats and water sports equipment can be rented.

During summer, Lake George village is packed with tourists, most of them families. After Labor Day, the place shuts down abruptly and remains shuttered until Memorial Day of the following year.

Lake Excursions

Brave the hordes of tourists and take a cruise on Lake George. Though the boats are highly commercialized, they do take you out into deep, dark blue waters framed with moody forests and peaks.

Affiliated with Shoreline Restaurant, **Lake George Shoreline Cruises** (2 Kurosaka Ln., 518/668-4644, www.lakegeorgeshoreline.com, May-Oct.) offers day and evening cruises on board two different boats. **Lake George Steamboat Cruises** (Steel Pier, 57 Beach Rd., 518/668-5777, www.lakegeorgesteamboat.com, May-Oct.) offers sightseeing, dinner, and entertainment cruises on board three large boats, including a paddle wheeler.

Fort William Henry

In a small, hilly park, you'll find the largely unexcavated ruins of the original Fort William Henry, along with plaques explaining various aspects of the 1757 battle. The original fort was built in 1756 by British general William Johnson, the man responsible for naming the lake for King George III. The fort was attacked in 1757 by 1,600 French soldiers and 3,000 Native Americans under the command of General Montcalm. James Fenimore Cooper based *The Last of the Mohicans* on the incident. Picnic tables throughout the park offer good lake views.

Nearby is **Fort William Henry Museum** (48 Canada St., 518/668-5471, www.fwhmuseum.com, May-Oct. daily 9am-6pm, adults $19.50, seniors $15, children 5-15 $8, children under 5 free), a facsimile reconstruction of the fort. Featured are some French and Indian War artifacts and life-size dioramas and demonstrations of cannon and musket firings.

The fort museum does not present much

Lake George Village

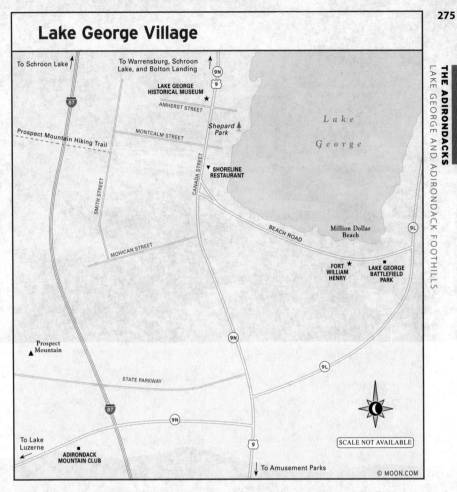

To Schroon Lake

To Warrensburg, Schroon Lake, and Bolton Landing

9N
9

87

LAKE GEORGE HISTORICAL MUSEUM ★

AMHERST STREET

Prospect Mountain Hiking Trail

MONTCALM STREET

Shepard Park

Lake George

SMITH STREET

CANADA STREET

▼ SHORELINE RESTAURANT

BEACH ROAD

Million Dollar Beach

9L

MOHICAN STREET

FORT WILLIAM HENRY ★

LAKE GEORGE BATTLEFIELD PARK ■

Prospect Mountain ▲

STATE PARKWAY

9N

9L

87

9N

To Lake Luzerne

ADIRONDACK MOUNTAIN CLUB

9

To Amusement Parks

SCALE NOT AVAILABLE

© MOON.COM

that's original (and tours offer sensationalized accounts of the history); it's better to save your money for the considerably more authentic Fort Ticonderoga, located at the northern end of Lake George.

Lake George Historical Association and Museum

Housed in the Old Courthouse, the **Lake George Historical Association and Museum** (290 Canada St., 518/668-5044, www.lakegeorgehistorical.org, days and hours vary seasonally, free) has three floors of exhibits on the history of Lake George.

Of particular interest are the jail cells in the basement (circa 1845), an exhibit on lake shipwrecks, photos from the steamboat era, and an elaborate, doll-size wooden church carved by convicted murderer George Ouellet in 1881. After finishing his church, Ouellet sold it for a sizable sum, hired a new lawyer to appeal his conviction, and was acquitted.

Prospect Mountain

For a terrific view of Lake George and the southeastern Adirondacks, drive up **Prospect Mountain Veterans Memorial Highway** (formerly Prospect Mountain State Parkway),

which intersects with Route 9 just south of the village. The 5.5-mile (8.6 km) drive leading up the 2,030-foot (620 m) mountain offers 100-mile (161 km) views of five states. Park your car near the top and board one of the "view-mobiles" to travel to the mountain's crest.

An easy 1.6-mile (2.6 km) hiking trail, marked with red blazes, also leads to the summit. To reach the trailhead from Lake George village, take Montcalm Street to Smith Street and turn south. The trail begins midway down the block and follows the roadbed of an old cable railroad, believed to have been the world's largest. Experienced cyclists can also ride to the summit on a 5.5-mile (8.6 km) trail.

Amusement Parks

Lake George wouldn't be Lake George without its amusement parks. Five miles (8.1 km) south of the village is the largest of them, **Great Escape & Hurricane Harbor** (1172 Rte. 9, 518/792-3500, www.sixflags.com, late June-Labor Day daily, hours vary, adults $65.99, children under 48 inches $49.99, children under age 2 free), offering over 135 rides, shows, and attractions, including Steamin' Demon Loop Rollercoaster and the Sasquatch drop ride.

Three miles (4.8 km) south of the village, **Magic Forest** (1912 Rte. 9, 518/668-2448, www.magicforestpark.com, late June-Labor Day daily 9:30am-5pm, $19.99 adults, seniors, and children, children under age 2 free) offers 24 rides, most of them for kids.

Adirondack Mountain Club (ADK)

Also to the south of Lake George village, near the intersection of Route 9 and Route 9N, is an **information center** run by **Adirondack Mountain Club** (ADK, 814 Goggins Rd., off Rte. 9N west of I-87, 518/668-4447 or 800/395-8080, www.adk.org, Mon.-Sat. 8:30am-5pm), a nonprofit organization dedicated to broadening the public's appreciation of the

Adirondack wilderness. Stop here for information on hiking trails and camping areas. The center also has a bookstore where you can buy maps and guidebooks or make a purchase from a limited but carefully chosen selection of gear. Experts are on hand to answer questions. Take Exit 21 to reach the center directly from I-87.

Hiking

Buck Mountain is on the southeastern shore of Lake George. A well-marked, 3.3-mile (5.3 km) hiking trail leads to the summit and great views of Lake George, Lake Champlain, the Adirondacks, and Vermont's Green Mountains. To reach the trailhead, head east from the village to Route 9L. Turn left and continue for about 7 miles (11.3 km) until you see a turn for Pilot Knob and Kaatskill Bay. Follow this road about 3.5 miles (5.6 km) to the trailhead, marked with a large sign and parking lot. The easy-to-moderate round-trip hike takes about four hours.

Stewarts Ledge is a gentle hike on Lake George's eastern side, ideal for travelers with young children. It also ticks other family-friendly boxes: the hike is short, about 30 minutes to the top, and still yields impressive views of Lake George itself.

Pilot Knob Preserve Hike is another family-friendly trail, a 20-30-minute walk that keeps young ones moving forward because of ever-improving views of a waterfall. Need more to encourage everyone to make it to the summit? There's a gazebo at the top of the trail, where you can enjoy panoramic views of the mountains and lake.

Food

A number of fast-food and sandwich shops are located along Canada Street and Beach Road. Among them is **The Garrison Restaurant and Bar** (220 Beach Rd., 518/685-3013, www.thegarrisonlakegeorge.com, Mon.-Sat. 11:30am-10pm, Sun. noon-10pm, $20), serving burgers, sandwiches, and simple entrées.

For finer dining, try the airy ★ **Shoreline Restaurant** (2 Kurosaka Ln., 518/668-4641,

1: Hudson River in the town of Lake Luzerne
2: historic steamboat on Lake George

The Birth of the Park

In 1872, years after explorers had discovered the sources of the Nile and various rivers out West, a young surveyor named Verplanck Colvin finally traced the Hudson River to its mysterious source. Starting in the Champlain Valley, he and his party hiked from peak to peak until reaching Mount Marcy and what is now known as Lake Tear of the Clouds. "Far above the chilly water of Lake Avalanche," Colvin later reported to the state legislature, "at an elevation of 4,293 feet (1,310 m), is *Summit Water*, a minute unpretending tear of the clouds as it were—a lonely pool, shivering in the breezes of the mountains, and sending its limpid surplus through Feldspar Brook to the Opalescent River, the well-spring of the Hudson."

From that expedition on until 1900, Colvin surveyed the entire Adirondack region. Often financing his own expeditions, he sent back frequent reports to the state legislature, passionately arguing for the creation of a park to preserve the forest and its watershed.

Few listened at first, but as the century wore on, downstate New Yorkers began to worry about their water supply, and businesses worried about the buildup of silt in New York Harbor. Protecting the forests would help solve both problems and create a giant "pleasuring-grounds for the people." Largely because of the businessmen's influence, the idea took hold, and in 1885, the state passed an unprecedented bill establishing a 681,374-acre Adirondack Forest Preserve. This law, strengthened in 1892 and again in 1894, even went so far as to dictate that the preserve remain "forever wild," a phrase that has created considerable controversy ever since.

www.lakegeorgeshoreline.com/restaurant, Memorial Day to Labor Day, daily 11am-10pm, $24), which looks out on a small marina. Menu selections range from fresh fish to chicken teriyaki. Sit on the deck and enjoy live entertainment in summer. Also overlooking the water is the big, boisterous **Boardwalk** (2 Lower Amherst St., 518/668-5324, www.lakegeorgeboardwalk.com, $30), offering burgers and sandwiches at lunch, and considerably more elaborate entrées at dinner.

Accommodations and Camping

This area is best appreciated for the natural beauty of the lake and surroundings, so consider camping or look farther up the lake for accommodations. If you prefer being in the heart of a town with tourist services, consider a chain, as the franchises are most likely to provide the expected level of quality. Dozens of small motels are located along Routes 9 and 9N, many of them classic Adirondack 1950s-style properties. Ask to see the room before committing; many are outdated or well-worn from waterlogged families making themselves at home over the years. Value is

questionable, and the level of service and amenities often does not match the rates.

Six Flags Great Escape Lodge (89 Six Flags Dr., 518/824-6060, www.sixflagsgreatescapelodge.com, $149-239) boasts the kid-friendly amenity of an indoor water park. The hotel's 200 reasonably priced rooms are clean and comfortable and offer a microwave and fridge; some are even Adirondack-themed, with kid-friendly cabins inside the oversized suites. The attractive Adirondack-style lobby with its massive stone fireplace is a nice contrast to the area's largely motel-style offerings. The 1950s diner chain, Johnny Rockets, with dancing servers, cheese fries, and malteds, is on the property, as well as several other restaurants. This resort is one of a few that are open year-round. In winter, it offers Holiday in the Lodge packages, which include entrance to the theme park's ice-skating, sledding, live music, and holiday light festival.

For camping, visit the 68-site **Lake George Battleground State Campground** (2224 Rte. 9, 518/668-3348, www.dec.ny/gov/outdoor/24453.html, reservations 800/456-2267, $22/night for New York residents, $27/night for nonresidents) or the 250-site

Hearthstone Point (3298 Lake Shore Dr., 518/668-5193, reservations 800/456-2267, www.dec.ny.gov/outdoor/24470.html, $22/night for New York residents, $27/night for nonresidents).

LAKE LUZERNE

Take Route 9N out of Lake George village to reach Lake Luzerne, a quieter resort community about 10 miles (16.1 km) away. The village, bounded by two rivers, consists of a few small streets crowded with Victorian homes. Lake Luzerne traditionally has been known for its dude ranches, which is why you'll notice signs pointing to Big Hat Country along the way. Though the dude-ranch business is not what it once was, the country's oldest weekly rodeo still takes place weekend nights in summer at Painted Pony Ranch (703 Howe Rd., 518/696-2421, www.paintedponyrodeo.com).

The free Lake Luzerne Chamber Music Festival (203 Lake Tour Rd., 518/696-2771, www.luzernemusic.org), featuring members of the Philadelphia Orchestra, takes place on Monday nights during the summer at the Luzerne Music Center.

Water Sports

The Hudson River flows along the east side of town, where bubbling Rockwell Falls rushes downstream through a small park. At the western end, the Sacandaga River attracts white-water rafters and canoeists. Rental equipment and guided white-water raft trips down Sacandaga's Class II and III waters are offered by Wild Waters Outdoor Center (518/494-4984, www.wildwaters.net) in nearby Warrensburg.

Hiking

Although Hadley Mountain is just under 2,700 feet (820 m) high, it affords magnificent views from its summit. To the north loom the High Peaks, to the south are the Catskills and Great Sacandaga Lake, and to the east are Lake George and the Green Mountains. The Adirondack Mountain Club considers the 4-mile (6.4 km) round-trip hike to the summit easy-to-moderate in difficulty. The hike should take about three hours.

To reach the trailhead, take Route 9N north of Lake Luzerne to Hadley and head north on Stony Creek Road. Continue 3 miles (4.8 km) to Hadley Hill Road and turn left. Proceed slightly over 4 miles (6.4 km) to Tower Road, turn right, and continue another 1.5 miles (2.4 km) to the trailhead on the left, marked with a sign.

Accommodations and Camping

For camping, visit the 174-site Luzerne State Campground at Fourth Lake (Rte. 9N south of the village, 518/696-2031, reservations 800/456-2267, www.dec.ny.gov/outdoor/24480.html, $22/night for New York residents, $27/night for nonresidents).

The gracious Lamplight Inn B&B (231 Lake Ave., 518/696-5294, www.lamplightinn.com, $175-250 summer, about a third less other seasons) is an award-winning 1890 inn featuring eight bedrooms, most with fireplaces. A carriage house and cottage on the property are also available for rental.

BOLTON LANDING

Back along the shores of Lake George, about 10 miles (16.1 km) north of Lake George village, is Bolton Landing, a congested tourist town. Traffic here is bumper to bumper during summer.

For many visitors, Bolton Landing's main attractions are its gift shops, most along Main Street, which are a step up in class from Lake George village offerings. Bolton Historical Museum (4924 Main St., 518/644-9960, www.boltonhistoricalmuseum.org, July 4-Labor Day daily 10am-4pm, spring and fall Sat.-Sun. 10am-4pm, free), housed in a former Catholic church, includes a collection of photographs by Seneca Ray Stoddard and an exhibit on sculptor David Smith, who once lived in the area.

Sagamore Resort (110 Sagamore Rd., 518/644-9400, www.thesagamore.com), isolated on its own private island at one end of the village, opened in 1883 and is now listed in the National Register of Historic Places. The columned, gabled hotel remains a luxurious year-round resort. Features include eight restaurants and cafés, a full-service spa, tennis courts, playground, nearby golf course, and a sandy beach with great views of Lake George. Cruises on the lake are offered by *The Morgan*, a replica of a 19th-century touring boat (sightseeing cruise included in resort fee).

The Sembrich

Marcella Sembrich, a soprano who sang with the Metropolitan Opera, summered in Bolton Landing from 1921 to 1935. In those days, the village was a favorite resort of opera stars, and Sembrich brought several students with her each year. Today, the diva's former studio **The Sembrich** (4800 Lake Shore Dr., 518/644-2431, www.thesembrich.org, June 15-Sept. 15 daily 10am-12:30pm and 2pm-5pm, free, donations accepted) houses her sizable collection of music, along with her costumes, furniture, and other memorabilia.

Food and Accommodations

Across the street from the Sembrich estate is **Ballymore Guest Cabin at Hilltop Cottage** (4825 Lake Shore Dr., 518/644-2492, www.hilltopcottage.com, $100, May 1-Oct. 31 only). Marcella Sembrich's opera students stayed in the cottage back in the days when she was teaching here.

The ★ **Sagamore Resort** (110 Sagamore Rd., 518/644-9400, www.thesagamore.com, $229-335 off-season, $389-659 summer) offers 100 luxurious rooms and suites in the historic main hotel and 240 private lodge rooms. The Sagamore Resort has a variety of **restaurants** (hours vary). **Mr. Brown's Pub** ($24) serves sandwiches and salads; the **Pavilion** ($38) has a similarly casual menu, with meals served lakeside. **Club Grill Steakhouse** ($45) serves steaks at dinner. **La Bella Vita** ($35) specializes in Italian cuisine.

The casual **Algonquin Restaurant** (Lake Shore Dr., 518/644-9442, www.thealgonquin. com, hours vary seasonally, $28), built over

the water, is a local favorite for lunch and dinner. On the menu is everything from burgers to fresh fish.

NORTHERN LAKE GEORGE

Route 9N continues north of Bolton Landing into much wilder countryside. Tourist centers are left behind as you veer away from the lakeshore, beyond the Tongue Mountain Range, and then return to it once again, passing the isolated resort communities of Sabbath Day Point, Silver Bay, and Hague.

Scenic Route 8 heads west out of Hague to Brant Lake, about 10 miles (16.1 km) away. En route, lookouts offer great views of the High Peaks. In the fall, the surrounding Dixon Forest turns vivid hues of red, yellow, and orange. Mohawk legend describes this as the land of Broken Wing, a crippled brave who saved his village and is remembered every autumn by the turning of the leaves.

About 2 miles (3.2 km) north of Hague on Route 9N are **Indian Kettles,** shallow glacial potholes 1-3 feet (0.3-0.9 m) in diameter said to have been used for cooking by Native Americans.

Rogers Rock State Park

Just north of Indian Kettles, **Rogers Rock State Park** (Rte. 9N, 518/585-6746, camping reservations 800/465-2267, www.dec.ny.gov/outdoor/24493.html, $22/night for New York residents, $27 for nonresidents, parking $6-8) offers a 332-site campground, beach, and bathhouse, along with a 2.5-mile (4 km) hiking trail that leads up 500 feet (150 m) to Rogers Slide. At first, the trail winds mostly uphill and northerly, but then it flattens out to run along a ledge and open expanse. Keeping to the right at a fork just past the ledge will bring you to cliffs overlooking Lake George.

Accommodations and Camping

Forty-eight of the islands dotting Lake George are available for camping, though you'll need a boat to pack in and out. The gorgeous

Beneath the waters of Lake George lie approximately 300 shipwrecked vessels in three "submerged heritage preserves" that are open to the public. Two of the three sites date to the mid-18th century French and Indian War. The third submerged heritage preserve is an underwater classroom for scuba divers who want to learn more about the lake's ecology and these sunken treasures.

Among the wrecks are bateaux, flat-bottom boats that were part of a large fleet deliberately scuttled by the British and the American colonists in 1758 to protect the craft from the French and Native Americans. The British returned to the lake in 1759 and raised close to 200 of the ships. No one suspected the remaining bateaux still existed until two teenage divers discovered them in 1960. That same year, three of the boats were raised from the lake; one was put on exhibit at the Adirondack Museum, which has the second-largest watercraft collection in the country.

Yet another ship was discovered in 1990, a 52-foot (16 m) radeau (seven-sided battleship) named the *Land Tortoise*. Also part of the scuttled fleet, this fragile vessel is North America's oldest intact warship. It is also one of the country's few shipwrecks designated as a National Historic Landmark. Divers can only approach this wreck with advance registration.

To learn more about Lake George's Shipwreck Preserves, contact the **Department of Environmental Conservation** (518/897-1276, www.dec.ny.gov).

---

setting, absolute privacy, and crystal clear swimming make these an obvious draw. For more information, contact the **Department of Environmental Conservation** (518/623-1200, www.dec.ny.gov).

One of the last of the old lakeside hotels that once flourished in this region is **Northern Lake George Resort** (Rte. 9N, Silver Bay, 518/543-6528, www.northernlakegeorge.com, $99-260). It was built in 1896 and originally called Hotel Uncas. The resort has been altered over the years but still features an old-fashioned rustic lobby complete with stone fireplace and high ceilings. Accommodation options include lakeside villas and motel rooms.

SCHROON LAKE AND VICINITY

Schroon Lake, a quiet resort community with a laid-back Main Street and good-size public beach, is situated west of Lake George. During the summer, one-hour narrated cruises of the lake are offered by **Schroon Lake Boat Tours** (518/532-7675). The area is also home to the **Seagle Music Colony** (999 Charley Hill Rd., 518/532-7875, www.seaglecolony.org), a music retreat founded by concert baritone

Oscar Seagle in 1915. The colony stages opera concerts and musical theater July-early August.

Natural Stone Bridge and Caves

At the lake's southern end, near Pottersville, lies **Natural Stone Bridge and Caves** (535 Stone Bridge Rd., off Rte. 9, 518/494-2283, www.stonebridgeandcaves.com, hours vary seasonally, adults $14, children 5-12 $8.50). Formed by the Ausable River, this geological park features odd-shaped rock formations, waterfalls, and potholes large enough to park a truck in.

Hiking Pharaoh Mountain

To the east of Schroon Lake rises Pharaoh Mountain, surrounded by the Pharaoh Lake Wilderness Area. The splendid views from the mountaintop, covered with open rock, take in nearby ponds and craggy hills, as well as the more distant High Peaks. The 9-mile (14.5 km) round-trip hike is of moderate difficulty and takes 4-5 hours.

To reach the trailhead, head north of Schroon Lake on Route 9 about 2 miles (3.2 km). Turn right onto Alder Meadow Road and continue 2.2 miles (3.5 km) to a fork. Bear left on Crane Pond Road and travel 1.4 miles (2.3 km) to a parking lot. Continue on the road on foot 1.9 miles (3.1 km) to Crane Pond, where the trailhead begins at the end of another parking lot (parking is not permitted here).

Detour to North Hudson

On the edge of the High Peaks region about 7 miles (11.3 km) north of Schroon Lake village is North Hudson, a tiny mountain hamlet surrounded by ponds and wilderness; its year-round population is about 240. The place is well worth a detour for the magnificent views along the way.

Blue Ridge Road (Rte. 2) heads west out of North Hudson to skirt the southern edge of the High Peaks. The route runs alongside the Branch, which flows between Elk Lake and Schroon River; about 3 miles (4.8 km) from the village cascade the lovely **Blue Ridge waterfalls.**

Food and Accommodations

One of the finest restaurants in the area, specializing in innovative American dishes, is the rambling Civil War-era ★ **Friend's Lake Inn** (Friends Lake Rd., 518/494-4751, www.friendslake.com, Fri.-Sun., 5:30pm-8pm, $32), about 7 miles (11.3 km) south of Schroon Lake in historic Chestertown. The wine list alone runs about 25 pages long. A full menu of New American fare is offered at dinner only, though in summer, a bar and light lunch menu are also available. Upstairs and out back are 17 lovely guest rooms ($359-550, including breakfast and dinner; $319-510 breakfast only), all with queen-size beds and private baths. Many rooms also have whirlpool tubs, and two have fireplaces.

Schroon Lake Bed and Breakfast (Rte. 9, 518/532-7042, www.schroonbb.com, $130-170) offers four comfortable guest rooms furnished with antiques. A breezy front porch provides good views of the lake and Adirondacks.

Tucked into the mountains north of North Hudson is ultrasecluded ★ **Elk Lake Lodge** (1106 Elk Lake Rd., 518/532-7616, www. elklakelodge.com, $125-210 pp, includes all meals). One of the finest rustic lodges in the Adirondacks, Elk Lake Lodge is situated on its own private lake surrounded by a 12,000-acre preserve. The main lodge, built in 1904, offers six rooms with private baths, as does the more modern Emerson Lodge. Eight cottages sit on the lakefront.

Champlain Valley

In 1609, 11 years before the Pilgrims landed in Massachusetts, French explorer Samuel de Champlain "discovered" the long, thin, sparkling blue lake that now bears his name. Shortly after his arrival, he encountered and killed two Iroquois, establishing the tenor of European-Native American relations for centuries to come.

Lake Champlain is 110 miles (177 km) long and in spots 400 feet (120 m) deep. Encompassing 490 square miles, it stretches from New York north into Canada and east into Vermont. Even bigger than the lake itself is the basin in which it sits. On the New York side, that basin extends as far west as the Adirondack Mountains and as far south as Hudson Falls. About 25 percent of Adirondack Park lies within the Champlain Valley.

Compared to Lake George, the shores of Lake Champlain appear sparsely forested and surprisingly undeveloped. The countryside becomes especially magnificent north of Port Henry, where the raw, jagged High Peaks of the Adirondacks rise to one side and the moody, rounder peaks of Vermont's Green Mountains to the other. Away from the shore, the valley opens into rich farmland.

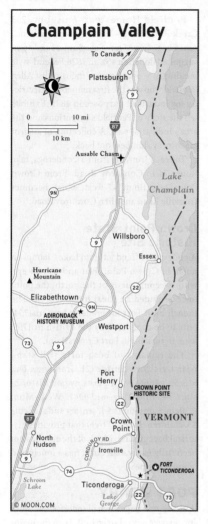

Champlain Valley

Red barns, silver silos, and a patchwork of green fields spread out over one gentle slope after another. Dairy farming is especially big business.

Pick up brochures and maps at **Lake Champlain Visitors Center** (814 Bridge Rd., 518/597-4649, www.lakechamplainregion.com, Mon.-Fri. 9am-4pm), which is near the Lake Champlain Bridge connecting New York with Vermont.

TICONDEROGA

Ticonderoga, the town and the fort, is sandwiched in the 2 miles (3.2 km) between Lake George and Lake Champlain. The town sits at the foot of Lake George; the fort overlooks Lake Champlain.

The Town

Sprawling, scruffy Ticonderoga centers around a historic downtown containing several interesting buildings. Among them is **Ticonderoga Heritage Museum** (Montcalm St. at Bicentennial Park, 518/585-2696, Memorial Day-mid-Oct., hours vary seasonally, free), which houses displays on the area's industrial history. Traditionally, Ticonderoga has been known for its pencil- and papermaking plants. The first commercial pencils, which bore the name "Ticonderoga," were produced in the area in 1840. The industry has not entirely disappeared; International Paper still operates in town.

★ Fort Ticonderoga

One of the Adirondacks' most popular visitor attractions, **Fort Ticonderoga** (100 Fort Ti Rd., 518/585-2821, www.fortticonderoga.org, mid-May-mid-Oct. daily 9:30am-5pm, hours vary off-season, adults $24, seniors $22, children 5-12 $12, children under 4 free), sits within a shade-filled park. Originally built by the French in 1755, the fort bore the nickname "Key to a Continent." Strategically located along the Canada-New York waterway, Ticonderoga was attacked six times during the French and Indian and Revolutionary Wars. Three times it held successfully, and three times it fell. Control changed hands among the French, British, and Americans.

Inside the fort are meticulously restored barracks, kitchens, stables, cannons, and artifacts from both wars. Among the more unusual items on display are a lock of George Washington's hair, a pocket watch once owned by Ethan Allen, and a rum horn given to General Schuyler by Paul Revere. Numerous special events are staged daily throughout the summer, including parades, cannon firings, and fife-and-drum musters.

America's Fort Cafe (518/585-2821, $13), on-site in the Log House Visitors' Center, serves reasonably priced soups, salads, and sandwiches and has great views of Lake Champlain and Vermont's Green Mountains.

Fort Ticonderoga Ferry

Continue east past the fort on Route 74 to reach a public boat ramp and dock for the **Fort Ticonderoga Ferry** (4831 Rte. 74, 802/897-7999, www.forttiferry.com, daily 7am-6pm, $12 per car with up to four passengers one-way, $18 round-trip; $2 per bicycle and rider; $1 per pedestrian, cash only), in operation in one form or another since the mid-1700s. From May to October, the flatbed ferry crosses whenever there's traffic to Shoreham, Vermont. The low-key journey only takes a few minutes.

CROWN POINT

About 8 miles (12.9 km) north of Ticonderoga is the village of Crown Point, not to be confused with the Crown Point State Historic Site a few miles farther north. The village of Crown Point was once known for its iron industry. The remains of two forts are at the historic site.

Ironville

Hard as it is to believe today, the quiet, near-deserted area just west of Crown Point was once a major industrial center filled with dirty, clanking machinery. A rich bed of iron ore was discovered here in the early 1800s, and throughout that century, the region teemed with mines, forges, and railroads. The high-quality ore attracted the U.S. Navy, intent on securing iron to build its first ironclad warship, the Civil War-era *Monitor*.

Crown Point's industrial activity centered around the company town of Ironville, now a village so small it's all but disappeared. In its heyday, Ironville boasted a company store, company housing, and company script. Today, it's an exceptionally lovely hamlet with a strong New England feel.

Penfield Homestead Museum (703 Creek Rd., 518/597-3804, www.penfieldmuseum.org, June-Oct. Sat.-Sun. 11am-4pm, suggested donation $5), an 1828 Federal-style building, was once home to industrialist Allen Penfield who was the first man to use electricity for industrial purposes in 1831. Exhibits tell the story of Penfield's inventions and the area's industrial past. A collection of ancient machinery slumbers out back.

To reach Ironville from Ticonderoga, take Route 74 to Corduroy Road. From Crown Point, take Route 47 west, which becomes Ironville Road and then Corduroy Road.

Crown Point State Historic Site

A pudgy spit of land juts into Lake Champlain north of Crown Point. Flat and windswept, with sweeping views of the north, the point once provided an ideal lookout spot. The French built Fort St. Frederic here in 1734, only to be conquered by the British in 1759, who, in turn built, Fort Crown Point.

The remains of both forts still stand near a **visitors center** (21 Grandview Dr., 518/597-4666, www.parks.ny.gov/historic-sites/34, mid-May-mid-Oct. Wed.-Mon. 9:30am-5pm, adults $4, seniors and students $3, children under 12 free) that provides historical background. Much of the area has not been fully excavated, but it has a lonely and haunting appeal.

PORT HENRY

Port Henry, a large town of redbrick buildings spread over several steep hills, is on the mainland just north of Crown Point State Historic Site. Like Crown Point, Port Henry was once known for its iron industry, which peaked here during World War II. A giant 18-million-ton mountain of ore tailings that's visible for miles around is just west of town.

"Welcome to the Home of the Champ" reads the sign at the town's entrance. A cheerful green serpent with a zigzagging tail stands nearby. **The Champ** is a legendary monster purported to live in the depths

The Adirondack Ecosystem

The Adirondack forest supports over 70 different species of trees, most of which are in the spruce and fir, or beech, birch, and maple families. White pines grow at the park's lowest elevations in the Champlain Valley, while spruce grows above 2,500 feet (760 m). In between thrive spruce swamps and hardwood forests.

Woodland wildflowers such as dewdrops and lily of the valley flourish in the lower Adirondacks, while bright specks of alpine flora, mosses, lichens, and other hardy plants grow on the peaks. Several good guides to the park's flora and fauna are published by the Adirondack Mountain Club.

As for mammals, the Adirondacks are home to 53 species, including raccoon, porcupine, weasel, mink, otter, bobcat, fox, coyote, white-tailed deer, and black bear, as well as the elusive moose and lynx, which were reintroduced into the forest in the 1990s.

Birdlife in the park ranges from the very small (chickadees and nuthatches) to the very large (grouse and osprey). More than 200 species have been spotted, including hawks, kingbirds, peregrine falcons, and bald eagles. One of the most characteristic sounds of the Adirondacks is the haunting call of the loon.

Eighty-six species of fish swim in Adirondack waters, including trout, salmon, northern pike, and small- and largemouth bass. The region also supports 35 species of reptiles and amphibians. Pesky blackflies thrive in the mountains in late May-June, and mosquitoes are plentiful throughout the summer.

---

of Lake Champlain. Stories about him have circulated for hundreds of years, first among the Iroquois and later among explorers and settlers. In 1609, Samuel de Champlain reported seeing the 20-foot-long (6 m) creature in the lake. Since then, there have been over 300 reported sightings of the Champ, many near Port Henry. Although there is no concrete proof that the Champ exists, the legislatures of both New York and Vermont have passed resolutions encouraging scientific inquiry into the depths of the lake.

WESTPORT

Lying on a natural terrace above a deep bay, the tidy Victorian village of Westport has been a favorite stopping-off place since steamship days, when families traveling north on Lake Champlain debarked here to catch stagecoaches for points farther west. Later, Westport became a destination in its own right, as evidenced by the elegant homes along Route 22. Today, Westport remains one of the few villages in the Adirondacks that's accessible by rail; Amtrak travels through here on its way between New York and Montréal.

Westport is known for its historic inns and

Depot Theater (6705 Main St., 518/962-4449, www.depottheatre.org), which presents professional summer stock in a restored 19th-century railway station. A busy marina, where boats can be rented, and a public beach are on the lakeshore.

Food

For casual dining at the marina, try **The Galley** (20 Washington St., 518/962-4899, www.westportmarina.com/galley, hours vary seasonally, $22), which offers pasta, fish, and burgers. Live bands play on weekend nights in the summer. The **Westport Lakeside Hotel** (6691 Main St., 518/962-4501, www.thewestporthotel.com, Mon.-Fri. lunch and dinner, Sat.-Sun. breakfast, lunch, and dinner, $24) runs a tavern whose walls were made from wooden siding reclaimed from an area barn. The stone bar and cozy fireplace also contribute to the authentic Adirondack ambience.

Accommodations

The clapboard **Westport Lakeside Hotel** (6691 Main St., 518/962-4501, www.thewestporthotel.com, $65-150) dates to 1876, the same year that the railroad came to town.

Inside are 11 guest rooms nicely outfitted in early Americana; outside is an inviting wraparound porch.

The stately 1855 **Inn in Westport** (1234 Stevenson Rd., 518/335-1966, www.innwestport.com, $130-205, with breakfast), situated across the street from the town library, features 12 spacious guest rooms with period furnishings, each named after a famous writer. A sitting room with a fireplace, a bookstore styled like a personal library, and an outdoor deck are common areas enjoyed by guests.

ESSEX

The loveliest village along the Lake Champlain shore is Essex. Filled with trim, white pre-Civil War buildings, the entire village is in the National Register of Historic Places. The Adirondacks' dramatic High Peaks rise to the west; to the east sparkle the blue waters of the lake, offset by the dusk-blue mountains of Vermont.

Essex, founded in 1765, was one of the earliest European settlements on Lake Champlain. The community was completely destroyed during the American Revolution but soon rose again to become a prosperous shipbuilding center and lake port. By 1850, Essex was one of the largest and busiest towns on the lake, with a population of 2,351.

Then came the Civil War, the opening of the West, and the building of the railroads, all of which drew commerce away from Lake Champlain. Essex's economy suffered and its population dwindled. There was little money for building; standing structures had to suffice. And so it remains today.

Essex centers around two parallel streets, Main and Elm, both just two blocks long. Excellent examples of Federal, Greek Revival, and Victorian architecture abound, while a park and small marina stretch along the waterfront.

Lake Champlain Ferries (802/864-9804, www.ferries.com, car and driver $10.75 + $4.50 per adult passenger and $2.25 per child passenger, cyclists $5.50; prices quoted are one-way) dock at the northern end of the village, crossing between Essex and Charlotte, Vermont. The ride takes 20 minutes one-way.

Food and Accommodations

At the heart of Essex sits the 200+-year-old ★ **Essex Inn** (2297 Main St., 518/963-4400, www.essexinnessex.com, $195-395, with full breakfast), which was fully renovated in 2010 and has 14 guest rooms. Breakfast and dinner ($22) are served outside in warm weather.

ELIZABETHTOWN

Elizabethtown, the Essex County seat, is about 10 miles (16.1 km) west of Westport and Lake Champlain. Settled in 1791 by pioneers from Vermont, Elizabethtown was at first known for its lumber mills and later for its resort hotels.

Essex County Courthouse

Essex County Courthouse (7551 Court St.), where the body of abolitionist John Brown lay in state on the way to burial in nearby North Elba, is in the town's center. Brown's wife and other members of the funeral entourage spent the night at the town's Deer's Head Inn while four young men from the village stood guard over the body. Today, the courthouse features a mural of Brown speaking in his own defense at his 1859 trial in West Virginia. Another mural depicts Samuel de Champlain firing his arquebus at the Iroquois.

Adirondack History Center Museum

Housed in a big old schoolhouse on the edge of town, the laid-back **Adirondack History Center Museum** (7590 Court St., 518/873-6466, www.adkhistorycenter.org, Memorial Day to mid-Oct., Tue.-Sat. 10am-4pm, Sun. noon-4pm, adults $5, seniors $4, children 6-16 $2, children under 6 free) corrals an enormous hodgepodge of exhibits. A re-created log-cabin kitchen and artifacts from an iron mine take up one floor; on another is an exhibit on the Iroquois and displays about the lumbering industry. A light-and-sound show offers some perspective on the

French and Indian War, while Adirondack guide boats, early farm implements, antique bobsleds, and a roomful of dolls tell stories of everyday Adirondack life.

Hiking

On the north side of Route 9N, 6.8 miles (10.9 km) west of Elizabethtown and 1.6 miles (2.6 km) past Hurricane Road, a small parking area and sign point the way to **Hurricane Mountain.** The red-marked trail passes through a pretty coniferous forest before heading up a ridge to the rocky summit pass. Superb views of the Jay Range, the Green Mountains, Mount Marcy, and Whiteface Mountain await at the top. The Adirondack Mountain Club lists the moderate-to-difficult hike as 5.3 miles (8.5 km) round-trip, averaging about 4.5 hours.

KEENE

Route 9N leads northwest from Elizabethtown to Keene, the "Town of High Peaks." Completely surrounded by jagged mountaintops, Keene's main street is lined with white frame houses, white picket fences, and tourist-oriented shops. Most noticeable among them is **North Country Taxidermy and Trading Post** (Main St./Rte. 73, 518/576-4318), with stuffed bears and wolves out front. The shop stocks a wide array of North Country souvenirs, including antlers, stuffed birds, mounted heads, leather goods, and bearskin rugs.

Route 73 climbs west out of Keene to Lake Placid. For much of the way, the route follows the riverbed of the wide Cascade Brook. En route you'll pass two sparkling lakes ringed with trees.

Food

A Keene Valley landmark, **Noon Mark Diner** (1770 Main St./Rte. 73, 518/576-4499, www. noonmarkdiner.com, daily 6am-10pm, $12) is the place to go for homemade fruit pies, as well as homemade doughnuts, soups, and bread. Chili, burgers, and simple dinners are also on the menu. Another popular spot is

Lisa G's (6125 Sentinel Rd., 518/523-2093, www.lisags.com, daily lunch and dinner, $19), a friendly place serving "comfort food with a twist."

Accommodations

Keene Valley Lodge (Rte. 73, Keene Valley, 518/576-2003, www.keenevalleylodge.com, $80-325), housed in a lovely Italianate building, is a B&B offering a variety of rooms, some of which share baths; others are suites. Guest rooms are furnished with antiques. Common areas include a den with fireplace and the inn's wraparound porch. Another excellent option is **The Snow Goose Bed & Breakfast** (1433 Rte. 73, 518/576-9460, www.thesnowgoose. com, $125-140), a comfortable B&B with three rooms. The property is set on 13 acres, and hiking trails begin practically just outside the front door.

NORTH TO AUSABLE CHASM

Continuing north of Essex on Route 22, you'll hug the lakeshore for a few glorious miles before heading inland to **Willsboro,** which is on the Bouquet River. Continue another 13 miles (20.9 km) north and you'll bump into **Ausable Chasm** (2144 Rte. 9, 518/834-7454, www.ausablechasm.com, spring, fall, and winter daily 9am-4pm, summer daily 9am-5pm, adults $17.95, children 5-12 $9.95, children under 5 free). Carved out by the Ausable River over the past 500 million years, this massive stone gorge stretches out over 1.5 miles (2.4 km). It is 20-50 feet (6-15 m) wide, 100-200 feet (30-60 m) deep, and filled with odd rock formations, caves, rapids, and waterfalls. After the serene back roads and peaceful vistas of Lake Champlain, this place comes as a shock.

Ausable Chasm is one of the oldest tourist attractions in the United States, opened in 1870. Count on dozens of tour buses crowding its parking lot. A 0.75-mile trail leads through the gorge to Table Rock, where visitors can opt to take **rafts** (adults $12, children 5-12 $10, children under 5 $5) the rest of the way.

Forever Wild

During the past 100 years, numerous land purchases by the state have increased the Adirondack Forest Preserve from its original 681,374 acres to its present size. The park's Blue Line—a term derived from the color ink used in 1884 to delineate the park's boundaries on a map—now encompasses nearly six million acres.

With this growth has come conflict, exacerbated by increased tourism and a boom in second homes. The conflict has pitted conservationists concerned about the park's ecological future against those advocating varying forms of economic development.

The conflict reached one early crisis point in the late 1960s, when the building of I-87 opened up the region to yet more visitors. As a result, Governor Nelson Rockefeller appointed a state commission to study the future of the park in 1968. Among the commission's proposals was the establishment of an Adirondack Park Agency (APA) to encourage wise land-use planning.

Duly established in 1971, the APA has since instituted zoning laws for both the park's state *and* private lands. This has infuriated many residents who feel that the state has no right to tell them what they can or cannot do with private property. Many also feel that zoning laws, along with the original "forever wild" clause, are inhibiting economic growth in an area already suffering from out-migration and severe unemployment.

For conservationists, of course, there is no real debate. In a world of ever-decreasing blank spots on the map, the park must be preserved.

NORTH ON 9N

Heading into the High Peaks region from Ausable Chasm on Route 9N, you'll pass through **Au Sable Forks,** once home to illustrator Rockwell Kent, and tiny **Jay,** beautifully situated on the East Branch of the Ausable River. Several old-fashioned country stores and **Jay Craft Center** (Rte. 9N, 518/946-7824, www.jaycraftcenter.com), housing a pottery studio and a gift shop, are located in Jay. A few miles south in **Upper Jay** are **antiques shops** just waiting to be browsed.

From Jay, take Route 86 west to reach **Wilmington,** a small ski town huddled at the base of towering Whiteface Mountain, or keep heading north for Plattsburgh.

PLATTSBURGH

The small industrial city of Plattsburgh played an important role in both the American Revolution and the War of 1812. In 1776, the British won the Battle of Lake Champlain off Plattsburgh's shores. In 1814, American commodore Thomas MacDonough defeated a British fleet from Canada here by using an intricate system of anchors and winches that enabled him to swivel his vessels completely around.

Plattsburgh-North Country Chamber of Commerce runs a **visitor information center** (off I-87 heading south between Exits 41 and 40, 800/487-6867).

Riverwalk Park

Historic Plattsburgh centers around **Riverwalk Park,** which runs along the banks of the Saranac River downtown. The park begins at Bridge Street and extends to the Champlain Monument at Cumberland Avenue. Sights worth noting along the way include the 1830 **Trinity Episcopal Church** (Trinity Pl.); the 1917 **City Hall** (City Hall Pl.), designed by John Russell Pope; and the **Champlain Monument** (Cumberland Ave.), a gift to the city from France in 1909, commemorating the tercentenary of Samuel de Champlain's voyage.

Kent-Delord House Museum

The city's foremost visitor attraction, **Kent-Delord House Museum** (17 Cumberland

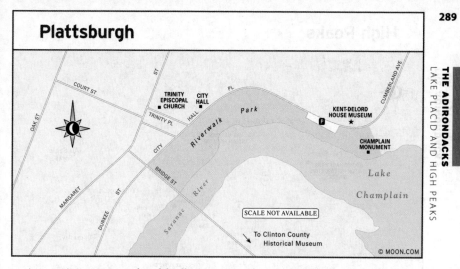

Plattsburgh

Ave., 518/561-1035, www.kentdelordhouse.
org, May-Oct., hours vary seasonally, adults
$5, children under 12 $3), stands across from
the Champlain Monument. Built in 1797 and
enlarged in 1811, the gracious house was com-
mandeered by the British during the War of
1812. Home to three generations of the Delord
family, the house contains nine period rooms
and an interesting collection of portraits. Of
special interest is an exhibit on Fanny Delord
Hall, a self-taught healer who in the late 1800s
patented and marketed her own home remedy,
Fanoline, "a healing, antiseptic and curative
ointment, in cases of Eczema, Fever-sores,

Catarrh, Salt-rheum, Piles, Sore Nipples,
Burns, Blisters, Scratches, Corns, Sore Eyes,
Chapped Hands, and Lips."

Clinton County Historical Museum

To learn about Plattsburgh's history, visit the
Clinton County Historical Museum (98
Ohio Ave., 518/561-0340, www.clintoncoun-
tyhistorical.org, Wed.-Sat. 10am-3pm and
by appointment, adults $5, seniors $3, children under 12 $2), which presents exhibits on
North Country themes, including mining and
other local industry.

Lake Placid and High Peaks

Though it was known to avid hikers and skiers, it wasn't until the 1980 Winter Olympics
that Lake Placid transformed from a sleepy
town to a destination on the state map. Today,
almost everyone who visits the Adirondacks
visits Lake Placid, which centers on one long
and sometimes very congested Main Street
running alongside the lake. The village draws
almost as many visitors because of its upscale
shops and restaurants as it does for its lonely,

mountainous countryside. Even the former
Olympic sites have become popular tourist
attractions.

Keep in mind that Lake Placid is not actually on Lake Placid, but on Mirror Lake. Lake
Placid, a much larger body of water, lies to the
immediate north of the village.

The term "High Peaks" generally refers
to the heart of the Adirondacks, where 46 of
the region's highest peaks can be found. Just

High Peaks

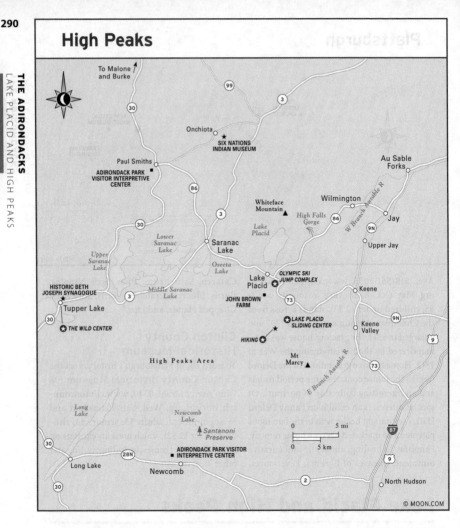

© MOON.COM

west of the Champlain Valley, the High Peaks are loosely bounded by Elizabethtown to the east, Wilmington to the north, the Franklin County line to the west, and Newcomb to the south. Lake Placid lies at the center.

Many hikers come to the High Peaks region intent on climbing all 46 of its highest summits and thereby becoming "46ers." The tradition dates back to the early 1920s, when two young brothers, George and Robert Marshall, climbed to the top of Whiteface Mountain with their guide, Herb Clark. Upon reaching the summit, they made a pact to climb all the peaks in the park measuring 4,000 feet (1,220 m) or more in height. Later, it turned out that some of the peaks on their list were under 4,000 feet (1,220 m), but no matter, a pattern had been set. Today, hikers come from all over the country to carry on the tradition. If you intend to join them, Adirondack Mountain

1: Olympic Center in Lake Placid 2: Lake Placid Sliding Center 3: ferry on Lake Champlain 4: Fort Ticonderoga

Club has a special website devoted to the 46 Peaks (www.adk46er.org), which is rich with information, including a list of the peaks, their elevations, and hiking tips.

SIGHTS AND RECREATION
Olympic Center

Olympic Center (2634 Main St., 518/523-1655, www.whiteface.com), built for the 1932 Winter Olympics and renovated for the 1980 Games, stands at the entrance to the village. The center still houses four Olympic ice-skating arenas (three indoor, one outdoor), which are open for public skating. In Olympic Center, Lake Placid Olympic Museum (www.lpom.org, daily 10am-5pm, adults $8, seniors and children 7-12 $6, children under 7 free) has an extensive collection of Olympic memorabilia.

Lake Placid-North Elba Historical Society Museum

Now occupying the old Lake Placid railroad station, the eclectic Lake Placid-North Elba Historical Society Museum (242 Station St., 518/523-1608, www.lakeplacidhistory.com, May-Oct. Wed. 10am-6pm, Thurs.-Sun. 10am-4pm, adults $5, seniors $2, children free) houses everything from antique sporting equipment to mementos of conductor Victor Herbert, who once summered on the lake. Exhibits on the experimental colony for former enslaved people, founded in 1849 by abolitionist John Brown, are especially interesting.

John Brown Farm State Historic Site

In 1849, abolitionist Gerrit Smith, later joined by John Brown, established a farming community for free Blacks and escaped enslaved people in the Adirondacks. Each new farmer was given 40 acres to till, but since few came prepared to cope with the region's harsh climate, most left within a few years. The area is now designated the John Brown Farm State Historic Site (115 John Brown Rd.,

518/523-3900, www.parks.ny.gov/historic-sites/29/details.aspx, May-Oct. Wed.-Mon. 10am-5pm, free). Brown himself lived on the farm for several more years, in a cabin that has been nicely restored. He erected his own gravestone on the grounds.

Brown was executed in Charlestown, Virginia, on December 2, 1859, following his seizure of the U.S. Arsenal at Harper's Ferry. His body was shipped north to New York City, where his coffin was exchanged for a new one so he would not be buried in Southern property. At each stop along the way upstate, his entourage was greeted with sympathetic crowds and tolling bells.

★ Olympic Ski Jump Complex

If you approached Lake Placid from the east on Route 73, the first thing you undoubtedly noticed were the stark towers of the Olympic Ski Jump Complex (5486 Cascade Rd., 518/523-2202, www.whiteface.com, daily 9am-4pm, $40 for Olympic Sites Passport), looming out of the landscape like giant misshapen thumbs. The site still serves as a training center and is open year-round, thanks to plastic mats, water ramps, and snowmaking machines.

Upon entering the complex, stop first at the freestyle aerial facility, where—with any luck—you'll see athletes practicing their maneuvers by sailing off water-filled ramps and over pools. Next, visit the main lodge to view a photo exhibit on the history of ski jumping, and catch the chairlift to the 90-meter jump. If training is taking place, you can watch from an observation deck. If not, take the glass-enclosed elevator to the top of the 120-meter jump for great views of the High Peaks.

★ Lake Placid Sliding Center

South of the ski jumping complex rises Mount Van Hoevenberg, site of Olympic bobsled, luge, and skeleton runs at Lake Placid Sliding Center (518/523-4436, www.whiteface.com, daily 9am-4pm, $40 for Olympic Sites Passport). The track measures almost a mile long. Passenger rides on bobsleds are offered year-round.

The excellent **Olympic Cross-Country Biathlon Center** (www.whiteface.com), also on Mount Van Hoevenberg, offers a 31-mile (50 km) system of trails. In winter, trails are groomed frequently and open to cross-country skiers of all levels. In summer, trails are used by mountain bikers and horseback riders. Skis and bikes can be rented on-site, and guided horseback rides are available.

★ Hiking

Mount Marcy, elevation 5,344 feet (1,630 m), is the highest mountain in the Adirondacks, and the one that draws the most hikers each year. In 1872, Verplanck Colvin first hiked the mountain and discovered **Lake Tear of the Clouds,** the source of the Hudson River. "But how wild and desolate this spot!" he wrote. "It is possible that not even an Indian ever stood upon these shores. There is no mark of ax, no barked tree, nor blackened remnants of fire; not a severed twig or a human footprint?"

Since that day, many have followed in Verplanck's footsteps; an estimated 45,000 people make the 7-mile (11.3 km) trek annually. Anticipating the problems that come with overuse, park personnel urge hikers to shy away from famed Mount Marcy and tackle lesser-known peaks instead. **Adirondak Loj** (1002 Adirondak Loj Rd., 518/523-3441, www. adk.org), 8 miles (12.9 km) south of Lake Placid, is the starting point of many trails that ascend into the park. It's also the site of a first-rate information center, staffed by the nonprofit **Adirondack Mountain Club,** which can help you choose the hike that's right for you.

Also on Averyville Road, 1.2 miles (1.9 km) past the intersection with Old Military Road, is a blue-marked trail that leads to **Wanika Falls.** The 13.4-mile (21.6 km) hike takes about seven hours, but the terrain is easy, and the waterfalls make the trip worthwhile. According to the Adirondack Mountain Club, the route leads through some of the finest forest in the region before ascending an old road leading to Chubb River and cascading falls, several hundred feet high. The trail is part of the much longer Northville-Placid Trail laid out by the Adirondack Mountain Club in 1922 and 1923.

Boating

A small **public beach** (Parkside Dr., off Main St., 518/523-2445, daily dawn-dusk) is situated south of Olympic Center. Just

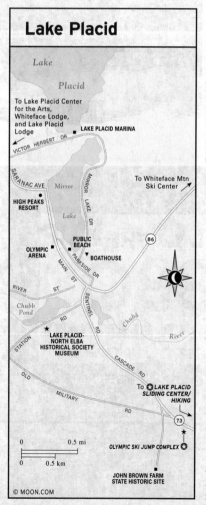

Lake Placid

Lake

Placid

To Lake Placid Center for the Arts, Whiteface Lodge, and Lake Placid Lodge

LAKE PLACID MARINA

VICTOR HERBERT DR

SARANAC AVE

Mirror

MIRROR LAKE DR

HIGH PEAKS RESORT

Lake

To Whiteface Mtn Ski Center

PUBLIC BEACH

86

OLYMPIC ARENA

BOATHOUSE

PARKSIDE DR

MAIN ST

RIVER ST

SENTINEL RD

Chubb Pond

Chubb

River

STATION RD

★ LAKE PLACID-NORTH ELBA HISTORICAL SOCIETY MUSEUM

CASCADE RD

OLD MILITARY RD

To ◑ LAKE PLACID SLIDING CENTER/ HIKING

73

0   0.5 mi
0   0.5 km

OLYMPIC SKI JUMP COMPLEX ◑

© MOON.COM

JOHN BROWN FARM STATE HISTORIC SITE

beyond the northern end of Mirror Lake lies Lake Placid and **Lake Placid Marina** (Mirror Lake Dr., 518/523-9704, www.lakeplacidmarina.com), where one-hour lake cruises depart May-October.

Canoes, kayaks, and other boats can be rented at **Captain Marney's** (35 Victor Herbert Dr., 518/523-9746, www.boatrentallakeplacid.com).

Winter Recreation

Some of the best outdoor winter activities are to be found in the Adirondacks region, though not all of these are geared toward novices. **Ice climbing** is one such activity, and Lake Placid's **Multiplication Gully** (Rte. 86) is one particularly beautiful, challenging spot for experienced climbers. The 225-foot (70 m) climb is up a long, vertical crevice between two large, tall rock faces, with three pitches and other challenges presented by the gully's narrow width. Climbing pros from **High Peaks Mountain Guides** (2733 Main St., Lake Placid, 518/523-3764, www.hpmountainguides.com) offer guide services to this and other climb sites. Their climber to guide ratio is low, and services come with all gear included, as well as instruction. Half-day trips start at $300, with $100 per additional climber (up to four people total).

Cross-country skiing is an ideal sport for people of all skill levels, and plenty of trails crisscross the Adirondacks, leading across frozen lakes and mountainous terrain. One of the most popular routes is the Northville-Placid Trail (www.nptrail.org), which was laid out beginning in 1922 and now spans more than 130 miles (209 km). Making use of now-defunct logging roads, the NPT, as it's called locally, winds through wilderness and towns, with the highest elevation topping out at just over 3,000 feet (900 m). Full thru-trail hikes are best saved for summer months, but shorter jaunts via skis are ideal for winter, when the trail turns into a snow-covered wonderland.

1: Olympic Ski Jump Complex 2: Mirror Lake 3: Tail O' the Pup between Lake Placid and Saranac Lake

Guides and Tours

Bear Cub Adventure Tours (30 Bear Cub Rd., 518/523-4339, http://www.bearcubadventures.com) offers guided canoeing, kayaking, fishing, backpacking, and hiking trips.

For a scenic flight over the High Peaks, contact **Adirondack Flying Service** (Airport Rd., off Cascade Rd., 518/523-2488, www.flyanywhere.com).

ENTERTAINMENT AND EVENTS

Lake Placid Center for the Arts (17 Algonquin Dr., 518/523-2512, www.lakeplacidarts.org) presents music, dance, theater, film, and special events throughout the year. The 18-piece **Lake Placid Sinfonietta** (Mid's Park, 518/523-2051, www.lakeplacidsinfonietta.org, July-Aug. Wed. evenings) performs free concerts.

Figure skating, hockey games, and speed skating events take place in the **Olympic Center Ice Arena** (2634 Main St., 518/523-1655) throughout the year.

SHOPPING

Main Street heads north of the Olympic Arena past about 100 shops, some of them one-of-a-kind, others ubiquitous chains. One must-see is **The Adirondack Store** (2024 Saranac Ave., 518/523-2646, www.theadirondackstore.com), which sells everything from hand-knit sweaters to Winslow Homer prints.

FOOD

For tasty scones and other baked goods, step into **Bluesberry Bakery** (2436 Main St., 518/523-4539, www.lakeplacidbakery.com, Thurs.-Tue. 7:30am-5pm). For mouthwatering barbecue stop at **Tail O' the Pup** (Rte. 86, 518/891-0777, www.tailofthepupbbq.com, mid-May-mid-Oct., hours vary seasonally, $18), a classic roadside eatery halfway between Lake Placid and Saranac Lake. **Lake Placid Pub and Brewery** (813 Mirror Lake Dr., 518/523-3813, www.ubuale.com, Mon.-Thurs. 11:30am-9pm, Fri.-Sat. 11:30am-10pm, Sun. noon-9pm , $17) is a popular spot, offering pub food upstairs and a boisterous bar below. At **Nicola's on Main** (211 Main St., 518/523-5853, www.nicolasonmain.com, daily 5pm-9pm, $24), you'll find an upscale Italian menu with pasta, fresh fish, veal, and pizza baked in a wood-fired oven. **Great Adirondack Brewing Company** (2442 Main St., 518/523-1629, www.adksteakandseafood.com, Tue.-Wed. 4pm-close, Thurs.-Sat. noon-close, Sun. 10am-close, $28), in addition to serving locally raised beef and seafood flown in from Boston, has its own on-site brewery.

High Peaks Resort is home to the casual restaurant, **The Dancing Bears** (2384 Saranac Ave., 518/523-4411, www.highpeaksresort.com, daily 7am-10pm, $26), which claims to serve the coldest beer in Lake Placid. The evidence? Draught beers are encased in ice blocks.

ACCOMMODATIONS

Luxury Inns and Lodges

High Peaks Resort (2384 Saranac Ave., 518/523-4411, www.highpeaksresort.com, $149-269) features a choice of private dock or three pools for swimming, as well as a health club and full-service spa. The resort also offers four on-site restaurants.

Entering the large, heavy-beamed lobby of the all-suite **Whiteface Lodge** (7 Whiteface Inn Ln., 800/582-0505, www.thewhitefacelodge.com, $400-488), guests are greeted with that quintessential Adirondack scent of woody goodness. Resort offerings are extensive, including top-rated restaurant Kanu, large, luxurious suites, romantic surroundings, a movie theater, full-service spa, indoor/outdoor pool, lake swimming, canoeing, kayaking, and paddle boards. Guests can also enjoy cigars and cognac in outdoor lean-tos.

Posh ★ **Mirror Lake Inn Resort and Spa** (77 Mirror Lake Dr., 518/523-2544, www.mirrorlakeinn.com, $240-350 for rooms, $420-660 for suites in summer, about a third less off-season) is a grand colonial-style structure that was rebuilt after a 1988 fire. Also on-site at this AAA Four Diamond resort are **The View Restaurant** (Sun.-Thurs.

5:30pm-9pm, Fri.-Sat. 5:30pm-9:30pm, $42), **Taste Bistro** (Sun.-Thurs. 5pm-9pm, Fri.-Sat. 5pm-9:30pm, $25), a bar, cozy lounges, a spa, tennis courts, indoor and outdoor pools, and a private beach.

On the shores of Lake Placid lies secluded **Lake Placid Lodge** (144 Lodge Way, 518/523-2700, www.lakeplacidlodge.com, $440-900), an authentic great camp complete with a stone fireplace and moose head. Now a member of exclusive Relais & Chateaux, the lodge boasts 30 guest accommodations, ranging from lodge rooms and suites to private cabins and cottages. Two restaurants are on-site.

The retreat of the Adirondack Mountain Club (ADK), **Adirondak Loj** (1002 Adirondak Loj Rd., 518/523-3441, www.adk.org, from $169 private rooms, from $70 bunk beds, from $60 pp lofts) is 8 miles (12.9 km) south of Lake Placid, high in the mountains on the shores of Heart Lake. Meals can be arranged for an additional fee ($9.50 for breakfast and lunch, $19.50 for dinner). You don't have to be an ADK member to stay here (though members get a 10 percent discount on lodging and meals), but you must make reservations well in advance—as far as a year ahead of your planned visit. The Loj is also the starting point of the Van Hoevenberg Trail, which leads to the summit of Mount Marcy.

Motels and Hotels

Lake Placid Inn (2050 Saranac Ave., 800/566-0363, www.lakeplacidinn.com, $125-175) may sound like a small and cozy full-service accommodation, but it's actually a property with several different types of accommodations, including comfortable self-catering apartments. Each apartment has wireless Internet, cable TV, and a full kitchen. There's a laundry room on-site as well, and grocery stores, restaurants, and services are a short walk or drive away. On-site parking is included in the reservation rate.

Wildwood on the Lake (2135 Saranac Ave., 518/523-2624, www.wildwoodmotel.com, $58-350) offers a cozy fireplace lobby, indoor heated pool, lakeside barbecues, and free boat rentals for guests. The picturesque locale is a 10-minute walk from the village.

Art Devlin's Olympic Motor Inn (2764 Main St., 518/523-3700, www.artdevlins.com, $78-200) offers friendly service and an easy location for wandering around town.

In the upscale motel category there is **Golden Arrow Lakeside Resort** (2559 Main St., 518/523-3353, www.golden-arrow. com, $129-220), offering excellent value accommodations. The resort, located on the lake as its name suggests, has its own small beach, which is equipped with boats (free for guests). Golden Arrow also has a heated indoor pool, sauna, restaurant, lounge, and nightclub.

WHITEFACE MOUNTAIN

From Lake Placid, take Route 86 northeast to reach Wilmington, a small ski town huddled at the base of towering Whiteface Mountain. The largest ski resort in New York, state-owned **Whiteface Mountain** (5021 Rte. 86, 518/946-2223, www.whiteface.com) boasts 90 trails, 11 chairlifts, and the highest vertical drop in the Northeast at 3,216 feet (980 m). The mountain attracts expert skiers, but intermediate and novice trails are also plentiful.

During the summer, the mountain's peaks are accessible via the **Whiteface Mountain Cloudsplitter Gondola Ride** (late June-early Oct. daily 9am-4pm, adults $24, seniors and children 7-12 $18, children under 7 free) and **Whiteface Veterans' Memorial Highway** (free with $40 Olympic Sites Passport). The chairlift leads to Little Whiteface Peak (3,676 ft/1120 m), while the highway leads to Whiteface Summit (4,867 ft/1480 m). Both afford superb views of the High Peaks to the south, Lake Champlain and the Green Mountains to the east, the St. Lawrence River and Canada to the north, and Saranac Lake Valley to the west. Of the Adirondacks' 46 High Peaks, only Whiteface is accessible by car.

Santa's Workshop

Near the entrance of Whiteface Veterans' Memorial Highway stands **Santa's Workshop** (324 Whiteface Veterans' Memorial Hwy., 518/946-2211, www.north-poleny.com, hours vary seasonally, theme park: adults $22.99, seniors and children 2-16 $20.99), a cheery red-and-white cottage surrounded by flowers. Inside is a post office/gift shop where visitors can send letters postmarked "North Pole" or buy "I believe in Santa Claus" T-shirts. Out back, a cozy, kid-oriented theme park includes amusement

halfway to the top of Whiteface Mountain

park rides, Santa's reindeer, and Santa's elves. Special events such as a Santa Claus Parade are presented daily.

Food and Accommodations

★ **Hungry Trout Motor Inn** (5239 Rte. 86, Wilmington, 518/946-2217, www.hungrytrout.com, $119-199) offers 22 comfortable motel rooms, all with picture windows, along with a pool and playground. The inn's restaurant (dinner only, $22), overlooking the churning white waters of the Ausable River, specializes in its namesake trout, prepared a myriad of tasty ways, along with continental fare.

Stop at **Country Bear** (5830 Rte. 86, Wilmington, 518/946-2691, Fri.-Tues. 7am-noon, $9) for a satisfying breakfast.

SARANAC LAKE

After the heavy tourist traffic of Lake Placid, Saranac Lake village comes as a relief. Although classified as a village, Saranac Lake is a sizable town (pop. 5,300), with a busy, unpretentious Main Street where stores, banks, churches, and supermarkets cater to residents, not tourists. It is not located on the shores of its namesake, but on smaller Lake Flower. A pleasant public beach (daily dawn-dusk) is on Lake Colby, just north of downtown. The Saranac Lakes—Lower, Middle, and Upper—are farther west. Upper Saranac Lake is famous for its rustic Adirondack architecture, best glimpsed by boat.

Settled in 1819 by Jacob Smith Moody, Saranac Lake soon established itself as a center for Adirondack guides. All of Moody's sons became guides, and their Uncle Martin once guided everyone from President Grover Cleveland to Ralph Waldo Emerson.

In 1876, Dr. Livingston Trudeau, suffering from tuberculosis, came to Saranac Lake to die. Instead, the fresh mountain air restored him, and in 1884 he opened the first outdoor sanatorium for the treatment of tuberculosis. By the early 1900s, Trudeau Sanatorium was famed worldwide, with thousands flocking to "The City of the Sick" to take "the cure."

The Legend of Whiteface Mountain

There once was a young brave who wanted to win the hand of a beautiful Iroquois princess. The princess asked him to prove his love by bringing her the skin of the Great White Stag who roamed the region's highest peak.

Armed with two magic arrows an old chief had given him, the brave went to the mountain. For weeks, he hunted for the stag in vain. At last, late one evening, he found him standing in the mist at the top of the mountain. The brave deftly shot his two arrows. One pierced the stag's neck, the second his haunch; but when the brave rushed forward to claim his trophy, he couldn't reach him—the mountainside was too steep. The stag remained pinned to a ledge by the magic arrows, just out of reach.

When the brave awoke the next morning, the stag had disappeared, but the rock where he had hung had turned white. From then on, the Iroquois called the mountain Whiteface.

Trudeau Sanatorium closed in 1954, after antibiotics were developed, but its legacy lives on in the Trudeau Institute, a scientific research institute. *Doonesbury* cartoonist Garry Trudeau is the great-grandson of Dr. Livingston Trudeau.

Robert Louis Stevenson Memorial Cottage and Museum

Among the pioneer "lungers" who came to Saranac Lake to take the cure was Robert Louis Stevenson. In 1887, fresh from the success of his just-published *Dr. Jekyll and Mr. Hyde,* the author rented a cozy cottage on a hill within easy reach of Dr. Trudeau. While living here, Stevenson wrote some of his best essays and started his long tale, *The Master of Ballantrae.* "I was walking on the veranda of a small house outside the hamlet of Saranac.

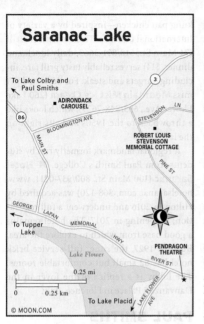

Saranac Lake

To Lake Colby and Paul Smiths

ADIRONDACK CAROUSEL

86

BLOOMINGTON AVE

MAIN ST

GEORGE

LAPAN

To Tupper Lake

MEMORIAL

STEVENSON

LN

3

ROBERT LOUIS STEVENSON MEMORIAL COTTAGE

PINE ST

Lake Flower

PENDRAGON THEATRE

RIVER ST

HWY

LAKE FLOWER AVE

To Lake Placid

0   0.25 mi

0   0.25 km

© MOON.COM

It was winter, the night was very dark, the air clean and cold and sweet with the purity of forests. For the making of a story, here were fine conditions," reads the quote by the door.

Today, the **Robert Louis Stevenson Memorial Cottage and Museum** (11 Stevenson Ln., 518/891-1462, www.robert-louis-stevenson.org/107-baker-cottage-saranac-lake, July 1-Sept. 15, Tues.-Sun. 9:30am-noon and 1pm-4:30pm, adults $5, children under 12 free) houses a large collection of Stevenson memorabilia, including his ice skates, playing cards, letters to Henry James, autographed first editions, and the velvet jacket that he always wore while writing. On the mantelpiece are Stevenson's cigarette burns, which he left everywhere he went.

Recreation

Saranac Lake is ideally situated between the High Peaks and the Northwest Lakes, which offer some of the best canoeing in the Northeast.

Large and friendly **St. Regis Canoe Outfitters** (73 Dorsey St., 518/891-1838, www.canoeoutfitters.com) is both a sprawling

retail shop and the place to go to set up a canoeing or kayaking trip. St. Regis rents boats and camping gear, provides instruction and trip-planning advice, and offers guided trips and shuttle services. Trips can be arranged for as short as one morning or as long as two weeks or more.

Adirondack Foothills (518/359-8194, www.adkfoothills.com) offers customized hiking, camping, canoeing, and fishing trips. **McDonnell's Adirondack Challenges** (518/891-1176, www.macscanoeadk.com) rents canoes and kayaks by the day or longer; staff can provide information about recommend canoe routes.

CANOEING

Choosing a canoeing route in the Adirondacks can be a challenge: With a landscape stippled with so many waterways, there are so many options. For paddlers who want to combine a day trip in the canoe with a primitive camping experience, the nearly 500-acre Follensby Clear Pond is an obvious pick. There are islands to explore, and carry paths allow you to expand your trip to other nearby ponds, such as Polliwog, Floodwood, and Little Square. Then, back at Follensby Clear Pond, you can choose from among 20 campsites, all tucked into the trees, and all featuring a waterfront view.

HIKING

Curiously named Ampersand Mountain (www.adk.org/ampersand-mountain) is a moderately difficult day hike just 8 miles (12.9 km) from Saranac Lake. The hike, which starts flat and smooth, involves a steady 1,300-foot (400 m) ascent toward the end. But patience and persistence will pay off with a 360-degree view of Saranac Lakes and the St. Regis ponds from the rocky summit.

BICYCLING

Mountain bikers should make tracks for the **Dewey Mountain Recreation Center** (277 Rte. 3, Saranac Lake, 518/891-2697, www. deweymountain.com, hours vary by season), which features more than 5 miles (8.1 km) of single-track trails ranging in difficulty from easy to extreme. Put your legs to the test as you pedal 450 feet (135 m) to the summit, which opens up to views of Saranac Lakes. Summer and fall are best times to visit, as the biking trails become ski trails in the winter.

Entertainment and Nightlife

Pendragon Theatre (15 Brandy Brook Ave., 518/891-1854, www.pendragontheatre. org) presents professional regional theater, performing both classic and contemporary works.

A number of popular bars, many hosting local bands on the weekends, hug Main Street near Hotel Saranac and along Broadway north of Main. Among them is the popular, teeming, indoor-outdoor Water Hole (48 Main St., 518/354-5441, www.saranaclakewaterhole. com), which offers live music several nights each week.

Traveling with little ones? Adirondack Carousel (2 Depot St., 518/891-9521, www. adirondackcarousel.org, summer daily 10am-5pm, winter Fri. noon-4pm, Sat.-Sun. 10am-4pm, $2.50 per ride) should definitely be a stop on the itinerary. Opened in 2012 after more than a decade of fundraising, the carousel features 24 animals that are all indigenous to Adirondack Park. Have the kids make a game of looking for the nine-spotted ladybug—New York's state insect—carved onto each animal, all of which were handmade by local artists. In addition to the carousel itself, the building where it's housed also has a charming play space where kids can dress up in costumes, play house, or spend some time with any number of fun toys. In warmer months, they can also enjoy the playground just outside.

Food and Accommodations

Blue Moon Cafe (55 Main St., 518/891-1310, www.bluemoonadk.com, days and hours vary by season, $18) serves an eclectic range of dishes—from Amelia Island gumbo to kung pao chicken—inspired by a variety of international cuisines. The Downhill Grill (74 Main St., 518/891-3663, daily lunch and dinner, $14) serves reliably tasty grill fare, including burgers and steak. For dessert, don't miss Mountain Mist Ice Cream (260 Lake Flower Ave., 603/848-7629), which looks like a throwback to the 1950s and sits right on the lake.

A regional landmark formerly run by students from Paul Smith's College, ★ Hotel Saranac (100 Main St., 800/937-0211, www. hotelsaranac.com, $68-120) was acquired by Hilton in 2016 and underwent a full renovation, reopening in 2017. The hotel remains a good base from which to explore the area. Built in 1927, the snug, full-service brick hotel has 82 small but comfortable rooms. The lobby is a replica of the foyer in the Danvanzati Palace in Florence, Italy.

PAUL SMITHS

About 10 miles (16.1 km) northwest of Saranac Lake lies the hamlet of Paul Smiths, named after Appollos (Paul) Smith, a famed Adirondack guide who established one of the Adirondacks' first hotels here in 1859. Charles Dickens once said of Smith, "He has no bad habits, and is, withal, the best rifle shot, paddler, and compounder of forest stews in the whole region." When Smith died in 1912, his funeral was the largest ever held in northern New York, drawing more than 700 people.

The original Paul Smiths hotel has closed, but its spirit lives on through Paul Smith's College (Rtes. 86 and 30, 800/421-2605, www.paulsmiths.edu), founded by the hotelier's son in the 1930s. The school is known for its degrees in hotel management and culinary arts. The college's 3,000-acre Visitor Interpretive Center (VIC, www.adirondackvic.org) offers free and fee-based sports, arts, children's, and nature-oriented activities throughout the year. Its expanse is spacious enough for 25 miles (40 km) of trails, many of which have comfortable walking surfaces and signage that explains the ecology of the area.

Almanzo Wilder, Farmer Boy

Fans of Laura Ingalls Wilder might want to head north of Paul Smiths about 35 miles (56 km) to the Almanzo Wilder Homestead (177 Stacy Rd., 518/483-1207, www.almanzowilderfarm.com, late May or early June-Sept. Mon.-Sat. 10am-4pm, Sun. noon-4pm, adults $10.50, seniors $9.50, children 6-16 $6.50), located in farm country east of Malone. Wilder's husband, Almanzo Wilder, grew up here, and the author based her book *Farmer Boy* on his childhood.

The trim, airy house has been carefully restored to reflect the book. Downstairs is the parlor where "Almanzo didn't mean to throw the blacking brush," and upstairs is his "soft, cold feather bed." In the kitchen are kerosene lamps, tallow candles, and a butter churn—all similar to the ones used by Almanzo—while out back is the red barn where he did his chores. In 2013, a replica schoolhouse opened on the grounds.

Ingalls Wilder, who met her husband in South Dakota, never visited the Wilder homestead, but according to family members, the house was "as described in the book." Photocopies of the sketches Almanzo drew for Wilder, along with several of her letters, are on display in the entrance hall.

White Pine Camp

White Pine Camp (White Pine Rd., a half mile east of the Rtes. 86/30 intersection, 518/327-3030, www.whitepinecamp.com, cabins $130-440 daily) served as President Calvin Coolidge's summer White House in 1926. Built in 1907, the camp overlooks Osgood Pond and contains about 20 asymmetrical buildings, complete with soaring rooflines, unusual angles, and skylights. In the main cabin, exhibits explain the site's history and architecture, while among the surrounding outbuildings are a tennis house, indoor bowling alley, and a Japanese teahouse. There are also cabins and cottages available for rent by the week.

Tours (late June-late Sept. Wed. and Sat. 10am and 1:30pm, adults $12, children $6, cash only) of the camp are offered and reservations are not required.

ONCHIOTA

"Leaving 67 of the friendliest people in the Adirondacks (plus a couple of soreheads)" reads the sign at the northern end of Onchiota. No one seems quite sure exactly who those soreheads are, but to meet the first variety, stop into the one-of-a-kind Six Nations Indian Museum (1462 Rte. 60, 518/891-2299, www.sixnationsindianmuseum.com,

July-Aug. Tues.-Sun. 10am-5pm, adults $4, children $2). From the outside, the museum looks much like an ordinary house. Inside, though, you'll find yourself surrounded by a kaleidoscopic array of pictographs, paintings, basketwork, beadwork, quillwork, pottery, canoes, masks, drums, and lacrosse sticks, all very neatly arranged to cover virtually every square inch of wall and peaked wooden ceiling. The museum is the creation of one man, Ray Fadden, a Mohawk who drew most of the elaborate pictographs himself. The works tell traditional Iroquois tales.

Fadden, who spent much of his life as a teacher, began fighting for the preservation of Iroquois culture as early as the 1940s. Back then hardly anyone listened, but Fadden never faltered and eventually was instrumental in the founding of numerous Iroquois heritage programs. Many of his former students are now major leaders in the Mohawk Nation.

The museum is run by Fadden's son and daughter-in-law. Visitors are warmly greeted at the door and taken on personalized tours. To reach Onchiota from Paul Smiths, take Route 86 east to County Roads 31 or 30 north (not to be confused with State Route 30, which leads to Malone). The museum is in the hamlet's center and easy to find.

Central Adirondacks

Nestled into the center of Adirondack Park are more still blue lakes, encircled by densely packed forests and small to moderate peaks. The climate here is not as harsh as it is farther north, and the landscape has a more human-size feel. Some sections of the Central Adirondacks, such as Indian Lake, attract only a handful of visitors; others, such as Old Forge, are overrun with vacationers.

LONG LAKE

Heading south from Tupper Lake on Route 30, you'll come to Long Lake, a 14-mile (22.5 km) stretch of water that is really just an engorged section of Raquette River. At the intersection of Routes 30 and 28N is the village of Long Lake, dominated by the rectangular Adirondack Hotel, an 1870s lodging with wide verandas. Just across Long Lake bridge from the hotel is a **public beach** (Rte. 30, just south of the bridge, daily dawn-dusk, with year-round heated bathrooms) and boat launch.

One of the region's most popular **canoe trips** begins at Long Lake launch and heads north along Raquette River through the High Peaks region. Past the High Peaks, paddlers can choose to continue on Raquette River to Tupper Lake or portage to Upper Saranac Lake. Either way, the trip covers about 40 miles (64 km) and takes about four days. Boats and canoes can be rented at **Long Lake Marina** (Rte. 30, 518/624-2266, www.longlakemarina.com), in the village center. To take a scenic seaplane flight, contact **Helms Aero Service** (Rte. 30, 518/624-3931, www.americade.info/helms.htm, May-Oct. daily).

Hiking

At the southern end of Long Lake ascends the double-peaked **Owls Head Mountain.** The well-marked, 3.5-mile (5.6 km) trail leading to the top is of moderate difficulty and takes about four hours to hike round-trip. Along the way you'll pass streams, valleys, a fire tower, Lake Eaton—a good place for a swim—and good views of the High Peaks. To reach the trailhead, take Route 30 for 1 mile (1.6 km) north of Long Lake village to Endion Road and watch for signs.

Shopping

You can't miss **Hoss's Country Corner** (1142 Main St., 518/624-2481, www.hosscountrycorner.com), a big, square emporium built in the classic Adirondack style. Inside, you'll find everything from groceries and clothing to handicrafts and a good selection of regional books.

Food

Long Lake Diner (1161 Main St., 518/624-3941) serves breakfast and lunch. ★ **Adirondack Hotel** (1245 Main St., Rte. 30, 518/624-4700, www.adirondackhotel.com, $23) holds a popular café open for breakfast, lunch, and a light dinner; the hotel's more formal dining room, The Victorian Room, serves full-course dinners.

Accommodations and Camping

Two miles (3.2 km) north of the village is 135-site **Lake Eaton Campground** (Rte. 30, 518/624-2641, reservations 800/456-2267, www.dec.ny.gov/outdoor/24464.html, $20/night for New York residents, $25/night for nonresidents). Five miles (8.1 km) west of Long Lake is 80-site **Forked Lake Campground** (381 Forked Lake Campground Ln., 518/624-6646, reservations 800/456-2267, www.dec.ny.gov/outdoor/24467.html, $18/night for New York residents, $23/night for nonresidents).

On the shores of the lake is ★ **The Long View Lodge** (681 Deerland Rd., 518/624-2862, www.thelongviewlodge.com, $100-160, with breakfast), a comfortable, low-key place with guest rooms, cottages, and a private

Central Adirondacks

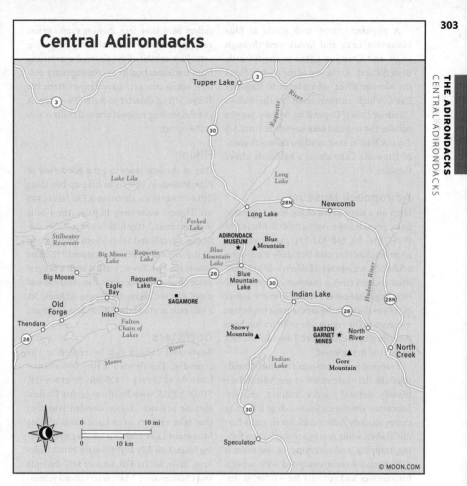

© MOON.COM

beach equipped with canoes, kayaks, and other boats.

Though now better known for its restaurants than for its guest rooms, **Adirondack Hotel** (1245 Main St., Rte. 30, 518/624-4700, www.adirondackhotel.com, $85-250, some rooms share baths) still accommodates overnight visitors. Rooms are spartan but clean.

BLUE MOUNTAIN LAKE

One of the loveliest lakes in all the Adirondacks is dark, spring-fed Blue Mountain Lake. Situated 1,800 feet (550 m) above sea level, the isolated lake is dotted with small islands and flanked by towering Blue

Mountain, a moody peak that the Iroquois once called "Hill of Storms." The lake, one of a chain of three, is stocked with bass, whitefish, and trout.

The village of Blue Mountain Lake sits at the water's southern edge, along Routes 28 and 30. Though home to only about 100 permanent residents, the village is a major cultural center, thanks to the presence of the renowned Adirondack Museum and the much smaller Adirondack Lakes Center for the Arts. A postage-stamp-size **public beach** (off Route 28, July-Sept.) is situated in the heart of the village, and several crafts galleries are located along Route 30.

A popular canoe trip starts at Blue Mountain Lake and heads west through Eagle and Utowana Lakes to the 0.4-mile Bassett Carry. At the end of the portage flows the Marion River, which leads to Raquette Lake, which in turn leads to the Fulton Chain of Lakes. Depending on how far you paddle, the trip can take anywhere from 1-5 days. A lean-to is situated on the north shore of Utowana Lake about a half mile above the dam.

Adirondack Museum

High on a slope overlooking Blue Mountain Lake presides the Adirondack Museum (9097 Rte. 30, 518/352-7311, www.adkmuseum.org, late May-mid-Oct. daily 10am-5pm, adults $20, seniors $18, children 6-17 $12, children under 6 free), a compact complex of 22 buildings that covers virtually every aspect of Adirondack life. By far the most important museum in the region, the complex has been described by the *New York Times* as "the best of its kind in the world."

Featured in the museum's two main buildings are first-rate exhibits on Adirondack history, natural science, culture, and art. Dioramas simulate scenes such as a logging camp, an early Adirondack hotel, and a hermit's cabin, while nearby are displays on fishing, trapping, and surveying. In one room is a Victorian hearse equipped with wheels for summer and runners for winter; in another, over 800 wooden miniatures carved by one man.

Smaller buildings focus on specific themes. The Boat Building is packed with dozens of sleek wooden vessels; the Transportation Building has 50 horse-drawn vehicles and a private railroad car. At the Photo Belt, visitors watch historic photographs slide by on a moving belt.

Adirondack Lakes Center for the Arts

The inviting Adirondack Lakes Center for the Arts (3446 Rte. 28, 518/352-7715, www.adirondackarts.org, Thurs.-Sat. 10am-4pm, gallery admission free, evening events prices vary) presents both visual and performing arts. Past exhibits have covered everything from traditional quilts to contemporary pottery, while concerts have ranged from the Tokyo String Quartet to Aztec Two-Step. A gift shop selling regional arts and crafts is also at the center.

Hiking

One of the best ways to get a good view of Blue Mountain Lake is to hike up brooding Blue Mountain, elevation 3,750 feet (1,140 m). Though quite steep in parts, the 4-mile (6.4 km) round-trip hike is of moderate difficulty overall and takes about three hours. At the summit gleams the restored 1917 Blue Mountain Fire Tower, staffed with a ranger/guide on summer weekends. The trailhead and a well-marked hiking trail begin off Route 30, a half mile north of the Adirondack Museum.

Outfitters

Boats and canoes can be rented at the friendly, family-run Blue Mountain Lake Boat Livery (3429 Rte. 30 at Rte. 28, 518/352-7351, www.boatlivery.com). Docked outside are two classic wooden launches that take visitors to isolated parts of Blue Mountain Lake and two smaller neighboring lakes. Low-key sightseeing tours (July-Sept. daily, adults $20, seniors $18, students and children over 3 $15, reservations recommended) are filled with interesting historical information.

Blue Mountain Outfitters (144 Main St., 518/352-7306, www.adirondacksonline.com/bluemtoutfitters) rents canoes and kayaks, sells outdoor gear, and offers guided canoe trips.

INDIAN LAKE

Southeast of Blue Mountain Lake lounges long, skinny Indian Lake, named after Sabael Benedict, an Abenaki and the area's first settler. A hamlet of the same name clusters around the intersection of Routes 28 and 30 at the lake's northern end, while to the east stretches Siamese Ponds Wilderness Area.

Siamese Ponds Wilderness Area

Covering an area of 112,000 acres, the Siamese Ponds region is roughly bounded by Route 28 to the north, Route 30 to the west and south, and Route 8 to the east. Often overlooked by vacationers, the area encompasses gentle mountains, dense forests, crystal clear ponds, and rushing streams. In certain sections, you can hike all day without encountering another person.

Thirty-three miles (53 km) of marked hiking trails and many more unmarked ones run through the wilderness. Major trailheads are located at the end of Big Brook Road (off Rte. 30 a half mile south of Indian Lake village); at Thirteenth Lake and the end of Old Farm Clearing Road (take Rte. 28 east to Thirteenth Lake Rd.); and on Route 8 about 4 miles (6.4 km) west of Bakers Mills.

Hiking

One of the trails at the end of Big Brook Road leads up **Chimney Mountain,** named after its unusual central bulwark of layered gneiss, granite, and marble. The mountain is also known for its many crevices and caves. These should be explored by expert spelunkers only. Most visitors shouldn't proceed further than shining a flashlight down into the depths. The round-trip hike up and down Chimney Mountain covers 3 miles (4.8 km), takes 2.5 hours, and is quite rugged in spots. From up top are good views of Kings Flow, Round Pond, and the High Peaks.

The tallest of the southern Adirondacks, **Snowy Mountain** (3,899 ft/1190 m) offers a long, challenging climb best suited for hikers in good condition. The hike to the summit, which offers excellent views of the surrounding lakes, is about 7 miles (11.3 km) round-trip and takes about five hours. Steep sections are located near the trailhead and again near the top, while in between are rolling terrain and a sparkling brook that follows the trail for close to a mile. To reach the trailhead, take Route 30 south of the hamlet of Indian Lake 6.5 miles (10.5 km). Watch for a sign marking the trail on the right and a paved parking area on the left.

Rafting Trips

White-water rafting trips down nearby Hudson River Gorge and Moose River are offered by **Adventure Sports Rafting Co.** (6127 Rte. 28, 518/648-5812, www.adventuresportsrafting.com) and **Adirondac Rafting Company** (Rtes. 27 and 30, 518/523-1635, www.lakeplacidrafting.com).

NORTH CREEK

Off Route 28 midway between Indian Lake and Warrensburg in the southeastern Adirondacks lies North Creek, a small town wedged between mountains and the **Hudson River Gorge.** Towering over North Creek to the south is Gore Mountain; to the north flows the Hudson River and a 16-mile (26 km) stretch of white water that's considered the finest rafting run in the east.

The Hudson River Gorge begins east of Indian Lake, just beyond the confluence of the Indian and Hudson Rivers. During the spring, the water runs high, with near continuous Class III and IV rapids. The river should be tackled by experts only; a number of deaths have occurred here over the years.

Gore Mountain

One of New York's largest ski resorts, **Gore Mountain** (793 Peaceful Valley Rd., 518/251-2411, www.goremountain.com) particularly attracts intermediate skiers. Featured are 110 trails, a vertical drop of more than 2,500 feet (790 m), and 15 ski lifts. The **gondola ride** (July 4-mid-Oct., adults $22, seniors and kids 6-11 $12, children under 6 free) operates to the summit, offering bird's-eye views of the countryside.

Barton Garnet Mines

On the back side of Gore Mountain lies **Barton Garnet Mines** (Barton Mines Rd., North River, just north of North Creek, off Rte. 28, 518/251-2706, www.garnetminetours. com, days and hours vary by season, adults

Happy Goats, Great Cheese

At **Nettle Meadow Goat Farm and Cheese Factory** (484 S. Johnsburg Rd., Warrensburg, 518/623-3372, www.nettlemeadow.com), you'll see a sign with these words: "Happy Goats. Great Cheese!"

A tour of the picturesque farm affirms that both statements are true. It would be hard to find a better place to be a goat . . . or a cheese lover. The farm is a goat's utopia, with a designated retirement home for old milk-goats no longer able to produce, as well as a bachelor pad housing the male goats born on the farm. The pampered goats—all of which are called by their own name—munch on organic feed made of wild herbs, nettles, garlic, kelp, and wild raspberry branches.

Determined to keep from the slaughterhouse the young males they bottle-fed by hand as babies, owners Lorraine Lambiase and Sheila Flanagan allow the goats to roam the land until they can find them a good home as a pet or 4-H project. Nettle Meadow's no-kill policy even extends to the wolves and coyotes that threaten the herd. Finding the idea of shooting the intruders repugnant, they hired a top-of-the-line security force of no-nonsense llamas.

To outsiders, it probably seemed unlikely that a business that spoils its goats so and ladles (as opposed to drains, which is less time-consuming) the product to protect the architecture of the curds could survive. But its cheeses have won lots of awards, and Nettle Meadow's unique organic Kunik cheese, a goat milk-cow's cream blend, has even been listed by the celebrated Murray's Cheese as one of the World's Best 300 Cheeses. It is also featured in many top New York City restaurants, and respected New York City cheesemonger Anne Saxelby has declared, "It may well be the sexiest cheese in the U.S.A."

Farm and rescue sanctuary **tours** are available at noon on Saturdays. The farm is open for cheese sales daily from 10am-4pm.

$14.95, seniors $13.95, children $10.95), a sprawling operation that produces 90 percent of the world's industrial garnet. Garnets are also New York State's stone. During the summer, visitors can tour the open-pit mines with guides who explain the area's geology and history.

Outfitters and Guides

One of the oldest rafting outfitters in the state, **Hudson River Rafting Company** (1 Main St., 518/251-3215, www.hudsonriverrafting.com) offers guided trips down the Hudson River Gorge and along the Moose, Black, and Sacandaga Rivers.

Food and Accommodations

At the ★ **Copperfield Inn** (307 Main St., 877/235-1466, www.copperfieldinn.com, $159-285) you'll find 31 spacious rooms with plenty of amenities, a heated pool, health club, hot tub, and tennis courts. Also on the premises is **Trappers Tavern** (hours vary seasonally, lunch $13,

dinner $24), serving casual meals like pizza and chili.

NORTHWEST ON ROUTE 28N

Scenic Route 28N heads out of North Creek in the southeastern Adirondacks to skirt the southern edge of the High Peaks region. Along the way you'll pass one splendid lake and mountain vista after another. The ride is especially magnificent in autumn.

Adirondack Park Visitor Interpretive Center

In Newcomb, the Adirondack Park Agency maintains the **Adirondack Park Visitor Interpretive Center** (5922 Rte. 28N, 518/582-2000, www.esf.edu/aic, Tues.-Sat. 10am-4pm, free), which offers an excellent introduction to the park. Exhibits range from the region's logging history to local flora and fauna. Print out free information about trailhead locations and canoe routes at one of the touch-screen stations, or follow one of the interpretive trails outside. Trails lead onto a peninsula in Rich Lake, past beaver ponds and old-growth hemlocks.

Camp Santanoni

Deserted Camp Santanoni, one of the old great camps, stands on the shores of Newcomb Lake. Built in 1892 by Albany industrialist Robert Pruyn and surrounded by 12,900-acre Santanoni Preserve, the eerily empty camp built of massive logs includes a central lodge, boathouse, studio, and guest cottages. To explore the grounds, you'll need to hike in 5 miles (8.1 km) along Santanoni Road. Another option is to take a horse-drawn carriage. For information about this option and about current preservation efforts, visit the website of Adirondack Architectural Heritage (www.aarch.org).

The road is located on the north side of Route 28N, about a mile east of Adirondack Park Visitor Interpretive Center. A parking area is near the camp's gatehouse; beyond stretch fields crisscrossed with stone fences. About 1.5 miles (2.4 km) in is a deserted farmstead that once provided the great camp with its provisions.

A yellow-marked trail runs north of the great camp along Newcomb Lake. Here you'll find several remote campsites with their own private beaches.

For more information, inquire at the Park Visitor Interpretive Center.

RAQUETTE LAKE

Heading west of Blue Mountain Lake on Route 28 instead of east, you'll come to Raquette Lake. It was here that W. W. Durant built Camp Pine Knot, the first Adirondack great camp, in 1877. Durant combined elements of the Adirondack log cabin and the Swiss chalet, a style that continues to predominate in the Adirondacks. Camp Pine Knot still stands near the lake, along with four other great camps: Camp Echo, Bluff Point, North Point, and Sagamore. Only Sagamore is open to the public, but you can glimpse the other four by touring Raquette Lake by boat.

At the southwestern edge of Raquette Lake lies a hamlet of the same name, equipped with three marinas and little else. At the lake's southeastern edge stretches Golden Beach State Park (Rte. 28, 315/354-4230, www.dec.ny.gov/outdoor/24468.html), offering a swimming beach, good fishing spots, hiking trails, boat rentals, and a 205-site campground (May-Sept., $20/night for New York residents, $25/night for nonresidents).

Great Camp Sagamore

A self-contained rustic village hidden deep in the woods, Great Camp Sagamore (Sagamore Rd., off Rte. 28, 315/354-5311, www.sagamore.org, tours given late May-mid Oct., hours vary seasonally, adults $18, seniors $16, children $10) was built by W. W. Durant in 1897 and sold to Alfred G. Vanderbilt Sr. in 1901. Considered the prototypical great camp, Sagamore centers on a seemingly indestructible main lodge built of huge dark logs, while outbuildings house a dining hall, guest cottages, boathouse, horse barn, icehouse, and bowling alley.

One of Sagamore's most interesting buildings is the casino playhouse, the walls of which are covered with animal "trophies" killed by generations of Vanderbilts. The camp was once known as the "headquarters of the gaming crowd," and the Vanderbilts entertained lavishly, inviting everyone from Gary Cooper and Gene Tierney to Lord Mountbatten and Madame Chiang Kai-Shek.

Now a National Historic Landmark owned by the Sagamore Institute, Sagamore hosts weekend and weeklong learning vacations focusing on such subjects as wood carving, storytelling, and folk music. You can also book a simple "Outdoor Weekend" with no classes. Summer weekend packages start at $385 per person.

Outfitters

Boats, canoes, and water sports equipment can be rented at Bird's Marine (179 Rte. 28, 315/354-4441, www.birdsmarine.com).

Raquette Lake Navigation Co. (254

Antlers Rd., 315/354-5532, www.raquettel-akenavigation.com, June-Oct.) offers lunch, dinner, sightseeing, and moonlight cruises. Brunch cruises are also offered on Sundays.

Shopping

Inside the sprawling **Raquette Lake Supply Co.** (1 Main St., 315/354-4301), owned by the same family since the late 1800s, you'll find everything from a post office and launderette to groceries and fishing supplies.

OLD FORGE AND THE FULTON CHAIN

Nestled in the western foothills of the Adirondacks, the Fulton Chain is a series of eight lakes, flanked by long ridges. None of the ridges reaches higher than 600 feet (180 m), but they feature steep, glaciated cliffs that drop dramatically down into the lakes. Excellent bird's-eye views can be had by hiking up Bald Mountain or by taking a ride up the McCauley Mountain chairlift.

Heading west from Raquette Lake on Route 28, you'll come first to Eighth and Seventh Lakes—the most pristine of the Fulton Chain—and to the attractive hamlet of Inlet. About 2 miles (3.2 km) beyond Inlet is Big Moose Public Road (County Road 1), a wooded back lane that leads north 4 miles (6.4 km) to Big Moose Lake. So far, so good. But then, about 10 miles (16.1 km) beyond Inlet lies Old Forge. After the relative solitude of Blue Mountain Lake, Indian Lake, and even Raquette Lake, built-up Old Forge and much of the Fulton Chain may come as a surprise. The towns here have a number of souvenir shops, motels, and attractions, including the theme park **Enchanted Forest/Water Safari** (3183 Rte. 28, 315/369-6145, www.watersafari.com, early June-early Sept., $36.95-37.95 adults, $32.95-33.95 kids, the lower price is for tickets purchased in advance online; the higher price is for tickets purchased on-site), a total kid-pleaser.

If you're keen to get back into the wilderness, take heart: One of the Adirondacks'

most famed and popular **canoe trips** begins in Old Forge and proceeds north through the Fulton Chain to Raquette Lake, Long Lake, and the Raquette River. Canoeists can then head to either Saranac or Tupper Lakes. The entire route is about 100 miles (161 km) long, involves about 9 miles (14.5 km) of portage, and takes about six days. To canoe just the 18-mile-long (29 km) Fulton Chain, from Old Forge to the Eighth Lake Campground, takes a full day and involves 1.7 miles (2.7 km) of portage.

Detour to Big Moose Lake

Located off the beaten tourist track, Big Moose Lake is worth a detour, especially for fans of Theodore Dreiser's novel *An American Tragedy* or its 1951 film adaptation, *A Place in the Sun*. Dreiser based his classic on an actual tragedy; it was in the lake's South Bay that Chester Gillette drowned Grace Brown. Bear left on Big Moose Road upon reaching the lake and you'll come to the old railroad station (now Big Moose Station Restaurant) where Gillette and Brown disembarked. Bear right and you'll reach the former site of the Hotel Glennmore, where the couple registered and rented their boat. The hotel is gone now, but several outbuildings remain.

Dreiser wrote: "The quiet, glassy, iridescent surface of this lake . . . seemed, not so much like water as oil—like molten glass that, of enormous bulk and weight, resting upon the substantial earth so very far below . . . Everywhere pines—tall and spearlike. And above them the humped backs of the dark and distant Adirondacks beyond."

View

The oldest multi-arts center in the Adirondacks, **View** (3273 Rte. 28, Old Forge, 315/369-6411, www.viewarts.org, daily 10am-4pm, $10) began its life in the early 1950s as the Old Forge Arts Center. It occupies a 28,000-square-foot facility with performance, gallery, and studio spaces. The galleries feature work inspired by the Adirondacks. Film, concert, and lecture series

The Tragedy That Became
An American Tragedy

On July 11, 1906, a young man named Chester Gillette overturned a rowboat in the middle of Big Moose Lake, drowning—accidentally or deliberately?—his pregnant girlfriend, Grace Brown. The case riveted the nation and became the basis for Theodore Dreiser's novel *An American Tragedy.* Dreiser stuck surprisingly close to the facts of the case. Like Gillette, Dreiser's protagonist, Clyde Griffiths, grew up in a religious family that roamed the West; he traveled east to work in his uncle's skirt factory and was desperate to achieve the American Dream no matter what it took.

Gillette was arrested the day after the drowning and incarcerated in the Herkimer County jail. Visitors lined up around the block to walk past his cell, and reporters flocked there from all over the country. Among those covering the case was ex-lawman Bat Masterson, who had become a sportswriter for the *New York Morning Telegraph*. Masterson was one of the few to question whether Gillette could receive a fair trial in Herkimer County, a charge that infuriated local officials.

Several buildings connected with the Gillette case still stand. In Cortland, south of Syracuse, is the rooming house where Gillette lived while working at his uncle's factory. In Herkimer, in the Mohawk River Valley, stand the courthouse and jail in which he was tried and incarcerated. And the railroad station through which the couple passed just hours before the fateful event remains in Big Moose Lake.

Chester Gillette was found guilty of first-degree murder and was electrocuted at Auburn State Prison on March 30, 1907.

---

are presented throughout the summer, along with crafts workshops, children's programs, and nature hikes.

Hiking

Bald Mountain, which offers superb views of the Fulton Chain for surprisingly little effort, is 4.5 miles (7.2 km) east of Old Forge. From the well-marked parking lot at the foot of the mountain, the trail climbs only 400 feet (122 m) in less than a mile. To access the trailhead, turn left on Rondaxe Road, just north of Old Forge off Route 28, and follow signs for the trail.

The trailhead leads into the woods and then, ultimately, to a scramble over craggy bedrock. The heavily-visited trail may not leave you feeling like you're in the wilderness, but fellow hikers are, like you, in this for the views of multiple lakes in the Fulton Chain. You can spot these as you're hiking the trail itself, but their full glory spreads out before you upon summiting. For an even better bird's-eye view, you can climb the restored Rondaxe Fire Tower at the top.

Outfitters and Guides

In Old Forge, boats and canoes can be rented at **Rivett's Marine** (102 Lakeview Ave., 315/369-3123, www.rivettsmarine.com). **Adirondack River Outfitters** (800/525-7238, www.aroadventures.com) conducts guided rafting trips down the Hudson, Moose, Black, and Salmon Rivers. **Tickner's Moose River Outfitter** (113 Riverside Ln., 315/369-6286, www.ticknerscanoe.com) offers guided canoe and kayak trips, along with instruction, rentals, and sales.

Shopping

Old Forge Hardware (104 Fulton St., 315/369-6100, www.oldforgehardware.com) bills itself as the "Adirondacks' Most General Store." Inside, you'll find everything you could possibly need, from snowshoes and camp stoves, to plenty of things you don't, like paperweights. Also on Route 28, **Mossback Traders** (2664 Rte. 28, Thendara, 315/369-6091, www.mossbacktraders.com) stocks classic Adirondack gear.

Food

Big Moose Station (2138 Big Moose Rd., Eagle Bay, 315/357-3525, www.bigmoosestation.com, daily breakfast, lunch, and dinner, $22), in the old Adirondack Railroad station, serves American diner-style food.

In Thendara, the 1893 **Van Auken's Tavern and Inne** (108 Forge St., 315/369-3033, www.vanaukensinne.com, Tues.-Sun. dinner, $22) serves contemporary American and continental fare. The menu includes everything from grilled veal chops to fresh fish.

Accommodations

Van Auken's Inne (108 Forge St., Thendara, 315/369-3033, www.vanaukensinne.com, $90-130), with its long, two-tiered porch, contains 12 renovated guest rooms with private baths. Some open out onto a breezy second-story balcony. On the ground floor are a comfortable lobby, tavern, and restaurant, all filled with antiques.

Northwest Lakes

The northwestern section of the Adirondacks is a sparsely populated area often overlooked by vacationers. Much of the land here is quite flat and covered with hundreds of lakes and ponds, along with seemingly endless unbroken forest. Though the region is primarily a canoer's paradise, thanks not only to the massive amount of water, but also the well-developed carry and portage paths that allow maximum opportunities for exploration, it also has much to offer in the way of easy-to-moderate hikes.

TOP EXPERIENCE

★ ST. REGIS CANOE AREA

To the immediate west of Paul Smiths begins the St. Regis Canoe Area, a 20,000-acre region encompassing 58 lakes and ponds. St. Regis Mountain stands alone at the area's northern edge, offering wide-angled views of the watery terrain.

St. Regis Canoe Outfitters (Floodwood Rd., at Long Pond Portage, 518/891-8040, www.canoeoutfitters.com), one of the area's largest outfitters, based in Saranac Lake, maintains an outpost in the canoe area at Lake Clear. To reach the outpost and several good boat-launch sites, take Route 86 north from Saranac Lake to Route 186. Turn left and follow Route 186 west to its end and junction with Route 30. Continue straight, past the junction, for 5.5 miles (8.9 km), crossing the Saranac Inn Golf and Country Club. Just beyond the course, at a paved four-way intersection, turn right on Floodwood Road. Continue straight ahead 4.1 miles (6.6 km) to the base.

Food, Accommodations, and Camping

Just west of St. Regis Canoe Area is the classic **Lake Clear Lodge & Retreat** (6319 Rte. 30, 518/891-1489, www.lodgeonlakeclear.com, $189-289), where you can choose among guest rooms filled with Adirondackiana, chalets, or suites with whirlpool tubs. The snug lodge is also home to an on-site speakeasy, which requires you to furnish a password for entry.

Sunday Pond B&B (5544 Rte. 30, Saranac Lake, 518/891-1531, www.sundaypond.com, $99) is tucked into the woods near a fish hatchery. It's a simple, Adirondack-style lodge with three guest rooms, a sleeping loft that's good for families, and a lean-to. All rooms have private baths. The proprietors also offer lunch and dinner for an additional fee.

The region's most exclusive accommodations can be found at **The Point** (Upper Saranac Lake, 518/891-5674, www.thepointresort.com, $1,250-2,500), an ultraluxurious great camp once owned by the Rockefellers. Now open to the public, The Point features

Northwest Lakes

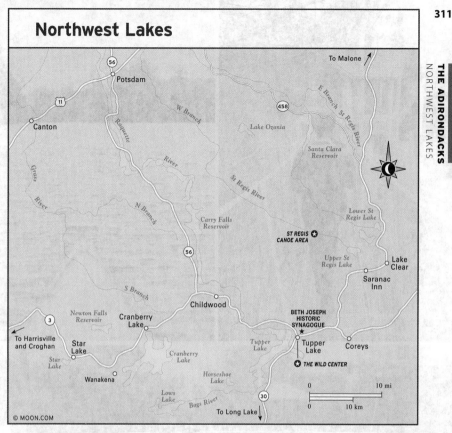

© MOON.COM

---

the absolute utmost in hedonistic delights, with the Relais & Chateaux stamp of approval.

Secluded **Fish Creek Pond Campground** (518/891-4560, reservations 800/465-2236, www.fishcreekpond.com, $22/night for New York residents, $27/night for nonresidents), with more than 300 sites, and 287-site **Rollins Pond Campground** (518/891-3239, reservations 800/465-2236, www.dec.ny.gov/outdoor/24494.html, $20/night for New York residents, $25/night for nonresidents) sit off Route 30 between the St. Regis Canoe Area and Tupper Lake village.

TUPPER LAKE

Once a major industrial center known for its lumber and paper mills, as well as its woodworking factories, Tupper Lake is made up of early-20th-century brick buildings, with a downtown that remains small, tightly knit, and compact. Many of the street names bear evidence of the town's French American heritage.

Raquette River Outfitters (1754 Rte. 30, 518/359-3228, www.raquetteriveroutfitters.com) rents canoes, provides car shuttles, and offers guided canoe trips.

★ The Wild Center

The best thing to happen to Tupper Lake in, well, forever, **The Wild Center** (45 Museum Dr., 518/359-7800, www.wildcenter.org, closed Apr., hours vary by season, $22 adults, $20 seniors, $15 ages 5-17, children under 4 free) has been a magnet for visitors to the Adirondacks since it opened in 2006. Inside

the state-of-the-art, highly interactive museum are 54,000 square feet of exhibits begging for hands-on engagement, including stations where kids can make nature-inspired art or explore the Naturalist's Cabinet, a high-ceilinged room with drawers filled with curiosities from the natural world that kids can touch and play with. Outside, there are 81 acres through which visitors can wander, with a playground for little ones and an imaginative "Wild Walk"—a whimsical aerie complete with a simulated eagle's nest into which guests can climb. It's easy to spend an entire day here, learning about the flora, fauna, and habitats of the Adirondacks.

Historic Beth Joseph Synagogue

The oldest synagogue in the Adirondacks, Historic Beth Joseph Synagogue (2026 Rte. 30, 518/359-7229, July-Aug. Tues.-Fri. 11am-3pm, Fri. services 7pm, free), is an architectural gem built in 1905 by Russian Jewish immigrants who came to the region as peddlers. At its peak in the mid-1920s, the synagogue served about 35 families but was closed in 1959 due to a dwindling congregation. Now in the New York State Register of Historic Places, the synagogue functions as a small museum. All fixtures and furnishings are original, and the vestibule houses an exhibit on the town's early Jewish community. A small art gallery is downstairs.

Canoeing

From day excursions to multi-day trips, Tupper Lake offers many opportunities to get out on the water and appreciate the Adirondack scenery. For less experienced paddlers or folks with limited time, a half- or full-day trip on the Raquette River Loop is recommended; the route shows off the diversity of the region's landscape, with part of the paddle cutting through tall grasses. Those with more experience and time might want to take a guided tour with Raquette River Outfitters to explore Lake Lila; motorized vehicles are prohibited and wildlife abounds, including bald eagles.

Food

The options for eating well in Tupper Lake are limited. At local favorite Larkin's Deli and Bakery (58 Main St., 518/359-9000, www.larkinsdeliandbakery.com, breakfast, lunch, and dinner), you can buy fresh homemade doughnuts, among other delights.

Check out ADK Food Hub (320 Park St., 518/359-5112, www.adkfoodhub.com, Mon.-Wed. 11am-7pm, Thurs.-Sat. 7am-9pm, Sun. 7am-7pm, $16), which has a farmer's market and prepared food options, mostly featuring grab and go favorites—perfect for an ADK picnic.

CRANBERRY LAKE

Mostly state-owned, Cranberry Lake has been virtually bypassed by civilization. Its 11 square miles include 55 miles (89 km) of shoreline. A village of the same name sits on Route 3 at the eastern end of the lake. To the west of the village is a boat launch, and to the east, the public Cranberry Lake Campground.

One of the area's most popular canoe trips begins at Inlet, off Route 3 southwest of the lake, and continues 16 miles (26 km) along Oswegatchie River to the lake itself. An easy hiking trail up Bear Mountain on the east side of the lake begins at Cranberry Lake Campground. The hike is 3.6 miles (5.8 km) round-trip, takes about two hours, and offers good views of the lake.

Recreation

The Adirondack region's third-largest lake, Cranberry Lake is also one of the area's remote lakes, part of the 107,230-acre Five Ponds Wilderness Area. Seven thousand of those acres are the lake itself. Outdoor enthusiasts in search of backcountry adventure head here for primitive camping (there are 46 campsites), hiking (a 50-mi/81-km trail circles the lake), and, of course, canoeing.

1: Wild Walk at the Wild Center 2: St. Regis Canoe Area 3: the Spider's Web at the Wild Center

Frequent paddlers on Cranberry love the lake for its size and features, namely, lots of flows, coves, and bays where one can boat and explore in relative solitude. Those who enjoy fishing also appreciate that they can cast a line for trout or bass. They warn, though, that the surrounding topography—the mountains—and the weather make for some interesting conditions on the water. Wind, in particular, can kick up suddenly and create hazards for inexperienced boaters, especially in the lake's center, where one lacks the protection of a cove, for example.

Food and Accommodations

There are 171 sites at **Cranberry Lake Campground** (Long Pine Rd., off Rte. 3, 315/848-2315, reservations 800/465-2267, www.dec.ny.gov/outdoor/24460.html, $20/night for New York residents, $25/night for nonresidents). Campers who prefer to rough it can row out to one of 46 primitive tent sites designated with yellow markers along the lake's shoreline. If you'd prefer a motel, try the simple but comfortable **Cranberry Lake Lodge** (7209 Rte. 3, 315/848-3301, www.cranberrylakelodge.com, $68-195),

which also has a family-style restaurant ($8) and lounge.

WEST ON ROUTE 3

From Cranberry Lake, Route 3 heads west through flat, woodsy, isolated countryside. Harrisville, built on the banks of the Oswegatchie River, is just over the St. Lawrence-Lewis County border, about 35 miles (56 km) from Cranberry Lake.

If you head north of Harrisville on Route 812 about 50 miles (81 km), you'll arrive in the Thousand Islands region. If you continue south about 14 miles (22.5 km) along Route 812 toward Croghan, you'll come to the hamlet of Indian River and an astonishing outdoor **Concrete Sculpture Garden.** Created by the late Veronica Terrillion, a folk artist, the park is alive with over 400 brightly painted statues of animals, people, and religious figures. Zebras, leopards, and a giraffe are poised near the driveway; a boat transporting the figures representing Terrillion's family floats in a small lily-filled pond.

Visitors are welcome to stop and take pictures of the park from the road, but please keep in mind that this is private property.

The Thousand Islands

Watery landscapes await in the Thousand Islands, an archipelago in the St. Lawrence River that separates New York and Canada. There are actually far more than 1,000—1,864 in all. Some are inhabited and can be visited, while others offer barely enough room to stand. To be counted among them, an island must be at least one square foot in size, support at least one tree, and remain above water year-round. Many scions of industry built lavish vacation homes here, including Boldt Castle, now one of the region's top tourist attractions. In the early 20th century, wealthy families from northeastern and midwestern cities would decamp to the Thousand Islands to escape the pressures of urban life and revel

in the calm, unhurried pace of the islands. Despite over a century of tourism, that slower pace remains today.

Most attractions lie along the Seaway Trail, which hugs the shores of the St. Lawrence and Lake Ontario. From the trail, views of the river and its bypassing boat traffic are outstanding. The 1959 completion of the St. Lawrence Seaway—a series of connecting channels and locks—made this river the longest navigable inland water passage in the world, stretching over 2,300 miles (3700 km).

New York and Canada share the islands. Canada's oldest national park east of the Rockies, Thousand Islands National Park, is here, where the Canadian Shield mountain

The Seaway Trail is a 520-mile (840 km) scenic highway that parallels New York's northern coastline along the St. Lawrence River, Lake Ontario, the Niagara River, and Lake Erie. Marked by green-and-white route markers, as well as brown-and-white War of 1812 signs, it is the longest national recreational trail in the United States.

In the Thousand Islands region, the Seaway Trail runs from Oswego in the south to Akwesasne in the north along Routes 104, 3, 180, 12 E, and 37. More parks and beaches are located along this section of the trail than anywhere else in New York State. In total, the Thousand Islands region boasts 45 New York and Canadian state parks; two of the largest are Wellesley Island and Robert Moses.

Seaway Trail, Inc. (401 W. Main St., Sackets Harbor, 315/646-1000, www.seawaytrail.com) publishes a free annual magazine, available in most regional tourism offices, and helpful touring guides. Among them are *Seaway Trail Bicycling,* which outlines some of the region's excellent bike routes, and *Seaway Trail Lighthouses.* Their website is a rich resource, with detailed maps available for download.

---

range connects across the river with New York's Adirondack Mountains. As a result, the region attracts as many Canadian visitors as American visitors. The Thousand Islands International Bridge (an extension of I-81) crosses over the St. Lawrence River near Alexandria Bay; the Prescott-Ogdensburg Bridge connects the two cities, and the Seaway International Bridge spans the river near Massena.

OSWEGO

Straddling the mouth of the Oswego River and overlooking Lake Ontario, the small city of Oswego (pop. 17,465) operated as an important fort and trading post throughout the 1700s. During the American Revolution, Oswego served as a haven for Loyalists fleeing the Mohawk Valley, and remained in British hands until 1796. Named the first freshwater port in the United States in 1799, Oswego protected the supply route to the naval base at nearby Sackets Harbor during the War of 1812.

Today, Oswego continues to function as a Great Lakes port and is a major sport-fishing center.

Fort Ontario State Historic Site

Fort Ontario State Historic Site (1 E. 4th St., 315/343-4711, www.parks.ny.gov/historic-sites/20/details.aspx, days and hours vary by season, adults $4, seniors and students $3, children 12 and under free) continues to stand sentinel over Lake Ontario, nearly 200 years after it was built. Originally built by the British in 1755, the site was attacked and re-built four times, with the present-day fort constructed between 1839 and 1844.

During World War II, Fort Ontario served as a sort of emergency refugee center/internment camp for victims of the Holocaust. The only one of its kind for European refugees in the country, the center invited 874 Jews and 73 Catholics to relocate here, but upon arrival, the refugees were placed in a fenced-in compound and told not to leave. The shocked refugees were interned for a total of 18 months.

Today, Fort Ontario has been restored to its 1867-72 appearance. Costumed guides interpret the lives of soldiers and civilians who once lived here.

H. Lee White Marine Museum

The delightful **H. Lee White Marine Museum** (1 W. 1st St., at West First St. Pier, 315/342-0480, www.hleewhitemarinemuseum.com, Sept.-June daily 1pm-5pm, July-Aug. daily 10am-5pm, adults $8, children 13-17 $4, children under 13 free) is a sprawling, hodgepodge affair filled with everything from

Oswego

© MOON.COM

archaeological artifacts to mounted fish. One exhibit focuses on Lake Ontario shipwrecks; another on the city's once-thriving shipbuilding industry; a third on the legendary "monsters" of the lake; and a fourth on the region's strong abolitionist history. Most everything in the museum has been donated, which gives it a folksy appeal. Outside, a World War II tugboat and a derrick barge invite exploration.

Richardson-Bates House Museum

Built in the late 1860s, Richardson-Bates

House Museum (135 E. 3rd St., 315/343-1342, www.rbhousemuseum.org, Apr.-Dec. Thurs.-Sat 1pm-5pm, Jan.-Mar. by appointment, adults $8, seniors and students $5, children 6-12 $3, children under 6 free) is a regal Italianate mansion still equipped with 95 percent of its original furnishings. The five plush period rooms downstairs are arranged according to photographs taken around 1890, while upstairs, succinct exhibits explain the history of Oswego County. The museum is run by the Oswego County Historical Society.

Recreation

Selkirk Shores State Park (7101 Rte. 3, 315/298-5737, reservations 800/456-2267, www.parks.ny.gov/parks/84/) is on the lakeshore about 15 miles (24 km) northeast of Oswego. It has a beach, hiking trails, a 148-site campground (tent sites $21-27/night for New York residents, $26-32/night for nonresidents) and cabins ($406-644/week).

Food

The ever popular **Rudy's Lakeside Drive-in** (78 Rte. 89, 315/343-2671, www.rudyshot. com, Sun.-Wed. 10am-9pm, Fri.-Sat. 10am-10pm, $13), a quarter-mile west of the State University of New York (SUNY) College at Oswego, has been serving up fish-and-chips and fried scallops and clams since 1946.

EN ROUTE TO SACKETS HARBOR

The Seaway Trail (Rte. 104 to Rte. 3) heads north out of Oswego to Selkirk Shores State Park and the mouth of the Salmon River. Take a 2-mile (3.2 km) detour east on Route 13 along the river to reach the Salmon Capital of Pulaski, where almost everything caters to anglers.

Continue another 5 miles (8.1 km) east on Route 13 to reach Altmar and the New York State Salmon River Fish Hatchery (2133 Rte. 22, Altmar, 315/298-5051, www.dec. ny.gov/outdoor/21663, Apr. 1-Nov. 30 daily 8:30am-3:30pm, free). Over three million fish are raised here each year, including chinook and coho salmon and brown, rainbow, and steelhead trout.

From the mouth of the Salmon River, Seaway Trail continues north along the shores of Lake Ontario. It bypasses several more parks and then bumps into deep-blue Henderson Harbor, a perfectly shaped semicircle ringed with historic homes, vacation cottages, marinas, and shipshape small boats.

About a mile southeast of Henderson Harbor is the hamlet of Henderson, where Confederate general Stonewall Jackson came for medical treatment for a stomach ailment before the Civil War. Part of his cure was to walk between the hamlet and the harbor daily.

SACKETS HARBOR

About 45 miles (72 km) north of Oswego, or 8 (12.9 km) miles west of Watertown, lies picturesque Sackets Harbor. Built on a bluff overlooking Lake Ontario, Sackets Harbor is peppered with handsome limestone buildings that date back to the early 1800s. Though now primarily a resort village, Sackets Harbor remains for the most part undiscovered, which helps account for its charm.

During the War of 1812, Sackets Harbor dominated American naval and military activity. A large fleet was constructed in its shipyard and thousands of soldiers were housed in the barracks built on its shores. Heavy fighting between British and American troops took place on the bluffs.

The former shipyard and adjoining battlefield is now Sackets Harbor's foremost visitor attraction. It is located at the end of a short Main Street lined with cheery shops, cafés, and historic buildings; more historic buildings flank quiet, tree-shaded Broad Street.

Sackets Harbor Battlefield State Historic Site

The silent and all-but-deserted Sackets Harbor Battlefield State Historic Site (foot of Main and Washington Sts., 315/646-3634, www.sacketsharborbattlefield.org, grounds: daily dawn-dusk, buildings: May 24-June 30 Wed.-Sat. 10am-5pm, summer Mon.-Sat. 10am-4:30pm and Sun. 1pm-4:30pm, adults $3, seniors and students $2, children under 13 free) was once the site of intense fighting between American and British troops. Monuments and plaques commemorating the events are strewn here and there, but for the most part, the battlefield remains an idyllic park, set atop a lush green bluff with glorious lake views. The Battle of Sackets Harbor is reenacted here every July.

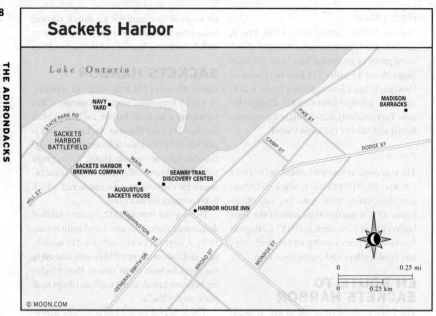

Sackets Harbor

© MOON.COM

Adjoining the battlefield is the partially restored Navy Yard, enclosed by a white picket fence. Built in the 1850s to replace the thriving shipyard once situated here, the yard contains a restored commandant's house and a museum showcasing exhibits on the War of 1812.

Madison Barracks

A mile or two east of the village center stand the former barracks, now known as **Madison Barracks** (85 Worth Rd., 315/646-3374, www.madisonbarracks.com), a converted complex holding apartments, restaurants, and a small inn. Visitors are welcome to explore the barracks' bucolic grounds, encompassing a parade ground, polo lawn, stone tower, officers' row, and military burial ground. Pick up walking tour brochures in the management office just inside the main gate.

Augustus Sacket Mansion

Housed in the handsome 1803 **Augustus Sacket Mansion** (301 W. Main St.) is **Sackets Harbor Visitors Center** (315/646-2321, www.sacketsharborny.com, hours vary seasonally), which contains three rooms of exhibits and an informative introductory video on the area.

Seaway Trail Discovery Center

One block away from the visitors center is the **Seaway Trail Discovery Center** (401 W. Main St., 315/646-1000, www.seawaytrail.com, hours vary seasonally, adults $4, seniors $3, children $2), housed in the old Union Hotel, which was built in 1817. Here, you'll find nine rooms of exhibits and lots of free literature on the historic trail.

Food

★ **Sackets Harbor Brewing Company** (212 W. Main St., 315/646-2739, www.sacketsharborbrewpub.com, daily 11:30am-10pm, $25) is housed in a refurbished railroad station in the heart of the village. Its historic location inspires the names of many of its brews, including War of 1812 Amber Ale and Grant's Golden Ale. On the dining room menu, find everything from fresh fish to potpies; a pub menu is also available.

Accommodations

In the heart of the village, three-story **Ontario Place Hotel** (103 General Smith Dr., 315/646-8000, www.ontarioplacehotel. com, $90-165) offers 28 spacious rooms and 10 suites with whirlpool tubs.

Also in the center of town, **Jacob Brewster House B&B** (107 S. Broad St., 315/646-4663, www.jacobbrewsterbandb.com, $100-125) is a renovated 1815 New England-style Georgian house with four guest rooms. Each has a private bathroom, a fireplace, and free wireless Internet.

WATERTOWN

One of the few towns in the Thousand Islands whose population has increased in recent years (just under 26,000), Watertown is named for the numerous falls of the Black River. Its proximity to so many waterways was, in large part, responsible for its industrial prosperity, a prosperity that was so robust that the town was said to have the most millionaires—at least per capita—in the United States at the beginning of the 20th century. That wealth helped Watertown develop infrastructure and architecture that were particularly remarkable given its size. It is the smallest town to have a park designed by Frederick Law Olmsted, Thompson Park, which is the location of the New York State Zoo.

The New York State Zoo at Thompson Park

Nearly a century old, the **New York State Zoo** (1 Thompson Park, 315/782-6180, www. nyszoo.org, Apr.-Oct. daily 10am-5pm, Nov.-Mar. Sat.-Sun. 11am-3pm, adults $10, seniors $8, children 3-12 $7, children under 3 free) is a 32-acre park that focuses on species that are native to New York. Some of the species are common, while others are rare, threatened, or endangered. Among them, expect to see bears, eagles, and wolverines. The zoo has a particularly strong educational and family program, so if you're coming with kids, be sure to see what activities are planned during your visit.

Recreation

If you're keen to get out on the river to run the rapids, **Adirondack River Outfitters** (140 Newell St., 800/525-7238, www.aroadventures.com, May-Oct.) will take you on a Black River white-water excursion. Expect 14 rapids ranging from Class II to Class IV.

Food and Accommodations

As Watertown's oldest restaurant, **The Crystal Restaurant** (87 Public Sq., 315/782-9938, www.thecrystalrestaurant.com, Tues.-Sun. 7am-9:30pm, $10) is an institution. Little has been done over the years to modernize the restaurant: the decor, the menu, and even the prices have refused to conform to trends. Service is generally excellent, which is one reason to visit. Another is the restaurant's contribution to cocktail culture: The Tom and Jerry, a Christmas holiday eggnog drink, wasn't invented here, but many locals claim it was perfected here. It's served only from Black Friday through New Year's Day.

Most lodging options in and immediately around Watertown are chain hotels, offering basic, reliable rooms and amenities.

CAPE VINCENT

Situated on a windswept spit of land at the mouth of the St. Lawrence River is Cape Vincent, "home of the gamey black bass" ("gamey" as in "feisty"). Cape Vincent has few tourist attractions, but it's a pretty village to drive through, with historic homes along Broadway.

The area's first European settlers were French, a fact that is celebrated every July on **French Heritage Day.** Real Street was once the location of "Cup and Saucer House," built in 1818 by Napoleon's chief of police, Count Real, in the hopes that the emperor could be rescued from the island of St. Helena. The building burned to the ground in 1867.

Sights

Cape Vincent Historical Museum (174 James St., 315/654-3094, July-Aug. Mon.-Sat.

10am-4pm, Sun. noon-4pm, free), in the heart of the village, showcases historical artifacts and a delightful collection of tiny figures created out of scrap metal by local farmer Richard Merchant. Not far from the museum is **New York State Department of Environmental Conservation's Research Station and Aquarium** (541 Broadway, 315/654-2147, mid-May-Oct. daily 9am-4pm, free), housing several hundred local fish.

It's also worth driving out to the 1854 **Tibbetts Point Lighthouse** (33439 County Rte. 6), several miles west of the village on the very tip of the cape. The lighthouse is not open for touring, but the drive along the shore road (Rte. 6) is outstanding.

Horne's Ferry

Cape Vincent is the only community left in New York State with a ferry to Canada crossing the St. Lawrence River. **Horne's Ferry** (855/442-2262, www.hferry.com, $15 for car and driver, one-way, $2 per extra passenger) operates May-October, and it takes 10 minutes to cross the river on the ferry.

Food and Accommodations

The boxy, brick **Roxy Hotel** (Broadway and Market St., 315/654-2456, www.theroxyhotel.com, $80) has operated continuously since 1894, with a brief break for renovations in 2011. Downstairs, an Irish pub offers beer and food; upstairs are 10 simple but adequate guest rooms.

CLAYTON

One of the most interesting villages along the St. Lawrence, Clayton contains four museums and the now-shuttered but still standing Thousand Islands Inn, where Thousand Island salad dressing was invented. The town spreads along the riverfront, with lots of park benches ideal for watching the swift current slide by. All along Riverside Drive stand sturdy brick storefronts, built in the late 1800s. An exception to the functional brick retail spaces is **Simon Johnston House,** a clapboard Italianate home with a widow's

walk and decorative eaves, located at the corner of Riverside Drive and Merrick Street.

Settled in 1822, Clayton soon developed into a major shipbuilding center and steamboat port. The St. Lawrence skiff, known for its sleekness and beauty, was first constructed here by Xavier Colon in 1868, and the 900-passenger *St. Lawrence,* the largest steamboat ever made, was built in the 1890s. During World War I, the Clayton shipyards produced submarine chasers and pontoon boats.

Tourists began frequenting Clayton in the late 1800s. Most came to fish and boat, and they stayed in huge wooden hotels—which have since burned down—along the waterfront. During Clayton's heyday, five express trains arrived here daily from New York City, and one hotel was equipped with a direct line to the New York Stock Exchange. Some vacationers even came during the winter, to ice-fish and watch the horse races run on the frozen St. Lawrence River.

Walking tour maps of the town are available at **Clayton Chamber of Commerce** (517 Riverside Dr., 315/686-3771, www.1000islands-clayton.com, July-Sept. daily 9am-5pm, Oct.-June Mon.-Fri. 9am-4pm).

Antique Boat Museum

Appropriately enough, Clayton has the finest collection of antique wooden boats in the United States. Among them are canoes, sailboats, launches, race boats, runabouts, and, of course, the famed St. Lawrence skiff. The gleaming boats, most built of highly polished woods and brass, are housed at the **Antique Boat Museum** (750 Mary St., 315/686-4104, www.abm.org, hours and admission vary based on activity) in a former lumberyard on the edge of town. There are over 300 vessels in all, spread out over eight buildings, along with a boatbuilding shop, almost 300 inboard and outboard motors, and thousands of nautical artifacts. The museum also contains extensive historical exhibits and during summer months, sails and lessons.

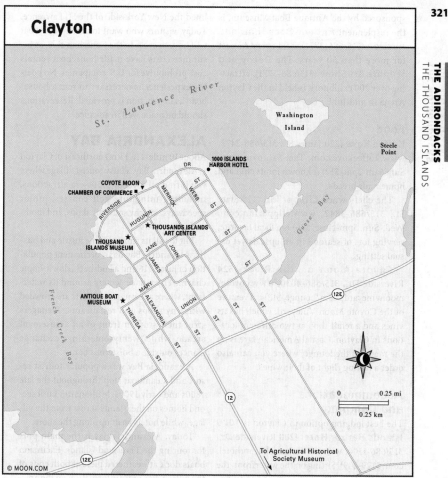

Thousand Islands Museum

Inside the eclectic **Thousand Islands Museum** (312 James St., 315/686-5794, www.timuseum.org, hours vary seasonally, free), you'll find the Muskie Hall of Fame, devoted to the region's most prized fish, and an enormous collection of hand-carved decoys, a popular North Country folk art. According to the exhibit, one riverman claims to have carved over 1,000 decoys, another about 5,000. Also on-site are re-created turn-of-the-20th-century storefronts, including a general store, millinery shop, law office, and old country kitchen.

Thousand Islands Arts Center

The **Thousand Islands Arts Center** (314 John St., 315/686-4123, www.tiartscenter.org, Mon.-Fri. 9am-5pm, free) began its life as the Handweaving Museum, but its name, mission, collection, and schedule of events and workshops expanded in 2009 to reflect a more diverse range of arts. Handwoven American textiles are still a specialty here, but photographs and other arts are exhibited and taught here as well.

Events

One of the region's most popular events,

sponsored by the Antique Boat Museum, is the resplendent Antique Boat Show and Auction (315/686-3771), held every August for more than 50 years. The Decoy and Wildlife Art Show (315/686-3771), attracting over 200 exhibitors, is held in the Clayton Arena in mid-July.

Food

Koffee Kove (220 James St., 315/686-2472, www.koffeekove.com, Tue.-Sat. 6am-8pm, Sun. 6am-2pm, $12) is known for its chili and homemade breads.

The chef-owned Clipper Inn (126 State St., 315/686-3842, www.clipperinn.com, Wed.-Sun. 5pm-close, $36) is a local favorite, serving lots of seafood in an upscale yet casual setting.

Coyote Moon on the River (524 Riverside Dr., 315/686-4030, www.coyotemoonvineyards.com/Lounge, $12) is a venture of the Coyote Moon Vineyard, which has its vines and a retail shop at two different locations in Clayton. Casual American fare is on the menu of the lounge, where you can also order a tasting flight of their wines.

Accommodations and Camping

The best lodging option in Clayton is 1000 Islands Harbor Hotel (200 Riverside Dr., 315/686-1100, www.1000islandsharborhotel.com, $129-209). Sitting on the waterfront, the property offers 105 rooms, as well as an on-site restaurant, indoor pool, gym, and wireless Internet throughout.

Campsites are available at 165-site Cedar Point State Park (36661 Cedar Point State Park Dr., 315/654-2522, reservations 800/456-2267, www.parks.ny.gov/parks/21, $18-34/night for New York residents, $23-39/night for nonresidents) and at three island campgrounds (www.1000islands-clayton.com/stay-thousand-islands/campgrounds) accessible only by boat.

Vacationing onboard houseboats is a popular activity in the Thousand Islands, and numerous houseboat-rental companies once lined the New York side of the St. Lawrence. Today, visitors who want to rent a houseboat will have to cross to the Canadian side, as insurance costs have made houseboat rentals cost-prohibitive for U.S. companies. No boating experience is necessary to rent a houseboat, as instruction is provided. Reservations should be made well in advance.

ALEXANDRIA BAY

About 10 miles (16.1 km) northeast of Clayton is Alexandria Bay, a busy tourist village where you'll find all sorts of 1950s-era attractions, including miniature golf courses, junior speedways, kitschy souvenir shops, and mom-and-pop motels.

But for all its summertime hustle and bustle, Alexandria Bay has a permanent population of just 1,116 and a laid-back, down-home charm. The village centers around its waterfront, where a few narrow streets are crowded with tiny shops and restaurants. Teenagers strut their stuff in front of an amusement arcade, while twentysomethings exchange glances outside a boisterous bar.

Alexandria Bay was a popular tourist resort and steamboat stop throughout the late 1800s and early 1900s. Millionaires built second homes on the islands across from the village, while hotels went up along the shore.

Today, Alexandria Bay is the main port for touring the Thousand Islands. Excursion boats dock at weathered piers at both ends of the village. For more information on the area, stop into the Alexandria Bay Chamber of Commerce (7 Market St., 315/482-9531, www.visitalexbay.org, daily 9am-5pm, with extended hours in July-Aug.).

★ Boldt Castle

Looming over Heart Island, across from Alexandria Bay, is a 127-room replica of a Rhineland castle. Boldt Castle (Heart Island, 315/482-2501, www.boldtcastle.com, hours vary seasonally, adults $10, children 5-12 $7, plus the cost of the boat ride over) was built by George Boldt, who came to the United States from Prussia in the 1860s. The son of poor parents, Boldt had tremendous industry and skill, and eventually became the most successful hotel magnate in the country. Both the Waldorf Astoria in New York City and the Bellevue Stratford in Philadelphia were his.

Boldt was deeply in love with his wife, Louise, and built the castle around the turn of the 20th century as a symbol of his love for her. The castle was to be their summer home, and he employed the finest craftspeople, instructing them to embellish the building with hearts wherever they could. Boldt even had the island reshaped into the form of a heart.

Then in 1904, when the castle was 80 percent complete, Louise passed away. Boldt sent a telegram to the construction crew to stop work immediately and never set foot on the island again. The castle was abandoned and allowed to deteriorate.

Finally, in 1977, the Thousand Islands Bridge Authority bought Boldt Castle, partially rehabilitated it, and introduced it to the tourist trade. Today, hundreds of visitors traipse through it daily, but all the activity in the world can't erase the castle's haunted, wildly romantic feel. In the former ballroom, exhibits explain the castle's history.

A shuttle boat operates from the castle to the **Boldt Yacht House,** perched on a separate island nearby. Completed before Louise's death, the boathouse contains three original spit-and-polish boats and restored living quarters furnished with handsome antiques. The Yacht House imposes a separate fee.

Excursion Boats

The only way to reach Boldt Island, as well as the other 1,800-plus islands in the St. Lawrence River, is by boat. Several boat companies offer tours, including **Uncle Sam's Boat Tours** (315/482-2611, www.usboattours. com), whose huge replica paddleboats dock at the eastern end of James Street. Uncle Sam's features an hourly **shuttle service** (adults $9.50, children 4-12 $7) to Boldt Castle that allows visitors to stay as long as they like, as well as various sightseeing and dining cruises.

Cornwall Brothers Store and Museum

Evidence of Alexandria Bay's early-20th-century heyday can be found at **Cornwall Brothers Store and Museum** (36 Market St., 315/482-4586, www.alexandriahistorical.com, May-Sept., days vary, 9am-5pm, donations accepted). Originally owned by the town's founder, Azariah Walton, the building

Boldt Castle

is now part museum, part re-created general store. Up front, choose from a nice selection of penny candy, vintage postcards, handicrafts, and books; in the back are historic photographs and artifacts.

Wellesley Island State Park

To reach Wellesley Island and Wellesley Island State Park (44927 Cross Island Rd., Fineview, 315/482-2722, www.parks.ny.gov/parks/52, parking $8) you must travel over the Thousand Islands International Bridge, a slim suspension expanse that seems to lead straight up into the sky. Built in 1938, the bridge extends over five spans and stretches 7 miles (11.3 km).

At the end of the first span lies the 2,636-acre state park, featuring hiking trails, swimming beaches, a campground, playground, and great views of the river. Covering 600 acres of the park is the Minna Anthony Common Nature Center (44927 Cross Island Rd., 315/482-2479, daily 10am-4pm, extended hours in summer, free), which includes both a museum and a wildlife sanctuary laced with trails. Live fish and reptiles, mounted birds, and an observation beehive are in the museum.

Thousand Island Park

South of the state park, at the very tip of Wellesley Island, lies Thousand Island Park (Wellesley Island, 315/482-2576, www.tiparkcorp.com), a quiet community filled with hundreds of wooden Victorian homes painted in luscious ice-cream pastels. Ornate carvings, shingled roofs, porches, turrets, and gables abound.

In the National Register of Historic Places, the park is largely privately owned, but visitors are welcome. The community has its own movie theater, post office, library, and playground.

Food

Numerous casual restaurants can be found on James and Market Streets downtown.

Among them is lively Dockside Pub (17 Market St., 315/482-9849, www.thedocksidepub.com, Mon.-Thurs. 11am-midnight, Fri.-Sat. 11am-2am, Sun. noon-midnight, $9), serving sandwiches, soups, and pizza in a setting near the water.

Hidden waterfront hot spot Foxy's (18187 Reed Point Rd., Fishers Landing, between Clayton and Alexandria Bay, 315/686-3781, www.foxys1000islands.com, hours vary seasonally, summer daily from 4pm, $24) is a small family-run eatery with great lobster bisque and an even better view of the sunset.

Windows on the Bay (17 Holland St., 315/482-9917, www.riveredge.com, daily 5pm-9pm, $22) in the Riveredge Resort serves creative American and French cuisine. The dining room offers fine views of Boldt Castle.

Accommodations and Camping

Campsites are available at the 73-site Grass Point State Park (42247 Grassy Point Rd., 315/686-4472, reservations 800/456-2267, www.parks.ny.gov/parks/139, $15-31/night) and the 432-site Wellesley Island State Park (Wellesley Island, 315/482-2722, reservations 800/456-2267, www.parks.ny.gov/parks/52, tent sites $18-36/night, cabins $266-294/week).

Capt. Thomson's (45 James St., 315/482-9961, www.captthomsons.com, $79-139) contains 68 standard rooms, some with balconies overlooking the river.

★ Riveredge Resort (17 Holland St., 315/482-9917, www.riveredge.com, $72-198) features views of the river and Boldt Castle. The hotel's rooms and suites are spacious and well-appointed; on-site are a health spa, indoor and outdoor pools, and a restaurant and lounge.

The sleek Bonnie Castle (31 Holland St., 315/482-4511, www.bonniecastle.com, $74-264) is the region's largest resort, equipped with 128 rooms and suites, a conference center, private beach, swimming pools, tennis courts, nightclub, miniature golf courses, and restaurants.

There Are a Thousand Stories in the Thousand Islands

The 1,864 islands of the Thousand Islands laze in the deep-blue St. Lawrence River like a "drunken doodle made by an addled cartographer," as one observer once said. Each and every one tells a story.

- The largest of the islands is Wolfe Island. The smallest is Tom Thumb. The only artificial island, Longue Vue Island, was formed by filling in the area between two shoals. As the story goes, Longue Vue was created by a doting husband who wanted to build a summer home for his wife. When he couldn't find a single island that suited her, he had one built, and then added a luxurious mansion atop it. His wife then ran off with another man.

- Devil's Oven on Devil's Island was the 1838 refuge of Canadian patriot Bill Johnston. After an aborted attempt to wrest Canada from the British Empire, Johnston hid out in the cave for nearly a year before surrendering to the authorities. He was later pardoned and appointed a lighthouse keeper.

- The Price is Right Island was given away in 1964 by Bill Cullen on *The Price is Right* TV game show. Deer Island is owned by the Skull and Bones Society of Yale University. Abbie Hoffman lived incognito—under the name Barry Freed—on Wellesley Island after jumping bail on cocaine charges in 1974.

- Florence Island, Arthur Godfrey's isle, was given to him as a gift by the Thousand Islands Bridge Authority in return for free advertising. Godfrey sang the song "Florence on the St. Lawrence."

- Grindstone Island was the site of the last existing one-room schoolhouse in New York State, in use until 1989.

- Ash Island has its own private railroad line running from the boathouse to the main house on the cliff.

- George Pullman of Pullman Car fame once owned Pullman Island and played frequent host to President Ulysses S. Grant.

- Calumet Island was once the property of Charles Emery, president of the American Tobacco Company.

- Picton Island was owned by M. Heineman, originator of Buster Brown Shoes.

- Oppawaka Island was owned by J. H. Heinz of Heinz 57 fame.

OGDENSBURG

The oldest settlement in northern New York, established in 1749, Ogdensburg is a busy port and industrial town at the juncture of the Oswegatchie and St. Lawrence Rivers. Downtown, Greenbelt Riverfront Park runs along the St. Lawrence, dotted with historical plaques that detail the War of 1812 Battle of Ogdensburg. A few blocks south of the park is the town's foremost visitor attraction: the Frederic Remington Art Museum.

Frederic Remington Art Museum

Artist Frederic Remington (1861-1909), best known for his paintings and bronzes of the American West, was born in the northernmost reaches of New York State. In his youth he made a total of 18 trips out West, collecting information and taking photographs that he would later use in his studio in New Rochelle, New York, to create his masterpieces. Remington never lived in Ogdensburg, but was born and is buried in nearby Canton. His wife moved to Ogdensburg after his death.

Housed in an imposing 1810 mansion, **Frederic Remington Art Museum** (303 Washington St., 315/393-2425, www.frederi-cremington.org, May 15-Oct. 15 Mon.-Sat. 10am-5pm and Sun. 1pm-5pm, Oct. 16-May 14 Wed.-Sat. 11am-5pm and Sun. 1pm-5pm, adults $10, students $7, children under 15 $3-7) contains the largest single Remington collection in the United States. On display are scores of oil paintings, watercolors, drawings, illustrations, and bronzes, including many small and relatively unknown gems. One room is filled with watercolors depicting the Adirondacks, another with a reproduction of Remington's studio. The most valuable Remingtons are kept in a locked gallery that is only open during guided tours, scheduled regularly throughout the day.

CANTON

About 20 miles (32 km) east of Ogdensburg lies Canton, artist Frederic Remington's birthplace. Settled by Vermonters in the early 1800s, Canton today is a busy small town (pop. 6,714), best known as the home of St. Lawrence University.

TAUNY Center and North Country Folkstore

It's worth a detour to Canton to visit **TAUNY Center and North Country Folkstore** (53 Main St., 315/386-4289, www.tauny.org, Tues.-Fri. 10am-5pm, Sat. 10am-4pm, donation), a unique arts gallery and gift shop located in a historic downtown building. North Country Folkstore offers buyable art made through traditional practices in the region. TAUNY (Traditional Arts in Upstate New York) Center exhibits detail-specific elements of local life, and a portrait gallery of North Country Heritage Award winners rounds out the facility, which also offers hands-on demonstrations and lectures by skilled artisans. Exhibits in the past have highlighted such subjects as St. Lawrence River fishing arts, Mohawk tourist arts, quilts and quilting bees,

and Old Order Amish crafts. Thoughtfully laid-out displays offer plenty of background information and photographs.

The gallery is also a good place to find out about folk arts events. Storytelling still thrives in the North Country, and there are occasional traditional music concerts and dance fests in the area.

Silas Wright Museum

Run by the St. Lawrence County Historical Association, the columned Greek Revival **Silas Wright Museum** (3 E. Main St., 315/386-8133, Tues.-Thurs. and Sat. noon-4pm, Fri. noon-8pm, donations welcome) once belonged to U.S. senator and New York governor Silas Wright. Regarded as an honest and intelligent man, Wright was so respected by his neighbors that he won his first election to the state senate in 1823 by 199 votes to 1; legend has it that he himself cast the one dissenting vote. The first floor of the house has been restored to its 1830-50 period appearance, while upstairs are local history exhibits. St. Lawrence County is one of the largest and least populated counties east of the Mississippi.

MASSENA

The main reason to make a stop in the small industrial city of Massena is to get a good look at the giant **St. Lawrence Seaway,** which connects the Atlantic Ocean with the Great Lakes. A joint project of the United States and Canada, the Seaway can accommodate ships up to 730 feet (220 m) long and 76 feet (23 m) wide. The public works project was formally dedicated on June 26, 1959 by Queen Elizabeth II and President Eisenhower.

Dwight D. Eisenhower Lock

Atop the long, spare **Dwight D. Eisenhower Lock** (Barnhart Island Rd., off Rte. 37, 315/764-3200) is a viewing deck from which you can watch ships being raised or lowered 42 feet (13 m) as they pass through the Seaway. The process takes about 10 minutes and displaces 22 million gallons of water. Ships pass through regularly, except in the winter when the St. Lawrence freezes over, but the viewing deck is only open June-September. Below the lock, a small interpretive center (315/769-2049, June-Sept. daily 9am-9pm) offers exhibits and a short film.

Robert Moses State Park and Campground

Adjoining the Power Project, Robert Moses State Park (19 Robinson Bay Rd., 315/769-8663, camping reservations 800/456-2267, www.parks.ny.gov/parks/51) is spread across the mainland and Barnhart Island. It is accessible through a tunnel beneath Eisenhower Lock and includes a swimming beach, bathhouse, boat rentals, picnic tables, playground, and great views of the river. The park also offers a 212-site campground ($18-34/night for New York residents, $23-39/night for nonresidents).

AKWESASNE

At the confluence of the St. Regis and St. Lawrence Rivers lies the St. Regis Indian Reservation, or Akwesasne (the name means "Where the Ruffed Grouse Drums"). Gas stations selling tax-free gasoline and mock tepees selling souvenirs line the roadsides. Signs along Route 37 include: This Is Indian Land; Private Property; No FBI, IRS, or Other Agencies.

Akwesasne is home to about 12,000 residents. The reservation straddles the St. Lawrence Seaway and the United States/Canadian border, and includes several islands.

In Hogansburg, about 10 miles (16.1 km) east of Massena, is the large and well-laid-out Akwesasne Museum (321 Rte. 37, 518/358-2240 or 518/358-2461, www.akwesasneculturalcenter.org, hours vary seasonally, adults $2, children 5-16 $1), housed in a big brown building that's also home to the Akwesasne Cultural Center and Library. The museum covers an entire floor and contains an outstanding collection of medicine masks, wampum belts, lacrosse sticks, carved cradle boards, water drums, Bibles written in the Mohawk language, beadwork, quillwork, modern artwork, historical photographs, and basketry.

Especially striking are the photography and basket exhibits. The photographs date back to the 1920s and depict a prosperous, pre-Depression Mohawk community bustling with shiny cars, sturdy baby prams, women in white dresses, and men in hats. The basket exhibit contains everything from a wedding basket, which looks just like a cake, to a thimble basket.

East of the museum is Akwesasne Mohawk Casino (873 Rte. 37, 877/99-CASINO, www.mohawkcasino.com, daily 24 hours). Opened in spring 1999, the casino offers blackjack, craps, and roulette tables, and hundreds of video lottery terminals.

Information and Services

The New York State Outdoor Guides Association (1936 Saranac Ave., Lake Placid, 866/469-7642, www.nysoga.com) provides a complete list of guides and outfitters operating in the Adirondacks.

For general information on the Adirondacks, contact Adirondack Regional Tourism Council (518/846-8016, www.visitadirondacks.com).

For more information on Lake George

and the southeastern Adirondacks, contact the Lake George Regional Chamber of Commerce (518/668-5755, www.lakegeorgechamber.com).

For more information on the Lake Champlain Valley and High Peaks region, contact the Regional Office of Sustainable Tourism/Lake Placid CVB (2608 Main St., Lake Placid, 518/523-2445, www.lakeplacid.com, www.roostadk.com).

Other useful area information centers include:

- **Oswego County Promotion and Tourism** (46 E. Bridge St., Oswego, 315/349-5239, www.visitoswegocounty.com)

- **Plattsburgh-North Country Chamber of Commerce** (7061 Rte. 9, Plattsburgh, 518/563-1000, www.northcountrychamber.com)

- **Town of Webb/Old Forge Tourism Department** (3140 Rte. 28, Old Forge, 315/369-6983, www.oldforgeny.com)

- **Warren County Department of Tourism** (1340 Rte. 9, Lake George, 800/958-4748, www.visitlakegeorge.com)

- **1000 Islands International Tourism Council** (Box 709, Wellesley Island, 315/482-2520, www.visit1000islands.com)

HIKING AND CANOEING

With 2,000 miles (3,220 km) of hiking trails and canoe routes stretching 100 miles (161 km) or more, the Adirondacks is an outdoor lover's paradise. Free, basic information on hiking trails, canoe routes, and tips for using the state's lands can be obtained from the **Department of Environmental Conservation** (DEC, 518/402-8013, www.dec.ny.gov).

Some of the DEC's brochures include enough information to actually embark on a hike or canoe trip, but many do not. The best source for more detailed information and maps—essential in many areas—is

Adirondack Mountain Club (ADK, 814 Goggins Rd., Lake George, NY 12845, 518/668-4447 or 800/395-8080, www.adk.org). ADK maintains visitor information centers at Lake George and Lake Placid and runs Adirondak Loj, a rustic lodge and campground at Lake Placid.

The Adirondack Mountain Club publishes a number of hiking and paddling guidebooks that are updated regularly. These guidebooks, along with detailed topographic maps of the region, are sold online through the club's store.

FISHING

Among the many fish swimming Adirondack waters are landlocked salmon, brook trout, lake trout, northern pike, pickerel, and small- and largemouth bass.

Fishing licenses are mandatory for everyone over age 16 and can be obtained in sporting-goods stores, bait shops, and town offices. Prices differ based on the length of time for which the permit is requested (one-day, seven-day, or year) and whether the person in need of the permit is a New York State resident or visitor. Once you've got your permit in hand, check with the **Department of Environmental Conservation** (www.dec.ny.gov), which maintains fishing hotlines dispensing information about good fishing spots. Call 518/402-8924 for current regional hotline numbers for the Adirondacks and High Peaks and northwestern lakes. The same information is also updated regularly on the DEC's website.

Getting There and Around

No major airports service the North Country, though there are regional airports in Lake Clear and Plattsburgh. The latter has limited commercial flights on Allegiant, Spirit, and United. Most visitors, however, fly to New York City, Albany, Syracuse, Boston, or Montréal, and then drive.

Amtrak (800/872-7245, www.amtrak. com) operates daily between New York and Montréal, with stops in Glens Falls, Fort Ticonderoga, Port Henry, Westport, and Plattsburgh. The scenery along the way is spectacular. In fact, the ride has been called one of the 10 most scenic in the world.

Trailways (800/776-7548, www.trailways.com) is the only bus company that provides service throughout the Adirondacks. Greyhound (800/231-2222, www.greyhound.com) travels to Glens Falls and Plattsburgh.

By far the best ways to explore the North Country are by car, canoe, and foot. The Adirondack North Country Association (ANCA, 67 Main St., Saranac Lake, 518/891-6200, www.adirondack.org) publishes a good map that outlines scenic and historic driving and cycling routes; copies can be picked up for free in most tourism offices.

The Finger Lakes

Syracuse 334
Skaneateles Lake 341
Owasco Lake 343
Cayuga Lake 347
Ithaca 353
Seneca Lake 359
Elmira 366
Corning 370
Keuka Lake 374
Canandaigua Lake 378
Rochester 385
Little Finger Lakes 394
Information
    and Services 396
Getting There
    and Around 397

This massive region, equal to New Hampshire or New Jersey in size, really seems to have it all: fascinating history, picture-perfect landscapes, farm-fresh food, and some of the country's best wines. And that's just for starters.

According to Iroquois legend, the Finger Lakes were created when the Great Spirit reached out to bless the land, leaving imprints of his hands. Six of his fingers became the major Finger Lakes—Skaneateles, Owasco, Cayuga, Seneca, Keuka, and Canandaigua. The other four became the Little Finger Lakes—Honeoye, Canadice, Hemlock, and Conesus. He must have had an extra finger, too; that one became Otisco.

Geologists have a different creation story. They say the long, skinny

Highlights

Look for ★ to find recommended sights, activities, dining, and lodging.

★ **Retreat to Skaneateles Village:** One of the prettiest of the Finger Lakes is anchored by this picturesque village, filled with cute shops, cafés, and a gazebo (page 341).

★ **Learn about women's rights:** The site of the first women's rights convention, **Women's Rights National Historical Park,** has an informative visitors center and historic sites (page 348).

★ **Sip wine:** Routes 414 and 14 are chockablock with **wineries,** with one tasting room after another tempting you inside to savor the flavor (page 362).

★ **Hike Watkins Glen State Park:** It's hard to believe that such incredible natural beauty is so accessible to the main drag. Hit the trail and feel the drops from an impressive waterfall stippling your face (page 364).

★ **See Mark Twain's Study:** Modeled after a Mississippi steamboat pilothouse, the stand-alone octagonal study holds the iconic writer's typewriter, hat, pipe, and other belongings (page 368).

★ **Soar over Harris Hill:** Climb into a tiny engineless glider and soar over the Seneca Lake Valley. The pilot tailors the flight to your tastes—from serene to exhilarating (page 369).

★ **Create a piece of art:** In addition to the remarkable collection at the **Corning Museum of Glass,** you can try your hand as a gaffer and make your own glass (page 371).

★ **Visit the Rockwell Museum of Western Art:** This fantastic museum features an exceptional collection of painting, sculptures, photos, and multimedia work from the American West. Special children's activities make it a must-visit for families (page 372).

★ **Play:** Kids won't want to miss the sprawling **Strong National Museum of Play,** where interactive exhibits and hands-on exploration are encouraged (page 387).

parallel lakes formed from steady progressive grinding of at least two Ice Age glaciers. As the glaciers receded, lake valleys filled with rivers that were backed by dams of glacial debris.

Depending on the weather, the water varies in hue from a deep sapphire blue to a moody gray. Along the lakes' southern edges, deep craggy gorges are sliced through the middle by silvery waterfalls. To the north are hundreds of drumlins, gentle glacier-created hills. All around lie fertile farmlands with fruit trees, buckwheat, and, especially, grapevines.

Scenic beauty is only part of the Finger Lakes story. The region's small towns abound with history. There's Auburn, home to abolitionists Harriet Tubman and William Seward; Seneca Falls, the site of the first women's rights convention; and tiny Palmyra, where Joseph Smith Jr. experienced his "First Vision," leading to the establishment of the Mormon religion. The region also holds a number of interesting small cities. Syracuse was once an Erie Canal boomtown. Ithaca, home to Cornell University, is surrounded by awesome steep gorges and waterfalls.

PLANNING YOUR TIME

The Finger Lakes make up one of the largest regions in New York State. Given the region's size, the number of historical and natural points of interest, and the variety of wineries in the area, one could easily spend a week or two exploring. If you don't have the luxury of time, you can still experience the best of the area. The Finger Lakes lend themselves to settling in a single town as a home base and exploring the wineries and natural features of the lake on which that town sits.

Most travelers will probably want to start their tour at Skaneateles, the prettiest of the Finger Lakes, which can easily be explored in an afternoon. Just down the road is Auburn, home to the fascinating house museums of abolitionists William Seward and Harriet Tubman. Beyond that is the town of Seneca Falls, a must-stop for anyone interested in women's history.

Outdoor lovers might want to focus on the southern side of the Finger Lakes region. Here, you'll find Ithaca, a university town surrounded by dramatic gorges and great hiking trails; Finger Lakes National Forest; and, at the far western edge of the region, Letchworth State Park, home to the "Grand Canyon of the East." There's also the little-known Finger Lakes Trail. More than 950 (1530 m) miles long, it runs from the Pennsylvania-New York border in Allegany State Park to the Long Path in the Catskill Forest Preserve. Branch trails lead to Niagara Falls, the Genesee River Valley, the Great Eastern Trail south of Corning, the central Finger Lakes, and Syracuse.

Wine lovers should focus on Hammondsport and Keuka and Seneca Lakes, which have an especially large number of vineyards, as well as lovely scenic vistas.

Culture buffs will want to spend one or two days in Rochester, which has an impressive children's museum and the George Eastman House, one of the finest collections of photography and film in the country. In Corning, the world-famous glass museum and Rockwell Museum of Western Art are must-sees. A visit to Corning can be paired with a stop in Watkins Glen, whose popular state park by the same name offers easy hikes with rewarding views of dramatic waterfalls and glacier-carved gorges.

Previous: peaceful afternoon in the Finger Lakes; view of Letchworth State Park; Watkins Glen State Park.

The Finger Lakes

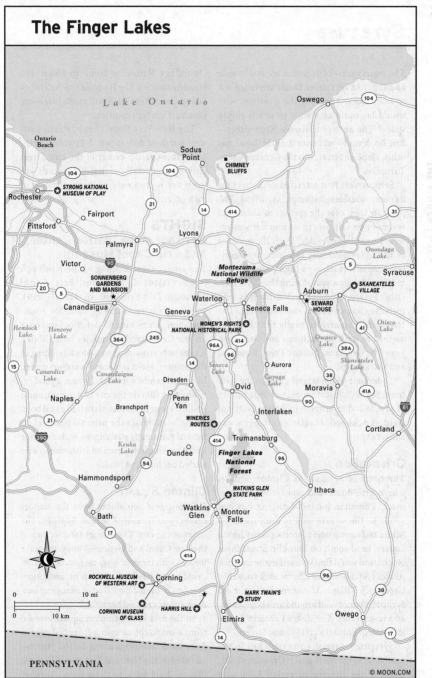

Lake Ontario

Oswego 104

Ontario Beach

Sodus Point

CHIMNEY BLUFFS

104

104

STRONG NATIONAL MUSEUM OF PLAY

Rochester

21

14

414

31

Fairport

Onondaga Lake

Pittsford

Lyons

Erie Canal

Palmyra

31

Canal

5

Syracuse

Victor

90

SONNENBERG GARDENS AND MANSION

Montezuma National Wildlife Refuge

Auburn

SKANEATELES VILLAGE

20 5

Waterloo

SEWARD HOUSE

Canandaigua

Geneva

Seneca Falls

41

Otisco Lake

Hemlock Lake

Honeoye Lake

WOMEN'S RIGHTS NATIONAL HISTORICAL PARK

Owasco Lake

38A

364

245

96A

414

Skaneateles Lake

96

38

15

Canandice Lake

Canandaigua Lake

14

Seneca Lake

Aurora

Cayuga Lake

Moravia

41A

Naples

Dresden

Ovid

90

81

21

Penn Yan

Branchport

Interlaken

Cortland

390

WINERIES ROUTES

Keuka Lake

414

Trumansburg

54

Dundee

Finger Lakes National Forest

96

Hammondsport

Ithaca

WATKINS GLEN STATE PARK

Bath

Watkins Glen

Montour Falls

17

414

13

ROCKWELL MUSEUM OF WESTERN ART

Corning

96

38

0   10 mi

MARK TWAIN'S STUDY

0   10 km

HARRIS HILL

CORNING MUSEUM OF GLASS

Elmira

Owego

17

14

PENNSYLVANIA

© MOON.COM

Syracuse

The main streets of Syracuse are oddly wide and flat, like fat rubber bands stretched out to their sides. They beg the question: who would lay out a city with so much empty space? The answer is simple. One street—Erie Boulevard—was once the Erie Canal, another, Genesee Street, was the Genesee Valley Turnpike.

Settlers were first attracted to the area for its many valuable salt springs. As early as 1797, the state took over the springs to obtain tax revenues on salt, worth so much it was referred to as "white gold." With the opening of the Erie Canal, the salt industry developed rapidly, reaching a high point of eight million bushels a year during the Civil War. Other Syracuse industries flourished as well, including foundries and machine shops. The Irish, who had arrived to dig the canal, remained to work the factories and were soon joined by Germans, Italians, Poles, Russians, and Ukrainians.

Today, one of the largest cities in the state (pop. 143,400), it still supports a wide variety of people and industries, including National Grid, Lockheed Martin, and Syracuse University.

Orientation

The heart of Syracuse is Clinton Square, where Erie Boulevard and Genesee Street meet. The main business district lies just south of the square and is dominated by Salina and Montgomery Streets. From Clinton Square, head south on Franklin Street three blocks, and you'll find yourself in the redbrick Armory Square District, Syracuse's answer to Greenwich Village. At one end hulks the old Syracuse Armory; all around are shops, cafés, and restaurants. The district centers on the junction of Franklin and Walton Streets.

Syracuse University sits on a hill to the southeast; to the northwest is Onondaga Lake. South of the city, the sovereign 7,300-acre Onondaga Nation is home to about 450 Haudenosaunee. The Iroquois Confederacy's Grand Council of Chiefs still meets here every year, as it has for centuries.

The New York State Thruway runs east-west north of downtown. I-81 runs north-south through the center of the city. Street parking is generally available. Sights downtown are within easy walking distance of each other.

SIGHTS

Heritage Area Visitor Center and Erie Canal Museum

The long, 1850s building of the **Heritage Area Visitor Center and Erie Canal Museum** (318 Erie Blvd. E., 315/471-0593, www.eriecanalmuseum.org, Mon.-Sat. 10am-5pm, Sun. 10am-3pm, $5 donation) was once an Erie Canal weigh station for boats. Today, it's the only remaining weighlock building in the country, and it is home to a visitors center, historical exhibits, a theater where a good introductory film on the city is screened, and a 65-foot-long (20 m) reconstructed canal boat. In the boat remain the original personal effects of some early passengers, including one heartbreaking letter from an Irishwoman who buried her husband at sea.

Clinton Square

Heading west two blocks from the visitors center, you'll reach **Clinton Square,** the heart of the city. The former intersection of the Erie Canal and Genesee Valley Turnpike teemed with farmers' wagons, peddlers' carts, canal boats, hawkers, musicians, and organ grinders in the old days. Today, many free outdoor events are held here.

In the mid-1800s, Clinton Square evolved from a marketplace into a financial center. Four bank buildings along Salina Street—all listed in the National Register of Historic Places—hark back to those days. Another

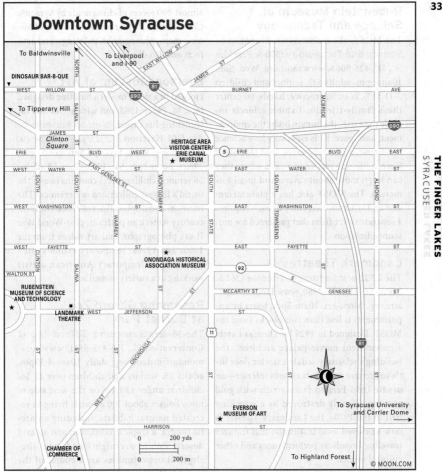

Downtown Syracuse

noteworthy historic item is the four-sided, 100-foot (30 m) clock tower on the 1867 Gridley Building, which was originally lit by gas jets.

At the western end of Clinton Square, near Clinton Street, stands **Jerry Rescue Monument.** The monument commemorates William "Jerry" McHenry, born into slavery in North Carolina around 1812. Jerry successfully escaped to Syracuse, where he got a job in a cooper's shop making salt barrels. He was discovered and arrested by federal marshals in 1851. A vigilante abolitionist group headed by

Gerrit Smith and Dr. Samuel J. May attacked the police station and rescued Jerry, who fled to Canada a few days later. That rescue, which challenged the Fugitive Slave Act of 1850, was one of the early events precipitating the Civil War.

One block farther west on Erie Boulevard at Franklin Street is the stunning **Niagara Mohawk Power Corporation** building. Completed in 1932, the steel-and-black structure is a superb example of art deco architecture. The edifice is especially worth seeing at night, when it's lit by colored lights.

Rubenstein Museum of Science and Technology

The MOST, aka Rubenstein Museum of Science and Technology (500 S. Franklin St., 315/425-9068, www.most.org, Wed.-Sun. 10am-5pm, adults $17, seniors and children 2-11 $15), is an interactive, hands-on center that's family-friendly. Exhibit subjects include the earth, the human body, the environment, and space. Kids especially love Science Playhouse, a climbing maze, and Discovery Cave, a life-size replica of a cave, where they can learn more about cavern and fossil formation. The MOST also has a planetarium and an IMAX theater; entry to each requires a separate ticket from that presented for museum admission.

Landmark Theatre

The 2,922-seat Landmark Theatre (362 S. Salina St., 315/475-7980, www.landmarktheatre.org, Mon.-Fri. 10am-5pm, tours by appointment) is less than two blocks from the MOST. Designed in 1928 by Thomas Lamb, a preeminent movie-palace architect, the building's relatively sedate exterior does little to prepare you for its riotous interior—an ornate Indo-Persian fantasy rich with gold carvings. Nearly destroyed by a wrecking ball in the 1970s, the Landmark Theatre is now a beloved local institution that features traveling Broadway performances and other cultural events.

Onondaga Historical Association Museum

One of the best county museums in the state, Onondaga Historical Association Museum (321 Montgomery St., 315/428-1864, www.cnyhistory.org, Wed.-Fri. 10am-4pm, Sat.-Sun. 11am-4pm, free, donations welcome) covers virtually every aspect of central New York history, from the Onondaga Nation and early African American settlers to the Erie Canal and the salt industry. Permanent exhibits include Freedom Bound: Syracuse and the Underground Railroad, Syracuse's Brewing History, and Syracuse China, which features almost 200 pieces of china made by Syracuse China over a 130-year period. A variety of historic maps, photographs, paintings, and artifacts are also displayed.

Everson Museum of Art

Housed in a sleek, modern building designed by I. M. Pei in 1968 and widely credited for launching his career, Everson Museum of Art (401 Harrison St., 315/474-6064, www.everson.org, Wed., Fri., and Sun. noon-5pm, Thurs. noon-8pm, Sat. 10am-5pm, $8 adults, $6 seniors, children free) contains one of the world's largest collections of ceramics. The museum also displays fine collections of 19th-century American portraits, post-World War II-era photographs, and art videos from the 1960s and 1970s. Temporary exhibits often focus on contemporary American artists working in a variety of media.

Rosamond Gifford Zoo at Burnet Park

The 36-acre Rosamond Gifford Zoo (1 Conservation Pl., 315/435-8511, www.rosamondgiffordzoo.org, daily 10am-4:30pm, adults $8, seniors and children over 12 $6, children under 13 free) on the west side of town houses about 700 animals living in re-created natural habitats, including an arctic tundra, a tropical rainforest, and an arid desert. Public overnights and meet-the-elephant opportunities are a couple of the zoo's highlights.

Tipperary Hill

West of downtown, at the juncture of West Fayette and West Genesee Streets, is the "Gateway to Tipperary Hill." Syracuse's oldest Irish neighborhood, Tipperary Hill is known for its upside-down traffic light, the only one in the country, at the intersection of Tompkins and Lowell Streets. When the stoplight was installed in 1925, right-side-up, members of the predominantly Irish neighborhood were irate: "British" red was placed above "Irish" green. Local boys protested by hurling stones at the light, breaking the lenses.

The People of the Longhouse

When French explorers first arrived in the Finger Lakes area in the early 1600s, they found it occupied by a confederacy of five Native American nations. The French called the Native Americans "Iroquois"; the Indians called themselves "Haudenosaunee," or "People of the Longhouse."

The Mohawk Nation (Keepers of the Eastern Door) lived to the east of what is considered the Finger Lakes region, along Schoharie Creek and the Mohawk River Valley. The Seneca (Keepers of the Western Door) lived to the west, along the Genesee River. In the middle were the Onondaga (Keepers of the Council Fire), and it was on their territory the chiefs of the Five Nations met to establish policy and settle disputes. The two other "little brother" nations were the Cayuga, who resided between the Onondaga and the Seneca, and the Oneida, who lived between the Onondaga and the Mohawk. A sixth nation, the Tuscarora, joined the Iroquois Confederacy in 1722.

During the Revolutionary War, all of the Iroquois except the Oneida sided with the British, as they had during the French and Indian War. Together with the Tories, they terrorized the pioneer villages and threatened the food supply of the Continental Army. In 1779, an angered General Washington sent Major General John Sullivan into the region, ordering him to "lay waste all the settlements around so that the country may not only be overrun but destroyed." Sullivan carried out his orders, annihilating 41 Iroquois settlements and burning many fields and orchards. By the time he was done, the Iroquois nation was in ruins. Thousands fled to Canada; others were resettled onto reservations in 1784.

City officials, realizing this was one battle they could never win, reversed the lenses in conciliation. Today, the green-over-red light remains, and a monument to the stone throwers sits at the same intersection.

Cashel House (224 Tompkins St., 315/472-4438, www.cashelhousegifts.com), packed with goods imported from Ireland, stands in the heart of today's Tipperary Hill. Across the street, Coleman's Authentic Irish Pub (100 S. Lowell Ave., 315/476-1933, www.colemansirishpub.com) has been serving Irish pub grub since 1933. Look for its "leprechaun doors" as you enter and leave the restaurant.

Salt Museum

To the north, in the suburb of Liverpool, lies lozenge-shaped Onondaga Lake, whose rich salt deposits first attracted settlers to the area. The lake is currently undergoing a major cleanup to remediate pollution. To one side stands Salt Museum (106 Lake Dr., Liverpool, 315/453-6715, www.onondagacountyparks.com/salt-museum, mid-May-mid-Oct. Sat.-Sun. noon-5pm, free), equipped with an original "boiling block." Brine was once turned into salt here through boiling

and solar evaporation. Battered antique iron kettles, wooden barrels, and other equipment, along with a fascinating collection of historic photographs, are on display.

The museum and lake comprise Onondaga Lake Park (www.onondagacountyparks.com), which also offers bicycle rentals, a tram ride, a playground, a skate park, and Skä·noñh—Great Law of Peace Center (6680 Onondaga Lake Pkwy., 315/453-6767, www.skanonhcenter.org, May-Oct. Mon.-Fri. 10am-4pm, Sat.-Sun. 11am-4pm, adults $5, seniors and children 9-17 $4, children under 9 free), which is focused on conveying Haudenosaunee (Iroquois) history and culture through exhibits and public programs.

Matilda Joslyn Gage House

History has all but forgotten Matilda Joslyn Gage, who doesn't enjoy nearly as much renown and recognition as fellow suffragettes Elizabeth Cady Stanton and Susan B. Anthony. The staff of the Matilda Joslyn Gage House (210 E. Genesee St., 315/637-9511, www.matildajoslyngage.org, hours vary seasonally, donations accepted), Gage's former home turned museum, is committed to doing their small part to restore Gage to history. Gage, a historian and scholar, was instrumental in drafting seminal documents of the suffrage movement; she was also an ardent abolitionist. Interestingly, she had another influence on American society as well: She was the mother-in-law of writer L. Frank Baum, famous as the author of *The Wizard of Oz*. Her life and work inspired Baum to explore the themes of courage and compassion that formed the crux of his most famous book.

At the Gage House, visitors can learn a great deal about 19th-century history in rooms that are devoted to the suffrage and abolition movements, as well as Iroquois influence on democracy and women's rights. There is also a room that interprets some of Baum's and Oz's history. Baum married Gage's daughter in this house, and he lived here for a short time. The house is part of the National Underground Railroad Network to Freedom.

RECREATION

Mid-Lakes Navigation (315/685-8500, www.midlakesnav.com) offers sightseeing and dinner cruises on the Erie Canal and Skaneateles Lake. The company also offers two- and three-day cruises and has boats available for weekly rental.

Take in a Syracuse University football, basketball, or lacrosse game at the 50,000-seat **Carrier Dome** (900 Irving Ave., 315/443-4634, www.carrierdome.com).

ENTERTAINMENT AND EVENTS

Performing Arts

Red House Art Center (400 S. Salina St., 315/362-2785, www.theredhouse.org) is a cultural center that presents many types of work, including theater, music, and visual art, year-round. Also housed on-site is **Open Hand Theater** (400 S. Salina St., 315/362-2788, www.openhandtheater.org), featuring giant puppets from around the world.

Landmark Theatre (362 S. Salina St., 315/475-7980, www.landmarktheatre.org) hosts concerts, plays, dance troupes, and classic movies throughout the year.

Syracuse Stage (820 E. Genesee St., 315/443-4008, www.syracusestage.org) is the region's premier professional theater and puts on up to seven plays and musicals annually.

Nightlife

The best source for what's going on where is *Syracuse New Times* (www.syracusenewtimes.com), a free alternative newsweekly published on Wednesdays, available throughout the city.

Many bars and clubs are located in the **Armory Square District** (www.armorysquareofsyracuse.com).

One of the liveliest music clubs in town is **Dinosaur Bar-B-Que** (246 W. Willow St., 315/476-4937, www.dinosaurbarbque.com), a friendly spot filled with dinosaurs and blues paraphernalia. Guests run the gamut from bikers to businesspeople. Live blues is performed most nights.

A good club in which to hear local bands is **Shifty's** (1401 Burnet Ave., 315/474-0048, www.shiftysbar.com), which has live music Wednesday-Sunday. On weekends, traditional Irish music can be heard at **Coleman's Authentic Irish Pub** (100 S. Lowell Ave., 315/476-1933, www.colemansirishpub.com).

Events

Syracuse Jazz Fest (www.syracusejazzfest.com) is the largest free jazz festival in the Northeast. The celebration usually runs for a couple of days in July, and features a wide variety of jazz events, artists, and styles. The city also hosts a smaller but growing **Blues Festival** (www.nysbluesfest.com)—also free—each summer.

One of the state's grandest parties is the **New York State Fair** (New York State

---

1: Rubenstein Museum of Science and Technology **2:** church on Skaneateles Lake **3:** Clinton Square in downtown Syracuse

Fairgrounds, 581 State Fair Blvd., Exit 7 off I-690, 315/487-7711, www.nysfair.org), featuring agricultural and livestock competitions, music and entertainment, amusement rides and games of chance, business and industrial exhibits, and talent competitions. The fair runs for nearly two weeks, ending on Labor Day, and has attracted as many as one million visitors in past years.

SHOPPING

If there's something you forgot to pack, it would be nearly impossible not to find a replacement at Destiny USA (9090 Destiny USA Dr., 315/466-6000, www.destinyusa.com), a six-story shopping mall with more than 250 stores. It's the largest mall in the state and one of the largest in the country.

FOOD

In the Armory Square District, try Pastabilities (311 S. Franklin St., 315/474-1153, www.pastabilities.com, Tues.-Sun. 4pm-8pm, $18) for Italian fare. Also in the neighborhood, Lemon Grass (238 W. Jefferson St., 315/475-1111, www.lemongrass-cny.com, Mon.-Thurs. 11:30am-2:30pm and 5pm-9:30pm, Fri.-Sat. 11:30am-2:30pm and 5pm-10:30pm, Sun. 4:30pm-9pm, $30) and Bistro Elephant Steakhouse (238 W. Jefferson St., 315/475-1111, Mon.-Sat. 5pm-close, $24) are owned by the same duo and share the same address and phone number. Lemon Grass is a Thai restaurant; Bistro Elephant is a steakhouse with some international influences.

★ Dinosaur Bar-B-Que (246 W. Willow St., 315/476-4937, www.dinosaurbarbque.com, daily 11am-9pm, $16), known statewide for its winning sauces, is awhirl with murals of frolicking dinosaurs. Business folks on lunch breaks slip past the row of Harleys parked out front to get their 'cue on. The fun, bustling hot spot serves straightforward barbecue dishes and home-style comfort foods for lunch and dinner; fried green tomatoes and pulled pork sandwiches are two favorites.

In its past life, ★ The Mission Restaurant (304 E. Onondaga St., 315/475-7344, www.themissionrestaurant.com, hours vary, $20) was a Methodist church, and today it still has a steeple and stained-glass windows. The church was also a stop on the Underground Railroad. Today, the repurposed building is a restaurant where Mexican cuisine is served.

The Clam Bar (3914 Brewerton Rd., 315/458-1662, www.theclambarrestaurant.com, Mon.-Thurs. 11am-10pm, Fri.-Sat. 11am-11pm, Sun. noon-9pm, $20), with a deceptively 1950s kitsch, dive-ish look, complete with knotty pine walls and motorcycle parking, fronts a family-owned place touted for the best seafood in town. This claim is backed up by the crowd, which you'll want to get here early to avoid.

In Tipperary Hill, Coleman's Authentic Irish Pub (100 S. Lowell Ave., 315/476-1933, www.colemansirishpub.com, bar open daily 11:30am-2am; dining Mon.-Thurs. 11:30am-10pm, Fri.-Sat. 11:30am-11pm, Sun. noon-9pm, $18) is a neighborhood institution. Its menu, written in both Gaelic and English, features lots of hearty Irish fare.

ACCOMMODATIONS

★ Barrington Manor B&B (1504 James St., 315/472-7925, $99-350) is in a lovely residential neighborhood just east of downtown. This stately English Tudor B&B offers five attractive guest rooms filled with antiques. There's a small garden out back, and a guest kitchen is generously stocked with snacks, beer, and wine.

Comfortable Craftsman Inn (7300 E. Genesee St., 315/637-8000, www.craftsmaninn.com, $99-180) is in Fayetteville, 10 miles (16.1 km) southeast of Syracuse. All 90 rooms and suites are furnished in Arts and Crafts style.

Downtown Best Western Premier Parkview Hotel (713 E. Genesee St., 315/701-2600, www.bestwestern.com, $129-675) features simple but comfortable rooms. Free breakfast and a complimentary shuttle to the airport, as well as to several stops downtown, along with free wireless Internet all add to the good value of this convenient downtown option.

★ **Jefferson Clinton Hotel** (416 S. Clinton St., 315/425-0500, www.jeffersonclintonhotel.com, $189-229), with warm, genuine service, impresses guests with little touches, from the rubber ducky atop the generous stack of bath towels to an omelet station at the complimentary hot breakfast buffet. Free Wii and X-box rentals, wireless Internet, and parking are added perks. What might be most winning, though, is the hotel's habit of scooting guests to their room on early arrivals whenever possible and offering free upgrades to available junior suites. The Armory Square location offers easy access to pubs, museums, and the large ice-skating pavilion during winter.

Hotel Skyler (601 S. Crouse Ave., 800/365-4663, www.tapestrycollection3. hilton.com/tc/hotel-skyler, $189-399) is one of Syracuse's most interesting accommodations, built in a former temple and theater in the middle of the Syracuse University campus. The hotel's 58 rooms are decorated in a contemporary style, and all have free wireless Internet. All guests enjoy complimentary access to the hotel's gym and business center, and breakfast and parking are both free, too.

Courtyard Syracuse Downtown at Armory Square (300 W. Fayette St., 315/422-4854, www.marriott.com, $199-249) is incredibly convenient to restaurants, shops, and other Syracuse attractions. The seven-story Marriott property has 96 rooms and six suites, all of which have free wireless Internet.

Skaneateles Lake

The farthest east of the Finger Lakes, deep-blue Skaneateles is also the highest (867 ft/260m above sea level) and most beautiful. Fifteen miles long (24 km) and 1-2 miles (1.6-3.2 km) wide, the lake is surrounded by gentle rolling hills to the south and more majestic, near-mountainous ones to the north. Iroquois for "long lake," Skaneateles is spring-fed, crystal clean, and clear. In the summer, its waters are specked with sailboats; in the winter, ice fishers build igloos.

The only real village on the lake is Skaneateles. Handsome summer homes placed judicious distances apart preside elsewhere along the shoreline.

★ SKANEATELES VILLAGE

The charming village of Skaneateles spreads out along one long main street (Rte. 20) at the north end of the lake. Graceful 19th-century homes, white-columned public buildings, and trim brick storefronts are everywhere and make for excellent strolling. Skaneateles

has been a favorite retreat among wealthy Syracusans for generations.

The first Europeans in Skaneateles were Moravian missionaries who visited an Onondaga village here in 1750. From 1843 to 1845, the village was the short-lived site of a utopian community that advertised in the newspapers for followers and advocated communal property, nonviolence, easy divorce, and vegetarianism. The area also served as a stopping place on the Underground Railroad, with English-born Quaker James Fuller spearheading the local abolition movement.

Clift Park, in the center of the village, is a waterfront refuge with a gazebo and wide-angled views of the lake. Docked at the end of a small pier are the two classic wooden boats of **Mid-Lakes Navigation Co.** (315/685-8500, www.midlakesnav.com, mid-May-Oct.). During warmer months, the family-owned spit-and-polish vessels offer enjoyable sightseeing and lunch and dinner cruises.

The Creamery

To learn about the lake's history, step into The Creamery (28 Hannum St., 315/685-1360, www.skaneateleshistoricalsociety.org, days and hours vary by season, donations welcome), a small, local museum housed in the former Skaneateles Creamery building. From 1899 to 1949, area farmers brought their milk here to be turned into buttermilk, cream, and butter. Displays include scale models of the boats that once sailed the lake, exhibits on dairy farming, and information about the teasel, a thistle-like plant once used in woolen mills to raise a cloth's nap. For 120 years, Skaneateles was the teasel-growing capital of the United States. The Creamery is run by the Skaneateles Historical Society (28 Hannum St., 315/685-1360, www.skaneateleshistoricalsociety.org), which also offers walking tours of the village.

New Hope Mills

For spectacular views of the lake, drive down either Route 41 to the east or Route 41A to the west. Route 41A veers away from the shoreline at the southern end and leads to New Hope Mills (181 York St., Auburn, 315/252-2676, www.newhopemills.com, store Mon.-Sat. 7am-4pm, café Mon.-Sat. 7am-3pm), an 1823 flour mill. Unbleached flours and grains are for sale in the mill's store, and coffee and baked goods are served in the café.

Events

Weekly sailboat races (2745 E. Lake Rd., www.skansailclub.com, June-Aug., check website for current schedule) take place throughout the summer, while free band concerts (W. Genesee St., across from the Sherwood Inn, www.skaneateles.com, July Fri. 7:30pm, Aug. Fri. 7pm) are held on Friday evenings in Clift Park. Polo games are played on Sunday afternoons in July and August at Skaneateles Polo Club (783 Andrews Rd., 315/685-8545, www.skaneatelespolo.com). Since 1980, the Skaneateles Festival (www.skanfest.org) has been bringing top chamber music artists to town in August. The town's largest event is the antique and classic boat show (north end of Lake Skaneateles, 315/685-0552, www.skaneateles.com) in early July.

But not all of the fun happens in the summer. The cold weather brings what Skaneateles calls "the world's smallest Christmas parade": Scrooge, Bob Cratchit, Tiny Tim, and a handful of other characters from Charles Dickens's A Christmas Carol kick off holiday festivities with a march around town. Dickens Christmas (www.skaneateles.com) has been celebrated every year for more than a quarter century. Beloved by locals and visitors alike, the festival features free horse and carriage rides, free roasted chestnuts, and free hot cider and doughnuts (or hot chocolate served by village Girl Scouts). There's also caroling on most every street corner, a sing-along in the village gazebo, Mother Goose story-time, and Father Christmas giving out free treats for the best little visitors. Live Dickens characters interact with townsfolk and visitors in the shops and along the streets and perform scenes from the Dickens classic. It's enough to warm the cockles of the Scrooge-iest visitor's heart.

Food

The laid-back ★ Doug's Fish Fry (8 Jordan St., 315/685-3288, www.dougsfishfry.com, daily 11am-9pm, $12) is a local favorite, renowned for its chowder, fried scallops, gumbo, and fish sandwiches.

Rosalie's Cucina (841 W. Genesee St., 315/685-2200, www.rosaliescucina.com, Sun. and Tue.-Thurs. 5pm-8:30pm, Fri.-Sat. 5pm-9pm, $29) offers first-rate Italian fare, ranging from pizza and pasta to grilled lobster tails, in an adobe tavern.

In addition to great accommodations, Sherwood Inn and Mirbeau Inn both have excellent restaurants. The restaurant at Mirbeau (851 W. Genesee St., 315/685-5006 or 877/647-2328, www.mirbeau.com, daily breakfast, lunch, and dinner, $34) serves creative American cuisine made with fresh local ingredients. Mirbeau also hosts special dinners with visiting chefs and special guests, as well as cooking classes. The restaurant at Sherwood Inn (26 W. Genesee St., 315/685-3405, www.thesherwoodinn.com, hours vary seasonally, $30) features traditional American fare. Check out Patisserie (4 Hannum St., 315/685-2433), which provides all the breads for the Sherwood Inn, a perfect stop for a great morning coffee and pastry.

Accommodations

Across from the park is the hospitable ★ Sherwood Inn (26 W. Genesee St., 315/685-3405, www.thesherwoodinn.com, $185-295), a rambling, colonial blue building that was once a stagecoach stop. The inn was established in 1807 by Isaac Sherwood, a man who began his career by delivering the mail on foot between Utica and Canandaigua and ended it as the "stagecoach king." Upscale yet casual, the inn includes a very popular restaurant, a tavern with frequent live entertainment, and 25 attractive guest rooms, all decorated with antiques. Contributing to the inn's relaxed atmosphere are a big screened-in porch with wonderful views of the lake, an outdoor patio for summer dining, lots of fresh flowers, and a snug lounge.

The Gray House (47 Jordan St., 315/685-0131, www.gray-house.com, $110-195), near the heart of downtown, is a welcoming B&B housed in a spacious Victorian home. It has five guest rooms, a large parlor, two breezy porches, and gardens.

Ultraluxurious Mirbeau Inn and Spa (851 W. Genesee St., 315/685-5006 or 877/647-2328, www.mirbeau.com, $185-385) is on the outskirts of Skaneateles. The elegant, European-style inn, complete with wall frescoes, waterfalls, soft lighting, and 18 spacious guest rooms, also has an on-site spa. The inn is also known for its serene restaurant.

Owasco Lake

The smallest of the major Finger Lakes, Owasco is 12 miles (19.3 km) long and 1.5 miles (2.4 km) wide at its widest point. Iroquois for "the crossing," Owasco lies 720 feet (220 m) above sea level. For great views of the lake, take Route 38 south, hugging the western shore, or Route 38A south, which travels high above the lake to the east. A few miles down, Route 38A bumps into Rockefeller Road, a shoreline route lined with 150-year-old camps and houses.

The city of Auburn (pop. 26,704) sits at the northern end of Owasco. At the southern end are the village of Moravia, birthplace of President Millard Fillmore, the Fillmore Glen State Park, and miles of farm country.

AUBURN

For a small city, Auburn has been home to an unusually high number of remarkable men and women: Logan, or Tahgahjute, Iroquois orator; Harriet Tubman, African American leader; William H. Seward, visionary statesman; Thomas Mott Osborne, pioneer of prison reform; and Theodore W. Case, the inventor of sound film. Tributes to all can be found in the city.

Auburn was originally a Cayuga village established at the junction of two trails. Revolutionary War veteran Colonel John Hardenbergh arrived in 1793 and built the area's first gristmill. By 1810, the village boasted 90 dwellings, 17 mills, and an incorporated library containing 200 books.

The opening of the Auburn State Prison in 1817 and the Auburn Theological Seminary in 1821 greatly stimulated growth. By the mid-1800s, Auburn was thriving. It even entertained hopes of becoming the state capital. The impressive public buildings on Genesee Street and lavish private homes on South Street date back to those heady days.

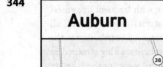

Auburn

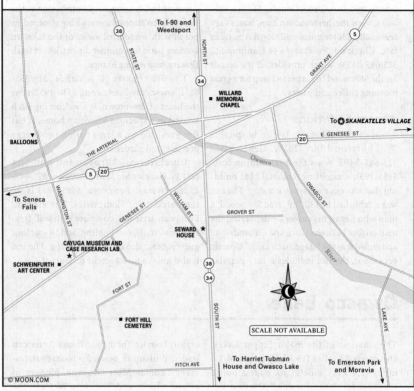

To I-90 and
Weedsport

STATE ST

NORTH ST

GRANT AVE

■ WILLARD
MEMORIAL
CHAPEL

To ★ SKANEATELES VILLAGE

E GENESEE ST

▼
BALLOONS

THE ARTERIAL

Owasco

To Seneca
Falls

5 20

WASHINGTON ST

GENESEE ST

WILLIAM ST

GROVER ST

OWASCO ST

River

SEWARD ★
HOUSE

CAYUGA MUSEUM AND
CASE RESEARCH LAB ★

SCHWEINFURTH
ART CENTER ★

FORT ST

38
34

■ FORT HILL
CEMETERY

SOUTH ST

LAKE AVE

SCALE NOT AVAILABLE

FITCH AVE

To Harriet Tubman
House and Owasco Lake

To Emerson Park
and Moravia

© MOON.COM

Seward House

One of the most interesting house museums in New York is **Seward House** (33 South St., 315/252-1283, www.sewardhouse.org, June-Labor Day Tues.-Sat. 10am-5pm and Sun. 1pm-5pm, hours vary off-season, closed Jan., adults $14, seniors $12, students $8, children under 6 free), a stately 1816 Federal-style home shaded by leafy trees. The house belonged to William H. Seward, ardent abolitionist, New York governor, and U.S. senator, best remembered for purchasing Alaska from the Russians in 1857. Seward also served as Lincoln's secretary of state and was almost assassinated by a coconspirator of John Wilkes Booth at the same time as the president.

Amazingly, almost everything in the

Seward House is original. Inside, you'll find not only Seward's furniture, but his grocery bills, top hats, pipe collection, snuffbox collection, 10,000 books, political campaign buttons, tea from the Boston Tea Party, personal letters from Abraham Lincoln, and calling cards of former visitors Horace Greeley, Frederick Douglass, Millard Fillmore, and Daniel Webster.

Seward first moved to Auburn for the love of Miss Frances Miller, whose father, Judge Elijah Miller, built the house. As a newly minted lawyer, Seward got a job in the judge's law firm and proposed to his daughter. The ornery judge allowed the liaison on one condition: Seward could never take his daughter away from him. Seward agreed and, despite his enormous worldly success, lived under his father-in-law's thumb for the next 27 years.

Excellent guides bring the past alive, and a fascinating collection of visiting leaders makes for a fun "Guess Who" game. Perhaps the most interesting aspect of the museum is the revelation and proof—in the form of photographs, news clippings, an eyewitness account, and a bloodied, rent garment—that Lincoln was not a solo target that fateful night in the theater.

Harriet Tubman Home

On the outskirts of Auburn, next door to the AME Zion Church, stands the **Harriet Tubman Home** (180 South St., 315/252-2081, www.harriettubmanhome.com, Tues.-Sat. 10am-3pm, adults $5, seniors $3, children $2), comprised of a brick house and adjacent white clapboard house wrapped with a long front porch. Known as the "Moses of her people," Harriet Tubman settled here after the Civil War, largely because her close friend and fellow abolitionist William Seward lived nearby.

Born into enslavement in Maryland in 1820 or 1821, Tubman escaped in 1849, fleeing first to Philadelphia and then to Canada.

Yet as long as others remained in captivity, her freedom meant little to her. During the next dozen years, she risked 19 trips south, rescuing more than 300 slaves. She mostly traveled alone and at night. Her motto was "Keep going; children, if you are tired, keep going; if you are scared, keep going; if you are hungry, keep going; if you want to taste freedom, keep going."

A visit to the Tubman property begins in the visitors center with interpretive panels that follow the timeline of Tubman's life and pertinent events. Afterward, a member of the AME Zion Church takes visitors on a tour of the clapboard house where Tubman tended to the elderly and where a few of her belongings, including her bed and Bible, are on display. Tubman herself lived in the brick house.

Fort Hill Cemetery

Harriet Tubman, William Seward, and numerous other Auburn notables are buried in **Fort Hill Cemetery** (19 Fort St., 315/253-8132, www.forthillcemetery.net, Mon.-Fri. 9am-4pm), on a hill to the west side of South Street. Native Americans used the site as burial grounds as early as AD 1100.

A large stone fortress gate marks the cemetery entrance; inside towers the 56-foot-high

the Harriet Tubman Home in Auburn

(17 m) **Logan Monument.** Erected upon a mound believed to be an ancient Native American altar, the monument pays homage to Logan, or Tahgahjute, the famed Cayuga orator born near Auburn in 1727. Logan befriended European settlers until 1774, when a group of marauding Englishmen massacred his entire family in the Ohio Valley. In retaliation, he scalped more than 30 settlers. Later that same year in Virginia, at a conference with the British, he gave one of the most moving speeches in early American history. "Logan never felt fear," he said. "He will not turn his heel to save his life. Who is there to mourn for Logan? Not one."

Cayuga Museum and Case Research Lab

Housed in a Greek Revival mansion, **Cayuga Museum** (203 Genesee St., 315/253-8051, www.cayugamuseum.org, days and hours vary by season, adults $7, seniors $6, children under 12 free) is devoted to local history. Exhibits cover early Native American culture, the Civil War, the Auburn Correctional Facility, Millard Fillmore, and women's rights.

Behind the museum mansion stands a simple, low-slung building known as the **Case Research Lab** (203 Genesee St., 315/253-8051, www.cayugamuseum.org, days and hours vary by season, suggested donation $3). Here, in 1923, Theodore W. Case and E. I. Sponable invented the first commercially successful sound film, ushering in the talking movie era. Displays include the first sound camera and projector, original lab equipment, and Case's correspondence with Thomas Edison and Lee De Forest, a self-promoter who claimed *he* was the inventor of sound film.

Schweinfurth Memorial Art Center

Next to the Cayuga Museum, **Schweinfurth Memorial Art Center** (205 Genesee St., 315/255-1553, www.schweinfurthartcenter.org, Tues.-Sat. 10am-5pm, Sun. 1pm-5pm, closed between exhibits, adults $10, children 12 and under free) features temporary exhibits by contemporary and classic artists. Shows feature everything from fine art and photography to folk art and architecture. Each winter the museum hosts a popular juried quilt show.

Willard Memorial Chapel

The only complete and unaltered Tiffany chapel known to exist, **Willard Memorial Chapel** (17 Nelson St., 315/252-0339, www.willard-chapel.org, Tues.-Fri. 10am-5pm, tours start every hour, on the hour, adults $8, seniors and students $5, children under 12 free) glows with the muted, bejeweled light of 15 windows handcrafted by Tiffany Glass and Decorating Company. Louis C. Tiffany also designed the chapel's handsome oak furniture, inlaid with mosaics, leaded-glass chandeliers, and gold-stenciled pulpit.

A visit to the chapel begins with a video on the chapel's history and the now-defunct Auburn Theological Seminary of which it was once a part. In July and August, free organ recitals and concerts are played in the chapel.

Food and Accommodations

One mile (1.6 km) south of Auburn, you'll find **Springside Inn** (6141 W. Lake Rd., 315/252-7247, www.springsideinn.com, $100-250, with continental breakfast), a striking red Victorian with big white porches. Upstairs are seven guest rooms furnished with antiques and nice touches like canopy beds and claw-foot or whirlpool tubs.

The Springside Inn is well known for its modern gastropub, **Oak & Vine** (6141 W. Lake Rd., 315/252-7247, www.oakandvine.com, Wed.-Sat. 4:30pm-9pm, Sunday 10:30am-1pm, $21), a local favorite for special occasions. The menu features American cuisine, including organic pasta and locally sourced organic produce.

Balloons (67 Washington St., across from the state prison, 315/252-9761, www.balloonsrestaurant.net, Tues.-Thurs. 5pm-9pm, Fri.-Sat. 5pm-10pm, $17) is a friendly spot with art deco decor, serving heaping platters of Italian American food since 1934.

The Restaurant at Elderberry Pond (3712 Center Street Rd., 315/252-6025, www. elderberrypond.com, mid-Mar.-Dec. Wed.-Sun. 11:30am-2:30pm and 5pm-8pm, $32) is surrounded by 100 acres of organic ingredients, from herbs to free-range meats, grown right on Elderberry Pond Farm. The menu changes daily; a sampling includes items like organic whole wheat pasta served with an assortment of daily garden pickings. The adjacent farm store, located in an 1800s smokehouse, is a good spot to pick up some favorites for the road (open seasonally, Saturdays only, 10am-5:30pm).

MORAVIA

At the southern end of Owasco Lake is Moravia, birthplace of President Millard Fillmore. Well off the beaten track, this small village boasts a number of handsome 19th-century buildings and the 1820s St. Matthew's Episcopal Church (14 Church St., 315/497-1171, Mon.-Fri. 8am-5pm, tours by appointment). The sanctuary's interior is covered with elaborate oak carvings

designed and executed in Oberammergau, Germany.

FILLMORE GLEN STATE PARK

Just south of Moravia lies the 857-acre Fillmore Glen State Park (1686 Rte. 38, 315/497-0130, camping reservations 800/456-2267, www.parks.ny.gov/parks/157, daily dawn-dusk, parking $7), centered on a deep, rugged ravine with five spectacular waterfalls. At the foot of the main falls is a geometric rock formation known as the Cowpens, and a popular swimming hole. Nearby are hiking trails, a campground ($15-27 for New York residents, $20-32 for nonresidents), and a playground.

The park also contains a replica of the tiny log cabin in which President Millard Fillmore was born. His actual birthplace lies about 5 miles (8.1 km) east of the park. Fillmore grew up dirt poor and went to work at an early age; he later described his upbringing as "completely shut out from the enterprises of civilization and advancement."

Cayuga Lake

The longest of the Finger Lakes, Cayuga stretches out for just under 40 moody miles (64 km), 382 feet (115 m) above sea level. It varies in depth from a few feet to 435 feet (130 m), and supports a wide variety of marine life, with carp and largemouth bass swimming in shallow waters and northern pike and lake trout inhabiting deeper ones.

Cayuga was named after the Iroquois nation that originally lived along its shores (the literal translation of Cayuga is "boat landing"). The Cayugas were called Gue-u-gweh-o-no, or people of the muckland, exemplified by the once-enormous Montezuma Marsh at the northern end of the lake.

Seneca Falls, the small industrial town where the first Women's Rights Convention met in 1848, sits just south of the marsh.

Anchoring the southern end of the lake is Ithaca, a friendly cultural center that's home to Cornell University, Ithaca College, and craggy gorges with waterfalls higher than Niagara. Along the lake's eastern and western shores are approximately 20 wineries; on the eastern shore is the historic village of Aurora.

SENECA FALLS

Seneca Falls owes its early development to a series of waterfalls dropping over 50 feet (15 m). The first gristmill was built here in 1795, and by the 1840s, the town supported dozens of water-powered factories. Many employed women worked 14-hour days for wages they had to turn over to their husbands. In 19th-century America, women were not allowed to own money or property or to even serve

Seneca Falls

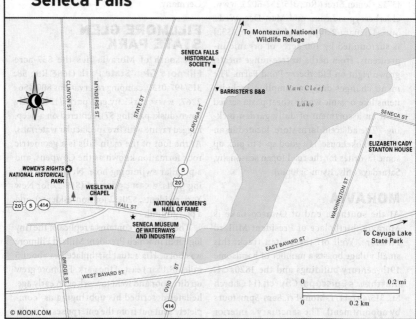

CLINTON ST

MYNDERSE ST

STATE ST

To Montezuma National
Wildlife Refuge

SENECA FALLS
HISTORICAL
SOCIETY ■

CAYUGA ST

▼ BARRISTER'S B&B

Van Cleef
Lake

SENECA ST

■ ELIZABETH CADY
STANTON HOUSE

WASHINGTON ST

WOMEN'S RIGHTS
NATIONAL HISTORICAL
PARK

WESLEYAN
CHAPEL ■

5
20

20 5 414

FALL ST

NATIONAL WOMEN'S
HALL OF FAME

★ SENECA MUSEUM
OF WATERWAYS
AND INDUSTRY

OVID ST

To Cayuga Lake
State Park

EAST BAYARD ST

BRIDGE ST

WEST BAYARD ST

0   0.2 mi

0   0.2 km

414

© MOON.COM

as legal guardians of their own children. This was the environment in which Elizabeth Cady Stanton gathered the historic 1848 convention that issued a Declaration of Sentiments calling for greater rights for women.

Today, Seneca Falls centers around Fall Street (Rtes. 5 and 20). Running parallel to Fall Street is the Seneca River and the Cayuga-Seneca Canal, which links Cayuga and Seneca Lakes. At the eastern end of town is the artificially constructed Van Cleef Lake.

Heritage Area Visitors Center

For a good general introduction to Seneca Falls, stop into the **Heritage Area Visitors Center** (115 Fall St., 315/568-1510, Mon.-Sat. 10am-4pm, Sun. noon-4pm, free). The exhibits cover virtually every aspect of the town's history, from its Iroquois beginnings and early factory days to its women's history and ethnic heritage, as well as the area's industrial past. Seneca Falls once held world fame for its knitting mills and pump factories.

Don't leave the center without learning about the destruction of the city's once invaluable waterfalls. The falls were eliminated in 1915 to create the Cayuga-Seneca Canal and, by extension, Van Cleef Lake. The flooding destroyed more than 150 buildings; today, many foundations are still visible beneath the lake's clear waters.

TOP EXPERIENCE

★ Women's Rights National Historical Park

Elizabeth Cady Stanton and her abolitionist husband Henry Stanton moved to Seneca Falls from Boston in 1847, a time when the town was both a major transportation hub and a center for the abolitionist movement. Often home alone, caring for her children, Stanton felt isolated and overwhelmed by housework. She also noticed the plight of her poorer neighbors: "Alas! alas!," she wrote in her autobiography *Eighty Years and More,*

"Who can measure the mountains of sorrow and suffering endured in unwelcome motherhood in the abodes of ignorance, poverty, and vice. . . ."

On July 13, 1848, Stanton shared her discontent with four friends. Then and there, the group decided to convene a discussion on the status of women. They set a date for six days thence and published announcements in the local papers. About 300 people—men and women—showed up. During the meeting, the group's Declaration of Sentiments was issued, calling for greater rights for women. Stanton and her friends deemed the convention a success. They were little prepared for the nationwide storm of outrage and ridicule that followed. Their lives, the town of Seneca Falls, and the nation would never be the same.

WESLEYAN CHAPEL AND VISITOR CENTER

The Wesleyan Chapel (126 Fall St.), where the historic 1848 convention took place, still stands. However, the structure is not entirely original. After suffering decades of weathering and vandalism, most of the chapel was in ruins. A restoration project improved the exterior, providing protection for some of the original elements of the architecture; National Park Service rangers now lead guests on tours of the chapel.

Nearby is a 140-foot-long (43 m) wall and fountain inscribed with the Declaration of Sentiments: "We hold these truths to be self-evident; that all men and women are created equal. . . ."

Next to the wall is the spacious, two-story Visitor Center (136 Fall St., 315/568-2991, www.nps.gov/wori, Wed.-Sun. 9am-5pm, free), managed by the National Park Service. Here, you'll find exhibits on the convention, its leaders, and the times in which they lived. Other sections focus on employment, marriage, fashion, and sports. There's a lot of interesting information, along with free handouts and a good bookstore.

ELIZABETH CADY STANTON HOUSE

Elizabeth Cady Stanton House (32 Washington St., tours June-Sept. daily, $1 pp) is about a mile from the visitors center on the other side of Van Cleef Lake. Stanton lived here with her husband and seven children from 1846 to 1862. During much of that time, she wrote extensively about women's rights.

Among the many reformers who frequented the Stanton home was Amelia Bloomer, the woman who popularized the clothing that bears her name. Though a resident of Seneca Falls, Bloomer did not sign the Declaration of Sentiments, believing it to be too radical.

The meticulously restored Stanton House is full of authentic, original ephemera from Stanton's life and era, including the bronze cast of Stanton's hand clasping that of Susan B. Anthony. Stanton met Anthony soon after the 1848 convention, and the women worked closely together throughout their lives.

In summer months, house tours are offered daily; visitors must sign up for the tours at the Women's Rights Visitor Center (136 Fall St., 315/568-2991).

Seneca Museum of Waterways and Industry

Housed in a historic building, the Seneca Museum of Waterways and Industry (89 Fall St., 315/568-1510, www.senecamuseum. com, Wed.-Sat. 10am-4pm, Sun. noon-4pm, free) is filled with exhibits on the history of the village and its surrounding waterways. A colorful 35-foot (11 m) mural lines one wall. The museum has antique fire engines, pumps, looms, and printing presses. One exhibit shows how the Erie Canal was built; another is a working lock model.

National Women's Hall of Fame

The National Women's Hall of Fame (76 Fall St., 315/568-8060, www.womenofthehall. org, Mar.-Oct. daily 10am-4pm, Nov.-Feb.

Wed.-Sun. 10am-4pm, adults $4, seniors and students $3, children under 5 free) bills itself as "the only national membership organization devoted exclusively to the accomplishments of American women." Enlarged photos and plaques pay homage to everyone from painter Mary Cassatt to anthropologist Margaret Mead.

Seneca Falls Historical Society

Seneca Falls Historical Society (55 Cayuga St., 315/568-8412, www.sfhistoricalsociety. org, Mon.-Fri. 9am-4pm, adults $15, students $10, families $25) is housed in a notable Queen Anne home, set back from the street behind an iron fence. Inside, 23 elegant rooms feature period furnishings, elaborate woodwork, and an extensive costume collection. A rare collection of 19th-century circus toys is strewn through the children's playroom.

Montezuma Audubon Center

Five miles (8.1 km) east of Seneca Falls is the Montezuma Audubon Center (2295 Rte. 89, Savannah, 315/365-3580, www. ny.audubon.org/montezuma, Apr.-Nov. daily dawn-dusk, free), a haven for migrating and nesting birds. Spread out over 6,300 acres of swamplands, marshlands, and fields, the refuge includes a visitors center, nature trail, driving trail, and two observation towers. Nearly 315 species of birds have been spotted in the refuge since it was established in 1937. Migrating waterfowl arrive by the tens of thousands in mid-April and early October. Late May to early June is a good time to spot warblers; in mid-September, the refuge fills with shorebirds and wading birds.

Before the turn of the 20th century, Montezuma Marsh was many times its current size, stretching about 12 miles (19.3 km) long and up to 8 miles (12.9 km) wide. The Erie Canal and Cayuga Lake dam projects greatly reduced its size.

Cayuga Lake State Park

Three miles (4.8 km) east of Seneca Falls

lies the 190-acre Cayuga Lake State Park (2678 Lower Lake Rd., 315/568-5163, camping reservations 800/456-2267, www.parks. ny.gov/parks/123, daily dawn-dusk, parking $7), offering a swimming beach, a bathhouse, hiking trails, a playground, and a 287-site campground ($15-25 for New York residents, $20-30 for nonresidents). In the late 1700s, the park was part of a Cayuga reservation, and in the late 1800s it was a resort area serviced by a train from Seneca Falls. The state park was established here in 1928.

Finger Lakes National Forest

The 16,212-acre Finger Lakes National Forest (National Forest Headquarters, 5218 Rte. 414, Hector, 607/546-4470, www.fs.usda. gov/fingerlakes) lies between Seneca and Cayuga Lakes and is the state's sole National Forest. Gorges, woods, pastures, shrublands, and many wildlife ponds are intermingled to provide excellent opportunities for wildlife-viewing and fishing. Over 30 miles (48 km) of trails, including the 12-mile (19.3 km) Interloken Trail, part of the Finger Lakes Trail, allow for hiking and horseback riding in the warm months and snowmobiling and skiing in the winter. Apples, raspberries, and other fruits are abundant throughout the forest, with five acres managed specifically for blueberry bushes. Inexpensive camping ($10-15/night) is available on three developed campgrounds on a first-come, first-served basis.

Events

Convention Days Celebration (315/568-8060, www.conventiondays.com), commemorating the first Women's Rights Convention, takes place each year on the weekend closest to July 19-20. Concerts, dances, speeches, historical tours, food, kids' events, and a reenactment of the signing of the Declaration of Sentiments form the schedule of activities.

Food and Accommodations

The large, historic ★ Barristers Bed and Breakfast (56 Cayuga St., 800/914-0145, www.sleepbarristers.com, $159-189), built by master craftsmen in the 1800s, features five spacious guest rooms furnished with antiques, a large front porch, cozy common room, and stone patio with a fire pit, perfect for sitting around on cool evenings. Guest amenities include a refreshment center.

The fresh, modern **Gould Hotel** (108 Fall St., 315/712-4000, www.thegouldhotel.com, $99-189) offers 48 rooms and suites with clean contemporary lines and extensive amenities (robes, Keurig coffee machines, iPod docking stations). A hipster-ish bar experience awaits downstairs.

Don't call it "just" a grocery store: **Wegmans** (1 Loop Rd., Auburn, 315/255-2231, www.wegmans.com, daily 24 hours) is a local institution. Visitors come to love it too because of sprawling hot and cold buffet bars, with a wide array of options for a quick, delicious, and healthy lunch.

WATERLOO

A few miles west of Seneca Falls on Routes 5 and 20 is Waterloo, a surprisingly busy village filled with aging redbrick buildings and shady trees. As a plaque along Main Street attests, Waterloo claims to be the birthplace of Memorial Day. Originally known as Declaration Day, the event apparently first took place here on May 5, 1866, in honor of the Civil War dead. Flags flew at half-mast, businesses closed, and a solemn parade marched down Main Street. In 1966, Congress and President Johnson officially recognized Waterloo as the birthplace of Memorial Day.

In the middle of town you'll find **Terwilliger Museum** (31 E. Williams St., 315/539-0533, Tues.-Fri. 1pm-4pm), which has a reconstructed Native American longhouse and village store, along with antique pianos, carriages, fire equipment, and a 1914 Waterloo mural.

You can also rent kayaks, canoes, and campsites from **Canal Side Experiences** (706 Waterloo-Geneva Rd., 315/781-6682, www.canalsideexperiences.com). If you prefer that someone else take the helm, you can hire them to take you on a canal excursion on one of their pontoon boats. The quirky one-stop shop also offers shopping, snacks, and entertainment. The owners operate a paint-your-own-pottery studio and rent time on their radio-controlled "theme park" with cars, trucks, and tanks you can drive around a homemade obstacle course.

Also on the canal, **Fuzzy Guppies** (1278 Waterloo-Geneva Rd., 315/539-8848, www.fuzzyguppies.com), rents canoes, kayaks, and paddleboats by the hour or the day, and welcomes campers who want to pitch a tent. You can also rent time in the "human waterball," a huge, inflatable ball bobbing on the water. Climb inside, try to walk on water—and see if you can keep your balance.

AURORA

Halfway down Cayuga's expansive eastern shore is picture-perfect Aurora, with its houses laid out like beads on a string. Most date back to the mid-1800s; the village is in the National Register of Historic Places.

Called Deawendote, or Village of Constant Dawn, by the Cayuga, Aurora attracted its first European settlers in the late 1780s. Henry Wells founded Wells College here in 1868, and the school—a premier liberal arts college for women, which only went coed in 2005—remains a focal point of Main Street.

Also in Aurora is **MacKenzie-Childs** (3260 Rte. 90, 315/364-7123, www.mackenzie-childs.com, daily 10am-5pm, free), a classy home furnishings-design studio best known for its whimsical terra-cotta pottery. The studio employs about 100 craftspeople, who design everything from glassware to lamps, and is housed on a 19th-century estate with great views of the lake. Though the studio itself is not open for tours, MacKenzie-Childs hosts a visitors center, where a video about the studio's craftsmanship is shown, and guests can take a free tour of the **Farmhouse,** a charming 15-room Victorian built in the 1800s. The tour features many MacKenzie-Childs products.

In the Tudor-style Aurora Free Library building, the charming, turn-of-the-20th-century **Morgan Opera House** (Rte. 90 at

Cherry Ave., 315/364-5437, www.morganoperahouse.org, May-Sept.) offers musical and dramatic events.

Food and Accommodations

One of the best options in the area is the lovely 1833 Aurora Inn (391 Main St., 315/364-8888, www.innsofaurora.com, $175-465). Inside, find 10 luxurious guest rooms furnished with antiques and Oriental rugs, a waterside restaurant (breakfast and dinner, hours vary seasonally, $30) with views of the lake, and a cozy tavern with a fireplace and mahogany bar. On the menu of the highly regarded restaurant is refined American cuisine inspired by the seasons and fresh regional products paired perfectly with Finger Lakes wines.

E. B. Morgan House (431 Main St., 315/364-8888, $165-390) rents rooms individually or all seven for larger groups. When the entire house is rented, a private epicurean dinner option for up to 14 is available.

ROMULUS

Midway down the west side of the lake lies Romulus, known for its vineyards and wineries. Two of the best wineries are only 5 miles (8.1 km) apart. A very large operation, Swedish Hill Winery (4565 Rte. 414, 607/403-0029, www.swedishhill.com, tasting room year-round daily 9am-6pm, $5 for wine flight, $3 for cider flight) produces about 30,000 cases of 25 different kinds of wines a year. Knapp Winery (2770 County Rd. 128, 800/869-9271, www.knappwine.com, Apr.-Nov. daily 10am-5:30pm, Dec.-Mar. Mon.-Sat. 10:30am-5pm and Sun. 11:30am-5pm, $5 tasting fee) is much smaller, but its wines are among the region's finest. Knapp's breezy Vineyard Restaurant (2770 County Rd. 128, 800/869-9271, days and hours vary by season, $17) emphasizes local produce.

OVID

Heading south of Romulus on Route 96, you'll come to the hamlet of Ovid, astride a small ridge surrounded by farmland. In the heart of the village stand three redbrick Greek Revival buildings known as the Three Bears because of the way they diminish progressively in size. "Papa Bear" was once the county courthouse; "Mama Bear," the village library; and "Baby Bear," the county jail. Today, the buildings house county offices.

Accommodations and Camping

Off Route 89 overlooking Cayuga Lake is Sned-Acres Campground (6590 S. Cayuga Lake Rd., 607/869-9787, www.snedacresny.com, tent camping from $25), a good place for families as it's equipped with a playground and miniature golf course.

Nearby is Driftwood Inn B&B (7401 Wyers Point Rd., 607/532-4324, www.driftwoodny.com, $140-195), offering six guest rooms in the main house, and four cottages, which are available by the week. Out front is a 260-foot-long (80 m) waterfront equipped with small boats and views of the lake.

TAUGHANNOCK FALLS

About 10 miles (16.1 km) north of Ithaca thunder Taughannock Falls, a skinny but dazzling 215-foot-long (65 m) stream of water flanked on either side by towering stone walls. Just 10,000 years ago, the falls cascaded straight down into Cayuga Lake, but erosion has moved them almost a mile inland. Thirty feet (9 m) higher than Niagara, Taughannock Falls are the highest straight falls east of the Rockies.

The falls are situated within the 783-acre Taughannock Falls State Park (2221 Taughannock Rd., 607/387-6739, camping reservations 800/456-2267, www.nysparks.com/parks/62, daily dawn-dusk, parking $8), which also offers lake swimming, fishing, boating, hiking, cabins ($210-238/week), and a 76-site campground (tent sites $18-28/night). Children will enjoy the park's imaginative playground, equipped with wooden towers and platforms. An overlook before the park gate offers a nice chance to see the falls without a commitment for those short on time. In July and August, free jazz, Latin, folk, and rock concerts take place weekly in the park.

Accommodations

A lovely option in Trumansburg, close to Taughannock Falls, is the best bet for this area. The proximity to Ithaca (10 minutes) makes this peaceful alternate locale worthy of consideration for a base to explore that city. **Inn at Gothic Eves** (112 E. Main, Trumansburg, 607/387-6033, www.gothiceves.com, $189-259) is an 1855 inn nestled in the heart of the tiny village. This unique property offers a selection of rooms, most of which are named after wines, and a true farm-to-table breakfast using eggs, berries, and local cheeses, often harvested that very morning. A can't-miss at this spot is a session in the outdoor wood-fired hot tub, which is included in the stay and stoked by the innkeeper by appointment.

Ithaca

Idyllically situated at the southern edge of Cayuga Lake, Ithaca is all but surrounded by steep hills and gorges. Three powerful waterfalls plunge right through the heart of the city and give Ithaca the tagline that it's used for years: "Ithaca is gorges." The small, progressive university town has a population of just over 31,000—which nearly doubles in size whenever its two colleges, Cornell University and Ithaca College, are in session.

Ithaca was originally a Cayuga settlement that was destroyed during General Sullivan's ruthless 1779 campaign. The first settlers arrived in 1788, but the town didn't really begin to grow until the opening of Cornell University in 1868.

For several years beginning in 1914, Ithaca was a center for the motion picture business. The Wharton Studios based itself here; *Exploits of Elaine,* starring Lionel Barrymore and Pearl White, and *Patria,* starring Irene Castle, were both filmed in Ithaca. The region's unpredictable weather proved less than ideal for moviemaking, however, and in 1920 the industry moved west.

Ithaca also claims to be the birthplace of the sundae, supposedly first concocted here in 1891. "As the story goes," writes Arch Merrill in *Slim Fingers Beckon,* "an Ithaca preacher came into C. C. Platt's drugstore, weary and sweating after the Sunday morning service. He asked the druggist to fix a dish of ice cream and pour some syrup on it . . . and thus another American institution was born."

Orientation

Downtown is small and compact. In its flat center lies **Ithaca Commons,** a pedestrian mall spread out along State Street. Perched on a steep hill to the east is Cornell University. The roller-coaster streets surrounding Cornell are known as **Collegetown.** On another hill to the south sits Ithaca College.

The best way to explore Ithaca and environs is by foot and car. Street parking is generally available, but there are also several municipal garages downtown.

SIGHTS
Ithaca Commons

The pedestrian-only Commons runs along State Street between Aurora and Cayuga Streets and along Tioga Street between Seneca and State Streets. Somewhat European in feel, it's filled with fountains, trees, flowers, and benches and flanked by shops and restaurants.

Most of the buildings along the Commons were constructed between the 1860s and the 1930s. Note the handsome Italianate building at **No. 158 E. State Street,** and the art deco storefront at **No. 152 E. State Street.** Just beyond the Commons, at **No. 101 W. State Street,** glows a 1947 neon sign of a cocky chanticleer.

The **Sagan Planet Walk** was built in memory of astronomer Carl Sagan, who was a resident of Ithaca. It starts at the "sun" on the Commons and continues on to visit nine

Ithaca

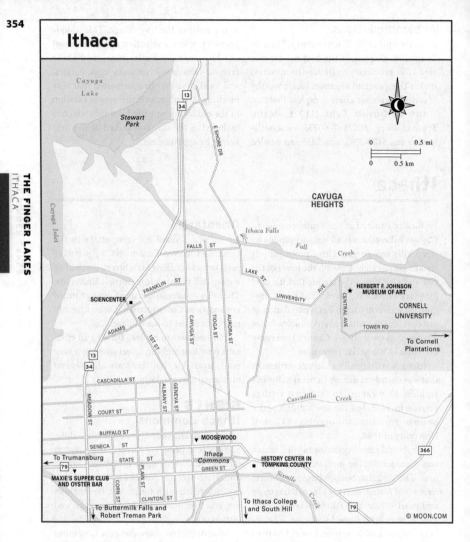

"planets" along a 0.75-mile route leading to the **ScienCenter Museum** (www.sciencenter.org). Visitors who get their "Passport to the Solar System" stamped along the way earn a free visit to the museum.

Historic DeWitt Park

The oldest buildings in the city are located on or near DeWitt Park, a peaceful retreat at East Buffalo and North Cayuga Streets, one block north of DeWitt Mall. Many buildings

in this National Historic District date to the early 1800s.

On the park's north side stands the 1817 **Old Courthouse** (121 E. Court St., 607/273-8284), thought to be the oldest Gothic Revival building in the state, and **First Presbyterian Church,** designed by James Renwick, the architect of St. Patrick's Cathedral in New York City. On the east side is the Romanesque **First Baptist Church,** built in 1890.

History Center in Tompkins County

Inside this large, renovated building you'll find the **History Center in Tompkins County** (401 E. State St., 607/273-8284, www.thehistorycenter.net, Tues.-Wed. and Fri.-Sat. 11am-5pm, Sun. noon-4pm, free), run by the DeWitt Historical Society. The society owns an impressive collection of over 20,000 objects, 3,000 books, and 100,000 photographs.

Permanent displays show the city's beginnings, its industries, and its surprising film history. Temporary exhibits have focused on such subjects as folk arts, alternative medicine, Italian immigrants, and Finnish American saunas.

ScienCenter

The hands-on **ScienCenter** (601 1st St., 607/272-0600, www.sciencenter.org, Tues.-Sat. 10am-5pm, Sun. noon-5pm, adults and children over 2 $8, seniors $7) primarily appeals to young ones, but adults can learn something here as well. Preschoolers can play in the Curiosity Corner, which has a water table and craft area, while older kids will probably head to the Animal Room or space exhibits. The museum has an extensive set of activities outside, too. In addition to minigolf, there's a "create your own waterfall" activity, a geometry climber, the world's only Kevlar cable suspension bridge, a giant lever, whisper dishes, and a "bubble-ology" section in outdoor Emerson Science Park.

Ithaca Falls

At the corner of Falls and Lake Streets thunder Ithaca Falls, the last and greatest of the six waterfalls along the mile-long (1.6 km) Fall Creek gorge. These "pulpit falls" are closely spaced rapids created by layers of resistant rock. To reach the site from Ithaca Commons—about a 20-minute walk—head north along Cayuga Street to Falls Street and turn right. To one side is a small grassy park and a wooded path that leads to a popular fishing hole.

Cornell University

Cornell University, built around a long, lush green lined with ivy-covered buildings, sits high on a hill overlooking downtown Ithaca. The views from here are especially fine at twilight, when Cayuga's waters glow with the setting sun and the gorges begin a slow fade into black.

Cornell was founded in 1865 by Ezra Cornell and Andrew D. White, who vowed to establish an "institution where any person can find instruction in any study." In so doing, they challenged a number of long-standing mores. Their university was one of the first to be nonsectarian; to offer instruction to all qualified applicants, regardless of sex, race, or class; and to feature courses in everything from agriculture to the classics.

Traffic and information booths are located at each entrance to the central campus. Except in a few metered areas, parking is by permit only; purchase a permit at the traffic booths. Visitors to the Herbert F. Johnson Museum can park in metered spaces out front. To tour the campus, contact the **Information and Referral Center** (Day Hall, Tower Rd. and East Ave., 607/254-4636, www.cornell.edu).

HERBERT F. JOHNSON MUSEUM OF ART

At the northern end of the Cornell campus is the **Herbert F. Johnson Museum of Art** (114 Central Ave., 607/255-6464, www.museum.cornell.edu, Tues.-Wed. and Fri.-Sun. 10am-5pm, Thurs. 10am-7:30 pm, free), housed in a striking modern building designed by I. M. Pei. The museum features especially strong collections of Asian and contemporary art but is also a teaching museum, containing a little bit of almost everything.

The Asian collection is situated on the 5th floor, where big picture windows open out onto 360-degree views of Cayuga Lake and the surrounding countryside. Among the many exquisite objects on display are funerary urns from the T'ang dynasty, silk paintings from 19th-century Japan, and bronze Buddhas from 15th-century Thailand.

WILDER BRAIN COLLECTION

Those interested in the odd and macabre will want to step into Cornell's **Uris Hall** (East Ave. and Tower Rd.) and ride an elevator up to the 2nd floor. In a small case are eight of the surviving stars of the Burt Green Wilder brain collection, which once numbered about 1,600 floating specimens.

Wilder, a former Civil War surgeon, was Cornell's first zoologist. He began assembling his collection in the late 1800s in the hopes of proving the size and shape of a person's brain were related to his or her race, sex, intelligence, and personality. Alas, his studies only disproved his theories, and in 1911 he rocked the scientific world by declaring that there was no difference between the brains of black and white men.

The pickled collection includes the extraordinarily large brain of criminal Edward Howard Ruloff, who was hanged in Binghamton on May 18, 1871. Ruloff allegedly killed his wife and daughter and was convicted of killing three men. He was also highly intelligent and had published several scholarly papers despite his lack of formal education.

Burt Green Wilder's brain is also in the collection. Considerably smaller than Ruloff's, it sits yellowing in viscous formaldehyde. The creator has joined his creation.

Cornell Botanic Gardens

Just north of the Cornell campus, 2,800-acre **Cornell Botanic Gardens** (124 Comstock Knoll Dr., 607/255-2400, www.cornellbotanicgardens.org, daily dawn-dusk, free) is an oasis of green. It encompasses a botanical garden, nature preserve, and arboretum, with specialty gardens devoted to everything from wildflowers to poisonous plants. Walkable nature trails wind through the Fall Creek gorge. Pick up maps in the **visitors center** (Tues.-Sat. 10am-2pm).

1: Taughannock Falls **2:** grounds of the Glenora Wine Cellars **3:** a marina on Seneca Lake **4:** Ithaca Falls

Sapsucker Woods Bird Sanctuary

At the eastern edge of the city lies a world-class center for the study, appreciation, and conservation of birds. Not everything is open to the public, but key attractions include 4.2 miles (6.8 km) of trails through the **Sapsucker Woods Sanctuary** and **Stuart Observatory,** which overlooks a waterfowl pond and bird-feeding garden.

The 230-acre Sapsucker Woods were named by bird artist Louis Agassiz Fuertes in 1901 after he spotted a pair of yellow-bellied sapsuckers—unusual for the region—nesting in the area. Sapsuckers continue to breed here each year. Near the woods you'll find a **visitors center** (159 Sapsucker Woods Rd., 800/843-2473, www.birds.cornell.edu, daily Oct. 1-Mar. 31 10am-4pm, Apr. 1- Sept. 30 10am-5pm, free), where you can pick up maps and view paintings by Agassiz Fuertes.

Buttermilk Falls State Park

Just south of downtown is **Buttermilk Falls State Park** (Rte. 13, 607/273-5761, camping reservations 800/456-2267, www.parks.ny.gov/parks/151, daily dawn-dusk, parking $8), plummeting more than 500 feet (150 m) past 10 waterfalls, churning rapids, sculptured pools, and raggedy cliffs. Alongside the falls runs a trail leading up to spire-like Pinnacle Rock and Treman Lake. At the base of the falls are a natural swimming hole, ball fields, and a **campground** (tent sites $15-19/night, cabins $210/week with 1-week minimum).

Robert H. Treman State Park

Robert H. Treman State Park (105 Enfield Falls Rd., 607/273-3440, camping reservations 800/456-2267, www.parks.ny.gov/parks/135, Apr.-Nov. daily dawn-dusk, parking $8), 5 miles (8.1 km) south of Ithaca, is 1,025 acres of wild and rugged beauty. Near the entrance is Enfield Glen, a forested gorge traversed by a stone pathway and steps. The steps lead to 115-foot-high (35 m) Lucifer Falls and a vista stretching 1.5 miles (2.4 km) down into a deep glen threaded by the Gorge Trail. A three-story 1839 gristmill, a natural swimming pool, and a **campground** (tent sites $18-28/night, cabins $210-400/week) are also on the grounds.

RECREATION

Circle Greenway is a 10-mile (16.1 km) self-guided walk or bike ride that leads to many of Ithaca's foremost natural and urban attractions, including gorges, the waterfront, Cornell, and the Commons. A free map can be picked up at **Ithaca/Tompkins County Convention and Visitors Bureau** (904 E. Shore Dr., 607/272-1313, www.visitithaca. com).

Ithaca Boat Tours (607/697-0166, www. ithacaboattours.com, prices vary by tour type) offers a variety of day and evening tours between May and October. A visit is especially enjoyable in the fall, when the changing colors of leaves are on full display.

ENTERTAINMENT AND EVENTS

Cornell's **Schwartz Center for the Performing Arts** (430 College Ave., 607/254-2787, www.pma.cornell.edu/schwartz-center) stages 6-12 plays September-May, along with the Cornell Dance Series and numerous guest performances. Professional regional theater is staged by acclaimed **Hangar Theatre** (801 Taughannock Blvd., 607/273-8588, www. hangartheatre.org, June-Aug.). The **Kitchen Theatre** (417 W. State St., 607/272-0570, www.kitchentheatre.org) presents contemporary theater year-round in an intimate space.

Among the groups performing regularly in the city is **Cayuga Chamber Orchestra** (171 E. State St., 607/273-8981, www.ccoithaca.org), the official orchestra of Ithaca. **Ithaca Ballet** (607/277-1967, www. ithacaballet.org) performs both classical and contemporary works.

Good club listings can be found in *Ithaca Times* (www.ithaca.com), a free alternative news weekly.

Many of the local galleries participate in the monthly **First Friday Gallery Night** (www.gallerynightithaca.wordpress.com), a free event that takes place 5pm to 8pm. Galleries and shops stay open late, inviting visitors to browse art and enjoy special exhibits and live performances.

SHOPPING

One block north of the Commons, at the corner of Seneca and Cayuga Streets, is **DeWitt Mall** (215 N. Cayuga St., www.thedewittmall. com). This former school building now contains about 20 shops, galleries, and restaurants. As its name suggests, **Ithacamade** (607/272-1396, www.ithacamade.com) is a gallery specializing in arts and crafts made by Ithacans. In addition to jewelry, pottery, and decorative arts, Ithacamade also has soap and snacks like macarons and biscotti for sale. Bibliophiles won't want to bypass **Buffalo Street Books** (607/273-8246, www.buffalostreetbooks.com, Sun.-Wed. 10am-6pm, Thurs.-Sat. 10am-7pm), which, true to local spirit, is a community-owned co-op.

Handwork (102 W. State St., 607/273-9400, www.handwork.coop, Mon.-Sat. 10am-6pm, Sun. 11am-5pm) is a craft co-op showcasing the work of over 30 local craftspeople. Here, you can find jewelry, clocks, glass, ceramic, fiber, and leatherwork, as well as home accessories, such as handmade wooden cutting boards.

FOOD

A number of casual eateries are located along Ithaca Commons. The 100 block of Aurora Street just off the Commons has one restaurant after another.

The cooperatively owned ★ **Moosewood Restaurant** (215 N. Cayuga St., DeWitt Mall, 607/273-9610, www.moosewoodcooks.com, Mon.-Thurs. 11:30am-3pm and 5:30pm-8:30pm, Fri.-Sat. 11:30am-3pm and 5:30pm-9pm, Sun. 10:30am-2pm and 5:30pm-8:30pm, $18) opened in 1973 and has been serving creative vegetarian cuisine ever since. It has made a name for itself worldwide for its best-selling cookbooks and natural foods. An outdoor dining area is open in summer.

Also serving contemporary American cuisine, as well as seafood, **BoatYard Grill** (525 Taughannock Blvd., 607/256-2628, www.boatyardgrill.com, days and hours vary by season, $22) overlooks the waterfront.

Just a Taste (116 N. Aurora St., 607/277-9463, www.just-a-taste.com, Sun.-Thurs. 5pm-9pm, Fri.-Sat. 5pm-10pm, tapa $8-10), Ithaca's wine and tapas bar, serves 50 wines by the glass and a menu inspired by Spain's small, shareable dishes, called tapas. Outside is a lovely garden.

Hot spot **Maxie's Supper Club and Oyster Bar** (635 W. State St., 607/272-4136, www.maxies.com, daily 4pm-10pm, $18) evokes New Orleans with its decor, attitude, and, of course, spicy Cajun cuisine and stick-to-your-ribs Southern soul food. Everything is homemade at this family-run affair.

Finally, if you're looking for breakfast, brunch, or something sweet, swing by **Purity Ice Cream** (700 Cascadilla St., 607/272-1545, www.purityicecream.com, Sun.-Thurs. 7:30am-10pm, Fri.-Sat. 7:30am-11pm, $10), which has more than cool, creamy treats on the menu.

ACCOMMODATIONS

As the teaching hotel of Cornell's School of Hotel Administration, the **Statler Hotel** (130 Statler Dr., 607/257-2500, www.statler-hotel.cornell.edu, $165-680) is Ithaca's hotel of choice for visiting parents, academics, and travelers. The hotel features 153 guest rooms, two restaurants, and a café and lounge; guests have access to most of Cornell's facilities, including the gym, pool, tennis courts, and golf course.

The very unique **Log Country Inn B&B** (4 Larue Rd., 607/589-4771, www.ithacabb.info, $70-150) may sound rustic, but it features soaring cathedral ceilings, fireplaces, a sauna, and 11 guest rooms, some with whirlpool tubs. Each room is named for a particular country or region of the world. A trip to the website is suggested to handpick a vibe of choice. Next door is a 7,000-acre forest, perfect for hiking and cross-country skiing. Some rooms share baths.

The picturesque **William Henry Miller Inn** (303 N. Aurora St., 607/256-4553, www.millerinn.com, $200-280) is an 1880 home and carriage house filled with stained glass and carved wood details. It has high-ceilinged rooms with private baths (some with whirlpool tubs) and modern amenities, warm service, evening dessert with coffee, and gourmet breakfast with offerings such as poached eggs with sun-dried tomato hollandaise or crème brûlée French toast.

For more bed-and-breakfast suggestions, contact the **Ithaca/Tompkins County Convention and Visitors Bureau** (904 E. Shore Dr., 607/272-1313, www.visitithaca.com) or **Bed & Breakfast of Greater Ithaca** (800/806-4406, www.bbithaca.com). You can also check room availability by visiting the visitors bureau's website, www.visitithaca.com.

Seneca Lake

At just over 36 miles (58 km) long and 618 feet (190 m) deep, Seneca Lake is the deepest lake in New York State. It seldom freezes over and is renowned for its superb lake trout fishing. Given to sudden, capricious gusts of wind, it's the most mysterious of the Finger Lakes.

Ever since the days of the Native Americans, area residents have reported strange, dull rumblings coming from Seneca's depths. The sounds are usually heard at dusk in the late summer or early fall and are most distinct midway down the lake. Native Americans believed the rumblings were the voice of an angry god. Early settlers considered them omens of disaster. Science attributes them to the popping of natural gas released from rock rifts at the bottom of the lake.

Whatever the cause, the dull rumbles—a sound much like gunfire—may have had some portent, for during World War II, a huge munitions depot was built along Seneca's eastern shore. The 10,500+-acre Seneca Army Depot remains, though it ceased operations in the 1990s and was shuttered in 2000. A herd of snow-white deer roam the grounds and can best be seen from Route 96A at dawn and dusk.

At the northern end of Seneca Lake lies Geneva, a historic town whose South Main Street has been called "the most beautiful street in America." At the southern end is Watkins Glen, a village known for the birth of American road racing. It's also home to a rugged, 700-foot-deep (210 m) gorge that's been turned into a natural theme park.

GENEVA

One of the larger towns in the region, Geneva is home to about 13,200 residents. Though overall a nondescript place, elegant South Main Street, lined with leafy trees, stately homes, and Hobart and William Smith Colleges, runs through its center.

Geneva was once a major Seneca settlement known as Kanadesaga. During the French and Indian War, the British erected a fort here from which they and the Seneca conducted murderous raids, only to be massacred themselves during the 1779 Sullivan campaign.

Soon after the Revolution, European settlers began to arrive. A visionary land agent laid out the town along a broad Main Street and a public green. This gave the place an air of dignity, which, during the 1800s, attracted an unusually large number of retired ministers and spinsters. Geneva soon earned the nickname "The Saints' Retreat and Old Maids' Paradise."

In 1847, the Medical College of Geneva College (now Hobart) received an application of admission from Elizabeth Blackwell of Philadelphia. The students and deans, assuming it to be a joke, laughingly voted to admit her. A few weeks later, to everyone's amazement, Ms. Blackwell arrived, and in 1849 she graduated—the first woman ever granted a medical diploma in the United States.

Rose Hill Mansion

Three miles (4.8 km) east of downtown lies Geneva's foremost visitor attraction, the 1839 **Rose Hill Mansion** (3373 Rte. 96A, 315/789-3848, www.genevahistoricalsociety.com, days and hours vary by season, adults $10, seniors $8, children 10-18 $6, children under 10 free), built in the Greek Revival style with six Ionic columns out front. The mansion was once home to Robert Swan, an innovative farmer who installed the country's first large-scale drainage system. Tours of the house take visitors past a fine collection of Empire-style furnishings. Next door is the former carriage house; out front, the green lawn slopes down to Seneca Lake.

Prouty-Chew House

Built in the Federal style in 1829 by a Geneva attorney, the **Prouty-Chew House** (543 S. Main St., 315/789-5151, www.genevahistoricalsociety.com, days and hours vary seasonally, $3 suggested donation) was enlarged several times in the 1850s and 1870s, which accounts for its eclectic look. It's now home to the Geneva Historical Society, which showcases changing exhibits on local history and art.

Wine Tasting

The regional wine passport program offers the best deal for tastings at wineries throughout the area.

Three Brothers Wineries & Estates (623 Lerch Rd., 315/585-4432, www.3brotherswinery.com, Apr.-Oct. daily 10am-6pm, Nov.-Mar. daily 10am-5pm, $20 "tasting passport" allows tasting in all three wineries and the microbrewery) offers three distinct wineries and one microbrewery. The tasting room of each has its own unique vibe. Stony Lonesome Estates is all hardwood and class, while Passion Feet is sexy with velvet accents, and Bagg Dare is down-home, kick-back casual.

Five bucks gets you five tastings at **Zugibe Vineyards** (4248 E. Lake Rd., 315/585-6402, www.zugibevineyards.com, daily 11am-5pm, $5). Take a seat on the porch and enjoy the unobstructed views of Seneca Lake while you sip your way through cab sauvs, gruner veltliners, and the lesser-known lembergers.

The tasting room at **Ventosa Vineyards** (3440 Rte. 96A, 315/719-0000, www.ventosavineyards.com, days and hours vary by season, $5 for tasting, $8 if you want a souvenir glass) opens up to beautiful lake views, but it's popular among oenophiles in part because it's open late on Friday, when it also hosts live music. The Italian café just off the tasting room serves light bites (daily, hours vary by season).

Food and Accommodations

Red Dove Tavern (30 Castle St., 315/781-2020, www.reddovetavern.com, Tue.-Sat. 5pm-9pm, $22) features American fare comprised of local ingredients. Entrées change weekly based on what's in season.

The extravagant, Romanesque **Belhurst Castle** (4069 W. Lake Rd., 315/781-0201, www.belhurst.com, $110-395, with breakfast) took 50 workers toiling six days a week for four years to complete. Finished in 1889, it features everything from turrets to stained-glass windows. Inside is **Edgar's Restaurant in the Castle** (Tues.-Sun. 5pm-8:30pm, $34), an upscale restaurant serving continental fare at dinner, and **Stonecutter's Tavern** (daily 11am-10pm, $14), which offers a tavern-style menu. Eleven modern guest rooms vary greatly in size and price. An on-site spa-salon pampers guests, and a winery offers tours and tastings. Out front are formal gardens and a lakefront beach. Also operated by Belhurst Castle are the lovely Georgian **White Springs Manor** (315/781-0201, www.belhurst.com, $110-395) and **Vinifera Inn** (315/781-0201, www.belhurst.com, $110-395).

The luxurious, all-suite **Geneva-on-the-Lake** (1001 Lochland Rd., 315/789-7190, www.genevaonthelake.com, $210-550, with continental breakfast) is especially popular among honeymooners. The property centers around a 1911 mansion built in the style of a 16th-century Italian villa. Each suite differs from the next. Outside are 10 acres of formal gardens. The **dining room** ($40), open to the public for lunch and dinner, serves classic cuisine that harkens back to an earlier time (think shrimp cocktail, filet mignon, and baked Alaska, set aflame at your table).

Stivers Seneca Marine (401 Boody's Hill Rd., Waterloo, 315/789-5520, www.stiverssenecamarine.com) offers a unique lodging alternative. You can remain docked at Stivers' own **marina,** which has a very good on-site restaurant, or choose to motor slowly along the canal on a multiday itinerary in the **houseboat** ($5,950/week), which has four bedrooms, a full kitchen, two full baths, a living room, a hot tub, and a slide.

DETOUR TO SODUS POINT

Sodus Point, which overlooks Lake Ontario, is worth a 30-mile (48 km) detour north of Geneva on Route 14. The village boasts gorgeous views and an inviting public beach.

Sodus Bay Lighthouse Museum

The handsome 1870 **Sodus Bay Lighthouse Museum** (7606 N. Ontario St., 315/483-4936, www.soduspointlighthouse.org, May 15-Oct. 15, Tues.-Sun. in May, Sept. and Oct. noon-5pm, in June, July, Aug. 10am-5pm, adults $6, children 8-17 $3) in a three-story stone block structure is dedicated to maritime and regional history. The lighthouse tower, about 50 feet (15 m) high, is open to visitors who can climb the 52 circular steps into the lens room. From there, it's a gorgeous view of the Lake Ontario shoreline.

Chimney Bluffs State Park

Located on the eastern side of Sodus Bay, the **Chimney Bluffs** rise 150 feet (46 m) above the lake like some giant confectionery delight. All pinnacles, spires, and peaks, they're part of a glacier-created drumlin that has been eroded, carved, and shaped by water, wind, and snow. Atop some of the pinnacles sit lone trees; below them extends a stony beach. Scuba divers exiting Lake Ontario are another unexpected sight on the beach.

Dozens of other drumlins (minus the pinnacles and peaks) can be found throughout this part of the Lake Ontario region. The only other places to view drumlins in North America are the areas bordering Lake Superior in Minnesota.

Chimney Bluffs and its beach form part of the undeveloped **Chimney Bluffs State Park** (7700 Garner Rd., Wolcott, www. parks.ny.gov/parks/43, daily dawn-dusk, $5 vehicle fee).

Alasa Farms and Crackerbox Palace

On your way to and from Sodus Point, you'll pass through farm country, heavy with rich black soil. Apples, cherries, and peaches thrive in this climate, as do corn, wheat, potatoes, onions, and lettuce.

Off Route 14 just south of Sodus Point lies **Alasa Farms.** Once a 1,400-acre Shaker religious community, the site passed into private hands in the 1800s. Throughout the 1920s and 1930s, the farm raised everything from shorthorn cattle and hackney ponies to timberland and orchards. Today, it's home to **Crackerbox Palace** (6450 Shaker Rd., Alton, 315/483-2493, www.crackerboxpalace.org, Sun.-Mon. 9am-noon, Tue.-Sat. 9am-3pm and by appt., $5 pp), a nonprofit farm haven that rescues and cares for abused and abandoned animals. Tours are available on Saturdays and by appointment.

Events

One of the region's foremost events is **Sterling Renaissance Festival** (800/879-4446, www. sterlingfestival.com), held in Sterling, near Fair Haven, about 25 miles (40 km) west of Sodus Point. For seven weekends in July and August, the fest celebrates the Middle Ages with music, jousting, outdoor theater, crafts, and food.

Accommodations

Several lovely B&Bs are in the heart of Sodus Point.

Carriage House Inn (8375 Wickham Blvd., 315/483-2100, www.carriage-house-inn. com, $120-190), an 1870s Victorian B&B, offers four guest rooms, all with king beds and private baths. Guests can walk along the beach for about a half mile to reach the Sodus Bay Lighthouse Museum.

Silver Waters B&B (8420 Bay St., 315/483-8098, www.silver-waters.com, $139) is a historic inn in the center of Sodus Point Village, featuring four guest rooms, each with a private bath. From here, it's a quick walk to the Sodus Bay Lighthouse Museum.

Situated on 5.4 acres with a combination of woods and 340 feet (105 m) of lakeshore, **The Cliffs at Sodus Point** (7961 Lake Rd., 315/483-4309. www.thecliffsatsoduspoint. com, $135-155) features five guest rooms with private baths. The B&B also has a gift shop on-site, where you can buy hand-painted wineglasses and handmade wine stoppers and jewelry.

★ WINE ROUTES

Heading south from Geneva on either side of Seneca Lake, you'll find a series of vineyards worth a visit. Route 14 runs south along the western shore of the lake, while Routes 96A and 414 run along the eastern shore. Both routes offer excellent wineries and scenic views, both from the vineyards and tasting rooms, as well as the roads you take to reach them. If you don't have time for both routes, choose the Route 14 wineries, which will allow the opportunity to pass through Watkins Glen and catch a view of its spectacular falls and gorges.

South on Route 14

From Geneva, Route 14 heads south along the western shore of Seneca Lake past two excellent wineries. **Fox Run Vineyards** (670 Rte. 14, Penn Yan, 315/536-4616, www.

The Vineyards of the Finger Lakes

The hills of the Finger Lakes, covered with vineyards, glow pale green in spring, brilliant green in summer, and red-brown-purple in fall. The conditions for ideal grape-growing were set into motion tens of thousands of years ago when retreating glaciers deposited a layer of topsoil on shale beds above the lakes, which create a microclimate that moderates the region's temperatures.

It wasn't until the 19th century, though, that winemaking began to take root in the Finger Lakes. A minister whose intent was to make sacramental wine planted some vines near Hammondsport in 1829. The yield was successful; soon, neighbors planted their own vines, and vineyards ringed the village. In 1860, 13 Hammondsport businesspeople banded together to form the country's first commercial winery: Pleasant Valley Wine Company. Dozens of other entrepreneurs soon followed suit.

For many years, the Finger Lakes vineyards produced only native American Concord, Delaware, and Niagara grapes, used in the production of ho-hum sweet and table wines. About 25 years ago, however, several viticulturists began experimenting with the more complex European vinifera grape. Today, a staggering number and variety of wines are produced here, including cabernet franc, cabernet sauvignon, Cayuga white, chardonnay, gewürztraminer, lemberger, merlot, pinot gris, pinot noir, riesling, seyval blanc, vidal blanc, traminette, and both ice and iced wines.

Called the "Napa Valley of the East," the Finger Lakes region currently boasts more than 100 wineries, most of which overlook Canandaigua, Cayuga, Keuka, or Seneca Lakes. Each lake has its own wine trail program, which publishes free maps and brochures and manages a "passport" program offering tasting discounts. Information about the wine trails can be found on the official Finger Lakes Wine Country website (www.fingerlakeswinecountry.com).

Most wineries are open daily 10am-5pm, year-round. Smaller wineries may close their tasting rooms in winter or reduce days or hours; call first. Tastings typically cost $2-5, an amount that's usually applied against your bill if you buy any bottles.

For a complete list of wineries, contact Finger Lakes Wine Country (607/936-0706, www.fingerlakeswinecountry.com).

foxrunvineyards.com, Mon.-Sat. 10am-6pm, Sun. 11am-6pm, $6) is housed in an 1860s dairy barn with sweeping views of the lake. Fox Run produces more than 90 wines, including ports. Anthony Road Wine Company (1020 Anthony Rd., Penn Yan, 800/559-2182, www.anthonyroadwine.com, daily 11am-5pm, $5-10) produces a variety of reds, whites, and dessert wines.

More good wineries are clustered near the lake's southern end. Among them is Hermann J. Wiemer Vineyard (3962 Rte. 14, Dundee, 607/243-7971, www.wiemer.com, Mon.-Sat. 10am-5pm, Sun. 11am-5pm, $8-12), founded by a foremost viticulturist who came from a family that made wine in Germany for more than 300 years. The winery is best known for its rieslings.

About 5 miles (8.1 km) farther south is Glenora Wine Cellars (5435 Rte. 14, Dundee, 607/243-9500, www.glenora.com, days and hours vary seasonally, $6). Established in 1977, Glenora is best known for sparkling wines. Its tasting room offers views of vineyards and Seneca Lake. The winery also runs Inn at Glenora Wine Cellars (5435 Rte. 14, 607/243-9500, www.glenora.com, $160-255), whose spacious rooms feature picture windows overlooking vineyards, as well as private balconies or patios. Whether you're a guest at the inn or just passing through, you can dine at the winery's restaurant, Veraisons (5435 Rte. 14, 607/243-9500, www.glenora.com, $30), where the specialty is "regional fusion" fare. In summer months, enjoy your meal on the restaurant's outdoor dining patio.

Fulkerson Winery (5576 Rte. 14, Dundee, 607/243-7883, www.fulkersonwinery.com, daily 10am-5pm, $10 tour includes tasting fee, $4 tasting only) has a large, light-filled tasting room, where staff will happily pour sips for you while sharing the Fulkerson family's fascinating history. Now in their seventh generation of farming, the Fulkersons trace their ancestry all the way back to the family's original farm . . . on New York City's Wall Street. Today, operations are firmly rooted in the Finger Lakes, where visitors can tour vineyards on foot or horseback or take a free winemaking class on weekends. An adjacent house owned by the family, and built in 1856, can be rented out by families or small groups. With four bedrooms, an enormous and fully equipped kitchen, large dining room and living room, and 2.5 bathrooms (plus a washer and dryer), the house is a fantastic home base for exploring the region.

South on Routes 96A and 414

From Geneva, Route 96A heads south along the eastern shore of Seneca Lake. About 10 miles (16.1 km) down is the 1,852-acre **Sampson State Park** (6096 Rte. 96A, 315/585-6392, camping reservations 800/456-2267, www.parks.ny.gov/parks/154, parking $7), once a naval station where thousands of service members trained during World War II. Today, the park is equipped with a marina, swimming beach, bathhouses, picnic area, playground, and 245-site **campground** (tent sites $15-31/night, cottages $300-350/night with 2-night minimum). South of Willard, Route 96A veers inland to Ovid, in the Cayuga Lake area, where it meets Route 414. Continue south on Route 414 to more small villages and a cluster of vineyards and wineries.

You'll find several wineries around the village of Lodi. Among them is **Lamoreaux Landing Wine Cellars** (9224 Rte. 414, 607/582-6011, www.lamoreauxwine.com, Mon.-Sat. 10am-5pm, Sun. noon-5pm, $10), housed in a Greek Revival building with great views of the lake. Lamoreaux produces everything from chardonnay to pinot noir.

A few more miles down the road sprawls **Wagner Vineyards** (9322 Rte. 414, 607/582-6450, www.wagnervineyards.com, daily 10am-5pm, $5). Its hub is a weathered octagonal building overlooking the lake. Established in 1979, Wagner produces over 30 different wines. On the premises is a **microbrewery** (www.wagnerbrewing.com) and **Ginny Lee Cafe** (607/582-6574, www.theginnylee.com, $11), open for lunch and Sunday brunch only. On summer Friday nights, Wagner hosts "Fridays on the Deck," a hugely popular live music series. Locals crowd the deck and the generous-size lawn to eat, drink, and dance.

WATKINS GLEN AND VICINITY

Watkins Glen, named for the astonishing gorge that cuts through its center, sits at the southern tip of Seneca Lake. The glen, which is a popular state park, is easily accessible from the main roadway, where you'll find many family-friendly restaurants and lots of shops.

From 1948-1952, the main street of Watkins Glen and the steep roads surrounding it were the speedway of the American Grand Prix. During the races, as many as 75,000 spectators descended on the village, whose year-round population was under 3,000. Today, world-class auto races take place at the **Watkins Glen International** (2790 Rte. 16, 607/535-2486, www.theglen.com), a racetrack 4 miles (6.4 km) south of Watkins Glen. The **Grand Prix Festival** (www.grandprixfestival.com) in early September commemorates the town's legacy, reenacting the 1948 American Grand Prix, complete with vintage vehicles.

TOP EXPERIENCE

★ Watkins Glen State Park

Created some 12,000 years ago during the last Ice Age, **Watkins Glen State Park** (off Rte. 14, 607/535-4511, www.parks.ny.gov/parks/142, daily 8am-dusk, parking $8) is a wild and raggedy gorge flanked by high cliffs and strange, sculpted rock formations. Glen Creek—which drops some 700 feet (210 m) in 2 miles (3.2 km) over rapids, cascades, and 19 waterfalls—rushes through its center.

Alongside the gorge runs the 1.5-mile (2.4 km) Gorge Trail, made up of 832 stone steps, stone paths, and numerous bridges. The trail leads past tunnels, caves, and a natural stone bridge, all carved out of the sedimentary rock by Glen Creek. If you hike the trail on a fine summer's day, you'll have lots of company, but the gorge inspires awe nonetheless.

The park also offers **campgrounds** (reservations 800/456-2267, tent sites $18-30/night, rustic cabins from $58/night with 3-night minimum).

Montour Falls

Route 14 leads south of Watkins Glen through narrow, winding Pine Valley to Montour Falls, a small industrial community surrounded by seven glens. In the middle of town is **Shequaga Falls,** plunging downward 165 feet (50 m) into a deep pool. The falls are illuminated at night; near the top is a pedestrian bridge.

Along Genesee and Main Streets you'll find a handsome **National Historic District,** known as the Glorious "T" District, composed of 24 brick buildings dating back to the 1850s. Among them is Memorial Library with its Tiffany windows and the Greek Revival Village Hall.

Recreation

World-class auto racing takes place April-October at **Watkins Glen International** (2790 Rte. 16, 607/535-2486, www.theglen. com). Ticket prices vary by event.

From early May until late October, 50-minute cruises of Seneca Lake are offered every hour on the hour by **Captain Bill's Seneca Lake Cruises** (1 N. Franklin St., 607/535-4541, www.senecaharborstation. com). Captain Bill also runs dinner cruises.

Another way to experience the lake by boat is to go on an excursion on the *True Love* (Dock at Village Pier, 607/535-5253, www.schoonerexcursions.com, $39-59 pp), a restored 1926 schooner made famous by its role in the movie *High Society,* which featured Louis Armstrong, Bing Crosby, Grace Kelly,

and Frank Sinatra. Morning, midday, afternoon, and sunset sails are offered early May-late October. Charter sails are also available.

If you're looking for a more active way to experience Watkins Glen, **Summit to Stream Adventures** (3192 Abrams Rd., 607/535-2701, www.summittostream.com) offers chartered fly-fishing and steelhead/salmon fishing excursions, as well as guided kayak and canoe trips and gear rentals.

Food

Classic Chef's (2250 Rte. 14, Montour Falls, 607/535-9975, daily 6am-8pm, $10) is a classic American eatery, now in its sixth decade. Come here for tasty pancakes or grilled cheese sandwiches.

Rooster Fish Pub (223-301 N. Franklin St., 607/535-9797, www.roosterfishbrewing. com, Sun.-Thurs. 11:30am-9pm, Fri.-Sat. 11:30am-10pm, $22) offers tasty organic fare, from creative sandwiches to hearty meals and fresh, house-made pizzas. Roosterfish ales are another big draw.

Chef-owned **Dano's Heuriger on Seneca** (9564 Rte. 414, Lodi, 607/582-7555, www. danosonseneca.com, Sun.-Mon. and Wed.-Thurs. noon-8pm, Fri.-Sat. noon-9pm, $20), with glass-walled lakeside dining, combines the tastes of a traditional Viennese wine restaurant with the Finger Lakes' best vintages. Charcuterie and schnitzel, authentic Viennese casual ordering style and Austrian traditions, like a festival celebrating the harvest with newly fermented wine, add to the charm. A chef's table is available on request for parties of six or more.

Blue Pointe Grille (16 N. Franklin St., 607/535-6116, www.watkinsglenharborhotel. com, daily 6:30am-11am, 11:30am-3pm, 5pm-9pm, $20-36) at Watkins Glen Harbor Hotel, is a casual fine dining restaurant where signature dishes include rack of lamb, eggplant Strato, and wild mushroom ravioli. The restaurant participates in Finger Lakes Culinary Bounty, a program where properties sign on to use freshly delivered locally grown products in their menus.

Nickel's Pit BBQ (205-207 N. Franklin St., 607/210-4227, www.nickelspitbbq.com, Wed.-Fri. 5pm-close, Sat.-Sun. noon-close, $19), located in the old Watkins Glen Fire Department building, serves authentic barbecue and craft beers. Its outdoor beer garden makes it an especially popular spot on weekends.

Village Marina Bar & Grill (Seneca Harbor Park, 607/535-7910, www.village-marina.com, hours vary seasonally, $13) is a hometown favorite on the shore of Seneca Lake. Burgers and other bar food can be paired with local beer and wine. Summer weekends see plenty of live entertainment here.

Accommodations

One of the more idiosyncratic lodging options in the area is **Seneca Lodge** (3600 Rte. 419, 607/535-2014, www.senecalodge.com, $70-200). A favorite haunt of bow hunters and race mechanics, the lodge centers around a restaurant and tavern whose back wall, bristled with arrows, looks like the hide of a porcupine and from whose ceiling hang NASCAR champs' tires and Formula One laurel wreaths.

Accommodations consist of basic camp-style A-frames, cabins, and motel rooms.

Magnolia Place Bed and Breakfast (5240 Rte. 414, Hector, 607/546-5338, www.magnoliawelcome.com, $140-190), an 1830 farmhouse about 7 miles (11.3 km) outside of Watkins Glen, offers five rooms and three suites overlooking Seneca Lake. Innkeepers talented in the culinary arts host wine tastings and create hot breakfasts of "Dutch babies" with cinnamon biscuits, or corn fritters with house-smoked salmon, crème fraîche, and a poached egg. They also provide homemade evening sweets and dinner or hors d'oeuvres on request.

Watkins Glen Harbor Hotel (16 N. Franklin St., 607/535-6116, www.watkins-glenharborhotel.com, $159-339), situated on Seneca Lake's waterfront, is a modern hotel that's a favorite of NASCAR drivers and their entourages during race weekends. Large, airy rooms feature lush bedding and spa-style baths. Lake-facing rooms, which have balconies, are particularly coveted. The hotel's dining options include alfresco in season, a classic country club sports bar, and Blue Pointe Grille restaurant.

Elmira

Elmira sits on both sides of the Chemung River, a few miles north of the Pennsylvania border. Some parts of the city are quite historic, with handsome stone and redbrick buildings.

Once the site of a Seneca village, Elmira was settled by Europeans in the 1780s. By the 1840s, the town was known for its lumbering and woolen mills, and by the 1860s, for its metal industries and iron furnaces. Elmira also served as a major transportation center, sitting at the crossroads of the Erie Railroad, the Chemung River, and the Chemung and Junction Canals.

Samuel Clemens, aka Mark Twain, spent

more than 20 summers in Elmira. His wife, Olivia Langdon, grew up in the area, and Twain wrote many of his masterpieces—including *Tom Sawyer* and *The Adventures of Huckleberry Finn*—while at the Langdon family farm.

Most of Elmira is north of the Chemung River. Exiting off Route 17 onto Route 352W (Church St.) will take you into the heart of the city. Route 14N runs past Elmira College and Woodlawn Cemetery (off W. Woodlawn Ave.).

In July and August, hour-long **trolley tours** (Chemung County Chamber of

1: Montour Falls **2:** Watkins Glen State Park **3:** Mark Twain's Study

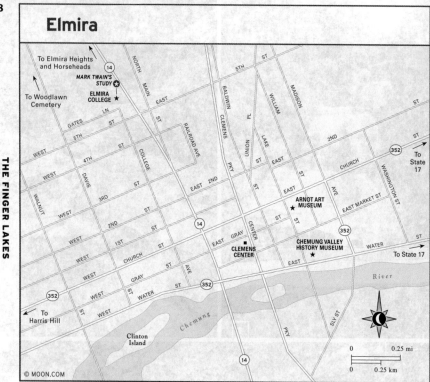

Elmira

Commerce, 607/734-5137 or 800/627-5892) of Elmira's historical attractions are offered.

SIGHTS

★ Mark Twain's Study

The story of Mark Twain and Olivia Langdon began in 1867 when Twain fell in love with her after viewing her portrait, shown to him by a friend as they were crossing the Atlantic. Upon his return to the United States, Twain immediately set up a meeting with Olivia. At first, she was not at all impressed. He was a rough-and-tumble self-made man; she was a refined young woman from a good family.

But Twain was stubborn. For the next two years, he visited Elmira regularly, and eventually won over the entire Langdon family. In fact, near the end of his courtship, Olivia, who was sickly and delicate, was only allowed to

visit with him for five minutes a day because she became so excited.

Mark Twain's Study (1 Park Pl., 607/735-1941, www.marktwainstudies.com, May-Labor Day Mon.-Sat. 9am-5pm, Sun. noon-5pm, Labor Day-mid-Oct. Sat. 9am-5pm, Sun. noon-5pm, free), modeled after a Mississippi steamboat pilothouse, was built for Twain by his sister-in-law. Twain once described it as "the loveliest study you ever saw. It is octagonal in shape with a peaked roof, each space filled with a spacious window and it sits perched in complete isolation on the very top of an elevation that commands leagues of valleys and city and retreating ranges of blue hill." In 1952, Twain's study was moved to its current location on the campus of Elmira College, one of the earliest colleges for women. The study's interior is simple and functional. A Remington Rand sits on a desk

(Twain was one of the first writers to submit a typed manuscript to a publisher) and a trunk inscribed with the name "Clemens" rests on the floor. The author's hat and pipe rest on a desk. A student guide is stationed at the study and offers details and stories about its history.

Twain fans will want to visit several other campus spots, including statues dedicated to Twain and his wife. The Center for Mark Twain Studies hosts visiting scholars and annual symposia about the author's life, work, and influence.

Woodlawn Cemetery and Mark Twain Burial Site

In **Woodlawn Cemetery** (1200 Walnut St., 607/732-0151, daily dawn-dusk), Mark Twain is buried in the Langdon family plot, along with his wife, his father-in-law, and his son-in-law, Ossip Gabrilowitsch, a noted Russian-born pianist. A 12-foot-high (3.6 m) monument commemorates the two famous men. Many visitors to Twain's grave consider their trip a pilgrimage and leave items like coins and cigars (Twain was known to smoke up to 22 cigars a day) on his tombstone.

Adjacent to the main cemetery is the **Woodlawn National Cemetery** (1825 Davis St., 607/732-5411, daily dawn-dusk), containing the graves of the 2,963 Confederate soldiers who died in the Elmira prison. Surrounding the Confederate graves are the graves of 322 Union soldiers. When families came north to retrieve their loved ones, they saw what respect had been afforded the soldiers, and many made the decision to leave them in their resting place.

Arnot Art Museum

Arnot Art Museum (235 Lake St., at W. Gray St., 607/734-3697, www.arnotartmuseum.org, Tues.-Fri. 10am-5pm, Sat. noon-5pm, adults $7, seniors and students $5, children under 18 free), in a restored 1833 neoclassical mansion, displays a fine collection of 17th- to 19th-century European and 19th- to 20th-century American paintings. At the heart of the collection are works acquired by Matthias Arnot

in the late 1800s. Among them are paintings by Brueghel, Daubigny, Rousseau, and Millet, hung floor to ceiling in the old salon style.

Behind the mansion, a handsome modern wing houses both temporary exhibitions and rotating selections from the museum's Asian, Egyptian, and pre-Columbian collections.

Chemung Valley History Museum

To learn more about Elmira's past, visit the **Chemung Valley History Museum** (415 E. Water St., 607/734-4167, www.chemungvalleymuseum.org, Mon.-Sat. 10am-5pm, adults $5, seniors $3, students 6-18 $1, children under 6 free). Exhibits on the Seneca, Mark Twain in Elmira, and the Civil War prison camp are featured. Trolley into Twain Country tours depart from the lobby throughout July and August. The tour is narrated by a guide.

★ Harris Hill

Unassuming Elmira has been known as the Soaring Capital of America ever since 1930, when the first National Soaring Contest took place here. Today at **Harris Hill** (57 Soaring Hill Dr., 607/742-4213 or 607/734-0641, www.harrishillsoaring.org), you'll find the **National Soaring Museum, Harris Hill Soaring Center,** and **Harris Hill Amusement Park.** At the Soaring Museum, visitors can learn more about the history and sport of gliding, while the Soaring Center provides the opportunity to experience gliding, either through demonstrations or a gliding excursion. Visitors who prefer to keep their feet on the ground can enjoy the rides and activities at the 27-acre amusement park, which features kiddie rides, batting cages, and go-karts. There is no admission fee; visitors pay by activity as they go along.

Wings of Eagles Discovery Center

Wings of Eagles Discovery Center (339 Daniel Zenker Dr., Horseheads, 607/358-4247, www.wingsofeagles.com, Wed.-Sun. 11am-3pm, adults $7, seniors $5.50, children 7-18 $4.50, children under 7 free) is a 25,000-square-foot hangar where you can walk among or climb aboard a wide range of military aircraft dating from World War II to the present. On-site Wings Cafe ($11) serves soups, salads, flatbread pizzas, and sandwiches, the latter named after famous aircraft and aviators.

FOOD

Charlie's Café and Bakery (205 Hoffman St., 607/733-0440, $20) offers sandwiches, salads, soups, pastas, and Finger Lakes wine and beer in a casual but elegant dining room. Leave room for the Finger Lakes Harvest Wine Cake, a specialty of the restaurant and region. It features local ingredients, including Finger Lakes apples and, of course, riesling.

Third-generation Hill Top Inn Restaurant (171 Jerusalem Hill Rd., 607/732-6728, www.hill-top-inn.com, Mon.-Sat. 5pm-close, $30) is just that and a friendly place to sit out on the large terrace and enjoy a gorgeous view of the valley below. It's just a stone's throw from the lookout where Mark Twain sat so inspired in the original location of his study. The spot is popular with locals and large loads of tourists stopping in as a midway point between Niagara and New York City. Fortunately, the establishment has the space to accommodate them all. Generous portions of items like haystack crab and a good-size wine list keep the crowd happy.

ACCOMMODATIONS AND CAMPING

A few miles south of Elmira lies Newtown Battlefield State Park (2346 Rte. 60, 607/732-6067, www.parks.ny.gov/parks/107, tent camping $15-25/night), where General John Sullivan won a decisive battle over a large force of Iroquois and Tories on August 19, 1779. Situated on a hilltop with wide-angled views of the Chemung Valley, the former battlefield is now a county park with hiking trails, a picnic area, and campgrounds.

Located between Elmira and Corning is Rufus Tanner House Bed and Breakfast (60 Sagetown Rd., Pine City, 607/732-0213, www.rufustanner.com, $140-155), a meticulously restored 1864 Greek Revival country home offering three spacious rooms with fireplaces and private baths. The B&B also has an outdoor garden and hot tub.

Corning

If good things come in small packages, Corning is indeed a gift waiting for visitors to unwrap. One of the most popular tourist destinations in New York State, Corning is home to two exceptional museums, Rockwell Museum of Western Art and the Corning Museum of Glass, which, contrary to popular belief, does not exhibit Pyrex measuring cups or Corningware baking pans.

Corning, current population 11,068, became a one-industry town not long after 1868, when the Flint Glass Company of Brooklyn relocated here. The company chose Corning largely because of its strategic position on the Chemung River and Chemung Canal, which allowed for easy delivery of raw materials.

In 1875, the company began to produce specialized types of glass, such as railway signal lenses and thermometer tubing. In 1880, the lightbulb division was developed in response to Edison's invention, and by the early 1930s, Corning was manufacturing 1,250,000 bulbs a day. In 1915, the company's research and development department invented Pyrex. In the early 1970s, a fiber optics division was established.

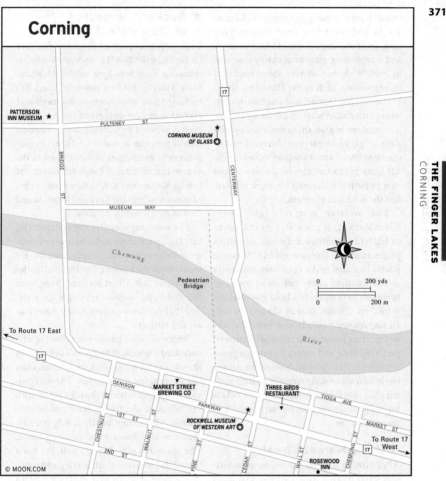

Corning

SIGHTS

★ Corning Museum of Glass

Billed as the world's largest museum devoted to glass, **Corning Museum of Glass** (1 Museum Way, 607/937-5371, www.cmog. org, early Sept.-late May daily 9am-5pm, late May.-early Sept. daily 9am-8pm, adults $19.50, seniors and students $20, children under 17 free) features thousands of objects—including more than 1,000 paperweights and, of course, plenty of examples of Tiffany lampshades and windows—spanning 35 centuries. The museum's Glass Sculpture Gallery claims to be the largest display of glass in the world, showcasing more than 10,000 glass objects at a time, many dramatically displayed in darkened rooms with spotlights. The oldest objects date back to 1400 BC, the newest seen in famous designers' contributions to constantly changing

© MOON.COM

installations. Among the many highlights are an iridescent vase from 10th-century Iran, an 11-foot-high (3.6 m) Tiffany window, and a table-long glass boat cut by Baccarat in 1900. With over 40 daily shows (included in admission), such as the Hot Glass Show, Flameworking Demos, and a demonstration where visitors can whip up a drawing and see it created out of glass in front of their eyes by a master gaffer, visitors can observe the art of glass up close. A **combination ticket** (adults $28, seniors $26, children free) offers admission to both the Corning Museum of Glass and the Rockwell Museum.

The massive nonprofit gift shop, **GlassMarket,** is populated by the works of individual outside artisans, as well as pieces made by museum gaffers. Museum guests can also make their own souvenirs at **The Studio,** where visitors as young as three can participate in a brief glassmaking workshop. Classes start at $23 and include an impressively sturdy and beautiful object to bring home, each tailored to visitors' preferred style and colors. Create gorgeous ornaments like colorful blooms on deceptively delicate-looking stems by pulling molten glass into flower petals. Purchase tickets for designated time slots on entry to the museum or online.

Historic Market Street

After visiting the glass museum, most visitors stroll down a wide walkway that leads to Corning's historic downtown. This 19th-century district, called Corning Gaffer District, was extensively restored following Hurricane Agnes in 1972, when the street was all but destroyed by the flooding of the Chemung River.

Today, Market Street is brick sidewalks, locust trees, and one bustling shop or restaurant after another. At one end are contemporary glass studios with artisans at work, including **Vitrix Hot Glass Studio** (77 W. Market St., 607/936-8707, www.vitrixhotglass.com, Mon.-Fri. 9am-6pm, Sat. 10am-6pm).

★ Rockwell Museum of Western Art

Rockwell Museum of Western Art (111 Cedar St., 607/937-5386, www.rockwellmuseum.org, daily 9am-5pm, adults $11.50, seniors $10.50, children under 17 free) has nothing to do with Norman Rockwell and everything to do with art of the American West. Collected by Corning denizen Robert F. Rockwell, this is said to be the most comprehensive assemblage of Western art in the eastern United States. A **combination ticket** (adults $28, seniors $26, children free) offers admission to both the Rockwell Museum and the Corning Museum of Glass.

The museum occupies the restored Old City Hall; permanent and temporary exhibits are well-curated in equally well-cared-for galleries. Works by Frederic Remington, Charles M. Russell, and Albert Bierstadt hang from the walls, and Navajo rugs drape the stairwell. Exhibit cases contain Native American art and artifacts.

Rockwell was a passionate collector who once used the walls of his father's department store to exhibit his artwork, and the museum has an engaging, personal feel. The staff provides children with backpacks filled with fun, educational activities developed for each exhibit. This exceptionally family-friendly museum also has a kids' drawing room. The museum's gift shop is small, but has a thoughtful selection of art, jewelry, and handcrafts, most of which were made by Western artists, many of whom are Native American.

Benjamin Patterson Inn Museum Complex

A half mile north of Market Street is **Benjamin Patterson Inn Museum Complex** (59 W. Pulteney St., 607/937-5281, www.heritagevillagesfl.org, Mon.-Fri. 10am-4pm, adults $4, seniors $3, children and students $2), peopled by guides in costume dress.

1: Hot Glass Show at the Corning Museum of Glass
2: Rockwell Museum of Western Art

Restored historic buildings include Benjamin Patterson Inn Museum, complete with a women's parlor, taproom, and ballroom, and the Painted Post-Erwin Museum, housed in a former freight depot.

FOOD

Visit Old World Cafe and Ice Cream (1 W. Market St., 607/936-1953, www.oldworldcafe.com, spring and fall Mon.-Sat 10am-6pm, winter Mon.-Sat. 10am-5pm, summer Mon.-Sat. 10am-9pm and Sun. noon-5pm, $10) for hearty homemade soups, sandwiches, salad, old-fashioned candy, and ice cream. If grabbing a slice is more your taste, try Atlas Brick Oven Pizzeria (35 E. Market St., 607/962-2626, www.atlaspizzeria.com, Mon.-Thurs. 11am-10pm, Fri.-Sat. 11am-11pm, Sun. noon-10pm, $12). In addition to pizza, Atlas sells calzones, pasta, salads, and sandwiches.

Tiny, hidden Bento Ya Masako (31 E. Market St., 607/936-3659, Tues.-Fri. 11am-3pm, $10) is tucked between two jewelry shops, up a flight of stairs, and marked only by a small "Open" sign half-covering a Japanese symbol on a nondescript door. First timers might be caught off guard by the open kitchen at the top of the stairs in what looks like an apartment with two women cooking away. Just grab a seat at one of a handful of tables and prepare to be surprised. This cash-only establishment has limited hours, but

offers authentic Japanese and sushi to those in the know.

Market Street Brewing Co. (63 W. Market St., 607/936-2337, www.936-beer.com, days and hours vary by season, $25) offers something for everyone, including rooftop and biergarten dining, dishes ranging from salads to steaks, a kids' menu, and, of course, fresh brews on tap. The casually elegant Three Birds Restaurant and Martini Bar (73 E. Market St., 607/936-8862, www.threebirdsrestaurant.com, restaurant: Mon.-Thurs. 5pm-9pm, Fri.-Sat. 5pm-10pm, martini bar: Mon.-Sat. 4pm-1am, $26) serves "progressive American fare" made with fresh local ingredients. It's also known for its popular martini bar.

The Cellar (21 W. Market St., 607/377-5552, www.corningwinebar.com, Mon.-Thurs. 5pm-9pm, Fri.-Sat. 5pm-10pm, Sun. 10:30am-3pm, $32) is an elegant wine bar and modern fusion restaurant, offering plates focused on locally sourced ingredients.

ACCOMMODATIONS

One of the area's most popular B&Bs, the handsome Rosewood Inn (134 E. 1st St., 607/962-3253, www.rosewoodinn.com, $110-185), is located close to downtown. The five guest rooms and two suites are outfitted with antiques and have private baths. Downstairs is an elegant parlor with a fireplace, where afternoon tea is served.

Keuka Lake

Gentle, Y-shaped Keuka Lake is the only one of the Finger Lakes with an irregular outline, made up of over 70 miles (113 km) of curving lakeshore scalloped with coves and bays. Its name means "canoe landing" in Iroquois.

At the southern head of Keuka Lake lies Hammondsport, site of one of the nation's first wineries, established in 1860. The small town Penn Yan occupies the lake's northern tip. Several Mennonite communities are

scattered throughout the Keuka Lake region. Driving south between Penn Yan and Dundee along Routes 14A or 11, or north of Penn Yan along Routes 14A, 374, and 27, you're bound to pass a horse and buggy or two clip-clopping down the road. Handwritten signs advertising Mennonite quilts, furniture, or produce for sale sometimes appear by the roadside, while more permanent shops are located near Penn Yan and Dundee.

HAMMONDSPORT

Nestled between steep, verdant hills and Keuka Lake, Hammondsport is a fetching Victorian village with a lively tourist trade. At its center lies the village square, anchored by a charming white Presbyterian church. Antiques shops, cafés, and restaurants line Shethar Street, the main drag. A park and two public beaches are along the lakeshore; the beach at the foot of Shethar Street is said to be the best. It is the local viticulture, though, that draws the most visitors. Tumbling down the surrounding hillsides are vineyard after vineyard, all supplying grapes for the area's 17 wineries.

Glenn Hammond Curtiss, the pioneer aviator, was born in Hammondsport in 1878. Though not as well-known as the Wright brothers, Curtiss made the world's first pre-announced flight on July 4, 1908, when he piloted his "June Bug" airplane over 5,090 feet (1,550 m) just outside Hammondsport. Curtiss developed the U.S. Navy's first amphibian airplane, opened the first flying school in the United States, and established the Curtiss Aeroplane Company—all in Hammondsport. During World War I, the Curtiss company manufactured the popular Curtiss Jenny airplane, which later became a favorite of barnstormers.

Great Western Winery Visitor Center

Even if you're the odd Finger Lakes visitor who isn't interested in wine, you might want to stop by the **Great Western Winery Visitor Center** (8260 Pleasant Valley Rd./County Rd. 88, 607/569-6111, www.pleasant-valleywine.com, Apr.-Dec. daily 10am-5pm, Jan.-Mar. Tues.-Sat. 10am-4pm, free, tours $5 pp), one of the largest tourist attractions in the region. The Pleasant Valley Wine Company, better known as the Great Western Winery, is one of the oldest continuous makers of wine in the United States, founded by a group of Hammondsport businessmen in 1860.

The visitors center holds exhibits that explain the history of the winery and the region, as well as an informative film, which is screened inside a 35,000-gallon former wine tank. A nearby working model train replicates the old Bath-Hammondsport Railroad, and a tasting room offers products for sampling. Winery tours are offered throughout the day. Take the hour-long tour through magnificent stone winery buildings, eight of which are listed in the National Register of Historic Places. The tour ends with a wine tasting.

Glenn H. Curtiss Museum

The cavernous hangars of the former Curtiss Aeroplane Company now contain the sprawling **Glenn H. Curtiss Museum** (8419 Rte. 54, 607/569-2160, www.glennhcurtissmuseum.org, May-Oct. Mon.-Sat. 9am-5pm and Sun. 10am-5pm, Nov.-Apr. daily 10am-4pm, adults $13.50, seniors $12, children 7-18 $10), devoted to both Curtiss and the early history of aviation. About a dozen spiffy antique airplanes crowd the main hall, along with antique bicycles, motorcycles, propellers, and engines. Curtiss's first interest was the bicycle.

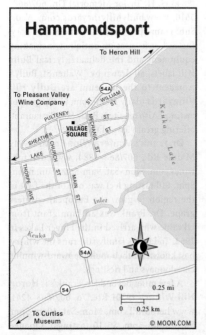

Hammondsport

To Heron Hill

To Pleasant Valley Wine Company

WILLIAM ST

PULTENEY ST

MECHANIC ST

SHEATHER

CHURCH ST

LAKE

THORPE AVE

MAIN ST

VILLAGE SQUARE

ST

Keuka Lake

Inlet

Keuka

0   0.25 mi

0   0.25 km

To Curtiss Museum

© MOON.COM

Among the Mennonites

A surprisingly large number of Mennonite and Amish Mennonite communities are scattered throughout the Finger Lakes and western New York. Some were established generations ago, but many others were set up more recently by people from Pennsylvania and Ohio who were attracted to New York by its numerous abandoned family farms.

The Mennonite religion is a Protestant sect, founded by Dutch reformer Menno Simons in Switzerland in the 1500s. The Amish are the Mennonites' most conservative branch, established in Pennsylvania in the 18th century. Both groups shun modern society and technology.

An especially large Amish population lives in Cattaraugus County in western New York, but a growing number of Mennonites are settling in Yates, Schuyler, and Ontario Counties in the Finger Lakes. Local residents estimate that the Mennonite population in these three counties—all centered around Keuka Lake—has increased exponentially since the late 1970s; in Yates County alone, there are more than 520 Mennonite families.

Throughout the region, you'll see Amish driving their horse and buggies, and you'll spot occasional signs advertising handmade quilts, furniture, or baskets for sale. Though not as organized as western New York, whose Amish participate in the Amish Trail program for visitors, the Finger Lakes' Amish and Mennonite communities are still accessible to visitors. Travelers can purchase goods at Amish farms throughout the region. Good places to stop include The Windmill Farm and Craft Market and Oak Hill Bulk Foods and Cafe, both near Penn Yan.

The Amish and Mennonites dislike having their pictures taken. Please respect their wishes. Also, be aware that they do not work on Sundays, so their farms and shops will be closed on that day.

One of his earliest planes, the Curtiss Pusher, looks just like a bike with double wings and wires attached.

A highlight of the museum is a replica of the famous "June Bug" airplane, built by volunteers in the mid-1970s. A Curtiss Jenny and delicate Curtiss Robin—resembling a giant grasshopper—stand nearby.

Wine Tasting

One of the odder tales in the chronicles of Finger Lakes viticulture is that of the battle waged over the name Taylor. Walter S. Taylor, a grandson of the founder of the Taylor Wine Co., was kicked out of the company in 1970. Subsequently, he and his father, Greyton, began their own winery high on Bully Hill. In 1977, Coca-Cola bought the Taylor Wine Co. and sued Walter for using his family name on his own labels. The case went to court and Walter lost, only to become a local hero. "They have my name and heritage, but they didn't get my goat!" he proclaimed and flamboyantly struck out the Taylor name on all his labels. "Branded For Life, by a man that shall remain nameless without Heritage"

reads the byline in his brochures. The **Wine and Grape Museum of Greyton H. Taylor** (8843 G. H. Taylor Memorial Dr., 607/868-3610, www.bullyhillvineyards.com, Wed.-Sun. 11am-5pm, free) tells little of this story. Instead, it focuses on antique winemaking equipment and the delicate, lyrical Bully Hill labels, all drawn by "Walter St. Bully." Adjacent to the museum are **Bully Hill Vineyards** (daily 11am-4pm, $1-5), open for tastings. Also on-site is Bully Hill Restaurant, offering great views of the lake.

Dr. Frank's Vinifera Wine Cellars (9749 Middle Rd., 607/868-4884, www.drfrankwines.com, Mon.-Sat. 9am-5pm, Sun. noon-5pm, $10 tasting fee) was one of the first in the region to grow the European vinifera grape. Dr. Frank was an immigrant from Ukraine who arrived in the Finger Lakes in 1962. Today, his family still runs the winery, best known for their multiple award-winning chardonnays and rieslings.

A few miles beyond Dr. Frank's is **Heron Hill Winery** (9301 Rte. 76, 607/868-4241, www.heronhill.com, Mon.-Sat. 10am-5pm, Sun. noon-5pm, $5-10 tastings). Opened in 1977, it specializes in chardonnays, rieslings, and Concord grape juice for the kids. Heron Hill also operates a café in the summer. Enjoy views of the lake and the vineyards from its deck.

Food

In addition to its mouthwatering ice-cream treats, cozy **Crooked Lake Ice Cream Parlor** (33 Shether St., 607/569-2405, www.crookedlakeicecream.com, daily 7am-2pm, $7-10) serves a good breakfast and lunch.

As its name suggests, **The Waterfront Restaurant** (12664 W. Lake Rd., 607/868-3455, www.waterfrontkeuka.com, Mon.-Fri. 4pm-close, Sat.-Sun. noon-close, $22) offers lakeside dining. Specials are featured every night of the week. The Original Clammin' and Jammin' happens on the dock every Sunday, Memorial Day through Labor Day, with fresh steamed clams and free live music.

Accommodations

Vinehurst Inn and Suites (7988 Rte. 54, 607/569-2300, www.vinehurstinn.com, $110-160) features spacious motel rooms, many with cathedral ceilings. Suites, including three for families and three with whirlpool tubs, are also available.

Lake & Vine Bed and Breakfast (61 Lake St., 607/569-3282, www.lakeandvinebb.info, $125-150), an 1868 Queen Anne home, offers four rooms, candlelit gourmet breakfast served with china and crystal, and many modern amenities.

Black Sheep Inn (8329 Pleasant Valley Rd., 607/569-3767, www.stayblacksheepinn.com, $169-289) is a five-room boutique inn, offering indulgent organic breakfasts utilizing local and organic products. This historic octagonal house also features an on-site spa.

PENN YAN

Named for its early Pennsylvanian and Yankee settlers, Penn Yan is an attractive small town (pop. 4,971) that serves as the seat of Yates County. Its claim to fame is the world's largest pancake.

Birkett Mills

On a windowless wall of **Birkett Mills** (1 Main St., www.thebirkettmills.com), an enormous griddle is mounted alongside the words: "The annual Buckwheat Harvest Festival. Size of big griddle used to make world record pancake, Sept. 27, 1987. 28 feet, 1 inch." What more needs to be said? Established in 1797 and in continuous operation ever since,

vineyards at Heron Hill Winery

Birkett Mills is the world's largest producer of buckwheat products and maintains a small **retail shop** (163 Main St., 315/536-3311) in its offices.

Oliver House Museum

Oliver House Museum (200 Main St., 315/536-7318, www.yatespast.com, Tues.-Fri. 9am-4pm, $5 suggested donation), housed in a handsome brick building, is run by the Yates County History Center. Permanent and temporary exhibits are on display, interpreting a variety of regional historical and cultural themes.

Events

Yates County Fair takes over Penn Yan fairgrounds in mid-July. On the Fourth of July and the Saturday before Labor Day, the shores of Keuka Lake glow with magical **Rings of Fire**, as in the days of the Seneca. The Seneca lit bonfires to celebrate the harvest; today, highway flares celebrate the holidays. For information about any of these events, contact the **Yates County Chamber of Commerce** (315/536-3111, www.yatesny.com).

Shopping

Midway between Penn Yan and Dundee is **Windmill Farm and Craft Market** (3900 Rte. 14A, 315/536-3032, www.thewindmill. com, late Apr.-mid-Dec. Sat. 8am-4:30pm), the oldest and biggest of several indoor/outdoor farm-and-crafts markets operating in the Finger Lakes. Every Saturday, from the last Saturday in April to the second Saturday in December, more than 200 local vendors set up shop in a large fairgrounds area off Route 14A. Produce, flowers, furniture, crafts, wine, antiques, and homemade food are among the goods for sale. Many Mennonite families operate booths here.

In Dundee, you'll find **Martin's Kitchen** (4898 John Green Rd., 607/243-8197), selling homemade pickles, pickled watermelon rinds, jams, apple butter, and other Mennonite specialties.

Food and Accommodations

Diner aficionados will want to stop by the classic **Penn Yan Diner** (131 E. Elm St., 315/536-6004, www.pennyandiner.com, daily 7am-2pm, $12), which dates back to 1925 and claims to serve "life-changing" pancakes.

Cozy **Laurentide Inn** (158 Main St., 315/719-3445, www.thelaurentideinn.com, $130-159), near downtown, is an 1820s Greek Revival home with five guest rooms and a carriage house loft. Common areas include a parlor with billiards table, a sitting room with a wood-burning fireplace, and a rose garden.

Canandaigua Lake

The farthest west of the major Finger Lakes, Canandaigua is also the most commercialized. Rochester is less than 30 miles (48 km) away, and the lake has served as that city's summer playground since the late 1800s. At the northern end of the lake is the historic city of Canandaigua, now largely a resort town. At the southern end is the village of Naples.

CANANDAIGUA

The city of Canandaigua has a wide, expansive feel. Busy Main Street, a four-lane thoroughfare lined with leafy trees and imposing Greek Revival buildings, runs through its center. The lake and City Pier are at the foot of Main. Tourist-oriented businesses dominate.

Following the Revolution, two New Englanders, Oliver Phelps and Nathaniel Gorham, purchased what is now Canandaigua, along with the rest of western New York, from the Native Americans. Settlers arrived in 1789, and shortly thereafter, the first land office in the United States

Canandaigua

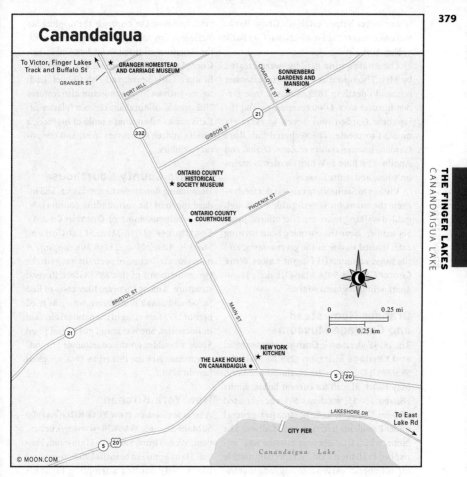

To Victor, Finger Lakes Track and Buffalo St
GRANGER ST
GRANGER HOMESTEAD AND CARRIAGE MUSEUM
CHARLOTTE ST
SONNENBERG GARDENS AND MANSION
FORT HILL
GIBSON ST
332
21
ONTARIO COUNTY HISTORICAL SOCIETY MUSEUM
PHOENIX ST
ONTARIO COUNTY COURTHOUSE
BRISTOL ST
MAIN ST
21
NEW YORK KITCHEN
THE LAKE HOUSE ON CANANDAIGUA
5 20
LAKESHORE DR
To East Lake Rd
5 20
CITY PIER
Canandaigua Lake
© MOON.COM
0   0.25 mi
0   0.25 km

was established near present-day Main Street.

On November 11, 1794, Seneca chiefs and General Timothy Pickering met in Canandaigua to sign what was later known as the Pickering Treaty. A document of enormous significance, the treaty granted the newcomers the right to settle the Great Lakes Basin. An original copy of the treaty can be found in the Ontario County Historical Museum.

Sonnenberg Gardens and Mansion

A serene 50-acre garden estate, **Sonnenberg**

Gardens and Mansion (151 Charlotte St., 585/394-4922, www.sonnenberg.org, May 1-Oct. 31, daily 9:30am-4:30pm, adults $15, seniors $13, students 13-17 $8, children 4-12 $3, children under 4 free), sits in the heart of the bustling downtown. The Smithsonian Institution credited the place "one of the most magnificent late-Victorian gardens ever created in America," thanks to its nine formal gardens, an arboretum, a turn-of-the-20th-century greenhouse, and a massive 1887 stone mansion.

Sonnenberg (German for "Sunny Hill") was once the summer home of Mary Clark and Frederick Ferris Thompson. Thompson, whose father helped establish Chase Bank, was cofounder of the First National City Bank of New York City.

The estate's nine gardens were created by Mrs. Thompson as a memorial after her husband's death in 1899. A classic rose garden features over 4,000 rosebushes, and the Japanese Garden took seven workers six months to create. The secluded Sub Rosa Garden contains statues of Zeus, Diana, and Apollo. The Blue & White Garden contains only blue and white flowers.

Visitors to Sonnenberg can wander freely—even the mansion is self-guided—though guided walking tours are also offered June-September. Near the entrance is an inviting café, housed in one of the greenhouses, and the huge, commercial **Finger Lakes Wine Center** (585/394-9016, May-Oct. daily 11am-4pm), selling regional wines.

Granger Homestead and Carriage Museum

The 1816 Federal-style **Granger Homestead and Carriage Museum** (295 N. Main St., 585/394-1472, www.grangerhomestead.org, May 1-Oct. 31, call for current hours, adults $6, seniors $5, students $2) once housed Gideon Granger, U.S. postmaster general under Presidents Jefferson and Madison. The home, which Granger once boasted was "unrivalled in all the nation," is especially notable for its elaborate carved moldings and mantelpieces, and for its fine original furnishings.

Dark, towering trees surround the house. Out back is a carriage museum, packed with about 50 spit-and-polish coaches, sporting carriages, sleighs, commercial wagons, and an undertaker's hearse.

Ontario County Historical Museum

To learn more about the history of Canandaigua, step into the **Ontario County Historical Museum** (55 N. Main St., 585/394-4975, www.ochs.org, Tues.-Fri. 10am-4:30pm, Sat. 11am-3pm, free, donations accepted), situated in a handsome

brick building. On display is the original Six Nations' copy of the Pickering Treaty with the signatures of Iroquois leaders Red Jacket, Cornplanter, Handsome Lake, Farmer's Brother, Little Beard, and Fish Carrier. Each signed with an X. The museum also features "life masks" of Abraham Lincoln (plaster-of-Paris masks taken from a mold of his face), a small children's discovery area, and temporary exhibits.

Ontario County Courthouse

Dominating downtown Canandaigua, and indeed much of the surrounding countryside, is the bulbous dome of **Ontario County Courthouse** (27 N. Main St., at Gorham, 585/396-4200, Mon.-Fri. 8:30am-5pm). A marvelous collection of portraits hangs in the two courtrooms of this 1858 Greek Revival structure. Among them are likenesses of Red Jacket and Susan B. Anthony, who was tried here in 1873 for voting in the national election in Rochester. She was found guilty and fined $100. A boulder on the courthouse grounds commemorates the Pickering Treaty, signed here in 1794.

New York Kitchen

A treat for foodies, **New York Kitchen** (800 S. Main St., 585/394-7070, www.nykitchen.com, Wed.-Thurs. and Sun. 11am-6pm, Fri.-Sat. 11am-8pm) is a beautiful 20,000-square-foot facility housing a tempting boutique with food products and kitchen tools for culinary-minded visitors. The center also has a glass-walled educational theater where classes and demos can be observed and the occasional food show is filmed. There is an impressive **Tasting Center** featuring the state's finest wines, beers, and spirits in a warm wood and stone setting. At **The Restaurant and Bar at New York Kitchen** (Wed.-Mon. 11am-3pm, Mon. and Wed. 5pm-8pm, Thurs.-Sat. 4pm-9pm, Sun.10am-3pm, $22), locally farmed ingredients come together in excellent meals with suggested wine and beer pairings that bring out the fullest flavors of the food. Visitors sticking around for a day or two can also sign up for a cooking class.

Live music makes weekend evenings a great time to visit for beer lovers, as a rotating selection of brews, chosen from New York's burgeoning number of craft breweries, are featured on tap (flight tasting available), as well as bottle choices from the state. New York State charcuterie sampler and artisan cheese plate are two good choices for nibbling.

Recreation

The *Canandaigua Lady* (205 Lakeshore Dr., 585/396-7350, www.steamboatlandingresort. com, May-Oct.) is a 150-passenger paddle wheeler offering lunch, afternoon, and dinner cruises.

For a more active experience on the lake, **Canandaigua Sailboarding** (11 Lakeshore Dr., 585/394-8150, www.cdgasailboard.com, summer daily 10am-5pm) rents kayaks, stand-up paddleboards, and water bikes. The staff also gives windsurfing lessons during the summer.

In winter, **Bristol Mountain Winter Resort** (5662 Rte. 64, 585/374-1100, www. bristolmountain.com), at 1,200 feet (370 m), claims to have the highest vertical rise between the Adirondacks and the Rocky Mountains. Thirty-eight slopes and trails represent a varied terrain, offering skiing and snowboarding opportunities for novices as well as experts. Several local hotels and bed-and-breakfast lodgings partner with the ski resort, offering free passes to Bristol Mountain with a one-night stay.

Seven miles (11.3 km) northwest of Canandaigua is **Finger Lakes Gaming & Racetrack** (5857 Rte. 96, 585/924-3232, www. fingerlakesgaming.com). Thoroughbred racing takes place April-November Friday-Tuesday. Also on-site are more than 1,100 gaming machines, as well as a bar and restaurant.

Entertainment

During the summer, Rochester Philharmonic Orchestra performs regularly at **Constellation Brands—Marvin Sands Performing Arts Center (CMAC)** (3355 Marvin Sands Dr., 585/394-4400, www. cmacevents.com), an outdoor amphitheater with 10,000 lawn seats and 5,000 covered seats. Rock, jazz, and pop music concerts are sometimes presented as well.

Food

Il Posto Bistro (137 S. Main St., 585/905-0535, www.ilpostobistro.com, Tues.-Thurs. 11:30am-2pm and 5pm-9pm, Fri.-Sat. 11:30am-2pm and 5pm-10pm, $18) is a small, intimate restaurant specializing in Italian cuisine. It has a robust wine list, though few of the wines are from the area; most are from Italy and France.

The Office Restaurant (2574 Macedon Rd., 585/394-8787, www.ericsofficerestaurant. com, Mon.-Wed. 11am-9:30pm, Thurs.-Sat. 11am-10pm, $22) serves burgers, bar fare, and heavier American entrées (think tenderloin topped with blue cheese).

Accommodations

The Canandaigua region is home to many luxury B&Bs. One of the best is the snug, colonial-style ★ **1795 Acorn Inn** (4508 Rte. 64, Bristol Center, 585/229-2834, www. acorninnbb.com, $195-295), which has achieved the AAA four-diamond rating for more than 20 years, a rarity for a B&B. Once a stagecoach stop, the inn now pampers guests with comfy canopy beds, luxurious private baths, an outdoor hot tub, and multicourse breakfasts.

Bristol Harbour Resort (5410 Seneca Point Rd., 585/396-2200, www.bristol-harbour.com, $195-495) is a 31-room, Adirondack-style resort that sits on Bristol Mountain, a perch offering spectacular lake views. The resort also has cottages and condos for rent. Golfers particularly enjoy this resort, as it has an 18-hole championship golf course designed by Robert Trent Jones. Other amenities and services include a spa, a restaurant, a private marina and beach, and a year-round hot tub.

VICTOR

About 10 miles (16.1 km) northwest of Canandaigua sprawls the village of Victor, worth visiting because an important Seneca village once stood here. The village was home to about 4,500 people; its palisaded granary stored hundreds of thousands of bushels of corn. All was destroyed in 1687 by a French army, led by the governor of Canada, who wanted to eliminate the Seneca as competitors in the fur trade.

Ganondagan State Historic Site

A visit to **Ganondagan State Historic Site** (1488 Rte. 444, 585/742-1690, www.ganondagan.org, Tues.-Sun. 9am-5pm, closed from mid-Jan. to mid-Feb., adults $6, seniors $3, children $1), which means "Town of Peace," begins with an interesting video that tells the story of the Seneca Nation and that of Jikohnsaseh, or Mother of Nations. Together with "the Peacemaker" and Hiawatha, Jikohnsaseh was instrumental in forging the Five Nations Confederacy; it was she who proposed that the Onondagan chief, who at first refused to join the confederacy, be appointed chairman of the Chiefs' Council. Jikohnsaseh once lived in the vicinity of Ganondagan and is believed to be buried nearby. No one searches for her grave, however, as a sign of respect.

Three trails that lead over gentle terrain past informative plaques begin just outside the visitors center. The Trail of Peace relates important moments in Seneca history. The Earth of Our Mother Trail identifies plants important to the Seneca. The Granary Trail re-creates the day in 1687 that Ganondagan was destroyed, through journal entries from the French forces. There is also a replica of a 17th-century bark longhouse on site.

Food

Warfield's (3 Coulter Ln., Clifton Springs, 315/462-7184, www.warfields.com, Tues.-Sat. 9am-9pm, $24) features seasonal "country

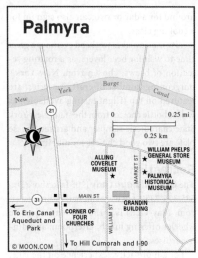

fare" inflected with Asian and European influences, served in a dining room with a pressed tin ceiling.

Lucca Wood-Fire Bistro (90 W. Main St., 585/924-9009, www.luccawfpizza.com, days and hours vary by season, $14) serves pizzas crisped to perfection in its wood-fired oven, as well as panini and salads.

PALMYRA

About 15 miles (24 km) due north of Canandaigua is Palmyra, an old Erie Canal town where Joseph Smith allegedly received a set of golden plates inscribed with the Book of Mormon from the angel Moroni. The Hill Cumorah Pageant commemorates that event every July.

Downtown Palmyra is small and compact, lined with sturdy brick buildings. A church stands at each corner of the intersection of Main Street and Route 21, a fact that once made it into *Ripley's Believe It or Not.* Just west of downtown is the graceful stone **Erie Canal Aqueduct,** off Route 31.

Three small museums run by Historic Palmyra sit side by side downtown. On the outskirts of town are the Hill Cumorah Visitor Center and Joseph Smith Farm, run by the Mormon Church.

Historic Palmyra

A **trail pass ticket** (adults $10, seniors and children $7, family $20) offers admission to all four historic Palmyra museums. **William Phelps General Store and Home Museum** (140 Market St., 315/597-6981, www.historicpalmyrany.com, May-Oct. Tues.-Sat. 10:30am-4:30pm, Nov.-Apr. Tues.-Thurs. 11am-4pm, adults $4, children $3) was operated by the Phelps family from the 1860s until the 1940s. The museum re-creates the general store of the 1890s and is an incredible untouched place to poke around, with excellent guides leading the way back into a simpler time. Shelves feature, among other items, spices and extracts that have retained their scents.

The **Alling Coverlet Museum** (122 William St., 315/597-6981, www.historicpalmyrany.com, Mon.-Sat. 1pm-4pm, adults $4, children $3) houses the largest collection of handwoven coverlets in the United States. Often referred to as the American tapestry, coverlets are ornate bedcoverings made out of wool, cotton, or linen.

The nearby **Palmyra Historical Museum** (132 Market St., 315/597-6981, www.historicpalmyrany.com, May-Oct. Tues.-Sat. 10:30am-4:30pm, Nov.-Apr. Tues.-Thurs. 11am-4pm, adults $4, children $3) occupies the former St. James Hotel. Exhibits here include 19th-century furniture, Erie Canal art and artifacts, children's toys, stern Victorian portraits, and a tour led by an expressive guide who brings the historic objects to life with animated anecdotes.

Palmyra Print Shop (140 Market St., 315/597-6981, www.historicpalmyrany.com, May-Oct. Tues.-Sat. 10:30am-4:30pm, Nov.-Apr. Tues.-Thurs. 11am-4pm, adults $4, children $3) features Palmyra-made printing presses and cutters with handmade type and print blocks from 1838 through 1972.

Hill Cumorah Visitor Center

A good place to learn about the Mormon religion is at the **Hill Cumorah Visitor Center** (603 Rte. 21, 315/597-5851, www.hillcumorah. org, Mon.-Sat. 9am-9pm, Sun. noon-9pm, free), 4 miles (6.4 km) south of downtown. Most visitors are Mormons, but non-Mormons are welcome and left more or less in peace to peruse the exhibits. A film provides a good introduction to Mormon history and beliefs, and exhibits tout the growth of the religion. There are currently about nine million Mormons worldwide, though only 1,500 live in upstate New York.

Behind the center stands Hill Cumorah, the drumlin where Joseph Smith is said to have found the golden plates on September 22, 1827. It took him years to translate the plates, and after he was done, he reburied them. A gold statue of the angel Moroni sits atop Hill Cumorah.

Joseph Smith Farm and Sacred Grove

Born in Vermont in 1805, Joseph Smith first came to Palmyra with his family in 1815. The Smiths were farmers, and Joseph—described by one contemporary as a "quiet, low-speaking, unlaughing" boy—lived in this simple, white clapboard house, now known as the **Joseph Smith Farm** (29 Stafford Rd., 315/597-5851, www.hillcumorah.com, Mon.-Sat. 9am-7pm, Sun. 12:30pm-7pm, free), until he was 22. He received his first vision in the **Sacred Grove** behind the house when he was only 14.

Events

The largest outdoor pageant in the United States, the **Hill Cumorah Pageant** (www. hillcumorah.org/pageant) commemorates Joseph Smith's visitation from the angel Moroni, which led to the founding of the Mormon religion. It's a spectacular performance with a cast and technological special effects worthy of Broadway.

Each August, Palmyra hosts the **Wayne County Fair** (www.waynecountyfair.org), one of the oldest fairs in the country, having originated in 1849. Livestock displays and beauty pageants are just two of the many activities at this beloved fair.

Palmyra Canaltown Days (www.palmyracanaltowndays.org) celebrates the town's historic connection to the Erie Canal. Held every September, the festival features craft and food vendors, and draws thousands of visitors.

Accommodations

A generous breakfast and kind hosts make **Liberty House** (131 W. Main St., 315/597-0011, www.libertyhousebb.com, $99-109) particularly noteworthy; the affordable rates don't hurt, either. Three guest rooms are available in this beautiful Victorian home with a wraparound porch.

Best Western Palmyra Inn & Suites (955 Canandaigua Rd., 315/597-8888, www.palmyrainn.com, $119-199) offers 60 rooms and suites, with kitchenettes in each room. Amenities include free wireless Internet access, a whirlpool tub and exercise room, and deluxe continental breakfast.

SOUTH ON ROUTES 364 AND 245

Heading south down Canandaigua's eastern shore, you'll pass through a series of picturesque valleys. At the southern end of the lake, the route skirts around South Hill and **High Tor Wildlife Management Area** (585/226-2466, www.dec.ny.gov/outdoor/24439). Hiking trails traverse the preserve, which is also one of the few places left in New York where you can still spot eastern bluebirds, the state bird. The main entrance to the area is off Route 245 between Middlesex and Naples.

NAPLES

Just south of Canandaigua Lake, surrounded by hills, lies Naples (pop. 1,020). A tidy village with a brisk tourist trade, Naples centers around a historic **Old Town Square.** Naples is one of the best places in the Finger Lakes to sample a sweet regional specialty: grape pie. The pies, made with dark grapes, are best during fall harvest season.

Cumming Nature Center

About 8 miles (12.9 km) northwest of the village lies 900-acre **Cumming Nature Center** (6472 Gulick Rd., 585/374-6160, www.rmsc.org, Wed.-Fri. 9am-3:30pm, Sat.-Sun. 9am-4:30pm, $3 per person or $10 per family donation), owned by the Rochester Museum and Science Center. A veritable outdoor museum, the preserve holds 6 miles (9.7 km) of themed trails leading through forests and wetlands. The Conservation Trail illustrates theories of forest management; the Pioneer Trail, complete with a reconstructed homestead, teaches about the early settlers' lives. The Beaver Trail focuses on the principles of ecology, and the Iroquois Trail focuses on Native American life. A visitors center is near the entrance.

Gannett Hill

Scenic Route 21 heads due north out of Naples to the highest point in Ontario County: Gannett Hill, 2,256 feet (690 m) above sea level. Now part of Ontario County Park, the hill offers bird's-eye views of the surrounding countryside.

Wineries

The local grapes are used for something more than pie. **Hazlitt's Red Cat Cellars** (5712 Rte. 414, 607/546-9463, www.hazlitt1852.com, Nov. 1-May 31 Mon.-Sat. 10am-5pm, Sun. 11am-5pm, June 1-Oct. 31 Mon.-Sat. 10am-5:30pm, Sun. 11am-5:30pm, $5) hosts wine tastings in its wood-paneled tasting room. **Inspire Moore Winery and Vineyard** (197 N. Main St., 585/374-5970, www.inspiremoorewinery.com, Jan.-Mar. Sat.-Sun. noon-4pm, Apr.-June Thurs.-Sun. 11am-5pm, Sat. 11am-6pm, July-Nov. Sun.-Fri. 11am-5pm, Sat. 11am-6pm, Dec. Thurs.-Sun. 11am-5pm, $5) has a casual restaurant next to the winery. **Arbor Hill Grapery** (6461 Rte. 64, 583/374-2870, www.thegrapery.com, Mon.-Sat. 10am-5pm, Sun. 11am-5pm, $5) features a shop and **Brew & Brats,** a restaurant specializing in exactly what its name suggests.

Entertainment

The only performing arts venue of its kind in the immediate area, **Bristol Valley Theater** (151 S. Main St., 585/374-6318, www.bvt-naples.org) is housed inside an old church. Music, theater, dance, comedy, and children's events are staged in spring, summer, and fall.

Shopping

At **Artizanns** (118 N. Main St., 585/374-6740, www.artizanns.com), more than 200 Finger Lakes artists and artisans exhibit their wares for purchase, with pottery, jewelry, photography, paintings, metalwork, and much more on display.

Food

Brew & Brats (6461 Rte. 64, 585/374-2870, www.brewandbrats.com, Fri.-Sun. hours vary by season, $9) specializes in local craft brews and nearly 10 kinds of bratwurst. Nondrinkers can enjoy nonalcoholic slushies made of locally crafted grape juice or root beer. Saturday nights feature live music.

Rochester

Rochester (pop. 208,046) straddles the Genesee River gorge just south of Lake Ontario and north of the Erie Canal. New York's third-largest city, Rochester has traditionally been known for its corporate high-tech industries, with Kodak, Xerox, and Bausch + Lomb being the biggest. Many major educational and cultural institutions are based here as well, including the Eastman School of Music, Rochester Philharmonic, The Strong National Museum of Play, and George Eastman Museum.

Established in 1803, Rochester became America's first boomtown with the opening of the Erie Canal, increasing its population 13-fold between 1825 and 1845. During the mid-1800s, Rochester was a hotbed of radical thought and social activism. Frederick Douglass, the escaped slave and abolitionist, settled in Rochester in 1847 and published his newspaper, the *Northern Star,* here for 17 years. One of his close associates was Susan B. Anthony, who was arrested in 1872 for daring to vote in a national election.

In 1881, a quiet young bank clerk named George Eastman patented and produced the world's first rollable film, an invention that changed Rochester forever. By the turn of the century, Eastman Kodak was Rochester's largest employer, and Eastman was a generous philanthropist. During his lifetime, he gave away over $100 million (more than $1 billion in today's economy), mainly to schools, parks, the University of Rochester, and local hospitals. "I want to make Rochester the best city in which to live and work." He succeeded: For much of the 20th century, Rochester was famed for its prosperity.

In more recent decades, the city has been forced to reinvent itself. As Kodak and other major employers have downsized or shuttered completely, laying off thousands of employees, Rochester's population has learned to take nothing for granted. Today, it's home to dozens of thriving but relatively unknown computer software, telecommunications, and medical equipment companies. Downtown Rochester is experiencing a renaissance, and many of the city's suburbs remain prosperous.

Orientation

Downtown Rochester is encircled by I-490, sometimes called the Inner Loop. Main Street runs east-west through the center of downtown, flanked by a mix of historic buildings and modern glass-sheathed skyscrapers. Clinton Avenue runs north-south. At the corner of Main Street and Clinton Avenue sprawls the 1962 **Midtown Plaza,** the oldest downtown shopping mall in the country. At the corner of Main Street and South Avenue stands the **Rochester**

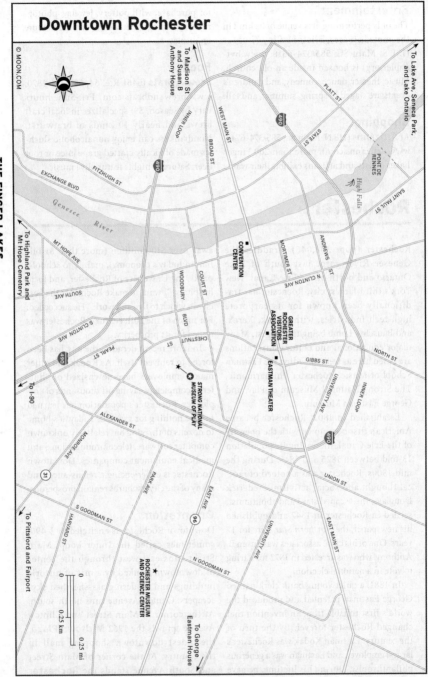

Downtown Rochester

© MOON.COM

To Madison St. and Susan B. Anthony House

To Lake Ave, Seneca Park, and Lake Ontario

PLATT ST

WEST MAIN ST

BROAD ST

STATE ST

INNER LOOP

FITZHUGH ST

EXCHANGE BLVD

SAINT PAUL ST

PONT DE RENNES

High Falls

Genesee River

MT HOPE AVE

MORTIMER ST

ANDREWS ST

N CLINTON AVE

CONVENTION CENTER

COURT ST

WOODBURY BLVD

SOUTH AVE

S CLINTON AVE

GREATER ROCHESTER VISITORS ASSOCIATION

EASTMAN THEATER

CHESTNUT ST

PEARL ST

GIBBS ST

NORTH ST

UNIVERSITY AVE

INNER LOOP

To I-90

STRONG NATIONAL MUSEUM OF PLAY

ALEXANDER ST

MONROE AVE

UNION ST

PARK AVE

EAST AVE

EAST MAIN ST

To Pittsford and Fairport

S GOODMAN ST

HARVARD ST

N GOODMAN ST

UNIVERSITY AVE

ROCHESTER MUSEUM AND SCIENCE CENTER

To George Eastman House

0   0.25 km

0   0.25 mi

To Highland Park and Mt Hope Cemetery

To Highland Park and Mt Hope Cemetery

Riverside Convention Center. Just west of South Street is the Genesee River. Graceful **Eastman Theatre,** with its rounded facade, is tucked onto Gibbs Street near Main Street, while the stunning art deco **Times Square Building** towers one block off Main Street at the intersection of Exchange Boulevard and Broad Street.

Major thoroughfares fanning out from I-490 include East Avenue, Park Avenue, Monroe Avenue (Rte. 31), and Mt. Hope Avenue (Rte. 15). I-90 runs just south of the city. Lake Ontario lies about 8 miles (12.9 km) north of the downtown.

The genteel southeastern quadrant of Rochester boasts four major museums, the University of Rochester, Mount Hope Cemetery, and Highland Park. Expansive **East Avenue,** peppered with stately mansions, gardens, and churches, runs through its center. Parallel to East Avenue runs **Park Avenue,** known for its classy boutiques, restaurants, and outdoor cafés. South of Park Avenue lies **Monroe Avenue,** a major commercial artery that's also one of the city's more eclectic neighborhoods. It's a haven for students, artists, performers, and activists. Most of the activity is centered between I-490 and Goodman Street.

You'll find several parking garages downtown, on or just off Main Street. Street parking is generally available elsewhere in the city. Downtown sights are within walking distance of each other and the major museums in southeast Rochester.

SIGHTS

High Falls and Brown's Race

Walk a few blocks north of Main Street and you'll see an enormous gaping gorge that rips right through the heart of the city, providing spectacular views. Brown's Race sits at the edge of wide, semicircular, 96-foot-high (29 m) High Falls. Cupping the falls to both sides, but especially to the east, are jagged brown walls streaked with dull red. A **pedestrian bridge** crosses the river just south of the falls.

Brown's Race is made up of four interconnected brick buildings that once contained water-powered mills. Extensively renovated in the early 1990s, it now features shops and restaurants. The word "race" refers to the diverted raceways that once harnessed the power of the falls.

★ The Strong National Museum of Play

The Strong National Museum of Play (1 Manhattan Sq., 585/263-2700, www.museumofplay.org, Mon.-Thurs. 10am-5pm, Fri.-Sat. 10am-8pm, Sun. noon-5pm, adults and children 2 and over $16, children under 2 free) is one of the largest children's museums in the country, with 150,000 square feet of exhibits. The National Toy Hall of Fame features new and historic versions of classic toys. Main interactive exhibits include Sesame Street, a kid-size supermarket, and a 1918 carousel.

Before her death in 1969, the museum's founder, Margaret Woodbury Strong, the daughter of wealthy parents, had amassed more than 300,000 objects, some of which she began collecting as a child. Often, during her family's many trips abroad, she was given a large shopping bag at the start of each day and told she could shop until she filled it.

Strong's many passions included fans, parasols, Asian artifacts and art, dolls, dollhouses, miniatures, toys, marbles, canes, paperweights, glass, pottery, samplers, figurines, kitchen equipment, and costumes. Her doll collection, numbering 27,000, is especially impressive. Many of these items remain on display.

Memorial Art Gallery

Connected with the University of Rochester, **Memorial Art Gallery** (500 University Ave., 585/276-8900, www.mag.rochester.edu, Wed.-Sun. 11am-5pm, Thurs. 11am-9pm, adults $15, seniors $12, students and children 6-18 $6) is a small gem, containing a little bit of everything, from pre-Columbian sculpture and ancient Chinese ceramics to American folk art and late-20th-century painting. The gallery owns more than 9,500 objects in all, spanning 5,000 years. A dozen or so temporary exhibitions are staged each year. In the center of the gallery is an enclosed, skylit sculpture garden filled with works by Henry Moore and Albert Paley, a Rochesterian.

Rochester Museum and Science Center

Like many other top science museums, **Rochester Museum and Science Center** (657 East Ave., 585/271-4320, www.rmsc.org, Mon.-Sat. 9am-5pm, Sun. 11am-5pm, adults $18, seniors and students $17, children 3-18 $16) houses plenty of fossils, dioramas, exhibits on flora and fauna, and prehistoric beasts.

What makes the place really special, however, is **At the Western Door,** a powerful exhibit about the Seneca Nation. The exhibit examines Seneca life from pre-European contact in the 1550s to the present. Separate sections, brimming with artifacts, focus on such subjects as the fur trade, the Iroquois Confederacy, the Sullivan campaign, and the sad history of broken treaties. As late as 1960, the Allegheny Senecas lost one-third of their reservation when it was flooded to create Kinzua Dam.

State-of-the-art **Strasenburgh Planetarium** (sky shows an additional fee) is also at the museum.

George Eastman House

Just east of the Rochester Museum and Science Center is the grand, 50-room **George Eastman House** (900 East Ave., 585/327-4800, www.eastman.org, Tues.-Sat. 10am-5pm, Sun. 11am-5pm, adults $15, seniors $13, students $5, children under 5 free), where Eastman Kodak founder George Eastman lived alone with his mother for much of his life. The Georgian mansion contains all the finest furnishings of its day, including Persian rugs, oil paintings, and carved mahogany furniture polished to a high gleam. But what makes the place interesting is the information and ephemera related to Eastman himself.

Born in 1854, Eastman left school at age 13 to help support his family. He worked first as a messenger boy, earning $3 a week, then as an accountant. He began taking photographs at age 23 while on vacation and started searching for an easier way to develop negatives. He spent three years experimenting in his mother's kitchen. By 1880, Eastman had invented a dry plate coating machine, the genesis of his Eastman Kodak Company.

Eastman's passions included music, fresh flowers, wild game hunting, and philanthropy. One year, he gave a free camera to every child in America who was turning 13. Then, at age 78, suffering from an irreversible spinal disease, he committed suicide in his bedroom. His suicide note read: "To my friends; My work is done—why wait?"

Also on-site is the Kodak photography collection, which features nearly half a million images and photography-related objects, including photos by the world's most renowned photographers.

Stone-Tolan House Museum

Continuing to the far eastern end of East Avenue, you'll come to the oldest structure in Rochester, the 1792 **Stone-Tolan House Museum** (2370 East Ave., 585/546-7029, www.landmarksociety.org, call for current days and hours, adults $5, children $2). A handsome, rustic building with wide floorboards, large fireplaces, and an orchard out back, the house was once both the Stone family home and a popular tavern. It is now owned by the Landmark Society of Western New York.

Highland Park

In 1888, Frederick Law Olmsted designed Highland Park, a planned arboretum bounded by Mt. Hope, Highland, and Elm Avenues and Goodman Street. One of the city's biggest celebrations, the Lilac Festival, takes place here every May, when the park's 1,200 lilac bushes bloom.

1: High Falls in downtown Rochester **2:** Middle Falls at Letchworth State Park

But lilacs are just the beginning. From early spring through late fall, Highland offers a riotous delight of Japanese maples, sweet-smelling magnolias, dazzling spring bulbs, delicate wildflowers, and 700 varieties of rhododendrons, azaleas, and mountain laurel.

In the center of the park reigns the 1911 **Lamberton Conservatory** (180 Reservoir Ave., 585/753-7270, daily 10am-4pm, adults $3, seniors and children $2). A tropical forest grows under the main dome, while other rooms contain orchid collections, banana trees, cacti, and house plants. Across from the conservatory is the 1898 **Frederick Douglass statue,** the first public statue erected to honor an African American.

Mount Hope Cemetery

From the corner of Mt. Hope and Elmwood Avenues extends extravagant **Mount Hope Cemetery** (entrance at 1133 Mt. Hope Ave.), a landscaped oasis of green strewn with knobby hills, ancient trees, marble tombs, and elaborate mausoleums. One of the oldest cemeteries in the country, established in 1838, Mount Hope contains the graves of every Rochesterian who was anyone, including Frederick Douglass and Susan B. Anthony.

An 1874 neo-Romanesque gatehouse marks the cemetery entrance, while just inside are a Gothic chapel and a white Moorish gazebo. The Douglass grave is off East Avenue near the northern end of the cemetery; the Anthony grave is off Indian Trail Avenue at the far northern end.

Maps to the cemetery are available at the Rochester Convention and Visitors Bureau. **Friends of Mt. Hope Cemetery** (585/461-3494, www.fomh.org) offers guided walking tours on Saturdays in the spring, summer, and fall.

Susan B. Anthony House

In a quiet, somewhat run-down neighborhood west of downtown stands the narrow, redbrick **Susan B. Anthony House** (17 Madison St., off W. Main St., 585/235-6124, www.susanb. org, Tues.-Sun. 11am-5pm, adults $15, seniors $10, students and children $5) that once belonged to the women's rights advocate. Simply furnished in the style of the late 1800s, the house contains much Anthony memorabilia, including her typewriters, clothes, letters, photos, and stuffed Victorian furniture.

Anthony, born in Massachusetts in 1820, lived in this house from 1866 until her death in 1906. It was here where she was arrested for voting in 1872, and here that she met and planned with fellow reformers Elizabeth Cady Stanton and Frederick Douglass. Together with Stanton and Matilda Gage, Anthony wrote her *History of Woman Suffrage* in the 3rd-floor attic, a wonderful hideaway now once again strewn with her books and papers.

Seneca Park Zoo

North of the downtown, along the Genesee River, runs the long, skinny **Seneca Park Zoo** (2222 St. Paul St., 585/336-7200, www.senecaparkzoo.org, Apr. 1-Oct. 31 daily 10am-5pm, Nov. 1-Mar. 31 daily 10am-4pm, adults $10, seniors $9, children 3-11 $7). About 500 animals from nearly 200 species live in the zoo, including polar bears, a Siberian tiger, and reindeer. Don't miss the aviary, where brightly colored tropical birds fly about freely. Younger kids will enjoy the barnyard petting area.

Ontario Beach Park

When in downtown Rochester, it's easy to forget that Lake Ontario is less than 15 minutes away. But indeed, north of the city along Lake Avenue, you'll soon find a land of wide-open spaces, beaches, and parks.

Just before reaching the lake, you'll pass the 1822 **Charlotte-Genesee Lighthouse** (70 Lighthouse St., 585/621-6179, www.geneseelighthouse.org, days and hours vary seasonally, adults $5, children 5-17 $2), now a small museum with exhibits tracing the history of lighthouses and lake transportation. Originally, the lighthouse stood on the lakeshore, but sand deposits have moved it inland.

Ontario Beach Park (Lake and Beach Aves., 585/753-5887) is a 0.5-mile-long beach with an aging art deco bathhouse and weathered fishing pier illuminated on summer nights. Around the turn of the 20th century, the park was the "Coney Island of the West," attracting tens of thousands of Rochesterians to its elephant shows, waterslides, and beachfront hotels. Harking back to those heady days is the park's still-operating 1905 Dentzel menagerie carousel, one of the oldest carousels in the United States. Stop by the locally famous Abbott's Custard (www.abbottscustard.com), at the park's entrance, for a sweet, creamy treat (don't call it "ice cream").

Seabreeze Amusement Park

From Ontario Beach Park, travel east about 5 miles (8.1 km) along Lake Shore Boulevard to reach Seabreeze Amusement Park (4600 Culver Rd., 585/323-1900, www.seabreeze. com, May-June hours vary, July-Aug. daily 11am-10pm). First established in 1879, the park has over 75 rides and attractions, including a water park. It's also the home of the oldest continuously operating roller coaster in the United States, the Jack Rabbit, which opened in 1920.

An unlimited Ride & Slide Pass is $35.99 for those 48 inches (122 cm) and taller and $28.99 for those under 48 inches (122 cm). A Spectator Pass allows access to the grounds, but no rides, and costs $13.99. Tickets are several dollars cheaper if bought in advance on the park's website.

RECREATION

The 49-passenger *Sam Patch* (585/662-5748, www.sampatch.org, May-Oct.), a replica packet boat, offers sightseeing and specialty cruises, as does the historic wooden boat, *Mary Jemison.*

ENTERTAINMENT

Classical Music

The renowned Rochester Philharmonic Orchestra (585/454-7311, www.rpo.org) performs at the Eastman Theatre October-May. One of the world's premier music schools, Eastman School of Music (26 Gibbs St.,

585/274-1000, www.esm.rochester.edu) stages over 700 performances annually by students, faculty, and guest artists.

Theater

Rochester's resident professional theater, Geva Theatre (75 Woodbury Blvd., 585/232-4382, www.gevatheatre.org) stages nearly a dozen productions annually. It's housed in a historic brick-and-limestone building that was once the Naval Armory. Downstairs Cabaret Theatre (20 Windsor St., 585/325-4370, www.downstairscabaret.org) produces popular comedies and musicals.

Rochester Broadway Theatre League (885 Main St., 585/325-7760, www.rbtl.org) presents touring Broadway shows and concerts, while Rochester Contemporary Art Center (137 East Ave., 585/461-2222, www. rochestercontemporary.org) is the place to go for performance art and avant-garde theater.

Live Music and Nightlife

The best music listings are published by *City Newspaper* (www.rochestercitynewspaper. com), a free alternative weekly.

California Brew Haus (402 W. Ridge Rd., 585/621-1480) presents a good dose of Southern rock in a space that is the longest continuously operated rock-and-roll bar in the city.

Rochester International Jazz Festival (downtown Rochester, www.rochesterjazz. com) is a massive event each June, held over the course of more than a week, featuring more than 300 concerts and 1,200 performers in nearly 20 different venues, all within walking distance of downtown's East End Cultural District. Options to attend include approximately 80 free performances, 40 headliner shows, over 180 club pass concerts, and dozens of late-night, no-cover charge jam sessions.

FOOD

For a quick lunch, visit DiBella's Old Fashioned Submarines (620 Jefferson Rd., 585/475-1831, www.dibellas.com, Mon.-Sat.

10am-9pm, Sun. 11am-7pm, $12), serving hot and cold subs on hand-shaped rolls since 1918. Another good lunch spot is Orange Glory Café (240 East Ave., 585/232-7340, www.orangeglorycafe.com, Mon.-Fri. 8am-3pm, $8), which offers tasty homemade organic dishes, gourmet sandwiches, and cookies. Head to this little eatery early for the best selection.

In the heart of downtown, Dinosaur Bar-B-Que (99 Court St., 585/325-7090, www.dinosaurbarbque.com, Mon.-Thurs. 11am-11pm, Fri.-Sat. 11am-midnight, Sun. noon-10pm, $17) offers great ribs and Cajun food, along with live blues on weekends. Romantic Tapas 177 Lounge (177 St. Paul St., 585/262-2090, www.tapas177.com, Mon.-Sat. 4:30pm-2am, Sun. 5pm-2am, $20) is a very popular spot, serving an eclectic menu by candle-light. The lounge also features a wide variety of martinis, salsa lessons, and live music on the weekends.

The spirits of generations of brewers permeate the cavernous Genesee Brew House (25 Cataract St., 585/263-9200, www.geneseebeer.com, Sun.-Wed. 11am-10pm, Thurs.-Sat. 11am-11pm, $14), one of the country's oldest continuously operating breweries. Expect typical American brew pub fare like burgers and wings, served alongside Genesee's own brews. A guest tap features other local beers.

For a simple salad or tofu burger, step into no-frills Aladdin's Natural Eatery (646 Monroe Ave., 585/442-5000, www.myaladdins.com, Sun.-Thurs. noon-9pm, Fri.-Sat. noon-10pm, $12). On Clinton Avenue, parallel to Monroe, is Highland Park Diner (960 S. Clinton Ave., 585/461-5040, www.highland-park-diner.com, Mon.-Thurs. and Sat. 7am-9pm, Fri. 7am-10pm, Sun. 7am-8pm, $10), a classic 1948 art deco Orleans diner.

On Jefferson Road, you'll find Raj Mahal (368 Jefferson Rd., 585/730-7360, www.rajmahalrestaurant.com, Mon. and Wed.-Fri. 11:30am-2:30pm and 5pm-9:30pm, Fri.-Sat. 5pm-10pm, Sat. 11:30am-3pm, $17), known for its tandoori and vegetarian dishes and fresh breads.

ACCOMMODATIONS

There are a handful of great places to stay, all in downtown Rochester. In a city of nearly all chain hotels, Inn on Broadway (26 Broadway, 585/232-3595, www.innonbroadway.com, $169-199) is a boutique hotel housed in the historic 1929 University Club of Rochester. Luxury rooms include polished hardwood floors and natural stone bathrooms with extra touches like multiheaded showers, whirlpool tubs, Keurig coffeemakers, and gas fireplaces. Complimentary continental breakfast is served in elegant Tournedos, a restaurant whose lunch and dinner menus feature in-house dry-aged beef, seafood flown in daily from Hawaii, and a wine list with over 550 selections.

One of the loveliest bed-and-breakfasts in Rochester is Dartmouth House (215 Dartmouth St., 585/271-7872, www.dartmouthhouse.com, $139-199), a spacious English Tudor home with a fireplace, window seats, very knowledgeable hosts, and four guest rooms equipped with private baths. The bed-and-breakfast is within easy walking distance of several museums and many cafés and shops.

Another good bed-and-breakfast choice is romantic Edward Harris House Inn (35 Argyle St., 585/473-9752, www.edwardharrishouse.com, $179-189), with nice touches like fresh flowers, robes and towel warmers, sunflower showerheads, all organic and natural breakfasts, and welcome snack baskets.

Just outside Rochester, Woodcliff Hotel and Spa (199 Woodcliff Dr., Fairport, 585/381-4000, www.woodcliffhotelspa.com, $156-540), is a perfect home base for exploring the surrounding area's attractions, including small canal towns like Fairport. The room decor runs the gamut from art deco to Southwestern to Asian. The expansive property has spa and a nine-hole golf course, as well as an on-site restaurant.

Genesee Country Village and Museum

Twenty miles (32 km) southwest of Rochester, world-class Genesee Country Village and Museum (1410 Flint Hill Rd., Mumford, 585/538-6822, www.gcv.org, days and hours vary seasonally, adults $18, seniors and students $15, children ages 4-17 $10) consists of more than 40 meticulously restored and furnished 19th-century buildings laid out around a village square, depicting life of three different historic periods. Among the buildings are an early land office, two-story log cabin, fly-tier's shop, octagonal house, Greek Revival mansion, Italianate mansion, bookshop, small-scale farm, blacksmith's shop, doctor's office, and pharmacy. Gravel walkways lead between the buildings; guides in period dress cook, spin, weave, and demonstrate other folk arts of the preindustrial age.

Near the entrance are a Carriage Museum and The John L. Wehle Art Gallery, which houses a world-class collection of wildlife and sporting art spanning four centuries of work by such artists as Audubon and Remington. An extensive renovation completed in 2012 also debuted a new exhibit: the Susan Greene Historic Clothing Collection, a remarkably intact representation of period clothing, unique for its pieces that represent both the working class (whose clothing was so well-worn that it rarely survived to be able to be exhibited) and the upper class.

Another delightful curiosity on the grounds is The Intrepid, a replica Civil War-era helium balloon. Its basket occasionally holds passengers, who soar up to 300 feet (91 m) over the Genesee grounds.

An heirloom garden provides blooms and seeds to be used in the village. To the north is a 175-acre Nature Center, networked with 3 miles (4.8 km) of hiking and nature trails.

VICINITY OF ROCHESTER

Pittsford

To the immediate southeast of the city, the canal town of Pittsford offers unique shops and cafés, some inhabiting historic buildings. The town's Lock 32 (585/328-3960, www.geneseewaterways.org, hours and prices vary seasonally) offers white-water kayaking in the spillway. Live music also rocks the locks, with a Summer Concert Series (Port of Pittsford Park, 22 N. Main St., www.townofpittsford.org, free), Positively Pittsford (Main and Church Sts., www.townofpittsford.org, free), and Pittsford Celebrates (www.townofpittsford.org, free), all filled with family entertainment and the occasional fireworks display.

Bushnell's Basin, a charming spot to dock just outside of the village, is home to one of Rochester's landmark restaurants, Richardson's Canal House (1474 Marsh Rd., 585/248-5000, www.richardsonscanalhouse.net, Mon.-Fri. 11:30am-2pm and 5pm-9pm, Sat. 5pm-9pm, $30), a restored 1818 Erie Canal tavern with its own secluded garden. Elegant and highly acclaimed, the restaurant serves French country and American regional fare by candlelight.

Macedon

Macedon's Mid-Lakes Erie Macedon Landing is the home marina to Mid-Lakes Navigation (315/685-8500, www.midlakesnav.com), where you can learn to drive one of the gleaming wooden canal boats that await visitors who come to relive a bit of history. These simple-to-pilot boats can be driven by anyone with a few lessons.

Nearby Long Acre Farms (1342 Eddy Rd., 315/986-4202, www.longacrefarms.com), a family farm with a Scandinavian jumping pillow (for all ages), gemstone panning, and the Amazing Maize Maze, attracts visitors. The town's annual mid-September Lumberjack Festival (Macedon Center Fireman's Field, Rte. 31 and Canandaigua Rd., 315/986-3732, www.macedoncenterfire.org) lets even amateurs unleash their inner Paul Bunyan with logrolling and team greased pole climbing.

Fairport

The bustling, canal-side community of Fairport can be explored with bicycle rentals from **RV&E** (40 N. Main St., 585/388-1350, www.recreationalvehiclesandequipment. com) or kayak rentals from **Erie Canal Boat Company** (7 Lift Bridge Ln., 585/748-2628, www.eriecanalboatcompany.com). For a more in-depth look at life on the canal, join an overnight excursion, which includes kayak rental, food, and an overnight campsite with sleeping gear. Paddling adventures with itineraries for up to 10 days are also available.

With any luck, a boater will need the **Lift Bridge** triggered, the only one of its kind on the canal system. With no angle the same, the irregularly constructed bridge once largely stayed raised in a crooked slant at its top 15-foot (4.6 m) height to allow for the high volume of traffic on the canal below. A pedestrian bridge was created to accommodate foot traffic in this raised position. Current times see more road traffic, so the opposite is true and the bridge is raised from its usual 6-foot-above-the-water (1.8 m) level only when a boat needs to pass.

Red Bird Market (130 Village Lndg., 585/377-5050, www.redbirdmarket.com, Mon.-Fri. 9am-6pm, Sat. 10am-4pm) is a good morning pre-paddle pit stop for baked goods and coffee. Afternoon cool downs can be had at **Donnelly's Public House** (1 Water St., 585/377-5450, www.donnellysph. com, Mon.-Sat. 11am-2am, Sun. noon-2am, $14), an excellent pub with 33 taps and good pub food.

Little Finger Lakes

West of the six major Finger Lakes extend what are known as the little Finger Lakes: Honeoye (pronounced HONEY-oy), Canadice, Hemlock, and Conesus. Honeoye sports a village of the same name at its northern end, and Conesus—closest to Rochester—is crowded with summer homes. Canadice and Hemlock, which serve as reservoirs for Rochester, remain largely undeveloped and comprise Hemlock/Canadice State Forest. Set in deep, wooded valleys with no towns nearby, these two Finger Lakes are totally undeveloped. As a state forest, they and their surroundings will remain "forever green." Fishing, boating, and hiking can be enjoyed in the area.

HONEOYE

At the southwestern end of Honeoye lies the largely undeveloped **Harriet Hollister Spencer State Recreation Area** (Canadice Hill Rd./Rte. 37, 585/335-8111, www.parks. ny.gov/parks/164, daily dawn-dusk). Set on Canadice Hill, the park offers great views of the lake and, on a clear day, the Rochester skyline.

Another quirky stop outside Honeoye is the unusual **Wizard of Clay** (7851 Rte. 20A, Bloomfield, 585/229-2980, www.wizardofclay. com, days and hours vary by season), where the Kozlowski potters use 100,000 pounds of clay each year, hand-throwing the family's functional creations. The workshop is open to tour and see each stage of the process, even that of the unique patented Bristoleaf collection, made by pressing locally collected leaves into the soft clay before firing, leaving the imprints to be glazed for a final vase or picture frame. A densely pinned map on the wall shows the hometowns of thousands of visitors.

LETCHWORTH STATE PARK

Along the Genesee River at the far western edge of the Finger Lakes plunges one of the most magnificent sights in the state: 17-mile-long (27 km) Letchworth Gorge, now part of **Letchworth State Park** (1 Letchworth State Park, Castile, 585/493-3600, camping reservations 800/456-2267, www.parks.ny.gov/parks/79, daily 6am-11pm, parking $10).

Dubbed the "Grand Canyon of the East," the gorge is flanked by dark gray cliffs rising nearly 600 feet (180 m). Dense, thicketed forest grows all around, and at the center of it all sparkle three thundering waterfalls. Excellent hiking and snowshoeing are available through the wild terrain.

Much of the Letchworth Gorge was purchased by industrialist William P. Letchworth in 1859. A conservationist and humanitarian, Letchworth bought the gorge both for his own personal use and to save the falls from becoming Rochester's hydroelectric plant. Before his death in 1910, he deeded the gorge to the people of New York to be used as a permanent park.

One main road runs through the park alongside the gorge, affording scenic views. Recreational facilities include over 25 hiking trails ranging from 0.5 to 7 miles (.8 to 11.3 km) in length, two swimming pools, 82 cabins ($132-512/week), and a 270-site campground (tent sites $24-26/night).

The park can be entered from Mt. Morris (off Rte. 36), Portageville (off Rtes. 19A or 436), or Castile (off Rte. 19A); Portageville entrances are closed in winter.

Letchworth Museum

At the southern end of the park stands the rambling Letchworth Museum (585/493-2760, May-Oct. daily 10am-5pm) with exhibits on the Seneca, William Letchworth, and the gorge's natural history. Note especially the exhibits relating to Mary Jemison, the "white woman of the Genesee."

The daughter of Irish immigrants, Jemison was taken prisoner by the Seneca at the age of 15 and lived the rest of her life among them. She married first a Delaware warrior and then, following his death, a Seneca chief; she bore seven children and became a Seneca leader in her own right. Under the Big Tree Treaty of 1797, she was granted close to 18,000 acres along the Genesee River. Eventually, however, Jemison was moved to the Buffalo Creek Reservation with the rest of her people, where she died at the age of 91.

Letchworth moved Jemison's remains to the gorge in 1910 when her grave was in danger of being destroyed, and today, the Mary Jemison Grave stands on a hill behind the museum. Also on the hill is the Council House in which the last Iroquois council on the Genesee River was held on October 1, 1872. In attendance were the grandchildren of Red Jacket, Joseph Brant, and Mary Jemison; and William Letchworth and Millard Fillmore.

Food and Accommodations

At the southern end of the park, across from the Letchworth Museum, the stately, yellow-and-white ★ Glen Iris Inn (inside Letchworth State Park, 585/493-2622, www. glenirisinn.com, $125-295) sits in a large flat field overlooking the 107-foot (33 m) Middle Falls. Once the home of William Letchworth, the Victorian mansion is now a modernized inn with 16 comfortable guest rooms, a library with a good collection of regional books, and a gift shop. The inn's bustling restaurant (Sun.-Thurs. 8am-8pm, Fri.-Sat. 8am-8:30pm, $29), flanked by picture windows, specializes in gourmet salads prepared tableside, seafood, and veal.

For a serene, scenic splurge, check availability for the signature Cherry Suite at the Glen Iris Inn (inside Letchworth State Park, 585/493-2622, www.glenirisinn.com, $270-295), which features patterned hardwood floors, a whirlpool tub, and a balcony overlooking the incredible Middle Falls. The balcony of the Cherry Suite, perched above the glass-walled restaurant, is a coveted spot for passersby. Four-bedroom The Stone House (585/493-2622, $440-480 for up to 8 people) is another option rented by Letchworth State Park, situated across from Inspiration Point overlook.

Information and Services

The **Finger Lakes Tourism Alliance** (309 Lake St., Penn Yan, 315/536-7488, www.fingerlakes.org) is a good central information source for the entire region.

Contact **Finger Lakes Wine Country Tourism Marketing Association** (1 W. Market St., Corning, 607/936-0706, www.fingerlakeswinecountry.com) for information about grape-growing regions around Keuka, Seneca, and Cayuga Lakes. Each of the lakes also has a "wine trail" website: www.keukawinetrail.com, www.senecalakewine.com, and www.cayugawinetrail.com.

Contact **The Landmark Society of Western New York** (585/546-7029, www.landmarksociety.org) for walking tours in Rochester. For self-guided tours, download maps on their website.

Several B&B registries operate in the Finger Lakes. Among them are **Finger Lakes B&B Association** (www.flbba.org) and **B&B Association of Greater Ithaca** (800/806-4406, www.bbithaca.com). Many counties, cities, and towns have their own visitor information centers. Most are open Monday-Friday 9am-5pm.

- **Greater Syracuse Convention and Visitors Bureau** (572 S. Salina St., Syracuse, 315/470-1910, www.visitsyracuse.org)

- **Skaneateles Area Chamber of Commerce** (22 Jordan St., Skaneateles, 315/685-0552, www.skaneateles.com)

- **Cayuga County Office of Tourism** (131 Genesee St., Auburn, 800/499-9615, www.tourcayuga.com)

- **Seneca County Chamber of Commerce** (2020 Rtes. 5 and 20 W., Seneca Falls, 800/732-1848, www.fingerlakesgateway.com)

- **Ithaca/Tompkins County Convention and Visitors Bureau** (904 E. Shore Dr., Ithaca, 607/272-1313, www.visitithaca.com)

- **Geneva Area Chamber of Commerce** (1 Franklin Sq., Geneva, 315/789-1776, www.genevany.com)

- **Finger Lakes Visitors Connection - Ontario County** (25 Gorham St., Canandaigua, 877/386-4669, www.visitfingerlakes.com)

- **Clifton Springs Chamber of Commerce** (2 E. Main St., Clifton Springs, 315/462-8200, www.cliftonspringschamber.com)

- **Victor Chamber of Commerce** (37 E. Main St., Victor, 585/742-1476, www.victorchamber.com)

- **Phelps Chamber of Commerce** (116 Main St., Phelps, 315/548-5481, www.phelpsny.com)

- **Steuben County Conference & Visitors Bureau** (1 W. Market St., Ste. 201, Corning, 607/936-6544, www.corningfingerlakes.com)

- **Corning and the Southern Finger Lakes** (1 W. Market St., Corning, 607/936-4686, www.corningny.com)

- **Canandaigua Chamber of Commerce** (113 S. Main St., Canandaigua, 585/394-4400, www.canandaiguachamber.com)

- **Wayne County Tourism** (9 Pearl St., Lyons, 800/527-6510, www.waynecountytourism.com)

- **Watkins Glen Area Chamber of Commerce** (214 N. Franklin St., Watkins Glen, 607/535-4300, www.watkinsglenchamber.com)

- **Visit Rochester** (45 East Ave., Ste. 400, Rochester, 585/279-8300, www.visitrochester.com)

Getting There and Around

Syracuse Hancock International Airport (www.syrairport.org) is serviced by **Allegiant** (702/505-8888), **American Airlines** (800/433-7300), **Delta** (800/221-1212), **JetBlue** (800/538-2583), and **United** (800/241-6522). American, Delta, and United also service **Ithaca Tompkins Regional Airport** (www.flyithaca.com). Allegiant and Delta fly into and out of **Elmira-Corning Regional Airport** (www.flyelm.com). Allegiant, American, Delta, JetBlue, **Southwest** (800/435-9792), and United

service **Greater Rochester International Airport** (www2.monroecounty.gov).

A taxi ride from any of these airports to their respective downtowns costs $25-30.

Amtrak (800/872-7245, www.amtrak.com) travels to Syracuse and Rochester. **Greyhound** (800/231-2222, www.greyhound.com) and **Trailways** (800/295-5555 or 800/776-7548, www.trailways.com) provide bus service throughout the region.

By far the best way to explore the Finger Lakes is by car.

Buffalo and the Niagara Region

Buffalo.................403

Vicinity of Buffalo 414

Niagara Falls 416

North of
  Niagara Falls.........422

Orleans County 428

South of Buffalo 430

Information
  and Services.........434

Getting There
  and Around..........434

Western New York looks and feels different from the rest of the state, shaped not only by distinct geographical features (proximity to two of the Great Lakes) and geological forces (glacial activity), but also by different historical influences and developments.

The region was first inhabited by the Seneca, who called the region the "Western Door." European settlers eventually made their way here, taking advantage of the boomtown opportunities that followed the Erie Canal's completion, as well as ample parcels of land that were—and remain—perfect for farming.

Western New York's two primary destinations are Buffalo and Niagara Falls, situated about 20 miles (32 km) apart along

Highlights

Look for ★ to find recommended sights, activities, dining, and lodging.

★ **Wander the waterfront:** Buffalo's revitalized waterfront **Canalside District** buzzes with festivals, concerts, recreation, and a naval and military park (page 404).

★ **Feel the falls:** Visit the famed waterfalls spanning the U.S.-Canada border at **Niagara Falls State Park.** Amp up the excitement by venturing behind the falls or sailing into the mist on a boat tour (page 416).

★ **Cruise the Erie Canal:** Rent a boat or let someone take the helm and explore historic towns along the canal. Landlubbers can take advantage of the nearly 400-mile-long multiuse Erie Canalway Trail (page 428).

★ **Sport your game face:** Known as the "Aspen of the East," **Ellicottville** offers lots of year-round recreation, including skiing, mountain biking, climbing, and zip-lining (page 431).

★ **Experience Amish culture:** See Old Order Amish communities along the **Amish Trail.** Purchase handmade toys, furniture, and other traditional goods (page 431).

Buffalo and the Niagara Region

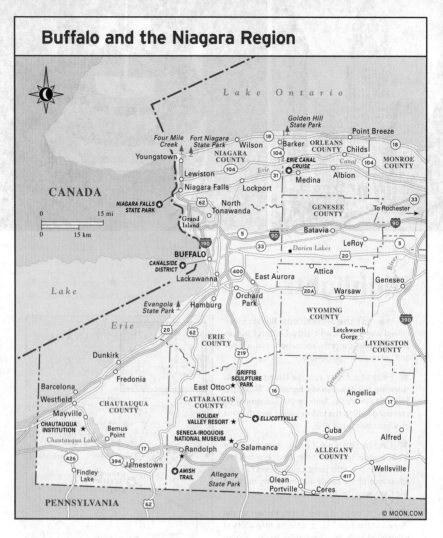

the Niagara River, across from Canada. At Buffalo's southwestern edge lies Lake Erie, while Lake Ontario presides north of Niagara Falls; both attract serious anglers keen to fish the Great Lakes.

Buffalo is the area's population center and New York's second-largest city. Seriously depressed following the decline of its steel industry in the 1970s, it still faces economic challenges but is in the midst of a surprising rejuvenation, with renovated waterfront and theater districts. To the north, south, and east of Buffalo extends especially fertile farm country, supporting Concord grapes, apples,

---

Previous: Niagara Falls; Buffalo City Hall; *Maid of the Mist.*

and a variety of produce. The Erie Canal snakes through this land, passing a number of towns still rich with history.

Niagara Falls has long been regarded as one of the world's great natural wonders. As far back as 1678, missionary Father Louis Hennepin wrote, "Betwixt the Lake Ontario and Erie, there is a vast and prodigious Cadence of Water. . . . The Universe does not afford its Parallel." Standing before Niagara Falls, you'll probably agree with Father Hennepin: The spectacular natural wonder really has no equal. The thundering sound of a massive volume of water cascading over three distinct falls—American, Bridal Veil, and Horseshoe Falls—will leave a lasting impression whether you choose to experience them from an observation deck, from an excursion boat, or via guided walking tour.

Most visitors to western New York include only these two destinations on their itineraries, but the region's people and attractions beg for more attention. The Amish Trail makes a relatively closed culture accessible to visitors. Historic lighthouses and hotels punctuate the Erie shoreline. Ski resorts and year-round outdoor recreation are the draws in places like Findley Lake and Ellicottville. And in a seemingly endless number of charming small towns, both transplants and families who have lived here for generations are coaxing Main Streets back to life.

PLANNING YOUR TIME

Visitors can make an easy one-week loop through this region. Spend a full day or two in Buffalo before heading north to Niagara Falls, where you'll want to budget another day to see the falls and the park and center for which it is named. Continuing north along Route 18, you'll drive through a series of small towns and attractions that sit along the Niagara River, including Lewiston, Youngstown, Fort Niagara State Park, Wilson, and Barker, all of which can be visited in a day. Lewiston makes a good home base; its Barton Hill Hotel and Spa sits right above the Niagara River.

After visiting these small towns, head south on Route 219, taking one or two days to explore the Amish Trail and nearby attractions, including the Sky High Climbing Forest and Aerial Adventure Park at Holiday Valley in Ellicottville. Holiday Valley has a variety of comfortable accommodations and on-site restaurants.

From there, head west on I-86 toward Jamestown, birthplace of beloved comedian Lucille Ball and home to a museum established in her honor. Continue on to Bemus Point and Chautauqua; followed by Findley Lake, known for its skiing and outdoor recreation; and Barcelona and Dunkirk, both with historic lighthouses. These towns are all clustered along Routes 430 and 394, two roads that form a ring around Chautauqua Lake and make for a pleasant drive. All of these towns along the lake can be visited in one or two days, depending on how much time you want to spend at the famed Chautauqua Institution or at picturesque Bemus Point. Rambling Hotel Lenhart in Bemus Point is a lovely place to stay, and that town also has several excellent restaurants. When you're ready to head back to Buffalo, continue north on I-90 from Dunkirk.

Buffalo

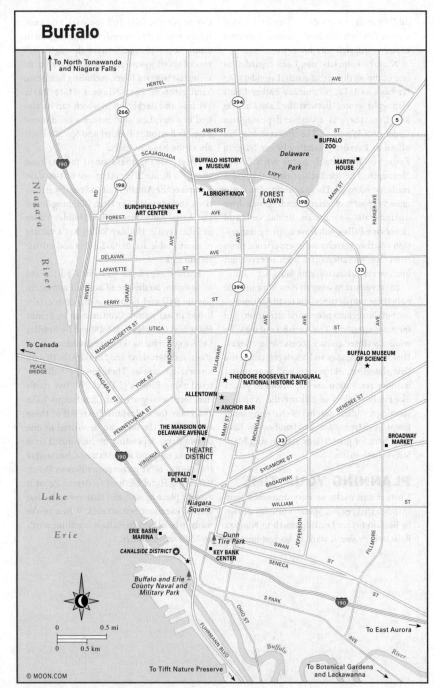

To North Tonawanda
and Niagara Falls

HERTEL   AVE

266   394

AMHERST   ST   5

BUFFALO
ZOO

SCAJAQUADA   Delaware
Park   MARTIN
BUFFALO HISTORY   HOUSE
MUSEUM

EXPY

198
FOREST   198
ALBRIGHT-KNOX   LAWN   MAIN ST   PARKER AVE

BURCHFIELD-PENNEY   AVE
ART CENTER

FOREST   ST

AVE

DELAVAN   AVE

LAFAYETTE   ST   GRANT   394   DELAWARE   AVE

FERRY   ST   33

RICHMOND   ST   AVE   AVE

UTICA   ST

MASSACHUSETTS ST

To Canada   5

BUFFALO MUSEUM
PEACE   OF SCIENCE
BRIDGE

NIAGARA   YORK ST

ST   THEODORE ROOSEVELT INAUGURAL
NATIONAL HISTORIC SITE   GENESEE ST

DELAWARE
ALLENTOWN

PENNSYLVANIA ST   ANCHOR BAR

THE MANSION ON   MAIN ST   MICHIGAN   BROADWAY
DELAWARE AVENUE   MARKET

190   VIRGINIA   THEATRE   33
DISTRICT   SYCAMORE ST

BUFFALO   BROADWAY
PLACE
WILLIAM
Niagara   ST
Lake   Square

JEFFERSON

FILLMORE
ERIE BASIN   Dunn
MARINA   Tire Park   SWAN
Erie   SENECA
CANALSIDE DISTRICT   KEY BANK
CENTER

Buffalo and Erie
County Naval and   190
Military Park

To East Aurora

0   0.5 mi

0   0.5 km   Buffalo

FUHRMANN BLVD   OHIO ST   S PARK   AVE   River

© MOON.COM   To Tifft Nature Preserve   To Botanical Gardens
and Lackawanna

190
RD
198
River
Niagara

Buffalo

Visiting Buffalo is like visiting an overgrown small town. People talk to strangers here and point to recent civic improvements with enormous, and quite justified, pride. After decades of economic decline, Buffalo's comeback is palpable, and it's attracting artists, do-it-yourselfers, and entrepreneurs who have defected from more expensive parts of the state to establish themselves here, where starting up is easier and the sense of community is often stronger.

Once the domain of the Iroquois, the Buffalo area was visited sporadically by French explorers in the 18th century. The origins of its name are disputed, but by 1832, Buffalo was incorporated as a city. The city's position between the Great Lakes and the canal made it thrive as a watery crossroads for commerce. Shortly after its incorporation, warehouses sprang up along the waterfront and thousands of immigrants, most from Ireland and Germany, arrived, helping fill the demand for laborers. By 1845, the city also boasted stove, nail, and cabinet factories, a bell foundry, and numerous other plants producing such products as mirrors, picture frames, and bathtubs. One of the railways, completed in 1873, connected Buffalo with the anthracite coalfields of Pennsylvania. That coal, together with Lake Superior iron ore and the newly developed Bessemer process, allowed for large-scale production of steel. More immigrants, this time from Poland and Italy, poured in; the newly rich built lavish mansions along Delaware Avenue.

By 1900, Buffalo was ready to show off its wealth and sophistication to the world. What better way to do so than to host the 1901 Pan-American Exposition? The expo covered 350 acres, attracted eight million visitors, and featured everything from columned temples to the latest scientific inventions. The glamorous event was tragically marred, however, by the assassination of President William McKinley, who was shot at the expo on September 6, 1901, by anarchist Leon Czolgosz. Following McKinley's death, Theodore Roosevelt was sworn into office as president in Buffalo. Today, you can visit the house where his swearing in occurred.

Buffalo reached its industrial zenith shortly after World War II. Relative prosperity continued, however, until the early 1970s, when newer, more efficient steel plants abroad caused a major shakedown of the steel industry. Buffalo's steel plants closed, the region's economy declined, and its population ebbed. During the 1980s, smaller manufacturing, finance, and advanced technology companies opened and flourished. In 1989, the U.S.-Canada Free Trade Agreement was signed and Buffalo became a center for American companies looking to expand into Canada. Today, Buffalo owes much of its economic base to that agreement.

Currently, revitalization is being driven by the arts, as new cultural organizations and institutions plant roots here. Visitors will find plenty to see and do, from open-air bus tours of the city's diverse and iconic architecture to unique, under-the-radar museums and attractions.

Orientation

Buffalo is a large city, and each of its neighborhoods has something distinct—whether in vibe or attractions (or both)—to recommend it.

The **Canalside District,** as its name suggests, sits along Buffalo's portion of the Erie Canal, and is a waterfront neighborhood that has been revitalized. Here, you'll find attractions where you can learn more about Buffalo's marine and industrial history, and if you're keen to experience the water yourself, you can kayak or take a boat ride. You can also rent and ride a bike on a lengthy trail that hugs the Outer Harbor. Canalside is also home to Buffalo's pro hockey team, the Sabres, who play at KeyBank Center, a sports complex ringed by a clutch of hotels and restaurants. The neighborhood is a particularly commendable attraction for families, as it has year-round outdoor activities, including ice biking and ice-skating in winter.

Downtown is home to some of Buffalo's loveliest buildings, many of which are significant to American architectural history. Downtown makes an excellent home base for visitors, with plenty of hotels and restaurants; in good weather, this neighborhood is easy to navigate on foot.

Buffalo's **Theater District** has a number of venues where live performances of all types—from American favorites to Irish classics—are staged. Many of these theaters are found on Main Street.

The neighborhoods of **Allentown** and **Elmwood Village** are hot spots for independent businesses, including boutiques, bookstores, and cafés and restaurants. You can also find fantastic art galleries and live music venues in these two neighborhoods.

Buffalo's **Museum District** is a leafy, peaceful neighborhood with large, inviting museums housing world-class collections. Two standouts are Albright-Knox and Burchfield-Penney.

Named for the Frederick Law Olmsted-designed Delaware Park, **Parkside** is the neighborhood where you'll find two top attractions: Buffalo's zoo and Frank Lloyd Wright's Darwin D. Martin House Complex. The neighborhood is best explored by car, with exception of the park, which calls for on-foot exploration.

Once the ethnic enclave of Polish and German immigrants, **The East Side** is particularly notable for a number of large, beautiful churches.

South Buffalo is home to several pretty outdoor spaces, including Cazenovia Park and Tifft Nature Preserve.

SIGHTS
★ Canalside District

One of Buffalo's most ambitious civic projects in recent years is the $295 million **Canalside District** (www.buffalowaterfront.com). The former western terminus of the Erie Canal, largely abandoned for years, has been spruced up considerably, turning a disused section of the city into a multiuse recreational area where more than 800 free events are held every year. In summer months, the area is buzzing with live music concerts, outdoor yoga classes, and kayak launches. A hockey complex and hotels round out the offerings.

Also part of this neighborhood is **Erie Basin Marina,** where hundreds of pleasure boats dock. One side of the marina features a pleasant park; on the other side, several restaurants overlook Lake Erie. At the end of the dock is an **observation tower** (716/842 4141, May-Oct. daily 8am-10pm).

Buffalo and Erie County Naval and Military Park (1 Naval Park Cove, foot of Pearl and Main Sts., 716/847-1773, www.buffalonavalpark.org, Apr.-Sept. daily 10am-5pm, Oct. daily 10am-4pm, Nov. Sat.-Sun. 10am-4pm, adults $15, seniors $12, children 5-12 $9) is also part of the Canalside neighborhood. The six-acre maritime park is dedicated to all branches of the armed forces.

Most of the exhibits, however, have to do with the U.S. Navy; three decommissioned ships are berthed here. Largest among them is the USS *Little Rock,* a 610-foot-long (190 m) guided missile cruiser outfitted much the way it was in the 1960s when 1,400 men lived onboard. Next door slumbers USS *Croaker,* a compact submarine that sank 11 Japanese vessels during World War II. Also seeing action in World War II was USS *The Sullivans,* a destroyer named after five brothers from Waterloo, Iowa, who died in 1942 when a Japanese torpedo sank their ship. Shamrocks

---

1: a tour of the Theodore Roosevelt Inaugural National Historic Site 2: Pearl Street Grill and Brewery 3: the Colored Musicians Club 4: fine architecture in Buffalo

1

2

3

COLORED
MUSICIANS
CLUB

4

on the destroyer's smokestacks pay tribute to the brothers' Irish heritage.

Downtown

Niagara Square centers around **McKinley Monument,** designed by architects Carrere and Hastings. The monument honors President William McKinley, who was assassinated in Buffalo while attending the 1901 Pan-American Exposition. Another significant structure on Niagara Square is the monumental art deco **Buffalo City Hall** (65 Niagara Square, 716/851-4200), erected in 1929. The hall's front entrance is lined with eight Corinthian columns three stories high; inside are vast, vaulted ceilings covered with sculpted figures and paintings depicting local history. An **observation deck** (716/851-4200, Mon.-Fri. 8:30am-4pm, free) on the 28th floor provides great views.

Old County Hall (92 Franklin St., 716/852-2356, Mon.-Fri. 9am-5pm) is where President Grover Cleveland got his start, first as a lawyer and then as mayor of Buffalo. Designed in the high Victorian Romanesque style, the 1870s building has a lavish lobby done up in marble and bronze.

Another block south, at the corner of Franklin and Church Streets, stands **Guaranty Building** (28 Church St., 716/848-1335, tours available by appointment), also known as the Prudential Building. Designed by Louis H. Sullivan in 1894, the 12-story terra-cotta-clad skyscraper is covered with elaborate ornamentation repeated on the elevators and mosaic ceilings indoors.

One block east, at the corner of Church and Pearl Streets, is **St. Paul's Episcopal Cathedral** (128 Pearl St., 716/855-0900, open to the public daily 9am-5pm). Designed by Richard Upjohn in the 1880s, the brown sandstone church features a front central tower topped with a tall, delicate spire.

Straddling both downtown and the Theater District are Main Street and Buffalo Place. In the late 1970s, downtown Main Street—semi-abandoned for years thanks

to urban flight—was transformed into a pedestrian thoroughfare named Buffalo Place. A sleek, above-ground section of the Metro Rail was built through its center, and business began returning downtown. Today, the pedestrian thoroughfare is being reverted to accommodate car traffic, but downtown is thriving.

Entering Buffalo Place from Church Street, you'll spot **Ellicott Square Building** (295 Main St.) on the southeast corner. When completed in 1896, this block-wide edifice was the world's largest commercial office building.

Two long blocks north, at Huron Street, is **M&T Bank Gold Dome Building** (Main St., at North Division, 716/852-2356), whose rotunda features some of the finest murals in Buffalo. On the north side is a scene depicting the city's harbor in the 1940s; the east side shows the Seneca, headed by Red Jacket.

Theater District

The restored Theater District is a 20-block area extending west as far as Delaware Avenue and north to Tupper Street. At least a half-dozen theaters and cabarets operate here, along with restaurants, galleries, and shops. Along Chippewa Street is **Chippewa District,** known for nightclubs.

Buffalo has an impressive theater history, which began in the mid-1800s, thanks to traffic along the Erie Canal. Dozens of theaters catering to travelers sprang up almost overnight; by the turn of the 20th century, Buffalo was one of the country's foremost drama centers.

The centerpiece of the district is **Shea's Performing Arts Center** (646 Main St., 716/847-1410, tours 716/829-1166, www.sheas. org), an opulent 1926 movie palace filled with marble and gilt. Saved at the last moment from the wrecking ball in 1975, Shea's is nearly fully restored and tours are given of the space.

ArtVoice (www.artvoice.com), an online publication, provides information on what's happening in the city arts-wise.

Allentown

Allentown, the nation's second-largest historic district, is just northwest of the Theater District. Streets here are lined with one Victorian structure after another, with all styles represented. Many of the homes have been converted into restaurants, art galleries, boutiques, and antiques shops.

Allentown is roughly bounded by Main Street to the east, Edward Street to the south, North Street to the north, and Cottage and Pennsylvania Streets to the west. Allen Street and Virginia Street run through its center.

Among the district's foremost architectural treasures are the typically middle-class **Tifft Houses** (Allen St. between Park and Irving Pl.); the extravagant **Williams-Butler Mansion** (672 Delaware Ave.), now housing the Jacobs Executive Development Center; and **Wilcox Mansion** (now the Theodore Roosevelt Inaugural Site, 641 Delaware Ave.). Mark Twain once lived at 472 Delaware Avenue, and F. Scott Fitzgerald spent part of his childhood at 29 Irving Place.

THEODORE ROOSEVELT INAUGURAL NATIONAL HISTORIC SITE

Theodore Roosevelt was formally inaugurated in the stately Wilcox Mansion, now the **Theodore Roosevelt Inaugural National Historic Site** (641 Delaware Ave., 716/884-0095, www.trsite.org, tours hourly Mon.-Fri. 9:30am-3:30pm, Sat.-Sun. 12:30pm-3:30pm, adults $12, seniors and students $9, children 6-18 $7), in 1901 after the assassination of President McKinley. "It is a dreadful thing to come into the Presidency this way," wrote the pragmatic Roosevelt shortly after the event, "but it would be far worse to be morbid about it. Here is the task, and I have got to do it to the best of my ability; and that is all there is about it."

Once owned by prominent lawyer Ansley Wilcox, the 1838 house is now run by the National Park Service. The library where Roosevelt was sworn in has been fully restored.

Museum District

Many of Buffalo's museums are clustered about 4 or 5 miles (6.4 or 8.1 km) north of downtown, near Delaware Park. To get here, take Delaware Avenue, a wide thoroughfare lined with mansions, most once owned by wealthy families and now home to law firms and the like.

ALBRIGHT-KNOX ART GALLERY

The centerpiece of Buffalo's art scene, **Albright-Knox Art Gallery** (1285 Elmwood Ave., 716/882-8700, www.albrightknox.org) is known around the world for its superb collection of contemporary art. Albright-Knox was the first museum in the United States to purchase works by Picasso and Matisse, and the first anywhere to present a major exhibition of photography, in 1910.

All major American and European artists of the past 50 years are well represented, including Van Gogh, Gauguin, Pollock, Miró, and Mondrian. The museum also presents 10 first-rate temporary exhibits each year and houses a solid general collection that spans the history of art. The Gallery Shop includes an extensive selection of art books.

The main museum will be closed until 2022 for a massive renovation and expansion project. In the meantime, a smaller, temporary space, referred to as Albright-Knox Northland (612 Northland Ave., Fri. noon-7pm, Sat.-Sun. 10am-5pm, pay what you wish), welcomes art lovers.

THE BUFFALO HISTORY MUSEUM

The Buffalo History Museum (1 Museum Ct., 716/873-9644, www.buffalohistory.org, Tues. and Thurs.-Sat. 10am-5pm, Wed. 10am-8pm, Sun. noon-5pm, adults $10, seniors and students $5, children 7-12 $2.50) is located within the only remaining permanent building from the 1901 Pan-American Exposition. Inspired by the Parthenon, the lovely structure once housed the New York State pavilion. Objects in the collection include items made in Buffalo during the industrial boom.

Twenty years ago, people betting on a bright future for Buffalo comprised a minority. Buffalo, New York State's second most populous city, was once the state's titan of industry and manufacturing. But the cumulative effects of the decline of canal and rail transport and the trend of moving American jobs offshore contributed to a sharp decline in Buffalo's fortune and a period of ambiguity about its future.

The mass exodus of traditional manufacturing businesses in the latter part of the 20th century left Buffalo with one of the highest vacant property rates in the country, and as businesses disappeared, so did jobs. Many of the newly unemployed left Buffalo, compounding the problems of abandoned property.

That would be a problem for any city—unoccupied buildings attract vandals and other social ills—but for Buffalo, it almost constituted a tragedy. The city is an architecture lover's trove; the 20th century's most illustrious architects all designed buildings for Buffalo, and nearly 100 of the city's buildings are listed in the National Register of Historic Places. Many also have National Historic Landmark status. What makes the collection particularly interesting is that the structures represent a vast range of styles, from art deco to Victorian, and take an equally vast number of forms, from family homes to mental hospitals to skyscrapers. Losing any of the city's iconic buildings would be a loss not just for Buffalo, but for architectural history. As *New York Times* architecture critic Nicolai Ouroussoff wrote in 2008, "Buffalo is home to some of the greatest American architecture of the late 19th and early 20th centuries . . . [having] shaped one of the grandest early visions of the democratic American city." The city, he wrote, "was founded on a rich tradition of architectural experimentation . . . among the first to break with European traditions. . . ."

Fortunately, a passionate group of preservationists, some with unlikely backgrounds, stepped up to save Buffalo's landmarks, fighting everywhere from newspaper columns to courts in an effort to preserve iconic buildings. Today, Buffalo is one of the country's most exciting—if not *the* most exciting—city for learning about historic preservation and enjoying American architecture's diversity. Here are some particularly interesting preservation projects, and a couple of ways to see preservation in action:

- **Babeville** (341 Delaware Ave., 716/852-3835, www.babevillebuffalo.com): Babeville, the nerve center for Buffalo native and folk rocker Ani DiFranco's music empire, is located in what was once Asbury United Methodist Church, built in 1876. Her offices are on an upper floor of the church, which she bought in 1999. A gorgeous event space (available to rent) occupies the former nave, and HallWalls, a contemporary art center, shares the same floor. The church basement has been converted into 9th Ward, an intimate live music venue.

- **Buffalo State Hospital** (400 Forest Ave.): This Revivalist Romanesque building was the

BURCHFIELD-PENNEY ART CENTER

Also near the Albright-Knox is **Burchfield-Penney Art Center** (1300 Elmwood Ave., 716/878-6011, www.burchfieldpenney.org, Tues.-Sat. 10am-5pm, Thurs. 10am-8pm, Sun. 11am-4pm, adults $10, seniors $8, children $5). Spread out over a few galleries, the center is a low-key affair dedicated primarily to Charles E. Burchfield, one of the 20th century's finest watercolorists. Originally from Iowa, Burchfield spent most of his life living and teaching in Buffalo. He was fascinated by Buffalo's streets and by patterns of fire and sound, which he depicted in a mystical, expressionist style.

The center owns the world's largest collection of Burchfield works, exhibited on a rotating basis. Works by other contemporary western New York artists are also exhibited.

Art lovers might also be interested in visiting the **Charles E. Burchfield Nature & Art Center** (2201 Union Rd., 716/677-4843, www.burchfieldnac.org, Mon.-Fri. 10am-4pm, Sun.

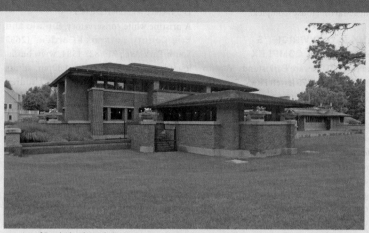

exterior of Frank Lloyd Wright's Martin House Complex in Buffalo

only hospital designed by 19th-century architect H. H. Richardson; it is also notable because its grounds were designed by foremost landscape architect Frederick Law Olmsted. The impressive, imposing building, which wouldn't look out of place in a gothic film, served as Buffalo's psychiatric center until the 1970s and was used for administration purposes until the mid-1990s. One of the most impressive fights for preservation was waged over this large property, which reopened as a hotel and conference center in 2017.

- **Frank Lloyd Wright's Martin House Complex** (125 Jewett Pkwy., 716/856-3858, www.martinhouse.org): Martin House is one of several structures in Buffalo designed by Frank Lloyd Wright; scholars consider this residence one of Wright's finest works. It underwent an extensive renovation between 1996 and 2016.

- **OpenAir Buffalo** (716/854-3749, www.openairbuffalo.org): Buffalo preservationist Tim Tielman leads a variety of preservation-focused tours on his OpenAir Buffalo bus. His firsthand experience saving some of the city's most important buildings makes for a lively, informative tour.

Tours of the city's extraordinary architecture are also offered by **Preservation Buffalo Niagara** (716/884-3138, www.preservationbuffaloniagara.org).

1pm-4pm, free) in nearby West Seneca, where Burchfield once lived. The center offers an exhibition area, nature trails, a meditation garden, and sculpture garden.

Parkside

Buffalo State College, the Albright-Knox, and The Buffalo History Museum all sit on the western edge of **Delaware Park**, a glorious, 350-acre expanse of green designed and laid out by Frederick Law Olmsted in the 1870s. Olmsted, who also designed Central Park in New York City, created an extensive park system throughout Buffalo that includes Front, Martin Luther King Jr., Cazenovia, and South Parks.

In the heart of the park, **Buffalo Zoo** (300 Parkside Ave., 716/837-3900, www.buffalozoo.org, daily 10am-4pm, adults $13.95, seniors $11.95, children 2-12 $10.95, parking $5) is one of the oldest zoos in the country, founded around the turn of the 20th century.

The Parkside neighborhood also includes Hertel Avenue, a vibrant shopping district for antiques, home decor, and clothing, and Buffalo's Little Italy, as well as Frank Lloyd Wright's Martin House Complex.

FRANK LLOYD WRIGHT'S MARTIN HOUSE COMPLEX

To the east of Delaware Park stands Martin House Complex (175 Jewett Pkwy., 716/856-3858, www.martinhouse.org, tours available). Dating to 1904, it's one of Frank Lloyd Wright's most important works. The long, horizontal building with its wide porches and few enclosed spaces is characteristic of the architect's early Prairie style. The pergola, carriage house, and conservatory have been brought back to life due to an inspirational restoration, much of it completed through the help of volunteers with a love of the master architect's work.

The Eleanor and Wilson Greatbatch Pavilion, designed by architect Toshiko Mori, functions as the welcome center and starting point for all tours of the Martin House. Check out the special tour packages, such as a combo tour of the multiple Wright structures in Buffalo.

BUFFALO MUSEUM OF SCIENCE

The four-story Buffalo Museum of Science (1020 Humboldt Pkwy., 716/896-5200, www.sciencebuff.org, Thurs.-Tues. 10am-4pm, Wed. 10am-9pm, adults $14, seniors $11, students and children 2-17 $11) is kid-friendly, with lots of interactive exhibits about the natural world. Three permanent exhibits provide information and insight into the ecology, geology, and archaeology of western New York.

BROADWAY MARKET

Though no longer the dynamic marketplace it once was, this old-world landmark, Broadway Market (999 Broadway, 716/893-0705, www.broadwaymarket.org, Mon.-Sat. 8am-5pm), founded in 1888 in the heart of Buffalo's Polish neighborhood, still sells fresh food year-round. Over 40 vendors hawk everything from homemade soups and potato dumplings to chickens' and pigs' heads.

South Buffalo

BUFFALO AND ERIE COUNTY BOTANICAL GARDENS

A pristine white conservatory, Buffalo and Erie County Botanical Gardens (2655 South Park Ave., 716/827-1584, www.buffalogardens.com, daily 10am-4:30pm, adults $12.50, seniors and students $11, children 3-12 $7, under 3 free) sits in Frederick Law Olmsted's South Park, all domes, semicircular windows, and sheets of glass. Designed by famed greenhouse architectural firm of Lord and Burnham in the 1890s, the conservatory is actually 12 small connected greenhouses. Each specializes in a different plant variety—bromeliads, orchids, cacti, fruit trees—with a pale-green glass dome crowded with palms dominating the center.

TIFFT NATURE PRESERVE

The 264-acre Tifft Nature Preserve (1200 Fuhrmann Blvd., 716/825-6397, www.tifft.org, grounds: daily dawn-dusk, free), administered by the Buffalo Museum of Science, is a peaceful area containing a 75-acre cattail marsh, a lake, several ponds, and 5 miles (8.1 km) of easy hiking trails.

RECREATION
Boating

Buffalo Harbor Cruises (Erie Basin Marina, 716/856-6696, www.buffaloharborcruises.com, adults $19-22, children $14) offer sightseeing tours such as Historic Buffalo River. Other cruise offerings include Spirit of Buffalo (www.spiritofbuffalo.com), Seven Seas Sailing (www.sevenseassailing.com), and Grand Lady Cruises (www.grandlady.com).

BFLO Harbor Kayak (1 Naval Park Cove, 716/228-9153, www.bfloharborkayak.com) rents boats and offers lessons for novices and tours for paddlers with some experience. The outfitter also rents boards for stand-up paddleboarding.

Spectator Sports

The Buffalo Bisons (1 James D. Griffin Plz.,

716/846-2000, www.milb.com, Apr.-Sept.), a AAA team for the Toronto Blue Jays, play at Sahlen Field. Tickets are generally available.

The National Football League **Buffalo Bills** (1 Bills Dr., Orchard Park, 716/648-1800, www.buffalobills.com, Sept.-Jan.) play at New Era Field. Tickets are available for most games, especially if you order a few weeks in advance.

The National Hockey League **Buffalo Sabres** (foot of Main St., 716/855-4100, www.sabres.com, Sept.-Apr.) play at KeyBank Center in Canalside. Tickets are generally available.

ENTERTAINMENT
Performing Arts

The renowned **Buffalo Philharmonic Orchestra** (716/885-5000, www.bpo.org) performs in **Kleinhans Music Hall** (3 Symphony Circle, 716/883-3560). The hall, designed by Eliel and Eero Saarinen, is one of the nation's best for acoustics.

Shea's Performing Arts Center (646 Main St., 716/847-1410, www.sheas.org) is a historic 1926 theater resembling a European opera house. Shows range from Broadway productions to opera and dance.

Theater District venues include 100-seat **Alleyway Theatre** (1 Curtain Up Alley, 716/852-2600, www.alleyway.com), **The Irish Classical Theatre Company** (625 Main St., 716/853-4282, www.irishclassical.com), **710 Main Theatre** (710 Main St., 716/847-0850, www.sheas.org/710-theatre), and **Town Ballroom** (681 S. Main St., 716/852-3900, www.townballroom.com).

Also in Buffalo is **Ujima Theatre Company** (429 Plymouth Ave., 716/281-0092, www.ujimacoinc.org), dedicated to works of African Americans. The nonprofit **African American Cultural Center** (350 Masten Ave., 716/884-2013, www.aaccbuffalo.org) presents dramas and other events in its Paul Robeson Theatre.

On D'Youville Square, northwest of downtown, is **Kavinoky Theatre** (320 Porter Ave., 716/829-7668, www.kavinokytheatre.

com), a beautifully restored 250-seat Victorian theater.

Nightlife

The best sources for information about Buffalo's music and nightlife are the Thursday edition of the **Buffalo News** (www.buffalonews.com) and **ArtVoice** (www.artvoice.com), an online arts publication. An ever-shifting array of nightclubs operates in the **Chippewa District**, along Chippewa Street downtown. Lively, upscale bars can be found on **Elmwood Avenue** near Buffalo State College.

A must-stop for jazz lovers is **Colored Musicians Club** (145 Broadway, 716/855-9383, www.cmctheclub.com, Thurs.-Sat. 11am-4pm, $10 for museum), a laid-back joint that was once the local union for African American musicians. Take a look at the excellent museum on the ground floor. The **Anchor Bar** (1047 Main St., 716/886-8920, www.anchorbar.com, Mon.-Thurs. 11am-10pm, Fri. 11am-midnight, Sat. noon-midnight, Sun. noon-10pm) in Allentown also presents jazz on a regular basis.

One of the oldest and best-known clubs in the city is laid-back **Nietzsche's** (248 Allen St., 716/886-8539, www.nietzsches.com, daily noon-4am), offering rock, country, reggae, blues, and folk. Live music is on the calendar every night.

EVENTS

Buffalo loves festivals. Favorites include **Allentown Art Festival** (716/881-4269, www.allentownartfestival.com) in June, showcasing work by over 400 artists and artisans. In mid-June the **Juneteenth Festival** (716/891-8801, www.juneteenthofbuffalo.com) takes place in Martin Luther King Jr. Park.

Also on Buffalo's festival roster is **Garden Walk Buffalo** (www.gardenwalkbuffalo.com), America's largest free garden walk, featuring about 400 private gardens open to view over the last weekend in July. Started as a neighborhood beautification project, the idea evolved and spread to the entire city; visitors can take organized garden walks, visit private homes' "open gardens," and take gardening workshops.

One of the nation's largest outdoor food fests is **Taste of Buffalo** (www.tasteofbuffalo.com), held in mid-July. Another food-focused festival is the **National Buffalo Wing Festival** (www.buffalowing.com), which celebrates Buffalo's contribution to pop food culture. Typically, it's held at the end of August or beginning of September.

For more information on these and other festivals, contact **Visit Buffalo Niagara** (716/852-2356, www.visitbuffaloniagara.com).

FOOD

Thanks to its diverse population, Buffalo has many inexpensive restaurants representing a range of cultural influences and flavors. The city is also the birthplace of two unique food specialties. One is **Buffalo chicken wings:** spicy wings served mild, medium, or hot, with celery sticks and blue cheese dressing, invented at Anchor Bar. The other Buffalo-unique nosh is the **beef-on-'weck sandwich:** thinly sliced roast beef piled high on fresh kimmelweck rolls sprinkled with pretzel salt and caraway seeds.

Downtown

In the Theater District, **Bijou Grille** (643 Main St., 716/847-1512, www.bijougrille.com, Mon. 11am-3pm, Tues.-Sun. 11am-11pm, $22), an Italian bistro, is a popular choice.

Try Buffalo's famous beef-on-'weck sandwich, along with a beer flight, at **Pearl Street Grill and Brewery** (76 Pearl St., 716/856-2337, www.pearlstreetgrill.com, Mon.-Sat. 11am-close, Sun. noon-close, $16).

Toutant (437 Ellicott St., 716/342-2901, www.toutantbuffalo.com, Thurs.-Mon. 5pm-midnight, Sunday brunch 11:30am-2:30pm, $22) takes a turn toward the south, with a menu featuring exceptional iterations of crawfish pie, jambalaya, and po'boys.

Other downtown options include

The Canalway Trail

The Canalway Trail is a network of more than 365 miles (590 km) of existing multi-use, recreational trails across upstate New York. Major segments follow remnants of the historic original canals of the early 1800s that have since been replaced with the working canal systems of today. **Erie Canal Heritage Trail** (518/434-1583, cycling maps available) connects with trails throughout New York State, providing one of the country's most extensive trail networks.

The canal system also offers excellent biking and walking. The **Erie Canalway Trail** (www.eriecanalway.org), a work in progress, is a nearly 400-mile-long (645 km), multiuse trail that, upon completion, will be the longest in the United States. Walking, running, hiking, cycling, and cross-country skiing are all allowed on the trail; some sections are paved and are safe for inline skating.

sushi at **SeaBar** (475 Ellicott St., 716/332-2928, www.seabarsushi.com, Mon.-Thurs. 11:30am-2:30pm and 4:30pm-9:30pm, Fri. 11:30am-2:30pm and 4:30pm-10:30pm, Sat. 4:30pm-10:30pm, $18) and steak at **Buffalo Chophouse** (282 Franklin St., 716/842-6900, www.buffalochophouse.com, Mon.-Sat. 4pm-10pm, Sun. 4pm-9pm, $46).

Allentown

Famed Buffalo institution the ★ **Anchor Bar** (1047 Main St., 716/886-8920, www.anchorbar.com, Mon.-Thurs. 11am-10pm, Fri. 11am-midnight, Sat. noon-midnight, Sun. noon-10pm, $20) is the friendly Italian restaurant where Buffalo chicken wings were invented in 1964 by Teressa Bellissimo, mother of the late owner Dominic Bellissimo. Live jazz is often featured on weekends.

At **Black Sheep Restaurant & Bar** (367 Connecticut St., 716/884-1100, www.blacksheepbuffalo.com, Wed.-Sat. 5pm-10pm, Sun. 11am-2pm, $28) you can taste the flavors of locally raised pork, as well as other meats, cheeses, and vegetables sourced in the region and New York State.

Greek American **Towne Restaurant** (186 Allen St., 716/884-5128, www.towneonallen. com, Tue.-Sat. 7am-11pm, Sun.-Mon. 7am-10pm, $18) is famed locally for its souvlaki.

Other Allentown picks are contemporary Italian spot **Tempo** (581 Delaware Ave., 716/885-1594, www.tempobuffalo.com, Mon.-Sat. 5pm-11pm, $34) and **Allen Street Hardware Café** (245 Allen St., 716/882-8843, www.allenstreethardware.com, Sun.-Thurs. 5pm-11pm, Fri.-Sat. 5pm-midnight, $18), with upscale comfort food and an extensive list of beer and wine.

ACCOMMODATIONS

To the east of downtown, in the suburb of Clarence (known for its many antiques stores), is acclaimed **Asa Ransom House** (10529 Main St., 716/759-2315, www.asaransom.com, $149-235, with breakfast). The 1853 inn features 10 spacious and lovely guest rooms and an excellent restaurant (Tue.-Fri. 5pm-8pm, Sat. 5pm-7:30pm, Sun. 4pm-8pm, $28) serving American fare by reservation.

A team of butlers awaits at ★ **The Mansion on Delaware Avenue** (414 Delaware Ave., 716/886-3300, www.mansionondelaware.com, $195-240) to offer complimentary touches like ushering you to your room after whipping up a welcome cocktail of your choice; shoeshine and pressing service; evening turndown service complete with homemade cookies; chauffeuring to and from local hot spots and eateries; or if the pull of the hotel makes a night in a temptation, they will arrange an order from any local restaurant, preparing a table either in your room or in the hotel's billiard room. European breakfast, a two-hour cocktail hour, whirlpool baths with multihead showers, and spa amenities all add to the good value.

The **Hotel @ The Lafayette** (391 Washington St., 716/853-1505, www.thehotellafayette.com, $195) is a centrally located downtown hotel, near many of the city's lovely, iconic skyscrapers. Though the lobby and hallways are dark, the hotel's large, comfortable rooms are filled with natural light. An upscale restaurant on-site gets rave reviews.

The 88 rooms at the **Hotel Henry** (444 Forest Ave., 716/882-1970, www.hotelhenry. com, $155) occupy what was once Buffalo's psychiatric hospital, which is surrounded by grounds designed by the same architects responsible for New York City's Central Park. The grounds have been updated with a small garden that supplies the on-site farm-to-table restaurant. The massive Gothic-style building has been completely renovated and, in addition to the hotel and restaurant, holds conference facilities and the Buffalo Architecture Center.

The 200-room **Buffalo Marriott at LECOM Harbor Center** (95 Main St., 716/852-0049, www.marriott.com, $299) is the best choice for visitors—especially families—who want to be close to the outdoor action of Canalside, which is literally just a few steps beyond the hotel's front door.

GETTING AROUND

Downtown Buffalo centers on Niagara Square and Buffalo Place. The **MetroRail** (716/855-7300, www.metro.nfta.com) runs along Main Street from the Buffalo River to the University at Buffalo South Campus. The system is above ground and free along Buffalo Place (Main St. south of Tupper St.); below ground, the fare starts at $2, is zoned, and can be complicated, but the $5 unlimited day pass is a good option. Tickets may be purchased from vending machines at all stations. Most downtown sites are within walking distance of each other. The downtown area has many parking lots. Elsewhere, street parking is usually available.

Vicinity of Buffalo

EAST AURORA

Along Route 20A southeast of Buffalo is East Aurora, an idyllic village surrounded by hilly dairy country. East Aurora was once home to President Millard Fillmore, and to Elbert Hubbard, a former soap salesman turned charismatic leader of the Arts and Crafts movement. "Conformists die, but heretics live forever," Hubbard was fond of saying. "Weep not peeling other people's onions."

Hubbard was the founder of an idealistic crafts community, the Roycrofters, whose Roycroft Campus (31 S. Grove St., 716/655-0261, www.roycroftcampuscorporation.com) still stands at the corner of Main and Grove Streets. Now a National Historic Landmark District, the 14-building complex still houses a number of artisans' workshops, along with gift shops, offices, a small museum, and Roycroft Inn.

At the heart of the campus, Copper Shop (31 S. Grove St., 716/655-0261) sells arts and crafts of Roycroft design. Down the street is the Elbert Hubbard-Roycroft Museum (363 Oakwood Ave., 716/652-4735, June-Oct. Wed. and Sat.-Sun. 1pm-3:15pm, $10), which documents the community's history. Nearby is Roycroft Inn (40 S. Grove St., 716/652-5552, www.roycroftinn.com).

Another must-stop is Vidler's 5 & 10 (676-694 Main St., 716/652-0481, www.vidlers5and10.com, Mon.-Thurs. 9am-6pm., Fri. 9am-9pm, Sat. 9am-6pm, Sun. 11am-5pm). A spiffy red-and-white awning flaps out front; inside are creaky wooden floors and display cases from the 1920s selling old-fashioned *stuff,* including penny candy, wooden animals, marbles, magic cards, Buster Brown socks, mousetraps, lace, and ribbon.

Just off Main Street is the 1826 Millard and Abigail Fillmore House (24 Shearer Ave., 716/652-4735, June-Oct. Wed. and Sat.-Sun. 1pm-4pm, adults $10, children 13-18 $5, children under 13 free), built by the future U.S. president with his own hands in 1826. Fillmore was then a young lawyer fresh off the farm.

Food and Accommodations

The handsome 1905 ★ Roycroft Inn (40 S. Grove St., 716/652-5552, www.roycroftinn. com, $195-350) is a one-of-a-kind place, filled with all original or reproduction Roycroft furnishings—mostly heavy, beautifully designed pieces in oak. All 28 suites have at least one sleeping area, a sitting area, and a whirlpool tub, while the common rooms feature fireplaces, rich wood paneling, and Roycraft lamps. The inn's restaurant (Mon.-Sat. 11:30am-3pm, Sun. brunch 10am-2pm, dinner Mon.-Thurs. 5pm-9pm, Fri.-Sat. 5pm-10pm, Sun. 4:30pm-9pm, $28) serves innovative American cuisine with a continental touch.

Just outside East Aurora sprawls Old Orchard (2095 Blakeley Corners Rd., 716/652-4664, www.oldorchardny.com, hours vary seasonally, $38), a historic farmhouse and former hunting lodge dating back to 1901, with large stone fireplaces. The menu features American/continental fare.

To the southwest of East Aurora is Colden Lakes (9504 Heath Rd., Colden, 716/941-5530, www.coldenlakes.com, $40), offering 140 campsites and some cabins. To the southeast is Sleepy Hollow Lake (13800 Siehl Rd., Akron, 585/542-4336, www.sleepyhollowcamp.com, $30-48), offering 200 campsites.

Locals love Rick's on Main (687 Main St., 716/652-1253, www.ricksonmain.com, Mon.-Sat. lunch and dinner, $35), which has plenty of surf and turf options. A favorite menu item is the restaurant's soup sampler, which includes small cups of three of its signature soups.

EDEN

As the self-proclaimed "Garden Spot of New York State," Eden, just about 30 miles (48 km) south of Buffalo on Route 62, is a pristine small town surrounded by farm country. The main attraction here is the Original American Kazoo Company: Museum, Gift Shop, Factory (8703 S. Main St., 716/992-3960, www.edenkazoo.com, Tues.-Thurs. and Sat. 10am-5pm, Fri. 10am-7pm, $2 for a guided tour). Established in 1916, the Original is now the only metal kazoo factory in the world. The company paid $5,000 for its first kazoo patent and still manufactures kazoos the way it always has, using die presses and sheet metal. On display is a wooden kazoo, similar to its African prototype, and liquor-bottle-shaped kazoos made to celebrate the end of Prohibition. The record for the most kazoos ever played at one time was set in Rochester on January 2, 1986, when 54,500 kazoo-ists performed.

GRAND ISLAND

Just north of Buffalo is Grand Island, the country's largest freshwater island. About five square miles larger than Manhattan, Grand Island was once intended to be a refuge for persecuted Jews and was also considered as a possible site for the United Nations; both plans were eventually discarded. Today, the island serves an entirely different purpose. Primarily a suburban community, Grand Island is also home to Fantasy Island (2400 Grand Island Blvd., 716/773-7591, www.fantasyislandny.com, hours vary seasonally, adults $25.95, seniors $17.95, children under 48 in/122 cm tall $20.95), an 80-acre theme park with thrill rides, live entertainment, and a petting zoo.

NORTH TONAWANDA

In the sprawling industrial city of North Tonawanda, directly across the river from Grand Island, is the old Herschell Carrousel Factory (180 Thompson St., 716/693-1885, www.carrouselmuseum.org, hours vary seasonally, adults $7, seniors $5, children 2-16 $3.50). In its heyday in the 1920s and 1930s, the plant produced over 50 carousels a year. Until 1928, all featured animals were carved entirely of wood; after 1928, the magical creatures were half-wood and half-aluminum.

Now both an informal museum and a workshop, the old factory contains a major exhibit on Allan Herschell, an expert woodcarver who was once the best-known carousel maker in the United States. Also on display are hand-carved animals dating back to the early 1900s and new carved animals in various states of completion. Adults as well as kids are invited to ride the working 1916 carousel that spins out back.

A landscaped Heritage Trail connects the museum with other locales of interest, such as the tiny Railroad Museum (111 Oliver St., North Tonawanda, 716/694-9588, June-Aug. Sat. 1pm-4pm, adults $2, children under 12 free) and the performing arts center of Riviera Theatre (67 Webster St., North Tonawanda,716/692-2413, www.rivieratheatre.org) near Gateway City.

Whimsical restaurant ★ Old Man River (375 Niagara St., Tonawanda, 716/693-5558, www.oldmanriverwny.com, hours vary seasonally, $12) sports a whale on its roof and washing machine fountains. On the menu is everything from Sahlen's hot dogs, a Buffalo specialty, to sweet potato french fries. Almost as quirky, and serving a similar menu, is Mississippi Mudds (313 Niagara St., Tonawanda, 716/694-0787, www.mississippimuddswny.com, hours vary seasonally, $12).

Niagara Falls

The name Niagara Falls refers to both the famed waterfalls and the city where they are located. The city is nondescript, surrounded by industrial plants and humming electrical wires; the Robert Moses Niagara Power Plant provides electricity for much of the northeastern United States. But the falls . . . ah, well, the falls. Despite the tourists, hoopla, and clichés, the falls are a sight to be seen. Stand in front of that white wall of water and you'll catch your breath. Guaranteed.

The falls began forming about 12,000 years ago at the end of the Ice Age. As the last glaciers melted away, huge torrents of water channeled along what is now the Niagara River, tumbling over the Niagara Escarpment. The water began eating away at the escarpment, and the falls slowly moved upstream. Today, the falls cascade 7 miles (11.3 km) from their original location through a canyon known as Niagara Gorge.

Located along the Niagara River between the United States and Canada, Niagara Falls are actually three falls: American Falls and Bridal Veil Falls on the New York side, and Horseshoe Falls on the Ontario side. The thundering water is on its way from four of the Great Lakes—Superior, Michigan, Huron, and Erie—to the fifth, Ontario.

NIAGARA FALLS, NEW YORK

The city of Niagara Falls has a compact downtown, adjacent to Niagara Falls State Park. While less commercialized than the Canadian side of the falls, the U.S. side is not without its tourist traps, including Seneca Niagara Casino. If the flash and dazzle of casino lights make you dizzy, stop by Niagara Tourism and Convention Corporation's Visitor Center (10 Rainbow Blvd., 716/282-8992, www.niagarafallsusa.com, June-mid-Sept. daily 9am-7pm, mid-Sept.-May daily 9am-5pm) to get oriented to the small city's other sites of interest. The staff can provide free maps and assist with booking tours.

TOP EXPERIENCE

★ Niagara Falls State Park

The falls and their accompanying attractions, including an interactive visitors center, are located on the western edge of the city in Niagara Falls State Park (off Robert Moses Pkwy., 716/278-1796, www.niagarafallsstatepark.com, parking $10). Established in 1885, it is America's oldest state park. The falls, which had been "remote as the moon" for most of the 18th century according to Canadian writer Pierre Berton, had by the turn of the century become a notorious tourist trap.

In the mid-1800s, the land surrounding Niagara Falls was privately owned and visitors who wanted to see the waterfalls had to pay clever entrepreneurs a fee to glimpse the mighty wonder. One traveler of the day griped, "I know of no place where one is so constantly pestered, where hackmen so incessantly worry you when you want to be at peace, where you are so dogged over every inch of ground you tread."

By the end of the 19th century, Niagara Falls would become no less of a tourist attraction, but it *would* become more accessible and the area around it more groomed, thanks to artist Frederick Church, landscape architect Frederick Law Olmsted, and the "Free Niagara" movement, established around 1870. For 15 years, the movement's proponents lobbied heavily to establish a park at the falls. Political opposition was enormous, but in 1885, Governor David Hill finally signed an appropriations bill that marked the beginning not only of Niagara Park, but also of the entire New York State Park System.

Today, Niagara Falls State Park receives millions of visitors a year. People come from

Niagara Falls

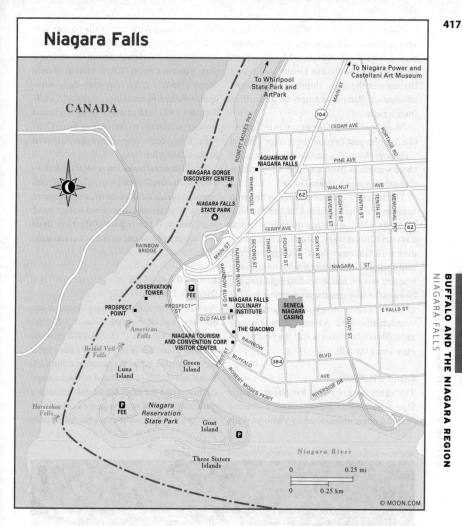

all over the world to stroll through the park, enjoy the gardens, and, of course, see the falls. Visitors can also board a **trolley** that makes stops at key sites throughout the park. *Maid of the Mist* and Cave of the Winds tours operate from the park; for visitors who don't want to get quite so close to the watery action, excellent views of the falls can be had from the park's **observation deck.**

There are two main **entrances** to the park. One is at Prospect Point, the other at Goat Island.

PROSPECT POINT

Prospect Point is the best place to view the falls on the New York side. The point sits at the edge of the American Falls' 1,100-foot (340 m) brink, where you can look straight down into the foamy, turbulent waters. Rainbows often form in the cataract's mist.

The **Visitor Center** (716/278-1796, daily 8am-6pm, with extended hours in summer, free) can also be accessed via Prospect Point; here, visitors can get information about the falls and the park's attractions.

Niagara Falls Scenic Trolleys (daily 9am-4:30pm, with extended hours in summer, adults $3, children 6-12 $2) depart from behind the Visitor Center and travel throughout the park, stopping at all points of interest. Riders can hop on and off at their leisure.

Niagara Falls Observation Tower ($1.25 pp) is just beyond the Visitor Center; it features dramatic, panoramic views of all three waterfalls from an open-air platform that extends over Niagara Gorge.

The tower's elevators also travel down to the foot of the falls, where *Maid of the Mist* (716/284-8897, www.maidofthemist.com, days and hours vary, adults $22.25, children 6-12 $13) boats dock. Visitors are given rain slickers before being herded onto sturdy wooden vessels, which head straight into the bases of the falls, passing almost close enough to touch. Spray stings, boats rock, and water thunders all around. A tourist attraction since 1846, *Maid of the Mist* is still the best way to experience the falls.

GOAT ISLAND

The other access point for Niagara Falls State Park is quieter Goat Island, a wooded flatland often overlooked by visitors. With Bridal Veil and American Falls on one side and Horseshoe Falls on the other, the island provides a very different view of the cataracts than Prospect Point. **Cave of the Winds tours** (716/278-1730, May-Oct. daily 9am-7pm, weather permitting, adults $11, children 6-12 $8) lead visitors along drenched wooden walkways to the base of Bridal Veil Falls. Thankfully, rain slickers are included in the ticket price.

Goat Island is flanked by several smaller islands, including **Three Sisters Islands,** surrounded on all sides by swift, white-capped waters. Step out onto these specks of land and you'll feel as if you're part of the river itself and about to be swept over the curved edge of the falls.

NIAGARA GORGE DISCOVERY CENTER

Perched on the edge of Niagara Gorge, at the northern end of the park, **Niagara Gorge Discovery Center** (716/278-1070, guided walking tours 716/745-7848, daily 9am-5pm, with extended hours in summer, adults $3, children 6-12 $2) is dedicated to the geological history of the falls. Highlights include a multimedia show on the gorge's formation and fossil and mineral exhibits. A footpath

American Falls is one of the three waterfalls that comprise Niagara Falls.

leads from the museum deep into the gorge; explore on your own or take a guided walking tour with a park naturalist. Hikes vary in length and difficulty.

Aquarium of Niagara

Open year-round, the **Aquarium of Niagara** (701 Whirlpool St., 716/285-3575. www.aquariumofniagara.org, daily 9am-5pm, adults $14.95, seniors $12.95, children 3-12 $10.95) features more than 125 species of marine mammals, birds, and reptiles.

Downtown Niagara Falls

TOP EXPERIENCE

NIAGARA FALLS UNDERGROUND RAILROAD HERITAGE CENTER

Opened in 2018, the Niagara Falls Underground Railroad Heritage Center (825 Depot Ave. W., 716/300-8477, www.nigarafallsundergroundrailroad.org, Tue.-Sat. 10am-6pm, Sun. 10am-4pm, adults $10, seniors $8, children 6-12 $6) is a vital addition to the cultural and historical offerings of the region, given that this area of the state was a primary waypoint (and last stop, in most cases) on the Underground Railroad. The center is located in the 1863 U.S. Customs House, which, while not a stop on the Railroad itself, was located next to the former International Suspension Bridge, which many freedom-seekers crossed. The center features an interactive permanent exhibit and "freedom conversation tours," which are included in the ticket price.

SENECA NIAGARA CASINO

Seneca Niagara Casino & Hotel (310 4th St., 716/299-1100, www.senecaniagaracasino.com, 24 hours a day) looms large as downtown's tallest building. The casino holds about 4,000 slot machines, plenty of games tables, and theater venues where pop stars and comedians perform. There are also a nightclub and several restaurants on-site.

NIAGARA FALLS CULINARY INSTITUTE

Niagara Falls Culinary Institute (28 Old Falls St., 716/210-2525, www.nfculinary.org, hours vary seasonally) opened in the fall of 2012 in a former shopping mall. Students in Niagara Community College's culinary arts, hospitality, and restaurant management programs take classes and fulfill their internships in the center, which houses a bakery, deli, and fine dining restaurant, all open to the public. The institute also operates a wine boutique specializing in New York State wines, and the country's only Barnes and Noble dedicated to food-themed titles.

Tours

Two of the most popular falls tours are offered by concessioners operating out of Niagara Falls State Park. *Maid of the Mist* (716/284-8897, www.maidofthemist.com, hours vary by season, adults $22.25, children 6-12 $13) is a boat tour with close-up views of the falls; **Cave of the Winds** (716/278-1730, hours vary by season, weather permitting, adults $11, children 6-12 $8) is a walking tour that takes visitors into the "stormy mist zone" behind Bridal Veil Falls. Visitors who purchase a "Discovery Pass" at **Niagara Tourism and Convention Corporation's Visitor Center** (10 Rainbow Blvd., 716/282-8992, www.niagarafallsusa.com, June-mid-Sept. daily 9am-7pm, mid-Sept.-May daily 9am-5pm) or in the state park can take both tours at a discount.

Other tour options include **Gray Line of Niagara Falls** (716/285-2113, www.graylineniagarafalls.com) and **Bedore Tours** (716/696-3200, www.bedoretours.com). For a different perspective on the falls, **Rainbow Air** (454 Main St., 716/284-2800, www.rainbowairinc.com) is available for helicopter tours.

Food

The 2012 opening of **Niagara Falls Culinary Institute** (28 Old Falls St., 716/210-2525,

www.nfculinary.org) was a boon for the downtown's struggling restaurant scene, where uninspired, mediocre menus were once the norm. Within the institute's complex are café-bakery **La Patisserie** (716/210-2587, hours vary seasonally) and the full-service, fine dining option, **Savor** (716/210-2580, hours vary seasonally, $25). Savor has a large, open kitchen where staff, including supervised culinary students, can be seen preparing meals; an advance reservation for the restaurant's chef's table can be made for groups of six or more.

The spectacular view of Horseshoe Falls is the main reason to eat at casual ★ **Top of the Falls Restaurant** (Terrapin Point, Goat Island, 716/278-0340, hours vary seasonally, $18), located within Niagara Falls State Park. It serves contemporary American cuisine, including lots of fish and pasta dishes, as well as salads, soups, and sandwiches. If you haven't yet tried the local specialty beef-on-'weck sandwich, you can do so here.

For burgers, there's the requisite tourist joint, **Hard Rock Cafe** (333 Prospect St., 716/282-0007, www.hardrock.com, daily 11am-midnight, $19), where you can also pick up your "Hard Rock Cafe Niagara Falls" T-shirt.

Accommodations

B&B options in the area include **Hillcrest Inn** (1 Hillcrest St., 716/278-9676, www.hillcrestniagara.com, $159-193), which has four guest rooms. A full, hot breakfast, served on the sunporch overlooking the river or in the Asian-themed dining room, is included.

Hotel Giacomo (222 First St., 716/299-0200, www.thegiacomo.com, $120-249) is a 39-room luxury boutique hotel in a historic art deco high-rise. Breakfast and valet parking are included.

The Seneca Nation of Indians is one of six nations that comprise the Iroquois Confederacy, which supports its communities with a variety of cultural and economic efforts. One of these is **Seneca Niagara Casino & Hotel** (310 4th St., 716/299-1100, www.senecaniagaracasino.com, $195-400). The property also offers a full-service spa in a modern, showy 26-floor, 600+-room casino hotel, with all the benefits and drawbacks that might entail.

If you prefer roughing it, the Niagara region has several excellent campgrounds, including **Golden Hill State Park** (9691 Lower Lake Rd., Barker, 716/795-3885, www.parks.ny.gov/parks/143, $15-31/night), on Lake Ontario's shore. The small campground has tent sites and trails for hiking and biking. It's a 50-minute drive from downtown Niagara Falls along the shoreline.

NIAGARA FALLS, ONTARIO, CANADA

Niagara's most spectacular cataract is **Horseshoe Falls,** best viewed from **Queen Victoria Park** (905/356-2241) over the Canadian border in Ontario. Though slightly shorter than American Falls—176 feet (54 m) as opposed to 184 (54 m)—Horseshoe Falls boasts a much wider brink (2,200 ft/670 m) and handles about 90 percent of the river's volume of flow.

Considerably more built up than the American side, the Canadian side is also more stylish and more commercial. **Rainbow Bridge,** near Prospect Point, crosses over the border into Queen Victoria Park. A passport is required to cross the border. The amount of time it takes to cross varies considerably, depending on the day and time of crossing, as well as the time of year. At peak times, it could take as long as an hour. For real-time border-crossing conditions, check www.ez-bordercrossing.com. There is a toll collected (automobiles US$4/CAN$5.25, pedestrians US$1/CAN$1).

Once on the other side, a **WeGo bus** operates among all points of interest. A 24-hour pass costs CAN$9 for adults and CAN$6 for

1: Cave of the Winds 2: view of Niagara Falls from the observation deck 3: view of Horseshoe Falls from the Canadian side 4: Niagara Falls State Park trolley

kids. For route maps and schedules, visit www.wegoniagarafalls.com.

A high point of a visit to the Canadian side is the **Journey Behind the Falls** (enter at Table Rock Welcome Centre, 6650 Niagara Pkwy., 905/354-1551, www.niagarafallslive.com, June-Sept. daily 9am-11pm, Oct.-May daily 9am-5pm, adults CAN$15 plus tax, children 6-12 CAN$10). Out come the big yellow slickers again, followed by a walk *behind* Horseshoe Falls.

Along nearby Clifton Hill stands one kitsch museum after another: **Guinness Museum of World Records** (4943 Clifton Hill, 905/356-2299, summer Sun.-Thurs. 9am-midnight, Fri.-Sat. 9am-1am, call for hours for other seasons, adults $16.99, seniors $14.99, children $11.99); **Ripley's Believe It or Not** (4960 Clifton Hill, 905/356-2238, www.ripleys.com/niagarafalls, Mon.-Thurs. 10am-midnight, Fri. 10am-1am, Sat. 9am-1am, Sun. 9am-11pm, adults $18.99, seniors $15.99, children $12.99) and **Louis Tussaud's Waxworks** (5709 Victoria Ave., 905/356-2238, Mon.-Thurs. 10am-midnight, Fri. 10am-1am, Sat. 9am-1am, Sun. 9am-11pm, adults $14.99, seniors $11.99, children $9.99).

A good restaurant offering buffet-style dining and superb views revolves atop the **Skylon Tower** (5200 Robinson St., 905/356-2651, www.skylon.com, daily 11:30am-3pm and 4:30pm-10pm, Sun. lunch in peak season only, CAN$60).

Those traveling with kids or fans of thrill rides might consider the **Great Wolf Lodge** (3950 Victoria Ave., 800/605-9653, www.greatwolf.com/niagara, $180-240), just over the border and minutes from the impressive Horseshoe Falls, as a place to stay. The lodge has good rooms and suites in a Northwood's theme, a full-service spa, two adults-only whirlpools (one, a year-round outdoor offering with indoor water entrance), wave pool, lazy river, and six giant grown-up-size tube or raft rides, including a water roller coaster. For children, there is a nightly cookies and milk bedtime story told next to the animal-covered clock tower in the lobby.

For more information about attractions on the Canadian side of the falls, contact the **Niagara Falls, Canada Visitors and Convention Bureau** (6815 Stanley Ave., 905/356-6061 or 800/563-2557, www.niagarafallstourism.com, Mon.-Fri. 9am-5pm).

North of Niagara Falls

WHIRLPOOL STATE PARK

Heading north of Niagara Falls on Robert Moses Parkway, you'll pass **Whirlpool State Park** (Robert Moses Pkwy., 716/284-4691, www.parks.ny.gov/parks/105, open year-round dawn-dusk, free), offering great views of a giant, swirling whirlpool, and **Devil's Hole State Park** (Robert Moses Pkwy., 716/284-5778, www.parks.ny.gov/parks/42, open year-round dawn-dusk, free), situated along the Niagara River's lower rapids. Both parks feature hiking trails.

NIAGARA POWER PROJECT

North of the parks reigns the immense **Niagara Power Project** (5777 Lewiston Rd., 716/286-6661, daily 9am-5pm, free), one of the largest hydroelectric plants in the world. During the tourist season, about half of Niagara River's water power (or 100,000 of 202,000 cubic feet) is diverted away from the falls for the production of electricity here and in Canada; at other times, that ratio rises to 75 percent.

The plant's visitors center does an excellent job explaining the principles of hydroelectric

The Underground Railroad

Michigan Street Baptist Church

From the early 1800s to the Civil War's end in 1865, the Buffalo-Niagara corridor, a collection of towns along the U.S.-Canada border, served as one of the last stops on the Underground Railroad for slaves traveling north toward freedom. Though few records were kept, it is estimated that as many as 30,000 people may have passed through the area on their way to Canada.

Today, there are several places where visitors can learn more about the region's role in the Underground Railroad:

- **Freedom Crossing Monument** (Lewiston Landing Park, Water St., Lewiston): This moving sculpture, crafted by local artist Susan Geissler, depicts a dramatic moment in the pursuit of freedom: Lewiston's Underground Railroad station master, Josiah Tryon, is handing a baby to its fugitive mother.

- **Michigan Street Baptist Church** (511 Michigan Ave., Buffalo): This small, modest church, built in 1845, hosted many of the abolition movement's luminaries, including Frederick Douglass, W. E. B. DuBois, and Booker T. Washington, and functioned as a station on the Underground Railroad. Though hours are irregular, visitors who happen to get lucky will be treated to a rich oral history narrated by clergy.

- **St. John's AME Church** (917 Garden Ave., Niagara Falls): St. John's was one of the first African American churches founded in Niagara County. Fugitive slaves could see the beckoning lights of Canada and freedom from the church's hillside location.

- **Thomas Root Home** (3106 Upper Mountain Rd., Pekin): Located midway between Niagara Falls and Lockport, the former Root home contains a trapdoor leading to a 5-by-10-foot (1.5-by-3 m) cellar. Here "volumes bound in black," as the coded messages once read, spent the night before being driven to the border, hidden beneath piles of vegetables. The house is now privately owned, but the station is set amidst a small row of pine trees accessible to the public.

power through hands-on exhibits and computer games. Also on-site are exhibits on Niagara Falls, past and present. Enjoy outstanding views of Niagara Gorge from the plant's observation deck.

CASTELLANI ART MUSEUM

Niagara University is home to **Castellani Art Museum** (5795 Lewiston Rd., 716/286-8200, www.castellaniartmuseum.org, Tues.-Sat. 11am-5pm, free). The museum's roomy galleries house work by contemporary artists, including big names like David Hockney, Charles Burchfield, Alexander Calder, Willem de Kooning, Cindy Sherman, and Nam June Paik. The museum's strong Folk Arts Program sponsors temporary exhibits on such subjects as Polish American Easter traditions, African American gospel traditions, and Halloween.

LEWISTON AND VICINITY

Continue north of the power project about 4 miles (6.4 km) to Lewiston. It's here where Niagara Falls originated thousands of years before glacial melt carved Niagara Gorge. It's here where the first significant battle of the War of 1812 was staged. And it's here where fleeing slaves made their final stop on the Underground Railroad before crossing the Niagara River and finding freedom in Canada. For more information on the history of the village, visit the **Historical Association of Lewiston** (469 Plain St., 716/754-4214, www.historiclewiston.org).

Freedom Crossing Monument

Local sculptor Susan Geissler created the **Freedom Crossing Monument** (Lewiston Landing Park, Water St.), drawing inspiration from real-life Underground Railroad station master Josiah Tryon, a Lewiston native, and from the children's book *Freedom Crossing*. The moving artwork shows Tryon handing a fugitive slave's child to its mother after Tryon ferried the freedom-seeking pair across Niagara River. Look carefully to find messages

and clues engraved on the figures; these tell more of the Freedom Crossing story. You'll notice quotes, Bible passages, and other cryptic engravings on each figure. The numbers on Tryon, for instance, are the GPS coordinates of his gravesite.

Artpark

The only state park in the United States devoted to visual and performing arts, **Artpark** (450 S. 4th St., 716/754-4375, www.artpark. net, daily 8am-dusk, parking $5-10, events vary in price) occupies 150 acres on Lewiston's southern edge. All sorts of events are staged during summer, including concerts, storytelling, acrobatics, and theater and dance workshops. Other park features include hiking trails; the 2,400-seat **Mainstage Theater,** which hosts national acts; and a burial mound dating back over 2,000 years to a time when the area was inhabited by the Hopewell. The mound, 30 feet (9 m) long by 20 feet (6 m) wide, is listed in the National Register of Historic Places.

Food and Accommodations

Lewiston isn't large, so lodging and food options aren't abundant; however, its location between Buffalo and Niagara Falls and its small-town, non-touristy vibe make the village a nice spot to overnight when you're exploring the Buffalo-Niagara area.

Niagara Crossing Hotel and Spa (100 Center St., 716/754-9070, www.niagaracrossinghotelandspa.com, $143-224) is a comfortable boutique hotel right near the waterfront, a three-minute walk to both Freedom Crossing Monument and adjacent restaurant and scoop shop, **The Silo** (115 N. Water St., 716/754-9680, www.lewistonsilo.com, May-Sept. daily 10am-10pm, $10). At The Silo, humble fare like burgers, fish and chicken sandwiches, and fries is complemented by excellent, close-up views of Niagara River. Save room for ice

---

1: Whirlpool State Park **2:** The Silo restaurant in Lewiston **3:** Old Fort Niagara in Youngstown **4:** Erie Canal locks in Lockport

Erie Canal

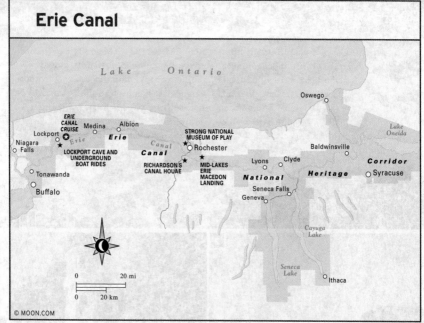

Lake Ontario

Oswego

Lake Oneida

ERIE CANAL CRUISE

Lockport   Medina   Albion

Niagara   *Erie*   *Erie*
Falls

LOCKPORT CAVE AND
UNDERGROUND
BOAT RIDES

STRONG NATIONAL
MUSEUM OF PLAY
Rochester

Canal   *Canal*

RICHARDSON'S
CANAL HOUAE

MID-LAKES
ERIE
MACEDON
LANDING

Lyons   Clyde

Baldwinsville

National

Seneca Falls

Geneva

Corridor

Syracuse

Heritage

Tonawanda

Buffalo

Cayuga
Lake

Seneca
Lake

Ithaca

0   20 mi

0   20 km

© MOON.COM

cream, which is served from the window of the caboose parked permanently next to The Silo.

OLD FORT NIAGARA

Even if you have no interest in military history, it's worth continuing a few miles north of Lewiston to Youngstown and **Old Fort Niagara** (off Robert Moses Pkwy., 716/745-7611, www.oldfortniagara.org, Sept.-June daily 9am-5pm, July-Aug. daily 9am-7pm, adults $15, children 6-12 $10). Strategically located at the mouth of the Niagara River, where it controlled access to the Great Lakes, the fort is a strikingly handsome place with commanding views of Lake Ontario.

Fort Niagara was established by the French in 1726, taken over by the British in 1759, turned over to Americans by treaty in 1796, recaptured by the British in 1813, and finally returned to American control in 1815. After these wartime transfers of power, Fort Niagara served as a peacetime border post and remained occupied by the U.S. military until

1963. Its oldest standing structure is the 1726 French Castle, a rectangular stone edifice equipped with a bakery, guardhouse, living quarters, and chapel.

During summer, visitors can witness daily military musters and fife-and-drum drills. **Fort Niagara State Park** (716/745-7273, www.parks.ny.gov/parks/175, hours vary seasonally, $8 vehicle entry fee), with easy hiking trails, playgrounds, and swimming pools, surrounds the fort.

WILSON AND BARKER

The towns of Wilson and Barker are a short drive east of Old Fort Niagara. Both are located on the shore of Lake Ontario in Niagara County. The towns are an ideal side jaunt for visitors interested in New York State's ever-growing craft beer and cider culture. Along the way, keep an eye open for some excellent examples of cobblestone houses, a unique form of architecture once popular in this part of the state. **Woodcock Brothers Brewery** (638 Lake St., Wilson,

Building the Erie Canal

Flour merchant Jesse Hawley was one of the first New Yorkers to articulate a vision for what would become the Erie Canal. Hawley, who had gone broke spending money to transport his goods across the state, wrote 14 newspaper essays from his debtor's prison cell promoting a canal. When President Jefferson first heard of the plan, he said, "It is a splendid project and may be executed a century hence … but it is little short of madness to think of it at this day." Not every politician shared Jefferson's skepticism; when the essays came to the attention of DeWitt Clinton, he became an enthusiastic promoter of the canal and was swept into the New York governor's office in 1817 on a pro-canal platform.

Work on the canal began that very year. An engineering marvel of its day, the canal was built almost entirely by shovel and pickax, by men who had no engineering experience. Many of the canal builders were recent Irish immigrants earning 80 cents an hour. They started in Rome, where light soil ensured rapid progress. In 1819, the first 15-mile-long (24 km) section of canal opened between Rome and Utica. Progress was slow, though; it would take another six years before the canal was completed, prompting naysayers to dub the canal "Clinton's Ditch" and "Clinton's Folly."

Work was grueling and often dangerous. Close to 1,000 men died of malaria while running the canal through Montezuma Swamp. Others died while constructing locks through the Niagara Escarpment—a solid wall of rock rising 565 feet (170 m) above sea level.

When the canal was finally finished in 1825, it was 360 miles (580 km) long, 40 feet (12 m) wide, and 4 feet (1.2 m) deep. A towpath for mules and drivers who pulled the barges before the advent of steam power ran alongside the canal.

The astonishing success of the Erie Canal sparked a canal-building craze, and between 1823 and 1828, several important lateral canals opened, including the Champlain, Oswego, and Cayuga-Seneca. The canals were enlarged three times over the years to accommodate larger boats, but by the 1950s, New York's canal system was all but obsolete when enormous St. Lawrence Seaway was completed.

For more information on cruising or biking along the canal, contact New York State Canal Corporation (518/471-5016, www.canals.ny.gov).

716/333-4000, www.woodcockbrothersbrewery.com, Tue.-Thurs. noon-9pm, Fri.-Sat. noon-10pm, Sun. noon-8pm) is the county's first brewery, housed in the old Wilson Cold Storage facility, where apples grown in the region were held before shipping. The cavernous interior of the on-site restaurant delights lovers of vintage design, as the owners preserved many original elements of the century-old building. Pizza from a wood-fired oven is the specialty here.

The first hard cider producer in Niagara County was BlackBird Cider Works (8503 Lower Lake Rd., Barker, 716/795-3580, www.blackbirdciders.com, days and hours vary by season), which has a small and inviting tasting room right on the edge of the cidery's orchard. On weekends, staff offers $3 and $5 tastings of ciders.

LOCKPORT

Just south of Wilson is the Erie Canal town of Lockport. Nearby, Locks District Museum (80 Richmond Ave., at Locks 34 and 35, 716/434-3140, May-Oct. daily 8am-5pm, free) documents the area's canal history, with photos from 1812 to the present. Down the street, Lockport Cave and Underground Boat Ride (ticket office at 5 Gooding St., 716/438-0174, www.lockportcave.com, hours vary seasonally, adults $15, children $10) takes visitors through five flights of locks, industrial ruins, and a 2,430-foot-long (740 m) tunnel blasted out of solid rock in the late 1850s.

Other area sites of interest include the art, education, and recreation facility, Kenan Center (433 Locust St., 716/433-2617, www. kenancenter.org, days and hours vary by season, free); **Erie Canal Discovery Center** (24 Church St., 716/439-0431, www.niagarahistory.org/discovery-center, adults $6, seniors $5, kids free with adult admission), which presents interactive exhibits highlighting the role Lockport played in opening the canal; and **Arrowhead Spring Vineyards** (4746 Townline Rd., 716/434-8030, www.arrowheadspring.com, daily noon-5pm, $5 tasting fee), which has a tasting room with friendly, knowledgeable staff.

★ Erie Canal Cruise

The construction of the Erie Canal catapulted New York into the industrial age; an explosion of trade between the East and Midwest occurred after its completion in 1825. Facilitating trade and transport, the canal's tolls had more than paid for the entire cost of its $7.7 million construction less than a decade after it opened. Pre-Erie Canal, New York City was the nation's fifth-largest seaport, behind Boston, Baltimore, Philadelphia, and New Orleans. Fifteen years after the canal's opening, New York was America's busiest port, moving tonnages greater than those of Boston, Baltimore, and New Orleans combined.

With the exception of Binghamton and Elmira, every major city in New York falls along the trade route established by the Erie Canal. While currently less than 100 commercial barges ply the waters between Buffalo and Albany each year, approximately 75 percent of the state's population still lives along corridors created by the canals and the Hudson River.

Today, the New York State Canal System primarily serves as a low-key, relatively unknown tourist attraction for boaters, bikers, and day-trippers. Two-hour cruises of the canal, highlighted by a trip through Locks 34 and 35, are offered by **Lockport Locks & Erie Canal Cruises** (210 Market St., 716/433-6155, www.lockportlocks.com, May-Oct., adults $18.50, children 4-10 $10). Macedon's Mid-Lakes Erie Macedon Landing is the home marina to **Erie Canal Adventures** (315/986-3011, www.eriecanaladventures.com), where you can learn to drive one of the gleaming wooden canal boats and relive a bit of history. These easy-to-pilot boats can be driven by anyone with a few lessons. Guided multiday tours are also available for those leery of taking the helm.

Orleans County

If you enjoy rural landscapes, unique architecture, and occasional stops at farm stands, a drive through Orleans County, east of Niagara, might be a fine way to spend a day in western New York. It's one of the flattest and quietest areas in the state, and agriculture is the number one industry here; enormous fruit and vegetable farms spread out along the area's highways and byways. Route 104, which cuts through the center of the county, is peppered with pick-your-own farms.

Albion, the county capital, and Medina, the main commercial center, are small historic villages along the Erie Canal. To the north are Lake Ontario and Point Breeze, a harbor known for its world-class salmon fishing. Orleans County is also the best place in the state to learn about cobblestone architecture, a building style that is all but unique to New York.

MEDINA

The main attraction in Medina is its wide, old-fashioned Main Street, flanked by mid-19th-century buildings. Many were built of local red sandstone and still house thriving small businesses such as bakeries, variety stores, and clothing shops.

Orleans County

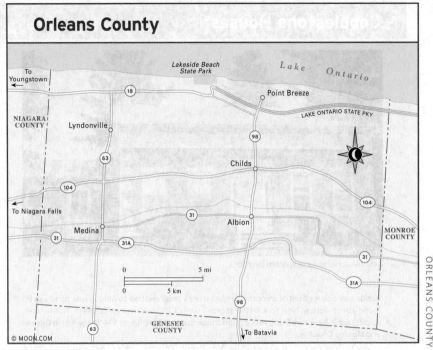

St. John's Episcopal Church (200 E. Center St., 585/798-3219) once listed in *Ripley's Believe It or Not* as "the church in the middle of the street," sits on East Center Street, just east of Main Street. At the north end of Main Street you'll find the Erie Canal and a boat basin in which canal boats once turned around. While driving through town, be sure to look up when on **Culvert Road**, where the road crosses *beneath* the canal.

The **Medina Railroad Museum** (530 West Ave., 585/798-6106, www.medinarailroadmuseum.org, Tues.-Sun. 11am-5pm, adults $9, seniors $8, children 13-19 $5), a century-old New York Central freight depot, houses an interactive exhibit based on HO scale trains. Admission is included with any of the many themed railroad trips aboard a 1947 vintage Budd passenger coach. Fall foliage, winery excursions, and family-friendly Polar Express trips depart from the museum (fares vary by tour).

CHILDS

If you were to speed through Childs, you likely wouldn't see anything worth stopping for. Slow down, though, and you might notice something that put Childs on the map: its cobblestone structures, whose unique architectural style also earned the town a listing in the National Register of Historic Places. The **Cobblestone Society Museum** (14393 Rte. 104, at Route 98, 585/589-9013, www.cobblestonemuseum.org, summer Wed.-Sat. 11am-5pm, Sun. 1pm-5pm, adults $10, seniors $8, children 5 and up $3) is housed in the basement of one of the oldest and best preserved of New York's 25 cobblestone churches, dating back to 1834. Simple exhibits explain the masonry's history and technique, while upstairs is an intimate sanctuary lined with wood. Next door stand two more cobblestone buildings—an 1849 schoolhouse and an 1840 house filled with Victorian-era furnishings. Also on-site are reconstructed blacksmith and print shops.

Cobblestone Houses

a cobblestone house in western New York

Handsome houses built of smooth rounded stones small enough to hold in one hand can be found across western New York. Of the approximately 1,200 cobblestone houses in North America, 800 are in New York State, with a good concentration along Route 104 (Ridge Rd.) in Orleans and Monroe Counties.

Cobblestone masonry is an ancient form of construction dating back to Roman times; it can be found in parts of England, Italy, and France. New York's tradition of cobblestone masonry began after the construction of the Erie Canal. Masons from Ireland and England who worked on the canal settled in the area, where they found abundant building material on hand.

There are two kinds of cobblestone houses: those made of rough ice-laid cobbles and those made of polished water-laid cobbles. The ice-laid variety can be found in glacially-formed "drumlin" areas between Rochester and Syracuse, while the water-laid variety—built of stones tumbled in Lake Ontario's waters—are found west of Rochester.

Many of New York's cobblestone houses were built between 1825 and 1860 in the Greek and Gothic Revival styles. Some featured meticulous patterns, such as herringbone or striped designs. By the late 1860s, cobblestone houses had become too expensive for the industrial age and the art died out.

South of Buffalo

The counties south of Buffalo—Cattaraugus, Allegany, and Chautauqua—are full of fascinating small towns that are overlooked by most travelers. While many of these towns and villages don't have headline attractions, they all have spots full of authentic local charm and residents who are thrilled to share their little piece of paradise with you. It's not uncommon, for instance, for someone to take a break from their work to show you a hidden historical treasure, to tell you a tale of the town's colorful characters, or to sit with you for a spell at his or her favorite watering hole.

The best way to experience these counties and their towns is by adding a few days to your road trip of the Buffalo-Niagara region.

Well-maintained state roads cut through and across these three counties, offering lots of lovely vistas along the way.

CATTARAUGUS COUNTY

Cattaraugus County is also known as the "Enchanted Mountains" region. A road trip affirms the aptness of the moniker. Departing from Buffalo on Route 219 South, you'll enter Cattaraugus and can take Route 242 to reach Ellicottville, one of western New York's principal ski destinations and a good place to eat and overnight. Along the way, there are plenty of other things to see and do.

Griffis Sculpture Park

Leave Buffalo on Route 219 South. Once you enter Cattaraugus County, you'll head west a few miles to the town of Otto, where **Griffis Sculpture Park** (6902 Mill Valley Rd., East Otto, 716/667-2808, www.griffispark.org, May-Oct. daily dawn-dusk, adults $5, seniors and students $3, children 12 and under free) awaits. The 400-acre spread is an outdoor home to more than 250 monumental works of art, ranging from the quirky 20-foot (6 m) figures from Larry Griffis Jr., the park's founder, to works from regional and international artists and changing exhibits in a lovely natural setting.

★ Ellicottville

From Otto, head back to Route 219 South and take that all the way to **Ellicottville** and its Holiday Valley Resort. Known for its winter sports, especially skiing, it's often called the Aspen of the East.

The best place to base yourself in Ellicottville is **Holiday Valley** (6557 Holiday Valley Rd., 800/323-0020, www.holidayvalley. com), the region's premier ski and snowboard resort. It has 60 slopes and trails and 13 lifts. It also offers snowshoeing, as well as tubing for those who prefer to plop and slide. This is the preeminent resort in the region.

During the rest of the year, people come to Holiday Valley for its **Sky High Aerial Adventure Park**, which features zip lines and obstacle courses ranging in difficulty. There's also an 18-hole golf course and 4 miles (6.4 km) of on-resort mountain biking trails that connect to 35 miles (56 km) of linked single-track running through a state forest.

Holiday Valley has a number of lodging options, from standard hotel rooms to three-bedroom condominiums, a spa and several indoor and outdoor pools, and an on-site restaurant, **John Harvard's Brew House**, which serves pastas and American comfort food.

Ellicottville Brewing Company (28 Monroe St., 716/699-2537, www.ellicottvillebrewing.com, daily 11:30am-2am, $18) is a pub located inside what was once a mill and carpentry shop on the town's main strip. Burgers, seafood, steaks, and, of course, beer, are on the menu here. During summer, the pub offers outdoor dining in its beer garden.

If you prefer staying in more intimate accommodations, a good option is **The Jefferson Inn** (3 Jefferson St., 716/699-5869, www.thejeffersoninn.com, $89-229), a Victorian bed-and-breakfast with four standard rooms and one suite. All have a private bath, free wireless Internet, and access to the outdoor hot tub.

★ Amish Trail

From Ellicottville, it's just a short jaunt to the south on Route 242 to the town of Randolph, the heart of New York's Amish Trail.

Western New York's Amish population is an Old Order community, upholding traditional, conservative values and family-centered life where traditional gender roles prevail. The Old Order Amish live without electricity, phones, and cars, and make their living farming and making handicrafts, furniture, quilts, iron, leather, woodwork, and jams.

Cattaraugus County has worked closely with the Amish over the past decade to create an "Amish Trail," along which visitors can get a glimpse of Amish life and purchase handmade Amish goods. Stopping at a few spots on the trail makes for a good half-day tour as you make your way to Bemus Point in neighboring Chautauqua County. A map of the **Amish Trail** (800/331-0543, www.amishtrail.com) is available at stops along the trail and can be downloaded from the website.

Visitors to the Amish Trail should realize that most of the participating businesses are run out of community members' homes rather than storefronts and many have no formal names. Amish businesses are not open on Sundays and credit cards are not accepted; transactions are cash only. Also, it is considered inappropriate to take photos of Amish people.

Many of the businesses along the Amish Trail are scattered around the county, rather than clustered in a single area; however, one place where visitors can see and purchase a few different types of goods is on Pope Road in the town of Randolph, just off Route 242. Here, you'll find **Hill Top Toy Shop** (11369 Pope Rd., no phone or website), which evokes yesteryear with handmade wooden toys like mini Amish buggies and wagons loaded with alphabet blocks. **A Slice of Heaven Alpacas and Simply Natural Alpaca Gift Shop** (11144 Pope Rd., Randolph, 716/358-5242, www.asliceofheavenalpacas.com) sells soft sweaters, scarves, hats, and socks made of alpaca wool. Between these two businesses is an unnamed **metalworking shop** (just below Hill Top Toy Shop), where light fixtures, hand-hammered hinges, wine racks, and sundries made of iron are all on sale.

Sprague's Maple Farms

If you're in Cattaraugus County during maple sugaring season (typically early spring), it's worth a short detour—especially at breakfast time—to **Sprague's Maple Farms** (1048 Rte. 305, 716/933-6637, www.spraguesmaplefarms.com, Sun.-Thurs. 8am-8pm, Fri.-Sat. 8am-9pm, $16), located in the town of Portville in the southeastern corner of the county and sitting almost right on the New York-Pennsylvania state line.

Visitors to Sprague's Maple Farms may be surprised to see so many people in what seems like the middle of nowhere. For locals and travelers in the know, Sprague's is an obligatory stop. Though this massive maple syrup producer hosts visitors for all sorts of seasonal events, including tapping and sugaring demonstrations, its restaurant is a year-round draw. Not surprisingly, maple dominates the menu and breakfast is served all day, every day. Surprisingly, you'll learn that maple's a lot like bacon: it tastes good in practically everything.

ALLEGANY COUNTY

No matter how you spell it (you'll see *Allegany* and *Allegheny*), Allegany County is a small but pleasant rural county in southwestern New York, whose foremost attraction is **Allegany State Park** (www.parks.ny.gov/parks/73, open year-round dawn-dusk, $6-7 vehicle entry fee), which is open year-round. The park, which will celebrate its centennial in 2021, offers 38 all-season, winterized **cottages** ($575-825/week) and about half of its 344 **cabins** ($154-456/week) are winterized as well. With three lakes, 99 miles (159 km) of coastline on the Allegheny Reservoir, a mountain biking and cross-country ski area, there's plenty to see and do here, whatever the season, and the park is quickly accessible from I-86.

CHAUTAUQUA COUNTY

After leaving Allegany or Cattaraugus County, head west on I-86 toward Jamestown, one of the larger burgs in Chautauqua County. Dominated by Chautauqua Lake, this county features the famed intellectual-cultural retreat, the Chautauqua Institution, and a number of picturesque small towns that sit along Chautauqua Lake and Lake Erie.

Jamestown

Jamestown is best known as the birthplace of Lucille Ball, who went on to great fame as a comedian in *I Love Lucy*. Fans can visit the **Lucy-Desi Museum and the Desilu Playhouse** (2-10 W. 3rd St., 716/484-0800, www.lucy-desi.com, Mon.-Sat. 10am-5pm,

Sun. 11am-4pm, adults $16, seniors $15, children $11), where Lucy memorabilia abounds.

Lucy isn't the only notable figure born in Jamestown. The **Roger Tory Peterson Institute of Natural History** (311 Curtis St., 716/665-2473, www.rtpi.org, Tues.-Sat. 10am-4pm, Sun. 1pm-5pm, adults $12, children $8) is a nature center and museum intended to further the legacy of 20th-century naturalist Roger Tory Peterson, renowned for his Peterson Field Guides. Exhibits and events are designed to foster curiosity about and appreciation for the natural world. If you want to overnight in the region, carry on to Bemus Point, home to historic Hotel Lenhart and several good restaurants.

Bemus Point

A few miles northwest of Jamestown is Bemus Point, which enjoys pride of place on the eastern shore of Chautauqua Lake. This small town is charming, especially in summer, when the Bemus Bay Pops Concert Series breathes life back into seasonal Bemus Point. Lawn chairs line the shore while local and national acts perform as the sun sets behind them. Those who aren't lucky enough to score seats can eavesdrop while having dinner at **The Italian Fisherman** (61 Lakeside Dr., 716/386-7000, www.italianfisherman.com, mid-June-mid-Sept. daily 4:30pm-close, $30), an excellent lakefront restaurant with ample outdoor seating (boaters can even pull right up to a lower-level dock and anchor).

Visitors who are so taken by the town that they want to spend the night should try for a room at historic **Hotel Lenhart** (20-22 Lakeside Dr., 716/386-2715, www.hotellenhart.com, Memorial Day-Labor Day, $90-185), which feels like your grandma's rambling summer home . . . if she had a rambling summer home and a family to fill it up. Kids play games in the downstairs parlor and run barefoot on the front lawn while adults sip on cocktails from the hotel's Lamplighter Room and enjoy the sunset from their rocking chairs on the front porch.

Chautauqua Institution

Leave Bemus Point by crossing the bridge over Chautauqua Lake; on the other side lies the county's best-known attraction. Since 1874, **Chautauqua Institution** (1 Ames Ave., Chautauqua, 800/836-2787, www.chq.org) has been operating as an "educational experiment in out-of-school, vacation learning" for adults, attracting luminaries from many fields, including the arts, science, politics, and philosophy. Located on spectacular, serene grounds on the shore of Chautauqua Lake, the institution is primarily active for just nine weeks each summer, hosting more than 100,000 visitors who attend one or more of the 2,200 events on campus. The grounds also feature a restaurant and lodging at **The Athenaeum Hotel** (www.athenaeum-hotel.com, $270-445). Even if you're not attending an event or staying over, you can purchase a day pass to explore the gorgeous, rambling grounds and plan to eat at one of the on-site cafes or restaurants.

Findley Lake

Due west of Chautauqua Institution, just off I-86, is Findley Lake. In winter, Findley Lake is a ski town. In summer, life centers around the lake, where boaters, water-skiers, and kids who fly into the lake from ropes tied to sturdy tree branches all enjoy the water. There is one lodging option: **Peek'n Peak** (1405 Olde Rd., 716/355-4141, www.pknpk.com, $149-354), a large resort that's popular with families. Dining is available on-site.

Barcelona and Dunkirk

Given its location on the shore of massive Lake Erie, it's hardly surprising that Route 5 is dotted with some spectacular lighthouses. Two of the most historic lighthouses are in Barcelona and Dunkirk. **Barcelona Lighthouse** was the first lighthouse in the United States to be powered by natural gas, but it didn't serve as a lighthouse for long. Built in 1829, it was decommissioned just 30 years later. Though it's now a private residence, it makes for a lovely photo and is easily seen from the road on Route 5.

Several miles to the north is **Dunkirk Historic Lighthouse** (1 Lighthouse Point Dr., 716/366-5050, www.dunkirklighthouse. com, hours vary seasonally, adults $10, seniors $8, children $3), which is open to the public. Not only can you ascend to the top for an unobstructed view of Lake Erie's vastness, but you can also learn what it was like to be a lighthouse keeper. The keeper's house, filled with memorabilia and period furniture and ephemera, is part of the tour. The upper floor of the house is also a military museum.

Information and Services

For general information on Buffalo, contact **Visit Buffalo Niagara** (617 Main St., Ste. 200, Buffalo, 800/283-3256, www.visitbuffaloniagara.com). For general information on the U.S. side of Niagara Falls, contact **Niagara Tourism and Convention Corporation** (10 Rainbow Blvd., 716/282-8992, www.niagarafallsusa.com), which operates an official **tourist information center** (June-mid-Sept. daily 9am-7pm, mid-Sept.-May daily 9am-5pm).

Several counties also operate their own tourism offices.

- **Allegany County Office of Tourism and Culture** (800/836-1869, www.wny-wilds.com)
- **Cattaraugus County Tourism** (303 Court St., Little Valley, 800/331-0543, www.enchantedmountains.com)
- **Chautauqua County Visitors Bureau** (716/357-4569, www.tourchautauqua.com)
- **Orleans County Tourism** (14016 Rte. 31, Albion, 800/724-0314, www.orleanscountytourism.com)

Getting There and Around

The region's largest airport is **Buffalo Niagara International Airport** (4200 Genesee St., 716/630-6000, www.buffaloairport.com), which is served by **American Airlines** (800/433-7300), **Delta** (800/221-1212), **JetBlue** (800/538-2583), **Southwest** (800/435-9792), **United** (800/241-6522), and **Sunwing** (877/877-1755).

Buffalo Super Shuttle (716/498-8700, www.buffalosupershuttle.com) offers service from the airport to Buffalo and Niagara Falls. **Niagara Frontier Transportation Authority** ("Metro" to locals) (716/855-7211, www.nfta.com) provides local bus and rail service, including transport to and from the airport.

Amtrak (800/872-7245, www.amtrak. com), **Greyhound** (800/231-2222, www. greyhound.com), and **Trailways of New York** (800/776-7548, www.trailways.com) all serve Buffalo and Niagara Falls. Many smaller towns are serviced by Greyhound and **Coach USA** (www.coachusa.com). The best way to explore the region, however, is by car. Major car rental chains have rental desks at Buffalo Niagara International Airport.

Background

The Landscape

The Landscape.........435

History and
    Government.........437

Geography has shaped the development of New York State more than any other single factor. Though bordered on the north, south, and east by mountains, lakes, and rivers, the state's central position between the Atlantic and the Great Lakes, along with its flat western terrain, made it a major thoroughfare for early settlers heading west. Highways were established through the Mohawk River basin and Finger Lakes in the late 1700s, followed in 1825 by the Erie Canal. The canal was largely responsible for New York's rise to prominence, and by 1900, four out of five New Yorkers were living along either the Hudson River or the Erie Canal.

Though New York ranks only 30th among the states in terms of area, it is one of the largest states east of the Mississippi and extremely diverse geographically. Mountains, plateaus, lowlands, forests, swamps, lakes, rivers, gorges, and beaches can all be found in the state, which was formed mainly during the last Ice Age, when a continental ice sheet up to two miles thick covered almost all of what is now New York. Today, most of the state is comprised of farmland, abandoned farmland, or semi-wilderness. While 85 percent of New York's population may be urban, 85 percent of its land is rural.

New York is bounded to the north by the St. Lawrence River and Lake Ontario, to the east by Lake Champlain and the Taconic Mountains, to the southeast by the Atlantic Ocean, to the south by the Delaware River and Allegheny Plateau, and to the west by Lake Erie and the Niagara River. The state's highest point is Mount Marcy (5,344 ft./1630 m)) in the Adirondack region; its lowest is the Atlantic coastline.

The Hudson River, which originates at Lake Tear of the Clouds atop Mount Marcy, flows north-south through the eastern end of the state. Running east-west through the center of the state is the Mohawk River, whose headwaters are in Oneida County, near Rome. Other important rivers include the Genesee and Oswego, which flow northward into Lake Ontario, and the Delaware, Susquehanna, and Allegheny, which drain the state's southern and western portions.

CLIMATE

Late spring, early summer, and early fall are the best times to visit New York City and much of the upstate. At these times, temperatures generally hover in the 70s, and you're more likely to wake up to one of the state's precious cloudless days. Midsummers in New York City and much of upstate tend to be hot and humid; winters are overcast, wet, and cold. Summer is the best time, however, to visit the more highly elevated regions of the Catskills and Adirondacks.

Average July temperatures range from 64°F (18°C) in the Adirondacks to 77°F (23°C) in New York City; average January temperatures range from 14°F (-10°C) in the Adirondacks to 33°F (1°C) on Long Island. The coldest winters occur in the central Adirondacks and St. Lawrence River Valley, where temperatures often drop below -10°F (-23°C). Expect snowy conditions—though dramatically varying accumulations—throughout the state in the winter months, especially in January and February. And rainy days can be expected in the spring months of late March through April.

Annual precipitation in the state is 32-45 inches (81-114cm), with the Catskills, Long Island, and Tug Hill (upstate, between Lake Ontario and the Adirondacks) receiving the most rainfall.

While the state is not impacted by hurricanes frequently, keep in mind that it does fall within the Atlantic hurricane area, and that hurricane season runs from June 1-November 30. Low-lying coastal regions, particularly those surrounding New York City, are likely to be most impacted.

PLANTS AND ANIMALS

Over half of New York State is blanketed with forests, in which over 150 kinds of trees grow. Among them are a few southern species, such as the tulip tree and sweetgum, and far more northern species, such as beech, sugar maple, red maple, hickory, ash, cherry, birch, various oaks, white pine, spruce, balsam fir, and hemlock. In the Adirondacks and Catskills, evergreens predominate, while elsewhere in the state, hardwoods are more numerous.

Among the state's most common

Previous: dock on Canandaigua Lake in the Finger Lakes region.

wildflowers are buttercups, violets, daisies, black-eyed Susans, devil's paintbrush, wild roses, and Queen Anne's lace. Bright specks of alpine flora can be found high on the Adirondack peaks, while woodland flora such as dewdrops and jack-in-the-pulpits flourish in the forests. Hundreds of species of shrubs, herbs, grasses, ferns, mosses, and lichens also abound throughout the state.

ENVIRONMENTAL ISSUES

As elsewhere in the northeastern United States, New York's great outdoors has been badly affected by industrial contamination. Chemical runoff from factories, intermittent oil spills, and shrinking space for solid waste are all problems that have affected the state in recent decades.

Despite those problems, there's plenty of good news to celebrate. Most of New York's rivers flow significantly cleaner today than they did just a few decades ago, when the Hudson, St. Lawrence, and Niagara Rivers were heavily polluted with PCBs, petrochemicals, and pesticides. The Clean Water Act of 1972, along with other state laws, and organizations such as Riverkeeper have helped reduce pollution significantly. And, of course, general improvements in social consciousness with respect to the reduce-reuse-recycle ethic have had a positive impact, too.

History and Government

HISTORY
Early Peoples

When Europeans first arrived in what is now New York State, they found it inhabited by two major tribes. The Algonquins lived near the Atlantic coast and along the Hudson River Valley, while in upstate dwelled the five tribes of the Iroquois: the Mohawk, Oneida, Onondaga, Cayuga, and Seneca. That New York of yore was a land of great abundance, filled with verdant forests and meadows, ice-blue rivers, lakes and streams, plump fish, and game.

Within a century after the arrival of settlers, the Algonquin population was decimated, due largely to virulent European diseases such as measles and smallpox. The Iroquois, however, thrived during initial contact. First the Dutch and then the French and British enlisted their help in the profitable fur trade, cultivating their friendship through gifts and the selling of firearms. During the French and Indian War, the Iroquois-British alliance against the French was instrumental in allowing England to gain control over North America.

The Iroquois did not fare so well during the American Revolution. Once again allying themselves with the British, they became the object of a ruthless 1779 campaign waged by American generals Clinton and Sullivan. By the time the campaign was over, the Iroquois nation was in ruins. Thousands fled to Canada; others were resettled onto reservations.

European Settlement

In 1524, the first European, Giovanni da Verrazano, arrived in what is now New York State by sailing into New York Harbor. However, due to a sudden "violent contrary wind [that] blew in from the sea and forced us to return to our ship," Verrazano never set foot in New York.

In 1609, Samuel de Champlain sailed south from Canada to explore the lake that now bears his name. That same year, Englishman Henry Hudson made the first of two voyages aimed at finding a northwest passage to the Orient. Backed by the Dutch West India Company, he sailed into New York Harbor and ventured halfway up the Hudson River before abandoning his quest and returning home. The following year, he returned as

The Native American Confederacy of Six Nations

Before the arrival of European settlers, Algonquin and Iroquois tribes lived freely in New York. The Algonquin resided in the south and along the Hudson River Valley, while the Iroquois spread out across the north.

The Iroquois were actually a confederacy of five tribes—the Mohawk, Oneida, Onondaga, Cayuga, and Seneca—who had banded together around 1570 to form the Iroquois League, an advanced confederacy with social laws and government institutions designed to promote peace among its members. Fifty sachems, chosen from the village chiefs, governed the confederacy, and each nation had one vote. A sixth nation, the Tuscarora, joined the Iroquois Confederacy in 1722.

The Iroquois survived through hunting, fishing, and the planting of the "Three Sisters"—corn, beans, and squash. Records were kept through storytelling and the weaving of elaborate wampum belts. Each of the Iroquois tribes was divided into matrilineal clans that took their names from birds and animals. Clans lived in longhouses comprised of 50-60 families, and all clan members were considered part of one family. Women selected clan chiefs.

The men responsible for founding the confederacy were a Huron, now known as the Peacemaker, and Hiawatha, an Onondaga chief. The two traveled from tribe to tribe for months, convincing their people to lay down arms and embrace the Great Law of Peace. The law gave equal voice to each tribe, guaranteed freedom of speech, set up a system for impeachment of corrupt chiefs, and outlined an amendment procedure.

Sound familiar? It's because the Great Law served as one of the models for the U.S. Constitution. No firm textual evidence exists, but several framers of the Constitution met frequently with the Iroquois after the Revolution, and Benjamin Franklin in particular expressed a wish to use their system as a model. In 1988, Congress passed a resolution acknowledging this Native American contribution to the U.S. Constitution.

Today, there are eight Iroquois communities located upstate, ranging in size from the 30,469-acre Allegany Reservation (Seneca) to the 5,700-acre Tuscarora Reservation.

captain of a British ship. This time he sailed into Hudson Bay, where the ship became icebound. Starving and doubting their captain's navigational abilities, the crew mutinied. They cast Hudson, his son, and several others adrift in a small boat, never to be seen again.

Though unsuccessful in his search for a northwest passage, Hudson was instrumental in drawing Europeans to the New World. His reports described the area's abundant natural resources, including a wealth of beaver and mink. In 1624, a group of Dutch merchants established Fort Orange, New York's first European settlement. Situated at present-day Albany, the fort served primarily as an outpost for the fur trade.

One year later, the Dutch established a similar outpost, Fort Amsterdam, at the foot of Manhattan Island. In 1626, Peter Minuit was appointed the colony's first governor. Almost immediately, he purchased Manhattan Island from the Algonquins for trinkets worth about $24. The Algonquins considered it a good deal at the time. Having a different sense of ownership than did the Dutch, they thought they were selling only the right to use land, not the land itself.

Unlike the dour religious colonizers of New England, the Dutch traders proved to be a fun-loving bunch who had to be constantly reminded by their governors not to play tennis when they should be working and not to drink on Sunday when they should be listening to sermons. Both men and women smoked, and as one observer of the day noted, "All drink here from the moment they are able to lick a spoon."

The last and most flamboyant of New

Amsterdam's Dutch governors was Peter Stuyvesant, in power from 1647 to 1664. Nicknamed "Old Peg Leg," due to a leg lost in battle, Stuyvesant was an arrogant, quick-tempered man with a puritanical streak. He ordered the taverns closed on Sundays and tried to prevent a group of Portuguese Jews from settling in the colony, an action for which he was swiftly reprimanded by his bosses back in Amsterdam.

For all his failings, however, Stuyvesant was responsible for turning New Amsterdam into a semblance of a town. He straightened streets, repaired fences, and established a night watch. And he was one of the few Dutch colonists who wanted to fight off the English. The rest of the colony didn't much care; the English, who had by this time established a strong presence in New England, had promised New Amsterdam residents that if they surrendered, their lives would go on as before. That was just fine with the Dutch merchants. As long as they were making money, it made no difference to them who governed the colony.

Enter and Exit the British

The British took over New Amsterdam in 1664, renaming the colony New York after the duke of York, who was later crowned King James II. The Dutch system of government was replaced with the British one, but for most colonists, life went on as before. The colony remained predominantly Dutch until the end of the century and continued to prosper and grow, with New York City reaching a population of 25,000 in 1750. In the New World, only Philadelphia was bigger.

For the colonists of African heritage, however, life under British rule became increasingly difficult. The trading of enslaved people was encouraged, and a slave market was set up on Wall Street. Some Black families who had owned land under the Dutch had their property confiscated; others lost it after passage of a 1712 law prohibiting Blacks from inheriting land.

The land-use system in upstate New York also continued much as it had before. The Dutch had used the patroon system, whereby an individual was given a large tract of land in return for bringing over at least 50 settlers to work that land. The English established a similar landlord-tenant arrangement whereby a few men were given enormous manor estates, which they then rented out in parcels to poor farmers. In some parts of the Hudson Valley and Catskills, remnants of this feudal-like system remained in effect until the 1840s.

By the time of the Revolutionary War, New York City had reached a population of 25,000. Albany and Kingston were thriving as river ports, and several smaller settlements, including Saratoga and Fort Stanwix, had been established as far north as Lake Champlain and as far west as Rome. Manor estates lined the Hudson River, and Long Island was peppered with productive farm communities.

When rumblings of revolution began, New York took a pro-Tory stance at first. Merchants and manor landlords intent on making money wanted nothing to do with war. "What is the reason that New York must continue to embarrass the Continent?" queried John Adams. As tensions escalated, however, New Yorkers changed their position and, after 1753, supported the Revolution wholeheartedly.

No state bore the brunt of the war more than New York. The earliest battles were fought in New York City—which remained in British hands throughout the war—and many of the later ones took place upstate. The Americans were badly defeated by the British at Oriskany, near Rome, in 1777. The British were unexpectedly defeated by the Americans at Saratoga, also in 1777. Benedict Arnold plotted to betray the Continental Army at West Point in 1780. General Washington declared victory over the British in Newburgh in 1781.

In 1789, Washington was inaugurated as the first president of the United States in Federal Hall on Wall Street, in New York City. The city served as the nation's capital until

1790, when the federal government transferred to Philadelphia.

Rise to Power

New York made a rapid recovery after the war. Upstate, settlers poured into the Mohawk River Valley and the Finger Lakes region. Many of the new settlers were Yankees, tired of eking out marginal livings on rocky New England soils. Attracted to New York's fertile farmland, they brought with them their strong work ethic, Protestant religion, and austere architectural styles, many examples of which still stand.

Settlers also poured into New York City. Between 1790 and 1830, the city gradually transformed itself from one of many important colonial centers into the largest and wealthiest metropolis in the new republic.

The factors leading to New York's ascendancy were many, but probably the most important was the opening of the Erie Canal in 1825. The hand-dug canal, stretching from the Hudson River to Lake Erie, established a water route to the West, thereby reducing the cost of transporting goods by a whopping 90 percent. Hundreds of thousands of small boats were soon plying the new route, carrying cargo to New York City for transfer onto oceangoing vessels. By 1834, the canal's tolls had more than paid for the entire cost of its $7.7 million construction. New York Harbor became one of the world's busiest ports, with grain elevators and warehouses sprouting up all along the docks.

The Erie Canal was the making of New York. It transformed New York City from one of many important colonial centers into the largest metropolis in the New World and gave rise to virtually every other major city in the state, including Syracuse, Rochester, and Buffalo.

About the same time, New York established the country's first regularly scheduled transatlantic shipping service. Previously, ships had sailed only when their holds were full. This innovation gave the metropolis a competitive edge for decades to come.

Manhattan's famous grid street system was established in 1811. All of the island that had not yet been settled was scored into 12 major avenues—each 100 feet (30 m) wide—and 155 consecutively numbered streets. Most of the streets were 60 feet (18 m) wide, but those that intersected the already established Broadway when it crossed an avenue were 100 feet (30 m) wide. Later, when the subway system was built, stops were placed along many of the wider streets.

In 1842, New York opened the Croton Aqueduct Water System, then the world's largest water system. The $12 million project dammed the Croton River, 40 miles (64 km) upstate, and brought water into the city through a series of reservoirs and aqueducts. New York thus became one of the first cities in the world to supply all its citizens—even the poorest—with clean, fresh water. As a result, outbreaks of cholera and other epidemic diseases were drastically reduced. Today, New York still has one of the world's best water systems.

Slavery and Civil War

Slavery had been in New York since 1626, when 11 African enslaved people were brought to New Amsterdam and forced to work as servants and craftspeople. Before the Revolution, New York had the largest number of enslaved people of any colony north of Maryland. Later, as a state conducting lucrative business with the cotton-growing South, New York often turned a blind eye to the cruelties of the "curious institution." In fact, New York was one of the last Northern states to abolish slavery, only doing so in 1827.

Despite this dismal beginning, New York played a critical role in the antislavery movement before and during the Civil War. Many of the country's most ardent abolitionists, including William Seward, Frederick Douglass, Gerrit Smith, and Martin Van Buren, lived upstate, and the Finger Lakes region was regarded as a hotbed of antislavery sentiment. Gerrit Smith and John Brown established a farm for escaped enslaved people near Lake

Placid in 1849, and Underground Railroad stations dotted the state, especially along the Niagara frontier. When escaped enslaved person William "Jerry" McHenry was arrested by federal marshals in Syracuse in 1851, he was promptly rescued by vigilante abolitionists. That rescue, which challenged the Fugitive Slave Act of 1850, was one of the early precipitating events of the Civil War.

The pre-Civil War years also witnessed the influx of the first great wave of immigrants that swept into New York City between the mid-1800s and the 1920s. From 1840 to 1855, over three million Irish and Germans arrived. Many of the Irish were escaping the potato famines; many of the Germans, the failed Revolution of 1848.

When the Civil War began, New York officially supported the Union. But the citizenry remained divided. The city's newest immigrants resented having to fight to free enslaved people, who might then come north and compete for jobs. In 1863, this deep-rooted discontent led to the Draft Riots, in which 2,000 people were injured or killed.

About 500,000 New Yorkers served in the war, and about 50,000 were killed. The state also contributed much in the way of supplies and weapons.

After the war, infamous William Marcy "Boss" Tweed rose to power in New York City. A tough street fighter, Tweed was America's first "political boss." He never held mayoral office, but he controlled the city from behind the scenes through the Democratic machine known as Tammany Hall. During Tweed's corrupt reign, from 1866 to 1871, he and his cronies pocketed as much as $200 million from padded or fraudulent city expenditures and tax improprieties. Eventually indicted, Tweed died in a Ludlow Street jail not far from his birthplace.

The Late 1800s

The Civil War put a temporary dent in New York's economy, but by the 1880s, it was back in full force. Corporations all over the state doubled, tripled, or even quadrupled in size,

with a corresponding explosion of activity in commerce, transportation, banking, and, especially, manufacturing.

New York City was in its full glory. In 1892, 1,265 millionaires lived either in the city or its suburbs. In 1895, the city housed nearly 300 companies worth over one million dollars—more than the next six largest cities combined. In 1898, New York annexed Brooklyn, Queens, Staten Island, and the Bronx, thereby increasing its area from 23 to 301 square miles.

The rich and the powerful flocked to New York City from all over the country, and the social elite were soon defined as the "Four Hundred"—the maximum number of guests who could squeeze into Mrs. Astor's 5th Avenue ballroom. Investment bankers such as J. P. Morgan and August Belmont became household names, as did leaders of commerce and industry such as John D. Rockefeller, Andrew Carnegie, and F. W. Woolworth.

New York City became the nation's cultural capital as well. Theaters sprang up along Broadway, and The Metropolitan Museum of Art and Metropolitan Opera opened their doors in 1880 and 1890, respectively. Walt Whitman sang the city's praises in poems such as "Leaves of Grass" and "Crossing Brooklyn Ferry," and Henry James and Edith Wharton reported on the lives of the upper crust in *Washington Square* and *The Age of Innocence.*

But the years surrounding the turn of the century also had a darker side. Between 1880 and 1919, a new wave of more than 17 million immigrants, this time mainly from southern and eastern Europe, swept into New York City. Many settled on the Lower East Side, where they worked miserable, low-paying jobs in the garment industry. Overcrowding became a serious problem; by 1900, more than two-thirds of the city's residents were squeezed into some 80,000 tenements in Manhattan and Brooklyn. The Lower East Side had a population density of 209,000 people per square mile, equal to that of today's Mumbai.

Immigrants who settled upstate to work

the region's many burgeoning factories suffered as well. Often illiterate and unable to speak fluent English, they were subject to exploitation, poor health and housing conditions, pollution, and increasing crime.

The larger the cities grew, the greater the need for improved transportation. Horsecars gave way to streetcars, and by 1900, nearly every city upstate had a streetcar system.

In 1904, Manhattan opened its first subway, long after London (1863) and shortly after Boston (1897). But New York's subway system would soon be distinguished for both its enormous size and its technological innovations. Within a year after opening, New York's subway—then just a single line running up Park Avenue, across 42nd Street, and up Broadway—was carrying over 600,000 passengers per day. By 1937, the city boasted over 700 miles (1130 km) of track handling 4.2 million passengers per day. Today, the subway system still has about 700 miles (1130 km) of track, and handles an average of 7.7 million passengers every weekday.

Reform, Depression, and War

At the beginning of the 20th century, New York was the most powerful state in the United States. Two-thirds of the nation's leading corporations were headquartered in New York City, and the state produced one-sixth of the gross national product. Ex-New York governor Theodore Roosevelt had just succeeded President William McKinley—assassinated in Buffalo in 1898—to the White House.

The Progressive Era in politics began to peak about a decade later, following the 1911 Triangle Shirtwaist factory fire that took the lives of 146 workers in Greenwich Village. Many progressive reforms were propelled through the state legislature by Democrat Al Smith, who later became one of New York's greatest governors. A self-educated man, born poor on the Lower East Side, Smith helped create dozens of monumental labor, safety, education, and housing bills.

After World War I, the United States emerged as a world power, and nowhere was this newfound status more evident than in dazzling New York City. Business and manufacturing flourished. The Jazz Age arrived and liquor flowed. F. Scott Fitzgerald came to town, and Jimmy Walker was elected mayor. A dandified gentleman with a taste for the good life, Walker spent most of his time visiting nightclubs, sporting halls, and showgirls. Thanks to his late-night carousing, he rarely appeared at City Hall before 3pm, if at all. "No civilized man," he once said, "goes to bed the same day he wakes up."

Strict new federal immigration laws of 1921 and 1924 slowed the influx of foreigners into New York to a trickle, but Harlem boomed as Black Southerners fleeing poverty took refuge in the city. In 1910, Manhattan was home to about 60,000 Blacks; by 1930, that number had tripled. Harlem became the center for African American culture, with the Harlem Renaissance attracting writers and intellectuals such as Langston Hughes and W. E. B. DuBois and jazz clubs and theaters attracting the likes of Duke Ellington and Chick Webb.

The Great Depression of 1929 hit New York State especially hard. By 1932, industrial production upstate had fallen by one-third, bread lines filled city blocks, and New York City banks shut down and reopened as soup kitchens. Scores of shantytowns called "Hoovervilles" dotted Central Park and other city parks upstate.

Enter Franklin Delano Roosevelt. In 1930, as governor of New York, he devised a five-point program to help the state cope with the economic disaster. In 1932, elected president of the United States, he applied and expanded his New York program into the national New Deal. New Yorkers went back to work on public works projects ranging from transportation to housing. Many were projects envisioned and developed by Robert Moses, the autocratic "master builder" largely responsible for the shape of modern-day New York.

However, like the rest of the nation, New York's greatest boon to post-Depression recovery was World War II. Overnight, the state's factories and shipyards thrived anew, producing arms, uniforms, and other items for the war effort.

During the war, Columbia University at 116th Street and Broadway was the site of a nuclear experiment conducted by Dr. Robert Oppenheimer. Code-named "The Manhattan Project," the experiment led to the creation of the world's first atomic bomb, dropped on Japan in August 1945.

Postwar Decline and New York City's Recovery

Despite prosperity brought to New York by World War II, the state reached its economic peak relative to the rest of the country around 1940. Thereafter, certain trends already in effect began to undermine both New York and the entire Northeast. These trends would not become visible for many years, but they were there, slowly eating away.

In 1880, 16 percent of all U.S. production workers lived in the New York metropolitan area. By 1900, that figure had fallen to 14 percent, and by 1990, it had fallen to 4 percent. Between 1956 and 1985, the New York City region lost over 600,000 industrial jobs; upstate lost hundreds of thousands more. Some companies left the region due to demographic shifts toward the South and West, others due to technological changes that allowed them to decentralize. Still others fled from the rising cost of doing business in New York.

In 1959, Nelson A. Rockefeller was elected governor of New York. An ambitious man with grand visions, Rockefeller greatly expanded the state university system and built Albany's impressive, futuristic Empire State Plaza. By the time Rockefeller left office in 1973, however, the state budget had grown 400 percent from its 1959 level and state debt had increased 14 times over.

During this same period, New York's once-thriving port also declined. The advent of container ships, which require large dockside cranes for loading, spelled its death. New York's old shipyards simply did not have the space needed to maneuver the cranes.

With these economic shifts came considerable social unrest. Urban race riots and antiwar demonstrations rocked the state. In 1969, the Woodstock Music and Arts Festival drew young people from all over the country to a dairy farm in the Catskills. Between 1950 and 1970, over one million families left New York City in the "Great White Flight." In 1971, a deadly uprising at Attica prison left 43 inmates and guards dead.

On the up side, New York City's cultural scene was thriving. The Guggenheim Museum opened in 1959, followed by Lincoln Center in the mid-1960s. Broadway was producing one great hit after another, including *My Fair Lady* and *West Side Story*. "Culture had become a commodity," wrote historian Harold Syrett, "and New Yorkers were its largest producers. Most other Americans had to be content with being consumers."

Things finally came to a head in New York City in 1975. Cultural attractions aside, the city was all but bankrupt. Banks shut off credit, and the city, in desperation, turned to the federal government for help. The famous *Daily News* headline "Ford to City: Drop Dead" caustically summed up Washington's stony response.

The city was temporarily rescued by the Municipal Assistance Corporation, put together by financier Felix Rohatyn and Governor Hugh Carey to issue city bonds and thereby borrow money. Washington was impressed enough by this effort to finally extend the city a short-term loan of $2.5 billion.

The city's recovery was further aided in 1978 by the election of Mayor Ed Koch. A onetime liberal from the Bronx via Greenwich Village, Koch helped set the city back on track through budget cuts and austerity programs. Brash, shrewd, and outspoken, Koch managed to play the city's various interest groups off one another to the general public's advantage, winning the respect of many New Yorkers in the process. Much of the 1980s construction boom, which included Trump Tower and the World Financial Center, was attributed to his efforts. Unfortunately, so was the city's steadily increasing homeless population.

Upstate, however, the economic picture remained gloomy. More jobs were lost throughout the 1970s and again in the early 1990s as companies moved from the Northeast to the South and West. Many New Yorkers blamed these industrial losses on the state's steep tax rate—among the highest in the nation—but the truth was, and is, that no amount of tax cuts can make New York the state it once was. The emergence of the Pacific Rim, the shift in the nation's demographics, and the rise of a global economy irrevocably altered New York's economic position.

The 21st Century

At the end of the 1990s, while much of upstate languished, New York City was riding the crest of the bull stock market. Dozens of new businesses, restaurants, bars, and shops were opening up daily, on even the most depressed of blocks. Rents were skyrocketing and streets teemed with well-dressed twentysomethings earning salaries their grandparents never even dreamed of.

In addition, New York was—and is—benefiting from the energy and spirit of yet another enormous influx of immigrants. Many had been steadily arriving since the easing of immigration quotas in 1965; others have come since the end of the Cold War, or following political upheaval in their home countries. Some 90,000 documented immigrants enter the city each year; one out of every three New Yorkers is foreign-born.

Then came the recession and the September 11 terrorist attack on the World Trade Center that killed about 2,700 innocent people in a morning that will be forever seared into New York's sense of itself. In a few short moments, the city was plunged into death, devastation, and unspeakable horror. But even as New Yorkers reeled with grief and fear, they also rose to meet the crisis. In

one of the city's finest hours, thousands of citizens quickly pulled themselves together to volunteer their time, donate their money, and keep each other's spirits up. The attacks unified the city under the leadership of Mayor Giuliani in a way never before seen in modern times.

Giuliani was unable to run for mayor again in 2001 due to the city's term-limits law. Michael Bloomberg, a billionaire businessman, succeeded him. Bloomberg quickly set about dealing with the aftermath of the attacks and reaching out to some of the cultural communities that Giuliani shunned. Though regularly criticized for his impatience and occasional tactless speech, as well as his tendency to introduce and champion causes that many citizens saw as invasive (such as the so-called "soda ban"), Bloomberg was reelected to a second term in 2005. Then, in a highly controversial move, Bloomberg led a successful campaign to change the term-limits law and ended up serving a third term as mayor, arguing that the continuity he represented and market astuteness he possessed were needed to shepherd the city through the global financial crisis.

The Bloomberg era ended in November 2013 with the landslide win of Bill de Blasio, a Brooklyn Democrat. Previously a councilman and the city's public advocate, he was viewed by many voters as a populist candidate who, along with his multiracial family (his wife is African American, their children are biracial), more accurately reflects the face of diverse New York than his predecessors. Since taking office, however, he has been viewed largely as an ineffective leader, his popularity has suffered some blows, and he has been in perpetual conflict with the state's governor. His final term will end in 2021.

GOVERNMENT

New York's state government is led by an exceptionally strong governor with power over hundreds of appointments and a legislature comprised of a 62-member Senate and 150-member Assembly. Members of both houses are elected for two-year terms, and each house has standing committees concerned with public policy issues. The governor also appoints non-legislative commissions to investigate such problems as education aid and welfare administration. The state's finances are overseen by an independently elected comptroller.

On a local level, New York is divided into 62 counties that are further subdivided into towns. The towns, which function as townships do elsewhere, contain cities and villages, most governed by a mayor and a council.

Essentials

Transportation.........446
Accommodations......448
Travel Tips.............449
Information
and Services.........451

Transportation

GETTING THERE
Air

Most major U.S. airlines and many foreign carriers offer regularly scheduled flights into New York City's **La Guardia** (LGA, Elmhurst, Queens, 718/533-3400, www.panynj.gov/airports), **John F. Kennedy** (JFK, Jamaica, Queens, 718/244-4444, www.panynj.gov/airports), or **Newark Liberty International** (EWR, Newark, NJ, 973/961-6000, www.panynj.gov/airports) airports. Several major U.S. airlines also fly to other cities in the state, including **Albany** (ALB, 737 Albany Shaker

Rd., Albany, 518/242-2200, www.albanyairport.com), **Rochester** (ROC, 1200 Brooks Ave., Rochester, 585/753-7000, www2.monroecounty.gov), **Islip** (ISP, 100 Arrivals Ave., Ronkonkoma, Long Island, 631/467-3300, www.macarthurairport.com), and **Buffalo Niagara** (BUF, 4200 Genesee St., Buffalo, 716/630-6000, www.buffaloairport.com).

Train

Amtrak (800/872-7245, www.amtrak.com) has several north-south and east-west routes running through New York State. Its *Empire State* service runs from New York City's Penn Station in the east to Niagara Falls in the west, making stops in Albany, Syracuse, Rochester, and Buffalo along the way. Amtrak also has the *Adirondack,* which runs from New York City to Montréal, stopping in Albany, and the *Ethan Allen,* which runs from New York City to Albany and onward to Rutland, Vermont. Amtrak's trains also depart Penn Station for other major cities in the northeast and mid-Atlantic, including Boston, Philadelphia, and Washington, D.C.

Metro-North (212/532-4900 or 800/638-7646, www.mta.info/mnr), a commuter railroad, offers service between New York City's Grand Central Terminal and the Hudson Valley region, while **Long Island Rail Road** (718/217-5477, www.mta.info/lirr) offers service between New York City's Penn Station and Long Island.

Bus

Greyhound (800/231-2222, www.greyhound.com) offers regular bus service to major cities and popular tourist destinations throughout the state. **Trailways** (800/858-8555, www.trailways.com) also services major cities, as well as a variety of rural areas. **Peter Pan Bus Company** (800/343-9999, www.peterpanbus.com) operates between New York City and a number of northeastern towns and cities and beyond, as do a number of budget-minded bus services, including **BOLT Bus** (877/265-8287, www.boltbus.com) and **megabus** (877/462-6342, www.megabus.com).

GETTING AROUND

Though New York City is best explored by foot, subway, bus, and taxi, upstate New York is better suited to travel by car. Outside New York City, public transportation is limited and infrequent.

I-87 is the principal highway running south-north from New York City to Canada. I-90 is the main highway running east-west, from Massachusetts and Albany to Buffalo.

The statewide speed limit for open highway driving is 65 miles (105 km) per hour. Speed limits for cities, towns, villages, and smaller roads are considerably slower. It is against the law to drive without using seat belts in the driver and front passenger seats, and all passengers under the age of 16 must be buckled in. Children eight and under must be in an approved car seat or booster seat. Unless otherwise noted by signage, a right turn on red is permitted almost everywhere except New York City. Throughout the entire state, it is illegal to talk or text on a mobile device while driving. For a full list of road rules and driver safety information, visit www.trafficsafety.ny.gov.

If renting a car, try to do so outside Manhattan. Rates are typically lower at airports, in outer boroughs, and elsewhere in the state. Major car rental companies operating in New York State include **Avis** (800/352-7900), **Budget** (800/404-8033), **Hertz** (800/654-3131), and **National** (800/468-3334).

Accommodations

CAMPING

Excellent campgrounds are located in most of New York's 180 state parks (reservations 800/456-2267, www.parks.ny.gov). For $12-34 a night, campers are provided with a tent site, table, fire ring, running water, flush toilets, and hot showers; RV hookups are extra. Some of the campgrounds also offer cabins, cottages, or lean-tos. Some parks offer gear (lanterns, bikes, kayaks) for rent piecemeal. Only a handful of campgrounds remain open through the winter.

YOUTH HOSTELS AND YMCAS

Hosteling International-American Youth Hostels (AYH, 240/650-2100, www.hiusa. org) offer clean accommodations for people of all ages. A hostel usually consists of dormitory rooms, a kitchen, and a common room. Sometimes, hostels have private rooms available for families. Hosteling International facilities are located in New York City. Overnight rates are $31-260 per person.

You must be a member to stay at many AYH hostels. Day-only memberships can be purchased for $4, annual memberships are $18, and lifetime memberships are $250. Membership cards are usually sold on-site or through the national office (240/650-2100). They can also be purchased online (www. hiusa.org). Reservations at all AYH hostels should be made well in advance.

The Young Men's Christian Association (YMCA) offers inexpensive, but not always clean, accommodations at five locations in New York City and several other urban areas throughout the state. For information on New York's YMCAs, which are coed, contact YMCA of Greater New York (212/630-9600, www.ymcanyc.org) or visit the website of The Alliance of New York State YMCAs (www.ymcanys.org).

MOTELS AND HOTELS

Motels and hotels offering anywhere from 6 to more than 200 rooms abound in New York State. Some are independent operations; others belong to nationwide chains and provide an especially good choice for families or travelers looking for affordable accommodations. Among the many chains are Four Points Sheraton (www.fourpoints.com), Holiday Inn (www.ihg.com), Marriott (www.marriott. com), and Wyndham (www.wyndham.com).

BED-AND-BREAKFASTS

B&Bs are a popular lodging option in New York State, especially in the Hudson Valley, Cooperstown, Finger Lakes, Saratoga Springs, Rochester, Ithaca, and eastern Long Island. Many are expensive and cater more to city folk looking for pampering than to budget travelers. Keep in mind, too, that rates vary considerably depending upon the season.

Check the I Love NY website (www.iloveny.com) for a list of B&B accommodations throughout the state.

Travel Tips

WHAT TO TAKE

Visitors to New York City will want to bring comfortable walking shoes, casual clothes, and a few items of sophisticated attire for evenings out. Since much of New York State is humid during the summer, with temperatures in the 80s and 90s (about 25-35°C), bring plenty of short-sleeved shirts. In fall and spring, you'll need a jacket, long-sleeved shirts and pants, and rain gear. In the winter, dress for cold winds and snow. A pair of sturdy shoes or sneakers come in handy for casual exploring. Insect repellent is a must, and sunscreen is essential in summer.

VISITOR INFORMATION

If you plan to visit multiple beaches, trails, state parks, and campsites in New York State, you might consider investing in an annual **Empire Pass** (www.parks.ny.gov, $80), which offers unlimited vehicle entry to most facilities operated by New York State Parks and the State Department of Environmental Conservation. A New York State driver's license or a non-driver ID is required.

New York State residents with disabilities should apply for the **Access Pass** (518/474-2324, www.parksny.gov), which provides free entry to most state parks and recreation areas. The **National Park Service** (NPS) issues a similar pass by the same name (www.store.usgs.gov/access-pass.html).

Help for disabled travelers is also available through **Society for Accessible Travel and Hospitality** (212/447-7284, www.sath.org), a nationwide, nonprofit membership organization that collects data on travel facilities around the country.

The **Golden Park Program** provides New York State residents age 62 or older with free entry to state parks and recreation areas any weekday, excluding holidays. Simply present your current driver's license or nondriver's identification card at the entrance.

Similarly, the NPS issues **Senior Passes** to people 62 years or older for national historic sites and parks. Senior Passes are $80 and good for a lifetime. They provide free admission to parks and offer up to 50 percent off certain NPS amenity, facility, and service fees. Senior Passes replace Golden Access and Golden Age Passports, which are no longer sold. If you have one of these, however, the NPS will continue to honor it. For more information, visit the National Park Service website (www.nps.gov).

Anyone over age 50 is eligible to join **AARP** (888/687-2276, www.aarp.org), which provides its members with hotel, airfare, car rental, and sightseeing discounts. **Road Scholar** (800/454-5768, www.roadscholar.org) offers educational tour packages in New York City and State for travelers who are interested in lifelong learning. Once aimed at budget travelers age 60 and older, the Road Scholar programs now have no minimum age limit, though they still tend to attract adults between the ages of 55 and 75.

The **Council on International Educational Exchange** (207/553-4000, www.ciee.org) provides information on low-cost travel and work-study programs in the United States, including New York State, for international students and professionals.

HEALTH AND SAFETY
City Safety

Though crime is no longer the problem that once gave New York City a terrifying reputation, use common sense to protect yourself, especially in cities. Carry small amounts of cash; ignore hustlers and con artists; keep a tight hold on your purse, camera, phone and other electronic devices; label and lock your luggage; lock your car; and avoid lonely and unlit stretches, especially after dark.

Outdoor Safety

Before heading into forests and semi-wilderness areas of New York State, be sure you know where you're going and what you're doing. Check with park officials and other knowledgeable outdoorspeople about trail conditions, weather, water sources, and fire danger. Be sure your equipment is functioning properly, and don't head out alone. If you're an outdoors novice, accompany someone with more experience.

Basic gear for day hikes includes a small knapsack, hat, sunscreen, lip balm, compass, whistle, insect repellent, multipurpose knife, good hiking boots, layered clothing, food, and an ample water supply. For longer or more demanding hikes, bring a butane lighter or waterproof matches, nylon rope, first-aid kit, "space blanket," extra socks and shoelaces, and a waterproof poncho or large plastic bag.

Lyme Disease

Anyone who spends time outdoors in New York should be aware of the symptoms of Lyme disease. The bacterium that causes the disease is carried by deer ticks, which are found in brush, meadows, forests, and even lawns. In early stages, the disease is easily treatable with antibiotics, but if left unattended, it can lead to serious neurological, heart, and joint problems.

Many of those infected develop a red circular rash around the bite location within three days to one month. The rash usually begins with a small red dot that expands to a diameter of 1-5 inches (2.5-12 cm). The expanded rash may feature a bright red border and a hard, pale center.

The rash is usually accompanied by flu-like symptoms. These include fatigue, nausea, vomiting, diarrhea, muscle and joint pain, stiff neck, swollen lymph glands, headaches, fevers, chills, sore throat, dry cough, dizziness, sensitivity to the sun, and chest, ear, or back pain.

Lyme disease was first identified in Old Lyme, Connecticut, in 1975, and quickly spread throughout New England. At present, New York has the highest number of cases of Lyme disease in the country. If you suspect you have Lyme disease, contact your doctor immediately.

Wear light-colored clothing to spot ticks easily, and long pants and long-sleeved shirts to discourage them. Tuck pants cuffs into socks, and use an insect repellent with a 25-30 percent DEET content around clothing openings and on exposed skin.

Use gloves and tweezers to remove ticks; grasp the tick's head parts as close to your skin as possible and apply slow, steady traction. Wash your hands and the bitten area afterward. Do not attempt to remove ticks by burning them or coating them with anything like nail polish remover or petroleum jelly. If you remove a tick before it has been attached for more than 24 hours, you greatly reduce your risk of infection.

Ticks do not jump, but usually crawl upward until they find exposed skin. Their favorite spots are the back of the neck, scalp, armpits, groin area, and the backs of knees. Not all bites result in illness.

If you plan to spend much time outdoors in New York State, you may want to read additional tips on the **Center for Disease Control** website (www.cdc.gov/lyme). At present, no vaccine is available for Lyme disease; it was discontinued in 2002 due to insufficient demand.

Information and Services

DOMESTIC TRAVELERS

As of October 2021, US citizens over the age of 18 will need a REAL ID, state-issued enhanced driver's license, or passport for domestic air travel.

VISAS AND OFFICIALDOM

Most foreign visitors entering the United States are required to carry a current passport, visa, and proof they intend to leave (typically in the form of a return plane ticket). It's also wise to carry proof of citizenship, such as a driver's license or birth certificate.

Since 9/11, the process of obtaining a U.S. visa has become more difficult and lengthy. Apply early to avoid disappointment. For information about how to apply or how to extend an existing visa, visit the website of the U.S. Department of State (www.travel.state.gov).

To replace a passport lost while in the United States, contact your country's nearest embassy or consulate; many consulates are located in New York City; call the city's information hotline, 311, for a consulate address and phone number.

Visitors to the United States do not need inoculations unless they are coming from an area known to be suffering from an epidemic such as cholera or yellow fever. Visitors with medical conditions requiring treatment with narcotics or the use of drug paraphernalia such as syringes must carry a valid, signed physician's prescription.

BUSINESS HOURS AND MONEY

Standard business hours in New York are Monday-Friday 9am-5pm. Banks are usually open Monday-Friday 9am-5pm, with some branches open Saturday 9am-1pm or 3pm. Most banks offer 24-hour ATMs.

Most shops are open Monday-Saturday from 9am or 10am to 5pm or 6pm. In New York City, Sunday afternoon and evening hours are also common, and many grocery stores and delis remain open 24/7. The state sales tax is 4 percent, with counties imposing an additional 3-5 percent.

With the exception of some inexpensive motels, restaurants, and shops, credit cards are accepted almost everywhere in the state, and are mandatory for renting cars and most sports equipment.

MEASUREMENTS, MAIL, AND AREA CODES

Like the rest of the United States, New York still eschews the metric system. See the U.S.-Metric Conversion Chart in the back of this book. New York lies within the Eastern Standard Time zone. Daylight saving time, which sets the clocks one hour ahead, goes into effect from spring to fall.

Normal post office hours are Monday-Friday 9am-5pm and Saturday 9am-noon.

New York State uses an ever-proliferating number of area codes. To obtain a number from directory services, dial 411.

MAPS AND TOURIST INFORMATION

The best source for general information on New York State is the official tourism department, the **New York State Division of Tourism** (800/225-5697, www.iloveny.com). It publishes a free *I Love New York* guide that's updated annually, as well as an official state map and a wide variety of brochures on specific regions, attractions, and interests. For an updated calendar of events held throughout the state, including New York City, call 800/225-5697. Most regions, cities, and towns also staff their own tourism offices and visitors centers. These are listed at the end of each region's chapter in this book.

For a free guide to New York's state parks, including hiking and camping information, contact **New York State Office of Parks, Recreation, and Historic Preservation** (518/474-0456, www.parks.ny.gov).

Excellent maps of New York State are published by the **American Automobile Association** (AAA, 1415 Kellum Pl., Garden City, NY, 516/746-7730, www.

northeast.aaa.com). The AAA maps are available for free to members at any local AAA office.

Look for regional maps at rest areas and welcome centers. In New York City, a hard copy of the subway map is available for free in most train stations, though many visitors use apps and online services to find their way around the city and beyond.

Resources

Suggested Reading

NEW YORK CITY
Fiction

Capote, Truman. *Breakfast at Tiffany's*. New York, NY: Vintage, 1993. The moving story of a glamorous madcap adrift on the Upper East Side in the 1950s.

Ellison, Ralph. *Invisible Man*. New York, NY: Vintage, 1995. The classic 1952 novel follows a nameless protagonist from his home in the Deep South to the basements of Harlem. A masterpiece of African American literature that chronicles effects of bigotry on victims and perpetrators alike.

Finney, Jack. *Time and Again*. New York, NY: Simon & Schuster, 1970. A cult classic that time-travels back and forth between the present and the 1880s, when New York was little more than an overgrown small town.

Hijuelos, Oscar. *The Mambo Kings Play Songs of Love*. New York, NY: Perennial Classics, 2000. A rich, deeply resonant novel that recreates the world of immigrant Cuban musicians living in New York post-World War II.

McCann, Colum. *Let the Great World Spin*. New York, NY: Random House, 2009. This National Book Award winner deftly depicts a diverse array of New Yorkers in the 1970s, each as believable as if they were real.

McInerney, Jay. *Bright Lights, Big City*. New York, NY: Vintage Contemporaries, 1984. A young man immerses himself in the excesses of 1980s New York—the clubs, the drugs, the after-hours hot spots—until he is brought to an abrupt reckoning.

Paley, Grace. *Enormous Changes at the Last Minute*. New York, NY: Farrar, Straus and Giroux, 1985. Quirky, funny, sad, combative, vulnerable Paley, who grew up in immigrant New York in the 1920s and '30s, captures the soul of New York in one of her best story collections.

Parker, Dorothy. *The Portable Dorothy Parker*. New York, NY: Penguin Books, 1991. Poems, stories, articles, and reviews by that most quotable of *New Yorker* writers.

Wharton, Edith. *The Age of Innocence*. New York, NY: Modern Library, 1999. The first book written by a woman to win the Pulitzer Prize is a subtle, elegant portrait of desire and betrayal in moneyed Old New York. Among Wharton's other books set in the city are *The House of Mirth, A Backward Glance*, and *Old New York*.

Nonfiction

Caro, Robert A. *The Power Broker: Robert Moses and the Fall of New York*. New York, NY: Vintage, 1975. Much more than a biography, this Pulitzer Prize-winning tome tells the fascinating and often scandalous story behind the shaping of 20th-century New York. Though over 1,000 pages, the book is a compelling page-turner.

Editors of *New York Magazine*. *My First New York: Early Adventures in the Big City*. New York, NY: Ecco, 2010. Everyone who visits or lives in New York City has a "my first time" story; this anthology compiles the stories of notable New Yorkers, including Nora Ephron, Liza Minnelli, and Diane von Furstenberg.

Grimes, William. *Appetite City: A Culinary History of New York*. New York, NY: North Point Press, 2009. The former *New York Times* food critic makes readers hungry not only for the city's iconic foods, but also for bygone chapters of New York City's history.

Gross, Michael. *Rogues' Gallery: The Secret Story of the Lust, Lies, Greed, and Betrayals That Made The Metropolitan Museum of Art*. New York, NY: Broadway, 2009. Worthy of a fiction thriller, this fascinating history of the backstory of the Met is really a history of turn-of-the-20th-century New York's robber baron-philanthropists.

Johnson, James Weldon. *Black Manhattan*. New York, NY: Da Capo Press, 1991. First published in 1930, this classic work paints one of the earliest portraits of lives of African Americans in New York City. Much more than a history, the book also illuminates the Harlem Renaissance, of which Johnson was a part.

Mitchell, Joseph. *Up in the Old Hotel*. New York, NY: Vintage, 1993. A reprint of four classics penned by the deadpan *New Yorker* chronicler of city life. "McSorley's Wonderful Salon," "Old Mr. Flood," "The Bottom of the Harbor," and "Joe Gould's Secret" are included.

Sante, Luc. *Low Life*. New York, NY: Farrar, Straus, and Giroux, 2003. A highly original and literate book that delves into the underbelly—opium dens, brothels, sweatshops—of Old New York.

Thomas, Piri. *Down These Mean Streets*. New York, NY: Vintage, 1997. This 1967 memoir by the famed writer of Cuban-Puerto Rican descent, who lived in El Barrio, tells of the neighborhood's challenges and dangers, including gangs and drugs.

Poetry

Among the many poets who have written extensively on New York City are Djuna Barnes, Hart Crane, Allen Ginsberg, Victor Hernández Cruz, Langston Hughes, Frank O'Hara, and Walt Whitman.

Specialty Guides

Federal Writers' Project. *The WPA Guide to New York City*. New York, NY: New Press, 1995. First published in 1939 and since reissued, the classic guidebook remains remarkably on target. It provides long and evocative descriptions of everything from long-gone Ebbets Field to the then-new Empire State Building.

White, Norval, and Elliot Willensky, eds. *AIA Guide to New York City*. New York, NY: Oxford University Press, 2010. The most important and entertaining book on New York architecture, organized as a series of walking tours. An urban classic, with over 2,000 photos and 100 maps.

BEYOND NEW YORK CITY
Fiction and Memoir

Banks, Russell. *The Sweet Hereafter*. New York, NY: Perennial, 1992. A horrific school-bus accident in Sam Dent, New York, results in the deaths of 14 children. Banks writes compassionately of how the small town responds and somehow moves beyond grief to redemption.

Dobyns, Stephen. *Saratoga Haunting*. New York, NY: Viking Press, 1993. Low-key detective Charlie Bradshaw, operating in the summer horse-racing capital of the United States, reopens two cases he thought he had solved 20 years earlier. The seventh of poet Dobyns's Charlie Bradshaw books; all are set in Saratoga.

Dreiser, Theodore. *An American Tragedy.* New York, NY: Signet Classics, 2000. The classic book on the dark side of the American Dream, set largely in the Adirondacks and central New York.

Fitzgerald, F. Scott. *The Great Gatsby.* New York, NY: Scribner, 1995. One of the finest works of 20th-century literature takes place largely on the North Shore of Long Island.

Gardner, John. *The Sunlight Dialogues.* New York, NY: Random House, 1972. A grand and complex portrait of the United States in the 1960s, set in the small, agricultural town of Batavia, New York.

Irving, Washington. *Rip Van Winkle and the Legend of Sleepy Hollow.* Tarrytown, NY: Sleepy Hollow Press, 1980. The first American literary writer of note tells tales of the Headless Horseman galloping through Sleepy Hollow and Rip Van Winkle awakening from his 20-year sleep.

Kennedy, William. *Billy Phelan's Greatest Game.* New York, NY: Penguin Books, 1982. The second, and arguably best, of Kennedy's triumvirate of novels set in underworld Albany chronicles the fall and redemption of a small-time hustler. The other two books in the cycle are *Legs* and *Ironweed*.

Luper, Eric. *Bug Boy.* New York, NY: Farrar, Straus, and Giroux, 2009. Jack "Shabby" Walsh, an apprentice jockey at Saratoga Race Course in 1934, introduces readers to the fascinating and hard-edged world of horse racing and the reality of Saratoga life in the Depression.

Oates, Joyce Carol. *Bellefleur.* New York, NY: Plume Books, 1991. The complex and opulent tale of six generations of Bellefleurs, a wealthy and notorious family who live in a region much like the Adirondacks. Other Oates novels set upstate are *A Bloodsmoor Romance* and *Mysteries of Winterthurn.*

Wilson, Edmund. *Upstate: Records and Recollections of Northern New York.* Syracuse, NY: Syracuse University Press, 1990. One of the rare books that examines the character of upstate New York, where Wilson and his family summered for generations. The first third of the book, covering various aspects of New York history, is especially astute; the rest is diary entries.

Zabor, Rafi. *The Bear Comes Home.* New York, NY: W. W. Norton, 1998. In this winner of the PEN-Faulkner Award, an intellectual, sax-playing bear, well versed in literature, jazz, and philosophy, fights to find his place in the world. A comic gem, with great insights into what it means to be an artist, set largely in New York City and Woodstock/Bearsville, New York.

Outdoor Guides

Card, Skip. *Moon Take a Hike New York City.* Berkeley, CA. Avalon Travel, 2012. This trail guide leads you turn by turn through 80 different hikes, all within two hours of Manhattan.

Densmore Ballard, Lisa. *Best Easy Day Hikes Adirondacks.* Guilford, CT: Morris Book Publishing. This selective, rather than comprehensive, guide focuses mainly on the High Peaks region of the Adirondacks. GPS coordinates help orient readers quickly.

New York-New Jersey Trail Conference, Inc. *New York Walk Book.* Mahwah, NJ: New York-New Jersey Trail Conference, 2001. This "hiker's Bible" reflects many (but not all) of the changes that have occurred in the region since the book was first published in 1923. Some of the old trails are gone, of course, but a surprising number of new areas have also opened up, thanks largely to the public acquisition of land. The book also features excellent sections on the history, geology, flora, and fauna of the regions immediately surrounding New York City.

Internet Resources

GENERAL TRAVEL

The Official New York State Tourism Website
www.iloveny.com

This official site is packed with information on all regions of the state. Recreational areas, accommodations listings, suggested itineraries, activities and events calendars, road maps, and state facts—they're all here.

RECREATION AND THE OUTDOORS

Adirondack Mountain Club
www.adk.org

Visit this site for detailed information on outdoor activities in the Adirondacks. All topics from camping and hiking to educational seminars are covered; books, maps, and gear can be ordered from the site as well. There's also a page where you can check rates and book reservations for ADK lodges, cabins, and campsites.

America's Byways
www.byways.org

This is a U.S. Department of Transportation site that offers descriptions and maps of the country's most scenic back roads. Three New York State byways are highlighted: Great Lakes Seaway Trail, Lakes to Locks Byway, and Mohawk Towpath Byway.

New York State Department of Environmental Conservation
www.dec.ny.gov

This is a first-stop site for information on hiking, canoeing, camping, and other outdoor activities throughout the state. News articles on environmental issues and special events listings are also included.

New York State Office of Parks, Recreation, and Historic Preservation
www.parksny.gov

Each state park and historic site has its own extensive page on this informative site. Search by region or by activity for information about facilities, features, and fees.

NEW YORK CITY

NYC & Company
www.nycgo.com

At the official website of New York City's convention and visitors' bureau, you can book a hotel, learn about attractions and special events, check the weather, search out the perfect restaurant, and create your own itinerary. It makes an excellent first stop for Big Apple visitors.

New York City Government
www1.nyc.gov

On the city's official government website, find information about local laws and government departments, including the Taxi and Limousine Commission, New York Police Department, and many others. The site also has an event listings page.

LONG ISLAND

Long Island Convention and Visitors Bureau and Sports Commission
www.discoverlongisland.com

Run by Long Island Convention and Visitors Bureau and Sports Commission, this site covers cultural attractions, recreation, golf courses, restaurants, shopping malls, and more. Information on hotels and special events is also included.

THE HUDSON VALLEY AND THE CATSKILLS

Catskills Region
www.visitthecatskills.com
This official tourism site covers the four counties of the Catskills. Category listings include lodging, camping, attractions, and activities.

Hudson Valley Tourism
www.travelhudsonvalley.com
This official tourism site provides information about accommodations, dining, events, and a "things to do" section about local outdoor and cultural attractions.

THE CAPITAL-SARATOGA REGION

Albany County Convention and Visitors Bureau
www.albany.org
Visitors to Albany might want to check out this official tourism site, with things to do, places to stay, and events listings.

Saratoga County Chamber of Commerce
www.saratoga.org
Here you'll find information on where to stay, eat, and play in the horse-racing capital of New York. If you're visiting in the fall, it also has a useful fall foliage report to keep you informed about peak leaf-peeping times.

THE ADIRONDACKS

Adirondack Regional Tourism Council
www.visitadirondacks.com
To help plan your trip to the North Country, visit this site run by the Adirondacks Regional

Tourism Council. A "trip planner" feature can assist you in setting up a personalized itinerary, and you can download free travel guides.

1000 Islands International Tourism Council
www.visit1000islands.com
Everything you wanted to know about the Thousand Islands, from where to stay or play golf to "1000 Things to Do." The Communities section offers profiles about each town and its attractions.

THE FINGER LAKES

Finger Lakes Tourism Alliance
www.fingerlakes.org
Visitors to the Finger Lakes will want to check out this site, run by the Finger Lakes Tourism Alliance. In addition to information on attractions, lodging, and restaurants, the site also recommends special interest itineraries concentrating on subjects such as nature, art, and history.

BUFFALO AND THE NIAGARA REGION

Buffalo Niagara Convention and Visitors Bureau
www.visitbuffaloniagara.com
Run by the Buffalo Niagara Convention and Visitors Bureau, this site covers attractions, hotels, restaurants, and events in western New York's two biggest cities. Information on regional driving tours and special packages is also included.

Niagara USA
www.niagarafallsusa.com
This site, managed by Niagara USA, maintains an up-to-date events calendar and provides all the usual visitor information, including things to do and places to stay.

Index

A

Abyssinian Baptist Church: 82
accessibility: 103
accommodations: 448
activism: general discussion 11, 443; Harriet
    Tubman Home 345; Museum of the City of
    New York 75; Niagara Falls Underground
    Railroad Heritage Center 419; Union Square 55;
    Women's Rights National Historical Park 348-
    349; see also environmental activism/issues
Adair Vineyards: 203
Adirondack Architectural Heritage: 307
Adirondack ecosystem: 285
Adirondack History Center Museum: 286
Adirondack Lakes Center for the Arts: 304
Adirondack Mountain Club (ADK): 277, 293
Adirondack Museum: 21, 304
Adirondack Park: 30, 268, 278, 288
Adirondack Park Visitor Interpretive Center: 306
Adirondak Loj: 21, 293, 296
The Adirondacks: 268-329; Central Adirondacks
    302-310; Champlain Valley 282-289; highlights
    269; information and services 327-328;
    itinerary 21; Lake George and Adirondack
    Foothills 272-282; Lake Placid and High Peaks
    289-301; map 271; Northwest Lakes 310-314;
    outdoor adventure 30; planning tips 17, 270-
    272; resources on 457; The Thousand Islands
    314-327; transportation 329
ADK Food Hub: 29, 313
Admiral George Dewey Promenade: 44-45
aerial tours: 295
African American history/sights: African
    American Museum of Nassau County 130;
    The Apollo Theater 80; Frederick Douglass
    statue 390; Freedom Crossing Monument 424;
    Hardenberg House 207; Harlem 80-82; Harriet
    Tubman Home 345; Jerry Rescue Monument
    335; John Brown Farm State Historic Site
    292; Juneteenth Festival 411; Niagara Falls
    Underground Railroad Heritage Center 419;
    Onondaga Historical Association Museum
    336; Orient 126; Seward House 344; slavery
    and the Civil War 440-441; Underground
    Railroad 423; Wall Street 43
African American Museum of Nassau County: 130
air museums: 130, 196, 369, 375
air travel: 104, 446
Akwesasne: 327
Akwesasne Museum: 327
Alasa Farms and Crackerbox Palace: 362

Albany: 231-241
Albany Distilling Company: 235
Albany Heritage Area Visitor Center: 20, 234
Albany Institute of History & Art: 235
Albany Riverfront Park: 237
Albright-Knox Art Gallery: 407
Alexandria Bay: 322-324
Algonquin Hotel: 23, 101
Algonquin tribes: 124
Alice in Wonderland: 69
Alice Tully Hall: 84
Allegany County: 432
Allentown: 407
Allentown Art Festival: 411
Alling Coverlet Museum: 383
All Souls Episcopal Church: 118
Almanzo Wilder Homestead: 301
Altamont Fair: 240
Amagansett: 148-150
American Falls: 416
American Folk Art Museum: 76
American Merchant Marine Museum: 112
American Museum of Natural History: 19, 76
Amish Trail: 431
amusement parks: 277, 391, 415
An American Tragedy: 309
Andre Monument: 178
Andrus Planetarium: 161
animals: 436-437
Annandale-on-Hudson: 198
Anthony, Susan B.: 390
Anthony Road Wine Company: 363
Antique Boat Museum: 320
antiques: Art, Craft & Antiques Dealers' Fairs
    177; Bridgehampton 142; Cooperstown 263;
    Hudson 225; National Bottle Museum 254;
    Rhinebeck 196, 197; Saugerties 207; Upper
    Jay 288
Aperture Foundation Gallery: 57
The Apollo Theater: 80, 83
Appalachian Trail: 30, 160
Appellate Division of the New York State
    Supreme Court: 55
aquariums: Aquarium of Niagara 419; Cold
    Spring Harbor Fish Hatchery and Aquarium
    115; Long Island Aquarium and Exhibition
    Center 120-121; New York State Department
    of Environmental Conservation's Research
    Station and Aquarium 320
arboretums: Bayard Cutting Arboretum 136-
    137; Highland Park 388; Mary Flagler Cary

Arboretum 191; Planting Fields Arboretum State Historic Park 114; Sonnenberg Gardens and Mansion 379
Arbor Hill Grapery: 384
architecture: Boldt Castle 322-323; Buffalo 406, 407, 410; Cathedral of St. John the Divine 78; Catskill 221; The Chrysler Building 61; City Hall Park 45; cobblestone houses 429, 430; The Dakota 76; Eldridge Street Synagogue 47; Ellenville 206; Empire State Building 63; Empire State Plaza 234; Federal Hall National Memorial 43; Flatiron Building 55; Gold Coast 111-112; Grand Central Terminal 59-61; Guggenheim Museum 73; Hurley Stone House Day 207; Landmark Theatre 336; Merchant's House Museum 51; Metropolitan Life Insurance Company 55; Mohonk Mountain House and Preserve 204; Morris-Jumel Mansion 82; National Museum of the American Indian 43; New York Life Insurance Company 55; New York Public Library 64; New York State Capitol Building 235; New York State Executive Mansion 237; Niagara Mohawk Power Corporation 335; Olana State Historic Site 224-225; Richard B. Fisher Center for Performing Arts 199; Saratoga Springs 242; Soho 50; Stanley Center for the Arts 265; St. John the Baptist Ukrainian Catholic Church 219; Thousand Island Park 324; Trinity Church 44; Upper East Side 70-71; Washington Square Park 53; White Pine Camp 301; Whitney Museum of American Art 58; Willard Memorial Chapel 346; Wing's Castle 191; Woolworth Building 45; see also Hudson Valley estates
area codes: 451
Arnot Art Museum: 369
Arrowhead Spring Vineyards: 428
art events and sights: Adirondack Lakes Center for the Arts 304; Albany Institute of History & Art 235; Amish crafts 432; Art, Craft & Antiques Dealers' Fairs 177; Artpark 424; best bets 22; Buffalo 407, 408; Catskill 221; Cedar Grove 222; Cooperstown 260; Corning glass art 372; Cunneen-Hackett Arts Center 188; Decoy and Wildlife Art Show 322; East Hampton 145; East Village 50; Edward Hopper House Art Center 176-177; Frances Lehman Loeb Art Center 190; Ithaca 358; Jay Craft Center 288; Kenan Center 427; Memorial Art Gallery 387; Munson Williams Proctor Arts Institute 265; Phoenicia 213; Piermont Flywheel Gallery 176; Pollock-Krasner House and Study Center 149; Roxbury Arts Group 212; Roycroft Campus 414; Soho 50; St. Mark's Church in-the-Bowery 50-51; Storm King Art Center 183; Tang Teaching Museum and Art Gallery 243; TAUNY Center and North Country Folkstore 326; Thousand Islands Arts Center 321; as a top experience 14; Union Church of Pocantico Hills 168; View 308; West Chelsea Galleries 56; Winter Garden at Brookfield Place 44; Wizard of Clay 394; Woodstock 209; Woodstock-New Paltz Art & Crafts Fairs 203; Yaddo 245-247
art museums: American Folk Art Museum 76; Arnot Art Museum 369; Asia Society 75; Brooklyn Museum 90; Caramoor Center for Music and the Arts 170-171; Castellani Art Museum 424; Cooper-Hewitt National Design Museum 73; Dia:Beacon 174; Everson Museum of Art 336; Fenimore Art Museum 262; Frederic Remington Art Museum 325; The Frick Collection 71; Guggenheim Museum 73; Herbert F. Johnson Museum of Art 355; Hyde Collection 272-274; International Center of Photography 43; Katonah Museum of Art 171; Kykuit 167; Long Island Museum of American Art, History and Carriages 119; The Metropolitan Museum of Art 71; Museum of Modern Art 66; Nassau County Museum of Art 112; Neuberger Museum 171; Neue Galerie 73; New Museum 43; Parrish Art Museum 140; Rockwell Museum of Western Art 372; Rubin Museum of Art 57; Schweinfurth Memorial Art Center 346; The Studio Museum in Harlem 80; Water Mill Museum 142; Whitney Museum of American Art 58
Artpark: 424
Ashland: 219
Ashokan Reservoir: 28, 211
Asia Society: 75
Athens: 223
At the Western Door: 388
Auburn: 343-347
Audubon Terrace: 82
Augustus Sacket Mansion: 318
Aurora: 351-352
Ausable Chasm: 287
Au Sable Forks: 288
authors: Almanzo Wilder Homestead 301; Cooper, James Fenimore 258; Irving, Washington 164; Mark Twain's Study 368; Stevenson, Robert Louis 298; Wharton, Edith 193; Whitman, Walt 117
Avery Fisher Hall: 84

B
Bald Mountain: 309
ballet: 84-85, 358
Ballston Spa: 254
banking: 451
Barbara Gladstone Gallery: 56
Barcelona: 433

Bard College: 198

Barker: 426

Barney Greengrass: 23, 96

Barton Garnet Mines: 305

baseball: Buffalo Bisons 410; Doubleday Field 260; National Baseball Hall of Fame and Museum 258-259; New York Mets 62; New York Yankees 62

Battery Park: 44

Battery Park City Esplanade: 45

Bayard Cutting Arboretum: 136-137

bay houses: 129

Bay Shore: 135-137

beaches: Amagansett 149-150; East Hampton 145; Fire Island 134; Heckscher State Park 136; Jones Beach 129-130; Lake George 274; Montauk 152; Orient 126; Southampton 142; South Fork 139; Sunken Meadow State Park 117-118; as a top experience 10; Wildwood State Park 120

Beacon: 174

Beacon Theatre: 83

Bear Mountain State Park: 21, 26, 30, 179

bed-and-breakfasts: 448

Beekman Arms: 194

Belleayre: 215

Belvedere Castle: 70

Bemus Point: 433

Benjamin Patterson Inn Museum Complex: 372

Bethel Woods Center for the Arts: 211

Bethesda Terrace: 69

Big Duck: 136

Big Moose Lake: 308

biking: Canalway Trail 412; Glimmerglass State Park 264; Hook Mountain State Park 177; Hudson River bridges 162; Mohonk Mountain House and Preserve 204

bird-watching: Central Park 70; Constitution Marsh Audubon Center Sanctuary 172; Elizabeth A. Morton National Wildlife Refuge 147; Fire Island 134; High Tor Wildlife Management Area 384; Mashomack Preserve 127; Merrill Lake Sanctuary 150; Montezuma Audubon Center 350; Orient Beach State Park 126; Piermont Marsh 176; Rockefeller State Park Preserve 168; Sapsucker Woods Bird Sanctuary 357; Theodore Roosevelt Sanctuary and Audubon Center 114

Birkett Mills: 377

Black Sheep Restaurant & Bar: 29, 412

Blue Hill at Stone Barns: 19, 29, 170

Blue Mountain Lake: 31, 303-304

Blue Ridge Road: 282

Blues Festival: 338

boating: Antique Boat Museum 320; Antique Boat Show and Auction 322; Buffalo 410;

Canandaigua Lake 381; Chittenango Landing Canal Boat Museum 266; Erie Canal 338, 428; Findley Lake 433; Great South Bay 136; Hudson River Adventures 184; Lake George 274; Lake Placid 293; Lake Superior State Park 211; Niagara Falls 418; North-South Lakes 216; Rochester 391; Schroon Lake 281; Seneca Lake 365; Skaneateles Lake 341, 342; Thousand Islands 323; wooden canal boats 393

Boiceville: 212

Boldt Castle: 322-323

Bolton Historical Museum: 279

Bolton Landing: 279-280

Booth Theater: 63, 84

breweries: Cooperstown 263; Sackets Harbor 318; Saranac Brewery 265; Wagner 364; Woodcock Brothers Brewery 426

Bridal Veil Falls: 416

Bridgehampton: 142-143

Bristol Mountain Winter Resort: 381

British colonization: 439-440

Broadway and Lower 5th Avenue: 55

Broadway Market: 410

Broadway shows: 23, 85, 98

Broadway street: 49

Bronx: 79

Brooklyn: 79, 90

Brooklyn Bridge: 21, 45, 90

Brooklyn Bridge Park: 90

Brooklyn Museum: 90

Brotherhood Winery: 185

Brown's Race: 387

Bryant Park: 64

Buck Mountain: 277

buckwheat: 377

Buddhist temple: 220

Buffalo: 403-413

The Buffalo History Museum: 407

Buffalo and Erie County Botanical Gardens: 410

Buffalo and Erie County Naval and Military Park: 404

Buffalo and the Niagara Region: 398-434; Buffalo 403-413; highlights 399; information and services 434; maps 400, 402; Niagara Falls 416-422; north of Niagara Falls 422-428; Orleans County 428-429; outdoor adventure 32; planning tips 17, 401; resources on 457; south of Buffalo 430-434; transportation 434

Buffalo Bills: 411

Buffalo City Hall: 406

Buffalo Museum of Science: 410

Buffalo Sabres: 411

Buffalo Zoo: 409

Bully Hill Vineyards: 376

Burchfield-Penney Art Center: 408

business hours: 451

bus travel: 447
Buttermilk Falls State Park: 357

C

Cairo: 220
Cambridge: 20, 252
camping: general discussion 448; Adirondack Mountain Club (ADK) 277; Cayuga Lake 352; Clayton 322; Cranberry Lake 313; Elmira 370; Fillmore Glen State Park 347; Greenport 125; Harriman State Park 179; Hunter Mountain 219; Lake George 278, 280; Lake Luzerne 279; Lake Taghkanic State Park 199; Letchworth State Park 395; Long Lake 302; Mills-Norrie State Park 193; Montauk 154; Mount Tremper 212; North-South Lakes 216; Old Bethpage Village 117; Robert Moses State Park 327; Saranac Lake 299; St. Regis Canoe Area 310; Taconic State Park 200; Wildwood State Park 120; Woodland Valley 213
camps, Adirondack: 307
Camp Santanoni: 307
Canalside District: 404
Canal Side Experiences: 351
Canalway Trail: 412
Canandaigua: 378-381
Canandaigua Lake: 378-384
Canastota Canal Town Museum: 266
Canfield Casino: 243
canoeing: see paddling
Canton: 326
Cape Vincent: 319
Cape Vincent Historical Museum: 319
Capital Region Scottish Games: 240
The Capital-Saratoga Region: 229-267; Albany 231-241; Central New York 255-267; highlights 230; information and services 267; itinerary 20; maps 232-233; outdoor adventure 31-32; planning tips 17, 231; resources on 457; Saratoga Springs 242-255; transportation 267
capitol buildings: 234, 235
Caramoor Center for Music and the Arts: 170
Caramoor Rosen House: 171
Carnegie Hall: 84
carousels: Adirondack Carousel 300; Central Park 68; Greenport 125; Herschell Carrousel Factory 415; New York State Museum 235; Rochester 391; Sea Glass Carousel 45
car racing: 262, 364, 365
carriage rides, Central Park: 68
carriages, historic: 119, 148, 380
Cary Institute of Ecosystem Studies: 191
Cascade Mountain Winery: 191
Case Research Lab: 346
Cashel House: 337
casinos: 247, 327, 419

Castellani Art Museum: 424
Castello di Borghese-Hargrave Vineyard: 123
Castle Clinton: 38
Castle Hotel and Spa: 19, 170
Catamount Ski Area: 200
Cathedral of St. John the Divine: 78
Catskill: 221-223
Catskill Fly Fishing Center and Museum: 218
Catskill Forest Preserve: 211
Catskill Mountain House Site: 216
Catskill Mountain Railroad: 21, 213
Catskill Mountains: 21, 28, 208-221
Catskill Park: 28, 30, 211
Cattaraugus County: 431
Cave of the Winds tours: 418
caves: Ausable Chasm 287; Chimney Mountain 305; Natural Stone Bridge and Caves 281; Schoharie County 257; Shawangunk Mountains 204
Cavin-Morris Gallery: 57
Cayuga Lake: 347-353
Cayuga Lake State Park: 350
Cayuga Museum and Case Research Lab: 346
Cedar Grove: 222
Center for Curatorial Studies: 199
Center for Photography at Woodstock: 209
Central Adirondacks: 302-310
Central Harlem: 80
Central Nassau County: 130-132
Central New York: 255-267
Central Park: 19, 23, 67-70
Ceres Gallery: 57
Champlain Monument: 288
The Champ: 284-285
Chapman Historical Museum: 274
Chappaqua: 171
Charles A. Dana Discovery Center: 70
Charles Department Store: 170
Charles E. Burchfield Nature & Art Center: 408
Charlotte-Genesee Lighthouse: 390
The Chathams: 227
Chautauqua County: 432
Chautauqua Institution: 433
Chelsea and the Meatpacking District: 18; accommodations 100; food 94-95; map 56; nightlife 86-87; shopping 89; sights 56-58
Chemung Valley History Museum: 369
Cherry Grove: 133
Chess and Checkers House: 68
Children's Museum of Manhattan: 78
Children's Museum of the Arts: 53
Childs: 429
Chimney Bluffs State Park: 361
Chimney Mountain: 305
Chinatown: 46, 92-93
Chinese American culture: 46

Chippewa District: 406
Chittenango Landing Canal Boat Museum: 266
Christ Episcopal Church: 260
Christmas events: New York City 64, 66, 83; Old
    Bethpage Village 117; Skaneateles Lake 342
Christopher Park and Sheridan Square: 53
The Chrysler Building: 61
Chuang Yen Monastery: 173
churches: *see* religious sights
cider, hard: 427
City Hall: 45
City Hall Park: 45
Civil War history: 440-441
classical music: Buffalo Philharmonic Orchestra
    411; Ithaca 358; Lake Luzerne Chamber Music
    Festival 279; Music from Salem 253; Rochester
    Philharmonic Orchestra 391; Skaneateles
    Festival 342
Clayton: 320
Clearwater Great Hudson River Revival: 188
The *Clearwater*: 188
Clermont State Historic Site: 199
Clift Park: 341
climate: 436
Clinton Academy: 143
Clinton County Historical Museum: 289
Clinton Square: 334
The Cloisters: 82
The Clothesline Art Sale: 145
Clove Furnace Historic Site: 180
cobblestone houses: 430
cocktails: 87
Coe Hall: 114
coffee: 97
Cold Spring: 172-174
Cold Spring Harbor: 27, 115-117
Cold Spring Harbor Fish Hatchery and
    Aquarium: 115
Cole, Thomas: 222
colleges and universities: Bard College 198;
    Columbia University 78; Cornell University
    355; Paul Smith's College 300; State University
    of New York at New Paltz 203; Stony Brook
    University 118; Union College 256; Vassar
    College 188
Colonel's Chair: 217
Colonial Street Festival: 202
Columbia County Historical Society Museum
    and Library: 227
Columbia University Area: 78
Columbus Park: 46
Concrete Sculpture Garden: 314
Congress Park: 243
Conservatory Garden: 70, 75
Conservatory Water: 69
Constitution Island: 181

Constitution Marsh Audubon Center Sanctuary:
    30, 172
Convention Days Celebration: 350
Cooper-Hewitt National Design Museum: 73
Coopers Beach: 142
Cooperstown: 32, 258-264
Cooper's Town: 260
Copake Auction: 200
Copake Falls: 200
Cornell Botanic Gardens: 357
Cornell University: 355
Corning: 370-374
Corning Museum of Glass: 371-372
Corning Preserve: 237
Corning Tower: 20, 234
Cornwall Brothers Store and Museum: 323
Cornwall-on-Hudson: 183-184
Council Rock: 260
Crackerbox Palace: 362
Cradle of Aviation Museum: 130
craft beer: 263
Cranberry Lake: 313-314
Crawford House: 184
The Creamery: 342
cross-country skiing: Adirondack Mountains 295;
    Finger Lakes National Forest 350; Mohonk
    Mountain House and Preserve 204; Olympic
    Cross-Country Biathlon Center 293
Cross Island Chapel: 266
Cross River: 171
Crown Point: 284
Crown Point State Historic Site: 284
cuisine, farm fresh: *see* farm fresh cuisine
The Culinary Institute of America: 19, 193-194
culture: Amish 431; French Heritage Day 319;
    Irish 221, 337; Iroquois 337; Latinx 75, 82;
    Mennonite 376; Shakers 239; Ukrainian 219;
    see also Jewish culture
Cumming Nature Center: 384
Cunneen-Hackett Arts Center: 188
Currie-Bell House: 124
Custom House: 147
Cutchogue: 122

D

D&H Canal Museum: 206
Dairy, Central Park: 68
The Dakota: 76
dance: National Museum of Dance and Hall of
    Fame 247; New York City 84-85; Saratoga
    Springs 253
Davenport Farms: 207
The David H. Koch Theater: 76, 85
Decoy and Wildlife Art Show: 322
Delacorte Theater: 70
Delamater Inn: 196, 197

Delaware Park: 409
Delord family: 289
Dering Harbor: 127
design museum: 73
Devil's Hole State Park: 422
DeWint House: 178
DeWitt Park: 354
Dia:Beacon: 174
Diamond District: 64
diamond mining: 265
Dickens Christmas: 342
Dirt Candy: 29, 93
disabilities, access for travelers with: 103
discounts, NYC: 98
Discover Albany Visitor Center: 235
distilleries: 185, 235
diving: 281
dog breeding: 253
domestic travelers: 451
Donald M. Kendall Sculpture Gardens at
    PepsiCo: 171
Doubleday Field: 260
downtown Buffalo: 406
Dragon Rock: 172
The Drawing Center: 50
Dr. Frank's Vinifera Wine Cellars: 376
drinking: 87
drive-ins: 221
driving: 447
dude ranches: 279
Dunkirk: 433
Dutchess County: 187
Dwight D. Eisenhower Lock: 326

E

East Aurora: 414
East Durham: 220-221
East Durham Irish Festival: 221
East End Seaport Museum and Maritime
    Foundation: 125
East Hampton: 143-146
East Hampton Town Marine Museum: 149
East Village: accommodations 99; food 93-94;
    map 51; nightlife 86; shopping 89; sights 50-51
economy, historic: 441, 443-444
Eden: 414-415
Edward Hopper House Art Center: 176-177
Egyptian collection: 71
Elbert Hubbard-Roycroft Museum: 414
Eldridge Street Synagogue: 47
Eleanor and Wilson Greatbatch Pavilion: 410
Eleanor Roosevelt National Historic Site: 193
Eleven Madison Park: 18, 95
Elizabeth A. Morton National Wildlife Refuge: 147
Elizabeth Cady Stanton House: 349
Elizabethtown: 286-287

Ellenville: 206
Ellicott Square Building: 406
Ellicottville: 431
Ellis Island: 18, 38
Elmendorf House: 207
Elmira: 366-370
El Museo del Barrio: 75
emergencies: 104
Emerson: 212
Empire City Casino at Yonkers Raceway: 162
Empire State Building: 19, 23, 63
Empire State Plaza: 20, 234
Empire State Railway Museum: 213
Enchanted Forest/Water Safari: 308
environmental activism/issues: general
    discussion 437; Adirondack ecosystem 285;
    Cary Institute of Ecosystem Studies 191; The
    Clearwater 188; Hudson Highlands Nature
    Museum 183; Hudson River 224; Pine Barrens
    120; Riverhead Foundation for Marine
    Research 121
Erie Basin Marina: 404
Erie Canal: 266, 394, 427, 440
Erie Canal Aqueduct: 382
Erie Canal Cruise: 428
Erie Canal Museum: 334
Erie Canalway Trail: 266
Escarpment Trail: 30, 215
Essex: 286
Essex County Courthouse: 286
estates, Hudson Valley: 165
European colonization: 437
European paintings at the Met: 71
Everson Museum of Art: 336

F

Fairport: 394
fairs: Altamont Fair 240; Columbia County Fair
    227; New York State Fair 338; Rhinebeck 196;
    Ulster County Fair 203; Wayne County Fair 383;
    Yates County Fair 378
Falaise: 112
Falcon Ridge Folk Festival: 200
fall foliage: Catskill Mountain Railroad 213;
    itineraries 24-26; North-South Lakes 216;
    Route 28N 306
family activities: American Museum of Natural
    History 78; Central Park 68; Children's Museum
    of Manhattan 78; Children's Museum of the
    Arts 53; Emerson 212; Fantasy Island 415; Fire
    Island 133; Herkimer diamond mining 265;
    Howe Caverns 257; Intrepid Sea, Air, and
    Space Museum Complex 63; Kids Night Out on
    Broadway 85; Lake George amusement parks
    277; Long Island Aquarium and Exhibition
    Center 121; Long Island Children's Museum

130; Museum of Innovation and Science 255; Museum of Mathematics 55; New York State Zoo 319; Quogue 139-140; Radio City Music Hall 66; Rubenstein Museum of Science and Technology 336; Santa's Workshop 297; Saratoga Spa State Park 248; ScienCenter 355; Seabreeze Amusement Park 391; The Strong National Museum of Play 387; Swedish Cottage 70; The Wild Center 311-313; *see also* carousels

Fantasy Island: 415

farm fresh cuisine: Blue Hill at Stone Barns 170; Briermere Farms 121; The Culinary Institute of America 193-194; New York Kitchen 380; Schenectady 257; Southold 123; Sprague's Maple Farms 432; as a top experience 15; Utica 265

farmers markets: ADK Food Hub 313; Bethel Woods Center for the Arts 211; Broadway Market 410; Rhinebeck 197; Windmill Farm and Craft Market 378

farms: Alasa Farms and Crackerbox Palace 362; Greig Farm 198; Long Acre Farms 393; Montgomery Place Orchards 198; Nettle Meadow Goat Farm and Cheese Factory 306; Stone Ridge Orchard 207

FASNY Museum of Firefighting: 225

FDR's Home, Library, and Museum: 19, 192

Federal Hall National Memorial: 43

Federal Reserve Bank of New York: 44

Fenimore Art Museum: 262

ferries: Ellis Island 38; Fire Island 133; Fort Ticonderoga Ferry 284; Horne's Ferry 320; Lake Champlain Ferries 286; New York City 107; Port Jefferson 119; Staten Island 38

Field Notes: 29, 257

5th Avenue: 19, 23, 66-67

film festivals: 210

film industry: 346

Findley Lake: 433

Finger Lakes National Forest: 31, 350

Finger Lakes Trail: 31, 350

Finger Lakes Wine Center: 380

The Finger Lakes: 330-397; Canandaigua Lake 378-384; Cayuga Lake 347-353; Corning 370-374; Elmira 366-370; highlights 331; information and services 396; Ithaca 353-359; Keuka Lake 374-378; Little Finger Lakes 394-395; map 333; outdoor adventure 31; Owasco Lake 343-347; planning tips 17, 332; resources on 457; Rochester 385-394; Seneca Lake 359-366; Skaneateles Lake 341-343; Syracuse 334-341; transportation 397

Fire Island: 16, 132-135

Fire Island National Seashore: 31, 132

Fire Island Pines: 133

fire museums: 50, 132, 225

fishing: Adirondack Mountains 328; Central Park 70; fly-fishing 218; Hunter Mountain 219; Lake Superior State Park 211; Long Island 154; Montauk 152; North-South Lakes 216; Nyack Beach State Park 177; Phoenicia 213; Saranac Lake 299; Ward Pound Ridge Reservation 171; Watkins Glen 365

575 Broadway: 50

Flatiron Building: 55

flightseeing: 295

fly-fishing: 218

folk art museum: 76

folk music: 200, 240

food trucks: 94

Fort Hill Cemetery: 345

Fort Niagara State Park: 426

Fort Ontario State Historic Site: 315

Fort Tryon Park: 82

Fort William Henry: 274

Fort William Henry Museum: 274

46 Peaks: 290-292

fossils: 241, 257

Fox Run Vineyards: 362

Frances Lehman Loeb Art Center: 188

Franklin D. Roosevelt Four Freedoms Park: 79

Franklin D. Roosevelt Presidential Library and Museum: 192

Fraunces Tavern: 43

Frederic Remington Art Museum: 325

Freedom Crossing Monument: 424

Freeport: 128-129

French Heritage Day: 319

The Frick Collection: 19, 71

Fulkerson Winery: 363

Fulton Chain: 308

F. W. Battenfeld & Sons: 198

FX Matt Brewing Company: 265

G

Gagosian Gallery: 57

Gannett Hill: 384

Ganondagan State Historic Site: 382

gardens: Admiral George Dewey Promenade 44-45; Buffalo and Erie County Botanical Gardens 410; Central Park 69, 70; Conservatory Garden 75; Constitution Island 181; Cornell Botanic Gardens 357; Edward Hopper House Art Center 177; Garden Walk Buffalo 411; Innisfree Garden 190-191; John Jay Homestead 171; Kykuit 167; Lamberton Conservatory 390; Manitoga 172; Mohonk Mountain House and Preserve 204; Nassau County Museum of Art 112; Old Westbury 113; Samuel Morse Historic Site 188; Sonnenberg Gardens and Mansion 379; Sunnyside 164; Union College 256;

Vanderbilt Mansion National Historic Site 193; *see also* arboretums
garnet mines: 305
General Grant National Memorial: 78
Genesee Country Village and Museum: 393
Geneva: 24, 360-361
geography: 435-436
George Eastman House: 388
Gibson-Mack-Holt House: 135
Gifford House Visitor and Education Center: 191
Gilboa Museum: 257
glacial potholes: 280
glass museum: 371-372
Glenn H. Curtiss Museum: 375
Glenora Wine Cellars: 363
Glens Falls: 20, 272-274
Glimmerglass State Park: 32, 262, 264
Goat Island: 418
Gold Coast: 16, 26, 111-112
golf: 220, 431
Gomez Mill House: 185
gondola rides: 297
Gore Mountain: 305
Gottesman Hall: 64
government: 444-445
Governors Island: 42, 79
Gracie Mansion: 71
The Graham & Co.: 21, 213
Gramercy Park: 55
Gramercy Tavern: 23, 95
Grand Central Oyster Bar: 61
Grand Central Terminal: 59-61
Grand Island: 415
Grand Prix Festival: 364
Granger Homestead and Carriage Museum: 380
Grange Sard Jr. House: 238
Grant, President Ulysses S.: 254
Grant Cottage: 21, 254
Great Camp Sagamore: 307
Great Depression: 442
Great Escape & Hurricane Harbor: 277
Great Lawn: 70
Great Neck Peninsula: 111-113
Great Western Winery Visitor Center: 375
Greene County Courthouse: 221
Greenmarket: 53
Greenport: 26, 125-126
Green River Cemetery: 149
Greenwich Village and West Village: accommodations 99; food 94; map 52; nightlife 86; shopping 89; sights 51-53
Griffis Sculpture Park: 431
Guaranteed Irish: 220
Guaranty Building: 406
Guggenheim Museum: 19, 23, 73

Guild Hall: 145
Guinness Museum of World Records: 422

H

Hadley Mountain: 279
Hallockville Museum Farm: 121
Hammondsport: 375-377
The Hamptons: 16, 137-155
hang gliding: 206, 369
Hans Christian Andersen statue: 70
Hardenberg House: 207
Harlem: food 96; map 81; nightlife 88; shopping 92; sights 80-82
Harlem Meer: 70
Harriet Hollister Spencer State Recreation Area: 394
Harriet Tubman Home: 345
Harriman State Park: 26, 30, 179
Harris Hill: 369
Harris Hill Soaring Center: 24, 369
hatcheries: 115
Haughwout Building: 50
Havens House: 127
Hayden Planetarium: 78
Hazlitt's Red Cat Cellars: 384
health: 449-450
Heckscher State Park: 135-136
Helen Hayes Theater: 63
Hempstead House: 112
Henderson: 317
Henderson Harbor: 317
Henry A. Wallace Visitor and Education Center: 192
Henry Luce Nature Observatory at Belvedere Castle: 70
Herbert F. Johnson Museum of Art: 355
Heritage Area Visitor Center: 242, 247, 334, 348
Herkimer: 265
Hermann J. Wiemer Vineyard: 363
Heron Hill Winery: 376
Herschell Carrousel Factory: 415
The High Line: 18, 57
High Falls: 21, 206, 387
High Falls Gorge: 25, 387
Highland Park: 388
Highmount: 215
High Peaks: 31, 289-301
High Tor Wildlife Management Area: 384
hiking: Adirondack Mountains 277, 293, 328; Bald Mountain 309; Bear Mountain State Park 179; Blue Mountain 304; Cairo 220; Chimney Mountain 305; Cranberry Lake 313; Escarpment Trail 215; Fillmore Glen State Park 347; Finger Lakes National Forest 350; 46 Peaks 290-292; Glimmerglass State Park 264; Harriman State Park 179; High Tor Wildlife

Management Area 384; Hook Mountain State Park 177; Hunter Mountain 217-218; Hurricane Mountain 287; Lake George 277; Lake Luzerne 279; Lake Taghkanic State Park 199; Long Lake 302; Manitoga 172; Mohonk Mountain House and Preserve 204; Nyack Beach State Park 177; Pharaoh Mountain 281; Saranac Lake 299; Siamese Ponds Wilderness Area 305; Snowy Mountain 305; Teatown Lake Reservation 168; as a top experience 9; Ward Pound Ridge Reservation 171; Watkins Glen State Park 365; Woodland Valley 213

Hill Cumorah Pageant: 383

Hill Cumorah Visitor Center: 383

Hillsdale: 200

The Hispanic Society of America Museum and Library: 82

Historic Beth Joseph Synagogue: 313

Historic Cherry Hill: 237

Historic DeWitt Park: 354

historic sights: Albany 237, 238; American Museum of Natural History 76; Beacon 174; Beekman Arms 194; Benjamin Patterson Inn Museum Complex 372; Buffalo 407; Canandaigua 380; Castle Clinton 38; Clermont State Historic Site 199; Cold Spring 172; Constitution Island 181; Cooperstown 260; Crown Point 284; Cutchogue 122; East Hampton 143-145; Ellis Island 38; Farmers' Museum 260; Federal Hall National Memorial 43; Fort Ontario State Historic Site 315; Fort Ticonderoga 283; Fraunces Tavern 43; Ganondagan State Historic Site 382; General Grant National Memorial 78; Genesee Country Village and Museum 393; Geneva 360; Gillette case 309; Governors Island 79; Grant Cottage 254; Hallockville Museum Farm 121; The Hamptons 139; Harriman mines 180; Hempstead bay houses 129; Hudson 224; Hudson Valley estates 165; Huguenot Street 202; Hurley 207; Hyde Park 192-193; Ithaca 353, 354; Katonah 170, 171; Kinderhook 226-227; Lake George 274, 275; Lake Placid 292; Matilda Joslyn Gage House 337; Merchant's House Museum 51; Montauk 151; National September 11 Memorial and Museum 44; New-York Historical Society 76; Niagara Falls Underground Railroad Heritage Center 419; Olana State Historic Site 224-225; Old Bethpage Village 117; Old Fort Niagara 426; Orient 126; Oyster Bay 114; Palmyra 383; Philipse Manor Hall State Historic Site 161; Rochester 388, 390; Roxbury 212; Sackets Harbor 317-318; Sag Harbor 146, 147; Samuel Morse Historic Site 188; Saratoga Springs 242; Schenectady 255-256; Seneca Falls

348-350; Shelter Island 127; Society for the Preservation of Long Island Antiquities Gallery 115; Southampton Historical Museum 140; Southold 124; South Street Seaport 45; Staatsburgh State Historic Site 193; St. James General Store 118; Stonewall Inn 86; Stony Brook 118-119; Suffolk County Historical Society 121; Tarrytown and Sleepy Hollow 164, 167, 168; Theodore Roosevelt Birthplace National Historic Site 55; Theodore Roosevelt Inaugural National Historic Site 407; Walt Whitman Birthplace State Historic Site 117; Watervliet Shaker National Historic District 239; William Floyd Estate 135; see also Revolutionary War sites

history: 437-444

History Center in Tompkins County: 355

Hither Hills State Park: 31, 152

H. Lee White Marine Museum: 315

Holiday Valley: 431

Home Sweet Home: 143

Honeoye: 394

Hook Mountain State Park: 177

horseback riding: Finger Lakes National Forest 350; Lake Luzerne 279; Montauk 152

horse racing: Finger Lakes Gaming & Racetrack 381; National Museum of Racing and Hall of Fame 244-245; Saratoga Casino and Raceway 247; Saratoga Race Course 245; season 248-249; Yonkers Raceway 162

Horseshoe Falls: 416, 421

Horton Point Lighthouse: 124

hostels: 448

hotels: 448

Howe Caverns: 32, 257

Hudson: 20, 223-226

Hudson, Henry: 437-438

Hudson-Athens Lighthouse: 223

Hudson Highlands: 30, 181

Hudson Highlands Nature Museum: 183

Hudson River: 224

Hudson River Adventures: 184

Hudson River Gorge: 305

Hudson River Museum: 161

Hudson River Way: 237

The Hudson Valley and the Catskills: 156-228; Catskill Mountains 208-221; highlights 157; information and services 228; itineraries 19, 21; Lower Hudson Valley 161-186; maps 158-159; Mid-Hudson Valley 186-228; outdoor adventure 30; planning tips 16-17, 160; resources on 457; transportation 228; Upper Hudson Valley 221-227

Hudson Valley estates: 16; Clermont State Historic Site 199; Kykuit 167; Locust Grove 188; Lyndhurst 164; Montgomery Place 198;

Philipsburg Manor 167; Philipse Manor Hall State Historic Site 161; Sunnyside 164; Val-Kill 193; Van Cortland Manor 168; Vanderbilt Mansion National Historic Site 193; Wilderstein 196
Hudson Valley Hot-Air Balloon Festival: 196
Huguenot Historical Society: 203
Huguenot Street: 21, 28, 202
Hunter Mountain: 25, 216-219
Hurley: 207
Hurricane Mountain: 287
Hyatt Times Square: 18, 101
Hyde Collection: 20, 272-274
Hyde Hall: 264
Hyde Park: 19, 192-194
Hyde Park Trail: 192

I

ice climbing: 295
ice-skating: Bryant Park 64; Central Park 68; Lake Placid 292; Mohonk Mountain House and Preserve 204; Rockefeller Center 66
Ichabod Crane School House: 227
immigrant culture, historic: 46
Indian Field: 151
Indian Kettles: 280
Indian Ladder Geologic Trail: 241
Indian Lake: 304-305
Innisfree Garden: 190-191
Inspire Moore Winery and Vineyard: 384
International Center of Photography: 43
international travelers: 451
Internet resources: 456-457
Intrepid Sea, Air, and Space Museum Complex: 63
Irish culture: 221, 337
Ironville: 284
Italian American culture: 46
Ithaca: 353-359
Ithaca Commons: 353
Ithaca Falls: 355
itineraries: 18-32, 90; best-of 18-21; Brooklyn day trip 90; fall foliage drives 24-26; NYC day trips 27-28; outdoor adventure 30-32

J

Jackson's Gardens: 256
Jacqueline Onassis Reservoir: 70
James Lane: 143
Jamestown: 432
James Vanderpoel House: 227
Jay: 288
Jean Hasbrouck House: 202
Jerry Rescue Monument: 335
The Jewish Museum: 73-75
Jewish culture: Eldridge Street Synagogue 47;

Gomez Mill House 185; Historic Beth Joseph Synagogue 313; The Jewish Museum 73-75; The Museum of Jewish Heritage 45
Jikohnsaseh: 382
John Boyd Thacher State Park: 31, 241
John Brown Farm State Historic Site: 21, 292
John Drew Theater: 145
John Jay Homestead: 171
Jones Beach: 16, 129-130
Journey Behind the Falls: 422
Junction Pool: 218
Juneteenth Festival: 411

K

Kaaterskill Falls: 25, 215
Kaaterskill Wild Forest: 25, 215
Karma Triyana Dharmachakra: 28, 209
Katonah: 170
Katonah Museum of Art: 171
Katz's: 18, 93
kayaking: see paddling
kazoo factory: 415
Keene: 287
Kenan Center: 427
Kent-Delord House Museum: 288-289
Keuka Lake: 374-378
Kinderhook: 226-227
Kingfisher Tower: 260
Kismet: 133
Knapp Winery: 352
Krasner, Lee: 149
Kykuit: 19, 27, 167

L

Ladies' Mile: 55
Lake Awosting: 206
Lake Champlain: 21, 31, 282
Lakefront Park: 260
Lake George: 21, 25, 31, 272-282
Lake George Historical Association and Museum: 275
Lake George Village: 274-279
Lake House: 238
Lake Luzerne: 279
Lake Luzerne Chamber Music Festival: 279
Lake Minnewaska: 204
Lake Placid: 21, 25, 30, 289-301
Lake Placid-North Elba Historical Society Museum: 292
Lake Placid Olympic Museum: 292
Lake Placid Sliding Center: 292
Lake Sebago: 179
Lake Superior State Park: 211
Lake Taghkanic State Park: 30, 199
Lake Tear of the Clouds: 293

The Lake: 69
Lake Tiorati: 179
Lamberton Conservatory: 390
Lamoreaux Landing Wine Cellars: 364
Landmark Theatre: 336
Lark Street: 238
lectures: 433
Lennon, John: 69
Lenz Winery: 123
Letchworth Museum: 395
Letchworth State Park: 31, 394-395
Lewiston: 424
Lexington: 219
LGBTQ+ events and sights: Albany 240; Fire Island
    resorts 133; New York City travel tips 103;
    Stonewall 53
libraries: 58, 64, 198
Lido Beach: 130
Lift Bridge: 394
lighthouses: Barcelona and Dunkirk 433;
    Fire Island Lighthouse 134; Horton Point
    Lighthouse 124; Hudson-Athens Lighthouse
    223; Montauk Lighthouse 152; Rochester 390;
    Sodus Bay Lighthouse Museum 361; Tibbetts
    Point Lighthouse 320
Lincoln Center for the Performing Arts: 75-76, 84
literature: see authors
Little Finger Lakes: 394-395
Little Italy: 46, 93
Livingston Manor: 218
Lockport: 427
Lockport Cave and Underground Boat Ride: 427
locks, St. Lawrence Seaway: 326
Locust Grove: 188
Locust Lawn: 203
Loeb Boathouse: 69
Logan Monument: 346
Long Acre Farms: 393
Long Beach: 130
Long Island: 26, 108-155; The Hamptons 137-155;
    highlights 109; information and services 155;
    map 110-111; The North Fork and Shelter
    Island 121-127; The North Shore 111-121;
    outdoor adventure 31; planning tips 16, 110-
    111; resources on 456; The South Shore 128-
    137; suburbs 133; transportation 155
Long Island Aquarium and Exhibition Center:
    120-121
Long Island Children's Museum: 130
Long Island Greenbelt Trail: 118
Long Island Maritime Museum: 137
Long Island Museum of American Art, History
    and Carriages: 119
Long Island Pine Barrens Society: 120
Long Island Rail Road: 130
Long Lake: 302-303

Louis Tussaud's Waxworks: 422
Lower 5th Avenue: 55
Lower East Side: accommodations 99; food 93;
    map 47; nightlife 85-86; shopping 88; sights
    46-47
Lower East Side Tenement Museum: 46
Lower Hudson Valley: 161-186
Lower Manhattan: accommodations 98-99; map
    42; nightlife 85; sights 38-46
Lower Plaza: 66
Lucy-Desi Museum: 432
Lumberjack Festival: 393
Luykas Van Alen House: 227
Lyme disease: 450
Lyndhurst: 19, 27, 164

M

M&T Bank Gold Dome Building: 406
Mabie House: 178
Macedon: 393
MacKenzie-Childs: 351
Madam Brett Homestead: 174
Madame Tussaud's New York: 63
Madison Barracks: 318
Madison Square: 55
Madison Square Garden: 83
Madison Square Park: see Union Square and
    Madison Square Park
Magic Forest: 277
MagnanMetz Gallery: 57
Mahayana Temple at South Cairo: 220
Maid of the Mist: 418
mail: 451
Main Reading Room, New York Public Library: 64
Majestic Theater: 63, 84
The Mall: 69
Manhattan: 40-41, see also New York City
Manitoga: 172
maps: 451
Marcus Garvey Park: 80
Marie's Crisis Cafe: 53
maritime museums: East End Seaport Museum
    and Maritime Foundation 125; East Hampton
    Town Marine Museum 149; H. Lee White
    Marine Museum 315; Long Island Maritime
    Museum 137
Mark Twain's Study: 368
Martin House Complex: 410
Martin Van Buren National Historic Site: 226
Mary Flagler Cary Arboretum: 191
Mashomack Preserve: 127
Massena: 326
Mathematics Museum: 55
Mather House Museum: 119
Matilda Joslyn Gage House: 337
McKinley Monument: 406

measurements: 451
Meatpacking District: see Chelsea and the
    Meatpacking District
Medina: 428
Memorial Art Gallery: 387
Mennonite communities: 376
Merchant Marines: 112
Merchant's House Museum: 51
Merrill Lake Sanctuary: 150
Metropolitan Life Insurance Company: 55
Metropolitan Opera House: 76, 84
The Metropolitan Museum of Art: 71
Mets, New York: 62
Mid-Hudson Valley: 186-228
Midtown and Times Square: 19, 23, 58-67;
    accommodations 100-101; food 95-96; map 59;
    nightlife 87-88; shopping 91
military sights: 181, 185, 404
Millard and Abigail Fillmore House: 414
Millbrook: 190-192
Millbrook Vineyards and Winery: 191
Mille Fleures: 112
Million Dollar Beach: 274
Mills Mansion: 193
Mills-Norrie State Park: 193
Minksoff Theater: 63
Minnewaska Lodge: 206
Minnewaska State Park: 30, 204
Mirabelle at Three Village Inn: 119
Miss Amelia's Cottage: 148
Mitchell Park: 125
Mohonk Mountain House and Preserve: 21, 204
money: 451
Montauk: 150-155
Montauk County Park: 151
Montauk Downs State Park: 152
Montauk Harbor: 150
Montauk Lighthouse: 152
Montauk Point State Park: 31, 152
Montezuma Audubon Center: 350
Montgomery Place: 198
Montour Falls: 365
Moravia: 347
Morgan Library: 58
Morgan Opera House: 351-352
Morris-Jumel Mansion: 82
Morse, Samuel: 188
motels: 448
Mother AME Zion Church: 82
motorcycle museum: 184
Motorcyclepedia: 184
Mott Street: 46
mountain biking: Ellicottville 431; Mount Tremper
    213; Saranac Lake 299
Mount Beacon: 174
Mount Gulian Historic Site: 174

Mount Hope Cemetery: 390
Mt. Lebanon Shaker Village: 239
Mount Marcy: 293
Mount Tremper: 21, 212
Mulberry Street: 46
Mulford Farm: 143
Multiplication Gully: 295
Munson Williams Proctor Arts Institute: 265
The Museum of Jewish Heritage: 45
Museum at Eldridge Street: 47
Museum District: 407
Museum Mile: 71
Museum of Chinese in America: 46
Museum of Innovation and Science: 255
Museum of Mathematics: 55
Museum of Modern Art: 19, 23, 66
Museum of the City of New York: 75
Museum Row: 130
Museum Shop: 124
music: Albany 240; Albany Riverfront Park 237;
    Amagansett 150; The Apollo Theater 80;
    Bard Music Festival 199; Beacon 176; Bemus
    Point 433; Buffalo 411; Canandaigua 381;
    Caramoor Center for Music and the Arts
    170; East Durham Irish Festival 221; Edward
    Hopper House Art Center 177; Falcon Ridge
    Folk Festival 200; Glimmerglass Festival 262;
    Jones Beach 130; Lake Luzerne Chamber
    Music Festival 279; Lake Placid 295; Maverick
    Concerts 209; New York City 83-84; Pittsford
    393; Rochester 391; Saratoga Springs 253;
    Seagle Music Colony 281; The Sembrich 280;
    Syracuse 338; Tarrytown Music Hall 167;
    Woodstock 208-209; see also classical music
Music from Salem: 253

N
Naples: 384-385
Nassau County: 130-132
Nassau County Firefighters' Museum and
    Education Center: 132
Nassau County Museum of Art: 112
National Bottle Museum: 254
National Buffalo Wing Festival: 412
National Museum of Dance and Hall of Fame: 247
National Museum of Racing and Hall of Fame:
    244-245
National Museum of the American Indian: 43
National Purple Heart Hall of Honor: 185
National September 11 Memorial and
    Museum: 44
National Women's Hall of Fame: 349
Native American history/sights: general history
    437, 438; Akwesasne 327; Council Rock 260;
    Ganondagan State Historic Site 382; Gomez
    Mill House 185; Indian Field 151; Iroquois 337;

Letchworth Museum 395; Logan Monument 346; Long Island Algonquin tribes 124; National Museum of the American Indian 43; Shako:wi Cultural Center 266; Shinnecock Reservation 142; Six Nations Indian Museum 301; Skä•noñh—Great Law of Peace Center 337; Southold Indian Museum 124; At the Western Door 388; Whiteface Mountain 297
Natural Stone Bridge and Caves: 281
NBC Studios: 66
Nettle Meadow Goat Farm and Cheese Factory: 306
Neuberger Museum: 171
The New Amsterdam: 63
The New Victory: 63
Newburgh: 184-186
New Hope Mills: 342
New Museum: 43
New Paltz: 21, 28, 200-204
New Skete Monastery: 20, 253
New Windsor Cantonment: 184-185
New Year's Eve celebration: 62
New York City: 33-107; accommodations 97-102; day trips from 27-28; discount weeks 98; entertainment and events 83-88; food 92-97; highlights 23, 34; history 441, 443; information and services 102-103; itinerary 18-19; maps 36-37; planning tips 16, 35; resources on 453-454, 456; safety 449-450; shopping 88-92; sights 38-82; skyline 38, 45, 63, 64; tours 102-103; transportation 104-107
New York City Fire Museum: 50
New-York Historical Society: 76
New York Kitchen: 29, 380
New York Life Insurance Company: 55
New York Public Library: 64, 91
New York Renaissance Faire: 180
New York State Capitol Building: 235
New York State Department of Environmental Conservation's Research Station and Aquarium: 320
New York State Executive Mansion: 237
New York State Fair: 338
New York State Museum: 20, 234
New York State Salmon River Fish Hatchery: 317
New York State Zoo: 319
New York Stock Exchange: 44
Niagara Falls: 14, 416-422
Niagara Falls Culinary Institute: 419
Niagara Falls Observation Tower: 418
Niagara Falls Scenic Trolleys: 418
Niagara Falls State Park: 32, 416
Niagara Gorge Discovery Center: 418
Niagara Mohawk Power Corporation: 335
Niagara Power Project: 422
Niagara Square: 406

nightlife: 137
Nipper: 238
The North Fork of Long Island: 121-127
The North Shore of Long Island: 111-121
North Country Taxidermy and Trading Post: 287
North Creek: 305
Northeastern Westchester: 170-171
Northern Lake George: 280-281
North Hudson: 282
North-South Lakes: 216
North Tonawanda: 415
Northwest Lakes: 310-314
Nott Memorial: 256
nurseries, commercial: 198
Nyack: 176-178

O

Ocean Bay Park: 133
Ocean Beach: 133
Octagonal House: 198
Ogdensburg: 325-326
Olana State Historic Site: 20, 224-225
Old Bethpage Village: 117
Old Dutch Church and Burying Ground: 27, 167
Old Erie Canal State Historic Park: 266
Old Forge: 308
Old Fort Niagara: 426
Old Hook Mill: 145
Old House: 122
Old Rhinebeck Aerodrome: 24, 196
Old Schoolhouse Museum: 122
Old Songs Festival of Traditional Music and Dance: 240
Old Town Beach: 142
Old Westbury: 113
Old Whaler's Church: 147
Oliver House Museum: 378
Olympic Center: 292
Olympic Cross-Country Biathlon Center: 293
Olympic Ski Jump Complex: 21, 292
Onchiota: 301
125th Street: 80
Oneida: 266-267
Oneida Community Mansion: 266
One World Observatory: 44
Onondaga Historical Association Museum: 336
Onondaga Lake Park: 337
Ontario Beach Park: 390
Ontario County Courthouse: 380
Ontario County Historical Museum: 380
Onteora Mountain House: 212
opera: 84, 262, 280
Opus 40: 21, 207
Orient: 126
Orient Beach State Park: 31, 126
Orient Country Store: 126

Original American Kazoo Company: 415
Orleans County: 428-429
Oswegatchie River: 313
Oswego: 315-317
Otsego Lake: 260
outdoor adventure: 30-32; hang gliding 206, 369;
    ice climbing 295; resources on 455, 456; safety
    for 450; Shawangunk Mountains 204; white-
    water rafting 279; wreck dives 281; *see also
    specific sport by name*
Outdoor Discovery Center: 183
outer boroughs: 79
The Outside In: 176
Overlook Mountain: 28, 209
Ovid: 352
Owasco Lake: 343-347
Oyster Bay: 27, 113-115
Oysterponds Historical Society: 126

P

Pace: 56
packing: 449
paddling: Adirondack Mountains 328; Blue
    Mountain Lake 304; Constitution Marsh
    Audubon Center Sanctuary 172; Cranberry
    Lake 313; Erie Canal 351, 394; Fulton Chain 308;
    Lake Luzerne 279; Lake Placid 295; Long Lake
    302; Phoenicia 213; Saranac Lake 299; St. Regis
    Canoe Area 310; Tupper Lake 313; Watkins
    Glen 365
Paine, Thomas: 53
Palmer Vineyards: 122
Palmyra: 382-384
Palmyra Canaltown Days: 384
Palmyra Historical Museum: 383
Palmyra Print Shop: 383
parks, urban: Albany Riverfront Park 237;
    Brooklyn Bridge Park 90; Bryant Park 64;
    Buffalo 409; Central Park 67-70; Christopher
    Park 53; Columbus Park 46; Cooperstown
    260; Fort Tryon Park 82; Franklin D. Roosevelt
    Four Freedoms Park 79; Gramercy Park 55;
    Greenbelt Riverfront Park 325; Greenport
    125; The High Line 57; Honeoye 394; Madison
    Square Park 55; Memorial Park 177; Montauk
    County Park 151; Plattsburgh 288; Riverside
    Park and the Boat Basin 78; Rochester
    388, 390; Syracuse 337; Union Square 53;
    Washington Square Park 52
Parkside: 409
Parrish Art Museum: 140
Paula Cooper Gallery: 56
Paul Smiths: 300-301
Paul Smith's College: 300
Peerless Pool: 248
Pelletreau Shop: 142

pencil manufacturing: 283
Penfield Homestead Museum: 284
Penn Yan: 377-378
Perennial: 29, 132
performing arts: Adirondack Lakes Center
    for the Arts 304; Albany 238; The Apollo
    Theater 80; Artpark 424; Bard College 199;
    Broadway shows 85; Buffalo 406, 411; Central
    Park summertime 69, 70; Cooperstown 262;
    Cunneen-Hackett Arts Center 188; East
    Durham 221; East Hampton 145; Ithaca 358;
    Lake Placid 295; Landmark Theatre 336;
    Lincoln Center for the Performing Arts 75-76;
    Naples 385; New Paltz 203; New York City 84;
    Poughkeepsie 190; Rhinebeck 196; Rochester
    391; Saranac Lake 300; Saratoga Springs 248;
    Schenectady 256; Stanley Center for the Arts
    265; Syracuse 338; Times Square 63; Westport
    285; Woodstock 210
Perkins Memorial Drive: 179
Pharaoh Mountain: 281
Philipsburg Manor: 167
Philipse Manor Hall State Historic Site: 161
Phoenicia: 21, 213
photography museums: 43, 209
Piermont: 176
Piermont Flywheel Gallery: 176
Piermont Marsh: 176
Piermont Pier: 176
Pilot Knob Preserve Hike: 277
Pindar Vineyards: 123
Pine Barrens: 120
Pine Hill: 215
Pine Neck Barn: 124
Pittsford: 393
planetariums: 78, 161, 255, 388
planning tips: 16-17
Planting Fields Arboretum State Historic Park: 114
plants: 436-437
Plattsburgh: 288
politics: 444-445
Pollack, Jackson: 149
Pollock-Krasner House and Study Center: 149
Polly Crispell Cottage: 207
polo: 342
Port Henry: 284-285
Port Jefferson: 119-120
Port Washington Peninsula: 111-113
postal services: 451
Poughkeepsie: 186-190
powwows: 142
preserves: Adirondack Park 278, 288; Constitution
    Marsh Audubon Center Sanctuary 172;
    Elizabeth A. Morton National Wildlife Refuge
    147; Finger Lakes National Forest 350; Fire
    Island National Seashore 132; High Tor

Wildlife Management Area 384; Mashomack Preserve 127; Merrill Lake Sanctuary 150; Mohonk Mountain House and Preserve 204; Montezuma Audubon Center 350; Piermont Marsh 176; Quogue Wildlife Refuge 139; Sands Point Preserve 112; Sapsucker Woods Bird Sanctuary 357; Siamese Ponds Wilderness Area 305; Smith Point County Park 135; Teatown Lake Reservation 168; Theodore Roosevelt Sanctuary and Audubon Center 114; Tifft Nature Preserve 410; Ward Pound Ridge Reservation 171; *see also* state parks
Prince and Spring Streets: 49
Prince Building: 124
Prospect Mountain Veterans Memorial Highway: 275
Prospect Point: 417
Prouty-Chew House: 360
Pugliese Vineyards: 123
Pulaski: 317
Purchase: 171
Purple Heart Hall of Honor: 185
Putnam History Museum: 172

QR

Quarryman's Museum: 207
"Queen of Greene Street": 50
Queens: 79
Queen Victoria Park: 421
Quogue: 139-140
Quogue Wildlife Refuge: 139
Radio City Music Hall: 66, 83
railroad sights: Catskill Mountain Railroad 213; Empire State Railway Museum 213; Long Island Rail Road 130; Medina Railroad Museum 429; Railroad Museum 415; Railroad Museum of Long Island 125
Rainbow Bridge: 421
Ramapo Mountains: 178-180
Ramble: 70
Randall's Island: 79
Raquette Lake: 307
Raynham Hall: 114
reading, suggested: 453-456
Red Falls: 219
Red Hook: 198
religious sights: Abyssinian Baptist Church 82; All Souls Episcopal Church 118; Buffalo 406; Cathedral of St. John the Divine 78; Chuang Yen Monastery 173; Cross Island Chapel 266; Eldridge Street Synagogue 47; 5th Avenue 66-67; Hill Cumorah Visitor Center 383; Historic Beth Joseph Synagogue 313; Ithaca 354; Joseph Smith Farm and Sacred Grove 383; Karma Triyana Dharmachakra 209; Mahayana Temple at South Cairo 220; Medina 429; Moravia 347; Mother AME Zion Church 82; New Skete Monastery 253; Old Whaler's Church 147; Plattsburgh 288; Rhinebeck Reformed Church 196; Riverside Church 78; St. John the Baptist Ukrainian Catholic Church 219; St. Mark's Church in-the-Bowery 50-51; Trinity Church 44; Union Church of Pocantico Hills 168; Wesleyan Chapel 349; Willard Memorial Chapel 346
Renaissance Faires: 180, 362
reserves, nature: *see* preserves; state parks
resources on: 128
Revolutionary War sites: Constitution Island: 181; Fort Ticonderoga: 283; Iroquois people: 337; Mount Beacon: 174; New Windsor Cantonment: 184-185; Perkins Memorial Drive: 179; Sackets Harbor Battlefield State Historic Site: 317; Saratoga National Historical Park: 253-254; Stony Point Battlefield: 180-181; Tappan: 178; Van Cortlandt Manor: 168; Washington's Headquarters State Historic Site: 184
Rhinebeck: 20, 194-198
Rhinebeck Reformed Church: 196
Richard B. Fisher Center for Performing Arts: 199
Richardson-Bates House Museum: 316
Rings of Fire: 378
Ripley's Believe It or Not: 422
Riverhead: 120-121
Riverhead Foundation for Marine Research: 121
Riverside Church: 78
Riverside Park and the Boat Basin: 78
Riverwalk Park: 288
Robert H. Treman State Park: 31, 357
Robert Jenkins House: 224
Robert Louis Stevenson Memorial Cottage and Museum: 298
Robert Moses State Park: 31, 133, 327
Rochester: 385-394
Rochester International Jazz Festival: 391
Rochester Museum and Science Center: 388
Rochester Philharmonic Orchestra: 391
rock climbing: 204
Rockefeller Center: 23, 64-66
Rockefeller State Park Preserve: 19, 168
Rockwell Museum of Western Art: 372
Rodgers Book Barn: 200
Rogers Mansion: 140
Rogers Rock State Park: 280
Roger Tory Peterson Institute of Natural History: 433
Romulus: 352
Ronald Feldman Fine Arts: 50
Roosevelt, Eleanor: 193
Roosevelt, Franklin D.: 192
Roosevelt, Theodore: 55, 114, 407

Roosevelt Baths: 247
Roosevelt Island: 79
Rosamond Gifford Zoo at Burnet Park: 336
Roscoe: 218
Rose Hill Mansion: 360
Route 3: 314
Route 9W: 203
Route 14: 362
Route 17 South: 179
Route 23: 219
Route 23A: 215-219
Route 28: 211-215
Route 28N: 306
Route 209: 206-207
Roxbury: 212
Roxbury Arts Group: 212
Roy K. Lester Carriage Museum: 148
RTA Building: 238
Rubenstein Museum of Science and
    Technology: 336
Rubin Museum of Art: 57
Rumsey Playfield: 69

S

Sacandaga River: 279
Sackets Harbor: 317
Sackets Harbor Battlefield State Historic Site: 317
safety: 449-450
Sagamore Hill National Historic Site: 27, 114
Sagan Planet Walk: 353
Sag Harbor: 146-148
Sag Harbor Whaling and Historical Museum: 146
Sailors Haven: 134
St. James: 118
St. James General Store: 118
St. John's Episcopal Church: 429
St. John the Baptist Ukrainian Catholic
    Church: 219
St. Lawrence Seaway: 326
St. Mark's Church in-the-Bowery: 50-51
St. Mark's Place: 51
St. Matthew's Episcopal Church: 347
St. Patrick's Cathedral: 23, 66-67
St. Paul's Episcopal Cathedral: 406
St. Regis Canoe Area: 310
St. Thomas Church: 67
Saltaire: 133
salt industry: 334, 337
Salt Museum: 337
Sampson State Park: 364
Samuel Morse Historic Site: 188
Sands Point Preserve: 26, 112
Santa's Workshop: 297
Sapsucker Woods Bird Sanctuary: 357
Saranac Brewery: 265

Saranac Lake: 298-300
Saratoga Casino and Raceway: 247
Saratoga Harness Hall of Fame: 247
Saratoga Monument: 254
Saratoga National Historical Park: 20, 253
Saratoga Race Course: 242, 245
Saratoga Spa State Park: 20, 247
Saratoga Springs: 20, 242-255
Saratoga Springs History Museum: 243
Saugerties: 21, 207-208
scenic drives: Ashokan Reservoir 211; fall foliage
    24-26; North Hudson 281; Prospect Mountain
    275; Route 23 219; Route 23A 215; Seaway
    Trail 315; Seven Lakes Drive 179; Skaneateles
    Lake 342; Storm King Highway 183; Whiteface
    Mountain 297
Schenectady: 255-257
Schenectady County Historical Society
    Museum: 256
Schoharie County: 257-258
Schoolhouse Building: 126
Schroon Lake: 281-282
The Schomburg Center for Research in Black
    Culture: 80, 92
Schubert Theater: 84
Schuyler Mansion: 237
Schuylerville: 253
Schweinfurth Memorial Art Center: 346
ScienCenter: 355
ScienCenter Museum: 354
Scottish games: 240
sculpture: Central Park 69; Concrete Sculpture
    Garden 314; Dia:Beacon 174; Donald M.
    Kendall Sculpture Gardens at PepsiCo 171;
    Griffis Sculpture Park 431; Opus 40 207; Storm
    King Art Center 183
Seabreeze Amusement Park: 391
Sea Glass Carousel: 45
Seagle Music Colony: 281
Sears-Peyton Gallery: 57
Seaview: 133
Seaway Trail: 315, 317
Seaway Trail Discovery Center: 317-318
Second House Museum: 151
Secret Caverns: 257
Selkirk Shores State Park: 317
The Sembrich: 280
Seneca Falls: 347-351
Seneca Falls Historical Society: 350
Seneca Lake: 24, 359-366
Seneca Museum of Waterways and Industry: 349
Seneca Niagara Casino: 419
Seneca Park Zoo: 390
September 11, 2001: 44, 444
1705 DuBois Fort Information Center: 202
The '76 House: 178

Seward House: 344
Shaker communities: 239
Shakespeare Garden: 70
Shakespeare in the Park: 70
Shako:wi Cultural Center: 266
Shawangunk Mountains: 30, 204-206
Sheep Meadow: 68
Shelter Island: 126-127
Shelter Island Heights: 127
Shequaga Falls: 365
Sheridan Square: 53
Shinnecock Nation Cultural Center and
    Museum: 142
Shinnecock Reservation: 142
Shubert Alley: 63
Shubert Theater: 63
Siamese Ponds Wilderness Area: 305
Silas Wright Museum: 326
Simon Johnston House: 320
Singer Building: 50
Six Nations Indian Museum: 301
Skä·noñh—Great Law of Peace Center: 337
Skaneateles Festival: 342
Skaneateles Historical Society: 342
Skaneateles Lake: 341-343
Skaneateles Village: 341-343
skiing: Belleayre 215; Bristol Mountain Winter
    Resort 381; Catamount Ski Area 200;
    Ellicottville 431; Gore Mountain 305; Hunter
    Mountain 216-217; Whiteface Mountain 288,
    297-298; Windham Mountain Resort 219
ski jumping: 292
Sleepy Hollow: 164-170
Sleepy Hollow Cemetery: 167
Smith Point County Park: 31, 135
Smith Point West: 135
Snowy Mountain: 305
Society for the Preservation of Long Island
    Antiquities Gallery: 115
Sodus Bay Lighthouse Museum: 361
Sodus Point: 361
Soho and TriBeCa: accommodations 99; food 93;
    map 49; nightlife 86; shopping 88; sights 49-50
Sonnenberg Gardens and Mansion: 379
Sound Avenue: 121-122
The South Shore of Long Island: 128-137
Southampton: 140-142
Southampton Historical Museum: 140
Southeastern Westchester: 171-172
Southold: 123-125
Southold Indian Museum: 124
South Street Seaport: 45, 84
spectator sports: Buffalo 410; Doubleday Field
    260; Lake Placid Olympic Museum 292;
    Mets 62; National Baseball Hall of Fame and
    Museum 258; Olympic Ski Jump Complex 292;
    as a top experience 12; Yankees 62
Sprague's Maple Farms: 432
springs: 242, 247
Spring Street, NYC: 49
Stanley Center for the Arts: 265
Stanton, Elizabeth Cady: 349
Staten Island: 79
Staten Island Ferry: 38
state parks: Allegany State Park 432; Bear
    Mountain State Park 179; Buttermilk Falls State
    Park 357; Cayuga Lake State Park 350; Chimney
    Bluffs State Park 361; Devil's Hole State Park
    422; Fillmore Glen State Park 347; Fort Niagara
    State Park 426; Glimmerglass State Park 262,
    264; Grass Point State Park 324; Harriman State
    Park 179; Heckscher State Park 135-136; Hook
    Mountain State Park 177; John Boyd Thacher
    State Park 241; Lake Superior State Park 211;
    Lake Taghkanic State Park 199; Letchworth
    State Park 394-395; Mills-Norrie State Park 193;
    Minnewaska State Park 204; Montauk 152;
    Niagara Falls State Park 416; Nyack Beach State
    Park 177; Orient Beach State Park 126; Robert
    H. Treman State Park 357; Robert Moses State
    Park 133, 327; Rockefeller State Park Preserve
    168; Rogers Rock State Park 280; Sampson
    State Park 364; Saratoga Spa State Park 247;
    Selkirk Shores State Park 317; Sterling Forest
    State Park 180; Sunken Meadow State Park 117-
    118; Taconic State Park 200; Tallman Mountain
    State Park 176; Taughannock Falls State Park
    352; Watkins Glen State Park 364; Wellesley
    Island State Park 324; Whirlpool State Park 422;
    Wildwood State Park 120
State Street: 238
Statue of Liberty: 18, 38
Stephen A. Schwarzman Building: 64
Sterling Forest State Park: 180
Sterling Renaissance Festival: 362
Stewarts Ledge: 277
Stillwater: 253
Stockade District: 255
Stock Exchange: 44
Stone-Tolan House Museum: 388
Stonewall: 86
Stony Brook: 118-119
Stony Brook Grist Mill: 119
Stony Point Battlefield: 180-181
Storm King Art Center: 21, 27, 183
Storm King Highway: 183
Strawberry Fields: 69
The Strong National Museum of Play: 387
The Studio Museum in Harlem: 80
Suffolk County Historical Society: 121
suffrage, women's: 337, 348, 390
Suits-Bueche Planetarium: 255

SummerScape SpiegelTent: 199
SummerStage: 69
Sunken Meadow State Park: 117-118
Sunnyside: 19, 27, 164
Susan B. Anthony House: 390
Swedish Cottage: 70
Swedish Hill Winery: 352
Swiss Hutte: 200
Syracuse: 334-341
Syracuse Jazz Fest: 338

T

Taconic State Park: 30, 200
Tallman Mountain State Park: 176
Tang Teaching Museum and Art Gallery: 243
Tannersville: 216
Tappan: 178
Tarrytown: 19, 27, 164-170
Tarrytown Music Hall: 167
Taste of Buffalo: 412
Taughannock Falls: 352
Taughannock Falls State Park: 352
TAUNY Center and North Country Folkstore: 326
taxidermy: 287
Teatown Lake Reservation: 168
temperatures: 436
Ten Broeck Mansion: 238
Tenement Museum: 46
Terwilliger House: 203
Terwilliger Museum: 351
Thayer Hotel: 27, 181
Theater District: 63, 406
Theodore Roosevelt Birthplace National Historic
    Site: 55
Theodore Roosevelt Sanctuary and Audubon
    Center: 114
Third House: 151
Thomas Halsey Homestead: 142
Thomas Moore House: 124
Thousand Island Park: 324
Thousand Islands Arts Center: 321
Thousand Islands Museum: 321
The Thousand Islands: 314-327
Three Brothers Wineries & Estates: 360
Three Sisters Islands: 418
Tibbetts Point Lighthouse: 320
Ticonderoga: 283-284
Ticonderoga Heritage Museum: 283
Tiffany & Co.: 23, 91
Tiffany glass: 346
Tifft Houses: 407
Tifft Nature Preserve: 410
Times Square: 62, 84; see also Midtown and Times
    Square
Times Square Museum and Visitors' Center: 62
Tinker Street: 209

Tipperary Hill: 336
Tivoli: 199
Top Cottage: 192
top experiences: 8-15; activism 11, 345, 419;
    Adirondacks hiking 293; arts, the 14, 22, 371;
    beaches 10, 129; Brooklyn Bridge 45; Corning
    Museum of Glass 371-372; cuisine 15, 29;
    Empire State Building 63; Erie Canal Cruise
    428; Finger Lakes wineries 362; fly-fishing
    218; Jones Beach 129-130; Long Island wine
    tasting 122-123; Niagara Falls 14, 416; Niagara
    Falls Underground Railroad Heritage Center
    419; NYC skyline 12, 38, 45, 63, 64; Rockefeller
    Center 64-66; Saratoga Race Course 11, 245;
    sports 12, 62, 258; Statue of Liberty 38; St.
    Regis Canoe Area 310; water sports 15, 218,
    319; Watkins Glen State Park 364; Women's
    Rights National Historical Park 348-349
Top of the Rock Observation Deck: 66
tourist information: 451
The Town Hall: 83
Town House, East Hampton: 145
trains: see railroad sights
train travel: 447
transportation: 446-447
travel tips: 449-450
TriBeCa: see Soho and TriBeCa
Trinity Church: 44
Trinity Episcopal Church: 288
Trophy Point: 181
tubing, river: 213
Tubman, Harriet: 345
Tulip Festival: 240
Tupper Lake: 21, 311-313
Tuxedo Park: 180
Twain, Mark: 368, 369

U

Ukrainian culture: 219
Ulster County Fair: 203
Underground Railroad: 423
Union Church of Pocantico Hills: 27, 168
Union College: 256
Union Square: 53
Union Square and Madison Square Park:
    accommodations 100; food 95; map 54;
    shopping 89; sights 53-56
United Nations Plaza: 61
universities: see colleges and universities
Upper East Side: accommodations 101; food 96;
    map 72; shopping 91; sights 70-75
Upper Hudson Valley: 221-227
Upper Jay: 288
Upper West Side: accommodations 101; food 96;
    map 77; nightlife 88; shopping 92; sights 75-78
Uris Hall: 357

U.S. Military Academy: 27, 181
USS *Slater*: 235-237
Utica: 265

V

Van Buren, Martin: 226
Van Cortlandt Manor: 168
Vanderbilt Mansion National Historic Site: 19, 193
Vassar College: 188
Ventosa Vineyards: 361
Victor: 382
Victoria Pool: 248
Vidler's 5 & 10: 414
View: 308
Village House: 126
Village Library: 122
visas: 451
Visitor Center and Museum Shop: 47
visitor information: 449, 451

W

Wagner Vineyards: 364
walking/biking trails: Albany Riverfront Park 237;
     Canalway Trail 412; Erie Canalway Trail 266;
     Heckscher State Park 136; Ithaca 353, 358;
     Long Island Greenbelt Trail 118; Pine Barrens
     120; Walkway Over the Hudson 188
Walkway Over the Hudson: 188
Wallace Center: 192
Wall Street: 43
Wanika Falls: 293
Ward Pound Ridge Reservation: 171
Warehouse District, Albany: 240
Warner House: 181
Warren Street: 224
Warwick Valley Winery and Distillery: 185
Washington, George: Beekman Arms 194; Federal
     Hall National Memorial 43; Tappan 178;
     Washington's Headquarters State Historic Site
     21, 184
Washington Park: 238
Washington Square Arch: 53
Washington Square Park: 51
Watch Hill: 134
waterfalls: Ausable Chasm 287; Blue Ridge Road
     282; Buttermilk Falls State Park 357; Fillmore
     Glen State Park 347; Ithaca Falls 355; Kaaterskill
     Falls 215; Montour Falls 365; Niagara Falls 14,
     416-422; Rochester 387; Taughannock Falls
     352; underground 257; Wanika Falls 293
Waterloo: 351
Water Mill: 142-143
Water Mill Museum: 142
Watertown: 319
Watervliet Shaker National Historic District: 239

Watkins Glen: 24-25, 364
Watkins Glen International: 365
Watkins Glen State Park: 25, 364
wax museums: 63
Wayne County Fair: 383
weather: 436
Webb House: 126
Wellesley Island State Park: 324
Wesleyan Chapel: 349
West 42nd Street: 63
West Broadway street: 49
West Chelsea Galleries: 56
Westchester: 170-172
Western art: 372
Westminster Kennel Club Dog Show: 83
West Point: 21, 27, 181-183
West Point Museum: 181
Westport: 285-286
West Village: *see* Greenwich Village and West
     Village
whale-watching: 152
The Whaling Museum: 27, 115
whaling museums: 115, 146
Whirlpool State Park: 422
Whiteface Mountain: 297-298
Whiteface Mountain Cloudsplitter Gondola:
     24, 297
White Pine Camp: 301
White's Drug and Department Store: 150
white-water rafting: Black River 319; Hudson
     River Gorge 305; Sacandaga River 279
Whitman, Walt: 117
Whitney Museum of American Art: 58
Wickham Farmhouse: 122
The Wild Center: 21, 31, 311-313
Wilder Brain Collection: 357
Wilderstein: 196
wildflowers: 168, 176, 285
wildlife viewing: 127, 140
Wildwood State Park: 120
Willard Memorial Chapel: 346
William Floyd Estate: 135
William Phelps General Store and Home
     Museum: 383
Williams-Butler Mansion: 407
Willsboro: 287
Wilmington: 288
Wilson: 426
Wilton: 254
Windham: 219
Wine and Grape Museum of Greyton H. Taylor:
     376
wine regions: Finger Lakes 363; Geneva 360;
     Great Western Winery Visitor Center 375;
     Keuka Lake 376; Long Island 122; Lower

Hudson Valley 185; Millbrook 191; Naples 384; New Paltz 203; Niagara Falls 428; Romulus 352; Seneca Lake 362

Wing's Castle: 191

Wings of Eagles Discovery Center: 369

Winter Garden at Brookfield Place: 44

Wizard of Clay: 394

Wollman Rink: 68

Women's Rights National Historical Park: 348-349

Woodcock Brothers Brewery: 426

Woodland Valley: 213

Woodlawn Cemetery and Mark Twain Burial Site: 369

Woodstock: 21, 28, 208-211

Woodstock Artists Association and Museum: 209

Woodstock Byrdcliffe Guild: 210

Woodstock Film Festival: 210

Woodstock Music Festival, 1969: 209, 211

Woodstock-New Paltz Art & Crafts Fairs: 203

Woolworth Building: 45

World Financial Center: 44

World War I: 442

wreck dives: 281

XYZ

Yaddo: 20, 245-247

Yankees: 62

Yates County Fair: 378

YMCAs: 448

Yonkers: 161-164

Yonkers Raceway: 162

Yunhong: 46

Zabar's: 19, 92

zoos: 319, 336, 390, 409

Zugibe Vineyards: 361

List of Maps

Front Map
New York State: 4–5

Discover New York State
chapter divisions map: 16

New York City
New York City: 36–37
Manhattan: 40–41
Lower Manhattan: 42
The Lower East Side: 47
SoHo and TriBeCa: 49
East Village: 51
Greenwich Village and West Village: 52
Union Square and Madison Square Park: 54
Chelsea and the Meatpacking District: 56
Midtown and Times Square: 59
Central Park: 67
Upper East Side: 72
Upper West Side: 77
Harlem: 81

Long Island
Long Island: 110–111
The North Shore (Western Section): 113
The North Shore (Eastern Section): 118
The North Fork and Shelter Island: 122
The South Shore (Western Section): 128
The South Shore (Fire Island): 132
The South Shore (Eastern Section): 134
The Hamptons: 138
Montauk: 151

The Hudson Valley and the Catskills
The Hudson Valley and the Catskills: 158–159
Lower Hudson: Westchester County: 163
Lower Hudson: Putnam County: 173
Lower Hudson: Rockland County: 175
Lower Hudson: Orange County: 180
Mid-Husdon: Dutchess County: 187
Mid-Hudson and the Catskills: Ulster County: 201
New Paltz: 202
Upper Hudson: 217

Upper Hudson: Columbia County: 222
Hudson: 223

The Capital-Saratoga Region
The Capital–Saratoga Region: 232
Albany: 233
Saratoga Springs: 244
Schenectady: 256
Cooperstown: 259

The Adirondacks
The Adirondacks: 271
Lake George and Southeastern Adirondacks: 273
Lake George Village: 275
Champlain Valley: 283
Plattsburgh: 289
High Peaks: 290
Lake Placid: 293
Saranac Lake: 299
Central Adirondacks: 303
Northwest Lakes: 311
Oswego: 316
Sackets Harbor: 318
Clayton: 321

The Finger Lakes
The Finger Lakes: 333
Downtown Syracuse: 335
Auburn: 344
Seneca Falls: 348
Ithaca: 354
Elmira: 368
Corning: 371
Hammondsport: 375
Canandaigua: 379
Palmyra: 382
Downtown Rochester: 386

Buffalo and the Niagara Region
Buffalo and the Niagara Region: 400
Buffalo: 402
Niagara Falls: 417
Erie Canal: 426
Orleans County: 429

Photo Credits

Title page photo: One Island in Thousand Island Region © Victorianl | Dreamstime.com
page 2 © Sborisov| Dreamstime.com; page 3 © Lightphoto | Dreamstime.com; page 6 © (top left) Francisco Collazo; (bottom) Francisco Collazo; page 7 © (top) CasualT | Dreamstime.com; (bottom left) Kirkikisphoto | Dreamstime.com; (bottom right) Zhukovsky | Dreamstime.com; pages 8-9 © Lhboucault | Dreamstime.com; page 10 © Rosemosteller | Dreamstime.com; page 11 © (top) Niagara Falls Underground Railroad Heritage Center/Kim Smith Photo; (bottom) Wingbeats551 | Dreamstime.com; pages 12-13 © (top) Jeffreymetcalf31 | Dreamstime.com; (bottom) Dleindec | Dreamstime.com;page 14 © (top) The Corning Museum of Glass (bottom) Cyscofinance | Dreamstime.com; page 15 © (top) Rmbarricarte | Dreamstime.com; (middle) 22tomtom | Dreamstime.com; (bottom) Peter Titmussi | Dreamstime.com; page 17 © (top) Francisco Collazo; page 18 © (left) Jamesandrews29 | Dreamstime.com; (right) Olli0815 | Dreamstime.com; page 19 © Demerzel21 | Dreamstime.com; page 20 © Jiawangkun | Dreamstime.com; page 22 © The Corning Museum of Glass; page 23 © Agaliza | Dreamstime.com; page 24 © Cllhnstev | Dreamstime.com; page 25 © Lightphoto | Dreamstime.com; page 26 © Brandon Klein/123RF; page 27 © Jaime Martorano/Historic Hudson Valley; page 28 © (left) Leesniderphotoimages | Dreamstime.com; (right) Indi Ericksen; page 29 © Francisco Collazo; page 30 © James Vallee| Dreamstime.com; page 31 © Haveseen | Dreamstime.com; page 32 © Indi Ericksen; page 33 © Mathiasrhode| Dreamstime.com; page 34 © (top left) Diegograndi | Dreamstime.com; (top right) Diegograndi | Dreamstime.com; page 39 © (top) John93 | Dreamstime.com; (bottom) Rumata7 | Dreamstime.com; page 48 © (top left) Lucie Ericksen; (top right) Agaliza | Dreamstime.com; (bottom) Pinkcandy | Dreamstime.com; page 54 © Sepavo | Dreamstime.com; page 58 © Francisco Collazo; page 60 © (top) Eriklichtenberg | Dreamstime.com; (left middle) Francisco Collazo; (right middle)Francisco Collazo; (bottom) Alexandre Fagundes De Fagundes| Dreamstime.com; page 65 © (top left) Lucie Ericksen; (top right) Francisco Collazo; (bottom left) Songquan Deng/123RF; (bottom right) Amadeustx | Dreamstime.com; page 69 © Chee-onn Leong| Dreamstime.com; page 74 © (top) Kmiragaya | Dreamstime.com; (bottom) Ahavelaar | Dreamstime.com; page 79 © Natalia Salomon; page 90 © Leobruce | Dreamstime.com; page 100 © Francisco Collazo; page 107 © Francisco Collazo; page 108 © Mnapoli501| Dreamstime.com; page 109 © (top left) James Kirkikis/123RF; (top right) Miles Astray| Dreamstime.com; page 116 © (top) Kirkikisphoto | Dreamstime.com; (left middle) David Wood | Dreamstime.com; (right middle) Francisco Collazo; page 123 © Kirkikisphoto | Dreamstime.com; page 131 © (top) Kirkikisphoto | Dreamstime.com; (bottom) Sylvana Rega | Dreamstime.com; page 136 © Littleny | Dreamstime.com; page 141 © (top) Francisco Collazo; (bottom) Francisco Collazo; page 144 © (top left) Francisco Collazo; (top right) Marlon Trottmann| Dreamstime.com; (bottom) Zhukovsky | Dreamstime.com; page 147 © Francisco Collazo; page 149 © pkhouse.org; page 153 © (top) Douglas Hockman| Dreamstime.com; (bottom) Francisco Collazo; page 156 © Ryan Deberardinis | Dreamstime.com; page 157 © (top left) Michael Kelsey/123RF; (top right) Colin Young | Dreamstime.com; page 166 © (top) Demerzel21 | Dreamstime.com; (left middle) Papabear | Dreamstime.com; (right middle) Francisco Collazo; (bottom) Kirkikisphoto | Dreamstime.com; page 169 © (top) Leesniderphotoimages | Dreamstime.com; (bottom) Jaime Martorano/Historic Hudson Valley; page 182 © (top) Mark di Suvero, courtesy the artist and Spacetime C.C., New York. Storm King Art Center, Mountainville, New York. Photo by Jerry L. Thompson; (bottom) Onpegasus | Dreamstime.com; page 189 © (top left) Francisco Collazo; (top right) Blogan1 | Dreamstime.com; (bottom) Cllhnstev | Dreamstime.com; page 195 © (top) Nancykennedy | Dreamstime.com; (bottom) Francisco Collazo; page 205 © (top left) Indi Ericksen; (top right) Indi Ericksen; (bottom) Alexkrassel | Dreamstime.com; page 210 © Indi Ericksen; page 214 © (top left) Francisco Collazo; (top right) Francisco Collazo; (bottom left) Francisco Collazo; (bottom right) Shabaana Hosein; page 225 © Unclejay | Dreamstime.com; page 229 © Sepavo | Dreamstime.com; page 230 © (top left) Bratty1206 | Dreamstime.com; (top right) Francisco Collazo; page 236 © (top) Demerzel21 | Dreamstime.com; (left middle) Francisco Collazo; (right middle) Francisco Collazo; (bottom) Sainaniritu | Dreamstime.com; page 243 © Francisco Collazo; page 246 © (top left) Francisco Collazo; (top right) Francisco Collazo; (bottom) Francisco Collazo; page 249 © Hollandog | Dreamstime.com; page 250 © (top) Sandrafoyt | Dreamstime.com; (bottom) Francisco Collazo; page 261 © (top) Wolterk | Dreamstime.com; (bottom) Francisco Collazo; page 268 © Aoldman| Dreamstime.com; page 269 © (top left) Indi Ericksen; (top right) Colin Young| Dreamstime.com; page 276 © (top) Colin Young | Dreamstime.com; (bottom) Bratty1206 | Dreamstime.com; page 291 © (top) Francisco Collazo;

Craft a personalized journey through the top national parks in the U.S. and Canada with Moon Travel Guides.

MOON
USA
NATIONAL
PARKS
THE COMPLETE GUIDE TO ALL
62 PARKS
BECKY LOMAX

ACADIA
NATIONAL PARK

ARCHES &
CANYONLANDS
NATIONAL PARKS

BANFF
NATIONAL PARK
HIKE·CAMP·KAYAK

DEATH VALLEY
NATIONAL PARK

GLACIER
NATIONAL PARK

GRAND
CANYON
HIKE·CAMP
RAFT THE
COLORADO RIVER

GREAT SMOKY
MOUNTAINS
NATIONAL PARK
HIKE·BIKE·CAMP

MOUNT RUSHMORE
& THE BLACK HILLS

ROCKY
MOUNTAIN
NATIONAL PARK
HIKE·CAMP
SEE WILDLIFE

SEQUOIA &
KINGS CANYON
HIKE·CAMP
SEE REDWOODS

YELLOWSTONE
& GRAND TETON
HIKE·CAMP
SEE WILDLIFE

YOSEMITE
SEQUOIA &
KINGS CANYON

ZION &
BRYCE

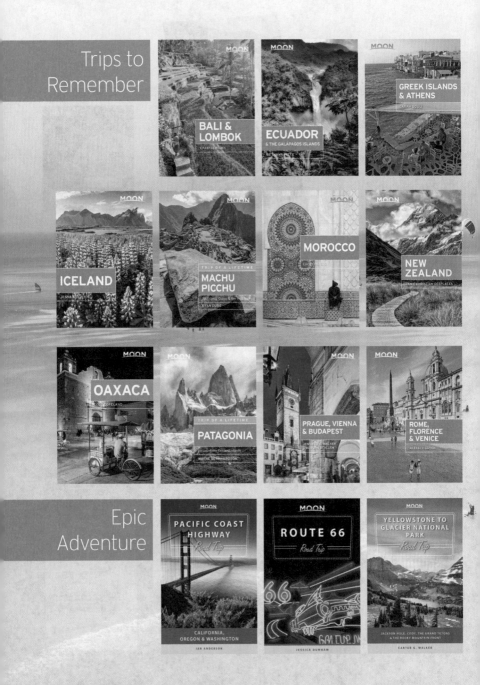

Trips to Remember

MOON
BALI & LOMBOK
CHANTAE REDEN

MOON
ECUADOR
& THE GALÁPAGOS ISLANDS
BETHANY PITTS

MOON
GREEK ISLANDS & ATHENS
SARAH SOULI

MOON
ICELAND
JENNA GOTTLIEB

MOON
TRIP OF A LIFETIME
MACHU PICCHU
CUSCO, LIMA, CUZCO & MORE
RYAN DUBE

MOON
MOROCCO

MOON
NEW ZEALAND
JAMIE CHRISTIAN DESPLACES

MOON
OAXACA
JODY COPELAND

MOON
TRIP OF A LIFETIME
PATAGONIA
Including the Falkland Islands
WAYNE BERNHARDSON

MOON
PRAGUE, VIENNA & BUDAPEST
JENNIFER D. WALKER
AUBEN STOLEN

MOON
ROME, FLORENCE & VENICE
ALEXEI J. COHEN

Epic Adventure

MOON
PACIFIC COAST HIGHWAY
Road Trip
CALIFORNIA, OREGON & WASHINGTON
IAN ANDERSON

MOON
ROUTE 66
Road Trip
JESSICA DUNHAM

MOON
YELLOWSTONE TO GLACIER NATIONAL PARK
Road Trip
JACKSON HOLE, CODY, THE GRAND TETONS
& THE ROCKY MOUNTAIN FRONT
CARTER G. WALKER

ROAD TRIPS AND DRIVE & HIKE GUIDES

MOON
Drive & Hike
APPALACHIAN
TRAIL

THE BEST TRAIL TOWNS, DAY HIKES,
AND ROAD TRIPS IN BETWEEN

TIMOTHY MALCOLM

MOON
BLUE RIDGE
PARKWAY
Road Trip

INCLUDING SHENANDOAH & GREAT SMOKY
MOUNTAINS NATIONAL PARKS

JASON FRYE

MOON
CALIFORNIA
Road Trip

SAN FRANCISCO, YOSEMITE, LAS VEGAS,
GRAND CANYON, LOS ANGELES,
& THE PACIFIC COAST HIGHWAY

STUART THORNTON

MOON
NASHVILLE TO
NEW ORLEANS
Road Trip

NATCHEZ TRACE PARKWAY • MEMPHIS
TUPELO • MISSISSIPPI BLUES TRAIL

MARGARET LITTMAN

MOON
NEW ENGLAND
Road Trip

BOSTON, ACADIA NATIONAL PARK, WHITE
MOUNTAINS, BERKSHIRES, NEWPORT, AND CAPE COD

JEN ROSE SMITH

MOON
NORTHERN
CALIFORNIA
Road Trip

SAN FRANCISCO, WINE COUNTRY, SONOMA, REDWOODS,
LAKE TAHOE, SHASTA, LASSEN, YOSEMITE, BIG SUR

STUART THORNTON & KAYLA ANDERSON

MOON
PACIFIC COAST
HIGHWAY

CALIFORNIA,
OREGON & WASHINGTON

IAN ANDERSON

MOON
Drive & Hike
PACIFIC CREST
TRAIL

THE BEST TRAIL TOWNS, DAY HIKES,
AND ROAD TRIPS IN BETWEEN

CAROLINE HINCHLIFF

MOON
PACIFIC
NORTHWEST
Road Trip

SEATTLE, VANCOUVER, VICTORIA,
THE OLYMPIC PENINSULA, PORTLAND,
THE OREGON COAST & MOUNT RAINIER

ALLISON WILLIAMS

MOON.COM | ROADTRIPUSA.COM

Road Trip USA

Covering more than 35,000 miles of blacktop stretching from east to west and north to south, *Road Trip USA* takes you deep into the heart of America.

This colorful guide covers the top road trips including historic Route 66 and is packed with maps, photos, illustrations, mile-by-mile highlights, and more!

MAP SYMBOLS

▰▰▰ Expressway	○ City/Town	✈ Airport	⚲ Golf Course
▬▬▬ Primary Road	◉ State Capital	✗ Airfield	Ⓟ Parking Area
▦▦▦ Secondary Road	✹ National Capital	▲ Mountain	◈ Archaeological Site
═ ═ ═ Unpaved Road	◎ Highlight	✦ Unique Natural Feature	⌖ Church
- - - - Trail	★ Point of Interest		🂠 Gas Station
·········· Ferry	• Accommodation	⬜ Waterfall	
■-■-■ Railroad	▼ Restaurant/Bar	⬆ Park	◌ Glacier
▨▨▨ Pedestrian Walkway	■ Other Location	㊙ Trailhead	▨ Mangrove
▥▥▥ Stairs	Λ Campground	🎿 Skiing Area	▧ Reef
			▭ Swamp

CONVERSION TABLES

°C = (°F - 32) / 1.8
°F = (°C x 1.8) + 32
1 inch = 2.54 centimeters (cm)
1 foot = 0.304 meters (m)
1 yard = 0.914 meters
1 mile = 1.6093 kilometers (km)
1 km = 0.6214 miles
1 fathom = 1.8288 m
1 chain = 20.1168 m
1 furlong = 201.168 m
1 acre = 0.4047 hectares
1 sq km = 100 hectares
1 sq mile = 2.59 square km
1 ounce = 28.35 grams
1 pound = 0.4536 kilograms
1 short ton = 0.90718 metric ton
1 short ton = 2,000 pounds
1 long ton = 1.016 metric tons
1 long ton = 2,240 pounds
1 metric ton = 1,000 kilograms
1 quart = 0.94635 liters
1 US gallon = 3.7854 liters
1 Imperial gallon = 4.5459 liters
1 nautical mile = 1.852 km

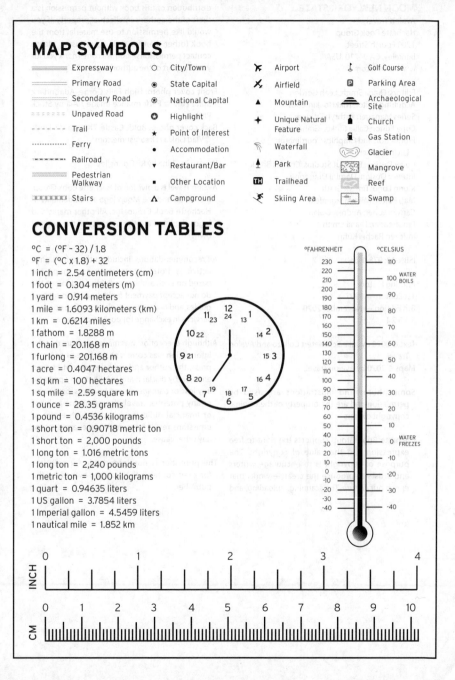

MOON NEW YORK STATE

Avalon Travel
Hachette Book Group
1700 Fourth Street
Berkeley, CA 94710, USA
www.moon.com

Editors: Diana Smith, Leah Gordon
Acquiring Editor: Nikki Ioakimedes
Series Manager: Kathryn Ettinger
Copy Editor: Callie Stoker-Graham
Production and Graphics Coordinator:
   Lucie Ericksen
Cover Design: Faceout Studios, Charles Brock
Interior Design: Domini Dragoone
Moon Logo: Tim McGrath
Map Editor: Mike Morgenfeld
Cartographer: Andrew Dolan
Proofreader: Diana Smith
Indexer: Rachel Kuhn

ISBN-13: 978-1-64049-829-7

Printing History
1st Edition — 1997
8th Edition — November 2020
5 4 3 2 1

Text © 2020 by Julie Schwietert Collazo and Avalon
   Travel.
Maps © 2020 by Avalon Travel.

Some photos and illustrations are used by
permission and are the property of the original
copyright owners.

Front cover photo: High Falls Gorge, Adirondack
State Park © Performance Image / Alamy Stock
Photo
Back cover photo: Boldt Castle, Thousand Islands
© Vlad Ghiea | Dreamstime.com

Printed in China by RR Donnelley